PADEREWSKI

THE STORY OF A MODERN IMMORTAL

Da Capo Press Music Reprint Series

MUSIC EDITOR
BEA FRIEDLAND
Ph.D., City University of New York

PADEREWSKI

THE STORY OF A MODERN IMMORTAL

BY

CHARLES PHILLIPS

WITH AN INTRODUCTION
BY EDWARD MANDELL HOUSE

DA CAPO PRESS • NEW YORK • 1978

Library of Congress Cataloging in Publication Data

Phillips, Charles Joseph MacConaghy, 1880-1933.
  Paderewski, the story of a modern immortal.

  (Da Capo Press music reprint series)
  Reprint of the 1934 ed. published by Macmillan,
New York.
  "A list of Paderewski's compositions": p.
  Discography: p.
  Bibliography: p.
  1. Paderewski, Ignacy, Jan, 1860-1941. 2. Musicians
— Poland — Biography.
ML410.P114P5 1978   786.1'092'4 [B]   77-17399
ISBN 0-306-77534-4

This Da Capo Press edition of *Paderewski: The Story of
a Modern Immortal* is an unabridged republication of
the first edition published in New York in 1934.

Published by Da Capo Press, Inc.
A Subsidiary of Plenum Publishing Corporation
227 West 17th Street, New York, N.Y. 10011

Manufactured in the United States of America

10-09-78

PADEREWSKI

THE STORY OF A MODERN IMMORTAL

IGNACE JAN PADEREWSKI
From a recent portrait by Casimir Klepacki.

PADEREWSKI

THE STORY OF A MODERN IMMORTAL

BY

CHARLES PHILLIPS

Author of "The New Poland"

WITH AN INTRODUCTION
BY EDWARD MANDELL HOUSE

NEW YORK

THE MACMILLAN COMPANY

1934

To

Paderewski's Friend

And Mine

SIGISMOND STOJOWSKI

Musician and Scholar

Without Whose Help This

Biography Could Not Have

Been Written

PADEREWSKI

Poland . . . and Music . . .

There was a silence as of death;
  The nations watched, the righteous mourned,
Where on her bier with hushéd breath
  Dear Poland lay, the wept—the scorned—

In all the darkened air no sound
  Save muffled drum and funeral bell;
Deep-chorded Chopin's anthem found
  Refrain but in the tears that fell—

Until the music of your soul,
  Great master of the harmonies,
Broke on her listening ear, to roll
  With echoing note across the seas.

Across the seas, across the years,
  With O, what hope renewed she heard
That summoning from night and tears,
  The voice of your rekindling word.

Mother to son she called; and son
  To mother hastening you came—
Now mark the mighty chords that run
  To music of her golden name!

Now mark the hand that strikes the chord
  And strikes the shackles off! O hand
Of filial love, of flashing sword
  That lifts and saves with one command—

What music ever man hath made
  Is like unto this music now
That rings with challenge unafraid
  Against the breakers of the vow?

What music ever heard of men
   Is sweeter than these chords that wake
Within her prisoned heart again,
   The sound of gyves that fall and break?

She rises, beautiful, renewed:
   She lifts her golden voice. She sings.
And in her song, sweet plenitude
   Of love, O son, your bright name rings!

INTRODUCTION

IN WEALTH of detail and in scholarly arrangement of the facts, no life of Ignace Jan Paderewski that has come to my notice equals this one written by Professor Charles Phillips. In writing it he has rendered a distinct public service, and Paderewski's many admirers in the English-speaking world will welcome this volume.

It is difficult to write of Paderewski without emotion. Statesman, orator, pianist and composer, he is a superlative man, and his genius transcends that of anyone I have ever known.

It has been my privilege to have many opportunities to fathom the man, and to look into the windows of a great soul. I have never found him guilty of an unworthy act. In international negotiations affecting the very life of his country and mine, it was enlightening to watch him overcome the opposition of those who tried to check the restoration of Poland. It was here that he appeared to best advantage. Time and again he brought to bear on those who represented the World Powers, the full force of his marvelous personality.

After finishing his work at the Peace Conference, Paderewski returned to Warsaw, and, as Prime Minister, welded together the new Poland. When this had been successfully accomplished, he went back to that kingdom of which he had been so long master, and received a welcome which must have touched and gladdened his heart. Absence in another field of endeavor had in no way lessened his musical genius, and his triumph was one of the most remarkable incidents in his career. The statesman, the executive, the diplomat and orator were now merged in the artist, the composer and the poet. Again the magic of his hands stirred the hearts of his audiences to rapture and to tears.

Those of us who love Poland are glad that she can claim him as a son, but let her always remember that Ignace Jan Paderewski belongs to all mankind.

EDWARD M. HOUSE

A NOTE ON POLISH PRONUNCIATION

Mr. Paderewski once told an amusing story of how he was introduced to a public gathering by a distinguished gentleman who was puzzled as to how to pronounce the artist's name. Before the introduction the speaker made inquiries, submitting to Mr. Paderewski four possible pronunciations. Which was correct? None of the four. Mr. Paderewski gave him the correct one: pronounce the name as if it were spelled "Pad-er-ev-skee", almost eliding the "v". But when the speaker rose he introduced the guest of honor as "Mr. Payderoosky."

The pronunciation of Polish words is not difficult if the following simple rules be observed: *j* is like *y; w* is like *v; g* is always hard (as in *go*); *cz* is like *ch* (as in *church*); *sz* is like *sh* (as in *show*); *rz* is like French *j* (as in *jardin*); *ch* is a pure aspirant, like *h* in house; *c* sounds like *ts*; the vowel *i* is like *ee*. Polish vowels all have the Latin sound.

Paderewski's baptismal names in Polish, Ignacy Jan, are in English Ignatius John, in French Ignace Jean. For euphony, and because custom has established the rule, the French form of the first name—Ignace—is used in this biography. Here also, in most cases, English phonetic spelling is used, as "Seym" for Sejm, "Vavel" for Wawel, "Volhynia" for Wolhynia, and so on.

CONTENTS

ILLUSTRATIONS

PADEREWSKI

THE STORY OF A MODERN IMMORTAL

I

TWO STORIES

ONE evening in midsummer of 1920 I stood in a wooded path
on the rocky slope of a mountain in southern Poland and looked
down at the town of Zakopané spread before me. Lights were
beginning to show in windows, supper-time smoke rose from
chimneys. The roof of the last villa on the edge of the town
was almost level with my feet, so steep was the sloping path
where I stood. But there was no light, no chimney-smoke from
this house; it was vacant and very still in the shadows of the
swift mountain dusk that was already filling the valley. The
last ashen rose of sundown was dying on the high Tatra peaks,
the shell-pink of their snowy ridges dimming to dove-gray
darkness. In a moment the stars would be out . . .

No stillness can be so sudden or so deep as the stillness of
a mountain valley with night coming down. Move one step,
displace a pebble in the path, and the sound breaks through the
silence with startling sharpness. I stood perfectly still. There
was no sound whatsoever. And then, not suddenly, not disturbing the silence but as if it were a part of it, music seemed to
come out of that empty house at my feet.

The house was the villa of Helena Modjeska. The music
was Paderewski's. Of course it was the familiar Minuet; and
of course I was imagining it. Helena Modjeska was dead and
gone; I had made a pilgrimage to her grave in Cracow the day
before. And Paderewski had left Poland after resigning his
post as Prime Minister of the Republic, and was even then preparing to resume his career as a musician.

All that the career of Ignace Jan Paderewski meant, both as
musician and as statesman, seemed to be summed up for me in

that hushed moment. Standing there on that mountain path in the free Poland that Modjeska had dreamed of and that Paderewski, by his music as well as by his statecraft, had helped to make an actuality, I could visualize her as I remembered her and I could see him as I had seen him and as she had known him, with a distinctness that made it easy enough to imagine his music drifting up in the stillness out of the chambers of the house in which she had once lived, and in which he had often played for her.

The first time I had seen Paderewski was in 1915 in San Francisco. But before that I had already made what seemed a personal contact with him through my friendship with Madame Modjeska. More than once she had mentioned him in her letters to me, and in her memoirs she had given a charming picture of him in the days of her Zakopané villa, when he was still only a young music teacher, his concert career ahead of him. "We had many chats," she wrote, "and I advised him to appear in public. I knew he would make a name and a fortune."

As an artist he had made both name and fortune that time I first saw him, thirty years after Modjeska's first meeting with him. But likewise, by 1915, he was already launched on a new career, one very different indeed from that of musician, a career in which he was to win strange laurels—and to lose his entire fortune. He was even then, thus early in the World War, one of the acknowledged leaders of the Polish people in their final struggle for freedom.

When next I saw Paderewski that new career of his in statecraft was become a brilliant reality, was in act at its pitch of achievement. That was scarcely five years later. But the history of a nation had been crowded into those five years. The famous mane of golden hair was now turned coppery gray; the tall figure that had gone out of Modjeska's villa to bow before the plaudits of hundreds of thousands seemed taller still as he greeted me in the Zamek Palace at Warsaw in 1919. And the strong hand that took mine, with its steel-like grip, the hand that had swayed the hearts of multitudes through music, was now firmly set to the helm of a nation whose thirty millions looked to him for their political salvation, for the restoration of their country to its rightful place in the ranks of the international world.

The story of Paderewski is two stories, or, as it were, the story of two men. The story of his artistic career belongs to the history of music; the verdict of that history places him among the masters of all time. I know that story from its beginning in many of its intimate details; I gathered much of it in Poland from among his friends. "You have evidently come across somebody who knows a great deal about my early youth," he once said to me, to which he added good-humoredly, "perhaps knows even too much!" But there is another story to tell of Paderewski, a story the living out of which, in great part, it was my good fortune to witness first-hand in the Poland of post-Armistice days. It is the story of his phenomenal success as a national leader and an international politician, a story that is not sufficiently known and yet one which illustrates the power of Paderewski's character fully as well as does the record of his triumphal artistic achievements. As a matter of fact, the one story is in its essentials no different from the other; the genius and character of the man comes out in both. Tireless, relentless, indefatigable patience, iron determination, merciless self-discipline, make the theme of both these stories. The youth who could practice at the piano seventeen hours at a time to perfect a pair of hands that had been laughed at by his fellows, and who could in the end develop in those hands a power of artistic magic that for nearly half a century has moved the soul of the whole music-loving world; such a youth could hardly escape the destiny of fame that Modjeska predicted for him, though she could not have dreamed how that destiny would work out in the end or what obstacles he would have to overcome. Include poverty and hardship among those obstacles, and we have, in the winning of a large fortune, another evidence of power, the power of level-headed practical common sense. Interrupt this story of fame and fortune with a cataclysmic war which not only turns the man face about from his artistic career to the wholly alien field of international politics, but at the same time strips him of his fortune; see him win as statesman a success as brilliant as that won by him in art; and watch him finally, over sixty years of age, his lifetime savings gone, return to his art, win a new fortune and make a new career: to follow Paderewski through such a story as this is to have beyond denial an extraordinary man to consider.

To the world at large, devoted for so many years to Paderewski as an artist, the most extraordinary thing that he did was to enter the field of international politics and become one of the great political leaders of history. But that extraordinary achievement of his is usually and very wrongly marvelled at as a mere freak of war-time change. While his musical genius is accepted as a patent fact, his eminence in statecraft is regarded as one of the accidents of history. Paderewski's career as statesman was not an accident. When one knows what Paderewski had to cope with as a political leader, and considers how the powers he had developed as an artist were applied to the problems of world politics, one realizes that the two apparently disparate careers were in reality one and the same, part and parcel of each other.

Paderewski's arrival in Poland in January 1919 had been preceded by some five years of political and philanthropic activity in America and Europe, raising funds with which to feed his starving people; inducing Woodrow Wilson to make the freedom of Poland one of the Fourteen Points; organizing Polish-American troops to fight for the Allies; securing a place for Poland at the Versailles Peace Conference. When I arrived in Poland in 1919 Paderewski was in the thick of his struggle to restore the nation to political unity. Poland had been liberated then for nearly a year, but in that time she had suffered such vicissitudes and such agonies of rebirth, after a juridical death of over a century, as would warrant any ordinary nation to drop back into chaos and ruin. The task of reconstruction and rehabilitation which Paderewski faced when he returned to his native land in 1919 was a task to stagger a giant.

Other countries, it is true, had, like Poland, been freed by

Wilson's peace terms and had set to work to reorganize themselves under their new found liberty. But none of them had come to that liberty as Poland had come, none had been so stripped, so torn apart, so stamped into political oblivion. Here was a nation that for over one hundred years had not only suffered the alien yoke of despotism and tyranny, but one that had been dismembered and as a political entity obliterated, not by one but by three despotisms. No longer was there a Poland to be restored; there were three Polands—Russian, German, and Austrian. Different tongues, different codes of law, different systems of education, different cultures, all these had been imposed upon that unhappy land, so that it had become literally true that Poland as a state, as a nation, had ceased to exist. "Poland is not yet dead!" had been the old rally-cry of the Dombrowski legions under Napoleon, as it now is the refrain of Poland's national anthem. But the Poland to which Paderewski came in 1919 was as dead as a cruelly dismembered body can be dead. Only her soul lived on, a disenthralled spirit, a wraith, separated from its body, living only in the hearts, the memories and the hopes of the people.

The practical result of the Polish dismemberment was this: The Polish people were no longer a united people. United they were, it is true, in their ideal of liberty as they had always been united in their hope of freedom. But they were sadly divided when it came to the question of how that freedom, now restored to them, was to be maintained and preserved. Not only was there no longer a Poland. There was no longer in actuality the Pole: there was the "Russian" Pole, the "German" Pole, the "Austrian" Pole. Not that the Muscovite had succeeded in Russianizing the Pole or the Prussian in Teutonizing him, or the Austrian in Hapsburging him. It was not that. But they had succeeded in sectionalizing the country and in making each section, when national issues were at stake, suspicious of the other. Who was to unify these separate parts? Could a "Russian" Pole do it, with the "German" Pole eying him askance? Or vice versa? That was not in human nature. And yet a man must be found, a leader of all, a champion in whom all would believe fully and heartily.

That man was found. He was Paderewski. He was a Pole of the Poles. He was neither "Russian" nor "German" nor "Austrian." He was just a Pole. By the providential circumstances of his life he had escaped the mark of sectionalism, and by reason of that fact he was assured a hearing at home as well as before the world.

More than that, Paderewski was "American". For some thirty years more or less he had lived in America, in a land that was a magic land to the Pole, a land to which the heart of Poland had turned in admiration and devotion ever since the days when Kosciuszko and Pulaski had crossed the seas to help us win our independence. Through all the generations of their own suffering in the cause of liberty, the Polish people had looked upon America as the one land where liberty really triumphed, where freedom was not a dream but a reality. And now, out of that land, returning to his mother land, rose up this son of Poland, Paderewski, the man who had been for half his lifetime the spokesman of Polish genius to the world at large, the unportfolioed ambassador of a lost nation to the courts and congresses of civilization. Such a man, one without a single tie of factionalism or sectionalism binding him, a man of international repute and with the prestige of America backing him, was the one man needed by Poland at that critical hour to seal the guarantee of her restoration and begin the building of her superstructure as a State on the foundations laid by his brother patriots.

Paderewski did it. He did it simply, nobly, practically. And yet, after all his long struggle in America gathering funds for the starving people of his country and raising troops for the Allies; after his still more difficult struggle to secure open avowal of the claims of his people in the peace terms of President Wilson, and an acknowledged place for a Polish spokesman at the Versailles Conference: after all this, his task was as yet only begun. He still had Poland itself to save, to save for itself and even from itself.

These were stirring days in Poland. The air was electrical with urgency. There was, as I have said, factionalism, sectionalism, division, dissension, on every side; for the harvest of division is dissension. Paderewski had to face all this, oppose it, fight it, reason with it, struggle night and day against it, laboring as perhaps no leader of a nation ever before has had to labor to save his country. And he had to carry on this struggle not alone against large divisions of partisan opposition but even against the sting of small personal attack, attack that stooped even to the intimacies of religious bigotry. Poland is distinctively a Catholic country, but it has not escaped the virus of Continental anticlericalism fostered by imported atheistic socialism. Paderewski's Catholic faith was seized upon by radical opponents as a means of rousing antagonism. I remember a postcard that was circulated against him, a picture representing him led by the traditional fox-faced monk of the anticlericals. Another, in kind, went further still, a mean cartoon that lampooned the noble and generous woman who is Paderewski's wife, a woman who was at that moment spending her utmost energies if indeed she was not permanently wrecking her health in service of the poor of her stricken country. There were many such attacks by cartoon and word of print in the "red" press, a press that gave plain evidence of enjoying Bolshevik subsidy from across the Russian border. Much of this sort of thing Paderewski had to suffer as he labored to draw his people out of the darkness of disunion—rather out of the blinding glare of new unaccustomed liberty—up to the plane of sober action, clear vision. But he had the vision, and he had the gift of ordered action and the power to lead others to see that vision and to act.

He did it. But he could never have done it if he had not already imposed upon himself the discipline that had perfected him in his art; if he had not developed in himself the smooth running machinery of controlled genius, of indefatigable, relentless, tireless patience, determination and self-criticism.

But that is not all of Paderewski's story as statesman. He did the great thing. And then he did a greater thing. He did one of

the greatest things that any man can do. He sacrificed himself.
His task of international recognition completed, his work of
national reunification launched, the machine assembled, the huge
and complicated engine of government set moving, he voluntarily stepped down from the engineer's seat, moved aside, made
way for others. Not too late and not too soon—although, in the
light of later events, it remains difficult for the American
observer not to believe that it would have been better for
Poland had Paderewski's distracted countrymen been possessed of just a little more of his broad vision, enough of it
to force him to remain. But the Polish democracy was no exception to the universal human rule: there was one spirit, one aim,
but there were divergent interests, opinions, convictions, pulling in opposite directions. Paderewski held and steered these
through the first crisis, through the "creative hour"; it was
the part of his genius to sense what that hour, that crucial
moment, was. Then, the crisis passed, he withdrew. He gave
over the wheel to others.

He might have staid on. He might have remained, keeping
to himself the glory of leadership, the honor of supreme office.
But it was not premiership or presidency that Paderewski was
working for. It was a free Poland he was working for, a strong,
self-controlled, self-functioning democracy, a Poland that
would be in plan, framework, and eventual operation as much a
harmony of accord as one of his own musical compositions. That
was his dream. Only the great make their dreams come true.
He had made his dream of music come true. Now, to make
his dream of a free Poland come true, a Poland harmonious
and accordant, he sacrificed himself. He had composed the
score, harmonized the furious fortissimo of its discords. That
done, he gave the composition to his people to play.

And yet no act of Paderewski's was less understood or less
appreciated than the act of his withdrawal from politics. "So
Paderewski failed?" If that question was asked me once, it was
asked a hundred times, when I came home from Poland. So
few in America had any grasp of the real situation in Poland,
of the real greatness of Paderewski. True, Americans never

disgraced themselves as some of the Prussian politicians did by ridiculing him as the "piano playing premier." Our people respected him too much and recognized his genius for statesmanship too readily for that. The unexpected does not surprise us; we are used to it, in a land where rail splitters become presidents. But nearly everyone here seemed to labor nevertheless under the impression that Paderewski's withdrawal from politics meant that he had failed.

He had not failed. As a matter of fact, no man in the war and the post-war history of Europe triumphed quite as Paderewski triumphed. He won back for his country its rightful "place in the sun" among the great nations. He did the one thing that had to be done to complete the restoration of Poland, the one thing that, as it happened, he alone at the moment could do. And if there be any today who still believe that Paderewski failed, all they need do is look across the sea to the new Poland of our time, that new Poland which, amidst all the ruin and confusion of post-war years has balanced her budget, established a soundly backed currency, exported more than she has imported, paid her bills and reduced her national debt to one of the smallest per capita public debts in Europe. That new Poland is built on foundations laid by Paderewski's hands. Whatever has happened since, whatever fame or glory others have won in the rehabilitation of Poland—they are many and they have won it justly and greatly—in the end as it was in the beginning the new Poland as a recognized entity in the world of nations, is Paderewski's Poland. The Poland that is, today, could not have been, certainly not within the time of living men, had not Paderewski come when he did, done what he did, and, in the wisdom of his unselfish foresight, quit when he did. Henryk Opienski in his biography quotes thus an eminent official of the Versailles Peace Conference: "Without his [Paderewski's] work in America none of the Allies would have dared to present the Polish question before the congress at Versailles as it was presented." Without Paderewski's work the Polish question would not have been solved in our day; it would have remained Europe's most despairing riddle.

So he quit the field of politics. But he did not quit his art. The strains of music that Paderewski makes are still heard as the pages of this book are written, as indeed they will be heard, in his compositions, for all time, as long as music exists on this earth. The "million dollar hands" that not only gave away their hard-earned millions to feed starving Poland, but that grasped and held the wheel of the nation and saved that nation from foundering, still strike music around the world. I know little about music; but Paderewski's playing has the power to draw me to the edge of my chair experiencing unimaginable things as I sit listening to him. As long as I live, I shall not forget his music. But whenever I hear it, whether actually as played by him, or in his compositions as played by others, or only in memory and imagination as I heard it that midsummer eve in 1920 —as if by some preternatural conjuring floating into the dusk out of the silence of Modjeska's empty house where often he played to the stars coming out over the snowy Tatras;—however and wherever I hear Paderewski's music, I shall not feel the artist only, I shall feel the impact of a strong and great man, a man endowed with genius, who played his part in the saving of a nation not in spite of his being an artist but exactly because he was an artist and by reason of no other fact. As Saint-Säens once remarked, "Paderewski is a genius who happens to play the piano."

Paderewski's story, then, is two stories, the story of an artist and the story of a statesman, the story of a genius of music and of a genius of statecraft. Which story should come first? Although he himself once wrote, "Fatherland before everything, art afterward" (*La patrie avant tout, l'art ensuite*), there is, nevertheless, no separating these two stories. They are woven and intertwined. Together they make a great symphony, an epic of ordered rhythm filled with mighty harmonies and contrasting dissonances, a story that is well worth telling; for in this story we have summed up a striking record of what man, raised to his highest exponent by virtue of character and will-power, can do and get done in this confused world where human ideals, even the ideals of civilization itself, are questioned if not repudiated. The achievements of Paderewski are an irrefutable demonstration of what Christian civilization means, a challenging and incontrovertible evidence of what the race at its best can produce.

II

BACKGROUNDS

"I DIE too soon," cried Paderewski's friend Sienkiewicz, the Polish novelist, as he passed away a little while before the flag of Poland once more rose over the Zamek, the ancient palace of the Polish kings at Warsaw. These, according to the report to me of one of Sienkiewicz's nieces who worked with us in the American Red Cross office in Warsaw in 1919, were the last words of the famous Polish author when he died the fifteenth of November, 1916. As history runs through its large cyclic spans, it was indeed "too soon", only a little while before the great change would come; yet the crash and thunder of war still rolled across the Polish plains when Sienkiewicz breathed his last. Plainly, nevertheless, he did not die in despair of that free Poland of which he had dreamed and for which he had striven, a Poland "soon" to rise out of its ruins. That deathless hope of his, deathless even in the face of death itself, was characteristically Polish. For more than a century alien rulers had usurped Poland's royal seat, an alien banner had flown from its flag-staff; yet no Pole had ever given up hope. Now, in 1919, as I looked for the first time at the Zamek from my vantage-point on the Praga Bridge, the cream-colored walls of the old palace tawny yellow in the sun under the rippling white and amaranth of the national colors, a Polish ruler once more occupied it. He was not a king but a civilian; yet he was a man who already, and for many years of his life, had won more acclaim in more of the capitals of the world than any monarch in history.

It was Sienkiewicz's friend Paderewski, Prime Minister of the Polish Republic, who occupied the Zamek now; Paderewski the musician, turned statesman and directing the destinies of a nation of thirty millions. This coming of an artist to the head of a people and their government was one of the greatest of all the surprises of that astounding post-war period of shocks and readjustments which followed the Armistice of 1918, a period in which only the extraordinary and the paradoxical could at all stir the war-jaded world.

Yet the coming of an artist to the leadership of the Polish people should not have astonished the outer world. For Poland is a land of surprises and paradoxes—and the greatest of these is the Pole himself. He is a puzzling mixture of human contradictions. As a fighter he is terrible; yet he can be happy only in friendliness. He is a poor hater; yet he is a dangerous enemy. He is very proud; yet his pride is humbled utterly before the shrine of human liberty. Fortune deserts him; but, deserted of fortune, he does not idle, he goes to work. Want haunts his steps; but no man on earth can share so graciously with others the hospitality of an empty cupboard; he is crushed under hopelessness, yet he hopes. One might continue drawing the portrait of the paradoxical Pole on interminable parallels of contradiction: He is gentle and wild, yet neither soft nor fierce. He is square, but circuitous. He is unequivocal, yet indirect. He is romantic, and a stark realist; he is a poet and a scientist in one. He is an innovator, and a traditionalist: above all Paderewski satisfies this paradoxical characteristic. Again, the Pole has Occidental energy and Oriental perseverance, the latter an attribute which has too often, to his discredit, been mistaken for indolence. He has a zest for life but he can die not only bravely but gayly; the art of life he understands so perfectly that he has forgotten it is an art.

It is from this Polish race that Paderewski comes. His racial origin helps to explain him.

"No one can study Eastern Europe," Ralph Butler writes of the Poles in his book "The New Eastern Europe" (Butler is an English critic inclined if anything to prejudice against the Pole) "without feeling that they are infinitely the most attractive of the peoples with which he has to do. They are the only

ones in whose composition there is included that subtle differentia which marks off the 'big nation' from the 'small.' In all
Europe there is no other people, with the possible exception of
the French, which is so naturally gifted." Paderewski himself
bears out this testimony not alone in his own largeness of character, but in the evidence of a striking passage which occurs in
one of his writings; in a speech, now famous, which he delivered many times during the World War when he was touring
the United States appealing for aid for his stricken country.
"Far from pretending that the Polish nation was made up
of angels," he said, "I willingly admit that my compatriots,
though exceptionally richly endowed, full of imagination, labo-
rious, brave, chivalrous, kind-hearted, broad-minded, were and
naturally still are extremely temperamental, excessively emotional, and consequently subject to passion, to errors . . . But
there flows throughout our whole history a stream of humanity,
of generosity, of tolerance, so broad, so powerful and so pure
that it would be vain indeed to look for a similar one in the
past of any other European country." "The Polish race, to those
who are acquainted with it," writes Arthur Symons, "is the
most subtle and the most delicate, and one of the noblest and
most heroic in Europe. Its existence should be as precious to
Europe, as that of a precious jewel." It has, in the words of the
novelist Reymont, "the beauty of an eagle, its passion for liberty, its desire of soaring up to the very sun, its pride, its love
of space."

All these acknowledged qualities of the Pole, however, no
matter how attractive and interesting they be, when taken together rather bewilder us. But the Pole has one attribute over
and above all others, or rather hidden under them and too
often not readily discerned, which commands the wholehearted respect of the practical world. It is his capacity for
getting things done in the end and at last, whatever the vicissitudes of the process. Underneath the Pole's cleverness, brilliance, what you will, lies the dogged determined will-power
of the man who never gives up; who fights on and on, inch by
inch, and who, even when winning, is never wholly satisfied

with himself. He is less inclined than any other man I know to fall back on his oars or rest on his laurels. He has in him the "divine discontent", the terrible urge of the idealist, with whom imagination and intuition, instead of being substitutes for precise knowledge, are simply means of achieving it. "Work will never take the crown from my brow," says an old Polish proverb. "Remember," Kosciuszko wrote to one of his compatriots, "thou hast done nothing so long as there remains anything to do." "Impervious against every temptation of ease" are the words in which General Nathaniel Greene of the American revolutionary army described that same Kosciuszko; and among "the perfect qualities of that Pole", as General Gates described him to Thomas Jefferson, was this: "If he has once promised we can depend on him." In any one of these phrases might be written a complete description of Paderewski's character and career.

And yet, the paradox again, this same dogged, determined Pole has never become a plodder. This is the reason why, in the long run of racial competition, by sheer basic superiority and "survival of the fittest", he has bested his antagonists in many of the contests in which Poland and her oppressors have engaged for a thousand years. Where the Prussian, for example, the Pole's most formidable antagonist, has been steady, powerful, self-righteous, self-satisfied, ponderous, the Pole has been dynamic, flexible, self-critical, idealistic and tenacious of his ideal. "What has Prussia to do with a race which it cannot understand, a race which desires only peace with freedom?" Arthur Symons the English critic asked in 1908, as Paderewski asked the same question in 1914. Paderewski's answer to the question was the freedom of Poland.

Chopin, Paderewski's illustrious predecessor in music, is an example of the Polish paradox. We need only read Chopin's biography to discover how truly and typically Polish he is; how, back of all the brilliance, the tragedy, the delicacy, the *zal*, the *tesknota*, the transcendant illumination of his music, is a force, a power of concentration, a capacity for tireless work, for infinite painstaking, for detailed and sustained effort, unsurpassed in the history of any other artist. Chopin lived but forty years, always in delicate health, but he left to the world a legacy of eight hundred pages of musical composition. "Chopin was an invalid, as you know," Paderewski once remarked, "but his music was volcanic." There is power in a volcano, and the surprise of action long prepared for.

This then is the surprise and the paradox of the Pole: the surprise of Chopin the fragile exquisite who in the space of one period of four years wrote fifty-three of his greatest compositions: of Madame Skłodowska-Curie the housekeeping scientist who helped discover radium not in five blazing seconds of a genius's leisure hour but after years of silent, tireless work: of Copernicus the astronomer who turned the world of the heavens inside out before he died, even though it took his whole lifetime to do it: of Conrad the novelist who, mastering the strange English tongue in his maturity, has given to English literature pages that rank with Shakespeare: of Matejko the half-blind painter, the delicacy of whose detail baffles the student: of Modjeska the actress who, unable to secure for herself the text of "Hamlet", copied out by hand the entire play; who at thirty was supreme in a repertoire of over one hundred classic characterizations and then, in four months, mastered English and appeared triumphantly in Shakespeare.

It is the surprise and the paradox of Paderewski, musician and statesman, who in the words of Frederick Martens has proved for all time "the falsity of Baudelaire's pessimistic theory that the artist cannot and should not share in the life and activities of the mundane world."

It is interesting to consider the racial and environmental factors which go into the making of a nature like that of Paderewski. Racially he is a Slav. That means a virgin strength the primitive force and elemental fecundity of which, it seems, cannot be devitalized by any of the fortunes of life, either by a surplus of oppression, war, hunger, disease, or by a surfeit of ease and luxury; for to all the Slavic peoples these fortunes in both extremes have come through the course of history; and yet they remain, all of them, whether Poles or Serbs, Russians,

Croatians, Czechs, what not, a peculiarly vital race. This basic quality of vitality has much to do with the makeup of the Pole and everything to do with Paderewski's story.

And yet, though the Pole is a Slav, we are forced to admit, on the evidence of his history, that Conrad's words are true: "Between Polonism and Slavonism there is . . . a complete and ineradicable incompatibility . . . The Poles, whom superficial theorists are trying to force into the social and psychological formula of Slavonism, are in truth not Slavonic at all. In temperament, in feeling, in mind, and even in unreason, they are Western, with an absolute comprehension of all Western modes of thought." A word like this explains what Washington found in Kosciuszko when he compared him to even so Western a type as the French military engineer Radière. The Pole was selected for the defense of West Point and the Hudson because in Washington's words, he was "better adapted to the genius and temper of the [American] people."

There are then, Slavs and Slavs, as there are degrees in kind. If the Slav peoples are strong, the Pole seems to be blessed with a superabundance of the vitality which is characteristic of his racial stock. "Misfortune is a hard school which may either mature or spoil a national character," Conrad tells us, "but it may be reasonably advanced that the long course of adversity of the most cruel kind has not injured the fundamental characteristics of the Polish nation which has proved its vitality against the most demoralizing odds." One realizes this when one compares him with his Russian cousin. The French critic de Voguë, writing of Gogol, the healthiest and most vigorous of Russia's literary artists, speaks of him as "the natural product of the land which gave him birth", and he describes that land, the Ukraine, thus: "This frontier country is subject to the contending influences of both north and south. For a few short months the sun revels there and accomplishes an almost miraculous work—an Oriental brilliancy of light by day, and soft, enchanting nights under a sky resplendent with stars. Magnificent harvests from fertile fields insure an easy, joyous life; all trouble and sadness vanish with the melting snow, and spirits rise to general gayety and enthusiasm." But, as the French scholar goes on, defining the characteristics of the Russian nature, "the boundless spaces, the limitless horizons of the sunny plains overwhelm the spirit; one cannot long feel joyous in the presence of Infinity. The habit of thought becomes like that of the eye; is lost in space, develops an inclination to revery, which causes the mind to fall back upon itself, and the imagination is, so to speak, thrown inward."

The French critic goes a long way not only in picturing for us the background, but in explaining the nature, of the Russian Gogol and his native brothers in art. Their spirits are overwhelmed, their imagination is thrown inward, they become, in the words of Conrad, "victims of disgust, of disenchantment . . . They detest life, the irremediable life of earth as it is." They suffer, the Russian Gorky tells us, from "the unhealthy ferment of the old Russian blood, envenomed by Mongolian fatalism and almost chemically hostile to the West with its untiring creative labor, with its active and indomitable resistance to the evils of life." Such words as those of de Voguë, then, explain the Russian Slav. But they do not explain the Pole, living alongside his Russian brother, even though they do accurately portray his background. He comes, the Pole, by the millions from like soil, from under like skies such as Gogol and Gorky and all their fellows knew; but he is wholly different, he is essentially Western. Paderewski was born in Podolia and for the most part raised in its neighboring province of Volhynia, regions which, so far as topography and climate go, are one with Gogol's Ukraine—the same endless levels of sky and plain. But whatever the limitless horizons of his native land did to Paderewski they did not overwhelm his spirit nor throw his mind back upon itself. In Paderewski the Pole proves true to his paradox by remaining "joyous in the presence of Infinity". It is his vitality that explains him, that vital stream of the life of hope and the hope of life which made the venerable Sienkiewicz, even while he cried, at seventy, "I die", still cry forward to the "soon" of his hope, a hope unquenchable even in death.

This vitality is temperamental, as Paderewski's own words describe it, "excessively emotional, and consequently subject to passion, to errors." There is, however, no question that the course of his own life, lived from early manhood away from the immediate influences of his oppressed people, lived freely and openly without the coercive contacts which Poles at home so long suffered, made Paderewski as the years passed more and more Western, more stable and evenly balanced. He was to realize this when, in the troubled days of reconstruction, he came into immediate contact with his own again and tasted of the bitter fruit of dissension that a century of partition had ripened in the Polish people. Nevertheless, realist as well as idealist, he was prepared for it, for he had always recognized the national fault, "our greatest demerit", he calls it, "the instability, the lack of perseverance with which we are generally credited . . . our, alas, undeniable incapacity for disciplined collective action." "Change follows change in us, almost without transition," he says; "we pass from blissful rapture to sobbing woe; a single step divides our sublimest ecstasies from the darkest depth of spiritual despondency. We see proof of this in every domain of our national life; we see it in our political experiences, in our internal developments, in our creative work, in our daily troubles, in our social intercourse, in all our personal affairs. It is palpable everywhere. Maybe this is only an inherent characteristic; yet when we compare ourselves with other happier and more satisfied races, it strikes us rather as being a pathological condition."

It is the true realist who can speak thus frankly of himself, of his own blood and race. This realistic frankness of Paderewski is one of the marks of his vitality, one of the secrets of his strength. Godlike is the strength of the man who knows himself. "From heaven descends the precept, know thyself." Paderewski learned the Delphian lesson early in his youth. That is why he understands and is at the same time a living example of that Polish vitality which is the keynote of his life; which he himself likens to "music which eludes metrical discipline, rejects the fetters of rhythmic rule, and refuses submission to the metronome as if it were the yoke of some hated government." "Our nation, our land, the whole of Poland," he declares, "lives, feels, and moves in *tempo rubato*."

And that, perhaps, is the greatest of all the Polish paradoxes of this typical Pole: born to the *tempo rubato* of the native temperament, he has risen above it. No matter how enchanting the *tempo rubato* of Paderewski's music, his life is a story of power realized through self-discipline.

III

1860: THE CRYSTAL HARMONICA

WHEN Paderewski was born, on the sixth of November, 1860, in the old manor house of Kurylówka in Podolia, Russia ruled his native province. Podolia had been one of the ancient palatinates of the old kingdom of Poland, but had been torn from the motherland in 1795 by the Third Partition, following the fall of Kosciuszko who, returning from his fighting for American independence, was aflame with ardor to free his homeland and establish her as a new America in old Europe. How far Kosciuszko's dream carried the Poles is perhaps best indicated in the words of the English statesman Burke who described the Polish Constitution of 1791 as "the most pure . . . public good which has ever been conferred on mankind." It was a noble as well as a notable document, "as well adapted", according to an American opinion "to meet the difficulties of the Polish state passing from mediaevalism into the new age as was its contemporary, the Constitution of the United States, to guide a people passing from dependency to independence." * But the scepters of tyranny had speedily put an end to Kosciuszko's dream. The Poles of the Podolia of Paderewski's boyhood were thus expatriates of the unhappiest kind, a people who, after centuries of native rule, had for three quarters of a century suffered the yoke not only of alien but of cruel suppression.

Knowing the nature of these people, their vitality, their courage and their optimism, it is not difficult to understand their temper at this time: They suffered. But they still sang

---

* "America and the New Poland" by H. H. Fisher. The Macmillan Co., New York, 1928.

defiantly the song of the Dombrowski Legions, "Poland Is Still Alive!" They still looked forward, still hoped. They could do nothing else, unless indeed race and nationality died wholly in them, for they had no frontiers to look across, no homeland to turn to in aspiration of being restored. Poland as a state, as a political entity, had actually ceased to exist. There was no Poland, there was only Russia, Austria, Germany. But neither race nor nationality passed from the Poles. They clung tenaciously to their proud origins. They remained Poles. Poland still lived. And their temper at the time, very soon in fact after the date of Paderewski's birth, manifested itself unmistakably in their participation in the "Rising of '63" which swept all Poland only to be crushed by the iron fist of the Czar. In that rebellion Jan Paderewski, Ignace's father, was arrested and for more than a year kept imprisoned because, as a member of the local committee of patriots, he had stored in his house arms and uniforms for the Polish regiments secretly organizing. And not only was he, as an insurrectionist leader, imprisoned, but Kurylówka village was burned to the ground, its defenseless inhabitants were whipped in herds by the brutal *nahajka,* the Cossack cat-o'-nine-tails, and scores of them were put to the sword and slaughtered in cold blood.

To thoroughly understand the Pole and his patriotism, and in particular to understand Paderewski and the impulses back of his lifetime activities, it is necessary to have a clear understanding of what this Rebellion of 1863, and the like uprising preceding it in 1831, really was. And first of all we must remind ourselves that Paderewski was born and raised in the central theater of the age-old Polish-Russian conflict, the borderlands, where, ever since the tenth century, two worlds, two civilizations, Rome and Byzantium, East and West, had confronted each other. As to the nature of this Polish-Russian conflict, which was both secular and religious, and the particular manifestations of that conflict in 1831 and 1863, Conrad in his "Personal Record" makes the matter plain. "Why the description 'revolutionary' should have been applied all through Europe to the Polish risings of 1831 and 1863," he writes, "I really cannot understand. These risings were purely revolts against foreign domination. The Russians themselves called them 'rebellions', which, from their point of view, was the exact truth. Amongst the men concerned in the preliminaries of the 1863 movement my father"—and here we may substitute "his" for "my", with Paderewski's father in mind—"was no more revolutionary than the others, in the sense of working for the subversion of any social or political scheme of existence. He was simply a patriot in the sense of a man who believing in the spirituality of a national existence could not bear to see that spirit enslaved." And literal enslavement was what the Russian power imposed on the Poles; for the immediate cause of the outbreak in which Paderewski's father participated was a particular and specific wrong, the conscription of Polish political suspects, who were not only forced into the Russian military service, but were sent to distant parts of the empire, a doubly yoked and doubly galling form of exile.

Paderewski, all his life, from the time he came to first know in his childhood what a struggle for national existence truly signified, and specifically during his years of activity in international politics, was inspired and impelled by exactly these sentiments which Conrad, speaking for all Poles, makes so clear—belief "in the spirituality of a national existence."

What actually happened there in Kurylówka when the elder Paderewski was carried off to prison, and the child witnessed the terrorizing invasion by the Cossacks of his father's home, can only be implied in the statement of arrest, of the burning of the village and the killing of its inhabitants. But the same Conrad who so clearly states the Polish case gives a detailed picture of the occurrences in one home in the same part of the country, a picture which may be rightly taken as a very fair report of the experiences in the Paderewski home. In that picture we can see the boy of three with his five-year-old sister clinging to his father, as they face the Russian soldiery.

"A squadron of scouting Cossacks passed through the village and invaded the homestead. Most of them remained formed between the house and the stables, while several dismounting,

ransacked the various outbuildings. The officer in command, accompanied by two men, walked up to the front door. All the
blinds on that side were down . . . The officer chose to enter
the room on the left and ordered the blinds to be pulled up
. . . The officer had been looking at the backs of the books
in the bookcases. Then he perched himself on the edge of the
centre table . . . sat there swinging his leg, very quiet and
indifferent . . . walked slowly through all the rooms of the
house examining them attentively . . . When he came back
to the study all the arms to be found in the house were lying
on the table . . . a pair of big flint-lock holster pistols from
Napoleonic times, two cavalry swords . . . a fowling piece or
two. The officer, opening the window, flung out pistols, swords
and guns . . . his troopers ran to pick them up."

Then came the mob; they "smashed everything in the house,
ripping with knives, splitting with hatchets so that, as the servant said, there were no two pieces of wood left holding together in the whole house. They broke some very fine mirrors,
all the windows, and every piece of glass and china. They
threw the books and papers out on the lawn and set fire to a
heap for the mere fun of the thing apparently."

These are mild and temperate words, but if they make the
heart of the reader burn with indignation it is not difficult to
feel how such outrages roused the people who suffered them
and inflamed them with the hope of liberation. Nor is it any
too difficult to realize what a scar they would leave on the
mind of a lively and sensitive boy like Ignace. It was such
scenes as these that wrung from the heart of the poet Kornel
Ujejski, "the Ukrainian Nightingale", the cry, "You ask a
song of charm and sweetness for your ears, but, oh! my compatriots, my only song for you is one that shall remind you of
the clanking of your chains."

Ignace was only three years old at the time, but he was old
enough to see, feel, and remember, as his great symphony,
composed forty years later, testifies. This symphony (B Minor:
Op. 24), one of the greatest of modern compositions, is of
monumental proportions; played in full it requires an hour

and a half to perform. But in that hour and a half is compacted a lifetime's experience for the hearer, the tragic history of a whole people, the universal cry of humanity for freedom. The frightening horrors of that childhood experience, the intimate recollections of it kept alive in the boy's mind by his family, the matured realization of all that it signified, are translated by Paderewski's symphony into music of such tremendous power and such ringing beauty that anyone who hears it not only can never forget it, but can never forget where it comes from—from the rockbound spring of Paderewski's earliest consciousness struck and opened by the brutal fist of a terrifying experience to pour forth in a fiery stream, a gushing column of symphonic force.

In his "Chorale", the noble strains of which were powerfully set to music by Josef Nikorowicz, Ujejski had sung, "With the smoke of the burning fires, with the dust soaked with our brother's blood, this voice, O Lord, beats up to thee. Terrible is this our complaint. Our hair grows white from such prayers as this. The crown of thorns has grown into our brows." Songs like these were among the first Paderewski was to hear. Ujejski's "Chorale" was perhaps the most popular of all national songs in the Poland of Paderewski's youth. Taught to children at home and in the church, sung in the churches and before the wayside crosses, printed and circulated secretly among the people everywhere, it was a real factor in the popular life, and it was bound to be an influence in the making of this boy's career. "Oh, Polish Mother," the national poet of Poland, Mickiewicz, had sung to an earlier generation, "when from thy son's eyes the light of genius shines, when from his childish brow the noble pride of the Poles of old looks forth: When spurning his little band of playmates, he runs to the aged man who will sing to him his nation's songs; when with bowed head he listens to the history of his sires: Oh, Polish mother, ill are these pastimes for thy son . . . Our Saviour, when a child in Nazareth, fondled a little cross . . . Oh, Polish mother, I would fain amuse thy child with his future playthings. So must thou early wreathe his little hands with chains, bid him be harnessed to the convict's barrow." It was such "playthings" as these, that Paderewski knew in his childhood.

Paderewski's mother, Polyxena Nowicka, of the good Vilna family of Nowicki, the daughter of a university professor, was a lady of high character and natural gift. His father, a gentleman of the landed gentry, poor in those times so difficult for the alien-governed Pole, but educated and refined, was the administrator of the estates of the wealthy family Iwanowski. This was the boy's natal background. But it was not alone such immediate experiences as those of his father's imprisonment and the burning of Kurylówka that colored young Ignace's first impressions. His mother's father had been banished from Poland to Siberia where he died in exile; his mother had been born in exile, in the Siberian town of Kursk, a favorite deportation station of the Czar in the days when Russian tyranny ruled by ukase and the Muscovite despot boasted of "making an example of the Poles." Thus it was that very intimately into Paderewski's earliest life, with the milk of his mother's breasts one might say, there came a sense of Poland's afflictions.

His mother, exile-born, died in his infancy. But the memory of such a mother, one who has seen her own father die in banishment and has come out of exile only to leave her son to the larger exile of orphancy, is perpetuated in unforgettable detail in the lives of those who care for her children. From his father and others of the family young Ignace must have heard many stories of his grandfather's and of his mother's sufferings in banishment. When his father on winter afternoons, looking out on the whitened roads and fields of the Podolian prairie, read to him from Slowacki's "Anhelli" or from Mickiewicz's "Ancestors", the dreary picture of the snowy Siberian wastes that his mother had known must have become very real to him. "What do I see? Long, and white is the course of the highway. So long are those roads we cannot see their end, over wastes, over snowdrifts leading on to the north. Onward, like streams they flow, they flow, on to a distant land. Straight runs that road to a gate of iron." Slowacki's "faces of prisoners, pallid and sorrowful, looking through gratings to the sky" must have stared the boy in the face as his father read to him.

But it was not always the father who read to the son. Sometimes the son read to the father. And thereby hangs a tale which serves not only to illustrate the lively capacities of the boy's mind and to bring him clearly to us as a lad of ten, but one which gives us likewise a key to certain sympathies and predilections of his which were to play a part in his political life many years later. This is the story:

Paderewski's father, recovering from an illness, found his eyesight so weakened that he could not read his newspaper. So to young Ignace was assigned the task of reading aloud the daily journal of events. Now this was in 1870; it was the time of the Franco-Prussian War, and from his French governess the boy had drawn a strong sympathy for the French arms, a sympathy of course already implanted in him, as in all Poles, including his father, through the Napoleonic tradition. But day by day the news from the war became more discouraging. The Prussians were defeating the French in more and more engagements. What to do? Excite his father, make him ill again by such disastrous news? That would never do. So the boy, reading the paper aloud, invented as he read. The French won the victories. Every day new triumphs crowned their arms. The father was happy, and the ten-year-old son was flushed with the success of his generous intrigue.

But one day soon afterward the father, going to a neighboring town on his first business trip since his illness, fell in with some acquaintances and began to discuss with them the course of events in France. Alas for those glorious French victories!— his views and opinions suffered a sudden and sensational upset. Doubtless he felt himself made a fool of; anyway he returned home prepared to have a quick accounting with his ingenious Francophile offspring. The offspring, foreseeing just such an outcome, had stuffed the incriminating newspapers into the stove; they were burning more fiercely than was the paternal anger when young Ignace was summoned. But destroying the evidence didn't help. With the threat of the family strap over his head, Paderewski junior was in for a bad quarter-hour. But a happy intervention came to his rescue in the humane pleadings of Sparitz, the Jewish barber who was on the ground. "Why punish the boy?" Sparitz argued. "If Ignace had read the truth from the papers his father might have wept from chagrin and thus more seriously than ever injured his ailing eyes. The impulse back of the boy's act was good, it was thoughtful, it was generous. He was guilty not of an evil act but of one of excessive good." Ignace Jan was pardoned. But he remained Francophile. He was to know one day what a friend to Poland was that same France that he, at ten, defended against the common Prussian enemy.

The impressions, the memories, the environment of Paderewski's boyhood, the knowledge of his country's sufferings, "the boundless spaces, the limitless horizons" of the scene in which he breathed, the literature which he knew: all these might have made a Gogol, a Gorky, a Tschaikowsky out of him, an apostle of despair. But he was not a Russian, he was a Pole, as different as was his own Chopin from what Paderewski describes as "the sombre and monotonous Russian Muse upon whose cheek no smile of humor or of happiness seems ever to have played . . . What an abyss between his yearnings, his griefs, the unfailing fitness of his tragic sense, and that withering despair which blows toward us as a blast frost-laden across steppes immeasurable, boundless, hopeless." He was a Pole; the vitality of his race, nurtured by suffering, was in him. It was in the food and sustenance with which his young intelligence was fed in poem, song and story. That was wholesome, invigorating food. "You are as men standing on the height!" cried Slowacki, wandering in exile. "The Pole," sang the poet Kaminski, "cries like a bird imprisoned in a cage; over and over he reminds himself that he once was free." But Kaminski's song does not conclude on that minor note. "Hope!" he cries. "Bright days will shine. You have brothers who are only waiting for the time." . . . If Kornel Ujejski cried out that he would sing only a song of chains, in the end, in his "Chorale", he sang of archangels leading to freedom. "God was, God is!" he shouted. If Mickiewicz wept with the Polish mother admonishing her to bind her infant's hands with gyves, in the end he echoes the cry of the Polish heart, "I am the master! I stretch forth my hands, even to the skies! I lay my hands upon the stars, as on the crystal wheels of the harmonica. Now fast, now slow, as my soul wills, I turn the stars. I weave them into rainbows, harmonies. I feel immortality! I create immortality!"

Given the elements of which Paderewski's being was compact—his blood, his native sensitivity, his childhood environment, his family traditions, and add to this the stirring in his consciousness of the impulses of genius, and we may hear even in his very young heart an echo of the cry of the poet striking the wheels of the crystal harmonica: "I feel immortality! I create immortality!"

IV

MUSIC ON THE BORDERLANDS

As IT was with the poetry and story that Paderewski first knew, so also it was with the music. There was vitality in that too, rally-call and challenge—and hope of better things.

There was music in the home that Paderewski was born in. That, however, is nothing exceptional among the people of Poland who are natural musicians, who traditionally, from time immemorial, have found their readiest expression in music, song, and dance. The common love of music among them is well known. The widely popular singing societies which the Poles foster in America are but a natural growth of the impulse which makes their "Lutnia", the communal singing societies of their native land named after the lute, one of the characteristic features of their life. They are a singing people, as any one who has lived among them knows. Soldiers sing day or night on their marches; peasants sing at their work in the fields; the choral singing in Polish churches is something to make one's heart beat fast. On the countryside they are fiddlers; some of their antique stringed instruments, handed down for generations and modeled after still older ones, are rare finds for the connoisseur. It would be difficult to find a peasant's cottage, even of the poorest, without its flute or violin. "One can scarcely believe what extraordinary fancies are invented by the Polish players of bagpipe and violin when they improvise between the dances," wrote Philip Teleman, a contemporary of Bach. "Someone who would take down the notes could, in a week, make a provision of ideas for a lifetime."

In the manor houses, in the homes of the educated such as Paderewski came from, fine music is an integral part of the culture. "No nation in the world," as he himself has said, "has reason to pride itself on greater wealth of mood and sentiment, on emotions more delicately tuned than ours." And Polish mood, sentiment, emotion, find their readiest and most characteristic expression in music. "The hand of God," as Paderewski expresses it in poetic phrase, "strung the harp of our race with chords tender, mysterious, mighty and compelling. Yearning maidenhood, grave manhood, tragic and sad old age, light-hearted joyful youth; love's enfolding softness, action's vigor, valiant and chivalrous strength—all these are ours, swept together by a wave of lyric instinct."

For the young Paderewski, then, to open his ears in this world to the strains of music was nothing unusual. Of him might be said what he himself said of Chopin: "Above his cradle orchestras of butterflies played to him in the sun . . . swarms of bees hummed to him their honeyed song . . . choirs of birds twittered to him softly." His mother was an accomplished musician, and although she did not live long enough to lead him to an instrument, she gave him music as a heritage. By the time he was three his inquiring young fingers had followed the inclination of his willing ears, he was finding out how music is made. At the age of six instruction in pianoforte had begun for him, although, as a matter of fact, his first teacher, Runowski, an itinerant instructor, was not a professional pianist but a violinist, an old man who came regularly to the house, and who was reputed to have made his studies in the Vienna Conservatory, which was as high a recommendation as anyone could ask.

Thus music was in Paderewski's life from his earliest days. As Conrad once said of himself that he was "a child who was never aware of learning to read", so Paderewski can say that he was a child who could not remember when music began for him.

Nothing is known of Runowski's method of instruction, but this we do know—he taught his young pupil how to work. The pupil, of course, did not like that. He liked to improvise; he would spend hours at that, freely and of his own will. But, boylike, he hated the tedious process of lessons and practice, and above all he hated the one thing that was yet to be his destiny and his life work—playing before an audience. Nevertheless this also he had to do under compulsion; for the music-master Runowski insisted on periodical exhibitions of Ignace Jan and his sister Antonina before the family and guests gathered solemnly in the drawing-room. It is not too difficult to believe that the young victims pounded out their duets sometimes with a vigor too rebellious to suit their teacher, or murdered the innocent Norma and the gallant Barber of Seville with a vicious glee that no aftermath of discipline could quite subdue in their outraged young bosoms. That Ignace, called to his lesson and "creeping like a snail unwillingly to school", would pounce on the keyboard like a swimmer taking a head-dive, is a matter of record.

When Paderewski was seven, the old master Runowski was succeeded by a more accomplished teacher, Pierre Sowinski, and under him what may be called the boy's first systematic training in pianoforte began and continued for four years. Sowinski was a capable instructor and bore a name not unknown; his brother was the author of the first Dictionary of Polish Musicians, published in Paris in 1856.

These were Paderewski's beginnings in music. Now, in the time of Paderewski's boyhood the proscriptive tyranny of the alien rulers of Poland had not only destroyed Poland as a state, but had bent every force to the destruction of her spiritual life. A native Polish art was impossible. No Polish painter could wield the brush freely, no sculptor carve unhindered; and as for literature, it had become, except in secret, an artifice of cunning, of "Wallenrodism" as it came to be called after Mickiewicz's poem "Conrad Wallenrod", the story of a Polish hero whose defense against deceit and oppression was "cunning for treachery". As a matter of fact the Poles had by this time developed in their writing an art of allegory, of veiled significance, which became the quintessence of symbolic double-meaning. It was their only safeguard against a censorship which threatened death not only to national authors but even to readers found possessing national writings. "The possession of Mickiewicz's 'Ancestors' sent a boy of seventeen to the dungeon where, maddened with terror lest under the knout he should betray the names of his companions, he burnt himself to death. Hundreds of young men went to Siberia for having read Krasinski's 'Temptations'." * Thus Poland had her Mickiewicz whose poems, their real significance hidden, were passed by the Russian censors only because the censors did not penetrate to their true meaning. She had her exiled Slowacki, the mystic of Siberia, and she had her Anonymous Poet, Krasinski, the authorship of whose writings, smuggled into the country from Switzerland, remained concealed for thirty years. Later on she had her Sienkiewicz who dared to tell his people their story only in terms of romance of the past; in whose "Quo Vadis", even, with its scenes of ancient Rome, the Pole read the interlineal record of his own struggle against Neronian tyranny. Poland has a vast library of *double entente* literature grown out of oppression and proscription. All the arts, insofar as they expressed or could be used to foster patriotism, were proscribed in Paderewski's youth.

But there is one art that cannot be proscribed. Music cannot be spied upon, hunted down. Where poet, novelist, dramatist, painter, sculptor, can be checked and suppressed by official prohibition, the musician remains free. Into the rise and fall of his cadenced notes, his harmonies and his dissonances, the musician may put the cry of his heart and not be silenced. He can utter the voice of his people in bar and scale and be heard and understood, and yet defy the censor. This is what Polish music did, the music that Paderewski knew from the beginning. It rang with the national spirit. In his own words: "All was forbidden to us; the language and faith of our fathers, our national dress, our songs, our poets—Slowacki, Krasinski, Mickiewicz . . . Chopin alone was not forbidden to us . . . in him we still could find the living breath of all that was prohibited . . . he gave all back to us, mingled with the prayers

---

* "Poland: A Study in National Idealism," by Monica Gardner. London: Burns and Oates, 1915.

of broken hearts, the revolt of fettered souls, the pain of slavery, lost Freedom's ache, the cursing of tyrants, and exultant songs of victory . . ."

Chopin's friend Witwicki once wrote these words to him: "The idea of nationality keep always in view, nationality and yet again nationality. There is national melody, just as there is national climate. The mountains, the forests, the waters and the prairies have their national voice, hidden underneath so that not every soul perceives it. Imbibe the vast treasures of Slav melody. Delve among the popular Slav melodies as the mineralogist digs among the stones and minerals of mountains and valleys." Chopin joyously put his creative genius to work in this direction. For him, as the French biographer Guy de Pourtalés writes, "Poland remained the living spring, the reflection of his dreams and his sentiments . . . the dynamo of his energies." Chopin was Paderewski's first love. Nurtured on such an ideal it is no wonder that he grew up to be not only an artist but a patriot whose soul burned with love of country and expanded with the buoyance of a deathless hope.

Paderewski, always original, one who never echoes other people's opinions, has his own views on nationality in music, views which might seem at first glance to contravene those theories of Chopin's friend, to which Chopin himself so faithfully adhered, although he too superimposed on them that unique personality which was Chopin. "Musical expression," Paderewski has said, "is never primarily national, but is personal and individual rather. It is so deep, so profound, that it goes beyond and below nationality and gives voice to the most private feeling. In music there is never exact heredity. Each man is an individual." Yet, as he shows further, the individual remains the child of his race, the inheritor of his national culture, the sharer of his national experience: "That which is the outcome of man's pure reason, Science only, knows nothing of national boundaries. Art, even Philosophy, in common with all that springs from the depths of the human soul and is the outcome of reason and emotion, bears the inevitable stamp of race, the hallmark of nationality." And the special mark of the Polish nationality, according to Paderewski, is best denoted in terms of Music. Poets could not express it fully, "they were hampered by limiting precision of thought, by strictness of words". But music, "music alone . . . could reveal the fluidity of our feelings, their frequent overflowings toward infinity, their heroic concentrations, their frenzied ecstasies."

The validity of music as an authentic expression of the Polish nature, especially of Polish national feeling in the face of suffering, is made clearer still by Paderewski: "It is a strange fact," he says, "that the greatest music is in the minor mode . . . Music expresses first of all sadness rather than joy. When people are sad and depressed, and therefore quiet and indisposed to activity, then they sing. Their state of quiescence, undisturbed by bodily motions, is favorable to song, and song is thus the natural means of expressing melancholy and grief. When people are full of joy, then they cannot sit still; they must let off their surplus energy by violent physical motion. But the quiet mood comes oftener than the lively one, and in music song comes before dance."

Paderewski speaking to the world as Chopin spoke, in the universal language of music which "goes beyond and below nationality", speaks nevertheless in his national accent. It was that accent, the Polish accent of purpose and hope as well as of sadness, that his young fingers, translating the impulses of his being, were to acquire in the beginning, and never lose. It was the same accent of promise and of unquenchable vitality that made the poets of exile and proscription end their song, no matter how minor chorded or tragic, on the suspended note of exaltation; Mickiewicz's ringing finale struck "on the crystal wheels" from the chordings of despair.

The very structure of Polish music reveals its national characteristics. "While the Poles sang in heroic tones of victories over Tatars, Cossacks, Swedes, or Muscovites," writes Jaroslaw de Zielinski, later events in their history "naturally saddened the voice of the people . . . Three musical elements enter into this characteristic, namely, melody, harmony and rhythm; forbidden progressions of intervals, such as augmented seconds, diminished thirds, augmented fourths, diminished sevenths, minor ninths, etc., are of common occurrence; the harmony is distinguished by successions of chords presenting no logical contradiction, and yet at variance with established usage." The effect of this is distinctively "nationalistic." "The closes of Polish music," as A. E. Tennant explains in her "Studies in Polish Life and History," * "are typical; melodies . . . do not close with ear-filling and soul-sating chords solidly founded and firmly sustained and emphasized in the bass." Instead, they are as it were etherialized; the spiritual exaltation is there, the rising above sadness and despair. "We do not feel that the drip, drip, drip, of the rain in Chopin's B Minor Prelude is doomed to continue forever." "Notwithstanding the melancholy which seizes you," as Kleczynski says in his interpretation of Chopin, "a feeling of tranquil grandeur revives you." This is true. In all the world there is no music so profoundly sorrowful as that of Chopin's "Funeral March" with its long series of indeterminate fifths alternating with fourths, every second chord being a six-four chord oddly placed upon weak beats, yet the cumulative strength and force of its slowly mounting climax does not end in the grave but in the skies. The voice of heavenly consolation, of Kornel Ujejski's "God was, God is", resounds through its trio. It is this trio, or middle section, which seems to reflect an upward gaze and brings a ray of hope with its sweet melody in the relative major key. Once I heard that magnificent pæan of heartsick lamentation, the Chopin "Funeral March", played over the ivy-wreathed coffin of a girl-soldier fallen on the battlefield, struck down by Cossack *nahajkas* and sabered to bloody death in the Bolshevik war of 1920. But when that sorrowful cortège had passed out of view, its mournful strains dying in the distance, my eyes were not on the grave, but on the Polish flag flying bravely though at half-mast over the Zamek where Paderewski had governed. I could still hear, overtoning above the sad funeral strains, the rousing fanfare of trumpets, joyous and jubilant, that Chopin put into

---

* "Studies in Polish Life and History," by A. E. Tennant, F.E.I.S. London: George Allen & Unwin, Ltd., 1924.

his Polonaise in A Major, just as, in the national anthem played everywhere in Poland on the Third of May, the anniversary of the establishment of the Constitution of 1791, I could hear the jubilation and thanksgiving of a whole people rejoicing over a new-found freedom.

Paderewski's earliest consciousness was stirred by the music of his people. Yet "joyous in the presence of Infinity", he responded to it in his own way as he lived out his boyhood on those same Ukrainian plains that turn the soul of his Russian brother inward. The suicidal finale of a Tschaikowsky's Pathetic Symphony was not in Paderewski's Polish lexicon of music. If he was born of an exile-mother, of a father imprisoned for patriotism, if Siberia with its chains and its gates of iron was something of his earliest intimate knowledge, he was still the son of a people whose special grace is the power to hope, to survive, and do. The national music with which he became familiar in his youth was an integral factor in the shaping and direction of his life, not alone as artist but as patriot. "The Pole, listening to Chopin," as Paderewski himself has said, "listens to the voice of his whole race." He heard that voice in his youngest days echoing the joyous refrain of Dombrowski's Song of the Legionnaires: "Have no fear! Have no fear! Poland is still alive. March on, March on, Dombrowski! It is joy to live, to sing, to fight! March on, March on Dombrowski! Poland is still alive!"

V

PRAIRIE BOYHOOD

ONE evening some years ago when Paderewski was the house guest of a physician friend, the doctor insisted on him staying indoors because of a heavy cold. The family went out and Paderewski was left alone with a little boy in the house. "Subjected to a volley of questions," as Paderewski himself tells the story, "I was finally cornered into admitting as the ultimate cause of my ailment and seclusion, 'I was foolish.' Whereupon my inquisitive little friend jumped to the conclusion, 'So you were small?'"

"Yes, incredible as it seems, Paderewski too has been small," as Stojowski observes in telling the story in "The Young Music-Lover". But that is incredible only to those who know him merely as a public figure. To his intimates he remains still a grown-up boy, a "larger growth" of the bright-haired youngster who lived out a happy, wholesome and not to any small degree a prankish country boyhood. The pranks are still played, as numerous stories told by his friends testify. He is a born tease, as Madame Modjeska used to say, relating the terrific scoldings he would give her for her bridge-playing. Guests who have been entertained at his Paso Robles ranch-house in California, guests in his home at Morges in Switzerland, know the jokes he would play on them—a favorite being the placing of a dummy under the covers of the guest-bed, the dummy fashioned of stuffed pillows and stockings—with the world-famous artist hiding behind the door, perhaps, to watch the comic effect of his surprise. Chopin, in his own way, had that in him, the saving grace of humor and playfulness.

Paderewski was a healthy boy and his life was the life of a

normal youngster, gay and alert, growing up in the customary environment of lessons and play. Family fortunes brought changes. After the tragedy of Kurylówka his father moved to Sudylków in Volhynia, to fill the post of administrator of the estates of Count Tyszkiewicz, while young Ignace Jan and his sister Antonina two years his elder, were sent for the time being to the home of an aunt at Nowosiolki, near Cudnów, to enjoy a riotous interim of no lessons and all play. They were inseparable companions, and such they have remained throughout the years, the sister returning to her brother in her widowhood to become in time the guardian angel of his home in Switzerland during the long absences of Paderewski and his wife on tour. During the trying years of the World War, when the Paderewski home at Morges became a refugee camp for fugitive Poles, Madame Antonina Wilkonska dispatched the management of the estate and its pensioners with a skill and tact worthy of her brother.

Established at Sudylkow, the father brought his motherless children to their new home. Later he remarried. Lessons were resumed. The old Polish system of home schooling, of governesses and tutors and parental instruction and discipline, was a rigorous one. It laid solid foundations in the elementaries; the Three R's were not neglected for fancy fads. The mind was trained and sharpened. It was such a system that made French a second mother-tongue for all educated Poles. Three languages were the ordinary equipment of Polish children in those parts, Polish, French and Russian, the latter of necessity; this same facility in tongues no doubt played a part in making possible later on such amazing achievements in English as those of Conrad. Paderewski's command of English fully equals Conrad's. His linguistic achievements, as a matter of fact, are remarkable. He is master of seven tongues—Polish, English, French, German, Spanish, Russian, and Italian.

But it was not all study for young Ignace. With whatever industry he applied himself to his books, or with whatever docility he submitted to his music lessons, he ran from the house when his lessons were done with all the untamed energy of a

healthy and energetic youngster. Sometimes when the old music teacher, Runowski, arrived, young Ignace "skived" and was
found hiding in a treetop. There were orchards to explore with
his playmates, the green leafy darknesses of willow-lanes to
penetrate, duck-ponds to paddle in, the stream to go swimming
in, winding footpaths to travel on through fields knee-high with
wildflowers, meadows red with wild strawberries. There were
stables and stable yards with stumbling calves and long-legged
plush-coated colts to be inspected, a flotilla of ducks on the
pond to be teased and fed, a flock of peacocks to be roused to
proud display;—a thousand things for a boy to do besides
study and practice piano scales.

Like all boys he had a special delight in playing soldier. This
was the favorite pastime whenever there chanced to be a group
of playmates in the house come to join him and Antonina for
an afternoon. On such occasions the guests were escorted to the
attic playroom, where, amidst the confusion of old trunks and
venerable pieces of discarded furniture, the miniature hostess,
with miniature cups of doll-china, served her tea in grandame
fashion, but where especially the lively young host soon had
his guests divided into opposing military camps, the Polish
camp and, of course, the enemy camp, invariably Russian.
There was a wooden hobby-horse, a noble steed for the commander to ride to battle. Mounted on this, a Polish *czapka*
with flaunting peacock feather jauntily set atilt on his ruddy
curls, a toy sword flourishing in his hand, Ignace Jan led his
forces. Sometimes the fray went hard and fast and always the
Russian army got the worst of it, but if more than once "the
enemy" went home battle-scarred, just as often Ignace bore
the proud marks of conflict. Always he saved Poland.

If Ignace had his first lesson in music he had likewise his
first lesson in horseback riding—something the Polish boy of
the countryside never misses—with the whole family out on the
veranda to watch him take the saddle, and all the prairie-like
expanses of the Volhynian plains to range over. And in winter
time, outdoors or indoors, things to do. It was not all tragic
reading from the heroic poets. There were thrilling stories of

the wild-boar hunt, the favorite sport of the Polish hunter, to listen to around the evening fire; there were festivals and parties, especially during Christmastide. Christmas brought the *kolendy*, the old-time Nativity carols, sung by everyone, sung along the roads on Christmas Eve by the countryfolk carrying their lighted *szopki*, miniature Bethlehem theaters, and sung again on Christmas day around the straw-strewn table, for, rich or poor, "Bethlehem straw" always bedecks the Polish Christmas table. Outdoors there was the fierce delight of ice-skating on the frozen duck-pond, the wild dash of shining sleigh-runners skimming over white roads to the clear jingle of harness bells, the dry white spray of snow stinging his rosy cheeks. Sleighing parties to neighboring houses—the traditional *kulig* —were likewise a part of the life of wintertime Poland, and if Ignace Jan was too young to join them, or his motherless home perhaps too modest to be included in them, he knew the sound of merrymakers' voices singing lustily under skies ablaze with blue-bright stars; such old fashioned *kuligs* as Modjeska tells of: "The night was dark. Over twenty tiny sleighs were waiting . . . at the side of each of them a man on horseback with a torch in his hand, and this train of sleighs headed by a small band of musicians. As soon as we started a jolly air of Krakowiak resounded in the air, filling the hearts with merriment. Many windows opened to see our folly, many people sent their laughing 'Hurray' after us . . . Then a wild ride . . . we were almost flying in the air . . . the snow sent up by the horses' hoofs was beating in our faces, the men with torches looked like demons on their nocturnal ride . . . We stopped at the door of a country house, the large hall brightly lighted . . . refreshments . . . the musicians . . . the air of a *valse* . . . and dancing began . . ."

Paderewski's native region is in what is known as the Black Earth country, one of the most fertile areas in Eastern Europe. Not even in sun-golden sea-washed Ireland have I seen such miles of lush green as spreads before the eye in that lovely country of rich undulating spaciousness, broken here and there, in Podolia, by wild ravines that canyon the level scene with a

romantic suddenness, giving a strange effect of skyey altitude
to the plateau-like plain. It is, in its own peculiar way, despite
its prairie-like expansiveness, a picturesque country; it has contours of interest, a romantic sweep, well designed to influence
the mind of an imaginative boy. The wind that blows over this
country from the south, up the Dniester Valley from the warm
regions of Crimea and the Black Sea, brings to these prairies
a caress and a sultry breath that makes them seem half tropical in summer. Its gardens are famous for their melons and
mulberries, its cherry orchards in blossom-time sweep the land
with a white tide of tangy perfume. It is here that that cherry
which Paderewski calls "the aristocrat of cherries" grows, his
favorite, the rich sour Lucullian fruit which he has imported
from Poland to cultivate in his Swiss orchard at Morges. But
the chief beauty of this breezy open land where young Paderewski ran and rode and filled his lungs and shouted . . . it
is easy to see the red gold of his radiant young head tossing
above the wild poppies in the wind-waving wheat field, his
dogs barking beside him; he is fond of animals and he adores
dogs . . . the chief beauty of the Ruthenian country in the wildflowers and the wild strawberries. Going through that country in June I have felt the breeze assail my nostrils with
such a laden sweetness from the wild strawberry beds that the
air seemed as stained with color as one's feet were, walking
through the red fields. The hot sun pouring down on the distant pine trees hemming the horizon distilled their resinous
essence and mingled it with the flavorous odors of the fields
until the senses were almost drugged, as with an airy tincture
of turpentine and honey. And all the time the eyes were rav-
ished with the variegated color of the flowers, a wilderness of
crimsons and yellows and purples moving with a million dap-
plings in waves of light. This is the land the boy knew under
skies of a dim mysterious blue, skies that are so cloudless and
expansive that the wide earth seems a part of the boundless
heavens. No wonder, with his vigor and his spirit, he was
"joyous in the presence of Infinity."

He was in no sense a prodigy. The gift of music bequeathed

him, in the most from his mother, was not at first regarded as
at all a mark of genius. He was, in fact, to paraphrase his friend
Henryk Opienski, of that type of true genius which reveals
itself, not in the cradle as the shining of a mysterious star which
burns out more quickly than it comes, but rather as the steady
growth and slowly ripening fruit of work. Beyond "an extraordinary force of mind every act of which bore the imprint of a
powerful lever", a force of mind easily mistaken in a boy for
mere wilfulness, he showed no signs of precocity and certainly
none of strangeness or of oddity. There are nightingales in
Podolia, to pierce the moonlight with their unearthly sweetness of melancholy; and if the cherry orchards sweep the land
in springtime with a whiteness equalled only by the snows in
winter, winter comes, nevertheless, and there are wastes of snow
to remind the son of a patriot father, an exile-born mother, of
Siberian loneliness; long dark snow-bound days with the world
buried in a drifted silence broken only by the whistle of the
wind. There is a graphic old Polish saying that gives us, better
than do a thousand words of description, the feeling of those
desolate wintry winds blowing across the Volhynian plains:
"Someone has hanged himself the wind is so high." But neither
moonlight nor nightingale nor the burden of snowy silences,
nor all the infinity of the Ukrainian plains, caused this boy to
be a mere idle dreamer. He was not a moody *Jean Christophe;*
he remained at all times normal, energetic, an able-bodied, active youngster.

Nevertheless all of the elements of his native scene were
working in him. We know, when we hear him play, especially
when he plays his Chopin, how they worked in him, and we
know it when we hear him speak of Chopin. It is not alone
the eloquence, the grace and power, of Paderewski's Chopin
eulogy, which in English is given us in the masterful translation of Laurence Alma-Tadema, that makes this a great utterance, a pure symphony of words, a masterpiece of Polish literary style. There is a further quality in it that gives it a
vibrating timbre. It is the nostalgia in it, the subdued undertone of unquenchable homesickness, the same quality that makes

Chopin's music, even in its most glorious bursts of energy, tremulous underneath. The Chopin oration, delivered in 1910 when Paderewski was fifty, was given in the then "Austrian" city of Lwów, a city which was an ancient capital of Polish culture, but one which, though it was near to his native region, he could scarcely know in his boyhood days, because those were the days of Cossack-patrolled frontiers when it was almost impossible for divided families to get permission to visit each other. Thirty-seven years had passed, in 1910, since he had left behind him the home scenes of his native Ruthenia, thirty-seven years of high adventuring around the world. But every word of that utterance chimes with an echo of his childhood: "Under the sad skies' vague blue he sees the wide plains upon which he was born, the dark edges of distant forests, plough-lands and fallow lands, fruitful fields and sterile sandy stretches. . . . A gentle hill has risen, at whose feet the twilight mists hover above the green hollows of the meadows; the gurgling of brooks reaches his ears, the scant leaves of the birch rustle tearfully, a soft wind plays in the tall poplars, strokes the green waves of yielding wheat; a perfumed breath blows from the ancient pine forest, wholesome, resinous . . . unearthly half-forgotten beings come to life in the spring night . . . phantoms without number haunt field and meadow . . ."

When we look back on Paderewski's past through his own eyes, when we listen back to it through the *intima* of his poetic language, we know what was happening to that ruddy golden-headed boy of the Polish countryside. Did the little fellow, we wonder, watch the guests in his father's house or in some neighboring manor, gathered in old Polish fashion to pace through the majestic measures of the native dance?—those measures which, in the *polonaise,* seemed to Liszt to be "the firm, the hard, the resolute tread of men bravely facing all the bitter injustice which the most cruel and relentless destiny can offer, with the manly pride of unblenching courage"? The *polonaise,* according to Brodzinski, a Polish authority, "is the only dance which suits mature age and is not unbecoming to persons of high rank; it is the dance of kings, heroes, and even of old men; it alone suits the martial dress. It does not breathe any passion, but is rather an expression of chivalrous and polite manners." When Liszt heard Chopin play the *polonaise* he saw in imagination what Paderewski's fathers had seen in reality, what Rubinstein called "a picture of Poland's greatness", a pageant of Paul Veronese figures "robed in the rich costumes of days long past . . . brooches of gold, velvets, damasked satins, silvery, soft and flexible sables, hanging sleeves gracefully thrown back upon the shoulders, embossed sabers, boots yellow as gold or red with trampled blood, sashes with long and undulating fringes, close chemisettes, rustling trains, stomachers embroidered with pearls, head-dresses glittering with rubies or leafy with emeralds, light slippers rich with amber, gloves perfumed with the luxurious attar from the harems . . . gorgeous carpets from Persia . . . filigreed furniture from Constantinople . . . ruby goblets embossed with medallions, wine from the fountains of Tokay . . . fleet Arabian steeds shod with silver . . ." All that Liszt pictures the *polonaise* to be I have seen and felt when the Poles danced it in antique costume— a dance that leaves in my memory one single recollection, the impression of a color-tone—purple; purple and regal; brave majesty.

"A way there," Paderewski cries, bringing it all back as he remembers Chopin and recalls his own boyhood days, "in the stately manor lights are flaring in the halls; great nobles, county electors maybe, are gathered here in a colored glistening throng. Music sounds. My Lord Chamberlain, or whoever present be most dignified to rank, steps forth to lead the *polonaise*. There comes the clank of swords, the rustle of brocaded silks against wide sleeves, purple lined. With dashing step the couples march on proudly, while soft, smooth words begin to flow towards fair cheeks and lovely eyes—the glib words of the old Polish tongue, well interspersed with manly Latin and with here and there a timid touch of French."

The Pole is born with his toes tingling. The dance is an integral part of Polish life, and young Paderewski, growing into his teens, came to know, whether in his father's house or in the houses of neighbors, or on the foot-beaten green before some peasant's thatched cottage, every step known to his people. "The dancing lilt of his native Mazurka . . . the crisp swing of the Krakowiak," the whirling Oberek, the stately *polonaise*, even the ancient "Song of the Hopvine", dating back to pagan times and still sung at peasant weddings; all of these native dances wove their measures into his receptive being and went into the shaping of his genius. And even in this music of pastime there was for him, though as a boy he was unconscious of the fact, a significance beyond that of mere pleasure. "The seeming gayety of Polish society," we are told, "—and nowhere, as Brandes points out, was the life of society so important as in that land where there was no other life—its dancing and music, were conscious manifestations of nationalism." Chopin's *mazurkas* are described by Ehlert as "pathetic dances in which the deepest, the most heartfelt sorrow has donned red buskins to weep itself to death amid a bacchanal tumult." "I have one of those in my mind now," Ehlert continues: "anything sadder you can scarcely imagine:—

> "*Ye still must dance, poor feet so weary*
>   *In gay shoes drest,*
> *Though 'twere for ye a fate less sad and dreary*
>   *'Neath earth to rest.*"

The soul of the boy Paderewski caught into itself this deeper meaning as surely as it fed on the rousing strains of the native poetry he heard. When he composes now, or plays, either Chopin or one of his own compositions, it is inevitably the things he knew as a boy, the native music and dance, that he is recalling and interpreting. When we listen to the brilliant and capricious two-four measures of Paderewski's Krakowiak (Op. 14, No. 6) with the lively motion of its fantastic accented and unaccented beats, peculiarly Polish; or to the slower three-four beat of his Mazurka (Op. 9, No. 4) with its curious syncopation, we are hearing more than a musical performance. We are dancing back to Poland, to the Podolian and the Volhynian prairies, with a Polish boy who has never really grown up.

"On a sudden, then, they thundered out an Obertas that made one quiver to the back bone." It is Reymont, the Polish novelist, describing such a wedding dance as Paderewski witnessed often in his boyhood. "Boryna leaped to Yagna's side, caught her in a mighty grasp, and at once started such a dance as shook the planks beneath them. He wafted her down the room—back again—clanged on the floor with his horseshoe heels—knelt suddenly to her and sprang up again in a flash—bore her about from wall to wall—roared out a solo which the instruments took up and accompanied, and still led the dance, while other couples imitated him, leaping, singing, stamping; no one could discern lass from lass in the swift rush—only rainbow masses flying about, driving as by a goad, with ever-changing tints, turning always, with greater and more impetuous speed . . .

> "*Lasses, lightly treading,*
>   *Come ye to the wedding,*
>   *Hear our gleeful tune!*
>   *Hear our voices' chorus*
>   *Join with flute sonorous,*
>   *Hautboy and bassoon!*
>   *Oy da dana dana,*
>   *Oy da dana dana,*
>   *Oy da dana!*"

That lively boy, ranging the countryside and the villages around Sudylków, looked on at and joined into many such a scene as this. He heard many a peasant orchestra of string and woodwind, fiddle and clarinet, play the old dances and songs with the ringing stroke of a rod on a scythe blade to give the percussion. He knew the ancient lute of the rural minstrels, the *geśla*, with its sweet-chorded plucking of ballads and old bardic songs. He knew what it was in the native dance to go, in the words of Rygier-Nalkowska, "careering in a tiny orbit toward the centre of which we lean all the time . . . turning round and round with vertiginous speed, like two planets run mad . . . locked in each other's arms, carried on by our own impetus, gliding along with half closed eyes, with a passive motion, as if by ourselves unable to keep so tremendous a pace . . . Around us we perceive only a confused mass of thick clotted brightness; the lights, the mirrors, the brilliant circle of lookers-on, are no longer distinguishable as they fly around us, all is merged in one maze of color." He had a relish for all of that, the relish of growing and glowing youth. He was very likely the last one to wish to go home; the "White Mazur" would be his claim, for "it is a custom in our country," Modjeska wrote, describing the Polish dancing parties, "to dance all night, and the feature of those balls is not a cotillion, which usually is danced at midnight, but the 'White Mazur', performed by daylight, if you please."

But when Paderewski looks back on his younger days and conjures them up in the name of Chopin, however madly, wildly, he may make the music of his native dances resound, memories and longings breathe their undertone up and down through his cadences. He is out on the Podolian plains, in the Volhynian fields, once more, and he dreams of the past, as he was dreaming of the future then: "Summer's breath on the fields of his fathers blows softly round his soul. The sea of golden wheat has dried away, the shocks and sheaves are standing, the sickle is at rest. Light quail and graver partridges are on the wing, searching the rich stores of the stubble. Waves of harvest song are on the air: from marsh and pasture comes the herdsman's pipe: not far away there is the hum and bustle of the wayside inn. The fiddlers play dexterously, they play by ear, thrusting in a frequent augmented fourth, familiar, racial; a rude bass viol supplies a stubborn pedal: and our folk dance briskly, stridingly, or sing slowly, musingly—a healthy folk, wayward, merry, yet soaked with melancholy . . . In the little church across the road an organ sounds, poor and humble . . . One hears the measured drops of the autumn rain, the soft thud of withered leaves falling to earth, the mournful rustle of the orphaned branches . . ." So does he tell the story himself in his beautiful eulogy of Chopin.

"Is this life's Autumn?" Paderewski asks, as he conjures up the scene. His answer is characteristic: "No; it is rather Autumn's life that here begins." If "the days are shorter, the light wanes," if "the old timepiece that measured fairer days for our grandfathers and great-grandfathers now solemnly strikes a late, a midnight hour," if "the gloomy wind howls in an empty chimney," if "the old graveyard is full of ghosts": though all this be true, and all too wistfully vivid to the man of years as he looks back upon his youth, still the boy remains, the bright-headed golden-haired country boy, busier at his play than at his books and his music-lessons.

By the time Ignace is twelve, however, Pierre Sowinski has convinced the father that his boy has exceptional talent. Jan Paderewski, the hard-headed, hard-working gentleman farmer has seen no marks of anything like precocity in his young son. And he is poor; a musical education, a career for Ignace Jan, seems something beyond his purse. That means sending him away to the Conservatory at Warsaw, an expensive luxury. And it means something more, the sending into the strange world of a large city an adolescent youth, temperamental, irrepressible, full of the warm sap of life; a very serious matter.

But the boy has caught fire now. He knows what he wants. He wants music. He wants to be a musician, he wants to be a composer of music—he wants to "make music". Doubtless Sowinski has had something to say on that score; he has seen the boy's gift and he counsels nothing but the best for him. If he is to go he must go to the top.

After nearly two years of debating and considering, the pressure on the father results in his consent. At twelve Ignace leaves the old home. . . . He is climbing up after his father into the seat of the *bryczka* to be driven off on his great adventure . . . he is looking back at the pillared porch among the trees where the family stands waving him goodby . . . there has been weeping; the old servants who have loved the noisy mischievous boy have embraced him with tears and blessings; Antonina, the sister and playmate that he loves so dearly, is looking bravely at him with wet eyes; the governess is openly crying; the old music teacher's eyes are glistening . . . Ignace Jan sees the roofs of home disappear among the treetops as the *bryczka* wheels gayly away down the dusty road. . . .

All the heartstrings pull tight in him at the last view of home; the strong hand of home affection strikes across them a chord that will vibrate through his being as long as he lives. But the sun is bright on his tawny head. . . . Warsaw is around the turn of the long road . . . great things are waiting . . . adventure, work, study, the world . . . music!

The twelve-year-old boy looks up with a manly smile into his father's face . . . but neither speaks. It is a big moment in the lives of both of them.

VI

FRIENDS AND INSPIRATIONS

IF IT was easy for us to see in our imagination the red-gold head of young Ignace bobbing over the poppied wheat as he ran at play in his native fields, we can see him now, a boy of twelve, as he arrives in Warsaw on an autumn day in 1872. He is almost twelve; his birthday is a few weeks ahead, in November. Doubtless, walking beside his father in the city streets, he feels very grown up.

Coming in at the Brest station, in the suburb of Praga, the boy soon caught an inspiring view of the capital—the broad Vistula with its bridges, the yellow walls and graceful cupola of the Zamek, the colorful skyline of spires and domes, the gay sprinkling of red-tiled roofs in the Staré Miasto, the old mediaeval city. Warsaw then, as now, was one of the real capitals of Europe, crowded, bustling, with fine broad streets, open squares, imposing public buildings. It was of course, in 1872, a "Russian" city, because Russia ruled it; but it was not Russianized. No better exemplification of what Conrad said about Poland belonging to the Western world could be found than in the makeup, the external apppearance, the atmosphere, the personality, of Warsaw. Myself, each time I have come out of Russia into Poland and have approached the Polish capital, I have felt almost as if I were returning home.

Young Ignace, rounding out his twelfth year, was a well grown boy, and a bright one. He missed nothing. What he saw that first day, sixty years ago, can of course be reconstructed only from memory; half a century has brought as many changes to the Polish city as it has brought to the Polish man—then a boy, but now, even yet, as Warsaw is still Warsaw, the same

Ignace Jan Paderewski who had just come up from the country, full of life and ambition. Perhaps we can find no better picture of the Polish capital of that memorable hour in his life than that given by his friend Madame Modjeska. She is writing of a time only three years earlier. She calls Warsaw "the heart of Poland". "No name," she says, "could better fit that city, throbbing with never extinguished love of the country and mutual love of people because of the chains, wounds, and constant terror which link that sensitive, warm-hearted imaginative mass of human beings so closely together that they seem like one body . . . 'Heart of Poland' indeed, for the blow at it disabled the whole body." Less than a decade had passed since the last blow had been struck in the crushing of the insurrection of '63, in which Paderewski's father had suffered imprisonment, in which Warsaw had been left torn and bleeding.

The picture that Modjeska gives of the Warsaw she first saw is, we may safely say, the Warsaw that the boy Paderewski saw when he stepped from the train and into the streets of the capital that day in 1872. "Streets, public squares, and parks swarm with people; young men with bright faces, latest fashions, and that nonchalance which can be seen only in large cities; beautiful women trotting on their small, perfectly shod feet, and shading their eyes with parasols often used as shields against the bold gazes of men; sweet-faced and white-haired matrons escorting their daughters; children; men and women of all stations; rich and poor; and among them, here and there, the brilliant uniforms of Russian gendarmes. But"—perhaps young Ignace had the same thought as he thrilled to the electrifying impact of a great city for the first time—"who cares if even a million official eyes are watching around? 'Life' seems to be written on every face, to vibrate in every countenance; the whole city is sparkling with it, and there is such a tremendous current of sympathy in the air that strangers meet each other with a smile upon their lips, ready to call each other friend."

We can be sure that life glowed in his young face, and just as sure that, though he was a stranger, he did not feel too strange. A nature of this kind has a genius for adapting itself to new environment. The winning charm of Paderewski's personality is known today in many of the capitals of the world; to it is often attributed a large portion of his success. It is a gift, and assuredly it worked in him as a boy when he came to the capital of his own land. In fact we know that it did, for we know that scarcely was he installed at the Conservatory before he had made fast friends.

The Warsaw Conservatory was an old institution, rich in tradition, when Paderewski came to it. Chopin had studied there. But it had been closed by the Russians during the revolution of 1831, and not reopened for thirty years, till 1860, so that now, in its new status, it was actually the same age as its newest and youngest pupil. Already, by the distinction of its teachers and the vigor of its direction, weathering successfully through the turmoil and ruin of the Uprising of '63, it had proved its standing and permanence. The teachers to whom the boy Paderewski was assigned were of the highest rank, although the school had just lost, a few months before through the death of Moniuszko, famous as the author of the opera "Halka", its most eminent figure. Ignace's first piano lessons at the Conservatory were from Sliwinski; from him he graduated to the direction of Schlözer, Strobl, and Janotha, the last named being the father of Natalie Janotha, a famous artist later a figure at the English court in Victorian days. In theory and composition he had an able and judicious mentor, Roguski, former pupil of Berlioz. He was in good hands, and he was quickly liked, not alone by his teachers but by the Director of the Conservatory, the well-known violinist Apollinary Kontski, and by the matron, the Director's wife, who was at once attracted to the radiant—and, as he turned out to be, the mischievous—boy from the borderlands.

But these were not the only friends he made on his arrival. "The closest, the dearest friend in my younger days," Paderewski has told me, "was Antoni Rutkowski, pianist and composer, who died in 1896." This gifted artist, whose creative powers were exceptional, lived long enough to see his boyhood companion reach the height of fame; but himself only in his thirties when he died, he might have achieved high rank, especially as a composer, had he been spared. Paderewski to this day laments his loss. And there was another friend. At the boarding-house where his father had established him he found a young violin student, Ignace Cielewicz by name. The two Ignaces quickly organized a partnership.

There was much for a boy in his teens, fresh from the countryside, to see in the capital, and although young Ignace could no longer, when the play spirit called him, perform gymnastics in a treetop to hide away from his lesson, he managed to do a good deal of excited exploring during those first days in Warsaw. With his chum Rutkowski as guide, what sights to see, what places to go! There was the broad Vistula flowing at his feet, "Our dear river" as the Poles call their historic stream and as the novelist Zeromski names it in the title of one of his books. There was the Belvedere, once residence of Polish Kings, set in its great park out beyond the lime-tree bordered Aleja Ujazdowska, one of the handsomest avenues in Europe; and in the old royal park there was the beautiful little Lazienki château of King Stanislas, mirrored in the golden waters of its lagoon; nowhere in the world is the gold of autumn leaves minted so lavishly as on the deeply tree-lined shores of the Lazienki Lake. There was Vilanov, another Versailles, the palace of King John, the brave Sobieski who, playing Poland's historic rôle of Christian barrier against the Eastern infidel, had saved Western Europe, driving the Turk from the beleaguered gates of Vienna.

Again there was, like an inspired symbol commingling all that Polish history and Polish art can mean to a Pole, the tiny shrine of the Mother of Sorrows, "the Queen of Poland", set amid the trees of a green triangle that faces the Zamek. John Sobieski put that shrine there. The blue perpetual flame of the little lamp that is kept burning before it, that had burned for two hundred years when the boy Paderewski first saw it, has in its steady glow more than the royal gesture and the deathless faith of the Pole. In its tremulous light the matchless "blue note" of Polish music, the note that Chopin first sounded, radi-

ates like the beam of a far off star. Soon after Ignace came to
Warsaw, winter came. In winter that blue flame turns the snow
around the shrine and the frosted branches of the trees that
shelter it to a magic web of light, light that is like that captured moonlight of a Chopin nocturne. Something like the pain
of star-points piercing his breast must have assailed the youth
as he stood before that shrine dedicated to the "Queen of
Poland", feeling its beauty and realizing what it signified of
Poland's past glories.

It is a characteristic of the people of oppressed nations that
they know their history. Young Ignace, like every other Polish
boy, was well versed in the story of Poland's past. "Whose
spirit there went past?" he asks in his Chopin eulogy. "Was
this Zolkiewski? Or Czarniecki's noble shade? Were those the
traitor brothers Boguslav and Janusz Radziwill? Or Radziejow-
ski of equal stain? Was this not the lofty figure of Kordecki?—
luminous still in this hour of darkness with the light of Jasna
Gora? Was this not Sicinski of dishonored bones? Here perhaps Rejtan the patriot or Potocki the renegade marshal of
Targowica. Here perhaps Bartosz Glowacki the peasant hero
or Szela the infamous . . . History, though she stands at the
threshold of immortality a fastidious guardian, admits to her
sanctuary good and bad alike, provided they be only great."

Here now in Warsaw that history, Poland's past, became for
him by the marks and monuments of its memories a living present. All that he had heard of and read about in his home in
the country became, in the city, reality, and he thrilled to its
impact. No matter if the houses of Polish kings were now the
residences of Russian governors. The Vistula still flowed from
the Tatras to Danzig on the sea and still sang its song, "Poland
is still alive!" The heart of King John Sobieski still reposed in
its gray marble sarcophagus beside the high altar of the Transfiguration Church which he had erected in 1693 as a votive for
his victory over the Turk. There too, urned in marble and
crowned with bronze, lay the heart of Stanislas Augustus,
last of the Polish kings, with its famous inscription, "What is
stronger than death?—Glory and love."

In the Palace Square, in the heart of Warsaw stands a column of Krakovian marble surmounting a fountain and topped by a bronze figure of King Sigismond III holding in one hand a sword, in the other a cross. I can see the boy Paderewski looking up at it as he hears its story. For during the days of Poland's travail, a story had grown around that monument erected to the King who, in the sixteenth century, had made Warsaw the Polish capital. The legend was in the manner of a prophecy: "When Sigismond shakes his sword Poland's freedom will come."

To the Pole, by some called superstitious, such things are possible and credible. They are credible and possible to him because, being at heart a mystic, he accepts the fact that life is full of wonders, revealed and unrevealed. Whether young Paderewski, fresh from the land and open-eyed at the marvels of the capital, believed literally or not in the legend of Sigismond's sword—I think he would have—is not so much to the point as is the fact that he did believe, ardently and wholeheartedly, in the moral of the story—that Poland would yet be free.

He could not have dreamed that day, a boy of twelve, that in Zamek Królewski, the royal palace which he faced as he looked up at the King's statue, he himself would yet be seated, the leader of a liberated Poland, its first Prime Minister.

Nor could he foresee the strange coincidence by which the prophecy of the legend would come true. For it did literally come true. And the happy irony of it is that it was the oppressors of Poland themselves who made it come true. When the Russians left Warsaw for the last time in 1915, pursued by the Germans who were in turn to be driven out, they blew up the great Poniatowski Bridge across the Vistula, a few streets away from Palace Square. The repercussion of the dynamite explosion shook the city. Sigismond shook his sword.

But the name of King Sigismond had for young Paderewski another significance beside that of a free Poland. Sigismond to him meant also music. There had been two Sigismonds, Kings of Poland, who had been famous as patrons of music, Sigismond the Old, the first to rule the land under that name, and his son Sigismond Augustus, whose royal chorus and orchestra had been considered the best in sixteenth century Europe. Music as an active tradition in Polish life was something that young Paderewski knew without being told of it; he felt it. From the earliest times the musician had been favored. A brilliant Polish school of ecclesiastical composers, now largely ignored or forgotten, had flourished. The University of Cracow, founded in 1364, had had an endowed chair of music. It was Poland that gave to the world of music, in 1627, the original form of the *concerto*, in which the composer Jarzembski made the first attempt to translate objective impressions into instrumental score. It was the Polish composer Gomólka who had introduced, even before the Italian Monteverde of Cremona, "the Wagner of the Sixteenth Century", the bold effects of unprepared sevenths and ninths, "exciting thereby", as de Zielinski tells us, "the wrath of the orthodox composers of the day." If Ignace Jan, returning to the Conservatory with his companion, often was silent walking the streets that had echoed to the tread of Polish kings, of free Poles and of Poles in chains, it might well be that he was dreaming of a new Sigismond yet to come, not only waving the sword of freedom, but the baton of music; a Polish ruler of the future returning to the Zamek . . . the picture of a regal train moving in stately procession to the strains of native music . . . a Zamek with its throne room reopened . . . the pageantry of a royal *polonaise* danced in the gala halls of the marble Bacciarelli ballroom of the old palace . . . a Poland restored under a patron of the arts . . . music . . . a royal commission . . . Who might the favored composer of the new Poland be? . . .

Boys' dreams . . . but no dream so fantastic as the undreamed dream that came true—the composer himself the ruler . . . the ruler-composer Ignace Paderewski himself in the Zamek palace.

Something more than a dream stirred the boy's heart when he stood for the first time before the old seventeenth century Church of the Holy Cross, an historic place where the people

had assembled by the hundreds in the days when the Rising of
'63 was afoot. It was not the graceful Italian lines of Giovanni
Bellotto's design, nor the fine Fontanna towers that held him.
It was a shrine in the crypt. The heart of Chopin is buried
there. Chopin's heart!—the flaming, tender, patriotic, music-
filled heart of the one artist who above all others has uttered
the cry and the song of Poland.

Everything that life could mean to such an ardent young
heart as Ignace Paderewski's vibrated to him out of that crypt:
Poland. And Music. To him the heart of Chopin was indeed a
veritable "cup of trembling", brimming over with love of
patria and love of art. He read with glowing eyes the inscription on the urn: "Where your treasure is, there shall your heart
be also."

Those stirring thoughts which Paderewski was to speak in
his Chopin panegyric nearly forty years later were even then
nursing themselves in his breast; they seem now like an echo of
his thoughts and feelings as he stood for the first time before
the urned heart of the master. "Here, at this very moment,
there rises amid us, above us, the radiant spirit of one who
Was. What light, what valor, what energy was in him!—what
strength of endeavor he showed in the midst of suffering!
Through trouble and affliction, through heartache, through
creative pain, he marked to his country's glory the burning
trace of his existence. By a bloodless fight fought on the plains
of peace he assured the victory of Polish thought." Here,
silent, but speaking to the embryo-artist with throbbing eloquence, rested the restless heart of that smuggler Chopin who,
in Paderewski's own later words, "in harmless rolls of music
carried contraband Polish patriotism to his brothers across the
border",—the priestly Chopin "who, to his fellows scattered
far and wide about the world, brought the sacrament of their
martyred home."

The eloquence with which Chopin's heart, silent but not
dead, spoke to young Paderewski had in it, even then perhaps,
that command which every Pole of his generation obeyed—the
command to go forth and carry to the ends of the earth the

story of Poland's wrongs and the light of Polish culture. "Then shoulder to shoulder!" was the cry of the national poet Mickiewicz in his *Ode to Youth*. "Let us engirdle the little circle of the earth with the chains that bind us to each other. To one end let us aim our thoughts, and to one end let us aim our souls. Hail, dawn of liberty, behind thee is the redeeming sun." Paderewski heard that cry, he set his eyes on that aim, he dedicated himself to that redeeming light. It may well be that his first moment before the shrine of Chopin's heart was his moment of dedication.

Whichever way he turned in Warsaw in those days the boy Paderewski faced memorials of his country's wrongs and monuments of her imprisoned greatness. He could not escape the command. He gave himself to it in the name of Chopin, his immortal compatriot who had "beautified and ennobled all that he had touched", who "deep down in Polish earth . . . discovered precious stones of which he fashioned the most priceless jewels in our treasury."

One more excursion for the boy to make, to seal the round of his inspiration during his first days away from home. A few miles outside of Warsaw, beyond the ancient Election Plain where for two hundred years the Kings of Poland were chosen, is the suburban village of Zelazowa Wola. There, close to the old-time manor, stands a little house that is a shrine of pilgrimage for every Pole, particularly for every Polish musician, as it is for all the music lovers of the world.* It is the house where Chopin was born. Screened by a cluster of shady trees that in autumn drop their bright patines of leafy gold like tributes of delicate music-notes on its modest roof, this cottage-like home, built in characteristic Polish style, gave to the world the genius whom Paderewski from the beginning has loved and venerated. The small one-story house is divided by a passage

---

* A plan is under way to transform the Chopin birthplace into a memorial museum, to surround it by a public park and to build on the spot a refuge for disabled or retired musicians. Funds for the memorial are to be raised by a committee, of which Paderewski is honorary president, Chopin festivals, concerts, contests, etc., being given; all this in connection with the project of bringing home from Paris to Poland and placing in the "Crypt of National Heroes" in the Cracow cathedral, the remains of Chopin.

which, at its further end, opens onto a court leading to the yards and fields. Three low-ceilinged rooms open to the right of this passage. In one of these humble rooms, early on a February evening in the year 1810—the date of February, the twenty-second, that had ushered into life the Washington who was to know Poland through Kosciuszko, the Washington whose country, through his successor Woodrow Wilson was yet to proclaim at Paderewski's behest a free Poland—Chopin was born. Young Paderewski could not but stand awed, with bowed head, in that room of miracle. He knew the story, told often to him at home, of how Chopin had, literally, been born into the world to the strains of music. At the moment Chopin was born a band of peasants, on their way to a wedding with their fiddles, were standing under the window of the cottage serenading the mother with rustic strains.

Poland. And Music . . .

Ignace Jan Paderewski, aged twelve, going on thirteen, new come from the borderlands to study at the Warsaw Conservatory, had there at the capital inspirations enough, artistic and patriotic, to beautify and ennoble all his dreams and all his efforts.

VII

1872: THE CONSERVATORY

"PIANO, marvellous instrument!" Chopin once exclaimed. Old timers in Warsaw told me more than one story of how people had tried to dissuade young Paderewski from his pianoforte ambitions when he began his studies at the Warsaw Conservatory. He was even advised, when he was assigned to the student orchestra, to take up the trombone! "You foolishly waste your time on that piano which will never bring you anything," the teacher of trumpet asserted, "when, with your good lips and lungs, you are sure to get a position in the band at the variety show." Others advised the flute. Others either made fun of, or condoled with him over, his hands. His hands are small; the third and fourth fingers of each hand are of almost equal length, the thumbs are short. Paderewski's hands are not, according to convention, the hands of a pianist; although, strangely enough, they are, if the dictum of the palmist means anything, the hands of a politician. A palmist once so read his hands. The palmist for once guessed at half the truth.

When Paderewski began his studies he could hardly span an octave. But the piano was his love, nevertheless, and the piano he would have. Perhaps it was as much the challenge in it as the beauty of its effect that attracted and held him. He may have felt that challenge instinctively, even in the beginning, even as a boy. To the true musician, the creative artist, the challenge of the piano is irresistible because it is so complete an instrument. It does not live on some fragment of melody, it does not sing with a single voice like the violin or any other stringed instrument, but like the organ or like the whole orchestra it is myriad-voiced. Whoever carries an entire world within his heart finds in the piano a world ready to take in and transmit every shade of emotion. The very fact that the piano is, of all the instruments, the most orchestral, may have drawn him; for in all of his keyboard compositions, as time more and more was to reveal, there is a strong orchestral inclination, an attribute in which he stands out in marked contrast with Chopin, although a French composer, George Migot, in an interesting essay, has called attention to the "orchestration" in Chopin's piano-style, too. This is only another way of saying that perhaps it was the essential largeness of the pianoforte, its self-sufficing quality with its "unity in variety", that moved Paderewski to his choice. What he himself has called "the fused sonorities which the use of the damper pedal and of sympathetic vibration gives to the piano" had magnetized him from the start. He is a devotee of polyphony, and the piano, alone among instruments, would give him polyphony in the full measure which his special genius demanded. He had too many things to say in music to find satisfaction in any but the most ample medium. That is where the satisfaction promised. But also, whereas in the orchestra each instrument lends individuality to the melody which it carries, in the piano all the instrumental differentiation must be accomplished by the performer. That is where the challenge lay.

But if one may speculate on Paderewski's choice of instrument—for in the end it must be all speculation, since that choice was so instinctive that even Paderewski himself could not explain it—there is another factor to consider, and it is the chief one. Paderewski is first, last, and at all times, a poet. It was the poet in him that made him desire from the beginning to compose music. The poet sings. Paderewski's avowed purpose, the whole motivation back of his entire pianistic career, has been and is to make song, to make his instrument sing. That is what he was doing as a small boy back home in the days when Runowski dragged him from his improvising to drive him to his practicing; he was singing, singing by himself, singing in his own language, which is music, the songs of his own inner being. That is what he has been doing all his life, singing, singing his own songs, singing the songs of other masters, making the piano sing. Finally, it was not really a matter of choice at all, except insofar as the boy did withstand the contrary counsel of others and insisted on going his own way. He was born for the pianoforte. It was instinct that first drew him to it, no matter what deliberation entered later into his realizing that to be a composer he must master the instrument of the master-composers. The remark often made by people after hearing Paderewski play, "He loves his piano", is literally true. "Assuredly the piano," he says himself, "is the greatest of instruments. Its powers—who has yet been able to test them to the full? Its limitations—who shall define them? No sooner does one fancy that nothing further can be done to enhance its possibilities than inventive ability steps forward and gives to it a greater volume, a more velvety smoothness of tone. It is at once the easiest and the hardest. Any one can play the pianoforte but few ever do so well, and then only after years and years of toil, pain, and study."

So he began his "years and years of toil, pain, and study"; so, in spite of adverse counsel and too-small hands he commenced his life work as a pianist. Work, practice, exercises, more work, more practice, more and more finger-stretching exercises; but before long there was an easy span to show; in time a whole decima. Now, perhaps, he began to appreciate the worth of his first master, the old teacher Runowski, who had forced on him such tiresome hours at the keyboard back in Sudylków. Runowski had taught him how to work.

The hours he spent at the Conservatory on muscular development alone were many, long, and arduous. Nor was this regulated labor merely a discipline to be dropped when a certain capacity was achieved. It was the beginning of a life-long discipline. Thirty years later Madame Modjeska, writing of a visit to Paderewski's home at Morges, in 1902, told how "he was never seen before luncheon, but we could hear the piano constantly. He was both composing and practicing. After lunch he retired for a short rest, and then the piano was again sending up its brilliant notes." From the beginning the fine-cutting to which he put his study of sound as music was remarkable: he would strike a note, listen intently to the vibrations which made its tone, then modify his touch over and over and over until he had these vibrations sounding exactly as his delicate sense of tonal beauty demanded. With Paderewski practice is, as it has been from the beginning, not alone time spent indefatigably, but concentration of the most intense kind. Seldom does he, even now, allow himself while practicing the relaxing interpolation of a single page of music. To this day he will deny himself such distraction while at practice; and even if he does relent to himself for a few moments, he returns almost at once to his phrasing, his staccato finger passes, his octave work. There have been times when Paderewski has practiced seventeen hours a day. Questioned as to this once, at the height of his "second" career in 1930, he admitted the fact. "Would you do that again if you had to?" he was asked. "It is appalling to think of the price you have paid and must pay, as long as you live, for your eminence. Has the game proved worth the candle?" The answer that Paderewski gave, not hastily but after reflection, is characteristic. He said very simply, "I can only tell you this: I've fought some good battles."

The ring of an iron will sounds in those words. They bring to mind a passage in Reymont's "Promised Land", a passage characteristically Polish and characteristically Paderewskian: "How terrible life is," Anka sighs. "No," comes the answer: "It is only our exactions of life that are terrible. It is only our impossible conceptions of beauty and good and justice that are terrible—because they never are realized, and at the same time they prevent us taking life as it is. That is the real source of all our sorrow and suffering." "*And of all our hope.*" That is the keynote to the *tempo rubato* of Polish life and to the life of Paderewski: "Conceptions of beauty and good and justice" which prevent men from submitting to life as mere existence, and drive them on to make life good and beautiful and just. The iron of Paderewski's will was already being tempered into steel during those first days at the Conservatory; he was learning to play on an even larger and more exacting instrument than the piano; on the manifold and terrible instrument of life's exactions and hopes that "prevent us from taking life as it is."

But this was only a boy of thirteen, and it was not in his nature that the discipline of the training which was now begun for him should make a drudge of him, suppress him. He was still the spirited youngster who back home in the country hid in trees to escape his music lesson. His young brain may have throbbed in his sleep at night with the hammer of ivory keys so that he heard their rhythmic beat pounding in his head, like an unbroken echo from the day before, when he woke in the morning to face again the new-old task of mastering himself and his instrument. But he could still play pranks and he could still run away, even if now, growing in wisdom as well as stature, it was from himself rather than from his teacher that he ran.

He didn't actually run away; but sometimes he ran wild. His capers soon made him notorious in the school. Pranks played on both teachers and fellow students gave him a name; but he had already won another name to balance it—everyone knew his goodheartedness, his generosity of spirit, his gayety and love of fun. Nevertheless, he got into trouble. Twice he was suspended for mischievous infraction of the rules, and it was only the charm of his winning personality that restored him to grace. Another time the disciplinary penalty was less severe but perhaps, to a boy in his teens, more painful. He was locked in a room by himself, condemned to solitary confinement and no dinner.

Now, no dinner was not exactly a new experience for Ignace Jan. He was poor; the allowance that his father could afford to send up from the country barely met necessities, and, boy-like, young Paderewski did not always spend his allowance on necessities. He had willingly sacrificed more than one meal for the sake of fun. Fun and meager funds had frequently reduced his ration to a glass of tea, and that is saying a good deal in behalf of fun for a boy with a healthy appetite. But to go voluntarily without dinner is one thing, to be denied it outright quite another. The wife of the Conservatory Director evidently knew this; she "knew boys", and she was fond of the auburn-headed Podolian. Ignace got his dinner, a secret feast with a few extras smuggled in by the kind-hearted matron.

He usually had companions in crime, his chums "Toni" Rutkowski and Ignace Cielewicz. The three became inseparable. They were seldom apart in their free hours; at least they were together as long as the occasion was one that left them clothes enough to go around. But when the occasion happened to be a formal one they were obliged to part, for there was not only a dire shortage of shirts between them, but only one entirely presentable suit of clothes. Short-rationed, but in their every-day garb, they could eat together; but often when it came to a good square meal they had to separate. Sometimes they took turns accepting invitations to dine out, again they drew lots to see who got the shirt and the suit—and the dinner. Comical situations with their attendant embarrassments grew out of this arrangement, stories of which Paderewski still relates with relish.

Those chance dinners which Paderewski and his chums enjoyed by turns in his first Warsaw days—in the days when he was learning how important the question of food really is—tasted good, we may be sure, to the growing boy from the Polish countryside where modest means had never meant a scant table. Food had a special flavor then as it had on a certain occasion many years later when, as he tells the story, his American chef gave him not only an exceptionally good dinner but also a very subtle rebuke. "My compliments to Copper," he said to the waiter. "Tell him the fish was superb, the entrée unsurpassable, the dessert a positive triumph." "Yes, sir." A few minutes later: "Did you give my message to Copper?" "Yes, sir." "What did he say?" "He said, sir, to please tell you that the soup was good, too."

In Warsaw young Paderewski had one elder friend who was wise enough to know that the boy needed something else besides encouragement in his art; who knew that growing boys not only can eat, but can't do well much of anything else unless they do eat. This friend was the well-known Warsaw piano-maker, Kerntopf, to whose wise patronage Paderewski senior had especially confided his son. "Edward Kerntopf was a real, good, true friend to me," Paderewski has told me. "While almost everybody was discouraging me, he believed in my future. I am more than glad to acknowledge my great indebtedness to this noble, generous, alas departed, friend." Kerntopf, in his close contact with the Conservatory, kept a careful eye on young Ignace. He was one of the first to recognize the unusual talent of the boy. He actively befriended him, interested himself in his welfare and his progress, took him into his home. The whole Kerntopf family speedily followed suit of the father in falling victim to his charm. There were young daughters in the house, there was comradeship and fun. And there were plenty of good meals. In no circles was Paderewski happier on his visits to Warsaw in later years than among these modest friends of his boyhood, and no friend of his lifetime has he mourned or missed so sincerely as Edward Kerntopf.

One story of Paderewski's Conservatory days, told in the Kerntopf household, gives a characteristic picture of the boy. Mr. Kerntopf had taken him to a certain music master to get a verdict on his talents. While the two men were conversing Ignace was left to busy himself over some music sheets. When the teacher asked young Paderewski to play, the boy went to the piano and executed a brilliant and elaborate *polonaise.*

"Splendid! This boy has genius," the music master exclaimed. "Whose music is it?"

"I think it is an Oginski Polonaise. It is an air well known in our home district."

When they had left the musician's house Mr. Kerntopf asked Ignace how he liked the teacher. "I liked him much, but——"

"But what?"

Ignace was giggling. "Well—he doesn't know what an Oginski Polonaise is."

"What do you mean? What are you laughing about? He praised you so beautifully."

"Yes, but while you were talking with him I read over his own Polonaise———"

"Well?"

"It was that that I played for him—with a few variations."

Pranks of this kind annoyed some of his elders, especially his temperamental music teachers who forgot sometimes that they were dealing with a mere boy. But there was one of his Conservatory masters, Roguski, the theory teacher who, no matter what tricks Ignace played, remained convinced of his gift and of his capacity for serious work. He encouraged him and he worked him hard.

He was still only a little fellow, twelve, thirteen, and it was indeed hard work. What was the boy doing? He was spending many solitary hours in the practice room struggling away at finger exercises. If, fatigued at times almost beyond endurance, his back aching, his fingers sore, his nerves taut, he looked up from the keyboard, it was only to see the hateful metronome staring him in the face. If he dared to look out the window it was to hear the voices of boys his own age at play—the jingle of sleigh-bells—or worse still, to see visions of the green countryside of home, of blossomy orchards and wild strawberry beds . . . the frozen duck-pond cleared for skating . . . voices under the window hallowing him to come out and play. . . .

"I can only say this—I've fought some good fights." He fought them with himself, and he fought them out on the keyboard of the piano, "marvellous instrument."

VIII

1876: YOUNG GROWTH

BUT he was doing something else besides drilling the raw forces of his talent, his small hands, his short fingers, into a regimented power of attack against the ivory enemy. He was living a life filled up more and more every day with a rich artistic experience. His friend Edward Kerntopf saw to that. Kerntopf was a leader in the artistic circles of Warsaw; and Warsaw was then, as it has remained, a musical capital. The Kerntopf home was more to young Ignace than a haven of good times and good meals. It was one of the central gathering places for the musicians of the city as well as for visiting artists. Too much cannot be said for the background of knowledge, criticism, encouragement and inspiration which that home gave him. When Paderewski, remembering his "Kerntopf days", says, as he once said to me, "I spent happy years in their house", he means more than just a boy's "good times."

Of visiting artists the greatest in the music world of that day came to Warsaw, frequently on their way to and from St. Petersburg, where the imperial patronage invited the élite of all the arts; we shall see later on how Paderewski's own invitation to the Czar's court developed into a dramatic incident. Thanks to Kerntopf, young Ignace not only heard some of the great ones in their public concerts, but met them. During the first four years of his Conservatory studies, Rubinstein, Hans von Bülow, Joachim, Wieniawski, Wilhelmj, Laub, were among those who stopped in the Polish capital. And above all there were the two greatest of celebrities from Vienna, two who were yet to play a large part in the making of Paderewski's first public triumph: Leschetitsky and his wife Madame Essipoff.

Besides all these, there were the leaders of Warsaw's own music world. There was Ludwig Grossmann, captain of Poland's Bohemia, whose overture "Marie" was based on a favorite poetic legend out of Paderewski's home country of Volhynia, and whose comic opera "The Ghost of the Voyevode" was a popular success. There was Zelenski, composer of operas and successor to Moniuszko of "Halka" fame, a Zelenski who, like Chopin, and like Paderewski, was known for his sense of humor, especially for his impromptu musical parodies, in which even the compositions of Chopin himself did not escape. There was Noskowski, illustrious student of Kiel at Berlin, who was in time to commend young Paderewski to the same master; and Zarzycki, for years director of the Conservatory, composer of popular songs, whose Mazurka has been played around the world by Pablo de Sarasate. There was Kasimir Hofmann, father of the famous Josef Hofmann, like his son a brilliant pianist. There were others, a galaxy of artists for the boy to hear, know and admire.

Ignace Jan lived and breathed in a world of music.

Warsaw is traditionally a home of the opera and preëminently the home of the ballet. In Paderewski's youth the opera was in its hey-dey. It flourished even at the expense of all other forms of musical presentation, and this fact played its part in deciding the direction of Paderewski's growth. He was to be a pianoforte composer and a virtuoso; nevertheless he was in due time to make his mark also in the field of opera. The influences he came under during these student days, when his friend Kerntopf took him to plays and operas, were to bear their fruit.

One of Kerntopf's friends was Adam Munchheimer, conductor at the Warsaw Opera House, composer of the music of "Mazeppa", under whose baton most of the native operatic compositions were presented, compositions which inevitably colored and directed the taste of the boy Paderewski. Among these native operas Moniuszko's took first place. There was his "Halka" to begin with, with its matchless weaving of native tale and native melody and the incomparable wistfulness and sweetness of its poetic refrains. There was the same composer's "The Gypsies", "The Haunted Manor", the gem of his creative output, his "Flis" ("The Boatman") and his "Hrabina" ("The Countess"), with the colorful pageantry of its stately *polonaise*. There were many others. It may be said that the hearing of these native operas in his boyhood had much to do with the ultimate making of Paderewski as an operatic composer. Inevitably they formed his taste and inspired him with the ambition to turn some day himself to the native theme for dramatic composition. Moreover they sharpened his critical faculty, as is witnessed in a later period when he wrote occasional criticism of native opera. Zelenski's "Konrad Wallenrod", based on the Mickiewicz poem of the same name, well known to Paderewski's boyhood reading, drew from him some years afterward a carefully balanced judgment when it received its première in the Grand Opera House at Lwow. Both he and his friend Gorski journeyed to the southern city for its première, along with many other musicians; for the first presentation of this opus, impossible under the censorship in "Russian" Poland, but allowed in the more liberal Austrian partition, was a national event.

But this is anticipating. To return to his school years at Warsaw, so formative and impressionable, we find him coming to a first-hand knowledge of the supreme music of the opera, the Italian. It is one thing for a boy to pound out the "Casta Diva" of Bellini's "Norma" as a keyboard exercise, to make the acquaintance of Donizetti and Rossini from the printed sheet of a piano score, quite another to see as well as hear their music on the boards of the stage, framed in its scenic picturing, vocalized and animated with dramatic action. The music rack and the stage of the opera house, as instructors in operatic music, can hardly be compared. For a boy of Paderewski's temperament, to move from the studio to the opera-auditorium was to be set afire by the fused flames of vocal, instrumental, and dramatic art. The great Verdi of "Rigoletto", "Trovatore", "Traviata", the Verdi of the then new "Aïda", produced for the first time in Poland during Paderewski's Conservatory days, was but one of the Ital-

ian masters who became factors in his inspiration in these early
years. Italy then, as now, ruled the world of opera. From these
Italian composers Paderewski learned his first boyhood lessons
in the making of opera, to be supplemented later, of course, by
acquaintance with French works and the discovery, momentous
to any musician, of Richard Wagner.

These, too, were the days of dramatic supremacy in Poland.
Zolkowski, ranking with the best comedians of the Comédie
Française at Paris; Rapacki, actor and playwright, whose Shy-
lock and Iago were known over the Continent; Jan Richter,
famous in Molière rôles: these and others of like rank were at
their height, and nothing that the boy Paderewski could have
seen of them could fail to quicken his artistic tastes. But more
important still these were the days of Modjeska. The queen of
Polish drama, the reigning ruler of the Polish stage, was at this
time in the zenith of her powers. The boy, entranced by the
music of her husky-sweet voice sounding the cadences of Slowacki's "Mazeppa" or of Shakespeare's poetic lines, enraptured
by her electrical grace, catching fire from the tragic beauty of
her eye and brow, could not dream that the day was ahead when
Modjeska would become one of his first patrons and dearest
friends; but inescapably the indelible imprint of her genius was
etched on his soul with its pencil of light.

The stage of Warsaw in Paderewski's Conservatory days was
not second to that of the Comédie at Paris or of the Burg at Vienna. It was a rich training ground in poetics, in scenic color and
dramatic rhythm for the impressionable boy, who came often
from the Grand Theatre so emotionally excited that he could
not sleep. It is to be remembered, too, that in those times the
great dramas were always presented with musical accompaniment. When Paderewski saw Modjeska as "Ophelia" he heard
likewise Moniuszko's "Hamlet" music, the same music that
Edwin Booth used for his presentations of the tragedy in
America. The boy's sense of the dramatic in music was thus fed
and quickened not only by opera but by drama. And here we
catch sight of still another thread just showing itself weaving
into the fabric of Paderewski's career: the thought of America,

the America which was to be the vital background of his later political life. In the fourth year of his study at the Conservatory, in 1876, an American actor, Maurice Neville, came to Warsaw and gave a series of Shakespearean performances in English, "Hamlet", "Othello", "The Merchant of Venice." It was Neville who encouraged Modjeska to study English and to come to America, as Wieniawski, who visited Warsaw in Paderewski's first "Kerntopf days", had already done, filling the hearts of Polish artists with dreams of the New World. Modjeska was to be a beckoning star for Paderewski a few years later, inviting him to his first venture overseas.

The emotional and artistic excitement of the boy in these days was high. There was, for instance, a certain memorable first performance of "Othello" in which Modjeska as Desdemona, became so frightened by the realistic acting of Leszczynski as the Moor that she shrieked and ran from him, precipitating at the finale of the tragedy a scene of such dramatic frenzy that the audience, first hushed with horror, went wild. It all ended with Modjeska carried about on the stage in triumph on the shoulders of her colleagues, Signora Mariani, a famous Italian opera singer, leading them, crying out "O bellissima Desdemona! Cara! Cara!"

It was in such an atmosphere as this that the boy lived; there was something after all to recompense a small boy for loneliness from home and tedious hours in the practice room.

Nor was the underlying, ever-moving spirit of nationalism and patriotism, which constantly stirred the bosoms of all Poles and perhaps especially the artistic circles of Warsaw, ever entirely absent. Paderewski's life motto, "Fatherland first, art afterward", experienced new strengthening daily. There was one occurrence a few years later, in the days of his first acquaintanceship with Modjeska, which made an indelible mark upon him.

A group of high-school boys, boys of about the age of Paderewski when he was completing his studies at the Conservatory, "put together their pennies", as Modjeska told the story, to purchase a bouquet for her to be sent over the footlights. They

tied their bouquet, a cluster of white roses, with a red ribbon—
and in that small circumstance rested the tragedy that followed.
Now, the Polish national colors are white and amaranth; and
the display of the national colors was forbidden by the Russian
police. Nevertheless the boys were given permission, by no less
a personage than the Chief of Police himself, to make their
presentation. The next day all of the seventeen boys were expelled from their school. The following night one of the boys,
hoping to exculpate his comrades and win their restoration to
school, shot and killed himself. All Poland was stunned.
Modjeska never forgot the shock of that tragedy. The thought
of that dead boy, a bullet through his brain, never quite left
her. With what bitterness must have Paderewski, himself burning with patriotic ardor, hearing Modjeska herself recount to
him that sad story—with what bitterness must he have said
then, as he was to say so often, "Fatherland first, art afterward."

Stirred thus, his spirit in constant artistic excitement, and as
constantly impinged upon by the ever present consciousness of
alien restraint, he developed rapidly. And more and more he
worked. Roguski at the Conservatory, training him in theory
and composition, was not alone by this time in recognizing his
unusual talents. Janotha, Strobl, and Schlözer likewise knew
that they had a pupil of more than ordinary promise. At the
close of the first year, thirteen years of age, he won the first
prize in composition and piano playing.

That gave him a new push. But the long hours of practice
were no less tedious than before, and as the next following years
of hard work and iron training put him more and more in harness, he was all the more at times inclined to rebel; perhaps still
more inclined to rebel just because of the prizes that he won and
the rapid progress that he made. Actually, with his friend
Cielewicz, he was concocting a scheme which he fondly dreamed
would once and for all put an end to his period of slavery and
launch him as a finished artist.

IX

1877: A RUNAWAY

JUST about this time, not far from the Conservatory, over at the Grand Theatre which houses both opera and drama under its capacious roofs, Modjeska was writing in the diary which she kept on the blank pages of a prompt-book: "Woe to those who rest, for the night will surprise them and they will lose their way . . . Do not pity those who fly, but rather deplore those who lose their strength, or discouraged, give up the fight." It was not that Paderewski had any intention of giving up the fight. Quite the contrary. The trouble was simply this: boy-like he thought the fight was already won. At any rate he felt that it was high time now to give over the perpetual drilling and regimenting of study and practice and to take the open field. Modjeska wrote in her diary, "Movement means life!"—and he wanted to move. She had written also, "Toil is life! Pain is life!" But young Paderewski had yet to learn that lesson. "It is a hundred times better to suffer and live than to sleep!" the diary exclaimed. But this youth, winning prizes, growing fast, growing ever longer of limb and quicker of mind, and chafing under the yoke of discipline, had begun to feel that he would indeed go to sleep, flat on the keyboard, that eternal, everlasting keyboard of practice, practice, practice, unless he got away.

After all he was only proving in himself, beforehand, the truth of words he was to speak many years later, when he looked back on his youth: "Times change, people change, thought and feeling take new shapes, put on fresh garments, sons bow their heads unwillingly to that which enraptured their fathers." His head was bowed unwillingly to the yoke of training. It was only the old story over again of youth straining at the leash; in his case, straining hard, thanks to that first unmistakable mark of genius noticeable in him in his earliest years, an exceptional force of will. "Every new generation," as he himself has said, "in its hour of dawn, filled with the dreams of youth, its thirsts, intoxications and enthusiasms, thinks itself called upon to impel humanity towards heights unmeasured, believes itself an appointed pathfinder, a thinker of thoughts, a doer of deeds greater than any of those which came before. Every new generation desires beauty, but a beauty all its own."

At sixteen he had reached this point. For the time being he could no longer find the beauty he craved in the mere task of mastering the old beauty of the old masters. It was his hour of dawn, and it was filled with youth's dreams, thirsts, intoxications, enthusiasms, and if he did not actually deliberate on the problem of impelling humanity to new heights, of a certainty he did ponder the problem of putting himself ahead.

So then, during his third year at the Conservatory he and Cielewicz, the violinist—both about the same age, actually a pair of youngsters—decided that it was time for them to begin their public careers. But there was a difficulty. It was forbidden students of the Conservatory to appear in public. By the characteristically devious reasoning of boyhood, however, they concluded that they could get around this difficulty and still keep within the law by carrying out their scheme during the free time of their winter holidays. The scheme was, to make a joint concert tour.

The boys apparently did not have complete confidence in their own reasoning away of the difficulty of regulation; at any rate they did not announce their scheme to the Conservatory authorities. They planned it in secret, and they started out in secret, after many whispered conferences and deliberations in the night and behind closed doors. They had no money, but they had a thrilling time getting the scheme launched, and if the enterprise had its disasters, in the end it bore its fruit of profit also, though not of the financial profit they had dreamed of. Of course they had heard numberless stories of the fabulous fees earned by famous artists; and they were both poor; and didn't they win prizes? One way or the other, they argued, they were safe—either they would win such fame and fortune that the Conservatory would beg to have them back, just so that it might bask in the reflected glory of their achievements; or they would win such fame and fortune as to make any such thing as return to a Conservatory superfluous and unnecessary!

So on tour the two Ignaces went.

They had no manager. They were their own managers, directors, booking agents, and cashiers. The tour of the two young concert artists, pianist and violinist, was thus of course poorly arranged. It reduced itself finally, from the ordered and triumphal progress from city to city which they had imagined, to an itinerant and haphazard course from one small town to another, wherever they could secure a hall and gather an audience. Into the Polish countryside, into Russia, even down into Roumania, they traveled. And they had many trying adventures, both domestic, so to speak, and professional. Their good beds back in Warsaw, and the good meals at the Kerntopf house, took on an undreamed-of charm as they struggled with comfortless quarters and scanty food in cheap taverns and rode slow primitive wagons through the back-country regions.

One of their adventures, decidedly a professional one, which Paderewski recounts with humorous relish is of a concert given in a small Russian town where everything was in order except the most necessary of all things. There was a hall, a stage, an assured audience. But there was no piano! That sleepy Russian community saw a spectacle that afternoon—a long-legged, wild-eyed, Polish boy with a tousled mane of red-gold hair, racing up and down the sleepy streets hunting for a pianoforte to be commandeered for the evening. Cielewicz had the best of him this time; he had his violin under his arm. And you can't carry a piano under your arm. Perhaps Paderewski wished for once that his medium was not Chopin's "marvellous instrument."

At last an instrument was found. One of the homes in the town yielded a piano. It was an old upright, one that looked so battered and worn that there was question as to whether or not it would stand being moved. But moved it was; with the hour of the concert almost at hand the upright was finally installed on the stage. And then—maddening discovery—the keys stuck, the hammers wouldn't move!

Nevertheless, the concert was given, and Paderewski performed. He hired a boy to stand beside the piano with a switch and whip the rheumatic hammers back into place whenever they refused to respond to the virtuoso's commanding strokes.

The munificent sum of one hundred and eighty roubles, about ninety dollars, was the profit from this first concert tour of Paderewski; and this profit had to be divided in two. So fortune did not come to him out of the venture, although the legend, often recounted, that Paderewski made his first appearance as a virtuoso while in his teens did thus find its origin in fact.

As a further matter of fact this boyhood tour actually introduced Paderewski as a composer, though not intentionally so. Although he was supposed to be playing selections from the masters, as it turned out he was really playing his own compositions; for every time he got stuck in a classic rendition, instead of giving up and stopping he would swing into an improvisation and thus carry the performance off with a dash. It was lucky, as he would say afterward, that critics were few and far between in the hinterlands.

Returned to Warsaw with their very small earnings, it was not the meager gain that was troubling him and his confederate. The question was, would he be allowed to return to the Conservatory? He had already been twice expelled for pranks. Now he wanted badly to return. And not alone because an irate father, down in Volhynia, having learned of the escapade, was threatening him with paternal anger: not alone because he wished to keep the good will of his masters, of his friend Kerntopf, of his inspiring teacher Roguski. There was another reason for Paderewski's desire to be reinstated in the school. He had learned a great deal on that concert tour. He had learned how much he had to learn, to be an artist. In short he had learned that he still could learn.

The one great lesson that Paderewski, aged sixteen, drew from that experience was the lesson of artistic responsibility.

The Director of the Conservatory, a wise man, knew that the boy would learn this lesson, as he likewise knew that it was a lesson that no instructor could teach to him or to anyone else, no instructor, that is, but Old Mother Experience herself. So he, the Director, said nothing. There was no reprimand, no punishment. He took the boys back. And from that day Paderewski had added to his artistic stature the good Biblical cubit of self-criticism, which is the corner-stone of the foundation of artistic responsibility.

Paderewski is temperamental; he could not be the artist he is and be otherwise. But sometimes during his career his temperament, the highstrung delicate sensitivity of his nature which makes his art possible, has been misunderstood. True, in his career there have been some startling exhibitions of nerves, as for instance an occasion in Manchester, England, when he was obliged to stop in the middle of Chopin's Ballade in G Minor and leave the stage because of the unseemly noise made by late-comers; or another and still more startling *crise de nerfs* at Philadelphia when the prolonged stamp and shuffle of feet in the audience sent him leaping from the piano to stamp, himself, up and down the platform, crying in exasperation, "You see, I too can walk! I can walk *out!*" In Paris once he used polite forbearance to silence certain late-comers in the parquet who insisted on exchanging greetings with friends in a box. "When you are through," he said with quiet and burning irony. But incidents of this kind have been rare and are easily understood; invariably on such occasions the audience is sympathetically with the artist against the thoughtless disturbers.

On the other hand, when audiences have been kept waiting, as they sometimes have, for the artist's appearance, the delay has been unjustly charged to "temperament", to that eccentric wilfulness which has unfortunately characterized a certain grade of artist, not always the highest grade. "Temperament" in such cases is often only bad temper, frequently an attribute, if not indeed merely an attitude, of pretentious second-rate people. There is not a grain of this, of attitude or of pretentiousness, in Paderewski's makeup. But he is temperamental, and his temperament has as its primary and governing force the highest attribute of the true artist, a sense of artistic responsibility. It is because this is so that Paderewski will never consent to give to his audiences anything but his topmost and absolute best, even though sometimes they must suffer a delay to be assured of it. A story will illustrate.

For many years it has been the custom of Paderewski to retire immediately before a concert to the dressing room of the stage where he appears, there to remain undisturbed for a space of time, that he may collect himself, compose himself, prepare himself in absolute silence and solitary self-communion for his performance. Habit of years has made this period of recollection twenty minutes. In that twenty minutes he relaxes from all thought that may intrude upon the task before him, withdraws from every outward distraction, summons all his inward forces to the focus of the music he is about to play. When his attendant takes him to that room and leaves him, he stands guard outside, to insure Paderewski against any interruption.

One day, when the twenty minutes was up and Paderewski was duly summoned by the faithful Joubert, for many years his "guide, piano-tuner, friend", his attendant forgot a step in the dark passageway, stumbled, fell, cried out a sharp warning. Paderewski did not speak. A more "temperamental" artist might have raged. He turned silently and reëntered the dressing room; he did not even mention the matter afterward except to ask his man, "Did you hurt yourself?" In his room he remained alone for another twenty minutes. The audience had to wait. Doubtless some complained, doubtless others spoke of "artistic temperament." They could not know that Paderewski, in that space of time which delayed the concert, was recovering himself from the rude shock which his nerves had suffered, which had broken the high tension of his absorbed concentration at the moment that he approached the piano. They could not know that he did this, that he has more than once done such a thing, simply because he would not trust himself before an audience unless he could give to that audience the perfect best that is in him. He loves his art, and he is too great an artist to discount the audience as an integral part of his art. He has a highly sensitized feeling of artistic responsibility.

He got his first lesson in artistic responsibility at sixteen when he made that wild runaway concert tour.

X

1879: ROMANCE

HE WAS growing fast in these Conservatory days, growing in mind and body. Boyhood and adolescence passed. All of a sudden, maturing rapidly, though not yet to his majority, the youth whose father had brought him to Warsaw, a boy of twelve, was a young man. A beautiful young man. We have record in pictures as well as in the testimony of friends of his remarkable physical beauty. All who knew Paderewski in his youth speak repeatedly and often of "the goodness that was in him"; and his looks were as good as his disposition. As a boy he was lively, irrepressible, mischievous, but a radiant kind of a boy with natural goodness, good nature, lovableness, shining in him. As a young man, sobering with growth, the goodness in him, framed in a physique of manly comeliness, became more and more a strength that made his personality peculiarly winning. About this time Modjeska writes of him: "Paderewski's head with its aureole of profuse golden hair and delicate almost feminine features, looked like one of Botticelli's or Fra Angelico's angels." The description measured by photographs of the time is not exaggerated, although the term "feminine features" might deter one from conjuring up a true picture of the young man. Noticeable in the Polish physiognomy, among both men and women, especially among those of the blond type, is a certain rather startling refinement of feature which is best described as "spiritual." It is, doubtless, a pure evolution out of generations of idealistic suffering, an inevitable refinement of nature under the denial and aspiration which has been the history of the Poles. There is something almost transparent about it, an effect of frailness. Paderewski had this in his young face; and as the pictures tell us, he had a very fine nose, an aristocratic nose, straight but neither too sharp nor too long. His blue eyes had blond lashes, accentuating his fairness as well as the depth of the eye. His brow, as the sculptor would put it, was nobly modelled, his chin good. This fine face, with its Slavic high cheek-boned contour giving the eyes a dreamy effect, crowned with thick golden-auburn hair that had a ringleted wilfulness to it; the slender figure, keeping for many years the supple length of a stripling's, all combined to make his person not only striking, but even arresting in its beauty, at once masculine and delicate.

This was the youth, now in his senior year at the Conservatory, who one day saw among his classmates a newcomer, a girl whose modesty and sweetness, and whose talent as he quickly came to know it, attracted him strongly. That attraction alone was proof of his impending maturity; he had left adolescence behind, had passed through the gangling boy-age when girls were only to be scorned. He liked this girl. When he learned her name a new attraction was added, for her name was the name of his sister, his dearest companion and playmate back in the Borderland home for which he often suffered a severe nostalgia. She too was an Antonina.

Paderewski fell in love with Antonina Korsak. The world suddenly turned upside down for him, and inside out, and the crashing dissonance of its upheaval resolved itself into a new, a tumultuous harmony, never heard before, in his heart. The echo of that harmony chimes down through the span of thirty years when he praises Chopin; he knows whereof he speaks when he speaks of the love-magic in Chopin's music: "Out in the garden where the air is sweet with the breath of roses, with sigh of jasmine and of lily, a lovely daughter of the house, under the shielding murmur of the limes, caught in a starry Nocturne, whispers to some sad youth the tender sorrows of the summer night . . ."

Nothing is easier than to smile knowingly at the coming of first love to youth. "They just think they are in love," the wise elders say, forgetting that to think you are in love is to be in love: the conjecture and the fact are one and the same thing, both beautiful and painful, and sometimes disastrous. For any youth this is an epochal event. For the youthful artist, above all for the superior and intricately compounded artist of the Paderewski nature, passionate, poetic, romantic, idealistic, it is a tremendous experience, a revolution, an upheaval. He is shaken to his foundations—and he shakes the stars down from heaven in the cataclysm; better still, he reaches to the stars, he strikes the crystal strings to make his song. Now nothing is beyond his reach, no work too arduous, no task too difficult, to win the way through life . . . because he loves. Young Paderewski in love, with the girl he loved daily by his side, went striding through his studies with a fiery ambition. At eighteen he was graduated from the Conservatory.

Now he knew what he wanted to do. He wanted to work, to earn, to make a home, to be great and famous and rich, to be everything that would make his love a proud fine thing. He wanted to get married. A position secured that would mean a regular income, he could soon save enough for marriage. The position was offered him at once upon his graduation. He was to teach in the Conservatory. He was given the instructorship in the intermediate piano courses.

That was something for a boy of eighteen; something to write home about with pride to his father; something to make the eyes of his love shine. True, the pay was small, beggarly small, scarcely enough to live on, even when augmented by fees for private lessons. Years later Paderewski referred humorously to these hard times. He was speaking at a banquet of the Music Teachers' Association in New York. "My pianistic wisdom," he related, "was available in Warsaw to private pupils at the handsome rate of twenty-three cents an hour." But no matter; it was work, pay, a start. He was on his own. But now, if he could have had one glance at Modjeska's diary, scribbled on the back pages of her prompt-book over there across the city at the Grand Theatre, he would have echoed the words she was writing: "When I struggle I know I live! Hamlet's 'To be or not to be'—I say 'To be, to be, to be! To gather all the strength of my will and go ahead farther and always higher!' "

Now he began really to strike the crystal harmonica to make his song, his own song. He began composing.

XI

1880: TRAGEDY

"Music," Paderewski tells us, "is the only art that actually lives. Her elements, vibrations, palpitations, are the elements of Life itself. Wherever Life is she is also, stealthy, inaudible, unrecognized, yet mighty. She is mingled with the flow of rushing waters, with the breath of the wind, with the murmur of the forest; she lives in the earth's seismic heavings, in the mighty motion of the planets, in the hidden conflicts of inflexible atoms; she is in all that lights, in all the colors that dazzle or soothe our eyes; she is in the blood of our arteries, in every pain, passion, ecstasy that shakes our hearts. She is everywhere, soaring above and beyond the range of human speech into unearthly spheres of divine emotion."

Above all, music is in Love, the consummation of all emotions, the divine emotion itself. Young Paderewski in love came to know this truth. And he began to utter it. He was only nineteen when his first composition was published, his "Impromptu in F Major", brought out by the Warsaw publisher Banarski in 1879; but already, thus early, as his friend and critic Opienski tells us, that poetic ideal which has moved the whole course of his career as virtuoso and composer, the ideal of song, "to make the piano sing", is evident. Already he was making the piano "ring with a melodious line, with a large and profound sonority." He was singing. And he was singing as he had never sung before—because he loved.

Paderewski's music is at all times deeply personal. We have already seen how strongly he feels on this point: "Musical expression is never primarily national, but is personal and individual. It is so deep, so profound that it goes beyond and below nationality and gives voice to the most private feeling." The earliest published compositions of Paderewski echo with the deep and joyous disturbance of his own private feeling. But they do more. They point the way already to the marked originality of his genius, to that characteristic which makes him, in the best sense, always modern, yet always a traditionalist; and never a mere "modernist". He abominates the insincerity of forced "originality", the gallery-posing of a certain type of "modern-istic" music, and he criticizes the "impressionist" apostles of such music vigorously. When Daniel Gregory Mason once suggested that there was something akin to modern French "Impressionism" in Paderewski's Variations, he not only repudiated strongly the suggestion, but he referred back to these first days of his earliest compositions, when he was already demonstrating his own originality. "I utterly repudiate any debt to the French impressionists," he declared. A master like Debussy he admires and plays, but, as he told Mason on that occasion, "I do not believe in the modern French school, because it is not founded on tradition. It is erratic, bizarre, wayward. It strives only for 'originality'; it has no true mastery. No, there is nothing French in what you call my impressionism. I used those effects of dissonance long ago, many years ago, before they had come into common use . . . I have written this way for years, and now you tell me it is French impressionism!"

Paderewski was never an impressionist in the sense of merely striving to make an impression, not even in the most impressionable days of his exuberant youth. But he has always been original and he has been distinctly modern, even to the point of rousing the indignation of old fogies who enshrine the dead bones of tradition at the expense of the life of art. The bold strokes of harmony in his youthful Violin Sonata, which invited the castigation of hidebound conservatives, is but one exemplification of this fact. In his early Variations, in the A Minor, Op. 11, and still more so in the magnificent and truly modern Variations and Fugue in E flat Minor, Op. 21, Paderewski, writing with the full-fledged mastery of maturity, has been a daring harmonist, an innovator and a pioneer. Some of his earliest com-

positions, such as "The Flood", written in his twenties and
based on a tragic inundation of the Vistula, show distinct impres-
sionistic traits and attempts at illustration; so also do his later
Toccata for piano, "In the Desert", and such songs as the exquisite "In the Forest", which latter drew from one French
singer the exclamation, "C'est presque du Debussy!" The whole
point of the matter of Paderewski as a modern is simply this:
he is actually "modern of the moderns", because he anticipated
many so-called "modern" harmonic innovations. But he used
them with the tact and discretion of the true artist and not with
the lavish extravagance of "stunt" composers who seek to make
an impression on the public by self-advertising themselves as
leaders of "trends" and "isms".

The impressionists, in Paderewski's opinion, try too hard to
be "original"; and he has never had to do that. He is original
without trying. "They are sometimes very extreme in their
search for 'originality'", he says of them, and as a result, he
adds, they produce only a "vicious mannerism", and so doing
fall short of the true greatness which the genius of music demands. "Nothing new [in art] was ever created consciously,"
Paderewski says. "True originality has its foundations in the
soul, not in the mind, and when there is an effort to create something different it is usually a failure. Beethoven or Schumann
or Chopin did not try to be original. They were original."

Discussing at one time this question of originality and referring to Emerson's definition of "genius", he applied it to
music, striking at the root of the matter. "The genius," he said,
"is the man who has genuine and deep human relations with
others, who does not cut himself off in the search for originality, but who realizes the value of artistic tradition." "Art is
great," he once declared, "only when it bears the stamp of the
individual." But, as he would explain, there must be a metal, an
alloy, on which the stamp is to be impressed, or as Dante would
put it, a wax. The metal, the wax, is tradition. "It is a mistake
to break with traditions," Paderewski tells us: "one then has no
foundation . . . Art must be a slow and normal evolution."

Tradition is the material of the evolution, the individual is the instrument.

The whole theory of true art, as opposed to the modernistic theory of separatism, of unique and exaggerated individualism, is set forth in these words of Paderewski. He recognizes not only the value of human relations in art, but recognizes also the fact that one of the artist's most effectual means of establishing human relations is to speak to others in the familiar language of artistic tradition. Dante's Nimrod was a giant who blew a giant horn, but he spoke an unintelligible jargon and made a fearsome noise.

"When I wrote that fifteenth variation," Paderewski told Mr. Mason, "I thought to myself, 'Presently some one will label that "French impressionism".' You say I use dissonances in a certain way. I do this because I am an accomplished musical scholar. The modern French are, many of them, not accomplished musicians. They have not mastered their art; they are in some respects amateurs . . . Originality, originality—is it original to drink like this?" and he picked up a glass, as Mr. Mason reports the scene, and held it in reverse position with the wrist strained backward.

The originality of Paderewski is interesting not only to the student of music but to the student of man, of nations and of national traits; for it is not alone the expression of a highly individualized artist, it is also in a measure a national, a Polish, characteristic. It is true, as Paderewski knew, that the Poles had from the beginning manifested in music certain dispositions toward the revolutionary, as in the case of the sixteenth century composers, an inclination to go their own way regardless of artistic orthodoxy. "The formulas prescribed by the tradition of the middle ages," as de Zielinski tells us, "were not acceptable to the Polish composers, for the temperament of the Slav does not tolerate oppression or even constraint; hence, while the attention of music students in other countries was centered on the artificial application of the principles of harmony, Polish musicians, without disdaining the rules of counterpoint, showed a freedom of form and variety of rhythm exclusively Slavonic and particularly Polish." The fact of interest is this: if Paderewski, even in his early compositions, was given to a new freedom, it was not because others before him had been original, but because he was what he was, a Pole, an artist who by his very Polish nature could not "tolerate oppression or even constraint." And the more he became "an accomplished musical scholar" the more original he grew.

But at nineteen, when his first composition was published, Paderewski, who was never a freak or a prodigy, was still an amateur, not yet the accomplished musical scholar who speaks strongly with authority. Already, however, he was original, and already he was feeling his strength to the point of asserting it. But he was not straining for originality; he was simply making the piano sing, and because he was in love it sang a joyous lyric song. So his first composition appeared. It was dedicated to his teacher Strobl. He felt a justifiable pride in the appearance of those first printed sheets bearing his name. He was a composer. He was arriving. He had steady, if as yet poorly paid, employment, a regular place on the Conservatory staff. Affairs were coming on for him. He decided to get married.

Not that matters, even counting the obvious difficulties, were all running smoothly. They were not. For one thing, taking the never enviable position of instructor who returns to teach in the school from which he has just been graduated, he was finding his situation anything but easy. "Of diverse voices," as Dante says, "is sweet music made." The student turned instructor in his own classroom is the proverbial prophet in his home city. He begins to hear discord in the diverse voices. Many of the old student crowd were gone. There were newcomers among the teachers also. All were his elders. Some patronized him, some envied him. He was experiencing now, in good earnest, that phenomenon of artistic circles, "artistic jealousy". "In every artistic career," Modjeska reminds us, "and especially when one has attained a high position"—and an instructorship in the Conservatory was a high position for a nineteen-year-old boy—"one is bound to meet with jealousy." If among a high-strung temperamental people like the Poles this "Platonic envy", as Paderewski's friend Sienkiewicz once called it, is intense, there was, according to Modjeska's argument, a reason for it. Poland's "sad political condition where government persecution penetrated into the most intimate recesses of private life, causing a continual nervous tension, could not exist without demoralizing effects." The youthful teacher was made to feel those effects. On occasion he was snubbed, "put in his place", even ridiculed. Those small hands of his were not forgotten. He was not thin-skinned, there was a quality of rugged strength in his nature that kept him from being over-sensitive, and he was blessed with a sense of humor. Nevertheless it was lucky for him that he was in love, and in love with a girl who not only adored him but who, with discerning insight, recognized his genius, believed ardently in his powers and in his future.

So they were to marry. There was opposition, of course; wise senior counsel was offered against this step so serious for such a pair of children. But the will of the nineteen-year-old lover prevailed. With no money, with nothing earned except the meager pittance of half a rouble per hour at the Conservatory and whatever small stipend might come in from published compositions, the boy and girl began their life as man and wife.

He stuck to his teaching position, distasteful and poorly paid as it was. At night he composed, studied, practiced without let-up, spurred on by his courageous partner. At the same time he attempted local concert work in the hope of adding to his small earnings. He began to be known a little as an accompanist and as a soloist. But here once more he encountered some evidence of *clique*; the prestige which his Conservatory association should have given him was not always forthcoming in the full measure that he might have expected. An unknown, unheralded boy of nineteen, aspiring to popular favor on the concert stage, without backing or funds, what hope is there ever in the field of art for such a figure . . . unless, indeed, he be a transcendent genius?

But he was happy, unimaginably happy, and the domestic felicity which he now experienced—even though he and his wife were living in the pinching economy of a single room for housekeeping and more than once were speaking the words Chopin spoke in his cold room in Paris, "It would be nice to be warm" —made him a man among his fellows, a leader in the small group of young musicians which at that moment was trying to animate the musical life of Warsaw with a new and decidedly nationalistic spirit. Whether or not there was anti-nationalistic design in the marked sponsorship which foreign music enjoyed in Warsaw just then at the hands of Russian officialdom, especially in the lavish concentration on imported opera, the fact remains that the field for Polish creative talent was a restricted one. The death of Moniuszko had removed the most popular figure from the native arena; his successors were as yet struggling to break through. Such gifted men among the younger artists as, for example, Julius Zarembski, had already sought other fields; Zarembski went to Belgium, to the Brussels Conservatory, only to die. Eugene Pankiewicz, another of the younger stars, seeking fortune in Russia, was also taken early by death. There was need of a young leader.

The nationalistic spirit, so strong in Paderewski since his earliest years in the Borderlands, central theater of the Polish national struggle, was an animating force in the life of the group. Already Zarembski had done some notable things in the utilization of native rhythms in composition. So also his elders, Moniuszko, Zelenski and Noskowski, had gone to the national dances of the Tatra peasants for inspiration. And of course there was always Chopin. This is what Paderewski also would do; he would, as it were, revive this impulse. He was alive with ambition. Neither success nor fame were yet come to him, but he was riding high on the wings of happiness. In his companions, especially in his friend Antoni Rutkowski, he had the inspiration of a comradeship fired by a common zeal; in his talented girl-wife, herself both student and artist, he had his greatest inspiration, the perfect joy of perfect understanding and of tireless encouragement.

And now the heart of the young artist swelled with a new zeal, a new pride. Soon he was to be a father.

The happy months flew by. The hour came. Then, without

warning, like an unnatural night in unbelievable reversal blackening the sunrise, came a terrible tragedy. Antonina, giving birth to her son, died.

In years still only a boy, not yet of age, Paderewski, husband, father, and widower at twenty, faced this crisis. There had been no preparation for it, no warning. The shock was terrible. All the consolations of friendship, all the steadyings of stern philosophizing, could not alter the fact that the girl he had loved so passionately, his wife, the mother of his child, was dead and laid in her grave . . . Nightingales haunt the treed spaces of the Povonzki Cemetery at Warsaw; on All Souls' Day that great graveyard turns to a wide garden of flaming flowers with the thousands of candles that the people light in memory of their dead; in winter it is as white with snow as the Podolian cherry orchards are with blossoms in April. Beautiful rest, muted song of nightingales on summer night, candle flower, and the hush of snow. But death . . .

The solemn tones of the requiem Mass chanted over Antonina's bier overflowed his heart, but in that darkened moment of eternity the light of his religious faith drew up the waters to distil them not into tears to burn his heart, but into a nourishing rain . . .

His infant son lived. There was the problem of the baby's care. There was the whole problem of an entire new adjustment to life.

One thing remained to him: the memory of his wife's faith in his genius. There had been no bounds to that faith. When they had married, her parents had given her a sum of money, a dowry for her first child. When she was dying she took this money and gave it to her husband with one last loving injunction. He was to use it to go on with his studies, to make his career. He must go abroad; she had always said it. "You have great genius. You must have the best teachers in the world. When you have won your success you will repay our son many times over." She exacted the promise that he would do her will.

So the idyl ended, and the great life, "the life that is toil, the life that is pain" began.

There is an old Polish saying, "I am grown not out of salt nor out of the soil but out of that which pains me." On one thing Paderewski was determined: he would not be among those of whom Modjeska had written in her diary, those to be deplored "who lose their strength", those to be pitied "who, discouraged, give up the fight." He would keep in mind the warning of one of his favorite poets, Slowacki, "Melancholy is the stone of the drowned or the wing of the great." He would be true to the historic motto of his Polish forefathers, the motto which his own father had lived by, *majestas infracta malis,* "majesty unbroken by misfortune." "Life," he would repeat with the poet Leopold Staff, "need not be happy but heroic." Also he would be sensible, keep his head, go on. Speaking once in later years of that difficult time, he said simply, "I was a teacher at the Conservatory and I had to work awfully hard. I gave lessons from morning till night. It was not interesting. In fact it was slavery. I asked myself why I followed such an arduous profession, and I decided to become a performer since in that way I should work hard a few years and afterwards have a life of ease, to devote myself to composition as I pleased."

XII

1884: MOUNTAIN INTERLUDE

THE one outstanding fact in the next chapter of Paderewski's career is that he has grown appreciably in self-criticism. In less than five years he has left far behind him the boy who virtually ran away from his Conservatory studies believing himself already ripe for a public career. Now every move he makes is self-critical, an extension of himself toward newer growth. Very early in life Paderewski learned that hard lesson of greatness which others like him have had to learn. In this he is peculiarly like Lincoln, another illustrious country boy, though differently endowed; from Lincoln, almost at the same age, though Paderewski was even younger, were taken all the dreams of young love, of self-satisfaction and self-ease. Both rose above the tragedy.

A boy of twenty, widowed and left with an infant child to care for, does one of two things: either he stops and drops to the obscure level of the mediocre wage-earner, finding himself less than his problem; or he is greater than his problem, he solves it and goes ahead. Paderewski solved his problem, though in the solution of it he learned his first hard lesson of greatness, that self-ease and self-satisfaction were not for him. When Saint-Saëns said that "Paderewski is a genius who happens to play the piano," what he meant was that Paderewski had brains. Art and brains do not always go together. Paderewski is a striking example of what happens when they do. He is the personification of Art and Brains. He used his brains in this crisis. Stunned by his bereavement, with what might have seemed a life of blank loneliness stretching before him, Siberian wastes for his soul to wander in, he sat down and faced his situation as a practical problem. Happily he had the affectionate support of such friends as the Kerntopfs and Rutkowski; and he had the living voice of his dead wife urging him on. He found means to arrange his affairs. He placed his infant son in the care of his father. For the time being he concluded his duties at the Conservatory, securing a year's leave of absence. He made the break, he left Warsaw. He departed for Berlin, there to take up his studies again. Once more he was a student.

Among Paderewski's friends at the Warsaw Conservatory were two of the professors of highest rank, Sigismond Noskowski, teacher of composition and director of the Musical Society, for a long period the central figure of musical life in Warsaw, and Ladislas Gorski, scholar and distinguished violinist, who exerted a strong influence on Paderewski at this time and who was at all times an ardent believer in the young artist's creative powers. Both Noskowski and Gorski were former students of the German master of counterpoint, Friedrich Kiel. With these and with others of his friends Paderewski had taken counsel, with the result that in Berlin he put himself under the instructorship of the famous specialist at the Royal Academy. He was determined to master the "science" of his art.

He spent the Berlin year in arduous study. Kiel was a hard taskmaster and his student's application was severe and close. Nevertheless he managed to do some composing and to make the acquaintance of Hugo Bock, head of the publishing firm Bote and Bock, which was soon to bring out some of his earliest compositions. Besides, he heard several celebrated artists, among them the one preëminent at that time, Rubinstein. Better than that he met Rubinstein, who had seen him in Bock's salon and had been attracted by his striking face. Better still, he played for Rubinstein some of his own compositions. Rubinstein was impressed. "That is new! That is good!" he exclaimed. And then he said something else that especially pleased the youthful artist. "You play like a composer." "I really listened to him as a composer," Rubinstein remarked to Stojowski years after: "I did not know at the time that he had any pianistic ambitions. But he must know his business. He has great successes, I hear, and the crowd does know." Herr Bock took delight in telling of his bringing young Paderewski to the attention of the great Rubinstein, and of Rubinstein's pleasure both in the youth's compositions and the highly musical, ingratiating way in which he performed them.

All this was encouragement. But when his Berlin year was up and he returned to Warsaw it was only to find himself still dissatisfied with his progress. The "divine discontent" of the artist, from the unease of which he has suffered all his life, was fastening itself more and more securely on him. It was not that Warsaw, limited though its opportunities at that moment might be, chafed his spirit. It was his own limitations that drove him on. He criticized himself; he recognized the justice of the criticisms of others. When one of the Warsaw critics, following a concert given the year of his return, amended his praise by saying that Paderewski's compositions "lacked naturalness" and were evidently "the fruit of an overflowing fancy"; and when another critic balanced his laudation with an appeal to the young artist—he was only twenty-one—that he "add to the richness of his text that richness of form which it demands and which comes only of work and experience"; when these honest criticisms came, Paderewski accepted them, and what is more he acted on them. He determined to return to his studies. He definitely severed his connection with the Conservatory and, once again a student, went back to Berlin. This time he was to devote himself to the special study of orchestration, placing himself in the hands of Heinrich Urban.

During all this time, one name, one figure, had loomed large in the aspirations of young Paderewski—Leschetitsky, the celebrated Viennese teacher, who with his wife, Madame Annette Essipoff, renowned likewise as teacher and virtuoso, had visited Warsaw in Paderewski's earliest Conservatory days, when his friend Kerntopf extended himself to insure the boy hearing and meeting as many artists as possible. Two objectives were Paderewski's aim, to be a composer and to be a virtuoso. Throughout these years of renewed study he was composing; that was his major ambition. But to prepare himself for the concert stage, he must study still more. It was Leschetitsky under whom he must study. Kerntopf especially encouraged him in this. "While almost everybody was discouraging me," Paderewski has told me, "he believed in my future, helped me to go to Vienna, to study there for a year and to start my pianistic career."

There is an interlude between Paderewski's concluding his studies in Berlin and his going to Vienna, which gives us an interesting picture of the young man debating his future course. He returned home to Poland, and while there he visited the beautiful Tatra mountain region in the south, that region which was to become the fountain source of new trends in Polish national music. Whatever his problem as to means toward the end of further study, Paderewski at this time was composing steadily, though not too freely, thanks to his own severe self-criticism; his publications were few and choice. And naturally, more and more, the native song and dance of the peasant, which had been Chopin's richest treasury of inspiration, attracted him. Chopin had already immortalized the Masovian plain, Moniuszko had drawn inspiration from the Ruthenian borderlands. In the Tatra country, living among the peasants, Paderewski would touch first-hand on an untapped source of original beauty in Polish music. His beautiful settings of folk melodies for piano four hands in the "Tatra Album" (Op. 12) were the result.

His own originality was consistently asserting itself in his compositions, in that quality of personal feeling, of poetic utterance, which is the greatest charm of his music. In his Elegy (Op. 4) the tragic bereavement which he had suffered in the death of his wife echoed his mourning; in his Songs of the Traveller (Op. 8) the melancholy of the homeless wanderer is heard; in the romantic scenes of his Maytime Album (Op. 10) the note of youth undaunted is again sounded under a smiling overtone of recaptured brightness. From Berlin, too, he brought a piece which was perhaps the first of many works of his, throughout his life, to be dedicated to the succor of others in distress: a piano composition, "Under the Waves", published in

Warsaw for the benefit of the victims of a disastrous flood which had ruined the Vistula country in 1884.

But it is to this interval between his Berlin studies and his going to Vienna, this period of sojourn in the Tatras, that we owe the first and some of the best of Paderewski's purely native Polish music, his Krakowiak (Op. 3), his Polish Dances (Op. 5 and Op. 9), including several Krakowiaks, Mazureks and a Polonaise. It is to this visit to the Tatras, likewise, that he owed the beginning of his friendship with Helena Modjeska. And more important still, it is during this visit that we hear the strains of a new romance which was to reshape his whole life.

Modjeska tells the story beautifully and reticently in her memoirs. She had returned that year to Poland from America, where she had won undreamed-of triumphs in Shakespeare on the English-speaking stage. Her return home was another triumph. "As we neared Zakopané many friends and mountaineers, mounted on horseback, met us and greeted us with cheers. We stopped our wagon, and a long while was spent in exchanging words of joy, embracing and kissing. While we were thus engaged, another wagon came up to us and also stopped. I heard a sweet voice from the depth of it, calling, 'Madame Helena! how do you do?' and the beautiful face of Madame Gorska appeared between the white canvas of the wagon . . . The beautiful creature, whose name is also Helena, looked at me with her wistful eyes and said: 'I envy you your going to Zakopané; you are going to meet one of the most extraordinary young men you ever met.' Then she sighed and said, 'And I must go away.' 'I must,' she repeated, lower. 'Good-by'."

The "extraordinary young man" was Paderewski. Modjeska met him the following day. "The very next day", as we have already heard her recount, Dr. Tytus Chalubinski introduced to her the "frail-looking young man": "I want you to know and love Ignace Paderewski, our second Chopin."

It is here that Modjeska gives us her memorable picture of the young musician who "looked like one of Botticelli's or Fra Angelico's angels." "He seemed so deeply wrapped up in his music," she tells us, "that this intensity was almost hypnotic.

He also phrased with so much clearness and meaning that his playing made an effect of something new and quite unconventional."

The village of Zakopané, where Paderewski now sojourned, devoting himself to a careful and sympathetic study of peasant music, is one of the most beautiful spots in the world. Nestling in a deep valley among the towering mountains of the Tatra, whose iron walls rise above the timber line to a chain of snow-clad peaks, with Gevont, Gerlach and Lomnica "kings of the valley", dominating all, the town breathes the breath of pines and sleeps and wakes to the music of rushing streams. Here, domiciled in a single room furnished only with a bed, a chair, and a piano, the young artist, poor in money but rich in resources and in friendships, spent epochal days. The illustrious Dr. Chalubinski, the man who had introduced him with such paternal love to Modjeska, was first among his Zakopané friends. A man celebrated for his charities as well as for his eminence in science, Dr. Chalubinski was a fortunate patron for the young musician to have at this critical moment of his life. Himself a student of peasant lore, known and loved by all the country folk, the doctor had become "the patron of the mountaineers", as Modjeska expresses it, had established for them a wood-carving school, as she herself had founded a school of lace-making for girls, and "they simply worshipped him. He discovered that these unlearned, uncultivated people had more inborn manner, more real artistic feeling, than any of the average city bred." Thus Paderewski had the happiest means of contact with the mountaineers, in whose music, in whose songs and dances, he was so vitally interested.

It was through Dr. Chalubinski that Paderewski met, among others, Bartek Obrochta, a "natural" violinist whose knowledge of the ancient music of tradition was invaluable to the young musician. Bartek was a real figure in the Tatra life. It is easy to imagine him, dressed in his picturesque peasant garb, white wool trousers, tight-fitting, brightly seamed and split at the ankle, embroidered blouse and richly patterned leather jerkin, small round hat rimmed with shells, his stout *ciupaga*, the mountaineer's walking stick with its eagle-shaped carven head, in his hand—until he put it by to take up his fiddle. "What a faculty he had!" Bartek once exclaimed, recalling Paderewski in these days when they spent hours together, going over the native airs. "No sooner would I finish a melody than he was repeating it. The moment a rhythm was finished, he had it. His fingers could hardly wait to run it over on the piano."

Now, when we listen to or when we ourselves play selections from Paderewski's Tatra Album (Op. 12) we can know where that music came from, directly from the people who made it perhaps a thousand years ago; we can see the auburn-haired young master, intense, vivid, electrified in his absorption, listening to old Bartek and transcribing from his antique fiddle to the ivory keyboard the rush of winds in the Tatra pines, the voice of waterfalls, the dance of gay feet stepping out native measures on the village green or on the beaten sod along some mountain roadside.

He spent happy hours at Modjeska's villa. They had endless confidences to exchange. She must tell over again to the "extraordinary young man" the story of her meeting with Helena Gorska on the road to Zakopané; she must tell him of America; and they had the whole artistic life of Warsaw to talk about, that stimulating life which his friend Kerntopf had taken care that he, though only a growing boy, should know. The young artist drank deeply of the wit and charm of the fascinating Pani Helena. His eyes blazed at her story of the Warsaw schoolboy driven to the martyrdom of suicide by the Russian police; his laugh rang out at her stories of adventure and misadventure behind the scenes—as when she recounted to him the ludicrous mishap of the actor who, as a Roman senator, made his entrance in a chariot drawn by "lions", only to find his impressive cue spoiled by a mischievous boy who had nailed the lions' tails to a post so that when they advanced they left their nether halves behind them and emerged as a pair of sweating stage-hands. That was the kind of prank Paderewski used to play. But whatever the entertainment, in the end it would be music. "It was impossible," Modjeska says, "to keep him away from the piano.

Sometimes he played long after midnight, and had to be taken from the instrument by force, when refreshments were announced."

All during this mountain interlude he was pondering his future course. The name of Leschetitsky in Vienna still magnetized him. But what to do? The way of the virtuoso was long, arduous, expensive, and he was poor, and more than that, ever self-critical and forever tormented by the desire of perfection, he had his moods of sharp self-appraisement and insecurity. Modjeska rallied him and helped him decide the question, and in her words of encouragement and challenge perhaps the memory echoed of that first hour spent before the urned heart of Chopin, when he had come as a boy to Warsaw, that hour of youthful dedication answering the summons which every Pole of his generation obeyed, Mickiewicz's command "Shoulder to shoulder! Engirdle the earth!" "Poland needs you," Modjeska told him. "Every man and woman of Polish blood must fall in line. This one as a soldier; that one as a nurse; the other as a writer; you as a musician." Her faith in him roused in his spirit a new determination. Twenty years later he had not forgotten this. In 1905, when a public testimonial was, at his instigation, given Modjeska in New York City, he said: "The first encouraging words I heard as a pianist came from her lips; the first successful concert I had in my life was due to her assistance, good, kind and generous."

"We had many chats," Modjeska has told us, "and I advised him to appear in public"—that is, to go on with his plans for a career on the concert stage. "I knew he would make a name and a fortune. His poetic face, combined with his genius, was bound to produce brilliant results. He hesitated, but finally made up his mind to go to Vienna and study with Leschetitsky." She did more than counsel with him and rally him; she helped him in a practical way to raise funds. "That same summer, after leaving Zakopané, he gave a concert in Cracow, at which I had the great pleasure of reciting. Then he departed for Vienna."

One memorable event signalized his departure for Vienna, following the Cracow concert. For the first time he appeared in Warsaw in a program exclusively of his own compositions. The concert attracted an immense audience, the critics were almost unanimous in their praise. He left for Vienna with renewed faith in his powers, and with funds with which to carry on.

Paderewski's departure for Vienna was a definite new step in his career, although he regarded it as only a return to the tasks of the studio. He was, in fact, on the way to an earlier realization of his dreams of success than he expected. He was only twenty-four.

XIII

1887: VIENNA

VIENNA in those days was the mecca of artists, the lode-star of the musician. From the beginning its fame and prestige had been of course familiar to Paderewski. In Warsaw during his student days, whenever technique and methods were discussed it was invariably "Vienna" that he heard as the ultimate word, especially when celebrities came to the capital to stir the life of Polish music circles to new ambition. Above all, Vienna had its Leschetitsky, the piano authority par excellence. Berlin had its Vater Kiel of contrapuntal fame, but Berlin was not Vienna, and Kiel was not Leschetitsky . . : Now he was on his way to Vienna; now he was in Vienna; now at last he was in the hands of the master.

A Pole felt more at home at that time in Vienna than he could ever feel in Berlin, and perhaps more at ease if not more at home than even in his own Warsaw. For Warsaw was still the Cossack-ridden capital of Russia's proudest and most unmanageable conquest. Czarist officialdom still patrolled the streets at every turn and irritated itself into the most private precincts of life. No one felt safe from the peering eye of the omnipresent under-cover man—as in the case of Witkiewicz, a young artist of Paderewski's time, who was all but hauled off to jail one day because, sitting innocently on a fence at the race-course sketching the horses, a group of friends gathered around to watch him. Spies were everywhere; a spy saw that group gather, listened to every word of conversation between Witkiewicz and his friends, and finally the police escorted his friends, when they left the artist, to their very door. Life in Warsaw was an irritation, especially for artists, for people of ideas. But life in Vienna was different. This was the capital of the least brutal of Poland's three alien captors; in "Austrian" Poland the Pole felt at least relatively free and in Vienna he was at home. Paderewski, after fifteen years in Russian-policed Warsaw and after two years in "iron Berlin" where the Pole was treated as an inferior, felt that he would be happy in Vienna.

Real happiness was in store for him.

His first encounter with Leschetitsky was a memorable one. It was not a stripling youth, but, despite his few years, a man with the mature stamp of experience already on his mobile visage, who presented himself for tutelage. Leschetitsky looked him over.

"But Mr. Paderewski, you are rather beyond the age—or perhaps this is only a whim?"

Paderewski stared at him, amazed. "A whim?"

"The question is, how much in earnest are you? Now—er— suppose I were to say to you, 'Jump out that window'——"

Paderewski knew his man. Apparently with dead earnestness, but perhaps with a glint of humor in his eye that the Viennese master did not detect, he moved with a stride of his long legs toward the window, exactly as if he were about to act on Leschetitsky's suggestion. "Hold on!" Leschetitsky cried in alarm.

"That is enough," he concluded decisively. "We will go to work."

They went to work. But to go to work under Leschetitsky virtually meant to go to war. He was the famous teacher of whom the American pianist Fannie Bloomfield-Zeisler once said, "Yes, Leschetitsky is awful to study with, but, were he to kick me down the front steps, I would crawl to him again up the back steps." Paderewski himself once told of a moment when, exasperated beyond endurance, he stormed out of the studio angry enough "to throw rocks"; he actually had the impulse to pick up a stone and send it crashing through the window. But he went back. Leschetitsky's war-like methods had a purpose. "I am a doctor," he once remarked, "to whom pupils come as patients to be cured of their musical ailments."

But if Leschetitsky was warlike, there is something Napo-

leonic in Paderewski's nature. At any rate the basis of his eminence, as it has been said, "is the elimination of the possibility
of failure", and that is a Napoleonic trait; that is how Napoleon
won his battles. In the battle of Vienna, for which he was now
set full tilt, Paderewski was determined to win, and not all the
stern searchings into his being of the omniscient Leschetitsky,
nor all the merciless self-searchings to which he put himself to
discover his faults, to undo old methods of technique which he
must discard, could flag his spirit. "The ultimate necessity," he
has said, "is the summoning of the mind and will to do their
duty." He was summoning all his forces now for this new uphill struggle toward complete mastery of his art.

What Paderewski learned from Leschetitsky could not, of
course, be put in words. The sum of it is in his playing. But the
sum of it, to be exact, is not of course a total of Leschetitsky,
but of Leschetitsky plus Paderewski, very much plus Paderewski. As a matter of fact, while Paderewski admired and appreciated the great teacher and learned from him many of his tonal
and technical devices, his artistic sensibility nevertheless was
often at variance with the Viennese master's taste. Because of
his superior musicianship, the sensitivity of his natural genius,
and his cultural attainments, Paderewski's insight far tran-
scended that of Leschetitsky. He rebelled, moreover, against
an approach to art which was rather that of the brilliant virtuoso than that of the deep musician. Paderewski, in truth, never
played quite as Leschetitsky wished him to. He always resisted
the virtuoso's true weakness, which is too great a concern with
the gallery. But, if the pupil disagreed at certain points with the
master, he never permitted himself, not for one moment, to
forget that it was for discipline that he had come to him. The
discipline he would have. He took it and abided his time.

Like Kosciuszko "impervious to every temptation of ease"
he settled in to his work. He began all over again the tedious
drilling of the schoolboy. Leschetitsky's system, in the words
of Finck, was to make his pupil, "take one bar or phrase at a
time and make it at once as perfect as he can, deciding on every
detail of fingering, touch, pedalling, accent. He must know this

so thoroughly that he can see in his mind what is written, each bar being engraved on it as on a map. One page a day." This system, which after all was not altogether new to Paderewski, as we know from the record of his Warsaw Conservatory days, meant that, literally, "on the education of every finger", as an English critic, Raymond, tells us, "was lavished as much pains as go to the instruction of the children of a good-sized township. The most repellent labor was faced, the most alluring temptations set aside, in order that the very maximum of digital dexterity—the rest was in the man's soul—should be obtained . . . The skill was largely a matter of sheer hard work, of self-discipline exceeding that of most old saints, of a savage energy which in another orbit might have guided half a dozen trusts."

As time was to prove it was an energy, trained, disciplined and perfected to guide more than "a dozen trusts"; for it was not alone his fingers that were being drilled, it was his mind, and that mind was to save, shape, direct and manage a nation.

Back then at his studies in Vienna, he worked without halt or rest, eight, ten, twelve hours a day. Of all Leschetitsky's pupils, according to the testimony of the teacher, Paderewski was the most docile. "There was no remark so insignificant, no detail so small, as to reserve less than his whole passionate attention." Then suddenly, after months of this intensive application, a surprise came, one for which he was entirely unprepared, and all the more unprepared because, in his own self-exactitude, he had not guessed how completely he had won the ever-exacting master. But Leschetitsky, from that first encounter, had understood; he also had known his man. He had recognized Paderewski's genius, had watched him closely, and had recommended him, without a word being said, to a position of importance. This was the surprise that came, the flattering offer of a professorship at the Conservatory of Strasbourg.

Paderewski could do nothing but accept; he did so gladly and gratefully. Nevertheless, with that constantly growing spirit in him of self-exaction he felt that it was a mistake, that he was not yet ready for the career upon which his mind was now set, for he had no intention of remaining a teacher. Certainly he felt that he was not yet ready to leave the hands of his Viennese master. When he left, it was with the secret determination of some day returning. Strasbourg at any rate would afford him not only experience but an opportunity to save money in order to still further pursue his studies.

A year later he was back in Vienna richer in experience and with money saved, for he had pinched and economized at every turn. But still the insatiable appetite for bettering himself was in him. He took up his modest two-room quarters again in the house at No. 46 Anastasius Grün-Gasse and went to work once more under Leschetitsky. The old master must have been proud of him.

How proud Paderewski was to be one of Leschetitsky's pupils comes out in a story told by Edwin Hughes. The incident occurred years later, on one of Paderewski's returns to Vienna. "It was after a concert in the Grosser Musikverein Saal, where Paderewski had received a stormy ovation from a crowded house. Leschetitsky had come to greet him in the artists' room, and in addition there were any number of others present for the same purpose, including a bevy of students eager for a nearer approach to greatness. Among the latter, one summoned up the courage to present her autograph album to Paderewski and to ask if he would not write in it. He took the proffered pen, and, to the great astonishment of the young lady, wrote the name 'Theodor Leschetitsky' in a hand that was strikingly like Leschetitsky's own. Leschetitsky was an amused onlooker at this exhibition of skillful penmanship. As soon as Paderewski had enjoyed for a moment the abashed face of the autograph-hunter, he took the book again, added an apostrophe and an 's' to Leschetitsky's name, two more words, and his own signature, so that the whole read as follows: 'Theodor Leschetitsky's grateful pupil I. J. Paderewski'."

Paderewski's strong sentiment for the memory of his Viennese days was demonstrated a few years later when he had left both obscurity and poverty behind. He took out a life-time lease on the house where he had lodged, to retain it as a souvenir of his most difficult years of struggle.

His resumed studies continued into the autumn of 1887, with the encouragement of Madame Essipoff, who admired and played his compositions, added to the supervision of Leschetitsky himself. He sought no spotlight, asked for nothing but time and more time for work. He scarcely left his piano. The streets of the beautiful Vienna that he had learned to love saw him seldom except at night when alone he took the air by the Gothic shadows of St. Stephen's spire, under the deserted colonnades of the Burg Theatre and the Opera House, or across the bridges spanning the "blue Danube." Then, one day in the fall of that year, it was announced that Paulina Lucca, celebrated Italian soprano, was to give a concert in Vienna, with Paderewski as soloist on the same program.

His chance had come at last. Perhaps he did not realize it. Inured to work, he may have regarded this opportunity as only one more step in the routine of his self-imposed task of perfection. But it was to bring him for the first time before the critical Viennese audience, and what is more, before the battery of Vienna's critics. He prepared for this concert as he always prepared, pledged to himself to give of himself the utmost best. However he regarded the engagement, he could not have expected it to turn out as it did. As a matter of fact, a pen-picture we have of him on this occasion seems to indicate that he took the whole affair as a matter of course. In the Countess Angela Potocki's biography of Leschetitsky we read: "I remember the night that Leschetitsky brought out his brilliant pupil Ignace Jan Paderewski. His performance of an original Theme and Variations was greeted with special favor ... Yet, as he stood nonchalantly in the passageway, his tawny head resting against the wall, those who foresaw his great future were probably few."

He was a sensation. There was one Viennese musician, however, who was not impressed; he remarked to Leschetitsky that in his opinion "the young man does not seem to promise so much."

"My dear sir," the teacher answered, "you will have to get used to hearing that young man's name."

XIV

THE POET AT WORK

WHAT did Ignace Jan Paderewski feel like when he woke up the next day to find himself a musical celebrity?—for the verdict of the critics in the morning confirmed the acclamations of the audience the night before.

And what was it that he had done to win this acclaim, both popular and critical?

He was happy of course, and proud too, proud to think of the joy the news would bring his old father back in Volhynia, and his playmate sister, Antonina, and happy thinking of what he could do for his folks at home if success really came to him. He was proud also thinking of what the news would mean to that ever more dear friend of his, the soft-eyed traveler on the Zakopané road who had whispered his name to Modjeska. And Modjeska herself, over in America, making the name of Poland proud—she had believed in him; and Kerntopf, and Rutkowski; all his warm circle of friends—he knew how they would rejoice. Deep down in his heart, too, he was proud with a wistful pride, remembering that other Antonina, his girl-wife, her faith in him; and glad to think of the things he could do now, with success in his hands, for his little invalid son, now a boy of six, but never to be strong and well. And finally, he was proud with a proper pride recalling those who had not believed in him. He wanted their faith too.

But the old unease of the poet's "divine discontent" was there to temper his pride. He had done this thing at last, he had uttered himself in his own language, fully, richly, unrestrainedly, with authority, and the world at last had listened, the world that counted. But what had he done, and how had he done it?

Was it, he asked himself, only a happy accident of favorable chance, sympathetic audience, generous critics? Or was it truly the fruit of a real gift and of a real mastery gained through the tireless drilling to which he had put himself? Could he do it again?

Every artist asks himself these questions after the first flush of the first triumph. And every artist gives himself the same answer that Paderewski gave himself that day in Vienna: Go on. Nothing to do but go on. Put yourself to another test. And another. And see what stuff you are really made of.

The great artist is the conscious artist. He knows his powers, knows what the deposit is whence he draws them, knows what he wants to do with them. And this knowledge makes him in the end not proud but humble. To be humbled before oneself is to be strong. In the midst of his triumph Paderewski, proud and happy but still dissatisfied, not with his success but with himself, went to work again, at once, to prepare himself for new tests, to correct imperfections which he recognized whether the critics did or not. Out of the sum total of the laudations given him he drew this conviction: that he had a gift, undeniable and unmistakable, a gift that could be developed and perfected by work; and that he must use this gift for two purposes. For his country. And for his art. Now another Polish name was being repeated abroad to confute that world, prejudiced and skeptical, which would have Poland a dead thing, not even remembered. He recalled Modjeska's words, "Poland needs you." And he said to himself, "La patrie avant tout, l'art ensuite."

His Vienna appearance had resulted in a sensation. What was the quality in Paderewski that made this possible? He had played the piano. But tens of thousands can play the piano. He had played the piano and a crowd of people had listened to him. But crowds of people had listened to others and had sat bored. The crowd that listened to him had acclaimed him. What had he done to them? Modjeska had said that when he played he did so with "an intensity that was almost hypnotic." She had said also that "he phrased with so much clearness and meaning that his playing made an effect of something new and quite unconventional." All that makes Paderewski's art what it is, is summed up in Modjeska's phrasing: his personality, "hypnotic"; his art, crystal-clear and luminous with meaning.

He was only at the beginning of his career that Autumn evening in Vienna in 1887, only twenty-six years old. He was to grow and grow and go on perfecting himself, through the years, studying, practicing, working, as he works to this day, never self-satisfied. But he was not to change. He was only to develop. What he is now he was then and what he was then he is now.

It is interesting to pause and consider what he is. It explains that first triumph in Vienna, as it explains his whole subsequent career as a musician.

First, he is a poet, a poet whose language is not words but music, a poet of "overflowing fancy", as one of his earliest critics had described him at twenty-one. "He possesses the true spark of poetry" another critic said three years later. "The character of his musical ideas is noble, his themes are beautiful." This is the true poet as Vienna heard him in 1887, and it is the same poet who nearly forty years later was described by Charles Buchanan, an American critic, as "the Paderewski of incredible Old World sighings, of lamentable far-off horizons and Once-Upon-A-Timeness, the one magician of our day who can, like some adroit Pied Piper, lure us out of 1925 into the fabulous, faded loveliness of Never-Never Land . . . No one has ever held the power, psychic, and occult beyond question, to sound the note of regret, of retrospection, as Paderewski sounds it."

Paderewski is first of all, then, a poet, the poet who, like all poets since man first sang, moves the hearts of people, draws them out of themselves, exalts them, makes them want to sit and listen to him by the hour so that they too may "feel immortality." "Look at concert audiences," exclaims Guy de Pourtalès in "Polonaise", his life of Chopin, after he has reminded us that "an analysis of music is the most futile of intellectual exercises, because it can build on nothing but emotion": "Concert audiences," he says, "are made up for the most part of lovers and old people. It is that they understand, remember, and seek again this powerful inexpressible thing on which they find the best that is in themselves." They find it evoked by the poet. Paderewski's first power, intrinsic in his being, is the poet's power.

In the exercise of this innate poetic force, called "hypnotic" by Modjeska, because it does actually hypnotize, all of Paderewski's personality projects itself. His noble head, his fine face, strong and sensitive, his eyes, his movements and gestures, the whole picture that he makes, all are brought into play and summed up in the revelation of what one critic has called "the apocalyptic spiritual stature of his nature." He is the poet. The poet sings. Paderewski makes the piano sing. "It is as a poet," Opienski declares, "that Paderewski has conquered the world." That was the first quality in him that Vienna recognized.

But he is more than poet, that is, more than merely the natural poet who sings as the birds sing. He is also the artist, the conscious artist, "the visible incarnation of an idea"; yet no one who has heard wild birds rehearse their song, trying it over and over, will say that he is any less the natural poet because he is also the conscious artist. It is not alone Paderewski's natural song that makes the masses listen to him entranced. It is also his art, for the masses know the art of song whether they know that they know it or not. They apprehend it and respond to it intuitively. A crowd of people listening to Paderewski is an elemental part of the universal harmony that makes the stars beat in their places. They give themselves involuntarily to the elemental rhythm that beats and pulsates out of his being. But that rhythm is not only elemental, it is also schooled, ordered, disciplined; and it is the critics, the students of the technique of music, who explicitly divine his power as artist. They divined it that night in Vienna. They have been responding to it ever since.

Gustave Doret, the Swiss composer, speaks of "the unity and firmness" of Paderewski's style, a unity and firmness "which no prank can weaken." That is the artist, master of his art. Krehbiel of New York turns to Paderewski as the best explanation he can find "of the magic force of music, of the fascination which an artist may exercise." "His name", says Alberto Jonas of Spain, "will stand out in the background of history above those of all other pianists because he has known how to weave the magic spell of tonal beauty, of digital splendor and of emotional intensity." We note that it is "because he has known how." He knows how because he is a trained and disciplined artist. The Vienna critics recognized this.

Poetry and artistry, a personality that is hypnotic and an art that has meaning: these two combined gave him at last this Vienna triumph, his first long-toiled-for victory. The working of the combination is clearly set forth, both its method and its effect, by his friend Alfred Nossig, author of the libretto of his opera "Manru." "Paderewski's technical ability," Nossig tells us, "is so perfect that the impression of the compositions which he is playing effaces consciousness of technique. The listener never thinks whether the piece is easy or difficult for the player and is therefore able to give himself up completely to its charm —the more so because Paderewski does not make the impression of being a virtuoso interpreting some composition foreign to himself: he seems to be a composer interpreting his own ideas. He plays everything with that spirit and warmth, with that love and coquetry, which other masters are able to develop when interpreting their own works only . . . The listener altogether forgets that a virtuoso in evening costume sits before him; he forgets that he has already heard the same composition innumerable times. It is as if the atelier of a composer had opened before him at the precise time when, struck by a new thought, the master utters it in tone, in the creator's complete ecstatic forgetfulness of the world . . . His is the gift of unveiling the deepest feeling and the highest flight of his artist soul to his hearers, while appearing entirely oblivious of their presence. At the moment when he is thanking his audience for its plaudits, the last notes of his music still ring in his ears, and his face, trembling and flaming with inspiration, betrays something of contempt for the noisy crowd . . . In all that he plays he remains the tone-poet that he was born . . . It would be a mistake, however, to conclude that Paderewski merely follows the elementary voice of his inspiration. On the contrary . . . he is an extraordinarily experienced artist, who knows his public thoroughly, and knows by what means to seize, warm, and transport it."

Nossig's term "contempt", it must be remarked, is unfortunate and not true.* Paderewski never shows any such feeling as contempt for his audience, for the simple reason that quite obviously he never has any such feeling. His acknowledgment of applause is not only at all times graceful but manifestly grateful. He is not only, in Nossig's words, "an experienced artist who knows his public thoroughly", but he is also very much of a human being who likes his audience. True, rising from the rapt concentration of a performance, his face will naturally betray something of momentary remoteness: he cannot at once tear himself wholly and completely out of the deep communion with his music. But "contempt for the noisy crowd" is as impossible to him as contempt for the music itself.

It was the craftsmanship of his art, his sympathetic response to and accord with his audience, above all it was the poetry of his being, that made the Vienna triumph possible. It was his trained capacity for work and for self-criticism, and the dedicated purpose back of all his work and his self-criticism, that made his progress beyond that first triumph inevitable.

Knowing what Paderewski was then, in 1887, we can understand the better the story of what followed.

---

* It may be due to mistranslation; the quotation is from Nossig's chapter on Paderewski in "Modern Music and Musicians," vol. I, p. 22 (The University Society, Inc., New York, 1908); but there is nothing to indicate whether the chapter was written originally in English or not.

XV

1888: PARIS

"A young man of from five-and-twenty to eight-and-twenty years of age, very thin, with blond hair, with a drawn face, who appears scarcely to have breath in his sunken cheeks"— so one of the Paris papers pictured Paderewski a few months after the Vienna début.

It is now March, 1888. The close application of his months of study in Vienna have told on his slender physique, but the steel-fibered wrist, the fine muscular fingers of the small hand, developed under practice to spring-like dexterity and strength, have kept pace with the tireless spirit. . . . The months between Vienna and Paris have been hard. There was not only endless rehearsal and practice but there was the task of practical arrangement of the tour which he had decided upon. It is no small thing for a young and hitherto unknown artist to face Paris and challenge it, even with Vienna backing him. Such an attack must be organized. . . . He is still the frail young man that Modjeska had described. He is virtually living on nerves. But at least he is no longer hungry.

For a hundred years Paris, called "the Polish capital" after the Uprising of 1831, was the traditional refuge of the Polish *émigré*. The inextinguishable flame of Poland's hope of resurrection was long fed by her exiles in Paris, from the days when Mickiewicz sang there his Messianic songs. Generations of Poles, sons of Poland who had never seen the motherland, lived an intense Polish life in the French capital. I knew the haunts of the Polish *émigrés* just before the World War, and I was astonished at the vitality of their national spirit. I remember one young man, a stripling not much younger than the

young Paderewski who had come now from Vienna, sending
me, after I had returned to America, a picture-postcard with a
sketch of a Polish uhlan, armed and mounted. *"This is what I
shall be like some day,"* is what he wrote on the card. Evening
gatherings on the Rue Jacob I never once saw concluded without the singing, all together around the piano, of the song of
Dombrowski's legionnaires, "Poland Is Still Alive!" This same
Paris offered to the newcomer from Vienna in 1888 a warm
circle of sympathetic friends, although he must always give to
them the old sad response, "It's just the same," when they
asked the inevitable question of the exile, "How are things in
the home country?"

The Poles of Paris welcomed him. But it was the critics of
Paris that he had to face. He wanted their verdict; it was for
this that he had come and he had his fears of them. Moreover,
the reception which his first rather small audience gave him in
the Salle Erard was for a short time puzzling to him, for it
was in this Paris début that he made his first acquaintance with
a French custom until then unknown to him. Tremendous applause greeted the closing of the first numbers of his opening
group of selections. "What will it be," he wondered to himself, "when I come to the end?" But when he came to the end,
when his recital was completed, instead of either applause or
the profound silence of responsiveness, there was only a seemingly indifferent hurry in the audience, apparently anxious to
go home. Had he failed? Had the early applause meant nothing? Was the verdict thumbs down from Paris? He went
through a frightening moment before he learned the custom of
French audiences—warm applause during the performance, little or none afterward. It was not really until the next morning,
when he read his press notices, that the fear of a Paris fiasco
was removed from him.

The next morning revealed that he had indeed conquered
the Paris critics. "I am embarrassed to praise him," wrote Ju-
lian Torchet. All of the critics were embarrassed because, as
Torchet admitted, they had indiscriminately used up their
superlatives, and now came one who left them beggared for

praise, one who could not be praised in the stock phrases of the critics' vocabulary. He appeared, in the words of Alfred Cortot "with the suddenness of a lightning stroke, making a blurring, an eruption in our hearts. Instead of a pianist, an inspired poet took possession of the keyboard."

The poet literally took possession of the critics. It was the poetic in his nature, glowingly uttered in his playing, that first captured his Parisian auditors. But the critics discerned in him something more than the poetic impulse. They saw in him an authoritative artist, a master of technique, a master of the art that conceals art. "He is always master of himself," one of them commented. "He phrases admirably, shades with simplicity, keeps measure with a rigorous exactness yet never shows stiffness. He obtains a large sonority by attack and enforcement. He knows his effects beforehand, and yet in spite of this assurance he seems to play as if by inspiration." "Free, inventive, audacious," were other terms used in the enthusiastic chorus of praise that Paris gave him.

But if the critics, like the audience, came quickly under his "hypnotic" spell ("He hypnotizes them," Henry Finck once commented, "by being seemingly hypnotized himself"), the critics were likewise not slow to analyze him and to define at least one of the secrets of his power. It was the secret of what has been justly termed "the superlative value of the pause in music." Paderewski, as we know from his Chopin panegyric and as we shall see in the developments of his political career, is a born orator as well as musician. As an orator he knows the value of the pause; he knows that the utterance of a speaker would make little or no impression, and perhaps only bore its hearers, were it delivered in a dead-level monotone accented only by formal punctuation. Edward Everett delivered his famous oration "The Character of Washington" a hundred and fifty times, but he never delivered it twice in quite the same manner. So with music; Paderewski is in a sense a "musical orator", clumsy as the term is; like the orator he delivers his message by playing upon the emotions of his auditors, using every facility of dramatic suspense, prolonging chords, making momentary silences that are the rich underscoring of sounds, silences that sustain sound and give the hearer time to take in all of its mingling implications of beauty. This fine detail of his art was natural to Paderewski, a part of the delicate instincts of his musical being; yet it is interesting to note that, as early as his first American tour, he was applying it outside of music; having taken pains to hear several great American orators speak, he commented on their skillful use of the oratorical pause.* In music he recognized instinctively "that a pause", as Mary Hallock expresses it in "The Elocution of Playing", "no matter how slight, but utterly empty of sound, is as telling as when an orator makes use of the same in a peroration." This the critics of Paris recognized at once as one of the unique gifts of Paderewski, his exquisitely delicate use of the pedal, of musical silences. "The reservoirs of silence lie far above the reservoirs of thought."

Of one other marked characteristic, one not unrelated to his striking use of the pedal, the critics made note: Paderewski's *tempo rubato*. This is not only an artistic, but, as he himself has said of Chopin, a Polish characteristic, the impulse toward free tempo; to live, as it were, as well as to play, unmetronomically; that is, finding liberation from the marked and measured time of the metronome. "Rhythm is the pulse of music," Paderewski tells us. "Rhythm marks the beating of its heart . . . Rhythm is order. But this order in music cannot progress with the automatic uniformity of a clock . . . Our human metronome, the heart, under the influence of emotion, ceases to beat regularly." So in music: "To be emotional in musical interpretation, yet true to the metronome, means about as much as being sentimental in engineering. Mechanical execution and emotion are incompatible . . . There are in musical expression certain things which are vague and consequently cannot be defined because they vary according to individuals, voices, or instruments . . . A musical composition, printed or written, is, after all, a form, a mold: the performer infuses life into it."

* His own comment on his return to Europe from his first American tour was that he had "learned from the American orators the great value of the pause."

It was the life that the new Polish artist infused into music that startled the Parisian audience with the first impact of his highly original and "personal" playing.

He conquered the impresarios also, and he conquered even those unconquerables of the modern music world, the conductors. The two most famous conductors of Paris, Lamoureux and Colonne, heard his first concert and at once asked to engage him. And he conquered the artists. Gounod came to him, presented him with his portrait inscribed, "*à mon cher, noble et grand Paderewski.*" Saint-Saëns came, the Saint-Saëns whose Concerto in C Minor, difficult and comparatively ungrateful as compared to the popular one in G Minor, Paderewski had included in his repertoire during his first Paris season, a rather daring venture for an introductory appearance with orchestra, executing it, in the words of Torchet, "in a superb and masterful manner." Paris was his. Another Paris concert, under Lamoureux, was still another sensation. On the heels of that he was honored with the distinguished invitation to appear as soloist at one of the exclusive concerts of the Conservatoire. No wonder the critics were embarrassed, and no wonder that some of them, even with the best of good will, could see in this sudden light bursting on the musical firmament like a new sun, sensationally beautiful and brilliant beyond any comparison, only a meteor, fated to burn out as quickly as it came. They did not know then the steel-forged frame, resilient and enduring, mental and spiritual as well as physical, that was back of Paderewski's brilliant performances.

He decided to make Paris his headquarters. This was his real world. He had found it at last, his own world, and he could not leave it. He felt as all artists do, but perhaps with a greater sensitivity than do most, the curious relaxation and at-homeness and at the same time the exhilaration and excitement with which Paris affects those whose interests reach beyond the common glare into the luminous penumbræ of life. Paris has a oneness, a unified wholeness, which draws the artist in, to be a part of it as naturally as rivers are part of the sea. The rhythmic line and symmetry, the color and tone, the expansive air of the capital of all the arts gave to the young Paderewski, achieving success at last after so long a struggle, an inspiring world in which to breathe and grow, the same world in which Chopin had flourished. He took a little ground-floor apartment on the Avenue Victor Hugo, No. 94, and this small bachelor establishment became his *pied-à-terre*. True, he gave no receptions there, spending most of his time when in the city either at the famous piano-house of Erard in the Rue du Mail or at the home of his Warsaw friends the Gorskis who had a short time before removed to Paris. It was to this home of these friends that he was very soon to bring his little son, to be mothered for the remainder of his life by Madame Gorska. The one-time Paris abode of Paderewski on the Avenue Victor Hugo, it is curious to note, in spite of its truly artistic memories, has since become a dog-and-cat hospital—the most ironic move imaginable from its historic atmosphere of harmony!

Just as the constant drilling of his school days at the Warsaw Conservatory could not make a drudge of the irrepressible boy who, metaphorically speaking, still climbed trees, so the drudgery of the long hours and long months of application that had brought him to Paris had not taken the edge from his sociable nature. "He was witty, alert, most kind-hearted, always interesting, always having a ready answer," Modjeska had said, describing him in his Zakopané days. He had not changed. His sense of humor as well as his breadth of mind, the humor which in boyhood found its expression in pranks, was an asset now to his social progress. "Gifted with a brilliant wit," Modjeska said of him, "fascinating in conversation, posted on every subject, he is a perfect entertainer, either as host or guest." Even in serious discussions of his art this humor comes to the surface, as when, describing Brahms, he once explained that it was "a sort of atavistic freak of nature, a hereditary trait" that made Brahms "abuse the bass" in his compositions: "His father, you know, was a contrabassist, and throughout his infancy Brahms heard constantly the *dum, dum, dum* of this instrument. Later, I suppose, an unconscious reaction made him try for contrast . . . very low and very high, without any middle at all. At some cradles, you know, the angels stand; but at others it is the contrabass."

Life in Paris was a tremendous new experience. He was a social success. But he was too wise a young man to let social success carry him off. He did not slack his work. He had ground himself down to a rule of practice, of review and preparation, that made him capable of a hundred iron "no's" when society flashed its dazzling temptations before his eyes. Nevertheless, he had a practical mind. He did not discount the value, to a rising artist, of the *soirée* and the *salon*.

One matter he had to make a decision about, once he had chosen Paris as his home. The question of teaching was bound to come up. Was he to teach? He had no love of teaching; he knew too well already, from his days at Warsaw and at Strasbourg, the drudgery of that way of earning a living; and he wished above all to compose, to "be himself" in the world of music. Pupils he might have had by the score. In fact, the pressure put on him in Paris to take pupils became embarrassing, especially when Erard's, thinking to find a solution of their own to the problem by quoting something like a prohibitory fee to the applicants who streamed in, succeeded only in complicating matters. Numbers would willingly pay the fee, any fee. But Paderewski stuck to his determination not to teach. True, as we shall see, because of personal interest he did later agree to instruct privately three—Ernest Schelling, Sigismond Stojowski, and Antoinette Szumowska, to whom was added at one time for a while Harold Bauer. From Madame Szumowska we have an interesting note on Paderewski in the rôle of teacher. "As in everything else," she once wrote, "he is superlative and exceptional in this capacity. He carries one into the higher realms of art, beyond the limits of technique, I mean the greater technique including rules of phrasing and so on, not mere finger dexterity. He takes the student into the sphere of nobility and beauty of expression." But, as she adds, to find the origins of his gift "we have to look deeper than into his mind, however fertile and brilliant that is. We have to peer into his soul's greatness, into an exceptional warmth and tenderness of heart." She relates a story of her own student days to illustrate:

"In a moment of youthful prank I disguised myself as an indigent old woman and made a tour of my friends in Paris, with a pathetic sob-story of a widow poor and sick, stranded in the city. The reactions of these various friends gave me an insight into their nature. Paderewski, to whom I also turned, listened to my tale of woe with eyes full of tears, then emptied his pockets of all the money they contained, deploring that they were not fuller. As I was taking my leave he saw me off to the vestibule with an attention and respect worthy of bestowal on a great lady."

From the point of view of Polish sentiment Paris had a special attraction for Paderewski. This was the Paris of Chopin, the young Chopin whose friends had once brought to him, as the most priceless gift, a silver goblet filled with Polish earth, that Polish earth which at his funeral a friendly hand had scattered over his coffin. The young Paderewski whom Chalubinski had called "our second Chopin" made his pilgrimage to the homes of Chopin, to No. 5 Rue Tronchet, to No. 27 Boulevard Poissoniere and to No. 5 Chaussée d'Antin, remembering his earlier pilgrimages to the shrine of the heart in Warsaw and to the cottage at Zelazowa Wola. He was stirred again with the feeling of his dedication . . . Poland . . . and Music. . . .

But he was not forgetting, either, that to appear in the Paris of Chopin meant that he, the Pole, was to be watched sharply and judged closely by every Parisian critic who heard him play the master's compositions.

In the history of music no question has been so much debated as that of the interpretation of Chopin, Chopin to whom the poet Mickiewicz, as reported by his daughter Madame Gorecka, had once exclaimed, "you have in your fingers an orchestra of butterflies." The "glittering iridescence that tops the deep wave" of Chopin's music gets the best of too many artists at the expense of "the deep wave"; too many of them go to sleep interpreting his dream. The temptation to morbid sentimentality which one quality of Chopin's music offers, that is, its exquisite tenderness, reduces the playing of many pianists to a blur of soft moonlight, poetically feminine. But there is more than exquisite tenderness in the Polish master. What Chopin needs for his proper interpretation, as he needed it when Paderewski came to Paris, is something masculine too, the vigor and boldness, boldness of design, of harmonic utterance, of musical fabric as well as of the spirit with its chivalrous flights, its passion and ardor and its truly Polish heroism. All of these are as genuinely Chopinesque as are those other qualities in him, too often overemphasized, of delicacy and exquisiteness and particularly of the famous and much overdone *zal*. Chopin's *zal* especially has been so long harped upon by sentimentalists, and their efforts to define it have been carried to such extremes, as to almost obliterate the virtue of Chopin's art. His French biographer, de Pourtalés, seeks to encompass the paradox of the term by calling it "sometimes every tenderness and all humility, sometimes only rancor, revolt and glacial vengeance." This does not satisfy. Another connotes it as "intensity, mystery, sadness, barbaric splendour"; but whatever of intensity, mystery and sadness is to be recognized in him, "barbaric splendour" can hardly be applied to that quintessence of aristocracy which was Frederic Chopin. Again we have Waldo Frank telling us that "Chopin is strained honey", and this, unless taken for a description of Chopin as interpreted by boarding-school girls, is the prime misconception, as is also Mr. Frank's "timid butterfly of music," too obviously a false echo of Mickiewicz's phrase. Even Polish musicians, better qualified than others to understand Chopin, have sinned in this regard, as Wanda Landowska does in calling him "a nineteenth century Couperin", a phrase which only magnifies Couperin as a musical genius and pioneer, but which does not properly characterize Chopin. Actually, Chopin the "volcanic", as Paderewski has called him, the gay, the richly varied, has been reduced to a filigree tinkle by lack of proper interpretation, and this was the condition he was in when Paderewski came.

He came, and against this misconception, shallow and one-sided, he established at his very first recitals in Paris a wholesome reaction. He had the *zal*, if that must be reckoned in the count, and he had another Polish quality, one which Modjeska called *tęsknota*, an untranslatable term which she, quoting Longfellow, described as a feeling that "resembles sorrow only as mist resembles the rain." But decidedly he had something else, he had the *vigor igneus*, the masculinity which is in Chopin's music and which must be in his interpreter if he is to be rightly enjoyed. "Chopin," Paderewski once said, "needs not my nor any defense; but a protest may be made against the legend of a spineless, effeminate, and self-pitying Chopin. How could the author of the 'F-Minor Ballade', the 'F-Minor Fantasia', the great, proud 'Polonaises', the spirited 'Mazurkas', the tragic 'Scherzos', and heroic Etudes (Chopin's Etudes I hold to be almost the most characteristic and original of his works)—how, good people, can he have been that? The frail body contained an heroic soul. The legend too, of a Chopin who was a mere melodist, with no real technical resources, may be corrected. Truly it is absurd. If one work were to be selected to refute it, I would name the 'F-Minor Ballade', with its subtle contrapuntal texture. The thought of Chopin's physical frailty brings to mind the demands, little realized by the lay public, which the musical career makes upon the strength of the body. How many women executants have had the keenest musical intuitions without the bodily strength to render them actual! A woman is, of course, frequently an excellent chamber-music pianist, but I call to mind only two of my time who had the strength adequate to the largest occasions—I mean Sophie Menter and Teresa Carreño—and, rather strangely, those so-to-say virile women lacked tenderness."

It is the overemphasis on the tenderness of Chopin to which Paderewski objects. In Warsaw there is Szymanowski's much admired monument to Chopin, on which the figure of the musician is represented as a youthful poet listening to the melody of the wind in the weeping willows. Paderewski does not like it. To him this concept of Chopin is distasteful because it serves to perpetuate the legend of an exclusively sentimental, eternally tearful Chopin, which is a treachery to Chopin's real spirit. Someone has listed the contradictory qualities which make up Chopin's music: laughter, and weeping, coquetry and gentle charm, irony and fury, badinage and gloom, ecstasy and despair. Taking such a list at its face value, one sees that a large genius, a deep human understanding, is required to apprehend these conflicting qualities, and likewise that suavity and energy are required to express them. Paderewski quickly revealed to the Parisian critics his power to understand and interpret. Thus he conquered them on the score of Chopin too. He rediscovered for them the lost vigor of Chopin. He was accepted as the authoritative interpreter of the Polish master. They acknowledged even thus early that he could, in the later words of Alexander Fried, "make magic with the evanescent lyricism of Chopin,"; that his playing, "technically clear and clean" yet also having "a color and a genuine emotional significance . . . is able to achieve the whole technical and poetic purpose" of the master composer. "His temperament is a mirror which sheds glory on the image."

But there was more than Chopin to his first Paris triumphs. "I do not speak of the Chopin interpretations alone," writes the French pianist Alfred Cortot, recalling years afterward those first Paris concerts, "but of his unforgettable interpretations of Beethoven, Schumann, Bach, the magnificent tones of which still ring in my memory." The master composers in Paderewski's voluminous repertoire have included Beethoven, Schumann, Bach, Liszt, Mendelssohn, Schubert, even Wagner, and the moderns . . . too many to name. Critics have at times disagreed on details, but in the end he is acclaimed the masterinterpreter of all the masters. Writing of his Beethoven, Vogel once said: "He knows how to unite the finest sensibility with the utmost sublimity of style."

Originality, as well as fine sensibility, was likewise recognized in his own compositions by the Paris critics. And here again the Chopin factor, just as he knew it would, entered into the calculation. Experience had prepared him for this. "The moment you try to be national," he once declared, "everyone cries out that you are imitating Chopin, whereas the truth is that Chopin adopted all the most marked characteristics of our national music so completely that it is impossible not to resemble him in externals, though your methods and ideas may be absolutely your own." A Polish critic had already passed judgment on this phase of his art some years before his Paris début: "Paderewski does not imitate Chopin. He knows how to find a new unbeaten path to the source." The French agreed with this verdict. More and more they acclaimed him for the vital originality of his music. Paderewski's philosophy of originality was demonstrated from the beginning in his Paris career, the theory of the traditional and the individual fused, and Paris accepted it, yet always with surprise. Jules Combarieu, writing in later years of Paderewski as composer and in particular of his Symphony, said: "Some of our Parisian masters declared that they were far from expecting such a manifestation of musical genius in an artist whom they held to be purely a virtuoso of the keyboard."

By this time not alone all Paris, but all of music loving France was talking about the romantic golden-headed Pole; for his Paris success was quickly followed by equal successes in the French provinces. They began to call him "the human chrysanthemum" because of that wild radiant mane of his tossing like a flame over the keyboard. They raved about his "transparent hands." He was followed in the streets. His lodgings were besieged. His fame got into the newspapers. There was a great deal of gossipy "keyhole criticism", to use his own term for the empty personalities which journalists foist on the public for the sake of sensation and which sometimes pass in the press for criticism. He despises this sort of thing as pointless and a waste of time. He once spoke warmly of this prying of the pseudo-critic into the intimate lives of artists. "Did Beethoven's deafness and all his other infirmities and worries," he asked, "prevent him writing sonorities of the most subtle, most imaginative kind? Chopin was an invalid, as you know, when he was living with George Sand, but his music was volcanic. What does this sort of criticism mean?"

So Paris became Paderewski's headquarters. The world of Paris was his. But there was a wider world waiting for him. Before long his name got across the channel. The London *Daily Telegraph* referred to him as "the lion of Paris." That was the first word of a call beckoning him to new worlds for conquest.

XVI

1890: ENGLAND

IT WAS a young English concert agent, employed at that time by a London impresario, who first noted the arrival of the newcomer with a view to bringing him to England. This was Daniel Mayer, later to be eminent himself as an impresario and as Paderewski's English manager.

Mayer was a "live wire" who kept his eye open for talent and followed carefully the affairs of the artistic world, especially on the continent. One day, scanning the newspapers, he saw a curious name mentioned in a Vienna musical criticism. "The only artist, aside from Stavenhagen and d'Albert who knows how to hold his public," remarked this critical note, "is Paderewski." "Paderewski"—the curious name arrested him. The fact stated by the Vienna critic was interesting enough, but it was the exotic connotation of that odd name, its suggestion of things strange and unknown from far away that held him. For some reason it "burned itself into his brain", as he once expressed it. "It was like the fire of a meteor streaking itself suddenly across his consciousness." He had to find out more about that name and the bearer of it. He did find out. By the time Paderewski had made his Paris début and had registered a Parisian triumph, Mayer knew a good deal about the Pole.

One morning in March, 1890, Mayer was calling on Arthur Chappell, the London music publisher. Chappell picked up a letter from his desk. "What do you think of the cheek of this youngster?" he said. "He writes asking me to arrange a series of concerts for him. Four, he wants no less than four!"

"What is his name?" Mayer asked, taking the letter.

"Pad—something. I can't quite make it out."

Mayer looked at the letter, at the signature first. It was "Paderewski," the strange name that he had first seen in the Vienna paper, that he knew well now from the Paris papers. He caught fire from the suggestion of a Paderewski appearance in London. He gladly took the matter out of Chappell's hands. Arrangements were made, and Paderewski was booked for his four recitals. When Mayer saw him for the first time a curious sensation struck him; he recalled the fiery meteor-like effect of that name when he had first seen it in print. There was something electrifying in the brilliance of the Polish artist's vivid personality, his flaming tawny hair.

The two men were at once attracted to each other. "You will have London at your feet!" Mayer exclaimed. "Go away, flatterer," Paderewski laughed back. Later, when *The Daily Mail* referred to him as "a lion", he asked Mayer amusedly, "Am I then out of a menagerie?"

Paderewski was more nervous about the London début than he had been about Paris. "The mere fact of knowing that a great audience waits on your labor," he once remarked, "is enough to shake all your nerves to pieces." And here the fact that the audience was one wholly new, in a strange land . . .

But there was no great audience gathered in St. James's Hall the evening of May 9, 1890, to greet Paderewski in London. Rain and wind had wrecked the day; the crowd was painfully small; the receipts were barely ten pounds, fifty dollars. And then the much-feared thing happened. Far from the Paris success being repeated, there was almost failure here. It was not alone the smallness of the audience, it was its attitude. It was unresponsive, coldly skeptical. "London cares little, as a rule, for what Paris thinks of new artists," Herman Klein wrote, recalling that occasion, "and it displayed anything but a burning impatience to hear Leschetitsky's latest pupil. A more coldly critical assemblage perhaps it would have been impossible to find. Not a soupçon of magnetic current was in the atmosphere —not even the quickened pulse arising from the anticipation of 'sensational effects'." Klein's picture of the new artist at that moment is graphic. When Paderewski appeared on the platform, he tells us, "there was a mild round of applause accompanied by an undercurrent of whispering and suppressed murmurs that had evident reference to his unwonted picturesqueness of aspect. The deep golden tinge of his hair seemed to accentuate the intense pallor of his countenance. One could plainly see that he was nervous; but in those deep thoughtful eyes, in those firmly-set lips, in that determined chin, one could read also the strong virile qualities of the self-contained, self-reliant artist, already accustomed to conquer audiences and to create magnetism in the most sterile space."

But this was a "sterile space" with a vengeance. The next morning the critics passed their sentence, and they were as the audience had been, cautious, reserved, on the whole decidedly unenthusiastic. True, there was praise of a kind, but it bordered closely on the faint praise that damns. Reading the papers the day after his début Paderewski could see little more than the blame. *The Times* thought that although "the amount of fire and passion he gave to three of Chopin's most difficult studies and to certain passages in Schumann's Fantasia in C Major produced a profound effect", nevertheless his "loudest tones were by no means always beautiful." *The Morning Post* said that his playing was "by no means conventional nor was it always artistic." Joseph Bennett in *The Daily Telegraph* did not "pretend to much admiration for Mr. Paderewski", and could see in him only "a monstrously powerful pianist" who might appeal to "the lover of marvels," because he played "with clang and jangle of metal and with such confusion of sound that trying to follow the working of the parts resembled looking at moving machinery through a fog." In the opinion of the *Telegraph* critic Paderewski's performance had been "the march of an abnormally active mammoth across the keyboard while the wondering observer expected the pianoforte to break down any moment." "Plainly we do not like Mr. Paderewski," the *Telegraph* critic concluded. "The result of his labors may be marvellous, but it is not music."

It was not only the artist's nervousness that served him ill that wet and windy evening. The effects of the sensational pub-

licity which the "keyhole" press of Paris had given him, and
which he detested, also were felt. The opinion of the London
Standard was colored by this; *The Standard* critic believed that
"the performer was more anxious to astonish than to charm."
"His rendering of a Prelude and Fugue in E Minor of Mendelssohn," this critic went on, "was utterly at variance with the
traditional methods of interpreting the music of this composer." "Much noise, little music" was *The Standard's* final
verdict: "That he is entitled to the higher rank of an artist is
more than can be said." *The Daily News* followed *The Standard* in unjustly crediting Paderewski's "leonine advertising" to
himself, and accused him of indulging in "extravagance" in his
performance. Klein, to quote once more from his recollections
of the *début,* says that "exactly how he played that day—
I mean, as compared with the Paderewski whose every mood
was by and by to become familiar—it is rather hard for me to
say. That he strove to be 'sensational' I do not believe now,
though at the time it was difficult to think otherwise. For surely
his contrasts were startling in their violence, and the instrument fairly thundered under his execution of a forte passage.
At times there seemed to be no restraint whatever. His magnificent technique enabled him to give free rein to his impulse
and imagination, and *laissez aller* was then the word."

Some of the things said by the London press the day following the début were "hard sayings", difficult for the young Pole
to take. The critics, almost to a man, were seemingly deaf to
the combined poetic tenderness and virile force of his Chopin
renderings and the romantic glow of his Schumann, and they
described as "eccentric" his Händel and Mendelssohn. They
preferred his interpretation of Liszt and Rubinstein. They
liked best of all his renderings of his own "Trois Humoresques
à l'antique," and the inevitable "Minuet", which had been enthusiastically encored. But such praises, when they were given
at all, did not console him much. True, there was one real grain
of comfort; his authority as an interpreter of Chopin was recognized by at least one critic. "It is in Chopin," said *The Times*,
"that Mr. Paderewski is at his best, and here not so much on the

sentimental side of the master's work as in his passionate and fiery moods." In the praise, too, one name stood out—George Bernard Shaw, in *The World*. Shaw was then beginning his work as a music critic, and, characteristically, he differed in opinion from all of his colleagues, finding Paderewski "alert, humorous, delightful, dignified, intelligent." How very characteristic this was of Shaw was revealed later when the story had changed and London critics had veered to uniform praise. To be his own contrary self, Shaw then could see Paderewski only as "sensational, empty, vulgar, violent."

However, no matter what chagrin and disappointment Paderewski suffered out of his London début, he was not beaten nor was he shaken in his own confidence in his powers. He went on with his recitals, four as originally scheduled. The critics began to modify their judgments. The public warmed up. The third recital altered the barometer from "change" to "fair"; his performance of Schumann's "Carnaval" and of Beethoven's Sonata in A flat, Op. 110, marked a real turn in the public's attitude. The fourth program, devoted entirely to Chopin, was sold out in advance. The receipts for the series had mounted from the beggarly ten pounds of the first recital to a total of two hundred and eighty pounds, some fourteen hundred dollars. These meager returns from Paderewski's initial London appearances are interesting when compared to the large fee paid a few years later by Robert Newman for one Paderewski recital in Queen's Hall, one thousand pounds, five thousand dollars.

The nervous strain of these days on Paderewski was heavy. Alone by himself he really was shaken. When Mayer came on the afternoon of the Chopin recital to tell him of the sell-out he found the artist in a little gloomy room practicing. Mayer told him his good news. Paderewski could hardly believe it. Tears came to his eyes, so sudden was the reaction from disappointment to success. To hide his feeling he pressed his hands to his face, bent over the keyboard, and said with a trembling voice, "Oh, I can't play at all! It's wrong. I can't take their money. I can't play at all!"

It was during his London début that he introduced himself to
England as a composer, giving his Concerto in A Minor, Op. 17,
written at twenty-eight. The critics accorded him at least originality as a composer and some few years later they were deeply
disappointed when the plans fell through for the première
in London of his opera "Manru". The negotiations for this
première had been made with Sir Augustus Harris, but Harris
required certain alterations in the libretto which at the time
Paderewski could not accept. It is interesting to note that in
the end most of these alterations were made when the opera
was originally performed at Dresden in 1901. In 1907 the
same London critics were excited over the prospect of a production of Paderewski's Symphony, which was to have been performed by the London Symphony Orchestra that season. When
it was finally given, with Arthur Nikisch conducting, an incident
occurred of the kind that makes understandable Paderewski's
strong hold on the musician as well as on the public. He attended a rehearsal of the Symphony, but he would not appear
at the performance. "No," he said, "that is to be Nikisch's day,
not mine." He knew that his appearance would make a sensation and he would do nothing to take the conductor's laurels
from him. He left London before the performance.

But now, in these first trying London days, if his fourth recital was a success, he was still not satisfied. He might indeed
remind himself that *The Globe* had said that "his mastery of
the keyboard is complete, his touch so exquisite both in *fortissimo* and *pianissimo* passages and in the three intermediate
gradations of tone that every shade of expression is at his command, and in the art of singing on the pianoforte he can only
be compared with Thalberg." Or that *The Saturday Review*
had called him "one of the most remarkable artists who have
been heard of late years." Again, recalling the accusations
of sensationalism that had been made, he might recall the
frankly appreciative words of the same critic of *The Globe:*
"There is no kind of *charlatanerie* in his playing; wrapped up
completely in the works he performs he devotes himself to
their exposition and while thus engaged appears to ignore the

presence of an audience." He might remember too that *The Daily News* critic had in the end credited him with "delicacy and poetical feeling," and that *The Standard* had agreed that "he plays fewer wrong notes than most pianists" and that "his tone in *pianissimo* passages is bell-like and delicate." But all this, good as it was, was not enough, it was not what he wanted. He wished to conquer London as he had conquered Vienna and Paris. He knew he could do it. Despite such moments of nerve-wrought discouragement as that when he had cried to Mayer "I can't play at all!" he knew he had the capacity, the power, to prove himself.

To conquer London he decided to attack England. Before leaving London, however, he gave in addition to the four recitals, an orchestral concert at which he played his own Concerto in A Minor, Saint-Saëns' Concerto in C Minor, and Liszt's "Fantaisie Hongroise", the conductor being Henschel. "And if it failed to arouse wide-spread interest," Klein writes, "this parting shot served to hit the mark so truly that I, for one, no longer hesitated to acknowledge Paderewski as a really great artist."

The London début had resulted, in Paderewski's mind, in a challenge. He would accept the challenge. He may be a Polish poet, but he can be a fighting Pole as well. He fought his London fight with the strategy of a commander and he fought it with the tactics of open fire; no ambush and no camouflage. He went to the provinces, and he heralded himself there with all the attacks and condemnations of the metropolitan critics.

This was his own strategy, for Mayer, disturbed by the London reception and fearing the effect of it in other cities, wished to delete from the reprints of the criticisms at least the most damaging passages. "No," Paderewski decided. "You will print in the advertisements for the provinces every word they have written about me. Unless this is done I shall be obliged to cancel the engagements." All of Daniel Mayer's eloquence, and he was an eloquent man, all his friendly sophistries, could not move the young pianist. Defeated beforehand, as Mayer thought, Paderewski went to the provinces.

He was received there enthusiastically, his success was immediate and unmistakable. Then, in 1891, he returned to London. And London reversed its verdict. His concerts created a furore, the acclaim was unanimous and even extravagant. "There had been opportunities in the meantime for reflection," as Klein tells us, "and the public was now beginning to scent a veritable musical 'lion'." "I used to receive letters from women readers asking all sorts of questions about the Polish pianist and begging for particulars that in no way concerned them," Klein continues. "These of course went unanswered; for the English journalist is less generous than his American confrère in dispensing information about the private lives of artists. But the very existence of such curiosity told a tale. There would be no more 'meager audiences' when Paderewski played. As a matter of fact, his Chopin recital at St. James's Hall in July drew the largest crowd and the highest receipts recorded since the final visit of Rubinstein. He also appeared at the Philharmonic, at a Richter concert, and at an orchestral concert of his own, when he was heard in the greatest two of all pianoforte concertos: the E flat ('Emperor') of Beethoven and the A Minor of Schumann. It was his superb rendering of these masterpieces that, in England at least, assured the fame of the gifted Pole."

Thus another score for the good name of Poland was marked on Paderewski's chart. During his tour of England, in 1894, he played in twenty-two cities, and in nearly every case the entire seating for his concerts was sold out two months in advance.

Paderewski became even a greater sensation in England than on the Continent. The cue that lined up before St. James's Hall for his recitals was often a block long and more than once scores of people stood in line all day long, bringing their breakfasts and their lunches with them in order to secure seats. Queen Victoria received him, showered him with honors, had him play before her court, presented him with a signed photograph; Victoria's daughter, the Princess Louise, an artist, begged the favor of painting his portrait. The boy from the Podolian farm was giving royal sittings. Two others of the greatest English artists asked the same privilege. Alma-Tadema and Burne-Jones both made portraits of him. Out of the Alma-Tadema sittings came one of his best life-time friendships. The brilliant daughter of the painter, Laurence Alma-Tadema, was so stirred by the genius of the Polish artist that from that time on her life was devoted to the Polish cause. She studied the language and became a champion of Paderewski's oppressed people. It is to Laurence Alma-Tadema that we owe the distinguished translation of Paderewski's Chopin Panegyric, the publication of which in English was characteristically devoted to the raising of relief funds for Poland. Six translations in verse of songs by Mickiewicz, set to music by Paderewski, made another of Miss Alma-Tadema's contributions to the Polish cause.

During his first London days Paderewski made the acquaintance of and formed friendships with many of the leaders of British thought who, in the strange weaving of the pattern of his life, were to stand by him in later years and support him in his struggle to free his country. Royalty, nobility, statesmen, artists, all were attracted to him and held by admiration. Among the artists none was so warm in regard as the English composer Sir Edward Elgar, famous for his setting to music of Cardinal Newman's "Dream of Gerontius." Elgar composed especially for Paderewski his "Polonia," a tribute that moved the Polish artist deeply not alone because it was dedicated to him but because it was inspired by his motherland.

In London Paderewski's Parisian social triumphs were repeated. With the Queen herself receiving him, every door was open to him. The thirty-year-old musician, extremely youthful in his appearance, charmed London society not alone with the unspoiled grace and simplicity of his personality, but with his breadth of mind. They discovered that, youthful though he was, he was a good deal more than merely an artist, in the popular term; rather, that he was the true artist who does not withdraw into the confining precincts of professionalism, but who makes contact with life at a hundred tangents, who lives a full life made only the fuller by his art. He fulfilled the old

Roman definition of the poet: *Humani nihil a me alienum puto*. He was the best of conversationalists, an easy listener with a ready wit and an unpretentious responsiveness. "He passed lightly from one subject to another," one English writer, Herbert Hughes, reports; "he spoke with an emphasis that indicated an intellectual authority belonging to a world of greater importance than the concert platform."

A little flash-light picture of young Paderewski in the drawing rooms of the British capital, which he now held so completely in his conquest, is found in the pages of Herman Klein's "Thirty Years of Musical Life in London," from which I have already been quoting. A warm friendship grew up between the artist and this critic, dating from that London orchestral concert, at which the Beethoven and Schumann concertos mentioned above were so superbly rendered. Paderewski's manager, Daniel Mayer, had requested Klein to undertake the writing of such brief analytical notes as the program required, and, instead of following conventional lines or of describing these familiar works in detail, Klein had contented himself with a more or less detailed contrast of the characteristic features of the two concertos. "This," says Klein, "appeared to have pleased and interested Paderewski; and when I was introduced to him after the concert he said some charming things in that charming manner which is so characteristic of the man. We quickly became close friends. I learned not only to appreciate the real magnitude of his gifts as a creative and executive musician, but also to gauge his rare intellectuality and to respect his broadminded views as cultured artist and man of the world. During his many visits to London we saw a great deal of each other, and more than once he testified to his kindly regard for me." Mr. Klein then gives us our flash-light picture of Paderewski among his intimates and away from the recital stage.

The date, fixed by the artist himself, happened to be a significant one. It was the Third of May, Poland's national holiday. The guests at dinner included Sir Arthur Sullivan, Sir Alexander Mackenzie, Sir Joseph Barnby, Klein's old master

Manuel Garcia, and the veteran 'cellist, Signor Alfredo Piatti. "I was especially gratified to be the means of bringing Paderewski and Sullivan together. They were acquainted, I fancy, but had not met frequently; at any rate, the former wrote me: 'Inutile de vous dire que je serai absolument enchanté de passer une soirée chez vous, avec vous, et de rencontrer Sir Sullivan [sic], que j'admire beaucoup.' "

"Just before dinner," Mr. Klein goes on with his story, "a quaint sort of letter was placed in my hands. It was from someone in the famous pianist's entourage, reminding me that Mr. Paderewski was very fatigued after his heavy work in the provinces and begging that I would under no circumstances ask him to play that evening. I was half amused, half annoyed by this unexpected communication, which, of course, I knew better than to regard as inspired by my guest of honor himself. However, I thought no more about it until after dinner, when I took an opportunity to inform Paderewski, in a whispered 'aside', of the strange warning I had received. I assured him seriously that I had not the slightest idea of asking him to play, and that my friends were more than satisfied to have the pleasure of meeting him and enjoying his society. He replied:

" 'Do you imagine I think otherwise? This is a case of "save me from my friends!" That I am tired is perfectly true. But when I am in the mood to play, fatigue counts for nothing. And I am in that mood tonight. Are you really going to have some music?'

" 'Yes, Piatti has brought his 'cello and he is going to take part in the Rubinstein Sonata in D.'

" 'Then I should like to play it with him; and more besides if he will permit me. Piatti and I are now old colleagues at the "Pops" and we always get on splendidly together.' "

So Paderewski played. "An unalloyed delight," says Klein, "was the performance of that lovely Sonata by the prince of 'cellists and the greatest of living pianists." Piatti was happier over it than anyone. "I have played the Sonata with Rubinstein many times," he told Klein afterward, "but it never went better."

The scene ends with Paderewski at the piano, all listening enraptured, and Sir Arthur Sullivan standing close beside him fascinated by the movement of his fingers. "Paderewski seemed inspired. Fatigue was forgotten." He seemed much fresher that night, after his long tour, than the night before at the Philharmonic when he had introduced to London his fine Polish Fantasia. The Fantasia had been first played in England in 1893, at the Norwich Music Festival, almost immediately after its composition during the summer of that year, while he was sojourning at Yport on the French coast; he had completed the composition in five weeks. He played on from one piece to another "with characteristic forgetfulness of self." It was well on to dawn before the company parted.

Sullivan standing by the piano was indeed fascinated by the magic of Paderewski's fingers. The others, seated about, held by the music, could not help but watch the movement of the pianist's romantic head, the enraptured expression of his face. It was the profile that Burne-Jones, the face that Alma-Tadema, has given us. A study of these two portraits makes a good composite picture of the artist as he was at the time of these first triumphs which established him as a world celebrity. The slender youth whom Paris had seen as a frail poet with sunken cheeks and face transparent in its spirituality, has now in his frame and his visage a new strength, even, as Opienski remarks, commenting on Alma-Tadema's more realistic portrait, something of that touch of irony of which Alfred Nossig once spoke, an expression which his audience has often seen on his face as he accepted its applause, the look of a dreamer being waked from his dream. If it is irony, it is not an irony that excludes the charm of high sentiment, of idealism and benevolence. All of that sentiment and its idealism glows in the poetic face that Burne-Jones presents. The Burne-Jones portrait, done in pencil and completed on the one sheet of paper without redrawing in a single sitting of only two hours, is in the opinion of James Huneker "the best and most spiritual interpretation we have had as yet of this spiritual artist. His life has been full of sorrow, of adversity; of viciousness never.

Nature points every meanness, every moral weakness with unsparing brush, and I suppose, after all, one of the causes of Paderewski's phenomenal success has been his expressive, poetic personality. His heart is pure, his life clean, his ideals lofty."

What strikes most forcibly those who know the early photographs, those of the Tatra period, is that this Burne-Jones portrait, made in the hour of laudation, of royal adulation and popular acclaim, is the portrait of a man unspoiled. He is still the young man of Modjeska's description, "one of Fra Angelico's angels." But he is decidedly a male angel. There is something ethereal, almost unreal, about this profile so rapidly sketched in what must have been an inspired moment for the artist. It is more like an ideal head than a portrait, more like a vision than a picture. It is full, strong, beautiful, a face with the fascination not alone of the spiritual but almost of the supernatural. There is something of the Viking in it, something of the keel of a ship. I saw the same look and the same light in Modjeska's face, as of a ship that breasts the gale and rides the wave, of a keel that if it is stormed by dark waters, those waters are starlit. Studying it, seeing Paderewski as Burne-Jones saw him in 1890, it is easy to understand how he came to fight for the conquest of England, and how he came to win the fight.

XVII

1891: AMERICA

THIS is the young man who was to come to America a year later. That Viking face was to feel the winds and the spray of the Atlantic as he made the long-dreamed-of venture over the ocean to the New World. He was to walk the deck at night and wonder what was in store for him. The sea and the stars and the ever widening distance from the solid earth of the only world he had known were to give him a strange new sensation, a feeling of tremendous pressure, and of tremendous release of new power, a new impulse toward achievement. He did not guess then that the New World was to become as familiar with his face as if it were printed on one of her postage stamps.

Paderewski's coming to America was inevitable. To begin with, he had dreamed of it, no matter how vaguely, from the days when he was a boy in Warsaw, the days when Wieniawski came home to Poland to thrill his compatriots with stories of the New World; when Maurice Neville came and told Modjeska that she must let America see her art; when Modjeska herself crossed the Atlantic and came back and talked to him, during those happy Tatra days, of her adventures overseas. Doubtless those incidents had played their part in bringing him here. But now America was inevitable, not alone because America demanded him out of the height of his European fame, but because, shaped by his genius to be the exponent of a universal art, he belonged no longer to Poland nor to Europe but to the whole world. A tour of the United States was the next logical step in the course of a career destined to be international.

The tour began in New York. On November 17, 1891, a few days after his thirty-first birthday, in Carnegie Hall, Pad-

erewski made his first American appearance. Three large concerts with orchestra were given, but so great was their success
that when, following them, he inaugurated a series of recitals
in the concert hall of Madison Square Garden, he was obliged
to move back to the larger auditorium, the largest in the city,
seating three thousand, to accommodate the crowds. This for
recital programs was at that time something phenomenal, the
soloist recital being then an innovation. Famous virtuosi who
had preceded Paderewski in America had invariably brought
assisting artists with them to give variety to their programs.
Rubinstein and Von Bülow, both with sensational successes in
their American record, had given their recitals thus. But Paderewski, to the surprise of all, was more than sufficient by himself alone. Returning to Carnegie Hall after five recitals in
Madison Square, he played ten times more, giving a total of
eighteen concerts in New York during his first season. The
whole tour totalled one hundred and seven recitals.

The immediate success of his first appearance was the beginning of a triumphal tour of the country, as it was the beginning
of a series of triumphal tours to follow, year after year for over
forty years. The history of those forty years makes an amazing
chronicle of figures and statistics. The young pianist landing in
New York in November, 1891, could not dream of the day
when he would look back on a record of more than fifteen
hundred American concerts. The vast expanses of the United
States and Canada lay before him, but he did not know then
that he was yet to play in over two hundred cities, that he was
to appear in every one of the forty-eight States of the Union,
and the Dominion Provinces, that he was to travel some three
hundred and sixty thousand miles, that more than five million
people were to hear him, and that he was to reap a great fortune from the piano on which he had been told as a boy in
Warsaw that he was "wasting his time."

Taken after-the-fact these figures, even though they be
amazing, make the record of Paderewski's American success
seem easy. But it was not as easy as it sounds. The simple statement of an instant success in New York and of continued

triumphal tours over the continent tells only half the story. There is much more to it than that. There was in the first place an adjustment to be made to life in this New World, which, in spite of the universal likeness of people in all countries, was very different from anything he had known. If Paderewski, arriving in America, experienced what all travellers experience on coming to a new land—that is, a certain sense of disappointment in finding that after all it is the same old world and that people are people wherever one goes—on the other hand he discovered that this was really a New World, a world wholly unlike the familiar world of Europe. Even the weather, the radical change of climate with its sudden temperatures, played its part, as he learned during his first stay in New York. There came a "nasty Saturday" shortly after his arrival which affected his nervous system noticeably, and consequently his playing. Even the English language, which he had fairly mastered before his coming, was not spoken as he had heard it spoken. Social customs, marked by the fine-cut differentia which emphasizes national cultures, were new to him. Business methods were new, management, the arrangement of concert bookings, railway travel, money, everything was strange.

There was also a whole world of new people to meet, and the ties with the old countries, with colleagues in Vienna, Paris, London, Warsaw, were few. True, there was Modjeska again reigning supreme on the stage in America, as she had reigned in Poland when he had gone to Warsaw as a boy. The de Reszke brothers and Marcella Sembrich, all compatriots, were among the stars of American opera; in the two de Reszkes, Jean the tenor and gigantic Edouard the basso, he found his happiest companionship in these first strange days, and he tells delightful anecdotes of the trio's foregatherings in New York. Josef Hofmann, whose father, one time teacher in the Warsaw Conservatory, had been one of Alfred Kerntopf's circle of musical friends, was the world's wonder-child at the piano. And there was a strong and influential body of Polish-American citizenry, with distinguished leaders, to welcome him. Nevertheless, this was emphatically a new world to which he must

PADEREWSKI ON HIS FIRST APPEARANCE IN AMERICA

adjust himself and for a time the nervous strain under which he lived was intense.

First of all he must adjust himself to that incredible colossus, New York, a city totally different from any other in his experience; and, even more difficult, to the still more incredible colossus, North America, the vast United States, the wide reaches of Canada, which at first appeared to him so large that even the dimensions of the Russia which he knew so well seemed dwarfed. Travelling at times some twenty thousand miles in a few months, from coast to coast and up and down, he asked himself in amazement more than once during his first American tours, "Is there no end to it?" Here, too, in this huge country, that sense of artistic responsibility which is so highly developed in him, suddenly took on the dimensions of a gigantic *noblesse oblige*. To cover the ground allotted to a tour, he must make his home in a railway coach, live in railway yards, yet be fresh and ready day after day, no matter what his fatigue or his nervous exhaustion. There were multitudes awaiting him at every turn, crowds the size of which he had not known before. And always there were the critics, all strange, some hostile. It was a tremendous experience.

The first practical problem he had to solve was how to arrange his manner of living in order to best carry on his work. His personal manager at that time was Hugo Gorlitz, an employé of Mayer's London concert bureau. To Gorlitz he entrusted the task of working out a schedule by which he could cover the great distances of American touring. Many things had to be talked over. Intermittent journeys with hotel lodgings were not practicable. There would have to be a private car. But even a pianist must eat, as Paderewski had learned as a boy in Warsaw. "Before starting on a tour," as Gorlitz once explained, "a series of menus was prepared, and, in accordance with the same, the car was provided with everything but fish and bread. These could be obtained at different stations by telegraphing ahead."

As a rule Paderewski while on tour takes his principal meal after his concert, usually about eleven o'clock at night. He has

had always to be careful of his eating, careful of every detail
that insures physical fitness, and in his early American days he
learned many things about the regulation of his diet and his
exercise. Especially he learned to protect himself from colds
so easily caught in the unaccustomed extremes of the American
climate, particularly when coming from a heated concert hall
after the heavy nervous and physical strain of a recital. During
his American visits his personal physician was for years Dr.
Francis Fronczak of Buffalo, Paderewski and Fronczak having
made a friendship while the latter was attending Canisius College, Buffalo, and working as a journalist to earn money for
his medical schooling. They met in 1891 when Fronczak was
sent by the editor of the Buffalo *Courier* to interview the pianist
on his first American tour. Paderewski's gift for sudden and
lasting attachments and for sympathetic interest in ambitious
and worthy youth came into play, and a life-long friendship
was formed. He told Fronczak, "If ever I need a doctor you
shall be the man," and he kept his word. Fronczak took very
seriously his mission of watching over the health of his illustrious patient. "Our acquaintance grew into friendship and
finally into a mutual love which has never been tarnished in all
these forty years," Dr. Fronczak told me in 1932. "I know of
no person who has been more friendly, more charitable, or who
has given impetus for greater and higher things than Ignace
Jan Paderewski."

In the matter of the preparation of food Paderewski is a
specialist. He believes rightly that food is one of the important
things in life—especially for artists, who often go hungry. He
has frankly criticized American and English cooking. Americans he once remarked, are indifferent to quality; "they are
rich, rich enough to spoil French cooking." "You have good
fruits, you have good meats, but nothing else is good except
the scallops, which are the best things you have. The fish is
abominable. You have destroyed your lobsters, your salmon,
your terrapin, your forests. You never think that another generation is coming." And England is worse than America—
"excellent foodstuffs but nothing tastes good."

A hearty eater who enjoys good food, Paderewski has never been stingy about sharing with others, as we know from the story told by Copper, his Pullman chef for many years. When Paderewski learned that there were some hungry tramps in the railroad yard where his car was sidetracked he instructed Copper to give to everyone that asked a good square meal. Copper obeyed, but the news spread too quickly; very soon the chef had to go to the master and complain that, if this kept up, he wouldn't be able to feed even Paderewski. "All right," Paderewski said. "Give each one that asks for food half a dollar." This was worse. The occasional hungry hobo grew into a small crowd. Copper then took matters into his own hands. With a frying-pan in one hand and a rolling-pin in the other he drove the beggars away. But all his life Paderewski has "fed multitudes", not always with Copper at hand to guard the larder. During his incumbency as Prime Minister of Poland and throughout his five years of political and diplomatical career Paderewski entertained lavishly, but he paid out of his own pocket, never out of the public treasury, for every dish that was served.

The securing of the private car was no off-hand matter. Paderewski had not yet made a fortune, and the cost was immense —twenty-five first class passenger fares over the entire routing for the privilege. But there was no other possible arrangement; and that arrangement made, there were a hundred other details to be settled. A piano had to be installed, an upright, to save space. And there must be a piano-tuner taken along to keep the instrument fit; for the daily practice, hours of it, must be kept up. At times stops were made in cities long enough for lodgings to be taken at a hotel, and in every such case a piano must be placed in the artist's rooms beforehand. "But sometimes," Gorlitz explained, "we would not leave the train for three weeks at a time." The piano on the train was indispensable. Incidentally that piano often attracted groups of workers in the railway yards, men who gathered around the Paderewski car to listen enraptured while he practiced for his recital of the day.

Some gorgeous Paderewski recitals have been given gratis on the switch-track.

There was one thing that has surprised all those who have had to deal with Paderewski from the beginning of his career in America. He is an artist, famous, picturesque, temperamental; but in business dealings he is at all times clear-headed, practical, definite. At his desk he knows exactly what he wants, just as at the piano he knows exactly what he is playing. "He is always sure of his notes," as George Bernard Shaw wrote of him in London. Likewise he is always sure of his wants. He has the statesman's gift of delegation; he trusts others, others trust him, and things are done. An engagement once properly fulfilled, all is arranged for all time between manager and artist. For many years his American manager was C. A. Ellis, manager of the Boston Symphony Orchestra. Ellis directed the Paderewski tours until his retirement. Later came George Engles. Since his first tour under Engles there have been no written contracts between them. "The arrangements for another tour are completed in ten minutes," says Mr. Engles. "At one time I received without previous warning a cablegram, 'What do you think of seventy to seventy-five concerts next winter?' In ten minutes my answer was on the wire, 'Tour all booked.' Actually, the complete bookings for that entire tour were closed in three days. That's the way he likes to do business. He detests letters or any form of written communication. As a matter of fact, he will not tolerate unnecessary transactions of any kind."

"Every manager wants him and adores him into the bargain," Engles says. "There is no artist more reasonable, reliable and considerate of the local manager's interests." He does more than make handsome profits for them. Once when a blizzard depleted the hall of a small-town manager Paderewski insisted on personally examining the box-office accounts to find out what deficit there was so that he might make it up.

There is never any doubt about his movements. "I may not hear from him for months," says Engles, "but I know that he will be on a certain ship, landing in New York at a certain time. And he knows that I will be with the hotel crew at the dock, that his seven pianos will be waiting for his examination and then routed over different parts of the country to meet him as he needs them;"—memories of that pianoless runaway tour of his when he was a student in Warsaw! "Also that his private train with its piano and its crew will be ready for him to occupy and live in during the tour."

If Paderewski is easy to get on with, however, he is not "easy." There is nothing negative in his make-up. He is a "positive." Frequently he has been likened to Liszt in his character of benevolent friend to everyone. But Liszt, according to Arthur Nikisch, who knew him well, never could learn to say "no"; fed up by adulation he retained in his old age a perpetually indulgent smile, his habit of universal benevolence prohibiting him to ever refuse anything. Paderewski, sharing with Liszt the attribute of generosity, seldom says "No" when his pocket is assailed; but in matters of art or affairs he can say his "No" as readily and as definitely as his "Yes". According to his friend Engles "he never repeats an order. If he found that he had to repeat an order he would get another manager." An English critic, Arthur Johnstone, once wrote of his art as having "a certain princely quality . . . indescribably *galant* and *chevaleresque*." This quality is in his person; his business orders are simply his wishes expressed. But they are the commands of a ruler.

A well-balanced personality such as this is assured beforehand of coming to his recital, in the words of Engles, "poised, composed, prepared." One thing that insures this is the rigorous regularity and the spartan-like sobriety of his daily routine. He is a good sleeper, he falls asleep easily. "After his labors," Harold Bauer wrote, recalling the days when he worked with Paderewski, "he would go to bed and sleep like a child." He often reads in bed; but his sleep he must have, either at night or by daytime. He usually rises late, at ten on days when he is not playing, at one when he has a recital. His morning repast, if he has an afternoon concert, is a cup of coffee or of tea, nothing more, not even bread or toast. But he is fond of his regular American breakfast of grapefruit and bacon and eggs.

On concert days he eats nothing before playing except one soft-boiled egg. During intermission in a concert he drinks a lemonade without sugar, and sometimes after the concert, before dining, a glass of champagne, preferring the sweet to the dry. He smokes; he must have his cigarettes and he likes others to smoke with him. And yet, simply to prove to himself that he was master of his habits, not his habits master of him, he quit smoking at one time and by sheer force of will refrained from tobacco for an entire year. Not until he was fully satisfied that he could control the habit did he take it up again.

Among Paderewski's intimates his devotion to gymnastic exercises is well known. "It is highly desirable," he has said, "that he who strives to attain the highest excellence as a performer on the pianoforte should have well developed muscles, a strong nervous system, and, in fact, be in as good general health as possible." It is not alone his "piano hands" that he cares for, although he does give them the greatest care; wrists and fingers are massaged daily, and he steeps his hands in very hot water before playing. As to practice, to avoid fatigue at the recital he reduces his usual five or six hours to two or three if he has an evening concert, and practices little or not at all if he has an afternoon program. He is strongly in favor of finger-exercises. "In thirty or forty minutes I can put my hands in better condition than by practising two hours on the music of my programs." Once he remarked, after his American tour of 1905, "I am afraid I have overdone the practice. Often I have spent the entire night on a Beethoven sonata. I must take more rest." "One uses his physical energy in music," he said during his 1927 American tour. "Decline or illness registers nowhere so quickly. When I begin to play badly, then I shall need no doctor to tell me I am not well."

He watches his whole physique, like a prize-fighter. "It might be thought," he says, "that practice on the pianoforte itself would bring about the necessary increase in muscular power and endurance. This, however, is not altogether the case, as it sometimes has a distinctly deteriorative effect, owing to the muscles being kept cramped and unused. The chief muscles actually used are those of the hand, the forearm, neck, small of the back . . . It is not so much that greater strength of muscle will give greater power for the pianoforte, but rather that the fact of the muscle being in good condition will help the player to express his artistic talent without so much effort. To play for a great length of time is often very painful, and you cannot expect a player to lose himself in his art when every movement of his hands is provocative of discomfort, if not of actual pain."

Harold Bauer has confirmed what Paderewski said about muscular strength aiding the artist to express himself more fully. His physical power, Mr. Bauer said, "gave Paderewski an enormous range of tone color possibilities. His palette was extremely broad. It was possible for him to go from gossamer effects to veritable storms."

Paderewski's friendship with Bauer, it is interesting here to note, began in a rather curious way. Bauer, as is well known, began his career as a violinist; until he was well past his twenties, after years of training, he did not dream of being a pianist. In the beginning he taught himself to play the piano simply because he was curious about it. Then came an opportunity to use his piano knowledge: in London Paderewski hired him to practice concertos with him, Bauer at a second piano reading off the orchestral accompaniment while Paderewski worked on the solo parts. After two or three turns at such practice Paderewski, impressed by the ability of his assistant, remarked, "You're too good to submerge yourself in other people's playing," and he asked him to play something for him. "Let me hear what you can do alone." "Gladly," Bauer replied. "But tomorrow." "To-morrow?" "You see, I didn't bring my instrument with me today." Paderewski was puzzled. "Didn't bring your instrument?" he exclaimed, glancing at the concert-grand piano. "But I am a violinist," said Bauer. And from that moment, it might be said, Bauer's greater career as a pianist, thanks to Paderewski, began.

Paderewski's amazing physical endurance is shown in his programs. He has at times played straight through for three hours. In his recitals the first group alone will include three gigantic compositions, such as a Bach Fantasy and Fugue, a big Beethoven Sonata and some other large work usually of the romantic type, such as a Schumann or Chopin Sonata or Carnaval, or Etudes Symphoniques; all this followed by an extensive Chopin group, and, on top of that, some shorter works, with a big Liszt or Wagner-Liszt to wind up with. This makes in substance two recitals in one, as compared with the programs of other artists; and a third recital invariably follows because of the clamoring of the audience and its refusal to leave. Truly, only a Hercules could stand such labor; the physical energy expended in one such program would express itself in tons.

He is an excellent swimmer and is fond of walking, taking a "constitutional", sometimes of several miles when opportunity allows; one of his favorite walks in America for years has been Prospect Park in Brooklyn, where, as the Pepys of the day, O. O. McIntyre, describes him, "he roams the unbeaten by-paths, knocking his head against the stars." Moreover, he knows how to walk—he is a "saunterer." Hurry is not in the lexicon of his legs. Thus he refreshes himself, thus he is prepared for the strain that a lengthy performance makes on arms, legs, feet and back. It was during his first American visit, before he had learned all the secrets of conserving himself, that he felt the severest effects of touring. "The nerves and muscles at the back of his neck and at the top of his shoulder-blades," Madame Paderewska once told, "would rise up in great knots and cause him intense agony, so that Mr. Gorlitz was compelled to massage his neck after each recital." "In the course of one hundred and seventeen days," as Paderewski himself recalled, "I played in one hundred and seven concerts and attended eighty-six dinner parties. Mon Dieu, but I was cross!" That was another thing Paderewski learned during his "railroading days"—to trim very closely on social engagements. So fond of company that while at home he keeps his house filled with guests, he discovered nevertheless that he could not stand the strain of entertainment while on tour. Often during his American travels he would refuse all but the most intimate invitations, excepting where children expected him. Then he would go, and for the children he would volunteer to play, although naturally at most social gatherings he preferred to be free of the piano for at least an hour or so.

Once while Paderewski was in London he became interested in the famous "strong man" Sandow and his physical culture movement, and he took this up with such earnestness that he was able to perform surprising feats of strength. According to Ernest Schelling he could stand erect, without support, with one leg held out backward, and support Schelling's full weight on the calf of his leg. Harold Bauer, relating some of his experiences during the days when he played in London with Paderewski, called him "a physical giant." "His endurance and strength were enormous. . . . When I was playing with him at Erard's he insisted upon having a chair that was especially heavy. It had a weight under the seat and stood like a rock in front of the keyboard. It must have weighed at least eighty or ninety pounds. I know, because my own traveling chair weighed forty-five pounds. Once I said to him, 'Move one of these chairs,' and he lifted it as though it were a slight bentwood chair."

His careful attention to exercise from the beginning of his career has kept Paderewski in remarkable health, so that after nearly half a century of strenuous living and beyond the three score and ten which means old age for most men, he is as vigorous as a well-preserved man of fifty. His rapid recuperation in 1931, at seventy, from an operation for appendicitis surprised his physicians at the hospital in Lausanne. He came back from that close call fresh and strong and made another triumphal tour of some eighteen thousand miles. Except for painful attacks of neuritis, due to the constant use of his arms, he has never been ill. In 1909 neuritis obliged him to cancel some of his recitals, and during the war, especially in Poland when I was there in 1919, he suffered severely. A serious phlebitis afflicted one of his legs in 1930, but this was completely cured by a French specialist from Orleans.

For the purpose of strengthening his arms Paderewski invented an apparatus of his own; besides this he uses light twelve-ounce dumb-bells. His gymnastic exercises he takes in the morning on rising, and anyone overhearing him from an adjoining room at that hour might think that he was counting piano scales, "one-two, one-two—one, two, three." Sometimes the narrow confines of his Pullman bedroom have come near to precipitating an accident, due to the danger of his crashing his hand through the window. "Oh, I am careful now!" he once exclaimed, "I came very near it the other day, when the train lurched." A Paderewski hand cut by window-glass would be an expensive accident.

Sometimes there are accidents. One serious one came very near costing him his life. As it was it cost him one of the greatest disappointments of his life, for he was on his way at the time to preside over a public testimonial to his friend Madame Modjeska, a testimonial which he had himself inaugurated. He could not appear. The accident occurred at Syracuse, N. Y., in April, 1905, and was due to a collision between Paderewski's train and the Buffalo Express. To avoid complete demolition the switchman of Paderewski's engine threw his train off the track, just in time to save his passengers from being cut to pieces. It was at night and Paderewski was at the table eating. The collision threw him with such force that his back was severely injured. Nevertheless he insisted on continuing. Some Canadian concerts following the accident he played in great pain. Dr. Fronczak was sent for; he joined him at Niagara Falls and remained beside him, traveling over the route with him for a fortnight, so dangerous was his condition. By the time Boston was reached, where on April 29 he was scheduled to give a benefit for the Orchestral Pension Fund, he was seriously disabled. His failure to help the fund, added to his inability to join in the tribute to Modjeska, according to his business manager, Julius Francke, "preyed on his mind for a long time." He sent a large contribution to the fund, but though he might have prosecuted the railway he did not do so. Rather, to avoid publicity, he accepted a nominal settlement which covered only his financial loss. With the known capacity of his hands to earn easily a million dollars a year he could have sued the railway for a fabulous sum.

There was another accident during Paderewski's "railroading days" in which he had no part, yet one which is remembered by others as a striking instance of his warmhearted charity and quick response to need. A poor Polish workman, going by foot from Savannah, Georgia, to New York, was run over by a train near Baltimore. The man had left his wife behind at Baltimore where she was trying to sell their last belonging, her most treasured possession, the feather bed which had been her dowry; they were that poor. The bed sold, the wife started out to rejoin her man at an appointed rendezvous, to find only his mangled body awaiting her. The shock prostrated her and brought on the premature birth of her child. She was taken back to Baltimore to a hospital. She could not tell her story, no one about her could understand Polish. The next day Paderewski entered the hospital unannounced, found the woman, and offered himself as interpreter. A brief item in a newspaper had told him of her misfortune. He had the woman and her baby taken on to New York and put in the Misericordia Hospital, and daily afterward while there he and Madame Paderewska visited her. Before he left New York Paderewski arranged a life-time financial provision for the woman and her child.

Still another train accident, this time without bad consequences but with some real drama in it and a little comedy, is recalled humorously by Paderewski. On the way from Toronto to Buffalo a heavy snowstorm held up his train for seven hours. His recital hour at Buffalo was eight o'clock, and he was due there at noon. When he saw that it was impossible to go ahead he wired to Buffalo asking that his audience wait one hour. This arrangement was made readily enough, but then it was discovered that his baggage had been moved into the Customs Office and the customs officers had locked up and gone home! He had to have his dress-suit for the Buffalo concert that night, so Hugo Gorlitz proposed a plan. He would break open one of the Customs Office windows, get in, secure the suit, lock the trunk, and get out. He did it, without being detected. When Gorlitz came back onto the train with the dress suit over his arm, Paderewski gave a mighty sigh of relief. He had suffered agonies of suspense while Gorlitz had been rifling the Customs Office. He had visualized the most horrible outbreak of newspaper publicity imaginable. He gave his Buffalo concert. And he spent most of the hours of that long wait by Suspension Bridge practicing for it.

It is not by long hours of manual practice alone, however, that Paderewski comes prepared to his recitals. He practices mentally also. He once told Henry Finck that he often lies awake at night for hours going over his program for the next recital, "note by note, trying to get the very essence of every bar, every subtle detail of accent and shading." In the daytime, too, these details haunt him. "If I walk or ride, or merely rest, I go on thinking all the time, and my nerves get no real rest." One pastime, however, gives him real relaxation, billiards. "When I play billiards I can forget everything, and the result is mental rest and physical rest combined."

Pastime or not, he plays billiards as he does everything else, intensely, with a tireless striving for the perfect angle and the perfect shot. Leschetitsky, who "finished" him at billiards as he "finished" him at the piano, once said of him, "He could have been successful either as a diplomat or as an actor if he had chosen." Or he might even have been a professional billiardist! Undoubtedly he would have been a champion.

The New World, when he came to it in 1891, was for him a very big and very strange place. But after forty years of "railroading" there is perhaps no native born American of Paderewski's years who knows the country, every square mile of it, as he does.

XVIII

THE CRITICS

WHEN he landed in New York he could not help but recollect what had happened to him when he had landed in London. What would the American critics do to him? What were the American critics like? Berlioz, the French musical genius, who had been the master of one of Paderewski's teachers, Roguski, had once described critics as being "like the vulgar birds that swarm in our public gardens and perch arrogantly on the most beautiful statues; and when they have befouled the forehead of Jupiter, the arm of Hercules, or the bosom of Venus, strut about with as much pride and satisfaction as if they had laid a golden egg." Paderewski had never felt quite that way about critics. But he wondered what he was facing in the new strange world.

The critics were ready for him. Music had by this time, the early 'nineties, become fairly well grounded in American life. America had gone a little way, at least, in developing her native art and a long way in developing appreciation. She had for years thrown open her doors to the best the Old World could supply. She had heard Rubinstein, de Pachmann, Joseffy, D'Albert, Rosenthal, Friedheim, Grünfeld, Rummel, Scharwenka, others. She had had her own Gottschalk, the first native pianist of eminence, whose tours had lasted till the close of the Civil War. She had criteria by which to judge the newcomer. Paderewski knew this when he came and he knew that he would be judged. During one of his earlier tours he commented on the widespread enjoyment of music in America. "It gratifies me deeply," he said, "to note that appreciation of the highest and best in music is becoming more general throughout America. In several of the Eastern cities and towns—more especially in New York, Philadelphia, Boston, and Worcester, to name but a few—a sincere and catholic musical culture is to be found. As to the cities of the Great West, Chicago is perhaps the most sensitively responsive to the charm of music, and the untrammeled enthusiasm of its audiences is uplifting, inspiring."

The most famous European pianist to visit America prior to Paderewski's coming was Rubinstein. He was still being talked about when Paderewski arrived. Paderewski had never forgotten that day in Berlin when Rubinstein had listened to him play. Rubinstein had encouraged him, and he, loyal to the memory of that kindness, had included Rubinstein's compositions in his programs, thinking them unduly forgotten, their value unjustly minimized. He recalled all this now as he faced the America that had gone mad over Rubinstein; he knew that comparison was inevitable.

He had reason to be nervous when the night of November 17, 1891, came. Perhaps never before had he felt quite so uncertain of himself: in spite of his phenomenal success in Europe he was still no veteran, and this New World adventure was after all something out of the ordinary. . . . The New York Symphony Orchestra had just closed the opening overture, Goldmark's "In Springtime"; Walter Damrosch, conducting, had moved his stand to the side of the piano and stood waiting for the entrance of the new artist, a Paderewski never seen before by a single eye in that audience. His picture had been displayed in old Steinway Hall and in the windows of a few music stores, but no one was prepared for the vivid and appealing figure that at last appeared as he threaded his way among the orchestra players toward the piano. The silence of that moment was dramatic. "A hush fell, almost painful in its intensity," wrote Harriette Brower recalling it. "What would he be like, this new genius? Would he really be great or only near-great?"

Slender and tall, his face pale under the bright mop of reddish-blond hair, he took his place at the piano, his face turned toward the director, waiting to begin. He seemed very slight and young, the low piano chair he used giving him an appearance of smallness. Saint-Säens' Concerto in C Minor was the first selection. The audience was impressed. But it was not until the Concerto was followed by a group of piano soli from Chopin that the full impact of the new artist was felt: "the effect was thrilling, electrical." When he followed the Chopin numbers with his own Concerto in A Minor, his conquest was complete. He received an ovation which lasted until he gave an encore. And then something unprecedented took place, a rush of hundreds down the aisles to keep him from leaving, clamoring for more. Thus was the custom of Paderewski's informal post-recital playing begun, and thus did Paderewski's first appearance in America become a popular triumph.

But what of the critics?

Paderewski has always respected the critics and appreciated the value of criticism. From the beginning of his career he has known his art, its demands and exactions, therefore he has known what valid musical criticism is. A true artist and a great one, he has never suffered the enslavement to the "press" which tortures and confuses the lesser artist; but he has looked eagerly for the opinion of the authoritative critic. On the morning of November 18, 1891, he was naturally both curious and anxious to learn what the verdict of critical New York might be.

There was of course a copious "press." Columns were printed about his American début. And there were names of importance in the American musical world attached to the notices. Those were the days of such major critics as Aldrich, Krehbiel, Henderson, Huneker, and the pianist William Mason. Paderewski knew beforehand the importance of their names. His whole American venture was still before him, and though the unmistakable enthusiasm of his first New York audience was more than gratifying, what the critics would say would mean much to the success of the country-wide tour which was before him. In England he had conquered London by going to the provinces, but he had no desire of facing the necessity of repeating that process in the New World.

Huneker's review appeared in the *Musical Courier*. This was an organ of influence; what it would say would unquestionably key much that would be said elsewhere. These are the words that the newcome artist read the day following the concert; the comparisons with other virtuosi, which Paderewski had expected, were made; moreover he was judged as a composer as well as a player:

Ignace Jan Paderewski played the piano last night at the new Music Hall, and played it in such a wonderful manner as to set a huge audience mad with enthusiasm and recall memories of Rubinstein in his prime, but a Rubinstein technically infallible.

In the dual role of a composer and virtuoso Mr. Paderewski won a triumph that was genuine and nobly deserved, for he is a new personality in music that will bear curious and close study. As to the physical side of his art, he is one of those virtuosi to whom the keyboard has no hidden secrets. His technical equipment is perfect and is used in such an exquisitely musical fashion that the virtuoso merges ever into the artist and mere brutal display and brilliant charlatanry are totally absent.

The two concertos selected by Mr. Paderewski for his debut were the fourth Saint-Saëns in C minor and his own A minor concerto, two well contrasted compositions which offered abundant chances for displaying the pianist's amazing versatility. The Saint-Saëns work is not the most grateful penned by its composer, for its first movement is more in the variation vein and episodical; in fact the concerto throughout lacks homogeneity, though the Celtic theme in the last movement is very characteristic. The composition was played by Mr. Paderewski with a sweep of style, a splendor of tone and with such fire and force as to be absolutely overwhelming. The octave passages were given magnificently; indeed the soloist's touch, so penetrating and so pure, his scale work so crystalline and his power so enormous mark him as a virtuoso among virtuosi. His own concerto in A minor is one of the significant works of modern times; in strict truth it is doubtful if among living composers there is anybody who could do just the things Mr. Paderewski does in this work. Dvořák's concerto in G minor is unplayable; the two Tschaikowsky concertos, despite their barbaric beauty, are written with a total disregard of the demands of pianism, and Rubinstein and Saint-Saëns and Sgambati have evidently done their best work. The Paderewski concerto which is new to New York (it was played in Boston last season by Mrs. Julia Rive-King), is a beautiful piece of writing, full of ideas, flavored perhaps by some modern composers, but in the main fresh and sparkling and treated in the most musicianly manner. Here the musicianship of the composer surprises us, for there is every evidence of profound knowledge of harmony, part writing, instrumentation, and all expressed in the most naïve fashion and with an utter absence of striving for effect.

Mr. Paderewski writes for his instrument as he plays upon it—superbly; he always gives one new passage work, harmonic surprises, and his orchestration is delightful in coloring and piquancy. As a composer alone he could stand comparison with many more celebrated names than his own. The second movement, a little spun out, is in C, with many abrupt harmonic transitions and replete with fine, cunning and subtle workmanship. In it the pianist showed his lovely cantilena touch—a touch that is golden in quality. He plays a melody with an unapproachable legato, and the crispness of his staccato is ever admirable. This quality of imagination Paderewski is the possessor of indubitably. There is a life about his work, a transfiguration of some simple musical idea, that is inspiration itself. His ability hinges perilously on the gates of genius. He is a veritable artistic apparition, and with that supremely magnetic personality, graceful and exotic appearance he naturally scored a success that was stupendous.

In the group of soli by his fellow countryman, Frédéric Chopin, Paderewski revealed himself as an interpreter who ranks as high as any Chopin player we have yet heard in this city. He has the true subtle poetic capricious spirit, the "zal" to use the Polish word, and his tender sadness and majestic sorrow in the great C minor nocturne were admirably expressed.

He played the A flat prélude, with its imploring cadences, and followed with the familiar C sharp minor valse, but not rendered familiarly by him. In point of finesse he vied with that arch master of finesse, de Pachmann, and in the C major étude (op. 10, No. 7) his lightness of wrist caused the double note figure to actually shimmer on the keyboard. That this self-same étude, which serves a technical purpose, was delivered so poetically proves Paderewski's innate musical nature.

He sang the lullaby of the F major ballade, so seldom played, charmingly, and thundered out its climaxes until the noble Steinway grand upon which he played sounded like a veritable orchestra. By the manner of his playing the A flat polonaise, which is topsy-turvied by most pianists in order to show how fast they can play, Paderewski administered a gentle reproof, for he took it at true polonaise tempo, a stately, dignified dance, and right chivalric he made its measures.

His octavo crescendo in the middle part was marvelous in its gradation of tone and elasticity of wrists. In fact his wrist work, notably in double octave trills, is herculean in its power and intensity. In response to overwhelming encores he played Liszt's "Campanella" in the daintiest style imaginable and made its crescendo formidable, and here the absolute surety and ease of the young man's skips were startling.

Indeed his grace and modesty are most commendable. After his own concerto, which he played wonderfully well, he was forced to play once more and play he did. He gave Rubinstein's "Staccato Etude," and made more of a wonder piece of it than did d'Albert.

Here again the coloring and variety of touches were noteworthy, and the étude became orchestral.

Paderewski is a great pianist, one of the greatest who has yet visited our shores, and his marked musical abilities as a composer, his superb skill as a virtuoso, when taken in conjunction with his age, concur in making him a youth favored by the gods.

This opinion of one of the foremost critics of the country, given within a few hours of his first hearing the new artist, was a good beginning. Today, when we turn to the same critic's recollections of this Paderewski concert, published twenty years later, we have the picture of the Polish artist's American début framed as it were in ripened and considered judgment: *

His tone was noble, his technic adequate, his single-finger touch singing. Above all, there was a romantic temperament exposed; not morbid but robust. His strange appearance, the golden aureoled head, the shy attitude, were rather puzzling to public and critic at his début. Not too much enthusiasm was exhibited during the concert or next morning in the newspapers. But the second performance settled the question. A great artist was revealed. His diffidence melted in the heat of frantic applause. He played the Schumann concerto, the F-minor concerto of Chopin, many other concertos, all of Chopin's music, much of Schumann, Beethoven, and Liszt. His recitals, first given in the concert hall of Madison Square Garden, so expanded in attendance that he moved to Carnegie Hall. There, with only his piano, Paderewski repeated the Liszt miracle. And year after year. Never in America has a public proved so insatiable in its desire to hear a virtuoso. It is the same from New Orleans to Seattle. Everywhere crowded halls, immense enthusiasms. Now to set all this down to an exotic personality, to occult magnetism, to sensationalism, would be unfair to Paderewski and to the critical discrimination of his audiences. Many have gone to gaze upon him, but they remained to listen. His solid attainments as a musician, his clear, elevated style, his voluptuous, caressing touch, his sometimes exaggerated sentiment, his brilliancy, endurance, and dreamy poetry— these qualities are real, not imaginary.

* In Huneker's book "Franz Liszt," published by Charles Scribner's Sons, New York, 1911.

No more luscious touch has been heard since Rubinstein's. Paderewski often lets his singing fingers linger on a phrase; but as few pianists alive, he can spin his tone, and so his yielding to the temptation is a natural one. He is intellectual and his readings of the classics are sane. Of poetic temperament, he is at his best in Chopin, not Beethoven. Eclectic is the best word to apply to his interpretations. He plays programmes from Bach to Liszt with commendable fidelity and versatility. He has the power of rousing his audience from a state of calm indifference to wildest frenzy. How does he accomplish this? He has not the technic of Rosenthal, nor that pianist's brilliancy and power; he is not as subtle as Joseffy, nor yet as plastic in his play; the morbid witchery of de Pachmann is not his; yet no one since Rubinstein—in America at least—can create such climaxes of enthusiasm. Deny this or that quality to Paderewski; go and with your own ears and eyes hear and witness what we all have heard and witnessed.

I once wrote a story in which a pianist figures as a mesmeriser. He sat at his instrument in a crowded, silent hall and worked his magic upon the multitude. The scene modulates into madness. People are transported. And in all the rumour and storm, the master sits at the keyboard and does not play. I assure you I have been at Paderewski recitals where my judgments were in abeyance, where my individuality was merged in that of the mob, where I sat and wondered if I really heard; or was Paderewski only going through the motions and not actually touching the keys? His is a static as well as a dramatic art. The tone wells up from the instrument, is not struck. It floats languorously in the air, it seems to pause, transfixed in the air. The Sarmatian melancholy of Paderewski, his deep sensibility, his noble nature, are translated into the music. Then with a smashing chord he sets us, the prisoners of his tonal circle, free. Is this the art of a hypnotiser? No one has so mastered the trick, if trick it be.

But he is not all moonshine. The truth is, Paderewski has a tone not so large as mellow. His fortissimo chords have hitherto lacked the fundamental power and splendour of d'Albert's, Busoni's, and Rosenthal's. His transition from piano to forte is his best range, not the extremes at either end of the dynamic scale. A healthy, sunny tone it is at its best, very warm in colour. In certain things of Chopin he is unapproachable. He plays the F-minor concerto and the E-flat minor scherzo—from the second Sonata—beautifully, and if he is not so convincing in the Beethoven sonata, his interpretation of the E-flat Emperor concerto is surprisingly free from morbidezza; it is direct, manly, and musical. His technic has gained since his advent in New York. This he proved by the way he juggled with the Brahms-Paganini variations; though they are still the property of Moritz Rosenthal. He is more interesting than most pianists because he is more musical; he has more personal charm; there is the feeling when you hear him that he is a complete man, a harmonious artist, and this feeling is very compelling.

On the whole the American critics accepted him warmly, some of them with the greatest enthusiasm, although a few were inclined to object to the "romantic ardor" of his Bach and Beethoven. And of course, not only in Huneker's review but in all of them, there were the comparisons which he had known would be inevitable. William Mason's judgment of him, in comparison with Rubinstein, serves to sum up the general verdict on that score: "As Moscheles played Bach half a century ago, and as Rubinstein played him later," wrote Mason, "so does Paderewski play him now—with an added grace and color. . . . Paderewski has an advantage over Rubinstein, however, in the fact that he is always master of his resources and possesses power of complete self control. . . . In Rubinstein there is an excess of the emotional . . . his impulsive nature and lack of restraint are continually in his way, frequently causing him to rush ahead with such impetuosity as to anticipate his climax, and, having no reserve force to call into action, disaster is sure to follow."

The London critics had not been able at first to see in Paderewski much more than "monstrous" physical energy. Bernard Shaw had described him as "an immensely spirited, young, harmonious blacksmith, who puts a concerto on the piano as upon an anvil and hammers it out with an exuberant enjoyment of the swing and strength of the proceeding. . . . His concerto was over, the audience in a wild enthusiasm, and the pianoforte a wreck." In 1901 Edward Baughan wrote that he had "no reserve force." But the Americans saw his reserve force, his emotional control. "Of five prominent pianists," wrote William Mason, "Paderewski may be classified as emotional-intellectual—a very rare and happy blending of the two temperaments." What Mason apprehended in Paderewski is what really explains the whole Paderewski and all his story as it has been lived out in his entire career: Art and Brains.

But all the critics had not the discernment of William Mason and James G. Huneker. Paderewski had a hard time winning some of them. The vitality of his personality has always made him live in a cross-fire of differing opinion, although the enfilade has at times been of the "sniping" order. Racial and political prejudice has sometimes prompted it. Again, his strong individuality, which consistently rejects and is immune to the excesses of the *Zeitgeist* and is not swayed by the winds of fashion, has more than once roused the ire of modernistic critics. This school of critics has been embarrassed by Paderewski's art; it has been too difficult for them to reconcile his traditionalism, on the one hand, and his bold treatment of tradition on the other. In his own words, in a remark commenting on the impressionism of the "iconoclast" Debussy, critics of this type have been wisely characterized: "They applaud and acclaim him because he tears down the great, because he is an iconoclast. If he himself were to become a master—an icon on his own account—they would be the first to turn upon him and tear him down."

The charge of "pounding" has been in America as in England one of the favorite accusations of Paderewski's adverse critics: "hitting the piano like an irate athlete", as one expressed it; or "Paderewski does not play any more, he pounds." This is not a late accusation; it has been made from the beginning. Baughan in London in 1901 called Paderewski's force "hysterical, an explosion of exacerbated nerves." Another English critic, Wortham, writing in the London *Daily Telegraph* in 1931 thus recalled his first Paderewski concert over thirty years before: "He sat down at the piano and then—I still shudder at the recollection of that moment—rattled off a number of commonplace chords *fortissimo*. He struck it almost viciously, as if there were nothing he hated more than a grand piano, and the harder he hit it the more hate he expressed. Many trials awaited me in that half hour. For after he had established the key of C Major with an emphasis quite unnecessary even in 1899, he began the 'Waldstein', and it all sounded oddly out of joint. Was he not forcing his tone? Were not the florid passages hard?

Should the second subject be taken at such a slow tempo, and be exaggerated by a rubato, and should the notes of a chord never be played together?"

Or here is an American critic, Charles Buchanan, who wrote of Paderewski in 1926, thirty-five years after the 1891 début, as "someone for three quarters of an hour playing the piano impatiently and exasperatedly . . . some of the worst piano playing this writer has ever heard . . . a frazzled, frayed Chopin, distorted, hurried through perfunctorily."

To understand these faults, as such critics have seen them, to appreciate Paderewski in the face of them, one must go back to his earliest days, to his choice of the piano as his instrument. He has been from the beginning another Liszt, a Liszt, "whose passionate soaring genius", in the words of Finck, "first sought to convert the piano into an orchestra." A London critic, likening Paderewski to Rubinstein, spoke of his "wielding his hammers with superhuman energy, making the pianoforte shake to its centre . . . transcending his exemplar in fury and force of blow." "Mr. Paderewski," the American critic Lawrence Gilman once remarked, "has often seemed to be in revolt against the natural limitations of the piano, as if he would compel its throat to be an orchestra's, myriad-voiced and thunderous." He has moments, in Gilman's opinion, "when he becomes the bardic rhapsodist filled with some urgent Ossianic fervor, or when he seems kin to the *uomo terribile* of the Renaissance as he flings his spirit against the ivory walls of that prisoning tower which often seems to constrain and cramp his far seeing imagination."

This is the "pounding" of which Paderewski has been so often accused, as he was accused when he first appeared in America. The same charge was brought against Rubinstein, and against Liszt. Liszt was even known to break two and three strings of his instrument during a performance, and Rubinstein kept two pianos on the stage as a provision against accident. The precedent, of course, as Paderewski himself would be the first to remind us, would not justify the act, that is, the act of actually breaking piano strings! But Paderewski's "pounding" has its explanation: "It is not his fault," Henry Finck avers, "but the fault of his instrument." "No piano has ever been built, or ever will be built" which can be converted into the instrument Paderewski demands "when he comes to one of his tidal waves of sound, his cyclonic climaxes." This is true, but it is equally true that no other pianist "has quite such limpid yet deep tone, a tone of such marvellous carrying power that its *pianissimo* is heard in the remotest parts of the house." As a matter of fact, critics when they echo the rather outworn charge of "pounding" forget, as did the first who made it, that it is to just such vigor of instrumentation that we owe the piano as it is today. The piano did not evolve of itself out of the harpsichord. It is the pianist who has made the piano. Liszt and Rubinstein in their day, forcing their tones as T. P. Currier points out in "Modern Music and Musicians", "compelled the makers to construct the larger, stronger, and fuller toned instruments which now respond so wonderfully to the demands of modern performance." Their predecessors did the same. "Genius experiments." The genius at the piano has to experiment to realize the full possibilities of that instrument's tonal effect.

In Paderewski's case there is still another factor to be considered—acoustics. Playing in the enormous concert halls that have had to be used to accommodate his public, he has been obliged to make continuous effort to fill them. His tours of America especially drew him into a study of this problem; but it would be humanly impossible for him to invariably and perfectly adjust himself to each particular auditorium in which he was playing. On the whole, as the American critic Henderson has concluded, while Paderewski may appear at times to make unreasonable demands on his instrument, the end has nearly always justified the means.

The same critic, Henderson, disposes of another favorite charge against Paderewski, that of "dropped notes." "Sticklers for accuracy will, of course, shake their heads," Henderson writes. "The same head-shaking was noticed when Rubinstein was engaged in thundering along the keyboard and dropping many notes under the piano. It may be well to remember that the scribes have never made habitual use of the words

'etched', 'cameo-cut', 'chiseled', in describing Paderewski's performances. He paints sometimes with a smear of the palette
knife, but what a colorist! Turner's drawing was more erratic
than Paderewski's ever was, but what a painter!"

Paderewski, whatever he has done to the critics with his
pianissimo, has, at *fortissimo*, worried them seriously. But what
really has troubled them most, perhaps, is the ordered authority
back of his asserted power. His personality is essentially masculine, independent, assertive, but at the same time it is disciplined
and controlled. When he is criticized he is only subject to the
fortunes of every artist, every man, of dynamic force. And in
the end, by reason of the very authority of his force, he usually
wins over to himself even the doubtful critic. The same London writer, Baughan, who had called him hysterical, once listed
all the faults he could find in him, and then concluded: "Is the
catalogue of defects full? If not, insert some more, and then—
why, then, I still assert that Paderewski is the greatest of living
pianists. I do not ask him to be anything but himself." "Even
when he treats a composition to a new, and, as it seems, a sensational performance," Mr. Baughan said further, "the conception is consistent throughout. And that is one of the reasons
why the pianist carries you away even when he runs counter to
theories or prejudices." Wortham, who recalled the "trial" of
his first half hour of Paderewski in 1899, concluded finally
that "possibly all this was done to relax the tension before the
atmosphere worked up to the fever heat it acquired later"; at
any rate "the real Paderewski" came in due time: "those lovely
half-tones, that unexampled power of crystallizing a simple
phrase began to subdue us. When it came to Chopin we were
ready to listen without equivocation, and at last the audience,
after an orgy of applause, laid siege to the platform." The
American, Buchanan, says quite the same thing: after "some of
the worst piano playing" he had ever heard, "then something
happened. As though an actual dividing line had been reached
—it happened to be the F Minor Ballade—the Paderewski of
incredible Old World Sighings . . . was with us once more. His
playing affected me hypnotically."

Thus the "hypnosis" that Modjeska recognized fifty years ago still weaves its spell. But Paderewski "hypnotizing" critics as well as audience is only exerting the real power that is his, the power of a master, of an authoritative artist who knows what he is doing. "He has the most extraordinary ability," says Edward Moore of Chicago, "in impressing the belief upon his hearers that an interpretation is the only correct and logical one because he has done it that way. In cold blood and away from the theatre one may venture to disbelieve this, but not at close range and under his dynamic spell." But a musician can hardly be judged at long range and "in cold blood." It is his "spell" that counts. Paderewski's own words are recalled: "A musical composition, printed or written, is, after all, a form, a mold: the performer infuses life into it, and, whatever the strength of that life may be, he must be given a reasonable amount of liberty, he must be endowed with some discretional power." Most of the critics, whether they have been "hypnotized" or not, have recognized this right in Paderewski, acknowledging his honesty as well as his power. "Your mind," as Mr. Baughan once wrote in London, "may be critically at work throughout the whole performance, but you feel at the same time that the player is not making a bid for the popularity of empty sensationalism."

From the beginning the body of American reaction has been, like that of Europe, an acclamation of Paderewski's genius. In America as in Europe, however, the critics were not always as ready as the people to accept him. In America it was the metropolitan critics who led the way to acclaim, instead of, as in England, the provinces. But in Germany, although the provinces, public and critics together, literally went wild over him, the Berlin critics refused to succumb in spite of his great success with his audiences. A genuine *cabale*, in which the press concurred, was organized against him in the Prussian capital. Later, some well-intentioned German critics, such as Otto Lessmann, August Spanuth, and others, protested the shabby treatment he had received, declaring that Berlin could never claim the status of a musical capital as long as it excluded such an artist as Paderewski. But he could not forget the *cabale* and he never returned to Berlin. The German critics who spoke for him really put their finger on the core of the matter. The real musical centers of Germany are outside of Berlin. They are in Munich, Leipzig, Dresden, Hamburg, Breslau. Berlin is the city where, to this day, Liszt is debarred in the Hochschule!

Not all the Berlin critics, however, refused to acknowledge him, at least "privately." An interesting story is told of one of them who came to Paderewski's room after a recital, his eyes filling with tears of delight as he praised the artist. But, ostensibly under editorial orders, the same critic the next day published a disagreeable comment. "He spoiled me by his call," Paderewski said, telling the story. "It is easy to be spoiled. But he was so pleased the first time, I felt sure he would come again."

If that Berlin critic whose writing belied his tears read his exchanges he must have been chagrined when he saw in the conservative *Leipziger Zeitung* the report that Paderewski's Leipzig recital was "a colossal success: not since Liszt has a pianist been received as Paderewski was"; or in the *Tageblatt* of the same city: "The public did not applaud, it raved." In Hamburg the eminent musical authority Ferdinand Pfohl, describing "the exultation, the enthusiasm of the audience", declared that "never before did an evening of two and a half hours at the piano seem so short." And from Munich, in a comment on his "extraordinary power over the multitude" came the tribute: "He is a poet of the pianoforte who dives below the usual level and reveals to the hearers things before hidden . . . he is a Chopin infinitely enlarged, a Chopin for the many." "Miracles still happen!" exclaimed the Breslau *General Anzeiger*, pointing to the crowds that packed the huge Concerthaus. "Not since Rubinstein have we heard such storms of applause."

If some critics have been hard to win, still harder have been some of the professional musicians. Finck quoted Alfred Reisenauer "who was furiously jealous of his Polish rival", as saying, when Paderewski's amazing general culture was mentioned, "Yes, he knows everything—except music." The magnetism of the man, too, that strong, attractiveness which not only draws thousands to hear him but holds them and makes them crowd around him for more, and still more—this also has aroused animosity. "Hysterical adoration" it has been called.

So, in America as elsewhere, the professional triumphs of Paderewski have not been triumphs thrown freely in the lap of the artist. They have been hardly won, not only by the tireless work of preparation back of them, but by sheer force of authentic power asserted against sometimes violent opposition. In the New World, too, as manifestly in Germany, from the time of his first coming to America one of the adjustments Paderewski had to make was to the voice of criticism not always based on the grounds of art. Racial prejudice has played its part, and this was a difficult thing for him to comprehend in a country which he considered as the fulfillment of the dream of that older Poland from which he came, that Poland which, when free, in the words of Robert Howard Lord, of Harvard, "in an age of religious persecution and chronic religious wars . . . offered almost complete toleration and an asylum to those fleeing from persecution in all western lands." We shall hear more of this when we read the story of Paderewski's career as statesman.

Allowing full margin for the honest conviction of valid criticism—for which Paderewski all his life has had the deepest respect, and to which many times he has avowed his debt—it can be said that, in the ranks of musical opinion that count, America has taken front place with the best in Europe in appreciating and honoring Paderewski's mastership. In America, as in Europe, an overwhelming critical majority has not only from the beginning acclaimed him, but has been, like the critics of Paris, "embarrassed for praise." Paderewski, looking back over the years and recalling the misgivings of those first days after he landed in New York, is not only grateful for the praise, but he has a keen appreciation of the critic's problem. He has realized, to paraphrase one of his own expresssions on the subject, that the business of the critic is to give *reasons* for his likes and dislikes and that thus, giving reasons, he is obliged to abandon for theorizing and rationalizing the proper field of feeling, in which music belongs.

The words of Richard Aldrich, dean of American music critics, may be taken as a summing up of critical opinion in America concerning Paderewski's art and his achievement. "The history of his conquest of America," says Aldrich, "has hardly been paralleled in the history of music. There came other artists before him, but Mr. Paderewski's achievements were of a different and a higher sort, more deeply grounded in the nobility, the poetry, the pure artistic quality of his musicianship. He touched the deepest and tenderest feelings and tugged irresistibly at the heart-strings of a whole people. He seemed to speak a new language in music; he raised its poetry, its magic, its mystery, its romantic eloquence to a higher power than his listeners had known. There was a beauty of line as well as of color and atmosphere, a poignance of phrase, a quality of tone, a lyrical accent such, so it seemed, as to make of his playing something never till then quite divined."

XIX

THE TEACHER

ALL artists are teachers, whatever their art. The musician playing the compositions of others is in some measure a critic as well
as a teacher; performing his own compositions he is at least a
teacher. Of formal instructing, Paderewski has done little since
his earliest days as Professor at the Warsaw Conservatory, days
which in his own words were days of "slavery." "Anyone,"
he once remarked, "who takes up piano playing with a view to
becoming a professional pianist has taken on himself an awful
burden. But better that than the drudgery of giving pianoforte lessons. The one is only purgatory, but the other is hell!"
    Of all the pianists who have come under his instruction or
influence, directly or indirectly, Paderewski acknowledges only
three—Sigismond Stojowski, Ernest Schelling, Madame
Szumowska. Stojowski met Paderewski first when, a little boy,
he attended Paderewski's first Cracow concert in 1884, the
concert which Madame Modjeska sponsored, and at which she
gave a reading, preliminary to Paderewski's going to Vienna to
study under Leschetitsky. But it was not until Stojowski had
completed his studies at the Paris Conservatoire that Paderewski
taught him. The younger Pole had just won a first prize at the
Conservatoire and had come eagerly to his friend and countryman for criticism. "You are an improviser," ran the master's
verdict, "with results good or evil, attendant upon caprice."
Lessons followed, revelations rather—generously proffered,
gratefully received—to the effect that discriminating thought
and controlled will held the key to mastery. Long hours of
work were capped with the remark: "I am trying to tell you
all." Ernest Schelling was accepted as a pupil by Paderewski,

after Paderewski had begun his American tours. Schelling had already studied under Mathias in Paris and Moszkowski in Berlin. Schelling, as an American, appealed to Paderewski's sense of obligation to America, which had so warmly welcomed him. The third pupil, Antoinette Szumowska, likewise accepted for personal reasons, was a cousin of Madame Gorska. These three have been Paderewski's only acknowledged pupils, unless we except Harold Bauer, mentioned in an earlier chapter, and certain special classes of young Polish aspirants in whom Paderewski has become interested and to whom he has given instruction in recent years during the summertime at his home in Switzerland. These classes, which last several hours at a time, while they find the boys who work in them periodically exhausted, leave the master as refreshed as when he began. Teaching and encouraging these youths is, for the man of seventy, merely a recreation.

And yet, though Paderewski has thus had in his lifetime only three pupils, actually he has had and has, unknown to him, hundreds, perhaps one might say thousands of other pupils, not in America only but all over the world. Wherever he plays, every teacher and student within reach hears him. Thousands call him "Master", among them many who have won fame. Edwin Fisher, the German pianist, once told of how, when he was a little boy, his mother promised him that if he studied well he might "go to hear him." Fisher's real musical education, he declares, began the day he did first hear him: "From that time, whenever the name was mentioned, I listened respectfully." Ernesto Berúmen of Mexico dates his best inspirations from the first time he heard Paderewski. Walter Spry, eminent American pianist at twenty, heard Paderewski play in Paris and determined from that moment to go to Vienna and study under Leschetitsky. "Without his knowing it he has been my teacher for years," says Madame Gainsborg. "I attended every concert which this Master played and drank in every nuance, each subtle tone color and thematic separation. I learned to know the beauty of a phrase completed."

For such as these Paderewski has done much, inspiring them

to go on aiming at his mastery, even though, in the opinion of one critic at least (Edward Baughan of London) his reading cannot always "be held up as a model to students" because, as he at least thinks, it is too subjective. William Mason the American pianist, author of "Touch and Technique", countered this opinion. Paderewski, he says "is so objective a player as to be faithful, true, and loving" to the composer he is rendering; "but withal," he added, "he has a spice of the subjective which imparts to his performance just the right amount of his own individuality." According to Currier, "while his extraordinary virtuosic flights have been and are beyond the pale of mere talent, the beautiful simplicity of his delivery of smaller pieces has well served as a perfect model in style and unaffected expression."

There have been teachers who professed to scorn Paderewski. There is record of a music teacher in St. Louis leaving the hall in the midst of a Paderewski recital, the "professor's" nose upturned in contempt of "this charlatan." Thus the back-fire of criticism goes on, and Paderewski's capacity for provoking feeling as well as for stimulating opinion, which is not the capacity of a negative nature, continues to be demonstrated. How quickly the answering gun is fired is shown in Henry Finck's comment on criticism of the petty kind: "A bit of advice to piano pupils: If your teacher sneers at Paderewski, leave him at once. An instructor who is not sufficiently musical to appreciate the playing of the greatest living pianist cannot possibly teach you anything worth while."

Paderewski's interest in music study and the problems of the music student is a practical as well as a sympathetic interest. Endowed schools of music enlist his warmest sympathy. "I do not believe, as do so many musicians," he once declared, "that genius should be left to fight its way to the light. Genius is too rare, too precious, to be permitted to waste the best years of life—the years of youth and lofty dreams—in a heart-breaking struggle for bread. To starve the soul with the body is to do worse than murder. Think, too, of what the public loses! Your colleges of music are carrying on a grand work, and it is to be devoutly hoped that they will multiply as the years go by and spread abundantly the gospel of good music."

Refusing the preëminent place which might have been his among the world's great music teachers, Paderewski has nevertheless his own philosophy of instruction, although he thinks that all theoretical teaching is fundamentally a mistake; "for when you have reasoned out an effect," he says, "you have lost that over which you reasoned. You must teach the student to feel." The burden thus rests in the end on the student. However, he has set forth in plain words his code. It is, obviously, based on simple elementaries.

"To teach or to learn to play the piano or any other instrument," says Paderewski, "we must commence at the beginning. The pupil must first be taught the rudiments of music. When these have been mastered he must next be taught the technique of his instrument, and if that instrument be the piano, or the violin, or the harp, or the violoncello, the muscles and joints of the hands, wrists, and fingers must be made supple and strong by playing exercises designed to accomplish that end. At the same time, by means of similar exercises, the pupil must also be taught to read music rapidly and correctly. When this has been accomplished he should render himself familiar with the works of the masters—not by having them drummed into him by his instructor, but by carefully studying them by himself; by seeking diligently and patiently for the composer's meaning, playing each doubtful passage over and over again in every variety of interpretation and striving most earnestly to satisfy himself which is the most nearly in harmony with the composer's ideas."

"The chief aim of every teacher of the pianoforte," according to Paderewski, "should be to impart to his pupils a correct technique and to enable them to play any composition at sight with proficiency and correctness; but how much, or rather how little of this kind of teaching is practiced by many so-called music teachers? Many really competent music teachers have assured me that of all the pupils who came to them from teachers of lesser reputation to be 'finished' there is not one in ten who has ever been taught to play all the major and minor scales in all the various keys."

Faithful and careful practice is Paderewski's first and last word to the student. "There is no other known method of finding out the inner meaning of a composition equal to that of playing it over and over again to one's self. New beauties present themselves; we get nearer and nearer to the mind of the composer; the process becomes one of continuous uplift." The memorizing of compositions by the masters is another point that Paderewski insists on. But, perhaps with recollections of his own boyhood days, he is careful to point out that the pupil must not be made mentally weary by overpractice: "physical weariness from too much practice," he declares, "is just as bad as mental. To overfatigue the muscles of the pupil is to spoil their tone, at least for the time being, and some time must elapse before they can gain their former elasticity and vigor." "When a pianist has overworked," he says, "he should not force himself to further effort. Instead he ought to stop practicing altogether and go out in the country and rest until his strained nerves and muscles become normal." With Paderewski the simple task of cutting the grass is a favorite form of relaxation.

But if Paderewski refuses to teach, he is inexhaustible in his sympathetic interest in those who wish to learn. He knows by experience the need of sympathy in the pursuit of art. "In the study of music moments of almost overwhelming discouragement come to all. Without sympathy of the understanding, helpful kind, many a one would lag by the way." Nothing makes a stronger appeal to him than a gifted child, and when he regards such a child, he has, with thoughts perhaps of his own musically gifted mother who died in his infancy, a sympathetic way of seeing, back of the child the child's mother. "To a child of pronounced talent for the art," he says, "a musical mother is a God-given aid. If we look but casually into the pages of musical biography we find the great and invaluable rôle which such mothers have played in the lives of master musicians. To the mother the world owes a great debt. Recognizing the precious talent which must receive very early and right cultivation to reach a high goal in the long, hard way of art, she has put no limit either on devotion or self-sacrifice that her child might be developed. The musically informed mother is of great aid in directing the earlier practice of her children in those years when little heads, not being old enough, can scarcely be expected to select as pleasantest the right way of doing things. This type of mother, too, knows her classics, and allows no sacrifice of time on the vapid and worthless."

To ambitious aspirants, listening to their stories as well as to their playing, advising them, encouraging them when he can honestly do so, Paderewski has always given freely of his time. Nor is it to musical aspirants alone that he lends his ear. Wherever he goes he is besieged by poets, composers, painters, writers, all eager to show him their efforts and to win his approval. But pianists most of all. The experience of one such will illustrate the care that he gives to the most humble. A boy of sixteen from the Middle West, talented but too poor to employ a teacher, took Paderewski as his model after reading in Henry T. Finck's book "Success in Music and How It Is Won" the story of the Polish artist's career. Through friends the boy secured work with a piano manufacturer in New York City, and toward the end of Paderewski's 1931 American tour he conceived the idea of writing a letter to the master asking if he might meet him. Paderewski stopped only a few days in New York before returning to Europe, and the boy's letter did not reach his hand until a few hours before he sailed. In the meantime the boy, watching every mail for a response, grew discouraged.

But one morning he received a telephone call—he was to come at once to Paderewski's hotel. He went with his heart beating fast. He was ushered into a room where there was a gathering of distinguished people come to say good-by to the pianist. A door opened and Paderewski, asking the others to wait, drew the boy in. With his hand on the boy's shoulder he ushered him to a chair, sat down, talked with him, questioned him, examined the boy's hand. "It is a good hand. You must cultivate a very firm nail joint with thumb brought out from the side of the hand and well rounded." He counselled him to practice scales, showed him how to arch his hand with curved fingers, and above all urged him to "put heart and soul into the music that you love." Paderewski gave a half hour of that crowded last morning to the unknown boy.

As it happened, Paderewski, obviously, told that boy nothing new, for he told him exactly what his teacher had been telling him. But it is easy to see with what renewed determination and with what new inspiration that youth returned to his studies.

Those very few who have had the privilege of coming under Paderewski's instruction, formal or otherwise, always remember two things: the direct, definitive lightning-like play of his explicit mind, and the inspiration that comes from personal contact with him. From Madame Szumowska, one of these, we have a detailed record of her experiences as a Paderewski pupil. She knows thoroughly his ideas and ideals as well as his methods. First of all, as she shows, Paderewski the teacher, the most individualistic of individuals, never forgot the individuality of his pupil. But he insisted on the pupil doing exactly as he, the teacher, directed until "with the growth of that understanding which thorough experience brings" the student's own individuality could be asserted. "If he is exacting he is at the same time most patient and most kind. His charming personality and power of persuasion are so strong that he makes you feel most convincingly that what he says is the right thing." With his sympathetic nature he quickly measured and weighed his pupil's character and capacities, even his physical capacities as regards practice. "Paderewski" [as we have seen already from his own words] "does not believe in too much practice." There is danger of the ardent pupil, hearing of Paderewski's own rigorous regimen, trying to emulate the master's practice-record without having his unusual physique. The thing to emulate is his will-to-practice. "By his advice," says Madame Szumowska, "the proportion of time daily to be given over to purely technical study and the interpretation of pieces is four hours. I studied about five hours a day under his teaching, but four hours' practice a day is all that the average pupil can do well. The first half hour of daily practice he apportioned me in scales and arpeggios. The mistake in giving too much time in practice of the purely technical kind is that it makes the player mechanical, and for that reason half an hour daily is sufficient."

All who have heard Paderewski play know that he abominates the purely mechanical, that what he lays most stress upon is, as Madame Szumowska says, "the producing of a beautiful large singing tone." He emphasized this in teaching, instructing the pupil to press down the key to its full depth to secure a perfect *legato*. "His method for securing a perfect *legato* was to follow the pressure touch, playing slowly and listening to the perfect binding of the notes." "Scales he advises played slowly, very *legato*, lifting the fingers as little as possible, but pressing the keys instead, listening always to the quality of tone produced . . . The touch used at all times was pressure on the cushion of the finger, never raising the finger, even in the case of accented notes, and with deep lingering stroke."

All exercises had to be played slowly at first; then once, only once, fast; then slowly again in the first tempo. Selections from the Finger Dexterity Exercises of Czerny, who was the teacher of Paderewski's teacher Leschetitsky, were used, practiced with a lingering touch, even in *piano*. "In following the expression marks I played with double the volume of tone indicated, *mezzoforte* for *piano, fortissimo* for *forte*."

Harold Bauer's story of Paderewski's low piano chair will be recalled. As to proper position at the piano "Paderewski", Madame Szumowska writes, demands "an easy position, no strain, sitting naturally on a chair and not on a piano stool. . . . Generally he used to sit at another piano while I played, at times letting me play the composition through without stopping me, that he might get my conception of it; but as a rule interruptions were frequent, and he would make marks and corrections, playing the phrase himself, then making me play it over and over. . . . If he criticizes severely he also encourages warmly, and arouses an enthusiasm that absorbs one completely."

In the selection of pieces for study Paderewski again kept in mind the individuality of his pupil. His plan was "to study the individual needs of the pupil, to give any good thing that was properly adapted to those needs . . . For instance, a young pianist with too strong a tendency to the emotional" was toned down "along the lines of the stricter classical represented by Bach", while one needing encouragement in the emotional was given Chopin. But he was always careful to vary, careful "that more than one kind be given" to build up a balance, and always with the view that any piece assigned "was sure to be a profit." Schumann, Beethoven, Chopin, Bach, as well as the modern composers, were among the sources used. For the study of the "singing quality" of tone, for which Paderewski is famous, he assigned selections from Mendelssohn's "Songs Without Words" and the Chopin Nocturnes.

Paderewski considers the pedal a study in itself, "an art in itself", and in this art, as all critics agree, he has developed effects never achieved by other pianists. He uses, Madame Szumowska tells us, "a great deal of soft pedal for *piano* passages. Sometimes he uses both pedals together, sometimes each separately. Almost never is a sustained melody, or a melody of any kind, played without the loud pedal, changing it with every change of harmony . . . and sometimes on every note when the melody and harmony demand it."

"It stands to reason", Madame Szumowska writes, "that Paderewski would dislike teaching." But it is in his nature to do everything thoroughly and to do it with enthusiasm. That is one reason why, as a virtuoso, he remains a great teacher. Very especially in America, from the time of his first coming, he has been followed in this regard. With his art, it has been said, he created in America a "Golden Age of piano playing." When he plays, the student can easily see, as Finck pointed out, that "he has no use for the left-hand metronome; his two hands go together, now faster, now slower, like the speech of an impassioned actor or orator." The student can, in fact, see a dozen things; how Paderewski pedals, how he gets full value out of the pause, his inspired use of *tempo rubato,* and so on. And if the student hear him more than once he can observe how Paderewski grows, how he is never done searching for new tone depths in the interpretation of the masters. Once, in Boston, praised for his rendition of the last Beethoven sonata, he only responded, "You heard me play it fourteen years ago." "But it is fine to have kept on growing." "Yes," he replied simply, "that's the thing to try for." But after all it is not so much what the student sees, that counts, as what he feels, when Paderewski plays: the impulse that he receives to go back to work and perfect himself.

Taking Paderewski in the rôle of teacher at recital, the only thing that he has been criticized for has been that he "does not sufficiently vary his programs", as Finck expresses it. Finck calls this "his only fault". Baughan in London once remarked that "Paderewski's repertoire is rather limited", and complained that "he never makes experiments with the compositions of new men." Regarding the "new men" Paderewski has his own sane view which easily disputes any implication of prejudice. "As to the general comparison of the music of the old composers with that of the moderns," he says, "what can one say but this: A man is not necessarily a master because he happened to compose two or three centuries ago. Much that was written then was worthless, and long since has gone down to dusty death; other things were truly fine and have survived. Let us beware of the worship of mere antiquity." "I am no prophet," he has said, speaking of the new and the old in music, "still I hardly think it probable that the future will witness any very radical change in the manner of expressing musical ideas. Sensuousness is a marked characteristic of a great deal of the music of our time, and that undoubtedly makes a potent appeal to a large section of the public. However, pure intellectuality in pianoforte and other music still finds its eagerly appreciative if limited audience."

The charge that Paderewski does not favor modern composers in his programs might be taken to imply that he holds them all in disfavor. From what we know of his views on a certain type of music, the charge would hold if the word "modernistic" were substituted for "modern", but not otherwise.

"A perplexed pianist," Sigismond Stojowski relates, "once confessed to Paderewski, 'I would rather not play that. You are playing it.' To which Paderewski replied, 'But I play everything.'" He does. His repertoire embraces the entire range of classical piano literature, "classical" being used in the sense of permanent value. Discussing this matter of the classical, Stojowski, so familiar with his ideals, expressed himself in words that one feels sure may be taken as those of Paderewski himself: "A milliner feels herself in duty bound to exhibit the latest Parisian fashions in hats. Along comes a customer to whom the new shapes seem rather odd. 'That's what they're wearing,' the saleswoman explains. And most of the time the customer is convinced and adopts the new fad. In matters of art things should be—though they not always are—quite different. Even in art fashion plays havoc with some people. It is scarcely to be avoided that the music-merchant display on his shelves not merely classical masterpieces but chiefly and principally the latest publications, regardless of whether they be worth the paper they are printed on. But the true artist is not a music-merchant, although, alas, there are among artists mediocrities and prophets of the new dispensation ready to serve and live on other mediocrities. But the *salon carré* of the Louvre is reserved for masterpieces only. The Louvre does not admit any living artists until they have served their time in the Musée du Luxembourg. Nor does the Luxembourg accept all the novelties and oddities of the annual *salons*."

The repertoire of an artist like Paderewski carries, in music, the responsibility that the Louvre does in painting. Paderewski feels this. But he does not cling rigidly to the classics as a Brahmin to his scroll. He plays mostly a classical repertoire because he and his audiences, as a matter of taste, prefer it. "The great familiar musical works," he has said, "are always greeted by the audiences as ever welcome and beloved friends." Furthermore, this love for the classical does not in the very least imply exclusiveness or narrowness nor a lack of interest in novelty or innovation. On the contrary, Paderewski, by the very nature of his highly original and inquisitive being, has always taken the liveliest interest in every new artistic manifestation. But his interest is discriminating. He will take a modern piece and study it—as he once did a certain sonata, a form of composition demanding a huge amount of work from both composer and performer—play it over and over again, only to exclaim in the end after many honest attempts, "What a pity I could not have talked this over with the composer before it was published! I would have had such a gorgeous new piece to play."

There are recognized composers who have talked things over with him, with the result that their compositions have been included in Paderewski's programs. No less a personage than the Director of the Royal Academy of Music at London, Sir Alexander Campbell Mackenzie, is one of these; his "Fantasy for Piano and Orchestra" owes its first presentation to Paderewski, as does a "Fantasy" by Sir Frederick Cowen, for many years Conductor of the London Philharmonic. Perilhou, a modern French composer, found the way to presentation in the same manner; so did Stojowski. "I want very much to have a novel piano-concerto to play," Paderewski once said to Stojowski. "It would please me enormously if it were to be yours." That is the way the commission was given—because Paderewski wanted something new, something modern. "Nevertheless," as Stojowski said, remarking on Paderewski's exacting demands of music whether new or old, "it took me a few years and quite a little talking over before I could produce a work that won his unstinted approval." But Paderewski gave more than his approval, once it was merited; he put all his energies into fostering the success of the piece upon which his friend and former pupil had worked so zealously and arduously. The crowning of these efforts was the American première of Stojowski's "Prologue, Scherzo and Variations" at Boston, in March, 1916, with the Boston Symphony Orchestra, Dr. Carl Muck conducting. Seven rehearsals were given to the new work, and after the performance Dr. Muck said to Paderewski, "We worked well for Art today."

Among contemporaries Paderewski has included in his programs the Russian Rachmaninoff, the American Schelling, the Pole Szymanowski, and many others. Szymanowski, whose opera "Hagith" I heard in Warsaw in 1922, is modern of the moderns. "Hagith" seemed to me the final word in modernistic composition, but Szymanowski has gone several strides further in modernism since then. New French composers have likewise frequently found place on Paderewski's programs; he once devoted an entire recital in Paris to contemporary French writers. Among the moderns Debussy, in particular, has figured on Paderewski's programs, even at a time when he was by no means universally acclaimed. "There is something in this man," Paderewski insisted. "I have learned to respect him through his piano-pieces," he said to Daniel Gregory Mason.

In his critical comments on composers, always interesting and instructive, Paderewski is again the teacher. He has positive opinions, and they are illuminating. We have heard already his views on the French impressionists. Debussy in his opinion stands head and shoulders over his followers and imitators, but he is nevertheless, "a man of great talent corrupted by his admirers", who writes operatic music "not for its own sake, but as a handmaid to something else. He aims at description, at philosophy, perhaps—yes, at realism even. Now, music is not a handmaid, a slave; it should not be made subordinate to poetry, to mere decoration; it should have its own form, its own meaning, its own *raison d'être*". In "Pélléas and Mélisande" he finds that "everything is subordinated to the text, nothing is musically salient." But he likes Debussy's piano music and admires his sense of color and knowledge of the instrument.

Among the elder French composers he bases Saint-Säens' greatness on his skill and versatility, which permitted him to achieve at least one masterpiece in every form. Saint-Säens, the man and the virtuoso, he warmly admired. That artist's superb playing in London of sixteen Mozart concertos from memory, four in each one of four concerts, at the age of seventy-six, Paderewski considers something memorable in the history of piano playing. Gounod's "Faust", with what he calls its "'immortally beautiful love music'", is for him one of the "eternal" compositions; like "Carmen", he says, "it can never grow old." He considers it superior to "Romeo et Juliette." Mefisto's song of the "Veau d'Or" he admires, but the famous "Soldier's Chorus" is to him uninteresting. Gounod, in his opinion, influenced Bizet and still more influenced Tschaikowsky, "who in all he wrote was dominated by Gounod." The "Faust" waltz colored Tschaikowsky's opera "Eugen Onegin" and even the second movement of his Symphonie Pathètique. Massenet's masterpiece, in Paderewski's view, is "Le Jongleur." Of Charpentier's "Louise" he speaks enthusiastically: "He treads in Wagner's footsteps in many places."

Paderewski the Pole is racially and temperamentally antipathetic to most of the Russian music; it is too gloomy, too despondent. When he heard Scriabin's Symphony No. 2 performed by Safonoff with the New York Philharmonic he exclaimed, "the first Russian musician with some sunshine in him!" "To know Tschaikowsky," he says, "is to know the whole Russian school, although the younger Russians repudiate him and Rubinstein . . . The last movement of Tschaikowsky's Symphonie Pathètique is sublime, the other three movements commonplace."

For Richard Strauss, although he considers his songs, with the exception of a few, much overrated, Paderewski has "great reverence . . . a man of remarkable talent, wonderful skill. Nevertheless he has few themes, few really musical ideas, and he develops these by an intellectual rather than by an emotional process. At least his development of them is not what I call creative. There are few lyrical melodies of deep emotional power in his works outside of his songs, some of which are exceedingly beautiful. In fact Strauss seems to be primarily interested not in emotional expression but in characterization."

Paderewski has an interesting comment to make on Mendelssohn. "Mendelssohn's use of the minor mode," he says, "may be connected with the Jewish tendency to complaint, which is in turn due to the trials and vicissitudes the race has suffered." He places Mendelssohn "very high". His Violin

Concerto he calls "one of the most perfect works in this form ever written." Ernest Bloch, he has said, is the first truly Jewish composer, that is, the one most faithfully expressing the trials and vicissitudes of the racial soul.

Speaking of Mendelssohn brings Beethoven to mind: "Beethoven I have always regarded as the most soul-satisfying of composers for the piano. He was the master harmonist, and we must all reverence his memory—no, not his memory, for how can it be said of such a towering genius that he is dead! Upon his brow there rests the fadeless garland of immortal fame. He speaks to us in music, he lives in sounds that ravish us to hear!" An anecdote will illustrate Paderewski's reverence for that master. Among the many pilgrims visiting Beethoven's home, where his piano is preserved, was a young American girl who breezed up to the instrument and nonchalantly dashed off on it an airy tune. "I suppose," the young lady remarked to the custodian, looking up from the keyboard, "I suppose you have many visitors here?"

"Yes, a great many."

"Many famous people, no doubt."

"Yes. Paderewski came recently."

"I suppose he played on this piano?" and her fingers ran a scale on the keys.

"No, Paderewski did not consider himself worthy to play on Beethoven's piano."

Paderewski adores Bach and Schubert and is a thoroughgoing Wagnerite. "Die Meistersinger" is to him "the supreme effort of the human mind. I constantly come back to it. I study it afresh each year and always find something new in it to admire." To properly hear "Meistersinger" he feels one must go to Vienna; for "Tannhäuser" to Dresden, for "Parsifal" or "Tristan" to Bayreuth. The best performance of "The Flying Dutchman" that he ever heard was in an obscure German city of thirty thousand population.

When one reviews Paderewski's relationships with critics, teachers and students, one sees that he has been, especially in America, a great stimulating force, a real teacher; and this not merely by the "accident of inevitability", but because he knows he is a teacher and realizes his responsibility as such just as surely as he realizes that scattered through every audience that greets him are numbers of eager aspirants. There can be no art without a criticism, no art without its teachers. And in all the varied ranks of the art-workers of the world none is singled out by Paderewski for a more devoted appreciation than the music teacher. "You have over a million music teachers in the United States," he says. "Financially most of them are in a bad way. The best artists have a hard time. Music as a profession has been hit on the head by the radio. Yet your music teachers, with a most devoted and admirable idealism, continue to spread the gospel of music. It is due to them that you still attract the best artists and that your orchestras are now the envy of the world. The little lady piano teacher of the little town does that. To her, music is not as much a profession as it is a religion."

The effect of Paderewski's recurrent appearances in America, as assuredly as in every other country he has played in, has been to keep musical criticism and the study of music, to use an Americanism, "on its toes." Certain words of Dr. Henry Noble MacCracken, President of Vassar College, expresses fully what Paderewski has done to stimulate culture and art in America. "In ancient Thebes," Dr. MacCracken said at the Paderewski testimonial tendered by the Kosciuszko Foundation in New York City in 1928, "it was fabled that Amphion raised the walls of the city with the music of his lute. Paderewski has raised with his music in all parts of this country an edifice more enduring than the walls of Thebes. He has given us again our heritage; he has restored to us the Kingdom of Art; he has given us in the United States a liberal culture . . . It is time that all Americans should recognize the great part which our citizens of Polish birth, led by Paderewski, are playing in our land. These people have brought with them from their country the same love of music and art that makes Paderewski supreme. In their meetings, in their societies, music is their channel of expression. They crowd our audiences. They help us to support orchestras and symphonies and operas, and if it were not for their enthusiasm and the like enthusiasm of other citizens of the older peoples who have brought to America this love of art, we should be barren indeed, famine stricken in this land, partitioned out in material things alone."

The final judgment on music of Paderewski the teacher is easily summed up in a glance at his various expressions. That judgment is, that music is essentially emotional. No matter to what degree the intellect is brought to bear upon the mastery of its technique, music remains primarily an art of the emotions. "It should," he says, "in the words of Mr. Gilder's beautiful poem on Chopin, have a voice, 'too tender even for sorrow, too bright for mirth'. It should sustain and cheer us, even while we are touched with a vague melancholy. It should ennoble." He agrees with his compatriot, Joseph Conrad: "Imagination, not invention, is the supreme master of art". "If I were asked to name the chief qualification of a great pianist, apart from technical excellence," Paderewski once said, "I should answer in a word, Genius! That is the spark which fires every heart, that is the voice which all men stop to hear! Lacking genius, your pianist is simply a player—an artist, perhaps— whose work is politely listened to or admired in moderation as a musical *tour de force*. He leaves his hearers cold, nor is the appeal which he makes through the medium of his art a universal one. And here let me say, referring to the celebrated 'paradox' of Diderot, that I am firmly of the belief that the pianist, in order to produce the finest and most delicate effects, must feel what he is playing, identify himself absolutely with his work, be in sympathy with the composition in its entirety, as well as with its every shade of expression. Only so shall he speak of that immense audience which ever attends on perfect art. Yet—and here is a paradox, indeed—he must put his own personality resolutely, triumphantly, into his interpretation of the composer's ideas."

XX

THE AUDIENCE

EXPERIMENT and experience served in due time to master the intricacies of American "railroading" life for Paderewski, so that, as Hugo Gorlitz once remarked, "Everything works like a machine." The test of time proved Paderewski's worth to even the prejudiced critics of this country, as it had so notably proved it to their colleagues in England. But very little time was needed to achieve the conquest of the American people.

It was not alone the new revelation of music he brought to them that made Paderewski popular. There was something in his character which immediately communicated itself to the people; by the processes of mass psychology they laid spontaneous hands of apprehension and appreciation on him and they have held him closely and strongly ever since. In America more perhaps than in any country in the world he became "the musician of the many." His name from the moment of his first arrival spread over the country like a fire; it was, one might say, as if that flaming head of his—actually it was the flame of his personality—had set a conflagration. When one reads through the files of the newspapers reporting his appearances from the time of his earliest American recitals, one is convinced that Paderewski was indeed a popular sensation. The public, as one chronicler reported it, "acted as if crazy with joy."

It was more than good management, good publicity, good showmanship that did this, more than the fame by which he had come heralded. Two things may be said to account for it all: the immediate attack, already mentioned, of his personality on crowds of people, and the steadily growing record of honesty and integrity which he built up in his relationship with the public. Of the first, this may be said: Paderewski not only has never stooped to his public ("he never stooped to conquer", as Finck remarked), but, he never assumed that he must stoop. The showy or the sensational he never foisted on his audiences, never "played down" to them, never treated them as "groundlings." He took his audiences as seriously as he takes his art. "An audience," in his opinion, "plays an important part in the actual work of the professional appearing before it. Sensitively developed, as the artist must be, properly to interpret his art, he feels subconsciously, while he is playing, the degree of sympathetic appreciation given by his hearers. If that appreciation is an ardent, understanding one, he is buoyed up by it, surpassing, perhaps, in spirit and interpretation, all bounds of his former achievements. The hearer, familiar with the contents of a composition, as he or she has found it individually, is able to appreciate the revelation of new and subtle expression and nuance. Such a hearer becomes, as it were, part of the performance, encouraging the artist, giving him freshened inspiration, and uplifting him in an answering enthusiasm of his own."

With feelings like this for his audiences, and invariably giving them the highest and the best on the assumption that they desired the highest and the best, Paderewski has appealed to the innate pride of people. This was, of course, the natural action of an idealistic spirit, human, sympathetic, genial, modest. de Pachmann once described Paderewski as entirely free from vanity, "the most modest artist he had ever seen." The people responded instinctively to this modesty, this absence of pretentiousness.

Paderewski's reputation for honest dealings with the public was rapidly established. His engagements, it was known, would be fulfilled; there would be no temperamental outbursts cancelling concerts. His sense of moral and artistic accountability makes him immovable in the face of circumstance when responsibility to his public is involved, even though the few may be at times inconvenienced and antagonized. I recall the incident of a newspaper writer who attacked him angrily in print because he, the writer, had been refused an interview when Pader-

ewski's train pulled into the station. It was in Minnesota, in
the depth of winter on a bitter cold morning, and the heating
apparatus of Paderewski's car had gone out of order. The artist,
easily a victim of neuritis, from which he has suffered so severely, was scheduled for a concert that day, a concert for which
some ten thousand people had paid their money in advance.
He would not expose himself in any way at the risk of jeopardizing his appearance or the quality of his performance. It is
the same spirit of accountability to his art and to his audience
that makes him insist on his twenty-minute seclusion and soli-
tude before he approaches the piano. "He knows," says Engles,
his manager, "what those twenty minutes mean. They might
wreck a whole career. The basis of Paderewski's eminence is
the elimination of the possibility of failure; therefore his instant refusal to go before his audience when the electric current of thought and creative power is interrupted. It takes courage and decision to say no in a moment of tension. When he
appears he will come poised, composed, prepared."

In 1893, during Paderewski's third American tour, an upset-
ting incident occurred, one that shows us how far he carries
his sense of obligation to his audience. Invited by Theodore
Thomas to take part in the opening concerts of the Chicago
World's Fair, he rearranged his tour, at great personal incon-
venience and considerable financial loss, in order to do so. When
he arrived to give his recitals, however, he discovered that the
piano which he invariably used, the Steinway, could not be used
according to a regulation of the Exposition officials, because
the Steinway manufacturers, not approving of the system of
awards at the Fair, were not exhibiting. The Board of Directors
informed Paderewski that he must play on an exhibiting instrument. He refused. He could not change his instrument at the
last minute. The matter got into the papers, but the publicity
resulted in the Exposition officials waking up to the fact that
an artist has rights which not even commercial exigency can
overrule. They backed down, and Paderewski played his own
piano. In the end the controversy drew from him a statement,
published in the press, which set right for all time the artist's

position in such a regard. He would not have made the statement had not one newspaper accused him of "selling himself to
a piano firm."

"I most emphatically deny," Paderewski wrote, "that I am
bound by contract or agreement, either in writing or verbally,
to the use of any particular make of piano. In this respect I am
at perfect liberty to follow my convictions and inclinations and
this privilege I must be free to exercise in the prosecution of
my artistic career. Throughout the wide world any artist is
permitted to use the instrument of his choice, and I do not
understand why I should be forced to play an instrument
strange to me and untried by me, which may jeopardize my
artistic success."

If Paderewski had to engage a special train to carry him over
the country in order to satisfy the popular demand for his
appearances, special trains also became a necessity to carry the
people to him. Every city where he played, every large town,
became a center attracting hundreds from outlying towns.
Whole schools traveled for miles to attend his recitals. Often,
when people could not hear him they came into towns from
the countryside to catch a glimpse of him as his train passed
through. Once, on a tour through a sparsely settled region,
after a painful injury to one of his fingers, regardless of discomfort he gave his recital before the injured finger was entirely healed. "But why did you do it?" he was asked. "I may
never come this way again," he answered. "I couldn't disap-
point them." In Minneapolis he heard of a cloistered order of
nuns whose vows prevented them from attending a public concert. But they loved music. Unadvertised, and unobtrusively,
in deference to their privacy, he gave them a recital all their
own.

Paderewski's agreeable generosity in giving encores is often
commented on; after a lengthy and trying recital of two hours
and a half he will sit for another hour, late into the night, playing informally for the people who crowd by the hundreds
around his piano. It was in America, during his first appearances in New York, that this custom, unprecedented in the his-

tory of concerts, came into being, a spontaneous outgrowth of the people's enthusiasm. Sometimes the lights have to be turned out or the stage-curtain lowered, to make the people go home and save the pianist from complete exhaustion. But people would not crowd around him, they would not approach him, they would go home and leave him, if it were not for that something-else in him besides picturesque figure and fame as artist. They don't want to leave him, they want more and more of him, because although they may not articulate the thought, or even be conscious of it, since it is a feeling more than a thought, that something in him which holds them is the best that is in themselves.

"It is like a football game!" one auditor at a concert in Milwaukee exclaimed, as he listened to the cheers that broke from the audience at the close of the recital. They would not go home. The people who leave him with regret receive him with joy. They stand en masse, hushed, when he appears, paying him the silent tribute of reverent affection. Then they break loose. "There is something exciting, even thrilling," one critic wrote, "in shouts of joy that go up, even from the staid and dignified Boston Symphony audience." This popular acclaim, it is true, has at times moved the press to scornful condemnation. They have referred to such demonstrations as "hysterical feminine adoration", yet the same newspapers, as Mr. Finck has pointed out, have given columns to the description of "soul-stirring" runs by a football player and the "delirious joy" of stadium crowds over a final goal-kick. Is not art, as those interested in it have asked, worthy of its enthusiasm?

Paderewski was once drawn into a remark on the often repeated slur of "feminine adoration." "It is natural," he said, "that women should make up the greatest part of my audiences, especially in America where the men do not have as much time to devote to music as women do. But the numerous stories about the ladies who have asked for locks of my hair and my photographs are pure invention." (There was a time during the war when Paderewski, deluged with requests for autographs, gladly gave them for a stated fee in order to raise money for the Polish Victims Relief Fund.) "Once, in America," he went on, "the papers said that a lady came up after the recital and seized my watch as a souvenir. But here it is, the same watch I've carried for fifteen years."

He has a deep respect for the women of his audiences. "But for women," he says, "there would be today no art in the world, not alone in America, but anywhere. The assertion may be a sweeping one, but I thoroughly believe it to be true. The women it is who, through inborn love of music and responsive, deeply refined feeling, encourage it in brave, practical, energetic ways. The women it is, too, who lead in the cause of its fostering, and influence by their supreme enthusiasm the men to follow."

If women have made up the greater part of Paderewski's audience, it has been in Germany, he says, that he has found the most musical women. "That," he explains, "is merely because the love of music is traditional in Germany and has now become a habit. But so far as the musical instinct is concerned," he declares, "the German women are no better off than the American, the French or the English."

Of course Paderewski was bound to suffer, as all artists must, from the celebrity-hunter, usually feminine, and sometimes he has been moved, being only a human being and a humorous one besides, to give the retort courteous a dash of "spoofing" in responding to the queries of curiosity seekers. To the eager lady who confused him with an international polo player, asking beamingly, "Are you the good soul who plays polo?" he responded, "No, madame, I am only the good Pole who plays solo."

Paderewski does not forget the so-called "unmusical" person in his reckoning of the audience. "We all know the story," he once said, "of the Emperor Ferdinand of Austria who boasted that he knew what was the imperial hymn and what wasn't. People who really dislike music are few—and they are suffering from an infirmity. Music is to them a vast desert, not because they lack sense of it, but because they cannot find their way to music, or music its way to them. I have noticed in in-

stances of those who profess not to understand it, or pose as
silent enemies to my art, that they were still extremely pleased
with pieces of their level. These people were attracted by some
frivolous rhythm or moved by some bars of simple touching
melody, and for this reason I am inclined to believe that some
music, like certain poetry, finds its appeal and way to all."

Paderewski's aim has been not only to give pleasure to those
who understand music, but to increase the capacity of all to
enjoy it. "You cannot meet a Beethoven, a Chopin, or a Schumann; yet when playing [or hearing played] the work of
these great masters, you live for a short moment, with mind
free, in the enjoyment of their society. And what it means to
be in contact with such spirits! It is a living with them, and a
something yet more. A poem you read silently, and often-times
it leaves you cold. It appeals to the mind, not to the emotions.
If you see a picture or a statue, and are without a knowledge
of pictorial or sculptural technic your impression is a minimum
one. But when you play [or hear played] a sonata with a certain degree of perfection, you not only know the composer, but
it uplifts you, puts you much higher than you were before."

The uninitiated can learn to enjoy the best music: "Those
who have suddenly found themselves in a strange country
whose language they cannot speak have confessed that at first
the foreign tongue spoken seemed like one single, long, unintelligible word; by degrees sentences as a whole became distinguishable, and finally the individual word grew to have its
rightful meaning. In a way this may be applied to one with a
little knowledge of music. Such a one finds the outline of some
work by a great composer growing gradually clearer from out
a general chaos; presently the individual phrase begins to reveal
itself, and from that point real comprehension is entered on.
Just as surely as every new language mastered opens up a new
world, so knowledge of a Beethoven, a Chopin, or a Schumann
opens up a new world in spiritual beauty and thought."

The audiences which gather to listen to music represent the
culture of a people or a country: "The culture of any country,"
in Paderewski's words, "is gauged first by its progress in art."

But culture is not a fungus that grows overnight. That process of learning, which Paderewski likens to the mastering of a strange language, is a slow process, and it must have its beginnings. "No people have sprung into greatness in any art without the slow, upbuilding process of preceding generations of striving. The first pipe fashioned from a reed meant, humble as it was, a stride toward the future evolution of music. The first rude attempt at recording notes was the forerunner of the elaborate orchestral score of to-day. Beginnings play their prized part in every finished human accomplishment, for beginnings mean the birth of added progress." The taste for art, like the talent for it, "small in one generation, is likely to be found more fully pronounced in the next. Men and women longing ardently to accomplish something in a given art, but failing in marked attainment, often realize in their children full possession of the gift in which they themselves fell short. Back to some half forgotten ancestor may oftentimes be traced a glorious talent enriching the world."

A wise head and a warm heart dictate such thoughts as these. William Mason, the American pianist, appraising Paderewski in his first appearances in this country, remarked that "he plays with a big warm heart as well as with a clear, calm, discriminating head", a verdict which only confirmed the tribute Mason paid Paderewski when he called him "an artist by the grace of God, a phenomenal and inspired player and, like all persons of large natural gifts, a simple, gracious and loving character." It is the "big warm heart" that has appealed to the masses. "The heartfelt sincerity of the man," Mr. Mason said, "is noticeable in all that he does, and his intensity of utterance easily accounts for the strong hold he has over his audiences." His playing "presents the beautiful contour of a living vital organism." To observe the functioning of that living organism at a recital is to become aware of the fact that at the piano Paderewski accomplishes a very strange feat. His effect on the crowd is not due to his working on the mass as a whole, but to his working on the individual. By the magic of his hands he separates from all the others each one of several thousand

people and holds that one apart, playing for him alone. But the hearer is not left alone with the player; he is left alone with himself, as he, Paderewski himself, seems to be alone.*
"His whole mind entirely absorbed in his playing," wrote Alexander Fried, "he looks up almost in fright at the irrelevant storm of applause."

The statistics covering Paderewski's American tours are, as we have seen, amazing. Over five million people in this country have heard him play. But mere figures give only a mathematical dimension to the story of his success. It has far wider and higher and deeper dimensions than that. It is not only that millions have heard him; there is something else—what he has done to those millions. A composite picture of Paderewski and his audience, made from the scattered record of some fifteen hundred recitals, tells the story better than figures can.

---

* Olin Downes, music critic of the *New York Times* felt this when he heard Paderewski playing Chopin in 1933: "It is one of the things so beautiful and poignant, so akin to what a human being most feels when he is alone, and knows his loneliness, far from all that is his." (*New York Times*, February 19, 1933).

XXI

PADEREWSKI PLAYS

"How Paderewski plays! And was it he
Or some disbodied spirit that had rushed
From silence into singing; that had crushed
Into one starved hour all life's felicity,
And highest bliss of knowledge—that all life's
grief, wrong
Turns at the last to beauty and to song!"
—RICHARD WATSON GILDER

THE hall fills up steadily. There is a large crowd outside, a long cue before the box-office getting last-moment seats, if there be any; others are dickering with people in the cue, trying to secure tickets. Perhaps the newspapers have announced a complete sell-out; nevertheless people come and try to get in. Numbers of them have gathered here to have at least a look at the crowd and possibly a glimpse of Paderewski. . . .

On the stage the piano waits for him; it seems in some strange way a sentient thing, silent until its master command from it speech and song. The master enters. The crowd, maybe five thousand, maybe ten thousand, rises to its feet to greet him, stands in a long silence before the welcoming applause begins. He bows, takes his place at the piano, waits for the audience to settle. He begins to play. For the time being, not as yet perhaps wholly rapt away by his music, he is still conscious of the presence of the audience, so conscious that there may seem to be in his eye a glance that commands absolute silence, forbids applause until the piece is ended.

The first selection closes. There is a silence, then the hand-clapping begins, bursts out suddenly to a roll of thunder; there are cries of "bravo!" breaking through the thunder. He waits. Silence again. He will play again. There is a feeling of intense suspension in this silence, communicated to the crowd by the strong hypnosis of the player's own intense concentration. The body, the noble head with its leonine mane, is still. Now it moves. Now his hand is lifted, it runs over the keyboard. His whole being is turning to music. He makes the piano sing. . . .

What is he playing? It may be Liszt's transcription of Schubert's song "Hark, hark, the Lark"—does the piano sing? "Literally," a critic once wrote, "he shames the human voice in its own sphere." "He alone, of all living virtuosi," Lawrence Gilman has said, "is able completely to convey, through the material agency of mere wire and wood, the illusion of an idealized living voice . . ." Selections from the masters . . . and he, the master interpreter, brings them one by one alive again, he reincarnates their souls, the songs of their wrath in thunder; of their pleading in melodic lines of pathos, tenderness; of their joy in lyric caprice, in the light treble of smiles, laughter; of their sorrow in lamentings, in tears that drop like fire on burning rock, or like cool rain on parched ground. . . . It may be Chopin's exquisite and familiar Butterfly Etude, or Schumann's fanciful "Papillons", or again the rousing sonorous Schubert-Tausig "Marche Militaire" with its triumphant cry of bugles. Perhaps it is a Chopin Scherzo, romantic, reckless, full of wild agitated runs streaming over the sweetness of wistful chordings; or the pure cradle-song tenderness of the Berceuse with its double chromatic runs, its far-off sound of a sunken bell. "And who," asks Gilman, "can play Chopin with Paderewski's flame-edged grace, his blend of fire and tenderness, his superb distinction of style? Who else can discourse to us with those strange accessions of divine madness that seize upon this uncompanioned artist?"

It may be Paderewski that Paderewski plays, although he rarely plays from his own compositions, and seldom if ever the older pieces. But suppose it to be the Cracovienne Fantastique: never elsewhere may we hear music more brilliant, more capricious and ingratiating. Or let it be his Nocturne in B flat, meditative, dreamy, rapturous, melodious, tender and full of wholesome sweetness, achieving what the moonlight itself achieves—elusiveness in its fragmentary melody, definiteness in outline with its *ostinato* accompaniment. Never is it saccharine or oversweet, always in every note and chord is it satisfyingly beautiful. Or let it be some of his own Variations. Or his Sonata. Or his Concerto. . . .

The Variations and Fugue on an original theme in E flat Minor (Op. 23) is one of his greatest piano-works, "a majestic theme", in the words of Abbie Finck, "upon which Paderewski has built one of the most splendid sets of variations in all music." "Rich color, masterly form, deliciously smeared with delicate dissonances," says Daniel Gregory Mason. "Astonishing sonority, pathetic mysterious emotions," in the description of Opienski, "sweet balancing of rhythms and of harmonies, firm design traced with entire mastership." All of these things and a thousand other things, to the critics, to those who understand the technique of music. But to the everyday auditor— just music!—music that rises and falls, sweeps and soars, rings and thunders, and sets the hearer on the edge of his chair magnetized, carried away, carried out of himself, he doesn't know why, he doesn't ask why. The only "Why" is that Paderewski is playing.

The Sonata? Now he is dramatic. He evokes in masculine chordings the heavy steps of a giant, a giant who treads on the hearts of his hearers; he passes to melodic melancholy, serenity, feminine graciousness; he tears the two apart, he brings them together, commingles them, fuses them; he ends in stormy passion . . . and a storm of applause, itself passionate in its delight, its satisfaction, its exaltation, answers the last crashing thunders of the keyboard.

The Concerto? If we could get a glance at the music sheets we should see a tell-tale phrase: "Dedicated to my master Leschetitsky" . . . those hard Vienna days that ended in the first triumph, in the first rise of that wave of success which swept him across the Atlantic, around the world, to South America, to Australia, to Africa, over the face of Europe from

St. Petersburg to Dublin, from Holland to Italy. He was only
twenty-three when he wrote the *allegro* of this Concerto. . . .
He gives the theme to the orchestra, he envelops it in piano-
cadences of "endearing arpeggios and gracious melodic illu-
minings." Then comes the slow movement of the dialogues
between oboe and piano, between violin and 'cello solos;
idyllic love-notes murmur over the rustling of April leaves
. . . over the soft monotone of running water. Then comes
the crescendo finale reëchoing the theme . . . life . . . overflowing joy. . . .

So Paderewski plays. So he holds and thrills multitudes of
people, thousands of them wholly unmusical in the technical
sense. "The test of a musician's genius is in his power over the
unmusical." How does the genius of Paderewski work on the
multitude? Is it mere virtuosity, mechanical adroitness, "stunt"?
"Of pure mechanical motion, where a tired mind wanders and
leaves nervous habit the only overseer of the hands," says
Fried—and he is writing of the "second" Paderewski, the
artist in his sixties who might well be tired—of pure mechanics
"there is not a moment in Paderewski's playing." What is his
secret then? "His strength lies not, like Samson's, in his hair;
that superstition was exploded long ago," writes Henry Finck;
"in fact, one can hardly see his hair in the religious light that
dims the stage while he plays. Nor does his strength lie in his
muscles, though his arms have the supple power of superfine
steel, as everyone knows who has had the honor of shaking
hands with him." His strength lies in his character, in the high
character of his art. "Never does he resort to clap-trap, tricki-
ness, or sensationalism in order to win applause. There are
successful pianists who draw attention to their skill by an obtru-
sive brilliancy of execution and a parading of difficulties. . . .
They try to show the public, not how beautiful the music of
the great masters is, but what clever performers they are. . . .
That is not Paderewski's way. . . . He has no looks, no gri-
maces for the audience. No public smile ever sits on his lips, yet
if you look closely you will observe subtle changes of expres-

sion on his features; he is listening intently to his own playing, and if the tone is as beautiful as he wishes it, an expression of pleasure flits across his features. He seems to be far away in dreamland, playing for himself alone; and his chief reward is not the applause of the audience but the delight in his own playing."

So he plays, and little by little we learn what his secret is. He loves his piano. He loves music. He makes us love it. He "makes the musical ideas he interprets absorbingly interesting to all classes of hearers."

So Paderewski plays. "So David's magic string," the Californian poet Ina Coolbrith sang,

> *Loosened the evil fetters of his King!*
> *So here—from what great star, divinely crowned,*
> *Rapt in whose ecstasy of perfect sound*
> *Each ivory key becomes a living thing!*
> *Aeolian murmurs of a mystic dream;*
> *The gathering tempest's mighty thunder-roll,*
> *A sob; a shivering sigh, just breathed and mute;*
> *Strife, triumph, rapture, peace of heaven supreme—*
> *All, all are his, the master's twin of soul*
> *With Israfel, 'whose heart-strings are a lute.'*

So Paderewski plays, year in and year out, and the people can never have enough of him. And whatever it be that he plays, holding us, doing unimaginable things to us, making us want more and still more, making us stand and wait and crowd around him . . . in the end it will almost surely be the Minuet. Everyone wants it, all are asking for it, waiting for it. We listen entranced to those simple familiar strains, naïve, melodious, they sway us in a gentle satisfying measure. . . .

We go home at last. And perhaps, after the silence that continues for a while—for Paderewski in music has the same faculty that the classic actress Margaret Anglin has in drama, the power of putting the quiet of the Greek *katharsis* on an audience—perhaps someone tells the story of how he came to compose that minuet; of how it came out of a kind of wager that no one in modern times could compose music like that of the old masters. One evening, so the story goes, during Paderewski's days as a teacher at the Warsaw Conservatory, he was at the home of the Polish writer Swiętochowski. The writer, who was an ardent admirer of Mozart, declared that no living composer could produce music with the simplicity and beauty of Mozart's compositions. Paderewski neither agreed nor disagreed, simply shrugged his shoulders and said nothing. The following evening, however, back again in Swiętochowski's house, he sat down at the piano. "You like Mozart," he said to his host. "May I play you a little thing that perhaps you do not know?"

His friend listened enraptured. When the piece was finished he thanked Paderewski and exclaimed, "Now you will perhaps agree with me! You will acknowledge that a piece like that could never be written in our time."

"Why not?" Paderewski responded, smiling up at his host. "That happens to be a minuet written by myself."

The captious may smile at that story and say that it can't possibly be true since no one could ever be fooled, anyway, into mistaking Paderewski's Minuet for a Mozart piece. The Minuet is Paderewski, pure and simple, with all the antique grace and stateliness and unquenchable gayety of his native Poland in it. But no matter. We have something worth while to talk about, and we have been happy. We have heard Paderewski play. Five million of us have heard him.

What has he done to us? It is impossible to put into words what the music of a master like Paderewski does to us. Only music itself could tell us. If it be in one moment a rousing force, a fiery passion, a kind of luminous ferocity, blood-tingling, frightening in its intensity, that sweeps through the hearts of people like the clear, roaring, smokeless flame of a divine conflagration, in the next moment it is a tenderness and a softness that has all poignancy, all sweetness in it, the weaving and commingling fall of the keys together making a murmur and a caress until there is nothing left but quiet and wistfulness, maybe an unwept tear-drop trembling in the center of a man's heart, and in the heart of that tear-drop a silence, a lovely, unearthly silence, deep down in the core of one's being . . .

What has he done to us? He has made us know, for a few moments at least, something wholly different from and something infinitely better than even the best that ordinary life can offer us, something which we have known is, but which we have not been able to touch, to grasp. He has made us aware, for a little while anyway, that man is a spiritual being. He has challenged us, struck at us, hurt us with the hurt of spiritual consciousness, spiritual growth; he has made our souls inside the crusted chrysalis of mere existence stir toward light. He has soothed us too, after the hurt, healed us, excited us, exalted us, bathed us in the refreshment of a luminous effulgence of harmony translated from light to sound, opening our inner eyes and making us see ourselves and others in a new *rayon* of beauty.

He is an adventurer and an explorer who takes us on great journeys. We move with him along tides of light, we draw near to mighty shores, pass up wide unknown rivers to splendid harbors into unknown lands and unknown worlds built of light and music—worlds unknown, yet somehow we recognize them, they are our homelands, they are not strange, they are beautifully familiar to us, we are happy in them. We rest.

These are some of the great and high things that Paderewski has done.

In the lesser sphere, to put it simply, he has given millions of people pleasurable relaxation, something stimulating and wholesome to enjoy, something worth while to talk about, something to be proud to remember. He has enriched us in experience. A moralist would say, he has made us want to be good. One of his intimate friends once said of him that his own greatest art is "the art of being good."

That saying somehow relates itself to the formula I have worked out for myself concerning the reason for Paderewski's effect on audiences. When I went to hear him once more, in

1933, I went in a kind of challenging mood. It was not Paderewski that I was challenging to judgment, it was my own memories and preconceptions of him. Perhaps the fear of being disappointed, disillusioned after all, let down after high impossible expectations, was at the base of my mood, which was deliberately skeptical. I had called him a superman, and then in cold blood I had told myself that that was not possible. He was only the man Paderewski; an artist true enough, the greatest of living artists, but I was not going to be fooled by the piled up clouds of aureate glory massed about his name and fame. I was going to start all over again, see him and hear him clearly, keep my eyes off the halo. . . .

There is an old Irish legend about a monk who listened to a skylark sing, and woke from his rapture to find that years had passed instead of moments. When the first part of Paderewski's program—it was all Chopin—was ended that day, and I came to, I looked at my watch. A whole hour had passed, an hour that had been less than a moment for me—and infinitely more—because it had been timeless. The challenge, the refusal, the skepticism, had all vanished in complete forgetfulness.

That recital began at three-thirty in the afternoon. At seven minutes to seven that evening the stage attendants came and took away the piano chair so that the four or five thousand people gathered in the hall would go home. What had happened to those people during those three hours of music? Why did they refuse to go? What had happened to me?

For myself, coming out of the trance into which the first hour of sound-magic had drawn me, I began, when the music was resumed, by looking about at the people around me. I did it deliberately. I wanted to see how they were behaving. There was as many postures of attention as there were people: some leaned forward eagerly, some held bowed heads in their hands, some rested their elbows on their knees cupping their chins, some leaned back against their chairs with closed eyes; many sat rigidly erect. I began thus, looking about. I have no idea how long I took to make my observations of the audience, for in what seemed only a moment I was observing Paderewski.

There were moments when he seemed wholly unconscious of hall, audience, even of piano; for he and his instrument were fused into one thing, man and instrument were at once part and entire whole of each other. His hands!—I remember this thought flashing through my mind: "I am *seeing* sound." The velocity, the rapidity, the electrical fluency, of the movement of those hands came nearer Dante's concept of the celestial immovable motion of the Primum Mobile than anything I had ever imagined. His face was lifted up at times in a kind of rapt exaltation, as if he were listening. But at other moments he turned his face to the audience—I felt that he turned to me—as if what he was listening to was a communicable thing; and yet that turning toward us was not a glance or a look. It was not as if he saw us clearly. . . .

Encore after encore; and after the applause for each succeeding encore those thousands of people rose to their feet and stood, stood in silence and remained standing—until he sat down again. Then they also sat again, relaxed, fell once more into their attitudes of rapt attention, gave themselves up to him and listened on and on. I don't know how many times this was repeated. It happened over and over until the whole thing became a massed unified series of risings and sittings, of listening silences broken only by punctuating applause. There was something vaguely stubborn and refusing in it, the refusal to be satisfied, to say "enough" and go.

Not until the piano chair was removed did the mood change; nor did it change suddenly. That mass of people had to come to, wake up, as I had. Then the ovation broke into rolling waves of hand clapping, cheering, waving of handkerchiefs, inarticulate cries. . . . A big six-foot man across the aisle from me was crying, tears wetting his cheeks.

What had happened? This is my explanation, my "formula":

The universe was created out of chaos into harmony. "Order is Heaven's first law." Man is a part of the created universe. The order of Heaven is in the beating of man's heart. He is part chaos, part harmony, he is matter and spirit; but order and harmony are the birthright of his higher self. His whole being needs order, harmony, concord; longs for it, craves it, desires it, is forever seeking its balance and equilibrium. Music is the language of order. Man has "intimations of immortality" when he listens to music. It is the language of his spiritual origin, of the far-off homeland of his soul. Seldom can he speak that language, but always he recognizes it when he hears it, and once recognized and listened to, he wants it more and more, he cannot give it up, he must have it, more and more of it. . . . Hearing it, he may not be able to answer, he may be struck dumb, but listen to it he will and must, once it has spoken to him.

Yet some creatures there are so attuned to primal order, so sensitive to the universal harmony of creation, whose heart-beats are so immediately out of the pulsation of the First Order Itself, which is God—some creatures there are who do speak the language of man's origin and birthright, who can and do listen back to the Nine Heavens, to the celestial spheres, to the very Primum Mobile, the source of all life and concord; and listening they can, and do, speak to us in our universal tongue. The moment they speak we recognize the tongue, the voice, the accent; quickly its phrasing begins to beat more and more familiarly on our attentive spiritual hearing . . . little by little and more and more we understand. Peace comes into us then, we are quieted, we rest. We are happy. But let that hushing concordant language of our souls, to which our souls so raptly listen, cease—up we rise, we stand up on our feet, we protest; it must not cease, it must go on. We are like children wishing for a familiar story to be told over and over.

When Paderewski plays he speaks the language of Heaven. To hear him is a spiritual experience. That is the secret of his effect on his audiences. And the secret of his life's success, of his world-wide influence for good, is simply this: He has a spiritual background. No man rises higher than his source. Paderewski draws off from a high and spiritual source. There-fore he rises high. And he lifts others up. As the American scholar and poet, John H. Finley, has said, addressing him:

Your touch has been transmuted into sound
As perfect as an orchid or a rose,
True as a mathematic formula
Yet full of color as an evening sky.
But there's a symphony that you've evoked
From out the hearts of men, more wonderful
Than you have played upon your instrument . . .

XXII

NATIONAL IDEALS

PADEREWSKI moved rapidly in his growth into American life, and it is interesting to note how rapidly he moved out of the orbit of visiting artist and became a kind of American institution. This fact has a bearing on his later career as statesman. If that peculiar something which happened between Paderewski and the American public had not happened, a different story would have been told when the World War came and he took his place among the molders of opinion in this country.

Hundreds of famous artists visit and have visited the United States, but most of them never become more than distinguished passersby. Paderewski's case was different. He became very American. In time he made a home for himself here and became an American farmer; for his establishing himself on a ranch at Paso Robles was not the mere setting up of a stopping-place this side the Atlantic. He was a real California rancher, seriously interested in his plantings and his crops. He was the son of his father, a Polish farmer.

Paderewski's American home, the Rancho San Ignacio, at Paso Robles, which he purchased in 1913, is about five miles from the Paso Robles Hotel, on the Adelaide Road. There are really two ranches, for near by is the Rancho Santa Helena, the property of Madame Paderewska. It was rest and the curative waters of the Paso Robles Hot Springs that first brought Paderewski there. Besides, it was the California of his friend Modjeska, a California that he had come to know well through his visits to her ranch, "Arden", at Santa Ana. He knew it so well, indeed, that he knew of other waters there besides those of the hot springs. He recalls one visit to "Arden", on his return from his first visit to Australia, during which he made an intimate acquaintance with the very cold waters of a Californian winter rain. He had cabled Modjeska from Sydney, and had arrived in California prepared for a full treat of the famous sunshine. But it was December, and as Modjeska related it to me in a letter of January 23, 1905, he came just in time for himself and his wife to make a twenty-three mile drive unprotected in a sudden chilling downpour. "They were shivering with cold when they arrived at Arden." This was bad for his neuritis, from which he was suffering and which so seriously affected his "piano hands."

The death of Modjeska, his life-long friend and patron, on April 8, 1909, Paderewski felt as one of his greatest sorrows and most severe losses. "Passing like an angel upon the Polish firmament of art," as the poet Tarasiewicz said, Modjeska had devoted her life to the cause that was Paderewski's: she had "revealed the lightning of Polish art to both hemispheres." He never forgot nor ever tired of speaking of the encouragement she had given him in his youth. With the poet he echoed the words of Tarasiewicz's panegyric at her grave in Cracow: "Queen of dramatic art and queen of the beautiful, rest in peace after thy work, thy battles, thy triumphs. Let thy genius be the guardian angel of the Polish stage."

But a mere rest cure in California could not wholly engage Paderewski; he must have work, something to do, even when he rests. He has an eye for business and soon after deciding on a Californian home he made large investments, not alone in fruit lands but also, in the Santa Maria district, in land that at the time of his purchase promised oil. He had not forgotten the slip of fortune which deprived him, on one of his earliest tours in the Southern states, of a handsome profit in Birmingham, Alabama, properties. He had foreseen the iron and steel future of "the Pittsburgh of the South", and had it not been for the miscarriage of a commission entrusted to another he would have established himself there.

As soon as he had secured the Paso Robles property he began planting, putting in some 250 acres of orchard, mostly almonds, diversified with pears and walnuts. He was, in fact, the pioneer almond grower of this district; the ranch now has twelve thousand bearing trees. Blooded live-stock is another of his hobbies. He rides his hobbies practicably, actually; a visit to his ranch means long hours spent among his workers in his orchards and fields. At the ranch or elsewhere, however, it is never all work with Paderewski. He likes to play. He has, for instance, a boy's delight in magicians' tricks, sleight of hand and all that. At Paso Robles, as well as at innumerable other places up and down the route of his American travels, whenever leisure permits, one of his favorite pastimes is going to the cinema. He is a "movie fan". Almost every evening at the ranch his guests are greeted with the invitation, "Let's go to the opera." The "opera" is the local movie-house. In New York too, in every city he visits, when time allows, he takes in a movie, with a special preference for "westerns", "horse operas" as he calls them in good American slang.

The Californian scene gave him delight. In the rich black-soil valleys of the West Coast, stretching for miles wide and level as prairies to the mountain ranges, he found an atmosphere redolent of the sun-drenched summer plains of his native southern Poland. Californian mornings in the spring intoxicate with freshness and color. Almond orchards in full blossom smoke with rosy fire in the drifting mists. The wind-washed skies that break through are pure virgin-blue. There are times when the lifting and moving of the mists around tinted acres of bloom make the valleys seem softly and coolly aflame. Orchards higher up on the slopes, half hidden behind white clouds of mist, or veiled in the gauze of fogs drifting in from the ocean, touched by the early sun look like smoking fires in the foothills. The twelve thousand almond trees of the Rancho San Ignacio, two hundred and fifty acres of fruit-bloom at sunrise, are a sight to see, one well calculated to give delight to a poet like Paderewski.

Living thus in America, instead of merely visiting it, and with a natural bent toward affairs as well as toward the soil, it was inevitable that American interests, American politics,

American public life, should engage him. Far from being merely a curious visitor, he became a student of American life. He read largely in American literature and studied it closely; Vernon Louis Parrington's "Main Currents of American Literature" is but one of the many books of the kind which he discusses animatedly, and he still talks about Frank Norris's "Octopus", which, with its Californian scene and its profound understanding of the wheat-grower's problem, was bound to interest him. Emerson became a favorite; Bryce's "American Commonwealth" became a text. Back of all this, all the time, was his deeply ingrained feeling for his home country. There was an impulse to check up his own country in his mind, measuring it by its potentialities against American achievement. He had day dreams in which he built up a new Poland, reconstructed it free and independent, saw it restored, its resources liberated for growth, its national life renewed. Related perhaps to a love of billiards as a recreation, for billiards means geometrical exactitude, or to his liking for cribbage, which means rapid calculation, Paderewski possesses a gift seldom found in the temperamental artist, a gift for mathematics. He could work out on the blank page of a music-sheet, as readily as Modjeska used to work out her thoughts in the diary she kept on the blank pages of her prompt-book, a complete scheme for the industrial, commercial and political rehabilitation of Poland, figuring everything, population, area, resources. His mind runs naturally to statistics, dimensions, and with no one is he happier discussing such matters as with the famous bridge-engineer, Ralph Modjeski, the son of his friend Madame Modjeska.

In one of her letters to me Madame Modjeska once wrote of a visit Paderewski made at her Californian ranch. Whatever they were doing, billiards, bridge, books, they were "always discussing politics." International politics was his hobby, and in all these discussions his knowledge of European affairs, of continental motives and movements, came into play and gave him what Americans, less familiar with the European checkerboard, might well have called a kind of prophetic insight.

Nor was, nor is, his interest confined to European politics.

Quickly enough he mastered the intricacies not only of America's political, but of its economical and industrial life as well, and this not alone through theoretical study, but by first-hand experience. He has only to refer to his own life as an American landholder and producer to speak with authority on questions of domestic economics. "In olden days, land was wealth. I own hundreds of acres of fertile land in California, almond groves, thousands and thousands of trees. But the more almonds those trees produce, the poorer I become! Today, should I be no longer able to play the piano, the almond groves I own would eat each other up, and me along with them. Too many almonds are being produced, too much wheat, too much corn, too much everything. Look at your wheat crops that rot away. Your land is too fertile. Your people are too industrious. Because you work too much there is no work. Because you produce too much your land impoverishes its owners instead of enriching them."

It is not work that Paderewski condemns, but the pace at which the American worker goes. And he recognizes the dire paradox in it all which, like the cross-breeding of antagonistic elements, produces only misery, dis-ease instead of ease. On the one hand, he says "man is naturally lazy, therefore he invents labor-saving devices. He even secretly hopes for some invention that will do his thinking for him. He is panic-stricken when he must think for himself. On the other hand, he is too energetic. He is too inventive. We have too many devices to save labor, to save time, and we have not yet learned how to manage the time we save. When America has learned that, it will become the most prosperous nation in the world." Paderewski, saying this, laughs at the thought of that millennial future and his own relation to it. "Will I live long enough to see it? Where will my almond groves be by that time? Will I be able to earn enough money to pay for their upkeep, or will the taxes eat them up? Every almond I eat now costs me twenty dollars!"

Paderewski is a thoroughgoing American when it comes to the question of taxes. He knows the pinch, as all do. But he is able to take a long view, too. What, he asks, is the basic cause of the situation which makes lands and people, not alone the American, self-devouring, so to speak? "The taxes everywhere in the world are confiscatory. Why? Because we have not yet devised an economical system of government." Over-industrialization, in his opinion, is at the root of this. "All industries try to manufacture their products at a minimum expense. The manufacturers install new labor-saving devices as fast as they are invented. The cost of government rises faster than the economies derived from such labor-saving machinery. While the overhead is being reduced in every industry, the governments increase their overhead. That means taxes and more taxes. Labor-saving devices throw men out of employment, lessen the earning power of the masses, make it impossible for them to pay the taxes levied on them. Your inventive genius is great, but nobody knows yet how to coördinate the inventions of your mechanics in such a way as to profit the whole country and not only the individual. You shall have to invent an economical way of administering your great country if you are to be happy. In the last analysis a government is a coöperative institution. If eight hours a day produce too much, work only six, only four. Otherwise half of the people will work and half stay idle. And the idle will have to be supported by the ones who work. Inevitably there is trouble in a situation like that. Revolutions are not made by the idle, but by those who work and cannot live by their labor. Too many unemployed cause the reduction of wages and of salaries, cause still higher taxes, and cause the incapacity to pay taxes. Ultimately America's greatest troubles will arise from high taxes."

With as clear an eye as he sees the domestic problem, he looks into America's difficulties in foreign relations, so closely related to the domestic. American commercial isolation is to him a prime source of trouble. Not forgetting, in his large view, that "intellectual isolation always follows commercial isolation", he says regretfully, "You have isolated yourself from the rest of the world commercially. You have raised commercial barriers after lending to Europe fifteen billion dollars for her industrial development. No one can sell you anything after paying your high duties, and profit from the transaction. Without the possibility of profit where is commerce? Your high tariff will not bring you in more money than before from customs duties. On the contrary, customs duties, when they are reasonable, help pay the government's expenses; when they are high they increase the taxes of the individual in order to pay the upkeep of government operations. It costs less money to collect ten million dollars in low duties than it costs to collect five million in high duties. Taxes. Taxes. Taxes again.

"Commercial isolation, high import tariffs, high taxes, these are responsible for economic depression in America. Your taxes grow. Your unemployment grows. The rich groan. The poor suffer. And you are so rich! Why should you be depressed? Your hand is not exhausted. You are not overpopulated. You have not been drained by wars." This brings him back to the European phase of the problem. "The cause of the depression in Europe is fear of war. Everybody talks peace and everybody is afraid of a war. Because of that fear no one invests more capital than is absolutely necessary for the moment. Because of that fear your investments in Europe are shaky, to say the least.

"The industrial possibilities of Europe are immense. Compared to the United States our industries are in their infancy. But who will invest capital in a country that may go to war tomorrow? The fortunes of war are capricious. Since the end of the Great War Europe has daily been on the threshold of war. The depression in Europe can end only when the cause of the fear of war has been eradicated. You must help Europe to shake off the fear of war if you want to retrieve your losses. A scared Europe is a liability."

This war-fear planted in the European mind, with its concomitant upkeep of armies, is, as Paderewski knows, a very real thing, but, as he shows, just as army upkeep is not the cause of depression in America, it is not the whole cause of Europe's economic depression. "You have no great army to support in your country, yet your taxes are unbearable. The increase of your taxes is entirely out of proportion with the increase of earnings in the last thirty years. People are being taxed out of their property. You can't blame everything on the cost of armies. It's bad enough, but it is not responsible for everything. Of course, if there were no armies, no dangers of war with near and distant neighbors, not only for Poland but for all countries, one of the biggest items of expenses of all governments would disappear from the ledger. That's true. But supposing that all of Europe's standing armies, at present five million men, were disbanded? They would be added to the number of unemployed. Directly, indirectly, the governments would have to support them. It's a question whether it would be cheaper to feed and clothe them as civilians than it is to feed and clothe them as soldiers. No. What causes higher taxes is, first, the uneconomical way of administering all countries; second, the uncertainty into which the world has been plunged by the last war. As the uncertainty increases the taxes rise."

Given the war-fear as a controlling factor in Europe, with its indisputable effects on American life, can this fear be removed? "Poland," he says, speaking for his own country, "has to keep up an army because of Germany and Russia. We have had one war with the Bolsheviks. You know what that cost us. On the other side is Germany. Prussia is our neighbor, the Prussia of which Mirabeau said 'War is the national industry of Prussia.' And when I say Prussia and the Prussians I don't mean Germany and the Germans. There are people in Germany, Germans, who groan as heavily under the Prussians as the Poles ever did. The Prussians rule Germany; have ruled it for more than a hundred years. They understand nothing but power. The Prussians loathe the Polish nation because they have never been able to digest it after they had devoured it. The Prussians believe that God had sent them here to lord over the world. All other peoples are but fertilizers. They want Poland for a fertilizer. They want to rule the world and pretend that the world will be, must be, benefited by their rule. 'God is always with the stronger battalions' is their slogan. Justice is on the side of strength, of power. So they have said. If ever the war-fear, with all its depressive effects of commercial and industrial atrophy, high taxes, and the influences of all these things on American life, is to be removed, Germany must be made to reach the conclusion that the territories that have been taken back from her will never again belong to her. Poland and other provinces that had been freed are free forever. That is that. It may take many years for Germany to learn that. Until then, unless worse happens, the rise of Communism, revolutions, civil war, Europe will not be able to shake off the depression. And America will continue to share in suffering the consequences." *

When Paderewski came to America he spoke English with a noticeable accent, with color added by his London associations. The accent disappeared. More and more he talked like a native American.† Now, in spite of the distinction of his speech, which is perfect English, it is noticeably American. In formal address his diction is flawless, in rapid-fire conversation the racy Americanisms pop out. He is discussing Liszt: "The Sonata is surely one of the summits of piano literature. You know, of course, how much Wagner pinched from Liszt." When he plays poker, although he never plays for money, he manipulates cards—and face—as a genuine native does. When he talks about the gangster problem, our political parties, the rôle of women in politics, one realizes that he knows his U. S. A. thoroughly. When he discusses the Irish policeman of New York you know that he knows his Manhattan. He tops that off with a humorous story. "There was a big traffic-cop on Fifth Avenue who halted

---

* From an interview with Konrad Bercovici in *The Pictorial Review*, New York, May, 1933, quoted by permission of the editor, Mr. T. Von Ziekursch.

† Arriving in New York for his 1933 tour, Paderewski was met by a delegation, among others, of Polish-Americans. The greeting of their spokesman and Paderewski's response were recorded in the movietone, and everyone remarked that, while the address of welcome was in a markedly foreign accent, Paderewski, "the foreigner", spoke perfect English.

a car that went through the stop-light. When he came up to the car he saw to his embarrassment that its passenger was a certain eminent Catholic bishop. 'Oh, I beg your Reverence's pardon,' said the policeman, 'I just stopped your car to tell you that the cop on the next corner is a terrible Black Protestant.' "

Paderewski's affinity for American life and ways recalls again Washington's preference for the Pole Kosciuszko over the French engineer Radiere, because, in Washington's words, he was "better adapted to the genius and temper of the [American] people." Paderewski, prairie born, bred on the Podolian plains and reared on the spacious levels of Volhynia, somehow found an affinity in the expanses of America; when he went to live in Switzerland it took him some little while to overcome the cramped feeling that the mountains gave him. But the relationship goes deeper than topography. In the large it is seen in the ready adaptability of the Polish immigrant to American life, an adaptability demonstrated from the times of the American War of Independence; since Kosciuszko and Pulaski, Polish names have figured in every department of American activity. The relationship, as a matter of fact, derives from a tradition inherent in the life of Poland from the Middle Ages, the tradition of political liberty, a tradition that Paderewski inherited from his mother's father, a political exile in Siberia, from his mother born in exile, from his father imprisoned in the Uprising of 1863. "A great enthusiasm for freedom in almost every branch of life, was possessed by the Poles in the Middle Ages," Dr. Robert Howard Lord, of Harvard, tells us in his "Some Problems of the Peace Conference": "the principle of the sovereignty of the nation, calling the citizens to participate in the responsibilities of government; the conception of the State as not a thing existing for itself, but as an instrument serving the well-being of society; aversion to absolute monarchy, standing armies and militarism; disinclination to make aggressive wars, but a remarkable tendency to make voluntary unions with neighboring peoples." These were the Polish ideals on which Paderewski had been nurtured. They are American ideals, and, possessing them, it is not difficult to understand how readily he fitted into the general scheme of life and thought in America.

"Nowhere in the world," Paderewski once declared, "could one observe such a strong influence of environment upon the intellectual and emotional molding of the individual as here in this wonderful country of yours. People of various races, languages and creeds, people born in the countries where a narrow and selfish nationalism has been prevailing as an almost religious dogma, after having been brought up here in America, or even after having spent a number of years in this atmosphere of freedom, of equal opportunities, of that large and broad equity which the English language calls 'fair play', acquire in a degree American mentality, American fellow feeling. It is the spirit of the country that compels them to think, to feel, to act that way. It is the spirit of the country which makes that mold into which must enter and to which must adapt himself everyone who aspires to become an American citizen. It is the spirit of the country, profoundly religious in its origin, supremely tolerant and liberal in its essence, that permits everyone to preserve the good characteristics of his own race while acquiring yours, and makes him twice human and twice humane." The problem of the Polish immigrant in America has naturally been of the liveliest interest to Paderewski, but he has taken far more than a sentimental interest in it. He knows from a practical point of view the intimate details of the immigrant's life, how he is housed, how he lives, how much he earns, how much he saves, how much he sends home to his people in the motherland. Above all, he knows why the Pole makes a good American.

Paderewski's growth into American life was not only sure and steady, but his apprehension of this country's ideals was quick; for as early as 1893, when he was still a newcomer and only on his third American tour, we hear him expressing it. "I loved your country before I knew it," he said in a speech at the Lotus Club in New York City that year, "for the very simple reason, allow me to tell you, that this country is the only one in which hundreds of thousands of Poles are living freely and enjoying liberty; the country in which every countryman of mine may speak whatever he likes of the past and future of his motherland without fearing to be arrested. A few years ago, at the same time that you were fighting the glorious fight against slavery, our poor nation made its last stand for liberty. [when his own father was imprisoned] You succeeded and we did not; but still you gave us a great deal of happiness in the feeling that we were not alone."

The tens of thousands of people who made up Paderewski's audiences, seeing him only as musician, hardly could have guessed that the man whom they saw only at the piano was dwelling on such thoughts as these. But being what he was and coming to understand America as he did, he could not escape such thoughts, any more than he could escape thinking, in contrast, of his own country, her sufferings, her lost freedom, her lack of opportunity. Nor could he help rejoicing in his own artistic triumphs as one vindication of the name of Poland before the New World as well as before the Old.

An incident happened during this third tour which sharpened his thoughts in this direction. The receipts of his first American tour from one hundred and seven concerts had been $95,000. On his second tour he had played sixty-seven times, the receipts aggregating $160,000; on his third tour, playing eighty-six times, the receipts had jumped to $248,000. With over two hundred cities visited and half a million dollars earned, he was indeed enjoying a triumph calculated to make the name "Pole" something to be noticed. He was feeling, and justifiably so, that he could in his own way demonstrate what the Pole can do, given a chance in a free land. So also was his friend Modjeska who had sent him to Vienna with the challenging counsel "Poland needs you." But Modjeska that year, invited to speak at the Chicago World's Fair, was proscribed by the Russian government because she had told her audience how Poland suffered under the Czarist yoke; she was prohibited to appear in her home land under penalty of expulsion, and as a matter of fact this decree was carried out, for when next she ventured to return to Warsaw she was literally run out of the country. Paderewski was deeply stirred by this incident, which so emphatically demonstrated the far-reaching tyranny which his people and his country endured. More than ever now he was out fighting for Poland in the only way he could fight, by spreading her good name. And more than ever his abiding interest in international politics was quickened, and his hope, the undying hope in every Polish heart for Poland's eventual freedom, strengthened by the public sympathy voiced on every side in America for his afflicted motherland.

If Paderewski grew rapidly and securely into the life of America it was because he brought to it an inherent understanding, seeing through its externals, sensing in it a spirit of idealism which Europeans have not always recognized. "Some people think," he once remarked, "that this huge country of yours, a country of enormous possibilities, of collossal enterprises, of titanic financial conceptions—that this is the country of the largest factories, of the longest railways, of the tallest buildings in the world, and of nothing else. They think that you are a great commercial and industrial people, of great engineers, of peerless inventors, fearless speculators—in business and banking superior to everyone. It may be true—it is true; but the truest of all is the fact that you are idealists to the core and that for ages you will remain idealists."

This was not mere praise by words. He substantiated his words by an act of faith in the artistic idealism of America. Nearly forty years ago, in 1896, he founded the Paderewski Award which by a gift of ten thousand dollars established a fund for the encouragement of American music. He had long been impressed by the growth of the communal orchestra in this country. "In the course of my American tours," he said, in 1900, "I have visited several cities which support a permanent orchestra. There I have always observed a heightened measure of appreciation of classic compositions and a lively interest in what is going on everywhere in the great world of music. Besides, these organizations foster civic pride, which is a virtue not to be lightly esteemed. For this reason, if for no other, are they worthy of encouragement. No city of importance can be said to be complete unless it has a permanent orchestra as a rallying-center for local music lovers and a means of presenting to the public the *chef d'œuvres* of the great composers of the past, together with the best that is given us by the moderns." The letter which he wrote announcing his American music foundation is a characteristic expression of his feeling as well as of his modesty; it is interesting too for its faint touch of Conradesque awkwardness in English, something scarcely to be found in his later utterances. He sent it to Mr. Steinway, April 21, 1896:

The generous support I have found in this country enables me to accomplish one of my most ardent wishes.

I do not intend to thank the American people for all they have done for me, because my gratitude to your noble nation is, and will be, beyond expression. But I desire to extend a friendly hand toward my American brother musicians, toward those, who, less fortunate than myself, are struggling for recognition or encouragement. To this purpose I send you herewith $10,000, asking you to accept, together with Col. H. L. Higginson, of Boston, and Dr. William Mason, of New York, the trusteeship of this sum.

Knowing the interest you take in public affairs, and your readiness to do good wherever you find an opportunity, I hope you will not refuse me this great favor, and will, after deliberation with the above-named gentlemen, invest this money in order to establish the following triennial prizes for the composers of American birth without any distinction of race or religion:

1—$500. for the best orchestral work in symphonic form.

2—$300. for the best composition for solo instrument with orchestra.

3—$200. for the best chamber music work; and the balance to be used for the expenses connected with the competitions for these prizes.

. . . I take no pride in making this endowment. The amount is a modest one, and my personality, in spite of all the success, is of little importance. I only hope that it will prove to be useful, and that your younger composers will not consider as a gift, but as a debt, this little encouragement coming from one who found in their land all happiness to which an artist can aspire.*

---

* One need only cite the names and records of those winning the Paderewski Award to realize the value of this contribution of his to American music. Among them have been the late Horatio Parker, composer of the opera *Mona,* the oratorio *Hora Novissima,* and of numerous other permanent compositions; Arthur Bird, composer of a symphony, the ballet *Rübezahl,* the comic opera *Daphne,* orchestral suites, much piano music; Henry Hadley, eminent among American composers, whose numerous works include three symphonies, two operas, lyric drama, cantata, overtures, etc.; Arthur Shepherd of the New England Conservatory, Boston, piano sonata, cantata, *Overture Joyeuse,* etc.; Walling-

Paderewski's faith in American idealism, American art, abides. Thirty-five years after he had founded his American award, while discussing the difficulties which art suffers in this "age of economics"—and "genius", as he had noted, "requires not only the divine spark, but also favorable conditions under which it may develop"—he said these words: "America may bring art back to the world, first, because wealth alone will permit it, and second because the standard of education in America is rising ever higher."

In those words Paderewski may be said to be the spokesman of the national ideals of both his own country and of the America that he so much admires: wealth and material prosperity dedicated to the people's spiritual betterment through education and art.

---

ford Riegger, Drake University, Iowa, chamber music; Hans Heniot Levy, Ravinia, Ill., orchestral work; Paul Allen, Boston, symphony; Rubin Goldmark, New York, David Stanley Smith, Yale University Music School, chamber music. In order to make the award immediately operative, William Steinway added $1500 for prizes for the first competition in 1897.

XXIII

FULL YEARS

THERE was a good deal of excitement in March, 1892, in the small Californian city of San Jose, a few miles down the peninsula from San Francisco, when advertisements appeared announcing that Paderewski was to play there. Up to that time the music lovers of San Jose and the Santa Clara Valley had gone to San Francisco to hear the famous artists who visited the Coast. Now some enterprising local impresarios had decided to bring Mahomet to the mountain.

Two young students of Leland Stanford University were the local impresarios. They were earning their way through college, and, thinking to do something big for themselves, for their school and for the town, they had undertaken to invite Paderewski to give a recital at San Jose. The terms arranged guaranteed a fee of $2000 to the pianist. It was a large undertaking, but the boys were confident of success. An unforeseen circumstance however, kept the box-office receipts down to $1600; no one concerned had, so far ahead, taken note that the date of the concert fell in Holy Week, notoriously a poor time for any kind of secular entertainment. The two students were in a fix. How to pay the rental of the hall, advertising and other expenses, out of $1600 and still have $2000 left for Paderewski, was too much of a problem for them, even allowing for the fact that one of them was an engineering student. But the pianist's fee must be paid and at once, and they were $400 short of it.

Deeply agitated the boys went to Paderewski's manager and asked if they might give their promissory note for the shortage, paying down the $1600, their total earnings from the concert.

The local account would have to be carried on credit, even though they remained in debt the rest of their college days. Paderewski sent for the boys. He told them that their arrangement did not suit him at all. He couldn't take their paper. They were in despair. "Go out and pay off your rental and other local expenses and come back," said Paderewski. They did so. When they came back he made them deduct $320, twenty per cent, from their gross receipts. "Now," he said, "that is your share. I shall take the remainder."

Paderewski's fee for that concert was about half the amount guaranteed. But he had his fun out of it. And, though he did not dream then of what he was doing, he won a friend, a friend who one day was to prove his gratitude, not by repaying Paderewski in money personally, but better still by befriending Paderewski's motherland. The friend, the young engineering student, was Herbert Hoover. Twenty-five years later Hoover helped Paderewski save the people of Poland from starvation.

This little incident, occurring when Paderewski first came to America as a pianist, and having its climax in the later days when, as everyone thought, he had closed his piano forever, spans twenty-five years of the artist's life, from 1892 to 1918. In 1918 the Poland that he had dreamed would be free was not only free, but was being fed and in large measure saved from ruin by the hand of the friend he made at San Jose in 1892.

In the meantime, touring America almost yearly, living a good part of his life here, and eventually establishing a home in this country, he had gone on adding to the dimensions of his world-wide fame both as virtuoso and composer. His London and Paris engagements became annual events. He toured Poland, England, France, Italy, Belgium, Russia, Holland, Germany, practically every country in Europe. During his German tours he gave in Leipzig a memorable concert as a contribution to the building of a monument to Liszt. He toured Australia, Africa, South America. His South American tour was a tremendous success; the receipts of his final performance in Buenos Aires were $12,000. This tour has one amusing memory for him. At a great fiesta given for him on a large plantation, he ate barbecued beef. And he didn't like it! But he ate it, and his host never knew. In South America he took a special interest in observing the agricultural riches of the country; he came back excited over the amazing natural wealth of the soil with its humus over a hundred feet deep.

His travels became triumphal progresses around the world. The crowds he attracted grew larger and larger; in New York in 1902 he broke all precedent by giving in one day two performances that filled to overflowing, with hundreds left outside disappointed, the two largest auditoriums in the city—a concert in Carnegie Hall, his opera "Manru" in the Metropolitan. Twenty thousand dollars is a conservative estimate for the Paderewski receipts on that one day.

But if he traveled, also he longed for a home life, and during these years he made more than one effort to establish himself in some permanent place where he could rest, compose, live something of a normal life, the life of a man with a house and a garden, with some other roof over his head beside that of a Pullman car. The garden was an essential. Paderewski has remained all his life a "born" agriculturist, as we know from his establishing himself as a rancher in his American home at Paso Robles, California.

His home ties in Poland grew stronger with the years. The joy that he had known on the morning of his first Vienna triumph had its fruition in the largesse he could now pour out for his father, his sister, his half-brothers and half-sisters. His father was established in a new home which the son built for him, although he did not live long to enjoy it. In 1894 he died. His father's death was not the only grief Paderewski suffered during these years. There was his son. Motherless from birth, the child remained frail, an invalid, throughout his short life. At the age of six the little fellow, troubled with a halt in his walk, had been taken to Paris by Sigismond Stojowski's father, to be placed in the home of Paderewski's friends the Gorskis, and there he was put under the treatment of a healer named Pomerol who gave every promise of a permanent cure. The first effect of the treatment was that the child ceased altogether to walk, but the *rebouteur* assured Paderewski that this was only an indication of response to the manipulations. Then Pomerol died. And Alfred never walked again. He was an exceptionally bright boy, keen and happy-natured, a great chess player, and his father worshiped him. He was an ardent champion of his father, very proud of his achievements on the piano. Once, when Alfred was very small, Gorski the violinist teased him, calling him "a little fool." "It doesn't take intelligence to play the *violin* well!" he promptly answered.

The helplessness of his son was a great cross to Paderewski. Nevertheless, out of that cross which the father, bereft at twenty, had to bear so long, came in time the greatest blessing of his life, the love of the one woman in the world best fitted to fill his life. She was the one who mothered his child. She was "the beautiful creature whose name is also Helena" that Modjeska had met that day on the Tatra mountain road when she was on the way to meet "one of the most extraordinary young men"—Helena Gorska, the Baroness de Rosen. The promise that the boy-husband had made to his girl-wife on her deathbed, to "make his career" and someday repay their son his dowry, had been fulfilled sevenfold. The gifts that the father laid at the feet of his child brought him finally the gift of a new marriage. In the sanctuary of the historic Cathedral of St. John of Warsaw, rich with relics of Poland's glory, later to be the scene of the consecration of Monsignor Ratti who as Papal Delegate to Poland was to be one of Paderewski's staunch friends during the war, and who still later was to become Pope Pius XI—in that fine old sanctuary with its royal box of former Polish kings, the marriage of Paderewski and Madame Gorska was celebrated in May, 1899.

In the end the son's life closed in tragedy. At the age of nineteen, still helpless in his wheeled chair but brilliantly educated and showing a promising literary gift, young Alfred heard of a specialist at Augsburg, Germany, who he believed could help him. His father sent him there; but on the way to Augsburg the boy caught cold and died of pneumonia. Paderewski, summoned by telegraph from Spain whither he had gone on a concert tour, reached him too late. His boy was dead. He grieved deeply; he was lost without Alfred in the house, where so often he had helped entertain his father's guests with original little comedies which his pen readily turned off. Thus Paderewski's earliest romance, marked by death from the beginning, ended in another death.

Paderewski had always wished for a Polish home. Before his marriage he had bought the property "Rozprza", near Piotrków, on the river Strawa. Piotrków, one of the oldest towns in Poland, with its ruins of a royal palace, the scene of the kings' elections under the Jagiello dynasty, was well designed to satisfy Paderewski's taste for artistic and historic associations. Later he added to this Polish property a country home in the south, "Biurków", near the ancient capital of Cracow, again in an atmosphere rich with satisfactions for the artist. Almost continuous travel, however, forced him to give up both of these places; he sold them in 1897. Married now, he found in the beautiful mountain district of the south an ideal place, Konsnia, and into this estate he put heavy investments, planning to make of it a model farm and even installing an elaborate fish-hatchery with the intention of restocking the neighboring streams. Konsnia was very large, a real domain; Paderewski used to be proud to tell that it took him four hours as the crow flies to walk across its acreage. But once more the demands of his career interfered with his dream of a Polish home; in this case he began to seriously lose money through the mismanagement of administrators left in charge of the estate during his long absences. Four years of expensive experimenting with agriculture and overseers ended finally in his selling the Konsnia property in 1903. He did so regretfully; he loved this place, its spacious fields, its broad river and old-fashioned bridge, its comfortable manor house with its homelike chimneys, vine-covered walls, old pillared frontage facing down a broad green slope. But he was at that time planning his first Australian tour, which was to occupy the whole of the year 1904, and he feared financial disaster if he left the estate in other hands.

In the meantime, after disposing of his first two Polish properties in 1897, and giving up his old summer quarters at the
French villa which he had leased on the shores of Lac du Bour-
get, near Aix-les-Bains, he had rented a villa, "Riond-Bosson",
the property of the Count Marois, situated on Lake Leman
near the little town of Morges, in Switzerland. Here, after
these various attempts to establish himself in a permanent
home, he found at last the place that filled his requirements: a
retreat where he could rest, compose, and prepare himself anew
for his tours; at the same time a retreat not too far removed
from the highways he was obliged to travel. In 1899, the year
of his marriage, he purchased Riond-Bosson which, from then
on, remained his home.

As matters turned out, the establishment of his home at
Morges, in the Switzerland that was to be the neutral center of
Europe during the World War, came to appear as almost a
Providential act. Here, at Riond-Bosson, the dramatic *entr'acte*
of Poland's restoration was to be staged.

Drama was in fact being enacted already. There was an incident in 1898, the year before his marriage, that had more significance than was dreamed of at the time. He was in Warsaw,
booked to give three large benefit concerts, and his appearance
was the signal for a public reception which changed into an
ovation, an ovation, however, which had serious political repercussions. The event was a memorable one, for it introduced Paderewski to the world in a rôle which he was destined later to fill
with historic consequences. On this occasion in Warsaw he made
his first appearance as an orator.

The speech he made was a stirring one, eloquent with patriotic fervor. His audience was roused to intense excitement. But
the Russian police were roused also. They were alarmed. Before the night had passed the edict had gone forth forbidding
the publication of a word of Paderewski's address. The Paderewski who before many years was to challenge the world of
Poland's enemies, had struck fire. Regardless of the censorship,
however, all of Poland heard of that speech. The country
hummed with applause. Forbidden print by the censors, manu-

script copies of the address were circulated throughout the country. People in the most distant provinces read it. The name of Paderewski, patriot, as well as of Paderewski, artist, was on everyone's lips. Behind the scenes of Russian and Prussian officialdom it was spoken of too, though not with applause.

This was the first sound of a new note struck in the music of the man called in a dozen countries "the Master." But the police-powers that ruled Poland could hardly yet suspect that that single note was to be in time not unlike Emerson's classic "Shot heard 'round the world." They still thought of him as "only a Polish pianist."

More than one echo of that 1898 speech was heard in the years following. Five years later, in 1903, it made a sharp repercussion. Paderewski had returned to Poland after new triumphs in America, England, France (the Colonne concerts), Germany (The Gewandhaus concerts at Leipzig under the direction of Nikisch). He was hailed now as one of the world's great composers, as well as virtuosi, because of his Concerto in A Minor, which he had played on his first appearance in America, and with which in 1901 he had inaugurated the Philharmonic Society of Warsaw. Now he was invited to Russia. The invitation alone was a triumph for him, a Polish triumph. The Imperial Society of Music in St. Petersburg was asking his favors.

But in the end the Russian concerts were all but cancelled. Following the invitation of the Imperial Society of Music came what is known in diplomatic language as a "command", an invitation from the Court to play before it. Queen Victoria had paid him this honor in England at the beginning of his career, and many such "command performances" had since been given by him. Now the Czar of All the Russias, titular of the throne that had so long oppressed Poland, but himself a kindly and friendly man, followed suit. The Czar, however, made a blunder, or some member of his chancellery did. When the "command" was communicated it offered the Polish musician a word of praise that Paderewski could not accept. "His Imperial Majesty," ran the word, "is pleased that the world's most eminent musician is a Russian." "His Imperial Majesty," Paderewski replied, "is mistaken. I am a Pole." *

Whatever Nicholas II thought of that, his consort, the Empress Alexandra, would not have it. The Czarina was a Hessian, notorious for such a hatred of all things Polish that not even a Prussian could equal. She interfered. Paderewski responded by refusing to appear, and by preparing to leave the city immediately. There was something nearing the proportions of a Court scandal when a delegation of the most eminent Russian artists came to him and begged him to reconsider. He gave the concerts. St. Petersburg raved over him as Paris and London and all the others had. Still another score for Poland was marked on his chart.

This was in 1903. Again, after another five years, that interdicted Warsaw speech of 1898 was to make an echo. In 1908 what seemed to promise a complete turn in Paderewski's career offered itself. He was suggested as the new head of the Warsaw Conservatory. He was now forty-eight years old; his fame was permanently established; his fortune was made; almost continuous travel over great distances for the better part of every year was interfering more and more with his love of composition. To come back to his own country, to have a Polish home, to return to his own school and have it placed in its entirety in his hands; above all to be free to carry on his work of composition: this was something to tempt any artist, especially one whose belief in the native genius of his country was a passion. Such an offer prompted dreams of making Warsaw in time the world's musical capital. It could be done; Warsaw could rival Vienna, Paris, any city in the world. He knew the great engine of artistic talent that moved and stirred under the surface of Polish life. He had instituted contests to stir and encourage that life. The first of these was held at Leipzig, its award going to Stojowski for a symphony which was first

---

* Elbert Hubbard, in "Little Journeys," XII, p. 101, adds a dramatic if apocryphal climax to the story of Paderewski's "imperial *rencontre.*" According to Hubbard's version the Czar said to Paderewski, "There is no such country as Poland. There is only Russia." "Pardon my hasty remark," Paderewski responded. "Your Majesty speaks the truth", *and then he played Chopin's Funeral March.*

played at the inaugural concert of the Warsaw Philharmonic.
In 1898, the year he had caused a sensation by his first appearance as an orator at Warsaw, Paderewski had founded another
prize for native composers, and already the board of international musicians making that award had chosen three whose gifts
were in themselves enough to warrant the highest expectations
of Polish music—Stojowski, Melcer, Fitelberg.* And it was
not of supremacy in music alone that Paderewski dreamed for
Poland. All the arts would flourish. Polish life would be renewed.

Paderewski expressed himself on the matter of the Poles
and music in an interview with James Francis Cooke of Philadelphia, in 1913. "You ask me whether the Poles are a musical
people. I can only say that one constantly meets in Poland
young men and women with the most exceptional musical talent—but what is talent without serious earnest study leading to
artistic and technical perfection? For more than one hundred
years Poland has been woefully restricted in its development.
Without national resources and with limited school facilities little progress of a broad character has been possible. In the Conservatory at Warsaw, for instance, we meet at once a decided
difference between that institution and the great music schools
at Moscow and St. Petersburg. In the Russian conservatories
general educational work goes hand in hand with music, and the
result is that the students receive a comprehensive course leading to high culture. If the same studies were introduced in the
Warsaw schools, instruction would have to be given in the Russian language and the Polish opposition to this is so great that
such a plan could only meet with failure. One can but take
pride in a nation that has been divided for a century, yet still
maintains the integrity of its mother tongue." "Even the scanty
instruction in the Polish language," as the Danish critic Georg
Brandes wrote in his "Impressions of Poland", "was given in
Russian . . . a boy of twelve years was shut up in the dark for

---

* Fitelberg, now director of the Warsaw Philharmonic, had one of his tone-poems, "Das
Lied vom Falken" performed by the Civic Orchestra of Chicago, conducted by Eric De
Lamarter, Feb. 26, 1933.

twenty-four hours because, coming out of school, he said to a comrade in Polish 'Let us go home'." The opposition that Paderewski spoke of is easy to understand.

The suggestion, then, that he take the Warsaw Conservatory in hand was a tempting one, and although we see from his own words that he did not minimize the difficulties of the position, nevertheless it offered a real opening for the revival and encouragement of a native art in Poland. He could see far ahead with a careful plan of procedure.

This offer was, moreover, in a sense surprising, yet it was an indication of the changed times that had come to Poland. To have the Russian authorities even show a disposition to invite a Polish artist to take this important position was significant. But the Russo-Japanese War had brought in its train a certain new, if only temporary, freedom to all the Russian dominions. Tragic events in 1905, such as the Warsaw massacre, when the square in front of the Opera House, where Paderewski as a boy had heard his first opera, had run with blood after the Russian military had charged the crowds with gun and saber; the student boycott of the same year demanding Polish education in the Polish tongue; the scandal of renewed Siberian terrors: these things had borne some fruit. The Russian bear, a little frightened, had drawn in his claws, and his victim was stirring with a movement of hoped-for liberty. Life was looking up. A letter which Modjeska wrote to me at this time speaks out of that past of a hopeful Poland: "Last Summer we spent in Austrian and German Poland; to enter Russian territory I am still not allowed, therefore we could not visit Warsaw and other cities of Russian Poland—'the heart of Poland' so to speak, and the largest part of our country. Nevertheless I lived through a few months of happiness and moved in an atmosphere of pure love of art and amidst the astounding literary movement which starts from every part of our unfortunate land. The vitality of the nation is enormous; the more it is oppressed the higher it rises."

Once it was known that the authorities were considering a Polish director for the Conservatory, public opinion at once demanded Paderewski for the position. He came to Warsaw to investigate the matter. He had an interview with the Governor General. He outlined to him his plans for the rehabilitation of the institution. The Governor General, the whole circle of Russian officialdom, appeared satisfied and pleased.

A striking and significant incident occurred during Paderewski's interview with the Russian Governor at Warsaw, General Skallon. The artist had laid down his conditions—a new building, an increased staff, better pay; he had the whole scheme of the institution at his fingertips. Then the conversation drifted to politics. Paderewski was fully as able to discuss practical politics as he was to set forth practical plans for the furthering of art. General Skallon's eyes opened wider and wider as he listened to the Polish artist's views. His keen insight into Russian affairs astonished him. "My God!" the Governor General suddenly exclaimed, "you're the kind of man Russia needs at the helm!"

The record of what happened after that interview is lost in the imperial Russian archives. Obviously General Skallon must have submitted his proposal to St. Petersburg. Perhaps in doing so he was a little too enthusiastic in his praise of the Pole. At any rate he never published his answer. There was only an unbroken silence in which the Poles were left free to speculate as they would on the intrigues of Czarina Alexandra in the imperial chancellery. The Hessian Empress, after waiting five years—ten years since that inflammatory Warsaw speech of 1898—at last had her revenge for the little affair of the concert in 1903, when Paderewski had balked her. Perhaps a more serious motive was back of the rude dismissal of the matter. Russia may already have begun to look on Paderewski as more than only a Polish pianist. There was something in him, backed by his world-wide prestige, that made him a Polish power, a power not to be encouraged.

At any rate, he did not become head of the Warsaw Conservatory. The story of this incident, read after the fact, makes one realize that in the large weaving of the pattern of his life it was necessary that that strand be rejected. Had Paderewski settled in Warsaw, no matter what he might have dreamed of accomplishing there, he could not have achieved what he did achieve otherwise. The same Providence which shuffled out of his possession one Polish home after another to bring him to Morges in Switzerland, now closed the half-opened door of the Warsaw Conservatory and kept him outside where, for a larger purpose, he belonged. Genius endowed with strong will and singleness of purpose—*"la patrie avant tout, l'art ensuite"* —genius of this kind projects out of itself an occult force which carries a man, through no matter what devious ways, to his ultimate goal. Paderewski's goal was *la patrie*—service to his country even above service to his art.

In 1910, two years after the Conservatory incident, the Polish power that was Paderewski again asserted itself; in his art he once more served his country, this time with a significance that seemed to her enemies to be a threat. Still another echo of the 1898 address that had disquieted the Russian officials was heard. This time there was greater alarm.

To understand that story we must go out of Poland with the artist, back to his home at Morges in Switzerland.

XXIV

GENTLEMAN AND FARMER

THE scenery around Lake Geneva—Byron's Lake Leman, from the French which preserves the Roman *Lacus Lemanus* —is some of the most beautiful in Switzerland. The lake, the largest of all the Swiss waters, lies in a long curve in the heart of the Alps; at one end is Geneva, at the other Villeneuve, with the forty-five miles of shore that stretch between, luxurious with vegetation and studded with beautiful villas. About midway on the north shore is Lausanne and a few miles from it the little town of Morges.

Morges is an old town. It has a ruined castle of the thirteenth century, an old seventh-century tower, a romantic atmosphere. When Paderewski decided to settle here his own romantic taste inclined him to the purchase of a certain ancient château, very picturesque. But the wise counsels of his wife prevailed against that. Riond-Bosson, the villa that he had previously rented from the Count Marois, a comfortable modern dwelling, was much better suited to the comfort which Madame Paderewska, woman-like, knew that he must have if he was to do his work. The house, well removed from the highroad, stands at the top of an open green that has a quiet inviting slope to it. Red brick, built somewhat in the manner of an Italian villa, with numerous verandas, balconies and awnings, and a friendly entrance, the Paderewski villa has a spacious, rambling, homelike air to it, and commands a superb prospect. To the south, across the lake, rise the magnificent ranges of the Savoyard Alps; beyond, plainly seen through the gap of the valley, the fifteen-thousand-foot splendor of Mont Blanc, monarch of the Alps, lifts its snowy spire in enormous majesty.

Memories of Gevont, Gerlach, Lomnica, Kings of the Tatras, rise in the heart of the Pole when he looks out on this splendid scene.

He did not altogether like it at first. With a romantic love of the mountains he felt nevertheless as all prairie-bred people feel when they come into a mountainous country; they feel shut in. Something crushing in this stupendous panorama; it takes a little time to adjust to it, to accustom one's eyes to that motionless heaven-high surf of glacial peaks breaking eternally in an eternal stillness against the sky. One of his house-guests tells of a little incident which illustrates Paderewski's feeling. His friend was standing on the terrace, gazing awe-struck at Mont Blanc revealed in all its majestic glory in the lights of a gorgeous sunset. Suddenly he felt a hand slipped under his arm and turned to find Paderewski, whom he had not heard approaching, standing beside him. The man was "raving", as he expressed it, over the spectacular beauty of the scene, but Paderewski shook his head. "Yes, that's fine . . . for Sunday," he agreed. "But come over here," and he led his companion over to the left-hand corner of the terrace. There they looked down on an inlet of the Lake, a quiet arm of still water that resembled a little river in the midst of green pastures, the bluish foothills of the Jura descending to it in gentle slopes. The picture was intimate, harmonious, reminiscent of Poland in its soft and mellow appeal. Paderewski stood silent contemplating the homelike loveliness of the pastoral scene.

Paderewski soon gave his own intimate touch to Riond-Bosson. New gardens were made. Greenhouses were built. Parrots in their cages—seven of them; canaries, a colony of cockatoos—on one trip from America he brought home seven. Noise! The screeching of the birds nearly drives him mad at times, but he likes his bird friends too well to throw them out. He has a curious fondness for noisy things; Adelina Patti was like that. And dogs. Paderewski loves dogs, has loved them since as a boy he played in the orchards and fields of Volhynia. There are numbers of dogs at Riond-Bosson, a dozen at least; several huge pure-bred St. Bernards that post themselves beside the old porter at the gate-lodge where there is a sign, "Do not enter without ringing; beware of the dogs." The St. Bernards are forever at Paderewski's heels, or by his chair receiving his friendly stroke. There are little dogs too, a very special pet "pug" and another very special Pekingese. They have the run of the house. . . . He has guests, he is playing for them in the salon. He has just thundered out his theme when suddenly two of the dogs begin a joyous romp through the room. "Paderewski's hands dropped from the keys," as the story of one such incident is told by Abbie Finck, "and the culprits were summarily put out, little realizing their sins. They reappeared at doors and windows, scratching and barking." But the master, once launched into his music, is too absorbed to notice anything. He plays to the end. . . .

Outside, a riot of verdure, a riot of color. Roses by the thousands. Paderewski is passionately fond of flowers; violets and roses are his favorites; but nearly every year, going away on tour, he misses spring and the violets, so he makes up for this in summertime with roses. Tall evergreens, big century-old lindens and chestnuts, border the wide lawns, for Riond-Bosson is an old place with its own romantic history. It was built during the French Revolution by the Marquis de Tournelles after he fled to Switzerland when Louis XVI and Marie Antoinette went to the guillotine. Later it became the property of Fouché, Napoleon's famous Minister of Police, and then of Fouché's widow the Duchess of Otranto. The trees as well as the walls of this house could tell a brilliant story. Over the walls of the terrace an immense glycene sprays cataracts of trifoliate verdure; in blossom time it makes gorgeous cascades of color. There are tubbed orange trees, hedges of pink geranium, odorous beds of mignonette and heliotrope, high fountains of purple wistaria dripping with clustered bloom; and always roses. There is not only a large formal rose garden with every imaginable species and color, but roses climb in profusion over the hedges, cover the fences, bloom even between the trees in the orchard. Bird-houses are at every turn, the place is alive with wild wings and song and restful with the murmur of fountains and the perfume of flowers.

The lawns, gardens and orchards occupy a great deal of Paderewski's attention. One of his favorite exercises at home is the commonplace task of cutting the grass. He does farm work too, puts on rough clothes and goes out with the men in the fields. In the orchard a place of honor is held by the sour cherry trees from Poland. Riond-Bosson comprises in all about sixty acres, field, wood and orchard, and the cherries are one of the most important items of the planting. There are four thousand bearing trees. From them Paderewski makes a *kirsch* that is in demand on the market for its flavorous quality. He knows all the secrets of distilling and bottling as well as of profitable marketing. His vineyards are known throughout Switzerland for their superfine table grapes. Between six and seven thousand gallons of superior wine are bottled every fall. Pears, peaches and apples are also grown for the market.

As a matter of fact, the boy off the Volhynian farm, grown into world fame, remains the thorough-going farmer. From the moment he arrives at home his practical supervision of his estate begins. His returns to Morges are always an occasion in the town; his picture is displayed in every window, flags are flown, the streets are bannered, the population turns out to greet him. But at Riond-Bosson there is for days ahead a thorough policing of everything from chicken-houses to sheep-pens.

Paderewski goes in for a little of everything in the farming line; fruit, poultry, blooded live-stock, including dairy cows, sheep, horses. Among his most treasured stock is a flock of sheep bred from six choice specimens from the royal stock farm at Windsor, presented to him by King Edward VII of England. One of this precious six, a ewe that Paderewski was very fond of, broke her forelegs, but she was not butchered, as the veterinary ordered; she was put to death with chloroform and buried, with a stake set up to mark her grave.

Bee culture is another of Paderewski's hobbies. In no land in the world is honey so much a food staple as in Switzerland,

and the product of the Paderewski hives is choice. He will tell you that the bees of this Salesian country are famous even in hagiology, for no less a person than Saint Francis de Sales, one time Bishop of Geneva, put them into sacred literature; in his "Introduction to the Devout Life" he tells of how the Alpine ancestors of these Swiss bees with curious wisdom saved themselves from the buffeting of the wind by carrying tiny pebbles as they went about their "honeyed toil." But it is perhaps of his hot-houses that the artist-farmer is proudest. Here he cultivates tropical fruits, bananas, pineapples, pomegranates, and above all grapes, a dozen varieties of grapes, chief of them the luscious black Hamburg with fruit as big as a man's thumb.

The chicken farm is almost a separate domain. With about one thousand fowls every known breed and cross-breed is here, from majestic Brahamas to snow-white Leghorns and American Plymouth Rocks. There are some magnificent golden pheasants. From America Madame Paderewska, whose special care is the poultry, at one time imported from the Kellerstrass Farm at Kansas City, Missouri, a rooster and two pairs of Orpingtons for which she paid the fabulous price of $7,500. The Paderewski poultry yard with its spotless white houses, its glass drinking-troughs, its continually changed gravel plots and sand, is one of the world's models. From it has gone a procession of prize-winning fowls to various international exhibits, as numerous cards and badges testify. A guest at Riond-Bosson was once shown a beautiful gold box, a souvenir of the première of Paderewski's opera "Manru", embossed with scenes from the opera. But this was not the reason for showing it. Inside was one of the prize eggs, laid by a hen that took first award at the Lausanne poultry show.

Paderewski moves about among these possessions of his, happy, relaxed, showing them to his guests with the unaffected pride of a husbandman. No guests does he enjoy more than those who understand his talk of crops and cross-breeding and new farm machinery, unless it be the children who so frequently visit him. The rabbit-hutches and the goat-pen are their special delight, and he delights in showing them. He belongs to that type of matured greatness which can take a child's hand and be led by it. He can be a child with children and laugh like a boy at the chattering of parrots and the comical popping of rabbits out of their hutches or the frisking of a kid on the grass. When his little godson Ignace Stojowski came to Riond-Bosson there were high times, such good times that the boy, who was five then, announced to his parents that he had no intention of returning to America; he had decided to stay with his godfather.

The son of Dr. Fronczak, for years Paderewski's personal physician in America, was one of the artist's special child friends. A strong tie bound them together and "Edziu", as Paderewski called his young chum, grew up to be one of the lights of his life, only, at twenty-four, to be taken by death. The last visit the two had together was when "Edziu" was eighteen, a strapping six-footer of fine character and manly bearing. He was at Riond-Bosson with his parents, and he and his great friend were inseparable, taking long walks over the farm, playing games together, deep in the happiest of companionships. Paderewski's tender thoughtfulness was revealed when, a few months after "Edziu's" death, his parents were again visiting at Riond-Bosson. With the bereaved father Paderewski talked long and affectionately about his son, who had come to be so much like a son of his own. But in order to spare the mother he gave instructions to every member of the household that in Mrs. Fronczak's hearing nothing be said.

The husbandman of Riond-Bosson keeps a keen eye to perfection in his tours around the farm, he misses nothing, neglects nothing. The kitchen garden with its vegetables and currant bushes is as important in his care as the Hamburg grapes in the hot-house. One corner of this garden especially interested him for a long time after a return from America. In America he grew to like "corn on the cob", and he brought some seed home with him. It was not a success. "The sweet juicy American corn," he explained, "will not, for some reason, grow in Switzerland, in spite of our mild early springs and hot summers." He is an expert on soils, weather, seed. He enjoys the "feeling" of actual farming, even the noises of the farm, the whinny of horses in their stalls, the lowing of cows coming in from the pasture at milking-time, the quack-quack of ducks going to the pond, the dusty rush of hens to their feed; but he farms practically. Never a dilettante at anything, he is not a "gentleman-farmer" merely in love with the pastoral, but a gentleman who really farms. If he raises pedigreed stock he also knows what it costs to raise crop to feed the stock. He talks of these things with as lively an interest as he discusses Bach or Brahms; in fact, he doesn't "talk shop" at home, he leaves his professional life to the studio. "Only once at Riond-Bosson," William Armstrong writes, "did I hear Paderewski speak of music, except passively; only once did he play, when the proofs of his new *Variations and Fugue* came from the publishers." On occasion, however—as at Herman Klein's dinner in London—he enjoys playing for his guests.

The cordial home-coming greetings that he receives from his townspeople in Morges are only one expression of the popular affection in which he is held at home. But it is Paderewski the man, not Paderewski the famous artist, who is loved. A local hotel keeper once remarked with an amusing air of family-indulgence, "Yes, he plays well I think. I have heard him. He plays well enough." But the same fellow-citizen said with glowing smile, "He drops in often to take a little glass with me." His picture is everywhere in the town; in the lobby of the Hotel du Mont Blanc a large photograph is on perennial display, and there is a small one in nearly every guest room. In the farmhouses in the country about, too, his picture is one of the principal home decorations.

The pride with which the people claim him is possessive. There is a kind of unspoken agreement in the commune to protect him from the curious. Evasive replies are given to unauthenticated strangers asking how to find him or his house, especially if they be armed with cameras. One friend of Paderewski's, arriving at Morges for the first time, had some fun with the natives by pretending never to have even heard of Paderewski. He was treated with scorn and indignation. Every-

where he goes the Master is greeted with affection and respect;
his bow to the salute of the postman, to the station-master, to
the agitated curtsies of children, is part of their life. When he
stops to talk they show their pleasure in their plain Swiss way
of democratic fellowship.

The sixty acres at Riond-Bosson, however, are not enough
to occupy this born farmer. He has another place, "a real farm"
as he calls it, "Les Avouillons", a few miles out from Morges,
and here, at the "ranch" as he sometimes calls it, with recollections of California, he gets his real rest and relaxation. A day
at Les Avouillons is a very domestic affair. Madame goes
ahead to prepare the meals in the little farmhouse that stands
under a big tree. The white-washed cottage is gay with wistaria
bloom clothing the spotless walls with the sumptuous color of a
polonaise. Along the warm south wall, rich green against the
white-wash, a choice pear tree is trellised to bear its special sun-
drenched fruit. Here too the trees are one of his loves. He talks
about the big trees beyond the line bordering the neighboring
property. They are not his. The owner wants to cut them down
for timber. Paderewski can't bear that. He will buy them. The
neighbor, scenting profit, demands a ridiculous price. He knows
he is dealing with an artist, and an artist about whose earnings
fabulous stories are told. "People think that an artist's money
comes easily, that he does not have to work for it. They forget
that he is productive for only a few years and that the foundation of it all is long preceding years of drudgery. Most of us
have a tendency to overlook the fact that a little while ahead
we can no longer earn big sums, and we go on, spend on, as if
it were to last for always, as if tomorrow would be just as good
as today."

Paderewski spoke those words in his sixties, when the fortune that he had built up had been swept away by the war—
rather, given away; for he spent it all for others. But he saved
the trees. He paid the neighbor's price for them. Then he
went out and made another fortune.

He is deeply attached to Les Avouillons and goes there to
get away sometimes from what he calls the "splendor" of

Riond-Bosson. "Never a thing shall be touched here," he says. "It shall be like a dear untroubled face that I shall always have to return to, no matter where my journeyings may lead me." And everyone in the neighborhood, including the thrifty owner of the trees, is attached to him, especially the children, and even the goats. Here is a picture drawn by William Armstrong in his "Romantic World of Music" which shows us how Paderewski is loved at home:

"While we were eating the luncheon that Madame Paderewska had prepared, a little goat sprang into the room. At the doorway at which it had entered two children's faces smiled . . . any excuse to get into a loved one's presence. The goat walked up to Paderewski and took as custom the lettuce leaves he fed to him. With exclamations of delighted surprise, as if the goat had never eaten before, the small conspirators tumbled in; they were in their best clothes, their faces shone with soap and water. [The word had spread quickly that the Master was at the farm.] Once inside, their shyness vanished. Both were telling Paderewski the goat's latest adventures. Madame Paderewska and me they looked upon as grown-up people, to be answered in monosyllables and with forced politeness. But Paderewski was regarded as one of themselves, sufficiently youthful and interesting to be taken as an equal. Until tea-time they and the goat tagged after him.

"It was during tea that Madame Paderewska asked the hour. 'Six o'clock, and we've missed the last train until nine,' her husband answered. 'With guests at Riond-Bosson!' she cried excitedly. 'And we cannot telephone them to have dinner served at eight. What shall we do!'

" 'Take the nine-o'clock train without fail,' said Paderewski, smiling. Handing me the strawberry tarts he went on jovially, 'Help yourself, we still have four hours until dinner.' "

It was growing dark when they left the farm. "The call of a cuckoo came from the wood in the still of the growing night; the blue Alps, pink at their snow-covered crests, were outlined mistily against a purple sky; green trees dotted the fields of billowing wheat; there was a scent of dew and flowers in the air. For some minutes Mr. Paderewski stood drinking it all in, then, sighing, turned to go."

They didn't get back to Riond-Bosson till ten. The guests declared that they had planned to dress in their night clothes to make an appropriate reception for the truants. As it was, midnight came before they left the dinner table to adjourn to the terrace.

Paderewski would have enjoyed the night-dress reception. On one occasion the matter of dress came near to embarrassing one of his guests, but he saved the situation with characteristic grace. A distinguished lady, the wife of a foreign minister at Berne, was invited informally to dinner at Riond-Bosson. The railway journey from Berne in midwinter was cold as well as rather long, so the Countess did not dress *décolleté*. She was dismayed on arrival to find the ladies of the party gowned formally, with jewels. She began to apologize to the hostess. "You said informal—I took it to mean *en famille*——"

"But one remembers," Paderewski himself interjected, "that even the most informal affair becomes an occasion when graced by the presence of Madame la Comtesse, whose gown is ever in the most perfect taste."

XXV

PHILOSOPHER AT THE KEYBOARD

HOME life for Paderewski is both play and work, although he is more inclined to forget to stop working than to stop playing. A few turns on the lawn at croquet with his valet, who is an accomplished linguist and who has refused flattering offers rather than leave Paderewski's service, may easily satisfy him, but when he gets to the piano . . . he forgets. Madame has to intervene sometimes, especially during Christmas holidays, when work is forbidden. One time when she was away from home he practiced until three in the morning. He got a round scolding for that.

A good part of his days at home will see him, as Modjeska saw him, "composing and practicing . . . the piano sending up its brilliant notes." He rises usually about ten, has his "first break-fast", and, if the farm does not engage him, remains in his studio. At luncheon, "second breakfast", he appears—looking to an American familiarly like pictures of Mark Twain, dressed all in white—gay, light-hearted, as refreshed as if he had just got up. If he goes back then to his music, after perhaps a turn at billiards or outdoors, he does not reappear till dinnertime. Sometimes he takes a drive or a long walk in the afternoon.

What goes on mornings and afternoons in that music room up on the second floor we shall see. If we listen now we shall hear. Either he is practicing as virtuoso, keeping fresh in the large repertoire of his recitals, experimenting with new pieces for it, or he is composing, trying out his own inventions, digging, delving, cutting deeper and deeper into the tonal secrets of some teasing phrase that, like the elusive word of the poet, strives for utterance. Perhaps it is some separate phrases from

Liszt's Sonata that we hear, some prismatic bars cut into filigree from the crystal ingots of Chopin, some bits of Debussy—
for, as we learned, whatever he has to say of Debussy's opera
he likes Debussy's piano music; or it may be some difficult passages from his own Variations. Hour after hour he works. He
refuses to spare himself. There are guests downstairs, there is
excursion and entertainment for them, there is the billiard
room to tempt him, there are the gardens and there is the farm
beckoning to him. There is everything and anything but practice. But he sticks to the piano. He conquers it daily. "I have
put up some good fights."

"People," he says, speaking of music students, "are far too
inclined to look upon music as a pastime rather than as a serious
study. This does not mean that the student should eliminate
joy or pleasure from his work at the keyboard, but he should
rather find his true happiness in labor of a more serious kind.
Students spend too much time in playing and too little in
work." They think, he says, that the hours upon hours they
must spend at the keyboard are hours thrown away, that nothing is accomplished. But, he says, "the very essence of success
is practice," and "system is the most essential thing in practice."
"Students who are gifted are very likely to be so enchanted
with a composition that they dream away the priceless practice
minutes without any more definite purpose than that of amusing themselves."

"Music study is work," he told James Francis Cooke in one
of his interviews with him. "Those who work are the only ones
who ever win the greatest awards. It is very delightful to sit at
the keyboard and revel in some great masterpiece, but when it
comes to the systematic study of some exacting detail of fingering, pedaling, phrasing, touch, dynamics: that is work and
nothing but work." "Art without technique," in Paderewski's
opinion, "is invertebrate, shapeless, characterless." And technique comes only one way, by systematic work.

The thing that Paderewski's intimates most remark upon,
however, is not so much his phenomenal capacity for work as
his ability to come from his work, reappear among his guests,

not fatigued but refreshed. Ready for play, he plays with a relish. He seems to have mastered the secret of shutting his mind to a given preoccupation, definitely and positively when the time comes, and of opening it freely to some other interest. Now, in his own home, he returns to his guests and takes them with pride through the house to show them his art treasures.

The interior of the Villa Riond-Bosson is roomy and comfortable and in spite of the fact that it is literally crammed with treasures it is furnished with a simplicity that is harmonious and uncrowded. A characteristic of the decoration is the amaranth tinting of the walls: amaranth is one of the Polish national colors. A lofty open staircase with light streaming from above, many fine mirrors, wide areas, room opening into room, all together give the house a spacious welcoming air. The walls hold some fine old tapestries, the collection of paintings and portraits is priceless. Here we recognize the Alma-Tadema portrait, and here the Burne-Jones profile. Emil Fuchs, the sculptor, whose bust of Paderewski is here at Riond-Bosson, agrees with James Huneker that the Burne-Jones portrait is the best of all the portraits of the artist, "the one nearest to the idealization that one would wish to see handed down to posterity." Few of the portraitists or the sculptors who have tried to portray Paderewski have succeeded. They have not caught "the essential man" who, as Fuchs has said, "so far transcends the frame and features which first meet the eye, that to exact a copy of his small chin and broad cheek bones, and such folds and wrinkles as he may have acquired with time" is to belie the real Paderewski.

The bust by Emil Fuchs seen here at Riond-Bosson has more of "the essential man" than most attempts, and this is perhaps because there is in it more of mystery and less of mere photographic representation of features than in others. In a portrait of Paderewski, Fuchs says, "there must be mystery, because mystery envelops the entire personality of the man and his music." Every feature in the face of a Paderewski portrait, in marble or on canvas, "ought to convey that high sensitiveness which is the chief charm of his art. That is what distinguishes him from all other musicians . . . An artist in reproducing the features of Paderewski must, first of all, stress the great forehead with the two marked eminences over the eyebrows, said to be the storehouse of music. Then there are the eyes, so captivating with their dreamy look, and peculiar for their combination of dark color and light lashes, with the lids so prominent that they give an effect of the impenetrable when they are really meant to look kind. An emphasis laid upon the sensitive mouth and the small mustache turned in at the corners would complete the picture of the man who is so remarkable a combination of knowledge, determination, patriotism and sublime poetry."

Among the portraits and sculptures of Paderewski at Riond-Bosson is a bust by his many-gifted friend Alfred Nossig; it is youthful and full of feeling. Nossig, author of the libretto of *Manru*, is not only a writer but a painter and a sculptor as well. Another of the more successful portraits is that by Styka, still another by Sigismond Ivanowski. Ivanowski once remarked on what a difficult subject Paderewski is: "a man of astounding gifts and kaleidoscopic moods, it is difficult to give any unified impression of him . . . He has a personality too large to be captured easily. My portrait of him is the outcome of five years' close and earnest study and literally hundreds of sketches."

There are scores of signed portraits at Riond-Bosson, a gallery of world celebrities all magnetized by the charm of the "genial" Pole, as Gounod called him in autographing his picture for him. Here are two Popes, Benedict XV and Pius XI, half a dozen kings and queens, among them Victoria and Edward VII of England, Margharita of Italy, Albert and Elizabeth of Belgium, two Presidents of the United States, Woodrow Wilson and Herbert Hoover (Paderewski's young friend of the San Jose concert), Mussolini, Venizelos, Marshal Foch . . . many others. Here is an exquisite photograph of Modjeska with her soft "Creole eyes"; another of Madame Paderewska as a girl, beautiful dreamy eyes, dusky hair, delicate features; and still another of Madame, a sketch by Siemiradzki, the Polish Alma-Tadema, who in this portrayal has caught the loveliness of her eyes as Modjeska saw them one day on a Tatra mountain road when they spoke together of a certain "extraordinary young man." The collection of Paderewski's signed portraits makes an interesting commentary on the man.

There are some very fine paintings by famous artists, the most striking of all of them Malczewski's "The Vigil of the Siberian Exile", which occupies an entire panel in the richly dark dining salon, a painting which, without a word being said, speaks volumes out of the past from which Paderewski came, the past of Poland's sad days, of his grandfather's banishment, of his mother's birth in exile. A carefully assembled collection of old Swiss prints is another of Paderewski's treasures, and a group of Fragonards, which have the place of honor in the salon and the drawing room. Upstairs, where the study is, and the library with its rare books and manuscripts, an exhibit of Chinese bronzes and vases gives us another angle on the artist's hobbies. This Chinese collection is one of his prides, and whenever he shows one particular piece in it he tells of an amusing coincidence which happened when he acquired it. It is a rare *cloisonné* image of a Chinese god. It was owned by his dentist, M. Foucou; but, curiously enough, the name of the god was the same, Fou-Kou, and the special mission of that god, according to antiquarians' belief, is to attract other works of ancient art. "As you may see," Paderewski remarks, "Fou-Kou does not fail in his mission." In the music room is another Oriental treasure, a collection of Chinese music-records. He is intensely interested in Chinese music, and whenever he visits San Francisco he spends time in the Chinese theaters listening to their puzzling cacophony, in which, according to the belief of some, lies the secret of the lost musical notation of the ancient Greeks. There is, of course, a complete collection also of Paderewski's own records, but some of these records of his own he does not enjoy listening to; the recollection of their making is too disagreeable, they had to be made over too many times before they satisfied him. He does not like making records, the acoustical difficulties are so great. They must be perfect or he will not release them. "I would rather play at twenty concerts than play once for a phonograph." Nevertheless his library of records now numbers fifty-six,* a collection which by itself will remain a monument to him for posterity to enjoy.

But if the host of Riond-Bosson makes a grimace at some of his own piano-records, he laughs heartily when he shows his guests his collection of caricatures. They are mostly of himself, and they picture him in every imaginable aspect and posture of the exaggerated. His famous hair especially has been the joy of the cartoonists.

Here is another room. It is a small drawing room now, and it is filled with mementoes of the artist's career, tributes and souvenirs showered upon him, the souvenirs and tributes that he laid at the feet of his son, among them the wreath given him by the Boston Symphony Orchestra. This was Alfred's room, the invalid boy whom Madame Helena mothered from childhood. For a long time after the boy's death this room was kept locked. Now it is filled with fresh flowers every day; and here is Alfred's wheeled chair, his table, all the things he loved, kept exactly as he left them. . . .

Paderewski's library gives us an entirely new side of him. He loves good books and is an omnivorous reader. As he himself has said, "But I play everything," so it may be said that he reads everything. Everything interests him, from poetry and novels to history and philosophy, and all of this in no less than eight languages; for, speaking seven, he has added to them a reading knowledge of Hebrew in order to indulge his taste for Biblical studies. During his earliest visits to England and America he made a thorough study of the English classics; that goes back to 1896. Since then the scope of his reading has embraced a huge and varied list. He likes Heine, he loves the Polish poets, especially Mickiewicz and Asnyk. Among his compositions are the settings for several of Asnyk's love lyrics. Asnyk, hearing him play some of them for the first time, exclaimed, "Ah, that man knows women!" But his reading of

---

* See Appendix B.

poetry goes far beyond the lyrical. He is a Dante enthusiast. He will discuss ardently the latest philosophers as well as the oldest. He once corrected a slip of memory of the great Bergson; Poincaré the mathematician, who, after the manner of Pythagoras, finds harmony and beauty in mathematical speculation, is a favorite topic; he smiles at the new French philosopher who argues that the world, to save itself, must return to Judaism; he raises a dozen questions over the latest philosophical speculations out of Spain.

Paderewski did not take up the study of Spanish until he was in his sixties, yet he speaks it fluently and reads Spanish works that even Spaniards find difficult. One of his favorite Spaniards is the Argentine novelist Enrique Rodriguez Larreta, one time Argentina's ambassador at Paris, whose "La Gloria de Don Ramiro", he especially likes. He has been enthusiastically recommending it to his friends ever since it appeared in 1908. The coloring of the book is one thing that fascinates him; he will quote for you the great scene describing the passage of the Grand Inquisitor Gaspar de Quiroga to the *auto-de-fe* at Toledo: "Coming after the gloomy procession, his crimson robes had the rousing effect of a blare of trumpets." That satisfies his sense of music as well as of color. He will roll off his tongue the mellifluous accents of Larreta's picture of a sunset at Avila: *El sol acababa de ocultarse, y blanda, lentamente, las parroquias tocaban las oraciones.* He will make you hear the rich vowel-music of *Era un coro, un llanto continuo de campanas cantantes.* . . .

It is a liberal education to spend an evening with Paderewski when he discusses literature, history, philosophy. A spirit definitely romantic glows back of the clear flashing of his brilliant mind. In politics he may be called a realist, because there he deals mercilessly with facts, yet at heart he is as much a romanticist in politics as he is in music. His career in statecraft as in art is a notable illustration of the power of intuition when reason controls it. He would argue that the true romanticist is the only true realist. His agreement would be with Newman, that there are "two modes of apprehending propositions, rational and real . . . real is the stronger . . . the more vivid and forcible . . . intellectual ideas cannot compete in effectiveness with the experience of concrete facts". Paderewski would stress the word "experience". He may quote Goethe writing to Ecker-man: "Understanding may serve to fix our affections when we already love, but the understanding is not that which is capable of firing our hearts and awakening a passion." Or Schlegel, say-ing that romanticism is love: *"Nicht ein Sinnliches, sondern das Geistige . . . Nein, es ist der heilige Hauch, der uns in den Tönen der Musik beruhrt"*—"not something sensual but the holy breath borne in upon us in the tones of music." The Saint of Geneva, Francis de Sales will speak for him: "The highest peak of the soul's activities [*extrémité et cime de notre âme*] is a certain pinnacle of reason and of the spiritual faculty [*certaine éminence et suprême pointe de la raison et faculté spirituelle*] guided not at all either by discourse or by the light of reason" [*qui n'est point conduite par la lumière du discours, ni de la raison*].

Paderewski goes deep into these thoughts. All life to him, but especially the life which finds its expression in culture, in art, in music, moves on the lines of St. Augustine's text: "Thou madest us for Thyself and our heart is restless until it repose in Thee." That to him explains the whole impulse back of mu-sic, back of all art; it is what, as he would show you, the Ger-man critic Walzel has called "the intense longing of man as a reasonable thinking being for the Endless and the Eternal." The artist is the one most tortured with this longing, but the one also given the gift of imagination, of seeing at least a glimpse of the way to repose. When Arthur Symons says that "imagination is sight, not wonder, a thing seen, not an opening of the eyes to see it", we understand how Paderewski sees and reveals life in music, and how he opens our eyes to a glimpse of the way. "Art," in Paderewski's own words, "is *the expression of the immortal part of man*. Art is the most important means of human culture. Culture begins the moment you start to work above your needs, and because of a something compelling you to work in that direction. *It is culture that makes man feel that he is made after God's own image.* Through art so many dark corners of the universe which human beings can only look into and conceive through emotion, are made more clear. And music seems the living art that creates the most powerful emotions." Here the philosopher at the keyboard might well quote Browning to us—music

> *. . . is earnest of a heaven,*
> *Seeing we know emotions strange by it,*
> *Not else to be revealed;*

but I prefer Paderewski's own simple words: "Art is the expression of the immortal part of man."

XXVI

HOME AND BEYOND

An hour of this kind of talk in the library with Paderewski is a rare treat. But he enjoys every kind of talk and every kind of company and gathers about him not only musicians, poets, painters, authors and statesmen, but old homebody friends who may never talk art or philosophy or politics. He is the most easily entertained man in the world and he relishes nothing better than an hour of stories or an evening of merry-making. For thirty years the villa has been a rendezvous for the famous and among them Paderewski is the perfect host, while Madame as hostess has always at her side Madame Wilkonska, Paderewski's sister, the sister Antonina who in pig-tails used to play duets with him under old Runowski. Now a widow, Pani Antonina, a handsome, distinguished woman, bears a strong resemblance to her brother.

No one who, even but once, has enjoyed Paderewski's hospitality at Riond-Bosson ever forgets the experience. It is a life-time event, something to be cherished dearly and talked over endearingly. In 1919 Camille Mauclair, the French literary critic, addressing a peroration to him, summed up all that everyone has felt who has had Paderewski as host. "I have not again seen you," said M. Mauclair, "since those happy afternoons when, during the year preceding the War, we wandered together in the gardens of your seigneurial domain at Morges. As an adolescent I had often applauded you without knowing that one day I would come to know you personally; and yet that day arrived. The charm of an exquisite *châtelaine* enhanced that of your Polish hospitality. You stood on the threshold of your flower-grown estate, at the head of a flight of steps where changing shadows marked the movement of the golden light among the leaves. The sun illuminated your auburn hair, your clear, fiery eyes and your face, worn, pale and delicate, whose nobility and individuality a Burne-Jones could reproduce to perfection. We talked of Beethoven and Chopin, whom your wonderful playing had gloriously evoked in the twilight hour. All was festive, all was sweet, friendly, sunny. The blue waters of Lake Leman lay beneath us . . . Now your head of ruddy gold has turned almost silver. In the shadows your glances divine a figure, that of Chopin. You sadly question the phantom. And then you once more play, play the 'Polonaises' as though you were praying, as though you were consulting an oracle. In their urgent and terrible rhythms you find once more the echoes of the battle-field. Time ceases to be. A mysterious synchronization turns you into Chopin himself, Chopin attaining his aim after the lapse of a century, a Chopin whose prayer has been granted, a Chopin avenged, trembling with joy in his tomb and rising from it to sing in triumph!"

It is at dinner, with his guests around him, that he is at his best, high-spirited, talkative, enjoying the give and take of conversation that touches on everything under the sun from American politics to cook-books. For a long time cooking was a favorite topic, because Madame was compiling a recipe-book, and, as Paderewski would laughingly remark, he had to have his finger in the pie. The Polish cooking in the Paderewski house is more than an expression of national feeling, it is an art. . . .

Guests and hosts rise from the dinner table that has in its generous length a feeling of the spacious hospitality of a Polish manor house; a mass of banked geranium blossoms or of roses makes a bed of color down its center, flowering branches radiating from it glowing under the shaded candle light. Now the light strikes Paderewski's hair, graying and leonine, leaving his face in shadow. They go to the broad stone terrace for their coffee; he leads them through the open French windows out into the moonlight, long shafts of light from the room following them as they emerge on the dark terrace. We can hear the low pleasing pitch of his voice. . . .

Someone has asked him to tell that story of Schumann and Wagner. "But yes!" he responds with a laugh, and he tells the story: Wagner came to Dresden; he called on Schumann. "Ach, yes," the German master said afterward, "he is a highly gifted man. But he is an impossible man! I told him about my experiences in Paris. I talked of the situation of music in France and Germany. I talked literature. I talked politics. And what? He remained as good as dumb for the whole hour, that Schumann! One can't go on talking to oneself for an hour! Dumb!" And Schumann of Wagner: "But yes, he is a very great man, a man of education, of spirit. But he is an impossible man! He talks incessantly. One cannot endure a man who talks, talks, talks, for a whole hour together!"

Paderewski is an excellent *raconteur*. He has a wealth of stories to illuminate his conversation. . . . But now, as the company comes onto the half-dark terrace, suddenly he lifts his hand, moves it in a quieting gesture, and looks without a word out into the splendid night. All eyes follow his, taking in in silence the superb scene spread before them, the never-tiring ever-new glory of the Alpine night. A clear moon is rising; it is so clear and bright that the lights in the villas below among the trees are dimmed. The moon is making a ribbon of rippling silver across Lac Leman. The distant peaks swim in the flooding mists. Mont Blanc stands aloof, Olympian, towering in frosted silver over the whole world. "Who," Paderewski asks, breaking the silence at last, "who could put that into music?"

Coffee in the moonlight on the terrace, subdued voices in the semi-darkness; then back into the house perhaps for improvised theatricals (for which his son Alfred used to write such clever little skits), or for games or gossip. Perhaps someone says "Bridge." To the cards, and Paderewski, playing his bridge-hand as he plies his billiard-stick, decisively, swiftly, accurately, teases his partner as he used to tease Modjeska with "terrific scoldings" for trumping an ace. He loves his bridge. There may be a subconscious reason for it beyond his enjoyment of recreation; when he is playing bridge he is playing a kind of music, thirteen cards in each suit for the thirteen notes of the chromatic scale, four suits in a deck played by two opposing hands, an octave . . . fanciful notion. "His patience at the music lesson," says Stojowski, "is inexhaustible, but not when he is teaching bridge! One evening he began on me, there was a second evening, a third—I gave up in despair!" . . . Bridge into the small hours, even till two or three in the morning; it is like a Polish dance—it waits for the White Mazur.

Or if not bridge far into the night, or hours of billiards or cribbage, which is another of his favorite pastimes, possibly because it means making rapid mathematical combinations, and he is champion at contriving "fifteens"—then a little music. In Paderewski's view, the home is the ultimate place where music belongs; in a sense that is its *raison d'être*, that the home may know it. "Far too many students," he says, "study music with the view to becoming great virtuosi. Music should be studied for itself without any great aim in view except in the cases of marvellously talented children. Music in itself is one of the greatest forces for developing breadth in the home."

This is one of Paderewski's favorite subjects, music in the home. "I cannot imagine a genuinely happy home without music in it," he has said. "Brightening, refining, it draws the members of a household nearer through a common emotional bond. As an offset to temptation, and an ennobling power, it is invincible. Early impressions are the strongest. Musical taste, founded early in the home circle and made part of daily life, grows in strength with growing years. The mother with a little knowledge of music, leading her small flock in the right way by gradually introducing them to good music, is performing a great work. Few children but have a latent love for music. It is far easier to direct a child of tender years in the right way in music than to wait until the many other things entering into its education and surroundings divide attention and leave the receptive faculties less keen."

It is because music in the home means so much to him that, to the surprise of many, he strongly endorses those mechanical inventions which bring good music into the home—"the best piano players with the best rolls and the sound-reproducing machines with the best records." He tells of a man of his acquaintance who learned this way to enjoy and appreciate good music. "At first he refused to have anything to do with music except that of the most popular description. Gradually his taste was revolutionized and now he will not permit any trashy music in his home." As for the radio, Paderewski has his views, of which we shall take later note. He has broadcast only once, in 1932, from Paris, on the hundredth anniversary of Chopin's arrival in Paris, when an international hook-up made it possible for all of Poland to hear him.

One can have music almost anywhere in Paderewski's home. There are seven pianos in the house. There are two right here in the drawing room. He will play tonight. If it be some selection which he has not played for months, perhaps years, and on which he has put only a little practice, he keeps the score before him, and Madame Helena turns the pages. But he hardly glances at them. . . . He plays. "From the very moment that he sits down at his instrument," as Emil Fuchs once said, "before he even touches it, the whole room is drenched in an atmosphere which is almost inexpressible, because it is so mysterious." He plays; and if you and I are outside in the moonlight, listening, with the glory of the Alpine night unfolding its white splendors out of deep darkness around us, the added glory of his music makes us feel that the whole world is, in Dante's words, "as a rose, when the consummate flower has spread its utmost amplitude." Something mysterious is happening, some kind of miracle, some mystic consummation . . . great waves of melodious sound spraying high lacy arpeggios of light . . . a wind of sound over waters of light . . . deep undercurrents of sound moving under and over tides of light . . . sound and light becoming one . . . sound flooding light, light flooding sound . . . a commingling of ethereal substances . . . universal rhythm uttered in a language that we understand though we cannot answer . . . "the holy breath that breathes on us in music" . . . *extrémité et cime de notre âme* . . . "a thing seen" . . . "an opening of the eyes" . . .

To bed, a jolly procession over the polished floors, the rich carpets, through the halls, up the stairways . . . and perhaps, a few minutes afterward from one of the rooms, a hearty laugh . . . the Paderewski who climbed trees on the farm and played pranks at school has put one of those fantastic dummies of his invention, a pillow buttoned into a coat, in the bed of one of his guests, some distinguished artist or some dignified and much mystified ambassador.

"Dobranoc!" which is "Good night" in Polish. Everyone to bed; but out of the silence of the still house a little later comes the muffled sound of music. He is at the piano again. Some recalcitrant phrase, some elusive chording that must be caught and conquered has teased him back to his instrument. He may be at it for an hour, for hours . . .

But he is fresh in the morning, up earlier sometimes than anyone else in the house if his mind be preoccupied with composition; out alone on the lawn, the dew on his shoes, or standing on the terrace watching the first snow-fire of day touch the Alpine crests with flame of rose. It is as if he were watching God create the world, the vast tumulus of silence and shadow resolving into familiar peak and range, woods and lake and town. Often back home in Poland, in the Tatras, he has watched God make the world in the morning. It is something to see! —the first arrow of fire winging from the ramparts of Heaven, striking the glacial peaks . . . the riven flush of answering light . . . the dark profound rising to be blessed and shaped by light . . . continents of cloud turning to islanded oceans . . . snow-crests, mountain slope, hilltop, forests, waters, one by one taking their place marshaled by the Hand of Light . . . universal order . . . harmony . . . something to put into music.

And it is something for us to see that solitary figure on the terrace watching the morning come, the contours of his leonine head, the strong lines of his face clear and forceful in the growing light. What are his thoughts? Chaffed once by a mature beauty for being sentimental, he answered, "Why not, madame? Sentiment does not suit a gendarme, but will you not allow a little of it to an artist?" Deep sentiment moves him as he beholds day come out of night, distantly with grandeur on the mountains, nearer and more intimately on the lake, among the tree-hidden villas of the town, in the gardens at his feet. Around him are his home acres, orchards in full bloom repeating in the growing light the smoky rose-fire drama of mist and sunrise in Californian valleys and foothills; better still scenting the fresh air with the tangy cherry-snow perfume of Volhynia in blossom time. Here is his home . . . across the seas and across America is his home . . . but beyond the Alpine wall is his real home. He is a Pole and an exile. Is it an eagle that wings its way across the white light . . . great white bird . . . White Eagle of Poland? Is he repeating the verses of the Podolian poet Goslawski:

> *Had I the royal eagle's wing*
> *How soon Podolia's air I'd breathe,*
> *And rest beneath that sunny sky*
> *Where all my thoughts and wishes wreathe.*
> *'Tis there I first beheld the light,*
> *There passed my happiest earliest years;*
> *'Tis there my father's ashes lie,*
> *Sunned with my smiles, dewed with my tears.*
> *Oh! were I but the regal bird*
> *I'd fly to where my steps once trod,*
> *Where buried are my highest hopes—*
> *Then change me to an eagle, God!*

Is it Maytime now, proclaimed by the white and amaranth of roses in his garden? So many Maytimes have passed, so many Thirds of May to remind a Pole of Kosciuszko and the Constitution, and the white and amaranth of the Polish colors. The year 1903 has passed with its fortieth anniversary of the last Polish struggle for liberty. His father suffered in that; he had seen him dragged to prison, he had seen Kurylowka burned, its defenseless people massacred. Nineteen-five has passed—

the Japanese war against Russia, with Poland stirring again, hopeful in her shackles. Now it is nearly 1910 . . . and something lies hidden for him behind the dark . . . he is beginning to utter himself toward it . . . the sun also rises over Poland. But when will the dawn of liberty that Mickiewicz sang of, "the redeeming sun", break over the motherland? . . .

The first sound of morning, greeting the first light—a bird note in the old linden tree, a cock crowing in the chicken yard. To work! To the piano!

All morning long the keyboard sounds, up in the study. Sometimes it is as if the light of day, breaking in beams across the Lake, and through the shutters of his room, were caught and held, made audible, tuneful. Now, though the sun is bright in the garden and the sky cloudless over the glittering Lake, the sudden thunder of a quick Alpine storm, rolling in a splendor of violet darkness down the valleys of the Savoys, sounds from the study windows. . . . Is it the Symphony? Is it the voice of Poland calling to God and the world God made, as it did call in the Symphony of 1910, when Russia heard still another echo of the speech of '98?

XXVII

THE COMPOSER

THE year 1910 stands out in Paderewski's life with a peculiar significance. In his activities that year the two forces motivating the whole course of his life, patriotism and art, seemed suddenly conjoined to operate in the open.

Back of 1910 lies a record of years of work as composer, much of it done at his home in Morges. It was not alone the natural love of home and domestic life, intensified by the fatiguing discomforts of almost perpetual travel, that made Paderewski long for a permanent establishment, a roof of his own over his head, a soil of his own to till. He desired and needed also a retreat where he could isolate himself and devote his whole time for long periods to composition. All through these years, scanning the record of his utterances, one finds this one desire most frequently expressed, the desire to compose. In his earliest period he thought of little else. The instrument was secondary, the utterance primary. Paderewski, whatever his powers and achievements as interpreter of music, is essentially a maker of music; he is a poet, and we remember that originally the poet was called "the maker." As Henry Finck expressed it, "Paderewski loves his piano; still, like Liszt and Rubinstein, he loves composing better." As a youth, from the days of his first boyhood attempts at improvising, he showed the strongest inclination toward original composition. At seven he was composing. At fourteen he had written a set of Polish dances. At nineteen he published his Impromptu in F Major. At twenty-three he had already written the *allegro* of his Concerto, one of the great modern compositions. By the time he was twenty-five he was the author of some thirty published compositions which have taken permanent place in musical literature. Primarily he is a creative artist, preferring, as an English critic once remarked, "to liquidate his debt to art by making music rather than by playing that of others."

"Paderewski's fame as a pianist," says Ossip Gabrilowitsch, "is such that nothing can be added to it. His accomplishments as a statesman and a patriot have also been universally recognized. It does not seem to me, however, that the importance of Paderewski as a composer has ever been given sufficient attention." This lack of attention to Paderewski's chief artistic gift Gabrilowitsch attributed to what he terms the "silly" modern view—an expression of our age of "specialization"—that "great pianists do not make great composers." "Liszt was one of the first victims of this 'begrudging' habit. All during his lifetime he was attacked by the insipid remark, 'Why don't you stick to your trombone?' Nevertheless," Gabrilowitsch continues, "Liszt went on composing and gave the world masterpieces . . . In my recitals I have frequently played works by Paderewski, and I claim that they deserve a permanent place in the repertoire of concert pianists."

Paderewski was twenty-five when he gave the first concert devoted exclusively to his own compositions, in Warsaw in 1885. Since then, despite the exigencies of his pianistic career, somehow, somewhere, year after year for a good many years he found time to withdraw and compose, although his musical friends and admirers have not ceased to bemoan the fact that being "on the road" so much has kept him from his writing desk. Nevertheless, today the library of his works, while not voluminous, is large and of the highest importance, including virtually every conceivable form of composition, from lyric melody to concerto, symphony, and opera.*

The characteristic note in Paderewski's compositions is the personal note. His strong individuality asserts itself. In the words of Henryk Opienski "he uses a musical language which is very personal; certain melodious and harmonic particular-

* See Appendix A.

ities characterize it—a preference for the diatonic style, a reaction against chromaticism which he avoids with care." "Strong
structure, elegant architecture, generous passion, rare and
healthy sensibility, a unity and firmness of style which no prank
can weaken," these, in the words of the Swiss composer Gustave
Doret, are his outstanding qualities.

It is difficult to find a term adequate to the description, or
rather to the classification, of such a composer as Paderewski.
He is both classical and modern, although never, and the point
cannot be overstressed, never "modernistic." True, he suffers
the fate of all original artists in this changing world, "seeming
like a classic today", as Opienski remarks, "yet in his time one
of the boldest of innovators." But, just as his boldest innovations have never been repudiations of the primary canons of art,
so his classicism has in it that quality which alone justifies the
term classic, the quality of life, the vitality of a strong personality. It is a pity that the word classic, in music as well as in literature, has, thanks to the remote erudition of the Brahmins,
taken on a glacial connotation, as of something mummified and
fit only to be exhibited in a museum. The classics are works that
have lived. They have lived because there is life in them. Enduring life means health. In much of the modernistic music of
the time there appears to be only the flushed and hectic life of
a fever that wastes the tissue and consumes itself.

Paderewski cannot understand this kind of music and when
he speaks of it he touches on that chromaticism which, as Opienski tells us, he carefully avoids. "I try to keep my mind open,"
he says, "but I cannot understand the meaning of most of the
music that is being written today. On my program are the
works of the best modern composers—but the average composer
today seems to be seeking color only, and color is not music."

"Art," in Paderewski's words, "has been on an orgy. Some
few years ago it went wild for color. Line was forgotten in
a mad desire for vivid colors. Today music is still in the state
that painting was in some few years ago. Color is the god
before which all modern composers are worshiping, but they
forget there are other gods than that. They have blinded their

eyes, if I may so express it, to the beauty of the simple lines of the classicist, and endeavor by effects of color to attain beauty without line. Light and shadow and the glow of color are wonderful, but they must have outlines to bound them, otherwise they are formless masses. And then, too, while I have been speaking of painting and music in similar terms, after all color is not music."

That there can be color in music in the proper sense, however, is attested by the first major work which Paderewski composed at his home in Morges. This is his opera, *Manru*, which has been described as the most inspired work of dramatic music since *Carmen*. He began work on this opera in 1897, when he first rented Riond-Bosson. He continued working on it for three years, completing it the year after his marriage, the composition being interrupted by annual tours to America and through Europe, as well as by that memorable visit to Russia which had had its political reactions.

It is interesting to note where Paderewski went for the story of *Manru*. He found it in a novel by one of his compatriots, Kraszewski, who though an over-prolific and therefore uneven artist, was in a peculiar manner endowed with something like the inexhaustible vitality of Paderewski's nature. This amazing writer published no less than five hundred volumes of writings, including novels, historical, satirical, romantic; dramas, essays, criticisms, political treatises, poetry. His energy was enormous, and so was his faith in Poland's future. It was his romantic novel "The Cottage Beyond the Village" that supplied Paderewski with the story for *Manru*. To his friend Alfred Nossig he entrusted the writing of the libretto.

The plot of *Manru* is somewhat like that of Jean Richepin's *Le Chemineau*, the story of a vagabond who loves but cannot stop too long, except that in *Manru* the chief character is a real gypsy. Manru, won by the charms of the pretty peasant maid Ulana, marries her, but he cannot abide domestic life. Asa, a gypsy princess wins him back to vagabondage, breaking Ulana's heart. Urok, a purely peasant folk-lore type, half wizard, half child, avenges Manru's desertion of Ulana by killing Manru;

and Ulana, loving Manru still, in despair throws herself into a mountain lake.

A story of this kind, set in the picturesque Tatras that Paderewski knows so well, affords opportunity for all the colors of romantic tragic music. The score is rich in its symphonic structure and full of bewitching melodies. The use of the violins and 'cellos is especially happy in the picturing of gypsy life. The songs and dances of the *tsiganes*, languorous and sensual and wild, contrasted with the vivacious native music of the Polish mountaineers, give the score a dramatic liveliness which grows into intensity as the pathetic fate of Ulana is depicted in conflict with the seductive charms of Asa, with Manru the tragic figure caught between two loves. A drama of passion, it is unfolded from an orchestration which Opienski characterizes as Wagnerian in force and at the same time wholly Paderewskian in originality. Especially successful with the public were the Gypsy March, the love-duet between Manru and Ulana, and again their duet when Ulana's lullaby is broken by the violent anvil-like protestations of Manru. Frederick Hegar's comment sums up as well as any the powerful and unified impression the opera made as a whole. "This music," Hegar said, "is astonishing in its steady growth, its climactic power; the first act full of charm with its choruses and stirring ballet, the second act lyrical and increasingly dramatic, the third act poignant and truly superb."

Manru was published in 1900 and had its première in Dresden May 29, 1901. Presentations in Nice and Monte Carlo followed, then Bonn, at the Beethoven Festival, with a concourse of German critics acclaiming it and its author, who was present for the occasion. In the meantime Paderewski, mindful as ever of his home country, had arranged for an early Polish production; this followed at Lwow only ten days after the Dresden première, and attracted the entire body of musicians and critics of all three Polands, who gave their compatriot an ovation. During the season following, *Manru* was brought to America, with Bandrowski, the original Polish Manru, in the title rôle, and Sembrich as Ulana. The Metropolitan production in New York was followed by presentations in Philadelphia, Boston, Baltimore and Chicago. Everywhere the opera was given to such crowded houses that it is difficult to understand why it is not more frequently presented. Gabrilowitsch, commenting on this asked, in *The Etude* of May, 1931, "May we know the reason why the Metropolitan Opera House in this year, when Paderewski attained his seventieth birthday, did not think it necessary to let us hear his opera *Manru* which was such a success in New York when it was first given?"

Wherever it was produced *Manru* provoked discussion. In New York the libretto was criticized, as it had been, as we already know, in London by Sir Augustus Harris. In America also some critics, detecting what they named a Wagnerian note in the prelude to the Third Act, cried "not original." This criticism drew from Paderewski one of his most characteristic and illuminating comments on the art of composing. "In music," he said, "absolute originality does not exist. It is the temperament of the composer that makes his work. In method one cannot help but follow those who have gone before. When a great genius like Wagner introduces a method that will give better expression to an idea it is not only not a sin to follow it, but it is a duty to follow it. In employing such a method it concerns not so much the idea as its treatment in a musical way.

"A piece of music must be built like a house or a church. You would not accuse an architect of being a copyist if he put windows in a house, would you? And yet he is merely doing what others have done. Likewise when you read the works of the great poets, you would not accuse Browning or Longfellow of plagiarism if they used the same style of verse as someone else? Their thoughts you would consider and not so much their method. Music, you see, is different from poetry. It appeals to the ears. In a musical work, a sound, or a combination of sounds, that has to do only with the method, may remind one of some other music, and the whole is set down as not original.

"Let us look at the prelude to the third act of *Manru*. There is one run, a little run, that reminds one of *Die Walküre*. I knew it, I tried to avoid it, but could not. Others heard it and they talk of the suggestion from *Die Walküre*. Yet, the first theme is not the same. The second theme is not the same, the orchestration is not the same. I defy anyone to show that anything except the one little run is borrowed. Yet for this detail of method the prelude is condemned. If I were to make an analysis I could show a likeness in method among the greatest composers. For instance, look at Schumann's Concerto in A Minor. The first theme is taken almost wholly in method from Mendelssohn. And Wagner in his first period, and even well into the second period, is not entirely original. One may easily find the influence of Weber and then of Meyerbeer. Beethoven was not free of the influence of other masters, for, in his works, we often find the suggestion of Mozart. And witness also the first Concerto of Chopin. Is it not suggestive very strongly of Hummel? And *Carmen*. Can we not find here an enormous influence exerted by Gounod? And it not only reminds you of Gounod, but some of the themes, as sung, are taken wholly from Spanish music. The 'Habañera' is not even Bizet's, but in all the scores that are published is shown to be taken from a composer who was alive when the opera was written."

Manru is Paderewski's only opera. In 1907 and 1908 it was rumored that he was working on another, but nothing more was heard of it, and Paderewski is one who never talks about what he is going to do. To choose from his compositions other works significant of his achievements as composer is difficult, his writings are so varied. Opienski, his best known Polish critic, selects four as typical, besides *Manru* and the Symphony; they are the Sonata, the Variations and Fugue (Op. 21), the Twelve Melodies for Verses by Catulle Mendes, and the Concerto. Besides these, as of real importance, should be mentioned the Polish Fantasy for Piano and Orchestra, a youthful work of mighty flight and glowing orchestral garb. The Polish Fantasy (Op. 19) cannot, in fact, be dismissed with a mere mention. It is one of those supreme compositions which most happily combine the sheer mastery of the composer with the irresistible appeal of free and spontaneous inspiration. Joseffy, hearing Paderewski play it, said that "it puzzled him because of its apparent simplicity of figuration," and in a burst of enthusiasm exclaimed, "Only a composer could have made it so wonderful!" Its colorful orchestration, its weaving together of the rhythms of Polish dances, its brilliant piano part, its flourishing and youthful ardor, all together make of it music which is pure delight.

The Sonata, in Opienski's description, is "the work of a poet who has suffered to the very depths of his soul, forever questing a high ideal." This work is in a style peculiarly appropriate to Paderewski, "marking as it does the continuous evolution of his thought as well as of his musical language;—he does not depart from classical forms, yet he advances the perfections of technique, refusing to remain in beaten paths." Of the Variations, twenty in number, which the American critic Daniel Gregory Mason says "combine in a remarkable degree the most various and interesting tendencies of modern music" (it was in these Variations, specifically in the fifteenth, "so deliciously *smeared*, with delicate dissonance," that Mason felt there was a touch of modern impressionism, Paderewski vigorously disclaiming it) —of the Variations, Opienski speaks particularly of their "originality, their technical perfection, their plastic character . . . effects of astonishing sonority . . . sweet balancing of rhythms . . . boldest dissonances . . . clear simplicity." It is "a work," again in Mason's words, "wherein the two essential characteristics of music, too often opposed to each other, meet for once in harmonious coördination."

The Melodies for Catulle Mendes are especially interesting as a revelation of Paderewski the poet whose originality asserts itself even when he draws on others for material. They were written in three weeks' time during the same year that he did the Sonata and worked out the sketch for the Symphony, that memorable writing which in 1910 was to play a dramatic, even a political, rôle in his career. How rapidly Paderewski works, once he reaches the actual point of writing, is shown in the fact that all three compositions here described, the Sonata, the Variations and the Melodies, appeared between February and June 1903. This was an especially fertile period; there was, according to Stojowski who spent that summer at Riond-Bosson, an almost daily birth of new song. But it is not the speed with which the Melodies were written that is significant, it is what the composer accomplished in setting the Mendes poems to music.

Apart from speed, it is interesting to note certain details of Paderewski's method of writing music. He is extremely careful about detail. In this sense he goes slowly; at times he achieves only a single page at a sitting. He has scored as many as five pages at a sitting. That is something to remember, and he tells of it with a humorous pleasure. "I was so proud of my five pages, even if they were all rests!" But when the task is completed he has the same impersonal attitude toward it that poets have toward their own verses: "I am not much interested in my compositions after they are done. When I play them in my recitals, I prepare them as carefully and conscientiously as I prepare everything, but I play them as if they were not my own. Composers are two kinds, you see: those who love their children and those who are indifferent to them. I belong to the latter class." "Yes," Madame Paderewska, when he made this remark, commented laughingly, "he is a stepfather, and a very naughty one!"

The rapidity with which Paderewski composes indicates the intensity with which he works. He does little practice when he is in the midst of composition. "When one wishes to compose, and feels that he has something to say, practicing appears irksome." At home in the country is where he likes best to compose, partly because he can get relaxation from manual labor. "Often I go out into the fields and labor for an hour or two—with bare hands. Of course they get stiff and sore. But when I return to the piano I feel invigorated. The stiffness soon wears off, and I can work again with clear and steady nerves. While learning my Sonata, which is difficult, I got very nervous at times, but work in the sun between hours would soon refresh me. I wish I could have such an opportunity for manual labor when on a concert tour. Its effect upon nerves and muscles is more restorative than anything else."

The third selection chosen here as representative of Paderewski as composer, properly should not be called melodies "for" the poems of Mendes, but "from". The great popularity of music written merely "for" familiar verses makes the distinction interesting. Paderewski gave to the French poet's lyrics a good deal more significance than they had in the original; he drew from the verses meanings which the author scarcely articulated. These Twelve Melodies might be taken as models of how this kind of composition should be done. The poems are little aquarelles with scenes "In the Forest", under "The Cold Moon", "The Heaven is Very Low"; among their *dramatis personæ* are "The Young Shepherd", "The Nun", "The Enemy"; they sing of "The Heart that is Pure Gold", "The Quarrel", "The Fatal Love". There is a cold and artificial detachment to the verses which changes under Paderewski's touch to something intimate and warm and even passionate. Their futile melancholy which grieves over things dead and gone becomes in his harmonic interpretation the sadness of things which though past may relive in memory.

The Twelve Melodies are not alone interesting in themselves, but interesting because they show the composer's development since he first essayed the composition of lyric music based on verse, nearly twenty years before. Among his earliest pieces were four lyrics from poems by the Polish poet Asnyk, already mentioned; these were followed by a set of lyrics from six poems by Mickiewicz, the first poet he knew in his boyhood reading.* The simple beauty of these earlier compositions is amplified in the Twelve Melodies by a force, a boldness of dissonance, a passion, that makes them, as Opienski remarks, "symphonies in miniature." In these compositions we see Paderewski true to his own dictum that music is an art by itself, separate and unique, "color is not music", music must always be written for its own sake, never as a handmaid to something else. "Music is not a handmaid, it should not be made subordinate to poetry."

The final work chosen as typical of Paderewski's composition,

---

* Both of these sets of songs, Op. 7 and Op. 18 are published with English text.

apart from the Symphony and *Manru,*—the Concerto (Op. 17)
—is one of the major contributions to modern music. It was
composed in 1888, and has won a permanent place in the literature of piano and orchestra. It found its first interpreter in
Madame Essipoff, and was first produced in Vienna under the
baton of Hans Richter. Although not then received with the
enthusiasm it merited, it has since grown steadily in esteem.
When Ernest Schelling played it in New York City a few years
ago, Paderewski, who was in the audience, was complimented on
its remarkable wearing capacity, its freshness and vitality after
a quarter of a century. "Yes," he responded, "it sounds fresh
today—but nobody liked it at first." It had its first American
presentation in 1893, with the Boston Symphony Orchestra,
on which occasion W. F. Apthorp, writing for the program, remarked thus on one of its special features: "It is worthy of note
throughout the Concerto how largely ornamental the piano part
is. Although the work was written by a pianist, by far the greater
part of its musical structure and development is confided to the
orchestra. But this does not mean that the piano is not almost
constantly doing something. In this the composer has followed
the lead of Liszt rather than that of Chopin and the older concerto writers. He invariably gives it that to do which it can do
best, and generally that which it alone can do."

Like all other Paderewski compositions, the Concerto is distinctively "personal", exemplifying in vigorous manner Paderewski's theories concerning music of this type. The complete
fusing of feeling and form is to him the *summum bonum* of
all music, which simply implies that perfect mastery of technique which leaves the composer free reign, within the frame
of his medium, for the emotional content of his composition.
"Even in Beethoven," he says, "we often see traces of a struggle
with form; joints and seams obtrude. In Mendelssohn this is
never the case. Everything is fluent, spontaneous and elegant.
The content of his music is sometimes weak, flat, lacking in
vigor, but the form is always consummate." To strike the
golden mean between the two, between form and feeling, and
to avoid the fault that he finds in the impressionists, lack of

concurrence in line: this is the composer's desidératum. Polyphony is the secret. "There cannot be true orchestral music without polyphony. Polyphony is absolutely essential to large works. If your piece is in a small frame you can get on fairly well without polyphony, but not if it has large proportions."

The Concerto has large proportions, force, nobility, brilliant orchestration and a piano style that is as simple as it is idiomatic. The first movement is classical in outline. The Romanza, with its mysterious recalls, its endearing arpeggios and ornamentations, deftly wrought around the solo-voices in dialogue, is an exquisitely poetic and original piece. The last movement is electrifying in its dash and brilliance. It is a great musical composition, a great poem. It stands in itself a complete evidence that Paderewski as composer can, as has been aptly said, "out of a maze of finely chiseled details construct an overwhelming arch."

XXVIII

1910: MUSIC AND PROPHECY

HE DID more than "construct an overwhelming arch" in the composition of the Symphony. It was in 1903, when Poland was remembering, forty years afterward, the Uprising of '63, that the first definite conception of this work came to him. He was full of the thought of his country's sufferings. Just then she was suffering anew, not only in the dominions under the Russian yoke, but especially in the parts ruled by Prussia. Of the two the Prussian yoke was the heaviest. A letter which Modjeska wrote me about this time (it is dated in January, 1904) gives an idea of the situation:

"The present Czar is a different man [from his father Alexander III] and though he cannot do much, being himself a slave to the system of government which it is not in his power to overthrow, yet he tries to bring relief whenever he is able to do so. The persecution of the Polish language is now much more severe in Germany [Poznania] than it ever was in Russian Poland. Imagine! the German government does not allow the Poles even to pray in their own language. Not very long ago in one of the villages a gendarme entered the Church during High Mass and took all the Polish prayerbooks out of the hands of the peasants and their children. Yes, such things happen in the twentieth century, under the reign of the civilized Emperor Wilhelm and his 'Kulturkampf' government. Culture indeed! What a derision! Believe me, we prefer the rude embrace of the Russian bear to these hypocritical descendants of the Knights of the Cross!"

It was the five-hundredth anniversary of the historic defeat of the Knights of the Cross at the Battle of Grünewald in 1410,

that Poland was now preparing to celebrate, and it was the
thought of this that precipitated finally Paderewski's conception of a great national musical composition. It was to be a symphony. He was four years writing it. He began it in 1903. Not
until 1907 was the composition and instrumentation of this
monumental work completed; although, as we have seen, during this time, within four months in 1903, three other major
compositions appeared. America, fittingly enough, the historic
friend of the Poland whose soul is articulated in this composition, was the first to hear the Symphony performed. Even the
date, accidentally enough, was appropriate, Lincoln's birthday,
February 12, 1909, and the place, Boston, the cradle of American independence. The presentation by the Boston Symphony
under the direction of Max Fiedler attracted critics and musicians from every part of the country.

If Paderewski can in music construct "an overwhelming
arch", the Symphony may be architecturally described as an
edifice not only richly arched but deeply based and spired with
a pinnacle of towering grace. It rises up and exalts, it surmounts itself, it is a great musical structure. Philip Hale, preparing the Boston program notes in 1909 from information
furnished by Paderewski, wrote of its patriotic character in
these words: "The Symphony is written as a patriotic tribute of
the composer to his native country, and it is directly inspired
by the fortieth anniversary of the revolution of 1863–64.
There is no absolute program for either the first or second
movement. The first movement is free, but classical in form.
It seeks to celebrate Poland's great heroic past. The themes,
though racial in character, are not based on popular melodies.
The same is true of the second movement, in which the composer endeavors to express the lyric nature of his race. In the
third movement Paderewski has followed a sharply defined
program. It is in effect a symphonic poem, and is peculiarly in
memory of the revolution of 1863–64."

The Symphony is in three parts. The first part, entitled "In
Memoriam", opens with a slow introduction which pictures a
vast landscape, the plains of Poland: the word Poland means

"the land of the plains". Against this background of horizon-less spaces comes an animated *allegro*, figurative of the life that peoples these plains, the vital force of the race, agitated and vigorous. The measures that follow the *allegro* are dark; and here for the first time Paderewski is introduced as an instrumental inventor. To procure an effect not possible through any existing orchestral instrument he devised what he calls the "tonitruone", a disc of carefully laid zinc designed to produce a thunderous sound, what Opienski describes as a "deaf" sound. Used at this point of the composition following the *allegro*, in conjunction with three "sarrusophones", an effect of menace and threat proclaims, "like the blows of a steel-gloved fist", the "enemy theme", the coming of an alien oppressor. A processional-like chording, organ-toned and grave, symbol of the prayers of the oppressed people, brings the first movement to a close:

> *O Lord, thou hast to Poland lent Thy might,*
> *And with a father's strong protecting hand*
> *Hast given fame and all its glory bright,*
> *And through long ages saved our fatherland:*
> > *We chant at Thy altars our humble strain,*
> > *O Lord, make the land of our love free again!*

> *O Gracious Lord! whose mighty hand doth hold*
> *The scales of justice o'er world-rulers vain,*
> *Crush out unholy aims of tyrants bold*
> *And hope awake in our poor souls again.*
> > *We chant at Thy altars our humble strain,*
> > *O Lord, make the land of our love free again!*

The second part, "Sursum Corda", builds its movement on the theme of hope. The dream of freedom muses through its melodic lines. There are rays of light . . . then sudden darkness again as the hammer-like blows of oppression break across the dream, the "tonitruon" muttering its somber menacing note.

In the third and final movement the composer deliberately abandons the beaten paths of classicism to create a true symphonic poem. What Paderewski really attempted here was a combination of the symphonic poem with the form of the symphony. The last movement could readily stand as a symphonic poem, yet it is the logical conclusion and crown of the whole edifice. In the opening there is the seething of discontent, the muttering of revolt. Then the music begins to rise and swell; there is the call of trumpets, alarm, conflict . . . but it is "the battle of vain hope" . . . vain because once more the oppression theme strikes in, increases in volume, surmounts, dominates, drowns, smothers, crushes.

But in the chaotic struggle, clash of battle, cry of dying soldiers, thunder of guns, although the force of the enemy-motive rises ever and ever more powerfully, and the death cries grow more faint and etherealized, the heroic strain persists:

> *Poland, shall the foe enslave thee*
> *Sadly and forever,*
> *And we hesitate to save thee?*
> *Never, Poland, never!*

Follows then a funeral march, slow, mournful, sorrowful . . . but it dies away and the echo of the song of hope sounds again, "Poland Is Not Yet Dead!" The coda of the Symphony gathers all its thematic strains together and closes in a mood of exaltation on a note of prophetic vision.

Strange as it may seem, the Symphony was not only in itself a prophecy, but certain words spoken by Paderewski in 1910 in conjunction with its presentation in Poland were still more explicitly prophetic. Still other words that he spoke the same year, another echo of his 1898 speech, gave genuine alarm to the alien governors of his country.

It is not difficult to imagine the effect of a piece of music like the Symphony on the Polish people. Poland did not hear it, however, until three years after its completion. America, as we have seen, heard it first. London followed, with Hans Richter conducting, then Paris, with Andre Messager, and with Saint-Saëns in the audience, surrounded by a galaxy of leaders from the French world of music. In America some of the critics questioned the "tonitruone" innovation, but everywhere the Symphony was accepted as one of the greatest modern contributions to music. In Paris nothing in the critical comments was so remarked as the striking originality of the composition. "Paderewski," said Jules Combarieu, "writes because he has something to say," and he quoted the composer as having once said to him, "I adore music, but I love my country more."

His country heard the Symphony in 1910. The historical coincidences of that year in Polish life are notable: it was not only the five-hundredth anniversary of the Battle of Grünewald, it was likewise the hundredth anniversary of the birth of Chopin. Thus Paderewski's life-theme, "Poland and Music", became the conjoined theme of popular thought. For the Chopin centenary a national music festival was arranged, to be held in the city of Lwow. Appropriately the Grünewald celebration, commemorating the victory of King Jagiello over the Hohenzollerns, was planned for the ancient capital of Jagiello, Cracow. It is noteworthy that both of these national celebrations took place in the Austrian partition of Poland. Nothing of the kind was possible in Prussian or Russian Poland.

The same year (1908) that Paderewski had been proposed for the directorship of the Warsaw Conservatory, with nullifying results, he met in Paris a young sculptor, Antoni Wiwulski, a friend of the granddaughter of Mickiewicz, the poet who had colored Paderewski's boyhood aspirations. Wiwulski, highly talented, was poor and sick. Paderewski, recognizing his talent and sympathizing with his situation, sent him to his home at Morges to recuperate as well as to afford him a place free of distractions to carry on his work. Already Paderewski had determined what his own part should be in the Jagiello celebrations: he would present to the city of Cracow a monument commemorating the victory of Grünewald. Who the sculptor should be was not decided. Paderewski made three requirements: the artist must be young, poor, and a Pole. In Antoni Wiwulski he had found the artist.

Cracow, ancient capital of Poland, is one of the most attractive cities in Europe. Ringed by its "Planty", a circular wooded park marking the line of the mediaeval walls, with the old towered gates still standing, it is very Italianate in appearance, and this aspect is emphasized by the graceful architecture of many of its old buildings, notably the fine Renaissance Cloth Hall, now a national gallery of art. The double spires of Panna Maria Church, built in 1276, rise in the center of the city; from one of these spires sounds the historic "hejnal", a bugle aria played every hour, after the bells have ceased their chiming, a custom centuries old and still unbroken. Dominating the city, which enshrines one of the oldest universities in the world, founded by Jagiello and his queen Jadwiga * in 1364, is the Vavel Castle, seat of the earliest Polish Kings and now Poland's pantheon, housing the tombs of her national heroes, among them that of Kosciuszko, whose sarcophagus is covered with the Stars and Stripes of America. Straight across the city from the Vavel Hill, in a direct line, and facing the Academy of Arts, is the equestrian monument of Jagiello. It stands in a square named for the artist Matejko. The monument is a massive conception of granite and bronze; four life-size bronze groups surround the base, representing four scenes of the battle; above rides Jagiello, armored, but with his sword at rest. The figure is forceful, daring. The image of the King's mount is exceptionally good, strong and vivacious.

Cracow was not large enough to hold the crowds that came on the tenth of July, 1910, to witness Paderewski's presentation of his gift to Poland. All Poland was there. And the ears of Poland's alien rulers were cocked to hear what he would say, for by this time he had taken on a significance, to them, greater than that of "only a Polish pianist".

If they were expecting an inflammatory speech from the man whose 1898 address at Warsaw they had suppressed, they were to be disappointed. Paderewski's utterance was a simple plea for peace. There was significance in the figure of the Teu-

---

* The romantic story of the "hejnal" is told in Eric P. Kelly's historical novel "The Trumpeter of Krakow" (New York: The Macmillan Company, 1931); the equally romantic story of Jadwiga and Jagiello may be read in Charlotte Kellogg's biography "Jadwiga: Poland's Great Queen" (New York: The Macmillan Company, 1931).

tonic Knight fallen in defeat on the Jagiello monument, but there was likewise significance in the sword-at-rest of the Polish conqueror. Paderewski, remembering this, standing on the platform erected beside the monument, spoke simply and unoratorically; but he spoke with a suppressed feeling that communicated itself to his audience the moment he rose to his feet. Dr. Fronczak, recalling the occasion, has told me that it was "a very wonderful piece of oratory, unforgettably dramatic." The tall bareheaded figure with its glowing crown of hair and its air of the apocalyptic messenger from far away, magnetized the huge crowd of people that packed the square and the tributary streets. The fine modulated voice, melodious and warm, strong and clear with great carrying force, held them in a spell. This is what he said:

"The achievement upon which we look today was not born of hatred. It was born out of deep love for our native land; not because of her great and glorious past, not because of her present helpless state, but because of a vision of her bright and powerful future. It was born out of love for and gratitude to our forefathers, who went forth to the fields of battle not for pillage and gain but in defense of a just cause, and were consequently rewarded with the sword of victory.

"The donor of this monument, and those who helped in this work, give it in thanksgiving as a votive offering on the altar of patriotism to the glorious memory of their forefathers, petitioning those exalted spirits, who ages ago were united with God, to inspire the children of earth with love and peace, to instill in their hearts faith, hope, tolerance and good will; without which, neither virtue nor valor can be attained.

"Let the Nation, at this time personifying sovereignty over all Polish lands, graciously accept this offering of our loving hearts.

"It is our ardent desire that each Pole and each Lithuanian, all the sons of Poland within her ancient boundaries as well as all the Poles across the seas, shall look at this monument as a sign of future unity, an evidence of universal glory, and, prompted by a strengthened faith, a prophecy of better times."

There was not much in that to cause alarm, unless indeed the oppressors of Poland, who had operated for a century under the old Roman policy of *divide et impera*, saw danger in Paderewski's summons to the Poles to unite, his promise of a "bright and powerful future", his prophecy of "better times". But Paderewski had not said his all in that brief address. At a reception given in his honor on this occasion, when most of the famous Poles of the time gathered to salute him, he spoke words which, though without the note of threat, were really prophetic. True, Russian and Prussian officialdom, no more than others, could then know how prophetic those words were. But the same bureaucracies that were, four years later, to plunge the world into its worst war, must have trembled at the clairvoyant power of a man who, seemingly knowing their secret hearts, could tell them to their faces, in 1910, what they were dreaming of. These were the words that Paderewski spoke at the reception:

"Brothers, the hour of our freedom is about to strike. Within five years a fratricidal war will soak with blood the whole earth. Prepare, compatriots mine, brother Poles, prepare, because from the ashes of burned and devastated cities, villages, houses, and from the dust of this tortured soil will rise the Polish Phoenix."

That was in July, 1910. He had said "within five years". Within four years, in July, 1914, the prophecy came true.

Paderewski's apparent gift of prophecy had its basis, of course, not in any occult power but in his knowledge of European politics. He knew what he was talking about, because he knew what was going on in the chancelleries of the Old World. He studied affairs as he studied billiards and bridge, as he studied the piano, thoroughly. That was why he could give his compatriots a word of hope as well as of warning in 1910; and that was why he could make his Symphony close, not so much on the rising inflection of a question as on the exalting note of a promise.

The year 1910 and the Cracow address signalize a definite turn in Paderewski's career toward politics. The 1898 speech at Warsaw had been undesignedly a warning of what might come, of what he could do. Now he was beginning to do it.

It was at Cracow, during the Jagiello celebration, that the officials in charge of the Chopin centenary to be observed a few months later invited Paderewski, who was their honorary president, to present the Symphony as the chief feature of the music festival at Lwów. It was at this festival, which gathered together the élite of the musical world, that the first Polish performance of the Symphony took place. It was given under the direction of Henryk Opienski and it created a sensation. On this occasion, too, Paderewski performed one of those many graceful acts which have made him loved. Unable to appear himself at the piano, for already he was a victim of that neuritis which more than once cancelled some of his recitals, he gave the place of honor to his American pupil, Ernest Schelling, who passed through the ordeal triumphantly. And it was on this occasion that he spoke his Chopin Panegyric, that matchless utterance of a man who by this time was recognized as a master of oratory as well as of music.

The opening of the Chopin speech sounds a note of challenge, and anyone reading it now who has seen him giving a public address can picture him as he appeared at Lwów that day in 1910. He has a way at moments while speaking of putting his hands in his pockets, the first two fingers, throwing back his head, and half closing his dark eyes with their blond lashes, that gives him a curious inscrutable air of daring, as if he were saying to his hearers, "I shall do what I shall do; it has been determined." He knew now, as he began to speak, what notice had been taken in official circles of his words at Cracow. As if to remind the enemies of Poland that he meant those words and was fully cognizant of their significance, he reverted to them. "Lately, in Cracow," he said, "on a luminous and unforgettable day in July, we paid homage to those valiant forefathers by whom our country was upbuilt; today we bring thank-offerings of love and reverence to him by whom it was enriched and marvelously beautified. We do this not only in remembrance of a dear past, not only in justifiable and con-

scious pride of race, not only because our bosoms are still quick
with sparks of that inextinguishable faith which was, is, and
always will be the noblest part of ancestor worship, but because
we are deeply convinced that we shall go forth from these
ceremonies strengthened in spirit, reinspired of heart."

That was the opening. But there was more to come of the
facing of realities. "We are in sore need of strengthening, of
re-inspiration. Blow after blow has fallen upon our stricken
race, thunderbolt after thunderbolt"—the thunderbolts of oppression that he had sounded so graphically in the Symphony;
—"our whole shattered country quivers, not with fear"—he
must have turned his voice toward Berlin and Petersburg as he
spoke that word—"but with dismay"; and there he faced Poland herself, and her enemies within the fold. "New forms of
life, which had to come, which were bound to come, have
waked us on a night of dreadful dreams. The same wind that
blew to us a handful of healthy grain has overwhelmed us in a
cloud of chaff and siftings; the clear flame kindled by hope of
Universal Justice has reached us fouled by dark and blackening smoke; the light breath of Freedom has been borne toward
us on choking, deadly waves of poisoned air.

"Our hearts are disarrayed, our minds disordered. We are
being taught respect for all that is another's, contempt for all
that is our own. We are bidden to love all men, even fratri-
cides, and yet to hate our own fathers and brothers should they
think otherwise, albeit no less warmly, than ourselves. Our new
teachers are stripping us of the last shred of racial instinct,
yielding the past to an indefinite future, thrusting the heritage
of generations into the clutches of that chaotic ogre whose
monstrous form may loom at any moment above the abyss of
time. The immemorial sanctuary of our race, proof until now
against the stoutest foe, is being assailed by brothers who bat-
ter at the walls, meaning to use our scattered stones for the
building of new structures—as if these poverty-stricken archi-
tects were unable to afford material of their own! The white-
winged, undefiled, most holy symbol of our nation is being
attacked by croaking rooks and ravens; strange, ill-omened

birds of night circle around her, screeching; even her own de-
mented eaglets defy her. 'Away with Poland!' they cry. 'Long
live Humanity!'—as if Humanity could live by the death of
nations!"

The chancelleries of Berlin and Petersburg must have
looked beyond Lwów with a kind of frightened wonder in the
direction of the Vienna which permitted the utterance of such
words as these, spoken publicly by a man whose power of leadership they already had reason to fear. "Why," they must have
asked, "does the Austrian government allow such things? Can
they not see that they endanger our future?"

But Paderewski was invoking the past; he knew what magic
word to speak to bind his compatriots together. "In such moments of distraction and turmoil," he told them, "we turn towards the past and wonder anxiously: is all that Was worth
nothing, then, but condemnation and contempt? Are only that
which Is, and that which May Be, worthy of regard and faith?
Blessed be the past, the great, the sacred past!"

It was out of Poland's past, the one common food on which
she could feed her heart in those times before her restoration
—the restoration that Paderewski more than any other one
man made possible—that he conjured up the figure of Chopin.
"Through long years of torment, martyrdom, and persecution,
our hounded thoughts encircle him with their most sacred
threads." But he did not forget what oppression meant to Chopin—"an oppression so ruthless and terrific that it can only be
accounted for as some wild delirious action of revolt against
the long-drawn Tartar yoke, falling in revenge upon the innocent"—nor how ineluctably Chopin had remained Polish in
spite of oppression. Then at last he named names. Russia. The
Russia that made Chopin an exile. "Not even that nation,
mighty in numbers, strong yet oceanless, which fain would create unto itself a sea engulfing all Slavonic streams, not even
that nation which has taken so much from us already, has yet
dared lift its usurping hand toward Chopin. He too was a Slav
—yet with how great difference! . . . What an abyss between
his yearnings, his griefs . . . and that withering despair which

flows toward us as a blast frost-laden across steppes immeasurable, boundless, hopeless . . ."

He invoked the past, but he did not stop with it. As at Cracow, so here at Lwów he spoke of the future too. The final words of this remarkable utterance, so daringly and challengingly spoken, calmly and forcefully in the face of Poland's oppressors, sound now, after the event, like a rally-call. "Let us brace our hearts to fresh endurance, let us adjust our minds to action, energetic, righteous; let us uplift our consciousness by faith invincible; for *the nation cannot perish which has a soul so great and immortal.*"

Some repercussion of such a public utterance, so fertile of defiance, was bound to be heard. So far as the Austrian officials were concerned, however, whatever their chagrin, nothing could be done. On no pretext could they punish the speaker, and it was too late to silence him. The words were spoken. And the whole country hummed with them. Nothing like them had been heard in Poland in a hundred years. But Prussia could forbid; and Russia, first permitting, could rescind or at least retaliate. She did so, and in a petty way. The following year, 1911, the Symphony, of which in a sense the Chopin Panegyric might be called the libretto, was presented in Warsaw. But the program-notes were sharply censored. No word expounding the thematic significance of the composition was allowed to be printed.

This was a foolish move on the part of the Russian police. It only intensified interest in the performance. And no Pole needed any program-notes, anyway, to explain Paderewski's Symphony. Every countryman of the composer knew what the "enemy-theme" was when they heard it, just as well as they knew the veiled strains of "Poland Is Not Yet Dead!"

In this year of 1910, with Paderewski's prophecy and summons, Poland was beginning, without being in the least conscious of the fact, to stir to a renewed life.

XXIX

1914: CHINESE DRAGONS

AMONG the Polish people the old Catholic custom is followed of celebrating one's anniversary not on the birthday but on the name-day, the feast of one's patron saint. Paderewski's patron is St. Ignatius Loyola, whose feast falls according to the Church calendar on the thirty-first of July. Ever since Paderewski's boyhood, when his name-day was a gala event in the home, the family tradition has been kept up. After his marriage to Madame Gorska it became literally a "double feast", for Madame Helena's anniversary came on the day following and the two were always celebrated together.

To see Paderewski on an occasion like this is to see him at his social best. For over thirty years, since he has made his home at Morges, the fête has been held; it has become virtually a local holiday, a gala event for the entire household, for neighbors residing in the vicinity, and for artists who live in the Lake Leman region. Josef Hofmann's European home is near Vevey, further along the Lake, Ernest Schelling's at Garengo, near Celigny, not far from Morges, Felix Weingartner's nearest of all, at St. Sulpice. They and their families are always present at the fiesta, as are also the brothers Morax, Swiss poet and painter respectively; Gustave Doret the composer and conductor; the De Coppet family with the famous Flonzaley Quartette from Chexbres; Marcella Sembrich, the Polish *diva*, and her husband, from Lausanne; several of the professors from the University of Lausanne . . . not to speak of others who came yearly from distant lands to join in the festivities; Miss Laurence Alma-Tadema and Paderewski's English managers, William Adlington, nicknamed "the Governor", and L. J. Sharpe from London, Mlle. Marie Mickiewicz from Paris, Henryk Opienski from Warsaw, Rudolph Ganz from Chicago, Sigismond Stojowski from New York. The Paderewski anniversary, in short, means a gathering of celebrities who join around their great friend from all parts of the world to honor him.

If Sembrich be present, she is the star of the festival. She sings; but that glorious soprano which has drawn thousands by its magic is not lifted up in arias from the operas, but in some newly improvised and very comical verses concocted for the occasion. Amid the laughter and applause that follows her gay performance the stately figure of Paderewski, the mere appearance of which on the stage has hushed thousands, tumbles elaborately to its knees before the *diva;* he is kissing Sembrich's hands with a tremendous flourish. One year, this was 1913, the Flonzaley Quartette gave a humorous Fantasy written by Ernest Schelling in burlesque of the futuristic fashions in music, whereupon Stojowski delivered a solemn and profoundly learned mock-lecture on the thirty thousand different noises in nature from which modernistic composers derive their instrumental effects. In connection with that mirth-provoking lecture a number of the guests illustrated, in a kind of musical charade with astonishing costumes, the capacities of various instruments. Josef Hofmann, Rudolph Ganz and Ernest Schelling appeared as piano movers. "Steinway & Co." was printed in large letters on their arm-bands, and they carried into the room an upright piano from which issued lively tunes played from the inside by an invisible player. The invisible player—and that was a surprise!—became visible while the piano was still in midair, when the beautiful and distinguished head of Madame Olga Samaroff emerged from the top of the instrument.

Innocent and hilarious fun rules the day. Everyone is young again; they sing together, they laugh till they weep. On one occasion a dignified Polish monsignor, prelatical in his purple, and a still more dignified American ambassador in full formal dress, the two having just met for the first time, were seen falling into each other's arms and embracing, weak with laughter.

After the entertainment come fireworks in the gardens, with the whole population of Morges out to see the place lit with rocketing cascades of colored fire. Then dancing in the salon, with such dance music as the gods never listened to. Six hands to each of the two pianos, Schelling, Samaroff, Stojowski at one, perhaps Hofmann, Ganz, Weingartner at the other; or even Sembrich, complementing her vocal program with a brilliant whirl at the keyboard.

In 1914 the usual procedure was slightly altered. Among the house guests was Roman Dmowski, leader of the National Democratic party in Poland, close friend of Paderewski and one with whom he had long advised about the political situation in the home country. Dmowski was obliged to leave Morges hurriedly; therefore, in his honor, the double celebration was begun a day before. There was good reason for Dmowski's hurry. Ever since the assassination of the Austrian Archduke Ferdinand at Serajevo in June of that year all Europe had breathed under a cloud of apprehension. No one knew what would happen, everyone feared that terrible things might happen. The diplomatic exchanges going on between Austria and Serbia, between Vienna, Berlin and St. Petersburg, had got on the nerves of Europe, and that nervousness had naturally invaded the precincts of Riond-Bosson. It was the cause of Dmowski's departure. He could not run the risk of being shut out of Poland by closed frontiers, and the frontiers might at any moment be closed and international railway communication stopped. He left for Warsaw the night of Thursday the thirtieth.

Paderewski's interest in Chinese music and art, of which, as we have seen, he is a connoisseur, had given his friends in 1914 a new idea to vary the annual program: they would make a Chinese fête of it. With Stojowski and Schelling as usual in the rôles of general managers they had transformed Riond-Bosson into a scene of Oriental enchantment. Lawns and terrace were changed into a garden of old Chinese loveliness for the night of July 31. Hundreds of paper lanterns made luminous garlands above the terrace and bloomed like big roses of

light among the trees. Townsfolk crowded around the park to
see the illuminations. Inside, the usual fun and play went on.
At her side as co-hostess Madame Helena had Madame Antonina since the boyhood of her famous brother a central figure in his family festivities; they were at their best, beautifully gowned and jewelled. It was a lively and colorful picture.

And yet the atmosphere of the occasion was different from
that of other years. Its spirit was a little forced. An invisible
cloud was hovering over the serene Alpine skies that night.
Alpine storms come suddenly, without warning; I have seen
the bronze walls of the mountains, brilliant in sunlight, grow
dark as iron, the blue lake turn black, almost as quickly as one
might raise his hand. But now there was a world-storm brew-
ing, and the slow rumblings of its thunder beyond the Swiss
frontiers were to be heard long before the tempest broke. If
gayety at Riond-Bosson was a bit self-conscious this year, it
was because all the people gathered there needed already to
escape, to escape from themselves, from something too terrible
to contemplate. Dmowski's hurried leaving had not lessened
this feeling. The guests from distant parts simply forced themselves for the moment to ignore the fact that they too might
have to watch the frontiers. Nor were the Swiss themselves in
any better case. The Swiss guests at Riond-Bosson that night
were deeply concerned about their country's neutrality. They
were at the call of their government in any emergency and this
assuredly was an emergency of the gravest kind. As it happened, the Swiss order of mobilization was issued that very
night and the next day disclosed a scene to be remembered in
the square facing the Morges Arsenal, when the peasants and
mountaineers of the region, garbed in their picturesque attire
and wearing their curious sabots, gathered with the townspeople
at the call to arms.

Paderewski felt as the others did, and, as it chanced by the
arrangement of the festival, he was given more of an opportunity to dwell on the situation than anyone else in the house.
He was locked in his room, alone. That is one of the features
of the party. It is a "surprise party", and to insure some of it

at least being a genuine surprise for Paderewski, it is always contrived sooner or later to get him to his study and lock the door on him while the entertainers rehearse their "show" downstairs in the salon and arrange the gifts which are heaped on a table in the hall. The gifts run from elaborate and precious souvenirs presented by Madame Helena and Madame Antonina to all sorts of laugh-provoking toys and contraptions brought by the guests.

In the meantime, while the "stunts" were being rehearsed, the prisoner upstairs was left to amuse himself as he might while he waited for the summons to join in the festivities. He would enjoy it all this year as he had other years, of course; he would play his part and be "surprised" and have a happy time. But he felt inwardly disturbed. Perhaps he felt more strongly than any of the others the sense of apprehension in the air. His talks with Dmowski during the past few days had not eased his mind. He had agreed that Dmowski must hurry away. Besides, he was tired at the end of his busy year. Thanks to the nervous strain under which he lived his old enemy neuritis had attacked him again; in March of this year, 1914, his recital of the 26th in New York City had been delayed forty minutes, due to the severe pain he had suffered. He had worked like an engine since the stirring times in Poland four years before. He had made his annual tours of America and Europe; in 1912 he had visited Africa. If, sitting now in his study, reviewing the year in recollection, he glanced at the piano or fingered music sheets, he was irked to think how more and more his compositional work had fallen off. That fact always had irked him. Actually he had composed scarcely anything during recent years; a Canzone for piano, and the sketches of a series of six piano Etudes, the latter even yet remaining unfinished or at least unpublished. The life of an artist is inevitably a life of "divine discontent", of a struggling against the circumstances which forbid him attaining the fullest reaches of his desire. From his earliest days, as we have seen, Paderewski had been by impulse and by wish a composer above all else; but the demands of his career as virtuoso had almost systematically interfered. He had never been able to reconcile himself to this and his friends had never ceased to deplore it. "He owes to the world all the music that is in him," Madame Trélat, the beautiful French singer to whom he had dedicated his lyrics from Catulle Mendes, had said, and there was not one who had ever heard a composition of Paderewski's who did not echo her sentiment.

But, after all, fatigue following a hard year, the recurrent sense of frustration, of things undone in his most chosen field of work—these were not new feelings to him. They could be thrown off. That was what this joyous annual fiesta meant, recreation, play, rest, freedom in his *asile* to do as he pleased. That is what it had always meant. Nevertheless, this year things were different. In the one place designed to be his retreat, his place of withdrawal from the world of the public, he had found withdrawal impossible. He breathed the disturbed atmosphere of Europe; there was dust in the air. With everyone else in that house at that moment he felt the shadow of the cloud, heard the rumble of the distant thunder.

Paderewski's feeling of apprehension during these midsummer days of 1914 was based on an exceptional knowledge of the European situation. Those startling words that he had spoken in 1910 at Cracow, warning his Polish compatriots that in five years Europe would be plunged into a war that would give Poland a new opportunity of freedom, had been uttered out of that knowledge. Paderewski knew not only the old axiom "when thieves fall out", but he knew that the thieves must soon fall out. He knew that this was inevitable, because he knew his Russia, he knew his Balkans and his Austria, above all he knew his Berlin. As for Russia, her war with Japan in 1905 had touched too closely on the nerve-center of his nationalistic sensitivity for him to escape its significance. During that war Joseph Conrad had written, "Europe is preparing herself for a spectacle of much violence and perhaps of an inspiring nobility of greatness." Paderewski might have been inclined to underscore Conrad's "perhaps", even though he must, like his compatriot, hope for the best, but he knew too much to have illusions. The Czar's abortive Duma gesture toward a degree of representative government and nominal liberty in Poland, when that gesture was made after the Japanese war, had not deceived him; and it had been with grave misgivings that he had watched at that time the romantic attempt of the Polish Socialist, Pilsudski, to raise a legion to join the Japanese against Russia. It was, he felt, such enterprises as this, more zealous than wise, that had in the past brought disaster to Poland. In that case even the Japanese, willing enough to welcome armed help in their struggle with the Russian colossus, had been wiser than the romantic Pilsudski; they had refused his aid. What Poland would have suffered, after the Peace of Portsmouth, had Pilsudski's picturesque scheme been carried out, would be impossible to imagine. To Paderewski the scheme, no matter how heroic, was a mad one, for as he could see from the beginning, whether that war ended in victory or defeat for Russia, Poland would for a time at least suffer dire consequences. Out of the Russo-Japanese war and its aftermath, however, Paderewski had made one deduction; the Russian colossus, long rotting at heart, was doomed soon to collapse—that Russia which his friend Sienkiewicz had described as "the race which does not know how to live and does not permit anybody else to live", the Russia which in Conrad's words "had no historical past . . . cannot hope for a historical future . . . can only end."

As for the Balkans, the word itself, ever since the Balkan war, had come to mean to Paderewski the ultimate distintegration of the Austrian Empire as surely as 1905 had pointed to eventual Russian collapse. The warning of the French writer Delaisi, who had even gone so far as to give to a book of his, published before the war, the title "From the Balkan War to the European War", and who had likewise said, as if prophetically, "the Balkan conflict becomes the European conflict"—that warning had meant something besides mere talk to Paderewski. He knew that Russia with her proposed Danube-Asiatic railway had been the real provoker of the Balkan war, and he knew that Germany's Bagdad railway was the answer to that Pan Slavic threat; that it was indeed more than answer to threat, but in itself a threat to British power in Egypt and India. All these interests must sooner or later come to an issue. Austria would break up. And Prussia?

Prussia at this moment, in July 1914, meant something very different. Prussia ruled the German people absolutely not only by force but by indoctrination, and she dreamed unquestionably of ruling Europe and the world, land and sea. Only a few weeks before, in June, she had opened, with a kind of universal detonation of jubilee, her war-like Kiel Canal which gave her navy the deep waterway she had long desired from the Baltic to the Atlantic. Her army was the most perfectly equipped and trained in the world, and, excepting the minority of Social Democrats, that army possessed the minds and hearts of the entire German people. "Other countries possess an army," a French military *attaché* had said in 1870, just before the Franco-Prussian war, "but in Prussia the army possesses the country." "War," Mirabeau had remarked during the French Revolution, "is the national industry of Prussia." The Prussia which Napoleon had described as having been "hatched from a cannon ball", the Prussia of July 1914, so busily engaged in the threatening conflict between her ally Austria and Balkan Serbia, had not changed since 1789 or 1870, had indeed only grown in power and arrogance. She still lived and breathed and had her being under the gospel of her hero Frederick the Great: "Nothing can confer honor and fame upon a prince except the sword; the monarch who seeks not his sole satisfaction in it must ever appear a contemptible character." Prussia, in short, in the midst of this cloud darkening Europe, meant vaunting power, force irresistible. Yet Prussia also was one of the thieves, one with Austria and Russia, now all but at each other's throats. The thieves would fall out. There was no doubt of it in Paderewski's mind. Only two years before, the thing had almost happened; in 1912 he had known that a war had been barely averted only because the Berlin bankers were not ready then to finance it. Were they ready now? The German Imperial Bank had increased its gold purchases from 174,-

000,000 marks in 1911 to 317,000,000 marks in 1913. Was this a war fund?

On June 28 of this year had come the Serajevo assassination, the match that had ignited this deadly fuse, the smoke of which all Europe was now smelling. Paderewski had not been surprised by the exaggeration of this "incident" in the war offices at Vienna and Petersburg and Berlin; their actions were too obvious. But he shrank at the thought of the possible and frightening consequences, and he discussed with his friends these possibilities and fears, especially in their relation to Poland, Poland caught in the claws of the double-headed eagle of the thieves. He could not help remembering that Mickiewicz, the national poet of Poland, the poet who had fed his spirit even in boyhood with hope for Polish freedom, the poet whose granddaughter was at this moment downstairs, a guest in his house, had once cried out, "For universal war for the liberation of all peoples, O God we beseech Thee!" Was it possible that now these rumblings of storm presaged the "universal war"? Unthinkable. And yet . . .

He had just been talking all this over with Dmowski, now hurrying back to Poland. Paderewski knew what was going on in Poland. He knew all about the work of the Austrophil Jaworski and all about the continued activities of the Socialist leader Pilsudski: all about his organization of Polish legionnaires, which at first had been secret; his frequent visits to Paris, the latest of these in January 1914, his failure there at that time to intrigue the French government into his support.

Paderewski was of course the last man to fail by one iota in active sympathy with any movement in Poland that looked toward her liberation. But twenty-five years of a public career, a career that had taken him not only into every corner of Europe, but better still into Europe's inner circles, had taught him a good deal about the arts of government and diplomacy. Above all it had taught him that if ever Poland was to be liberated she must be, when her hour of liberation came, more than merely a heroic figure struggling for her rights or a romantically pathetic figure downtrodden before the eyes of the world; she must be taken realistically and seriously as well as sympathetically. On two things Paderewski was determined; first, that whenever the hour did come, Poland must be free to free herself; that is, she must have credit among the nations as a responsible nation, with a credit unimpaired by rash and abortive internal attempts at liberty; second, that her people should be a united people, that her fight for freedom should not be a class war.

There was a menace to the realization of these ideals, if ever they could be realized, in the activities of some of the Polish partisans, especially those of the Socialists. They were the ones who, in the words of Sienkiewicz, "have undertaken the construction of a new house, forgetting that we live huddled together in a few rooms, and that in the others dwell strangers who will not assent to it; or rather on the contrary they will permit the demolition of those few rooms, but will not allow their reconstruction." Paderewski agreed with Sienkiewicz in this, and he agreed, in a measure at least, with Dmowski, who with him cherished the large view, the single objective, of ultimate Polish unity, whatsoever happened and whenever it might happen. But Paderewski's trend of thought regarding the then wholly problematical future of Poland ran counter to, or rather far beyond, that of others.

Two possibilities existed in the conjecture of others: unification of Polish lands achieved with the help of Russia, leading to some measure of autonomy under Russia's suzerainty—that was one; the other, the overthrow of Russia with the implied reunion of Austrian and Russian Poland under some kind of an Austrian-Polish-Hungarian trialism, an expansion of the Dual Monarchy, even though this should mean the sacrifice for all time of the German portion of Poland. But both of these possibilities were to Paderewski only compromises, compromises between the past and the future, the past imposing its already defined political boundaries, the future offering a liberty of imposed and limited autonomy, which at best could be only the shadow of a real liberty. "It should forever remain to Paderewski's credit and glory," as one of his compatriots has said, "that at a time when none of Poland's professional politicians could get away from or rise above either one of these two compromises, he and he alone saw, from the very outset, the inadequacy of both." The inspiration of a Russian compromise lay in the belief in Russia's invincibility. Dmowski believed in that invincibility, Paderewski did not. Since 1905 he had foreseen the collapse of Russia, therefore he saw no hope for Poland, ever, in a Russian compromise. Likewise he foresaw the disintegration of the Austrian Empire; therefore no hope could lie in that direction. The inspiration of the Austrian compromise rose out of the comparative leniency of Austria's rule over her Polish province: but if Jaworski, and Pilsudski with him, fostering the Austrophil sentiment, was moved by the axiom "In politics the first duty is to remember", in that remembering Paderewski saw; as he said later, something akin to the futile act of the Hindu widow throwing herself on her husband's funereal pyre.

These were some of the things that Paderewski was thinking of on the night of his party, the day after Dmowski's hurried departure for Poland. But they were not the things he would talk about when he came downstairs. No one at that time talked of Polish freedom or independence; that was too speculative a thing, too remote a dream to be commonly spoken of, something out of the range of probability. He put his thoughts away, deliberately and gladly; he dismissed them, falling back in his mind on the one resource that he could always invoke, his faith in the spiritual unity of the Polish people, a unity, a community of ideals, which made them one with the Western world. True, from that Western world he had to cancel that Prussian-ridden Germany which even now was showing her hand in the Austro-Serbian fracas. The unexpected return of the Kaiser to Berlin from a yachting cruise in the north, just a few days before, on July 26, following Vienna's ultimatum to Serbia on July 23, presaged trouble. That ultimatum was too deliberate a blow to have been aimed at the Balkan kingdom without prearrangement between Vienna and Berlin and the assurance that Wilhelm would sanction it. As a matter of fact Wilhelm not only sanctioned it but, according to subsequent revelations, demanded it, insisting, in a letter to his Chancellor, July 28, two days after his return to Berlin, on the occupation of Belgrade—in itself a virtual declaration of war on Russia. The imperious Hohenzollern, Paderewski felt, would "make matters boil", as the American Ambassador at Berlin, James W. Gerard, expressed it. But that the Kaiser would deliberately upset the whole world-kettle no one at that moment really believed, in spite of the well-known fact that he had been "boiling" now for six weeks, ever since, on May 20th, the Reichstag had adjourned amid an unprecedented scene, scandalous to the junkers, in which the Social Democrats, refusing to rise to salute the Kaiser's name, had instead booed and hissed it. This open threat to junkerdom had perhaps alarmed as well as angered the Kaiser. That was the kind of threat to drive a militaristic ruler headlong to war as the surest way of crushing domestic opposition and regaining popular sentiment.

But no matter . . . the storm might rumble, yet surely it would pass. At worst it would be localized between Belgrade and Vienna. And there still remained a stable Western world, despite Prussia, a world to which Poland belonged, a world which some day, God willing, though perhaps in the very far future, would welcome her to its free sisterhood. . . . Tonight was his "party night", his friends were gathering to honor him, he was tired of thoughts, he wanted to play. "Sufficient to the day——"

The fun really begins when the "prisoner" is released. Sometimes the guests greet him in the most fantastic of comic dress. One year Wiwulski, sculptor of the Jagiello monument at Cracow, designed an ingenious set of costumes all cut out of colored paper. Another year the costumes were designed by the sculptor Francis Black. This year, in keeping with the Chinese fiesta, the guests appeared in elaborate Oriental garb, the feature of the "show" being a procession of Mandarins and their ladies glittering in colors and tinsel and carrying terrifying paper dragons as they marched through the house, the kind of dragons that Chinese armies used to carry into war to frighten their adversaries.

On the signal, when his escorts released him from his room, Paderewski joined the festivities, the gayest of the crowd. Those terrifying, warlike Chinese dragons *were* a surprise! But they were an omen, too.

XXX

1914: THE UNIVERSAL WAR

PADEREWSKI is in his element with friends around him enjoying themselves. In a long life his relish for people has never left him. Amid the lights and colors of this Chinese *gala* he was the liveliest of all. There was a continuous fusillade of banter, wit, stories, laughter over the comical gifts. The Chinese lanterns that swayed in the breeze off the lake rivalled the white summer moon with a galaxy of multicolored moons. The fireworks were thrillingly beautiful; from the crowded terrace, standing among his friends, he watched the Roman candles and the rockets rise and burst with their soft luminous explosion, flooding the dark gardens with showers of colored stars. With the upturned face and the ecstatic "Ahs!" and "Ohs!" of a small boy he enjoyed himself. . . .

After the buffet supper, music and dancing. Paderewski and Madame Helena lead the dancing couples in the salon. . . . Some of the guests have scattered to the lawn; three or four of them make a small group in the garden . . . yes, they are talking about the war-cloud. They hear the music floating out on the summer air, they go back into the house to join the dancers. . . .

It is past midnight. The music and the dancing are at their height. . . . A servant appears—a telephone call. Mr. Paderewski's secretary goes to answer it. When he returns to the drawing-room he excuses himself to whisper a word to Mr. Paderewski. Paderewski's expression changes. He turns to his guests, his face is grave, there is solemn and intense excitement in his eyes and in his voice. He speaks: "This evening at seven o'clock Germany has proclaimed *kriegsgefahrzustand*—condi-

tion of danger of war." The announcement strikes through the
warm gay room as if a cold blast had blown suddenly through
an open window from the glaciers of Mont Blanc. Paderewski
speaks again: "Germany at the same hour has demanded that
Russia demobilize."

That ended Paderewski's name-day party, in the early hours
of Saturday, August 1. The gay Chinese lanterns of the fiesta
were soon mocked by the flash of headlights from the motor
cars of the departing guests. The sticks of the dead rockets of
the fireworks showed like the bones of dead men in the grass
when a shaft of light cut across the lawn. Those guests residing
in the region began to leave at once; those from outside of
Switzerland left as quickly because, like Dmowski the night before, it was too late. Only a few intimates remained for the
night.

Riond-Bosson slept in trepidation that night. The telephone
scarcely ceased ringing from the moment of that first call till
dawn of Saturday. Among the guests was Mrs. Robert Bliss,
who had come with the Schellings; her husband was the counsellor of the American Embassy at Paris. Mr. Bliss was anxiously 'phoning. In the meantime the Swiss guests were called
home individually, one after another, the Swiss government
having issued an order of immediate mobilization, perplexed
as it was because of its own neutrality, threatened by the stir-
rings across the frontier. Altogether, it was a night of alarm
and fear for all, but to no one did the news, so terrifying and
so startling yet after all so to be expected, come with such
ominous meaning as to Paderewski. A *kriegsgefahrzustand* bul-
letin from the German war office was virtually a declaration of
war. True, war was not yet declared. There still was hope. But
what he termed the "cheek" of Wilhelmstrasse demanding
demobilization of Russia certainly did not look very promising.

The next day, Saturday August 1, was spent in grave suspense. A gloom of fear, indescribable, almost palpable, had settled over the house that had a few hours before been so gay
with life and color. The garden and terrace were stripped of
their festive decorations. So they would have been in any case;

but now, with the air surcharged with a danger too vast to be contemplated, this and every other ordinary act seemed burdened with portent.

Paderewski's thoughts during that day of suspense were not confused, but even his well trained mind moved laboriously at first, ordering the details of the enormous significance of this crisis. Was it to be war, a big war, all of Europe perhaps at war—a world war? If it were to be that, then Poland was in the direst straits that any nation in history had ever been in, caught, absolutely caught, pinned in between the guns, the bayonets, the flying fists, the grappling limbs, of two giants, Germany and Russia. Would it mean death at last to Poland, complete extinction? Could she possibly survive the deadly onrush and death-dealing impact of two huge bodies at grips over her prostrate form?

There was grave and solemn talk that day at Riond-Bosson. And it was not alone of the larger problem, but of the personal: so many that they loved, their own people, over there in Poland—how would they fare if war came? What would happen to them? Could they get out? How could they be helped or saved?

Late that afternoon the final and now inevitable message came. At five o'clock, on the first of August, Germany's order for mobilization had been issued. At ten minutes past seven war was declared on Russia.

If the hours after the first alarm, before the actual declaration of war, were like hours spent waiting for the end of the world, the hours that followed were for Paderewski like hours spent waiting for the Last Judgment and the Resurrection. It was too soon yet for him or for anyone to speculate, to figure out details. The thing was too stupendous, too terrible, too frightening. But somewhere at the base of his consciousness was the conviction that the Mars who now blew the terrible bugle of war was also the Gabriel whose trumpet would summon Poland to life again. He felt this deeply. But as the feeling grew to thought, he was shaken with the terrifying question, "Would Poland rise?" This must be the resurrection of the body as well as the soul; and the body was dismembered and its parts broken with the fever of division. Was the disenthralled spirit still strong enough, still vivifying enough, to draw these parts together and make them rise?

He did not go near his piano that day. The piano was closed; soon it would seem that it was closed forever. Nothing so still in that still house in the months to come as that closed piano. But Paderewski was not idle. He was busier than ever before in his life.

During the next two weeks, while all of Europe, indeed the whole world, still staggered from the shock of the bursting of the black war-cloud that had so long impended, things were happening that made Paderewski and his compatriots, not alone those gathered around him but Poles throughout the world, live in the most painful suspense. The thing that the Swiss had feared, the violation of neutrality, had happened, and it had happened immediately, but it had not happened to them. Belgium was the victim. France had risen to arms, England had risen, the western advance of Germany had begun and had gone on. But Belgium was not the only victim. Another neutrality had been violated, the neutrality of defenceless Poland. There the eastern advance of the Germans had begun and the western advance of the Russians. In war, after its declaration, there is a thing more dreadful than the fire and blood of battle, and that is the moving of hostile armies toward each other. There is a kind of vast fearful silence to the advance of opposing armed forces soon to be locked in conflict. Battle, the opening of gunfire with its roar and crash and fiery shrieking of shells, even with its human cries of pain, comes at last as a kind of nervous relief, breaking the ominous rumble of preparation. To Paderewski and his countrymen, standing helpless on the side-lines, so to speak, watching their country turned into an open field of conflict, these days were days of severest trial. True, the Russian movement westward was slow and practically uncontested; into Austrian Poland the Czar's armies walked without firing a shot. But war can do other things besides destroy with cannonfire . . . and all the time steadily moving eastward was the huge enfiladed Germany that was yet to sweep Poland like a scythe of death.

In the most profound and painful suspense Paderewski watched the opening movements of the war. Then, some two weeks after the declaration of hostilities—to be exact, on August 16—came a turn of events that was of the greatest moment —Russia's proclamation of a re-united Poland, promulgated in the manifesto of the Grand Duke Nicholas Nicolaievitch. Paderewski was elated over this manifesto, and he was elated not because he appreciated the beauty of its noble phrasing, but because, while some Poles scoffed at it and others believed implicitly in it, he saw it rather on middle ground as a com-mital of Russia from which, whatever might happen, she could not withdraw, not even on the plea of having merely made a strategical move. The manifesto was too absolute for that. We have only to read it now to realize what Paderewski's reaction to it was at the time. "Poles!" it said, "the time has come when the dream of your fathers and forefathers will at length be realized." And it went on, in terms glowing with eloquence:

A century and a half ago the living body of Poland was torn in pieces, but her soul has not perished. She lives in the hope that the time will come for the resurrection of the Polish nation and its fraternal union with all Russia. The Russian armies bring you the glad tidings of this union. May the frontiers which have divided the Polish people be united under the sceptre of the Russian Emperor. Under this sceptre Poland will come together, free in faith, in language and in self-government. One thing Russia expects of you; an equal consideration for the rights of those nations with which history has linked you. With open heart, with hand fraternally outstretched, great Russia comes to you. She believes that the sword has not rusted which overthrew the foe of Tannenberg. From the shores of the Pacific Ocean to the Polar Sea the Russian War-hosts are in motion. The morning star of a new life is rising for Poland. May there shine resplendent in the dawn the sign of the Cross, the symbol of the Passion and Resurrection of nations.

Such a proclamation, issued at such a time, in the midst of terror, confusion and suspense, was well designed to appeal to Polish feeling, well calculated to raise hopes for the future. What that future was to bring—the downfall of the Russia which now promised freedom to Poland—was of course hidden to all men. In the meantime the devastation of Poland continued. Sienkiewicz, another Pole as world-famous for his writings, especially his "Quo Vadis?", as Paderewski was famous for his music, made a statement a few months later, in 1915, which gives us a picture of the almost unbelievable situation into which Poland found herself plunged. "She has nothing to do with the war," he said. "Conquered and partitioned, she is not one of the belligerent nations, and yet a million and a half of her sons are fighting fratricidal battles in the armies of three different warring states. Our country is made the cockpit of the battles of Europe and is devastated from end to end. Three-quarters of a million of our children are fighting in the Russian army, and another three-quarters of a million are bearing arms for Germany or Austria. Think what this means. When the order for a cavalry or a bayonet charge is given, hordes of soldiers rush on each other, and when they get to striking distance and commence cutting one another down they find that the language in which they are uttering their imprecations is the common national tongue—Polish! It frequently happens that when the Red Cross go out to collect the wounded from a battlefield they lift from a heap one man in German uniform, another in Austrian and a third in Russian, and discover that they are all—Poles!"

This was Poland's military situation, tragic and terrible. But worse still, the war, in Paderewski's own words, was "sweeping away every sign of civilization, destroying dwellings, devastating fields, gardens and forests, starving and exterminating human beings and animals alike. . . . In the desolated area, as large as the States of New York, Pennsylvania and New Jersey, more than 200 towns and 11,500 villages have been completely ruined. Losses to date in property destroyed and in agricultural, industrial, and commercial production paralyzed, amount to four billion dollars. The horrors of the gigantic struggle have overwhelmed more than eighteen million inhabitants, including nearly two million Jews. Fully eleven millions of helpless women and children, peasants, workmen, the very essence and strength of the nation, have been driven into the open. Thousands are hiding among ruins, in woods or in hollows, subsisting on roots and the bark of trees. Hundreds of thousands of once prosperous families are helpless, hungry, sick and succumbing." "Children raise their fleshless arms," said Sienkiewicz, "and cry to their mothers for bread, but the Polish mother has nothing to give them—nothing but her tears."

Within a few months of that first alarm in the night at Paderewski's home, of the eighty thousand square miles of Russian Poland alone, over which the German and Austrian armies passed back and forth four, five and six times, sixty-three thousand square miles had been left waste. More than two million cattle and over a million horses had been taken from the peasants; not a handful of grain, not a drop of milk, not a scrap of meat was left. There was no food. Of the ten million inhabitants of the occupied area four millions were menaced by death from famine. Over four hundred thousand workmen had been taken from their work. Agriculture and industry were demolished. This was the condition in Russian Poland, overrun by the German and Austrian armies.

In Austrian Poland the same conditions existed, the only difference being that here it was the Russian armies that over-ran the country. Of the total area of fifty thousand square miles, all but five thousand, around the city of Cracow, were in Russian possession. Two million head of cattle, nine hundred thousand horses, had been taken, the entire grain supply was gone. This region, rich in natural resources, was like a desert. More than a million of its inhabitants had fled, destitute.

It was to cope with this situation that Paderewski immediately busied himself at Riond-Bosson, from that first day of August when war was declared. If the Poles in tripartite Poland could do nothing but submit to conscription, he, outside the fiery ring of conflict, could and did find things to be done. Above all, something must be done for the Polish noncombatants now being ground under the spiked wheels of war. Some kind of relief organization must be effected. He had gone to work at once making plans, and in this, even misfortune was serving him, for the sudden declaration of war had left stranded in Switzerland a number of his compatriots who were thus ready at hand for consultation. From that time, in fact, Riond-Bosson become a kind of Polish refugee-camp, and for four years following it remained so. The house was filled with people; never less than fifteen, sometimes twenty, sat daily at Paderewski's dining table, often forty. Sunday afternoon gatherings, with scores assembled from all that part of Switzerland, became a regular institution. Paderewski, with Madame Helena and Madame Antonina at his side, was host to all.

Sienkiewicz was in Switzerland at this time, the most eminent of Paderewski's refugee compatriots. He was at Vevey, a short distance from Morges. Engaged when war broke out in the writing of a new novel, "The Legions", a story of the Napoleonic campaigns, he had managed to escape into Switzerland. There indeed he spent the remainder of his days, dying in the service of his country. As Paderewski gave up his piano, Sienkiewicz gave up his pen. "I die too soon," he said. "I shall not see Poland free." It was with Sienkiewicz as its head that Paderewski's relief committee was organized.

The problem which Paderewski and his countrymen faced in their determination to do something for Poland was one of almost insuperable difficulties. In the large view this problem had three aspects, the military, the social, and the political. Of the military, nothing could now be said; it was a *fait accompli*. The Poles, under the conscription of three alien governments, were, as Sienkiewicz's words have made clear, caught and helpless. As Paderewski put it, "We were compelled to fight each other, to kill each other; for the Poles, enlisted by force in three opposing armies, every battle was a fratricidal combat." The political phase, in Paderewski's opinion, was simply one that must be made ready for; its turn would come when the conflict ceased, although never for a moment might it be forgotten. The single and immediate problem, then, was the relief of the people; how to find food, shelter, clothing, medicine, for them. From the night of his name-day party at

Riond-Bosson on the last day of July, 1914, until on into 1915, as steadily as he had once worked at his piano, he worked now preparing himself for the task of raising funds to save his people.

It was not an easy task. The activities of the relief committee at Vevey, which the Poles began to call "the Polish capital", engaged all his forces of ingenuity and command. Gathered there on the neutral soil of Switzerland were numbers of Poles who represented the divergent political views of their home people. The difficulty was to get them to forget their differences, intensified in the heat of crisis, and make them concentrate on the one need of the moment, relief. Many a time Paderewski had to battle valiantly to make his larger view prevail, but little by little, with clear-sighted vision and unshakable confidence, he advanced his leadership. The Vevey relief committee was, in fact, the first testing ground of Paderewski's power as a national leader. He prevailed there; he steadily widened the area of his influence; in the end he prevailed in America, in England, at Paris, throughout the world. A remark made later by Dmowski, himself a strong man, who it will be remembered did not in all things agree with him, reveals Paderewski's unique power. "You cannot think as highly of my achievements as I do myself," Dmowski said to one of Paderewski's friends, "but after all I am merely one man in a row. Paderewski does not belong to any row. He stands alone with his genius."

He stood more alone now than even he guessed. That the leader, no matter how loyally supported, must always stand alone, he was to learn soon enough. But in Paderewski's case there was a special aloneness, for suddenly he had come to a turning point in his life and the new course that he faced led him away from everything that he had known, everything that had made up his life heretofore. His life had been the life of music, of the artist. Throughout that life he had been, it is true, an active patriot. The laurels of his achievements one by one had always been laid on the altar of motherland; and in recent years he had engaged himself openly on occasion in nationalistic affairs. Nevertheless his double-motivated career had run not so much on parallel as on conjointed lines, the one, Art, superimposed so heavily over the other that to the unobservant eye it obliterated the other. Yet all the time the other, Patriotism, had been the base-line. Now that base-line turned completely, led in an entirely new direction. He did not hesitate to follow it, uncertain though it might be, undefined in the confusion of this crisis, dangerous in its course and termination. He was no longer to be the musician, even though he still was to use his music for a time to further his new occupation. *"La patrie avant tout, l'art ensuite"* he had said so many times . . . and now it had become literally true.

But Paderewski the artist was nothing if not practical-minded. He had definite views about the place of art in life. "Which do you consider the greater," his American manager Engles once asked him, "the greatest artist or the greatest statesman?" "The greatest statesman," he answered unhesitatingly. "Of course you understand that I do not speak of all those who are called statesmen, but who are really nothing but maneuvering politicians. They are an entirely different subject. I speak of that man of state whose courage, morality and wisdom open for humanity a greater path of destiny; of those rare spirits which, voicing the innermost hopes and visions of the race, mold the future and hold up the torch for life." This is practical enough, assuredly; and yet it is the idealist speaking after all, the idealist who asks, "Are they not, the true statesmen, the greatest artists of all? And shall not all the others, great and small, spend their lives in interpreting directly or indirectly their conceptions?"

It was not, sad to say, the conceptions of statesmen that were now to preoccupy the mind of Paderewski, but the intrigues and machinations of some of the greatest and worst of the world's maneuvering politicians, the criminals of power who had plunged the world into a chaos of blood and fire, of ruin and starvation. It was them he had to cope with, against the evil consequences of their act that he had to plan and reshape his future.

By early January, 1915, affairs at Vevey were well organized, welfare work was launched, the political problem was in hand with couriers keeping the committee in constant touch with national leaders abroad. By this time too the important decision had been made that Paderewski must go to America. How thoroughly he prepared himself for his journey we learn from an interesting note made by Henryk Opienski who was present at Morges at this time. Master of English as Paderewski was, he was not satisfied. In the midst of the multifarious duties of his committee work he engaged a tutor, and twice a week he spent regular hours relearning the English language so that he would have fluent perfection in it. In January he and Madame Paderewska left Morges. To his sister he gave charge of Riond-Bosson to carry on the work of refugee hospitality.

In Paris Paderewski stopped to consult with the Polish National Committee there. In London he conferred with British leaders, Balfour, Asquith, Gooch, Chesterton, Wickham Steed, Belloc, others. He organized a relief committee, his British friends, headed by Laurence Alma-Tadema, daughter of the artist who had made his portrait fifteen years before, and such Polish leaders as Count Ladislas Sobanski and Kasimir Proszynski, rallying around him. With such personages as Father Bernard Vaughan, S.J., John Buchan, the Right Honorable Charles B. Stuart Wortley, M.P., in addition to those already mentioned, backing or serving on this committee, substantial and phenomenally rapid achievement resulted. Paderewski's plea published in *The Times*, and the work of this committee, brought in something like £50,000 within four months' time. A propaganda campaign was also launched, with August Zaleski, later to be one of Poland's Foreign Ministers, Dr. Rajchman, J. H. Harley and J. C. Witenberg, directing it and administering its publications.

In official government circles in London, however, he found his welcome as leader of his people, instead of as musician, not unlike the first welcome the London critics had given him twenty-five years earlier as an artist—skeptical. He had won the critics then. He must win the politicians and statesmen now. It was the politicians he feared. In London one day, at a luncheon of prominent men, he had his first encounter with Lloyd George, the wily Welsh politician whom he was to know better when peace had been declared. Paderewski did not say so, but in the light of later events we can imagine him in his mind classifying Lloyd George as "politician", over against his classic definition of "statesman". Lloyd George, he soon discovered, was not like Woodrow Wilson, whom Paderewski once described as a true statesman, "not a mind bound by seven and a half octaves." At this first London meeting Lloyd George seemed already bent on baiting the Polish leader. "Russia," he warned Paderewski, "is a steam-roller which will flatten all resistance and roll triumphantly into Berlin."

Lloyd George did not know Russia. Paderewski did. "Russia," he admitted later, recalling the early days of the war, "seemed then to stand firmly on her feet of clay. The tremors of revolution had not yet shattered the solid and once so mighty throne of the Romanoffs. The immense territory with its hundreds of races, of languages, of creeds, seemingly well cemented, was in all appearances still a tremendously powerful empire. Though no more a steam-roller, as it had been expected to be, it had millions of soldiers, abundance of resources and plenty of money."

What he said now, in 1915, to Lloyd George was: "The ball-bearings of that steam-roller are of wood, and its chauffeurs hail from Germany."

Having organized branches of the Polish Relief Committee at Paris and London, Paderewski sailed for America.

XXXI

1915–1918: THE STRUGGLE IN AMERICA—I

PADEREWSKI crossing the Atlantic early in 1915 on his new
mission to America, no longer the artist journeying to fill concert engagements, but the spokesman of a wronged and endangered nation, was by this time a seasoned sailor. He had already crossed the ocean back and forth some thirty times since
that first memorable journey in 1891. He had come then to a
new and unexplored world wondering how he would be received by its people and its critics. He had come many times
since, always with a high heart. He approached America now
as if returning home, yet his venture was so new and so strange
a one that he could not help but fear the outcome. He spent
hours in his stateroom preparing for the work ahead of him;
he spent other hours pacing the deck at night pondering his
task. He had no delusions. He knew that his way would be
beset with difficulties.

Waldo Frank, recalling those days of Paderewski's war-
time return to New York, gives us a picture: "In those early
days ere America came in, one saw him of an afternoon, walking in Central Park. Already the millions of Poles had made
him their leader. He strode silent between gesticulant friends.
His hands were clasped behind his back. His hair was still the
music-lion's mane. Upon it, incongruous, was a derby hat.
Why did the hat seem to mock the magnificent hair?"

Perhaps for the same reason that Clemenceau exclaimed over
Paderewski's changing from the world's premier musician to a
mere premier, "What a come down!" Or for the same reason
that another eminent publicist cried out later, on hearing of
Paderewski's leaving politics and returning to the piano, "What

a drop!" Impossible, apparently, for the world to reconcile brains and art or to accept the fact that Paderewski's music-mane and the derby hat of everyday business properly belonged together. "The world was astounded," said Walter Damrosch, "that a musician who had spent his public life for over thirty years in piano recitals and composition should demonstrate such remarkable gifts of statesmanship." But, as Mr. Damrosch adds, "the fact remains, he had prepared himself."

The days following his return to America were crowded with matter-of-the-hat, with practical business. Vast and confusing as the problem of the war had been, seen in its first impact at home in Morges, here in the then neutral America it took on new and bewildering dimensions. To the American people the war was still only a European war. At that it was bad enough, for the German outrage of Belgium and the attack on France had stirred deep feeling in the United States. But just because the most suddenly dramatic action of the whole horrible conflict had taken place in Belgium and France, the American people knew practically nothing of the war beyond the Western front. They had no conception of the immeasurable injury and suffering put on the peoples of the Eastern front, and it seemed impossible for a long time to get them to grasp the fact that Poland was as much a non-combatant and an invaded country as Belgium. Paderewski's task was to tell them these things, to make them see what he knew and feel what he felt.

The neutrality of the United States caused his situation to be a delicate one. He had made up his mind that he must come to America on this mission solely as an agent of relief. He represented no state, no government, but only the Polish people, outraged just as the Belgian people were. As a matter of fact, the nonexistence at that moment of a Polish state was an advantage to him in neutral America; it made it possible for him to come. In France and England it had been a disadvantage, because those countries were belligerents and Poland was still in part a Russian dominion, and Russia was allied with the French and the English against Germany. While it was easy enough for

PADEREWSKI AND HIS WIFE

From a war-time photograph taken by Hartsook Studios.

the French to appreciate Poland's situation as a noncombatant victim of the war, and easier for the English than for the Americans to comprehend this, there was at times, nevertheless, misunderstanding of the most painful kind, as when Lloyd George added to the bitterness of Poland's inhuman plight the galling sting of blame. With ridicule and raillery the British Prime Minister in one of his speeches attacked the Poles for "not knowing any better than to fight each other"! He could see the Czechs in their simplified position adroitly freeing themselves from the Austrian yoke, but of the situation of the Poles he betrayed an ignorance unpardonable in the public man whose utterances help to mold public opinion.

There was already a Polish national organization at Warsaw, established by Dmowski after his narrow escape from Morges on July 30, 1914, but in the complex situation of the moment this was of no advantage to Paderewski in America. Dmowski's political organization, for want of any other opportunity to advance the Polish cause, was still operating under the Russian régime. Thus for the time being Russian Poland was one of the Allies along with Russia that ruled her. But Paderewski must speak in America not only for the war-ravaged Polish masses, but eventually he must speak for a Polish state *in limine* if not *de jure*. And it was not only to a neutral America that he must speak, but to an America, as he discovered when he came in 1915, hopelessly confused and divided in sympathy. There was a strong pro-Allies feeling; but also, in spite of the Belgian outrage, there was also a strong pro-German sentiment. This was due to two causes: the large German population of America, and the fact that all the German news of the war came from the Over-Seas and the Trans-Oceanic press services, both controlled by the Krupp gun syndicate. What Paderewski had to tell the American people was in effect an indictment of both Germany and of the Allies, since both were wrecking Poland, the Allies in the person of Russia, and Germany in her own person.

Paderewski had therefore to proceed carefully, and all the more carefully since he must proceed with an eye to the future;

not only to the future of Poland as a state but to the future belligerency of America. Intimately acquainted with the disposition of Prussian motive and intrigue, he felt certain that America could not remain permanently neutral, would in the end be drawn into the conflict. As a matter of fact it may be said that in 1915 Paderewski knew more about the war, its inner momentum and its inevitable spread and growth, than any other man in America excepting perhaps President Wilson's adviser, Colonel Edward M. House. As Colonel House himself has written, "Sensing in advance of others of his kind that America would play the leading part before the world tragedy closed, it was here that he put forth his greatest endeavors; and it was here that he gathered his compatriots and planned a campaign which gave to the Poles freedom." But in planning that campaign he had to keep in mind at all times the officially neutral position of the United States.

Briefly, Paderewski's task in America was this: to acquaint the American people with Poland's distressful situation in order to get food for the starving; to rouse popular American interest in Poland's political problem and her hopes for the future; to open the way toward official governmental help for the solution of that problem; to unify Polish political sentiment. And all the time he must keep in trim for the piano, since it was his name as artist that was the magnet attracting the people to him.

If, as he knew so well, the exacting demands of professional life make mind and body wish at times to turn from their obligations, what he faced now, this triple task, of relief, politics, and music, was enough to appall him, to fatigue him even before he began. The prospect was discouraging. He realized now as he never had before that "the ultimate necessity is the summoning of mind and will to do their duty." More than that, as we know when we picture him walking in Central Park "between gesticulant friends", he knew that he was alone, that he must lead, that there was no one else. There must be some one man upon whom rested the responsibility of always speaking the final word and of acting upon it. And every word must be searched, weighed, measured. Incredible that he was the man. And yet, "already the millions of Poles had made him their leader."

Literally, as we shall see, this was not true. He was not yet, nor for some time was he to be, the acknowledged leader of all the Poles, and no one realized this better than he, as no one in the world knew better than he the grave divisions of Polish thought, the fruit of the Partitions which had almost succeeded in creating three Polands where once there had been one. But if the bulk of the American citizenry was so sharply divided on the war, it was not surprising that American Poles, reflecting the diverse sentiments of the Old World, should also lack unity of opinion.

Thus it was against heavy odds and a complexity of obstacles that Paderewski began his relief work in America. Happily, the ground was in part prepared for him. His old friend Madame Marcella Sembrich, of operatic fame, she who had so often joyously participated in the name-day festivities at Riond-Bosson, had already founded the American-Polish Relief Committee in New York City; in Chicago the Polish National Alliance had started a relief organization: and there was the Alliance of Polish Socialists, basically a political organization affiliated with the Socialist party in Poland and a partisan to the Pilsudski leadership in the home country. Paderewski found these societies functioning on his arrival in America. His part was not only to unify, harmonize, and coördinate their work, but to win the widest popular support for it from the American public as a whole. He had many helpers, an army of them, quickly organized into an active corps; some of them went far with him in the work, not the least among these being Michael Kwapiszewski, later to be *Chargé d'Affaires* and subsequently Counsellor at the Polish Legation in Washington under Paderewski's premiership.

"I have to speak about a country which is not yours, in a language which is not mine". It was with these words, eloquent in their simplicity, that he began his appeal to the American people early in 1915, when he opened the most unique tour of his career at San Francisco. It was with much inner misgiving that he appeared for the first time in the rôle of "beggar", as he called it. He was more nervous than ever he had been at the opening of a first recital in a new country. Certainly America was not a new country, it was one of his home-countries; but what would the American people think of him, how would they take him, in his extraordinary departure from his ordinary course? So much depended on the first trial. He put as much care into the preparation of his speech as if he were composing a concerto.

When Paderewski had left Morges in January to represent the Polish Relief Committee in America, no one, not even himself with all his knowledge of Europe and its war problems, dreamed that he would be gone from his home for over five years. Four of these years he spent in America, going up and down the country, visiting every State in the Union, playing and speaking, turning the golden notes of his music and the silver notes of his eloquence into food for his starving people, milk for babies, clothing for the naked. Into the coffers he himself poured all that he possessed; so much, in fact, that before the long strain was finally over his fortune was gone. The prewar securities which he had purchased were now either worthless or reduced to the minimum; one item of $380,000, paid for at above par, declined over two-thirds in value, dropping the first year to 32.

His addresses on behalf of his country created such an impression that they were talked of almost as much as his music. He spoke hundreds of times; many thousands of people heard him. Gutzon Borglum, the American sculptor, describes him thus as he heard him at Carnegie Hall in New York City:

"The representatives of the mid-European people had gathered there under the chairmanship of the Foreign Relations Committee of our Senate. Masaryk was to speak, also Paderewski. Masaryk had become the *de facto* president of the Czechoslovakians, recognized as a belligerent power by our government. Paderewski spoke just before Masaryk. He stood about five feet eight inches, solidly on his heels. He opened

with the usual acknowledgments of applause that always ac-
claims the artist. Then he began, much as he plays, though I
suppose few people thought of this. He massed his facts, built
up a background against which he placed the points that he
was to emphasize. He touched historically upon the sufferings
of his people; he referred to the great forces lying to the east
and the great forces lying to the west, and how they had fought
to possess Poland and how they had torn her to pieces; he told
how she had been invaded and quartered and how she had
suffered. He spoke little in praise of his own people. The laurels he placed on the brows of his brothers in the south, the
Czechoslovakians. He dwelt definitely upon them and recounted in detail the qualities that had brought them success.
He touched upon their wanderings, their sufferings, and how
they, too, had been all but extinguished as a people.

"His manner was simple and free from gesture, except an
occasional lifting of a hand, in a kind of plea or benediction,
or both. The management of his voice astonished me. Like
Demosthenes he had labored for months to free himself from
a slight accent and possibly a slight lisp. He had corrected both,
he told me with pride, and also in pride of how he had labored
for this result, 'because,' he said, 'I must face the councils of
Europe if I am to carry this fight to a finish.' As his nimble
fingers move up and down the keyboard, so ran his nimble
mind up and down the difficult and troubled frontiers of the
Russian and Teutonic peoples. . . . I felt that I was listening
to a great product of art, a gifted orator, telling the epic of a
people. By a curious magic of his personality, he had produced
a hush in that great hall and the audience listened with an attention that admitted no applause. I have heard nearly all the
great speakers of our time except Gladstone. I have heard none
that seemed to have the power that Paderewski exhibited that
day. He made me think of the great Greeks, and everybody
felt as I did. For forty minutes, without a halt, his fine voice
rolled on through that hall and filled it. One could have heard
a pin drop until he concluded, and then the auditorium rose in
unrestrained homage.

"Finally, when the applause had subsided, Masaryk stepped to the front. He was the speaker of the day and his oration was supposed to close the afternoon. Silent, pale, he looked at the chairman of the Foreign Relations Committee, at the audience, at Paderewski. Then he spoke: 'I know not what to say. I, too, have been carried away by the master speech of Poland's great leader and liberator. I came here intending to deliver these notes,' and he shook the written sheets he carried in his hand, 'but they are of no use now. As I sat and listened to the wonderful things Paderewski said I could not understand how he who had spent his life in the seclusion of his art could do this. Then it came to me. It is because he is a great artist that he can understand and know these things.' "

"Well do I remember that address," Samuel Vauclain, head of the American-Polish Chamber of Commerce, and father of the Kosciuszko Foundation,* said ten years later. "None was ever made like it. It is a question whether any will ever be made like it." It was thus that his speech affected American hearers. Those of Polish blood thrilled to another note: "It was the first plea I had ever heard freely spoken for Polish liberty," said Sigismond Ivanowski the painter. A great music critic, Richard Aldrich, heard him thus: "He took a unique part in the history of art . . . as an eloquent pleader for the rights of his native land in a speech of impeccable and burningly eloquent English."

It was necessary that he should be eloquent. It will be noted that he was likewise practical. In the emotional reaction of the time to the horrors of war, anyone, an artist above all, might have been excused for seeing only the horror and not beyond it. "It is not," he said, "the sight of the dead as they lie there. It is not even the cry of the wounded boys calling for their mothers—for there are thousands of mere boys among the wounded and often there is no one to do anything for them. No—the concentrated horror of it all is in the suffering, phys-

---

* The Kosciuszko Foundation, of the National Council of which Mr. Paderewski is a member, is an organization for memorial scholarships and the promotion of intellectual and cultural relations between Poland and the United States.

ical and mental, of these lonely, starving mothers, maddened by terror and pain, driven hither and thither in what was once the homeland—now charred and ruined. On them the hell-hail of war's torture never ceases to fall. The picture is too awful to paint." But Paderewski's balanced mind, shaken though it was by the cataclysmic ruin of his people, struck through the horror of the picture, through the smoke and blood of the moment, to the future; he saw more than the present need, more than the grain fields of Poland devastated. He saw them replanted. He was a farmer as well as a statesman. He asked not only for bread and that at once, but for seed for the Polish farmers, that there might be crops and bread in the future. "Thousands must die," he said. "Help cannot reach them in time. But the nucleus of a continuing Poland—a Poland, which, although now politically non-existent, has never ceased to live as a national spirit—we hope to save, we must save."

He had need to be eloquent especially on the political score. The work of more than a century of prejudiced misinformation about Poland had borne heavy fruit. Paderewski had nothing to overcome to open the hearts of the American people when he cried, "Is there anything more true than human pain? Is there anything more sincere than the cry for help from those who suffer? Only a great wave of mankind's pity can surmount an immense wave of human misery. In the name of Christian charity, in the name of common humanity give me some bread for the Polish women and children, some seed for the Polish farmers!" There was no resistance to this plea. But he had much to overcome to make Americans appreciate Poland's right to self-government. Not all were as ready as the artist Borglum to hear in his words the epic of a great people. "Official and officious historians of nations and governments, not precisely disinterested in the case," Paderewski said, "have been and still are writing profusely about Poland's inability to govern herself, about our dissensions, our anarchy. This distinctly immoral work of poisoning public opinion has been done for so long, so thoroughly and so effectively, that even a few of our own writers, brought up in Poland, but in foreign language and in foreign spirit, adopted the monstrous idea that our country's downfall was solely due to the people's own fault.

"Dissensions, anarchy, inability of governing ourselves! How do these things look in the light of positive historical facts? Our Statute of Wislica, established in 1347, was chronologically the first complete code of Christian Europe. In 1413 Poland concluded a political union with Lithuania. This act of free union proclaiming for the first time in history the brotherhood of nations, this act of union confirmed by a document of almost evangelical beauty, which lasted undisturbed till the very end of our independence, is one of the most glorious achievements not only of Poland but of humanity.

"Already in the fifteenth century a self-governing country, Poland became, in 1573, a regular republic, with kings elected. In 1430, consequently 259 years before the habeas corpus of England, and 359 years before the declaration of Human Rights in France, Poland established her famous law 'No man shall be detained unless legally convicted.' Our broad, liberal Constitution of 1791 preceded by 57 years the Constitution of Germany and Austria, and by 114 years the so-called Constitution of Russia. And all these momentous reforms, all these radical changes, unlike other countries, were accomplished without revolution, without any bloodshed, without the loss of one single human life. Does it prove our dissensions; does it prove our anarchy; does it prove our inability of governing ourselves?"

Facts such as these, affirmed with such eloquence, and confirmed before the eyes of audiences by the known record and acknowledged genius of the man who spoke, gradually opened the eyes of the American public. But they roused antagonism too; for here a new obstacle arose for him to overcome. Just as in music-criticism prejudice had entered, so now racial animosity showed itself, and the partisanship of war in this country was not beneath exploiting such animosity. When Paderewski proclaimed the fact that "Ever since the beginning of her political existence Poland has been a safe refuge for all oppressed people, a shelter for all persecuted religions and opinions"; when he reminded his hearers of the fact that "The persecuted Jews came to Poland from Germany in the eleventh century, and the first charter granting them the right of inhabiting Polish cities was issued by our King Ladislaus Herman from the city of Kalisch in 1096;" when he stated these facts, prejudice answered openly.

This prejudice was not a new thing. The year previous, during his American season of 1913-1914, there had been a dramatic moment in Paderewski's life when an accusation had been made that he was using money earned at his recitals for propaganda against the Jews in Poland. The accusation took a specific form: it charged him with having contributed $20,000 to the Polish newspaper *Dwa Grosze*, said to be devoted to anti-Jewish propaganda. Handbills, signed by Jewish associations, urging a boycott of Paderewski, threats of injury and even of death, followed. In several cities in which he appeared that year it had been necessary to guard the doors of the recital halls with detectives.

The canard was a ridiculous one on the face of it and was so regarded by all who knew Paderewski. Nevertheless it gained such notoriety if not credence that finally, to put an end to the talk, Paderewski, after as dignified a silence as any man could keep, went before a notary in San Francisco and took public oath that he not only had not done the particular thing of which he was accused, but that never had he contributed any money whatsoever to the newspaper in question or to any other organ of race prejudice.

Now, in spite of this, during these years of public appeal for the destitute in Poland from 1915 to 1918, more than one rumor of this kind was revived. Before his political career was closed, this strange prejudice, against a man renowned for his open mind and his total lack of prejudice, was to become a serious obstacle in his work, and it was to continue even after he had withdrawn from politics.* It did not avail that many of

---

* I had a personal experience with this prejudice when one reputable American publishing house offered to publish my book "The New Poland" on condition that I delete its

Paderewski's closest friends were Jews; it did not matter, for instance, that to a Jew had been awarded one of the music prizes he had established in Poland and another to a Jew in America. Nothing mattered, as nothing ever does matter when prejudice is based on religious feeling. It went hard with Paderewski, however, to be obliged to meet this kind of prejudice in "fair-minded America."

Sometimes there were recompenses for this kind of attack. There were Jewish men of eminence who were as disgusted as was everyone else with propaganda of this sort, men who would never dream of accusing Paderewski of anti-Semitic feelings; there were even Jews who claimed him as one of their own! An amusing happening occurred in New York City, one which incidentally showed Paderewski's gift for gracefully meeting what might have been an embarrassing situation. At an elaborate function given in his honor he was introduced to the company as a Polish Jew. When Paderewski rose to acknowledge the many complimentary things said of him by the toastmaster of the evening, he corrected this statement in characteristic manner. "I must tell you the truth—I am not a Polish Jew. But I have so many good Jewish friends that perhaps I might very well be called a Jewish Pole."

By the end of 1915 the first "begging" tour was completed. But the war was still going on, it had only begun, and the destitution of Poland was increasing to almost unbelievable proportions. In May, 1915, what has been called "the greatest military concentration that the world has even seen" had taken place on Polish soil, in the German drive against Russia and the Russian evacuation, with the result that millions of buildings were razed and many more millions of Polish peasants were scattered from their homes, driven into Russia and beyond, as far east as Armenia and the Caucasus. In this monstrous movement of men and arms the Russians had systematically laid the land waste in order to impede the German

chapter on Paderewski, while two others, equally reputable, mysteriously but perhaps conveniently "lost" the manuscript within a few weeks of each other.

advance, burning houses, stables, barns, haystacks, grain, until all Poland was a vast conflagration. On the Russians' heels the Germans completed the devastation. The German attitude was cynical. "Naturally we continued to make use of the country for the prosecution of the war," Ludendorff remarked later in his *Own Story*. When the Allies pleaded with their enemies for the proper administration of relief sent into Poland, the Germans refused and justified their refusal by stating that foreign relief was not necessary; this in spite of the fact that famine and misery in Poland had, in February 1915, moved even certain German leaders to pity, Prince Hatzfelt organizing a collection of funds for the destitute. At this time, as a matter of fact, not only America through Paderewski's activities, but the entire civilized world, was stirred to commiseration by the suffering of the Poles. From Rome Pope Benedict, sending a gift of twenty-five thousand crowns "with words of encouragement and hope", invited the Polish episcopate to appeal to all Christendom for moral and material help in "the lamentable situation."

This fearful catastrophe had a double effect on Paderewski's work in America. It not only increased the pressure for relief funds but it emphasized more than ever Poland's political misfortune. With Russia driven out of Poland, Poland was now helplessly in German hands. At the moment there might have been said to be an advantage in this: Poland was in a sense freed, momentarily at least, from the Russian yoke, and coming now wholly under the German yoke she could lay a new claim to Allied sympathy. The way was clearer now for the Allies to pledge Poland's freedom, at least her freedom from the German incubus. The question in Paderewski's mind however was, would the Powers wish to deliver Poland back to Russia, still their ally, when they had freed her from Germany? He must work against any such eventuality as that. "That Poland should have turned first against [Russia] the ally of the Western Powers, to whose moral support she had been looking for so many years," Joseph Conrad wrote, "is not a greater monstrosity than that alliance with Russia which had been entered into by Eng-

land and France." One of Paderewski's tasks was to make the
Allies see this. To this end, with the greatest foresight, he bent
every effort at this time to the winning of public opinion in
America toward a clearer view of Poland's situation, foreseeing
that American opinion would tip the balance when the final issue
came. He continued to raise funds, he extended more widely
than ever his field of speaking, but more and more he moved
along the line of political effort. He was tireless in searching
out opportunities to set the Polish problem before the people,
not alone at benefit recitals to large popular audiences attracted
primarily by his music, but to smaller groups, universities,
clubs, chambers of commerce, army cantonments. He left nothing overlooked. To spread the good name of Poland everywhere, to build up a body of public sentiment in the press,
among the people at every turn; in short to make the Polish
Question a World Question, this was his aim. He was preparing
for his attack on Washington which he knew must be made as
soon as America, already tried beyond endurance by German
impudence, joined the belligerents.

The social contacts that his career as artist had made in past
years became very valuable to his cause. Such men as former
President Taft, Thomas A. Edison, Frank A. Vanderlip, Her-
bert L. Satterlee, James M. Beck, Edward Bok, Cyrus Curtis,
Joseph Choate, Joseph Leiter, Melville Stone; eminent
churchmen such as Cardinal Gibbons, Bishop Wilson, Cardinal
Farley (in the death of Cardinal Farley, whose funeral he attended in New York, he lost a generous friend), Cardinal
O'Connell; prominent women such as Miss Anne Morgan,
Mrs. John Wanamaker, Mrs. Richard Watson Gilder and a
score of others;—all these rallied to his aid and served on his
Polish Victims' Relief Fund. His stepson, W. O. Gorski, acted
as secretary. Every contact that he had made in the past, every
kindness that he had done, his whole public life in America for
a quarter century, gave him a harvest of good will. Paderewski's welcome back to America in the rôle of "Polish beggar" is
as good a demonstration as can be imagined of how a man's past

will serve him. His unstained record, his integrity, were his best weapons in his fight for his country.

His capacity for administration came into action. He organized his Relief Fund; he then organized agencies in various cities throughout the country; he organized the presidents of these agencies into a body. He built up a smooth-running machine. "I don't know Paderewski well," said Borglum one day to Franklin K. Lane, Secretary of the Interior in Wilson's cabinet, when they were discussing the phenomenal activities of the Polish leader; "still I believe he is capable of rebuilding Poland—yes, of rebuilding Europe if the opportunity offered and the occasion demanded it of him." "Isn't he a wonder!" Lane answered. "He is the outstanding phenomenon of the war. He is the great surprise to all of us. The other characters are political or military. He alone represents the best in civilization's revolt against threatened imperialism that would seize the world and enslave us. He represents the culture of Occidental Europe, and, curiously enough, he is the leader of a great nation that has been dismembered for more than a century and divided among the three great empires, east, south and west, that dominate the continent. Artists always think in big terms. But there is a great practical side to the job of nation building. Paderewski has that also. That's why he is succeeding. He will become the liberator of modern Poland. Think of it—this artist."

Borglum took Lane up on the word "artist." "Yes," he replied, "but being an artist makes it logical, even makes it easy. One of these days you people will realize that the imagination and disinterestedness of the artist are powerful factors in the building of a state. The trouble with men generally in politics is that they are recruited almost wholly from the legal or commercial ranks and are mainly occupied with material values, and that not one per cent of our statesmen in public life determine in their careers to effect the happiness and the mental or social development of their community when they take up the duties of state."

Paderewski and Borglum liked to discuss this question of the artist in political history, often with a delighted listener in the person of Ivanowski, Paderewski's aide, who also had abandoned everything to serve Poland. "I have recently read," Borglum told Paderewski one day, "that Napoleon acknowledged that if he had taken Fulton's suggestions about the steamboat he would never have gone to St. Helena, but would have remained the master of Europe. Fulton was an artist, and it was Da Vinci who developed the plane, to which Wilbur Wright later added a gasoline engine."

It would not be long before Paderewski, on a memorable occasion, would recall those words about planes and gasoline engines.

XXXII

1915–1918: THE STRUGGLE IN AMERICA—II

IT WAS not all smooth running. Two major obstacles were ever present: the division among the Poles; the reluctance of American government officials to forget him as an artist and accept him as a statesman. The latter difficulty was emphasized by the former. American officials with the best disposition in the world could hardly be expected, as he himself felt, to accept Paderewski as the Polish leader while all of his own people did not.

"The war in Europe has done a very natural thing in America," President Wilson remarked in his Memorial Day address at Arlington in 1916. "It has stirred the memories of men drawn from many of the belligerent stocks. It has renewed in them a national feeling which had grown faint under the soothing influence of peace, but which now flares up when it looks as if nation had challenged nation to a final reckoning, and they remember the nations from which they were sprung and know that they are in this life-and-death grapple." In this regard the Poles in America were the same as others; but with this difference: they were divided, as their country was divided, not in allegiance but in belief as to how best their allegiance might be served. There were Poles in America who represented, sincerely and with feeling, in spite of their unity of ideal— freedom for Poland—the partisanships of their motherland. Both the Russian and Austrian "compromises of autonomy" had their adherents. Those who saw Russia alone as the enemy of Poland's past and future favored the Austrophils and, in a certain sense, Germany. Those who remembered Teutonic oppression faced the Russian way. This question of Polish division in America was, on the whole, Paderewski's most serious problem. Remove it, and he could progress toward American official support. It was not a mere polite difference of opinion; it was, at times, a thoroughgoing marshalling of organized force against him. In order to be a true harmonizer and a genuine leader he had to combat it not only with tact and persuasion but at moments with implacable refusal and command. It made enemies for him among those who could not see his larger view; they called him stubborn and egoistic and even questioned his motive.

Nor was it pre-war sentiment alone, carried over from the old country, that caused divided feeling among American Poles. The war itself had brought in new complications. From the earliest days of the war there had been the factor of Russia's proclamation, made on August 16, 1914, of a Poland "free in faith, in language, in self government." Paderewski, as we know, had regarded this manifesto, when it appeared, as a serious commital of Russia. In his London *Times* appeal early in 1915 he had said that "from the ancestral shores of the Baltic Sea to the southern slopes of the Carpathians every truly Polish soul was moved with gladness and hope" by the manifesto of Grand Duke Nicholas. But whatever its significance then, it now made for divided opinion among the Poles in America. Later on Paderewski had some diplomatic fun with the Russians out of that manifesto, holding them up when occasion offered to a sort of *noblesse oblige* on the strength of it. In Paris once, during the early days of war, the Russian Ambassador to France, Isvolsky, made some caustic remark about Poles, who had no court of their own, insisting on "hierarchical precedence." "But," said Paderewski with his most winning smile, "I understood that the Polish King-to-be was your own august sovereign?" M. Isvolsky could only bite his lip. This was the same Ambassador Isvolsky who, in the face of Russia's publicly avowed purpose of recognizing Polish autonomy, had received secret instructions from Petrograd to exclude all discussion of the Polish question from Allied deliberations at Paris and to place every obstacle in the way of Allied interest in that question.

Naturally, the interjection of Paderewski the Pole into international conversations nettled the Russian plenipotentiary.

Thus the Russian manifesto made a difficulty for Paderewski in America. Hundreds of thousands of Poles had believed in it as the solution in toto of their problems, and tens of thousands of these were in America. With Polish opinion divided; with Russia until its collapse in 1917 still one of the Allies, insisting to France and England that the Polish question was nobody's business but her own; with the Allies afraid to offend Russia by taking up the Polish cause; and with the American people divided in sentiment and the American government neutral, Paderewski, unsupported for a time by a united Polish sentiment and unrecognized as the accredited spokesman of his people, found his way a hard one. True, as we have seen, when the Russians were driven out of Poland in August, 1915, his argument of the Polish question as an Allied problem and not a Russian problem was advanced a little. Poland had been left then to the mercies of the common enemy, Germany, and could rightly call for allied deliverance. She had, in fact, suffered a new Partition by the Austro-German convention of December 14, 1915, which had cold-bloodedly sliced the country into a North and a South, with the German capital set at Warsaw and the Austrian capital at Lublin. But a year later, with the starvation problem intensified by the forced exportation of Polish foodstuffs out of Poland into Germany and Austria, and Paderewski deeper than ever into his work of raising relief funds and pushing the cause of Polish liberation, a new complication entered. The Germans now took their turn at trying to win the Poles over, attempting to alienate them from their natural protection of Allied support. Jointly with Austria they proclaimed, November 5, 1916, a Polish "independence", a new Kingdom of the Poles, carved out of Russian Poland.

This gave new momentum to the division of Polish sentiment in America. It strengthened the position of the Austrophils. But Paderewski was not deceived for a moment by the German manifesto. Its purpose was too obvious. Besides, he

knew exactly why Germany had made this move; she needed
recruits. General Sikorski (later to be Minister of War in
Poland, and at this time head of the military department of
the Austrophil "Supreme National Committee") had estimated
in 1915 that a million Polish volunteers to fight with the Central Powers against Russia could be secured. On the strength
of this estimate the German governor general at Warsaw, Von
Beseler, had advised Berlin in July, 1916, that an independence
manifesto, such as this now issued, would bring her from eight
hundred thousand to a million Polish volunteers, and a secret
protocol signed at Vienna on August 12 had laid the ground
for this manifesto. Ludendorff wrote to the German Foreign
Minister, Zimmerman—the same Zimmerman who was implicated in the historically absurd scheme to give part of the
United States to Mexico in return for Mexican aid in the war—
attacking what he called the "piggishness" of Austria, and arguing that for the Germans to mend matters and extricate themselves from the Austrian mess, a sop should be thrown to the
Poles. They were good fighters, he said, and they might come
over to the German side and hold the Russian line for her if
offered the proper bait. Thus Germany could reconcentrate on
the Western front and there crush the Allies. The German
knew well that there was plenty of young Polish manhood
available, and they knew too what a bait the word "independence" might be to the Poles. As the Polish deputy to the Russian Duma Szebeko eloquently expressed it, "One would have
to go through the Polish Golgotha in order to know the magic
power of that word 'Independence'." Now the Germans decided to try that magic.

Would it work? That was the question that Paderewski had
to face, the question he had to answer. He saw the grave danger: the German manifesto might work. The Poles in Poland,
war-worn, war-wasted, devitalized, desperate for any freedom
from the intolerable yoke that the war had put on them, blinded
and literally bled white, might be deluded into offering themselves wholesale to the German arms. True enough there were
certain reassurances. Pilsudski, whom Paderewski did not per-

sonally know, but with whose reputation as a patriot and as the organizer of the Polish legionnaire forces in Austria, he was entirely familiar, while still fighting in 1915 on the Austrian front against Russia, had gone secretly to Warsaw to discourage his compatriots from volunteering. "Today," Pilsudski had said at that time, "the Germans have taken the place of the Russians in Poland. We must resist the Germans." That was something to build hope on. True enough, also, there was the native instinct of the Pole working in his favor and against acceptance of the manifesto, an instinct sharpened by long contact with Teutonic aggression and by generations of first-hand acquaintanceship with German military stupidity; the same stupidity which had so grossly miscalculated a people's psychology as to lead Berlin to believe that the German army could pass through Belgium without resistance. All these things, happening overseas in Poland, were factors to reassure Paderewski in America.

But on the other hand there were factors to warn and disturb him. The answer that some Poles had made in 1915 to Pilsudski's protest against recruiting for the Central Powers had been one of puzzled dismay. "If we do what you wish," they had said, "we will simply be playing into the hands of the Russians"; and this view was still held by many. Moreover, the Supreme National Committee had actually organized at Warsaw propaganda to foster Polish volunteering. And what now would be the stand of Pilsudski, whose leadership of the legions already organized and fighting on the Austro-German side made his words the last word? * In the face of all this uncertainty Paderewski, alarmed by the dangers to Poland's future presented by this German independence manifesto, felt that he could take no chances, that he must weigh every possibility, even the possibility of the Poles having reached the

---

* Pilsudski, as matters developed within a few days, would go no further than to tell the legionnaires to "become soldiers again." He would not encourage enlistment. He was not taken in by fulsome expressions of German official praise such as that which appeared in Von Beseler's *Deutsche Warschauer Zeitung*, describing the November Fifth Proclamation as having "crowned the work of the great Polish patriot who was the true creator of the Polish Legions and who would be the father of the Polish Army."

point of saturation in hardship and suffering and of being consequently dulled and blinded to remote consequences. Again, there was another danger. Even if popular acceptance of the German "independence" did not eventuate, the manifesto itself immediately endangered Poland's situation with the Allies. The Allies could hardly be expected to trust the Poles to resist the German offer; in a Poland already taken over bodily by the Germans and now offered independence by them, they would see a Poland allied by circumstance, no matter how unwillingly, with German arms. They would cease to count Poland as one of themselves, and Allied lack of faith in the Poles would weaken Polish resistance. As long as the larger part of Poland still was fighting under Russian leadership the Allies numbered the Poles on their side. Next, with Russia driven out of Poland and the Poles put under the German yoke, the Allies could regard Poland as a land to be saved. But a Poland offered independence by Germany, and palpably too weak to reject the offer—this was something very different. Paderewski had a real issue to meet.

On the same day that the German manifesto was published in Warsaw Paderewski in America determined to act at once to counter the Prussian move. There was only one thing that could be done. The German offer must be immediately rejected by the Poles, the Allies must be told and told at once that it was rejected by them.

He must take instant action. But how? Whatever action was taken, he knew, would be futile were it merely the action of a separate group. It must be the action of all the Poles, the Poles in Europe, the Poles in America. Could acceptance of the manifesto in Poland be stopped? Could agreement be found in America to warrant action? Here was a moment in his life as leader when he must decide and act quickly and boldly.

It was in a crisis like this that Paderewski felt most seriously his ambiguous situation in the eyes of American government officials. His credentials of repute, his fame, his popularity, all these were negatived by the fact that he represented no state and only a disunited people. All doors in America were open to

Paderewski the man, Paderewski the artist; but for Paderewski the national leader, politician, diplomat, statesman, to break through the cold iron circle of government officialdom at Washington and be accepted as leader of the Polish cause, this was another matter, and an extremely difficult one. Robert Lansing, United States Secretary of State, telling in his book "The Big Four" of his relationships and experiences with Paderewski, makes us understand how difficult the Polish patriot's situation was.

Lansing's original impression of Paderewski, he tells us, "was not one of a complimentary nature, in view of the task which he had undertaken in behalf of his country"; and this was due undoubtedly, as he admits, "to the fact that he was a great pianist, the greatest, I believe, of his generation." "I felt," Mr. Lansing wrote, "that his artistic temperament, his passionate devotion to music, his intense emotions, and his reputed eccentricities indicated a lack of the qualities of mind which made it possible for him to deal with the intricate political problems which it would be necessary to solve in the restoration of Polish independence and the revival of Polish sovereignty. . . .

"When the famous musician came to see me in my office at the Department of State, I could not avoid the thought that his emotions were leading him into a path which he was wholly unsuited to follow. With his long flaxen hair sprinkled with gray and brushed back like a mane from his broad white forehead, with his extremely low collar and dangling black necktie accentuating the length of his neck, with his peculiarly narrow eyes and his small mustache and goatee that looked so foreign, he appeared to be a man absorbed in the aesthetic things of life rather than in practical world politics. My feeling was that I had to deal with one given over to extravagant ideals, to the visions and fantasies of a person controlled by his emotional impulses rather than by his reason and the actualities of life. I was impressed by his fervid patriotism, and by his intense devotion to the cause of Poland, but it was not unnatural to think that so temperamental a nature would be swayed by sentimentality in the advocacy of a course of action and would

give passionate support to his ideas with little regard to logic
or practical considerations. . . .

"I liked him personally," Lansing concludes. "I was glad to
see him enter my office, for I always found pleasure in talking
with him. . . . His cordiality of manner and address was very
attractive. He was a likeable, I think I may say a loveable man
in every sense of the term. Yet . . . there was the ever-present
sense that he lived in the realm of musical harmonies and
that he could not come down to material things and grapple
with the hard facts of life. It seemed as if he could not realize
the difficulties of the part which he had chosen to play in the
tragical drama of world affairs. In truth, I thought he was
making a mistake."

Others thought so, too. The feeling of the Secretary of State,
as he himself said, was "shared by many" who, like him, were
"not disposed to give weight to his [Paderewski's] opinions."
Not all at Washington felt as Franklin K. Lane felt, and even
if others at Washington could exclaim with Lane, "Isn't he a
wonder!" they still thought of him, as Lane did, as "only" an
artist. Besides, with America still neutral, Washington remained a center of international division. The ambassadors
and ministers of all the powers, belligerent and otherwise,
still contributed to the life of the American capital, still were
factors in the life of the State Department. Feeling ran high,
and if on the one hand Sir Cecil Spring-Rice, the British ambassador, and Colonel House, the adviser of President Wilson,
could quarrel, as they did, over the mere mention of the German ambassador's name, on the other hand pro-German sympathy could play its part; and all together they could make
neutral Washington not an advantageous place for a non-
portfolioed spokesman like Paderewski to fight his fight.

The Secretary of State, as we will see, changed his views
completely and in due time handsomely acknowledged that it
was he who was "making a mistake." But in the meantime here
was this serious obstacle for Paderewski to overcome. He was
determined to overcome it. He felt that if he failed in this, he
failed in everything. He had said to Borglum, "I must face the

councils of Europe if I am to fight this fight to a finish." But to face the councils of Europe he must first break into the councils of America. In November, 1916, suddenly brought short by the crisis of the German manifesto, he felt keenly the difficulty of his position.

There was one man in America, however, who differed from all the others in his regard for Paderewski, one who from the beginning, by the grace of a native insight and a wide knowledge of European affairs, had accepted him for what he was. This was Edward Mandell House, the man whom President Wilson had called his "second personality: his thoughts and mine are one." This natural-born Warwick, shrewd, discreet, "quiet voiced, quiet footed", who, in the words of Senator Gore, could "walk on dead leaves and make no more noise than a tiger", was more than a master politician. Clemenceau described him as a "super-civilized person escaped from the wilds of Texas, who sees everything, who understands everything . . . a sifting, pondering mind." But he was also an idealist, and Paderewski the patriot, the genius, but above all else himself the idealist *par excellence,* appealed strongly to him. House, like Leschetitsky thirty years before, "knew his man." And he knew Europe, especially the Europe of the World War. From 1914 to 1916 he had paid three visits to Continental capitals. He had been in Berlin in May, 1914, three months before the war began; he had been there again in March, 1915, and again in January, 1916. He knew what was going on. He was well equipped to be, as he was in actuality, the "international mind" of Woodrow Wilson.

Paderewski was as keen as anyone playing the great game of international politics. If his ideals were high, his methods were shrewd and practical. It was Wilson, President of the United States, that Paderewski was aiming to get to. From the hour that he had landed in America on this mission in 1915 he had determined that Wilson should hear Poland's case. He had been encouraged from the first. He knew that Wilson was open-minded as well as informed on the Polish question; as a matter of fact he knew that the President was a regular reader of the Polish propaganda publications issuing from London. And of course he knew Wilson's temper toward the German breaches of international law. Wilson's "solemn warning" to Germany had come on February 15, 1915, a few weeks after Paderewski's arrival. It had been followed by the "Odenwald note" of May 3 the same year, then by the three *"Lusitania* notes", then the Gerard note. In the spring of the same year the President had declared in a public address that he "deeply sympathized with Poland." On October 26, 1916, Wilson had said at Cincinnati that "America will lend her moral influence, not only, but her physical force, if other nations will join her, to see to it that no nation and no group of nations tries to take advantage of another nation or group of nations." . . . On November 4 the same year, the day before the German independence manifesto had brought Paderewski to face a crisis, Wilson had declared "the day of isolation is gone. . . . In the days to come men will no longer wonder how America is going to work out her destiny, for she will have proclaimed to them that her destiny is not divided from the destiny of the world, that her purpose is justice and love of mankind." These and various other utterances of the President and communications sent by Wilson to Berlin had made Paderewski little by little more and more sure of a sympathetic hearing in the highest quarter. His friendship with House definitely opened the way to that hearing.

As it happened, Wilson's regard for and confidence in House was based mainly on the fact that House was one man whose service was absolutely patriotic and unselfish, who not only sought no office but insisted on holding no office. Paderewski, exactly of like character, caring nothing for personal interest and everything for the cause at hand, could have found no better medium of approach to the President. In 1916 Wilson in his address to the National Press Club, said: "I can name two or three men with whom I have conferred again and again and again, and I have never caught them by an inadvertence thinking about themselves for their own interests, and I tie to those men as you would tie to an anchor. I tie to them as you would tie to the voices of conscience. Men who have no axes to grind! Those are the men, and nations like those men are the nations that are going to serve the world and save it." House was that kind of a man, so was Paderewski. Wilson may well have had them both in mind, and Poland as well, when he spoke these words.

So this friendship was formed between House and Paderewski, one of the finest and fastest-bound in Paderewski's life of many fine friendships. The two men understood each other from the first. They spoke the same language. They were bound together by the ideal of an unselfish cause, Paderewski's the saving of his country, House's the securing of peace and the freedom of an enslaved people. The American's admiration for the Pole, for his phenomenal gifts of mind and heart, was unbounded. "There is no man in public life I admire more than Ignace Jan Paderewski," Colonel House wrote to me in 1932. "It has always been the ambition of my life to find the one man my country needs," Paderewski said in a letter early in their friendship. "My ambition has been realized." In January, 1919, addressing the city of Warsaw when he was welcomed back to Poland, and later while speaking in the Seym or national assembly, he proclaimed to the Polish nation that it owed its independence to House, "my sincere friend, the friend of all the Poles."

In 1931 the world heard of a signal tribute and expression of gratitude being paid to the memory of Woodrow Wilson. A monument to him was erected in the city of Poznan. It was the gift of Paderewski. With characteristic grace and fitness he chose Poznan, the first place in Poland where he had spoken Wilson's message of Polish independence directly to the Polish people, as the site of this monument, and with equal grace he chose America's Independence Day for its dedication. One year later he repeated the gesture by putting the final public seal on his friendship with Colonel House by presenting to the city of Warsaw a monument to House, a magnificent life-size bronze figure, by the Polish sculptor Francis Black, which was unveiled July 4, 1932, in Paderewski Park in the Polish capital, a testimony for all time of the love of Poland for America as the two countries are personified by the two men. Paderewski's message on that occasion, read in his absence by his secretary, Mr. Sylvin Strakacz, contained some characteristic Paderewskian phrasing. Referring to his address in January, 1919, he reminded the audience that he had added to his tribute to House at that time the suggestion that his historic services to Poland should be commemorated. "My kind listeners, among whom I noticed the capital's most illustrious citizens, accepted my idea with enthusiastic sentiment. I remember them crying aloud, 'We shall erect monuments!' Years have passed. Our nation, sentimental and honest, never fails to pay its debts. But, impoverished by the war and preoccupied with economic reconstruction, it has been unable to erect monuments. What the nation is unable to do must be accomplished by its true servants. . . . To future generations it will be immaterial at whose expense this testimony of Poland's gratitude was erected, whether the nation's or an individual's. It will suffice that it was born in a Polish heart."

The story of how the friendship between Paderewski and House began makes a dramatic high-light in the life of the Polish patriot. It was Robert W. Wooley, Director of the United States Mint under Wilson, who brought them together. The beginning was a call made on Mr. Wooley early in 1916 by a friend of Paderewski's bearing a letter of introduction from Carl Vrooman, then Assistant Secretary of Agriculture. The letter asked Wooley to arrange a meeting between Paderewski and Colonel House. Vrooman knew of the friendship existing between Wooley and House.

Wooley agreed, but at the same time was forced to say that he could not make any promises. The demands on House at that time were enormous. Furthermore, Wooley was sufficiently in the Colonel's confidence to realize that there might be reasons of state which would cause him either to hesitate or refuse to grant an immediate interview involving the then acute and complicated question of Poland's plight. But Wooley himself was interested and sympathetic and he determined to bring the two men together if he could. The outcome of the call and of the Vrooman letter was that Wooley sent word from his office in Washington to Paderewski that he was to be in New York two days later and would communicate with him.

Paderewski's joy was great on receiving this news. Very seldom does he use the telephone; the experience of years has taught him to keep off the wire. But he lost no time now in calling Washington. "What a thrill his eager words gave me!" Wooley said to me, telling of that call. "The man was simply overjoyed at the prospect of at last meeting one who, he believed, could and would help to save Poland." But Wooley was still careful and uncertain; as a matter of fact, he had not yet even broached the matter to Colonel House. He suggested to Paderewski that his elation might be premature, and asked him to just stand by and await further word.

In New York Paderewski was lodged at the Gotham Hotel, only a few blocks away from Colonel House's residence at 115 East Fifty-third Street. When Wooley got to New York he went straight to House and told him his story. House pondered for a few seconds; then he said: "Yes, I will see him. I will see him today, this morning. But with one provision: you must be present at the interview." Happy over this progress in his mission, Wooley went next to the Gotham. Madame Paderewska greeted him excitedly. The tears came as she cried, "You are going to save Poland! You are going to save Poland!"

Wooley was amazed, a little disconcerted. "Why, Madame Paderewska," he replied, "I don't understand."

"You are taking Mr. Paderewski to see Colonel House," she persisted. "That is everything. Colonel House will do it. We know that."

Paderewski appeared almost immediately. They started out at once for Colonel House's apartment. "During our walk to the House apartment," Wooley relates, "Mr. Paderewski told me of the uphill fight he had made to raise funds through his Polish committee, and of his unavailing efforts to contact the Democratic administration at Washington. He showed me a list of this committee's personnel. Eminent lawyers, interna-

tional bankers, distinguished scholars, many college presidents
—and not a Democrat among them. Their power of attraction
or of influence had been practically nil." Wooley's own interest
and sympathy were well repaid in that short walk and talk.
"I have often thought since," he says, "what a privilege it was
to hear this remarkable man, this cultured scholar and great
artist, pour out his very soul in anticipation of a meeting which
he firmly believed was to mark the beginning of the rebirth
of the Polish nation. His poetic thoughts, his choice of words,
his beautiful phrasing, his perfect English were an intellectual
treat."

Colonel House had allotted a half hour for the interview.
Thus every second counted; discussion of the subject in hand
immediately followed the introduction. The conference was
held in the library, a small room not more than twelve feet
long by about eight feet wide. The Colonel and Wooley sat,
one in a chair, the other on a sofa. Paderewski refused to sit.
He paced back and forth, talking as he paced, driving home his
arguments with rapier-like incisiveness and with all the force of
unanswerable logic. It was a demonstration of eloquence, direct,
clear and forceful, such as a genius of the bar might have given
in the greatest case of his career.

When Paderewski came to the point of Poland's immediate
need and asked that the United States government make Poland a loan of a million dollars, Wooley interjected. "There
is no government of Poland," he said. "The United States
can't lend money to a mere committee." Paderewski wheeled
and turned on him, "fiercely", in Wooley's own words. "Can't,
Mr. Wooley?" he exclaimed. "The United States can do anything. She promised Cuba she would drive out Spain and set
Cuba free. She kept her word. No other country in the world
ever did such a thing. She won the Philippines at arms and then
paid Spain $20,000,000 for them. No other nation ever did
anything like that. She joined other powers in suppressing the
Boxer rebellion in China and then——"

"Let him go on," House said in a low voice to Wooley.

"Don't interrupt him." The logic and eloquence of Paderewski had already captivated the Colonel.

And he did go on. His plea piled up its arguments, pyramided one incontrovertible point on another. The allotted half hour was long gone by. An hour passed, and still he held forth brilliantly, fervently. It was one of the great hours of his life. It was "the" hour of his country's life. Plainly, as Wooley remarked afterward, Paderewski sensed in all its fullness the crucial importance of whatever was to happen in that small room that day. In the soft-speaking non-committal House he recognized the most formidable of adversaries to be overcome. No attorney ever had a greater case to plead than Paderewski had at that moment, his client a nation of thirty million people.

At last, with a simple gesture of finality, he ceased. He had done his utmost, shot all his bolts. What would the decision be?

Colonel House rose slowly from his chair. He extended his hand to Paderewski. He spoke quietly but with evident emotion: "You have convinced me. I promise you to help Poland if I can. And I believe I can."

Not often in any man's lifetime does a light come into his face such as suffused and paled Paderewski's expressive features at that moment. There was complete silence. "He was overcome," Mr. Wooley tells. By the time they got out on the street he had his balance again. He stepped quickly, lightly, his whole vigorous frame vibrating with joy and relief. "His words were as joyful as those of a boy at play."

Thus one of the historic friendships of modern times began.

To that little study in Colonel House's apartment on Fifty-third Street in New York, Paderewski made many visits. Always he went there with the knowledge that he would be received with complete understanding. Together the two worked out the plans for raising relief funds, discussed the knotty problem of the future Poland and its boundaries, weighed and measured every detail of this grave question which involved the lives of millions and the future peace of Europe.

On November 5, 1916, he hurried straight to Colonel House

when Germany and Austria proclaimed the *Zwei Kaiser* "independence" which the Central Powers had concocted.

Colonel House brought him immediately to President Wilson at Long Branch, New Jersey. That night Paderewski took his bold step. A protest against the German "independence" was drafted by him. The cables were got busy. The Polish rejection of the German offer, signed by Paderewski and indorsed by the Polish National Committee at Paris, by the Polish National Alliance at Chicago, by representative Poles of prominence, such as the President of the Academy of Sciences at Cracow, went over the wires to all the Allied chancelleries. For the first time since the war began, by the morning of November 6, 1916, which happened to be Paderewski's fifty-sixth birthday, the Allies became unmistakably aware of the fact that there was really a Polish Power, a potential if not a *de facto* Polish State, and that it had a leader. By this declaration they knew that the Polish Question was definitely an Allied Question and a World Question, and that they must now bid for Polish support, as Russia and Germany had bidden for it.

XXXIII

1915–1918: THE STRUGGLE IN AMERICA—III

PADEREWSKI enjoyed his birthday gift. He had taken Poland's fate out of the hands of Germany and had virtually delivered it over to the Allies. He had the Allied Powers turned at last in the right direction to insure their interest in the freeing of Poland. But he was not so sure as yet that he had all his fellow Poles with him. His leadership was now to be put to its final test. The bold step taken, he must win his compatriots' full endorsement of it. He himself was shrewd enough to realize that even this German "independence" move, rejected by him, could still be turned to Poland's advantage; but at the moment not all agreed with him. He knew that the idea of independence, which the Prussian military imagined they had so cleverly dangled before Polish eyes, could be made serviceable in the end. The word "independence" could not be bottled up after this, and Paderewski from that time on saw to it that it was not. Yet he was attacked in some quarters at first for having refused "independence." There were those who were short-sighted enough, against his far-sighted vision, to advocate the rule of "let well enough alone." Thus, the step taken, he had now to face the question of its support.

In spite of their former differences the Poles in America responded heroically to his action. Without dissent their organizations voted Paderewski their plenipotentiary, conferring on him their power of attorney to decide and act for them in all matters. This made Secretary of State Lansing sit up. "The first direct evidence of his capacity as a leader which impressed me," Lansing wrote, "was his successful effort to unite the jealous and bickering Polish factions in the United States and to obtain their common acceptance of the authority of the National Polish Council in Paris. Others had attempted the task and failed . . . I am convinced that Mr. Paderewski was the only Pole who could have overcome this menace . . . His powers of persuasion, which seemed to spring at once into being with his entry upon a political career, his enthusiastic confidence in the resurrection of Poland . . . his entire freedom from personal ambition, made him the one man about whom the Poles, regardless of faction, appeared to be willing to rally. It was a great achievement, a triumph of personality."

Looking back on this period of division and dissension, with its dramatic crisis in 1916, Paderewski's achievement is plain to see. By his clear thinking, persuasiveness, and eloquence—in short, by his wise and dispassionate leadership—he created in America a kind of political anchorage for all Polish feeling. The Polish masses within the war area, it must be remembered, could not be vocal. They could be vocal in America, but what they needed was a leader and a harmonizer. Unmistakably they were vocal even to the point of rousing certain American publicists. John Dewey, for instance, writing in *The New Republic*, tried to raise an alarm over what he called "self-determination in our midst." Yet the movement was not only legitimate and wholesome but it was, in the end, thanks to Paderewski's wise manipulation, a fortunate one for the Allies. Dmowski, organizing Polish action in Europe, was criticized for taking steps which engaged his country without his countrymen's support, but Paderewski won for him that support and thus with far-reaching effect advanced the Allied cause. No more positive evidence of what Lansing called Paderewski's "triumph of personality" could be asked than the great war-time Polish Assembly held in Detroit. To that assembly Dmowski was summoned from Paris, and from it, so to speak, he received the mandate of an at last united Polish people—united by Paderewski. This Detroit Assembly, moreover, did more than witness to Paderewski's leadership; it revealed, too, the man's supreme sense of patriotic loyalty and unselfishness. He stood aside. He presented Dmowski as the leader, demanded for

Dmowski and his Polish National Committee the support of all, and got it.

The far-reaching effects of Paderewski's harmonizing leadership, and particularly of his prompt and bold action in the crisis of 1916, were made manifest quickly and in a very practical manner to the Allies. While the Poles in America joined in a united front to back him, this is what happened then and afterward, in Poland: Word of the Polish declaration to the Allies rejecting the German manifesto penetrated the Prussian censorship. The carloads of German uniforms that had been shipped to Polish recruiting stations were left practically unused. The German military had, as a matter of course, handled the issue with characteristic tactlessness. Immediately on the issuing of the "independence" proclamation, so blunderingly eager had they been to roll up the Polish *Menschenmaterial*, they had opened recruiting stations for the so-called *Polnische Wehrmacht;* and not satisfied with that, they had insisted on all Polish recruits taking an oath of fraternity in arms with their German *Kamerads.* As a result, in the long run, up to midyear of 1917, they managed to get only 1,373 volunteers of the expected million. At the moment of the manifesto less than 300 took the bait. During the week following the manifesto there were popular demonstrations in Warsaw opposing the recruiting and demanding the formation of a Polish Government. By November 26 the Austro-German occupation authorities were forced to promulgate a statute instituting a Polish Council of State, the farce of which Berlin-controlled "government" for the new "Kingdom of Poland" ended eventually in the dramatic refusal by the Polish legionnaires, at Pilsudski's command, to take the Kaiser's oath, Pilsudski's resignation from the Council,* his arrest and impris-

---

* The statement made by Pilsudski, July 2, 1917, on withdrawing from the Council of State, makes plain in brief words the whole situation at home in Poland, which Paderewski in America was following in every detail: "Until now all attempts to form a Polish Army have had one characteristic trait in common, namely the Central Powers have always endeavored to exclude the interventions of any Polish organization. First, the Legions were incorporated in the Austrian Army; at present, according to the official text, they are associated with the German Army. The right to make decisions in this

onment in Germany, and the interning of all Polish troops. At the same time the Russian government, still hoping to regain Polish support, was busy. On November 15, 1916, it issued a new proclamation of its intention to restore Poland to freedom. Again, on Christmas Day, 1916, the institution of a free Poland was announced by the Czar in an Order of the Day to the Army.

Of course, since Russia was still one of the Allies, this reiteration of the Czar's "Polish sentiments" won applause among the Allies, and in the same measure added confusion to the Polish problem and to Paderewski's undertaking. France, even as late as March, 1917, was assuring Russia, through Ambassador Izvolsky at Paris, that the Allies still stood engaged to endorse Russia's disposition of the Polish question should the war be won by them. Nevertheless, in spite of confusions, the name of Paderewski now had a large credit with the Allies, in actual figures a credit of something like one million fighting men deducted from the German arms; for the success of the "independence" manifesto in Poland would of course have released whole armies to the Western front, there to put new pressure on the French trenches. From this time forward Paderewski was recognized more and more as the spokesman of a power. True, a long-continued and heroic effort was yet to be required to make the Allies commit themselves wholly to the freeing of Poland. The collapse of Russia and the pressure of America were to be needed to that end. But Poland and Paderewski were now become real factors in the World War.

In America his influence had steadily increased. During the winter 1915–1916 resolutions were introduced in Congress expressing sympathy with Poland. New Year's Day, 1916, was proclaimed "Polish Day" by President Wilson, who invited popular subscriptions to Paderewski's relief fund. Later the

---

matter is therefore in alien hands. Such a state of things has given us a fictitious army, Austrian yesterday, German today. If the Central Powers have acted in this way in a spirit of benevolence, they are mistaken in supposing that it is possible to form a Polish Army after that fashion. Since the Council of State, a Polish institution, can have no legal influence on the formation of a Polish Army, I, as representing that Army, can no longer remain at my post in the Council."

same year, on July 12, Wilson, addressing a group of Polish citizens at the White House, said—doubtless adverting in mind to his conferences with Paderewski: "It was not unnecessary that you should come. I mean I was not forgetful of Poland and was not likely to be forgetful of her. I know the terrible conditions, the tragical conditions, that exist there, and nobody could know them without feeling his heart torn with the knowledge." Paderewski's intimacy with Colonel House grew. That he exerted a real influence on House's thought is evident. When, for example, Lord Balfour, British Foreign Secretary, hesitated in 1917 about the restoration of Poland, still believing in revolutionary Russia, House, obviously moved by Paderewski's counsels, disputed this because, as he wrote in his diary, he "thought we had to take into consideration the Russia of fifty years from now rather than the Russia of today"—clearly an echo of Paderewski's thought, who knew, as no American could know, the Russian psychology. The conferences between House and Paderewski were numerous. "We poured over maps —his maps and mine—of Central Europe," writes House, "and together we traced what we thought should be a homogeneous Poland." The balance and wisdom of Paderewski's decisions in these conferences deeply impressed President Wilson's adviser: "The Poland we outlined, during those fervid war days, proved to be practically the Poland created by the Versailles Conference."

By the end of 1916 America's entrance into the war seemed unavoidable. Paderewski, working desperately now—and burdened by the loss of his old friend and co-worker in Europe, Sienkiewicz, who had died at Vevey November 16—knew that if Poland was actually to be freed, her name must be coupled with America's. He pressed forward into the new year, urged his claims more and more emphatically in his conferences with Colonel House. What was happening at this time and how it all came at last to a climax is told most dramatically by himself *:

---

* Address at Kosciuszko Foundation Testimonial, New York, May 16, 1928.

"On Monday, January 8th [1917] in the afternoon, Colonel House said to me, 'Next Thursday I am going to leave for Washington, and I wish to have with me your memorandum on Poland.' Terrified by the suddenness of that request, I exclaimed: 'But I have my recital tomorrow. I shall not be able to hold a pen in my hand for two days, and besides, it is impossible to prepare such a document without having the necessary data.'

" 'I must have the memorandum Thursday in the morning,' he answered, and it was the end of our conversation. I immediately returned to the hotel—and spent four solid hours in preparing the program for my recital. Only on Tuesday, after the recital, could I turn my mind to that new, very heavy task. It took me over thirty-six hours of uninterrupted work to prepare the document which was delivered, as requested, on Thursday, the 11th at eight o'clock in the morning.

"Led by the purest, by the noblest idealism, Colonel House made our cause his own . . . When about a week later I called on him, he was in a cheerful mood and said: 'The President was very much pleased with your memorandum. Now get ready. The first shot will be fired very soon, and it will take your breath away.' "

Paderewski could rest on that. But he would not have been human if he had not found the days succeeding that statement of Colonel House's to be days full of eager and anxious anticipation. He went on with his touring, giving recitals to raise relief funds, addressing thousands gathered to hear his plea for Poland, but day after day he watched for the promised developments. His travels took him into the South. On January 23 he heard the news. President Wilson, addressing the Senate January 22 on "The Essential Terms of Peace in Europe" had at last spoken the word that proclaimed the destiny of Poland before the nations. For the first time since the war began the name of Poland as a state was enrolled in the records of international debate. "No peace can last, or ought to last," Wilson had said, "which does not recognize and accept the principle that governments derive all their just powers from the consent of the governed, and that no right anywhere exists to hand peoples about from sovereignty to sovereignty as if they were property. I take it for granted . . . that statesmen everywhere are agreed that *there should be a united, independent, and autonomous Poland* and that henceforth inviolable security of life, of worship, and of industrial and social development should be guaranteed to all people who have lived hitherto under the power of governments devoted to a faith and purpose hostile to their own."

The shot was fired. "And, indeed," Paderewski said afterward, "it did take my breath away, for a long time." He was a breathlessly happy man that January day in 1917.

Not many weeks after Wilson's declaration of January 22, weeks spent arduously by Paderewski on tour and in his offices at New York, the culminating act came. On April 2, 1917, President Wilson called upon Congress to declare war against Germany. On April 4 the Senate adopted the war resolution. On April 6 the House of Representatives followed suit. War was declared. Every international obstacle to the proper consideration of Poland's status as a potential Allied state was now removed. America was at arms with the Allies against Germany, Poland was sponsored by America, and Paderewski heard with joy of how at Warsaw and other Polish cities the Poles had made a holiday, right under the German military nose, to celebrate America's entry into the war. Paderewski moved at once to take his next step toward consolidating Poland's position, a step which was to be not only a pledge of Polish devotion to the Allied cause but was to add another item to his credit with the Allies. They already had chalked up on his ledger a million recruits saved from the German force in Poland. Now they were to be strengthened in a positive manner by actual Polish arms. On April 4, the day that the United States Senate passed the war resolution, Paderewski moved the Union of Polish Falcons, in convention at Pittsburgh, to vote for the organization of "an army of Kosciuszko to fight by the side of the United States." The American declaration of war on April 6 cleared the way to carry this vote out.

This had long been a dreamed-of project of Paderewski's. "The necessity of an independent Polish army," he stated, "an army capable of demonstrating to the whole world that our nation at large was heart and soul with the Allied and Associated Powers, became both obvious and imperative." But while America had remained neutral and until she entered the war, nothing could be done. Man power by the thousands among Polish Americans above the draft age existed in the United States; only the call was needed, and permission of the government. To secure this official endorsement and to recruit his army were Paderewski's next moves.

The task, first of officially establishing a Polish army for the Allies, and then of recruiting it, was a slow and difficult one. In the beginning long negotiations with the French government had been entailed. They resulted finally in a favorable decree issued on June 5, 1917, the words of President Poincaré of France on this occasion being memorable as a succinct statement of the Polish question which Paderewski in America had made so clear to the world. "The number of Poles already taking part in the struggle for the right and the liberty of peoples," Poincaré said, "or who can be enrolled for service in the cause of the Allies, is sufficient to justify their being united in a distinct corps. Further, the intention of the Allied Governments, and in particular of the provisional Russian Government,* regarding the restoration of the Polish State, cannot be better affirmed than by permitting the Poles to fight everywhere under their national flag." Nor were the difficulties in the organization of Paderewski's army encountered in Paris only. Equally involved negotiations with the American government were necessitated. Finally, there was the raising of the troops. All of this took months and put a tremendous burden on him. The actual organization of the force meant, of course, a good deal more than a mere matter of calling for volunteers. The machinery of recruiting had to be organized, the record of every

---

* The provisional Russian government, following the Revolution of March 17, 1917, had, in March 29, proclaimed its recognition of a free Poland.

volunteer justified, a training camp had to be established, provision made for transport and feeding. Two camps were opened, one at Niagara-on-the-Lake for Canadian recruits, one at Fort Niagara, New York. Some twenty-two thousand men of overdraft age volunteered; and these in due time had added to their numbers some fifty-five thousand Poles who had been interned in France and Italy when taken as prisoners of war from the armies of the Central Powers. With further forces added in Europe, Paderewski's army, eventually placed under the leadership of General Josef Haller, one of the most daring and picturesque of Poland's heroes, totalled nearly one hundred thousand men. This leader of this Polish army, Haller, had had an adventurous career. He had appeared in France as a happy *deus ex machina* to fight on the western front only after a sensational escape into Russia following the heroic five-day battle of Kaniow in May, 1918, where he had hacked his way through the overwhelming superior German force. With a price on his head he had made his way to the Murman coast and thence had sailed to France to be appointed October 6 to lead the autonomous Polish force.*

The securing of the official endorsement of Paderewski's army from the American government was likewise a complicated process. There was opposition. Later, when the Paderewski Army was ready for service overseas, General Pershing in France opposed it, cabling his disapproval to Washington. There were lengthy deliberations between Paderewski and Colonel House, innumerable conferences with the State Department and the War Department. Long afterward, in an address in New York on the tenth anniversary of Polish independence in 1928, Paderewski referred humorously to those strenuous days when, as he put it, "someone"—himself—used to "molest" the War Department "at least twice a week." "If you do not guess who were the molester and the molested, then I shall confess, with a very slight touch of repentance, to having so

---

* The story of Haller is told in detail in my book "The New Poland", published in London (George Allen & Unwin), 1923; in New York (The Macmillan Company), 1924.

frequently bored your former Secretary of War. It was terrible boring and very deep, too, but I got oil anyhow."

Paderewski never forgot Newton D. Baker, Wilson's Secretary of War, and his service during those anxious times. "Burdened with the most tremendous responsibilities that could have ever confronted a member of the cabinet," he said of Baker, "he found it possible to surmount all these obstacles and difficulties of technical and political character and grant us that indispensable permission. Though overwhelmed with work, he always had a kind word and a friendly smile. When this body of men was officially recognized by the United States and by the allied governments as an autonomous, allied, co-belligerent Polish army, our status, our relation to the allied and associated powers became perfectly clear."

Secretary Baker, like everyone else in official Washington, came in good time to fully appreciate the character and ideals of the Polish leader. If the exigencies of office delayed him, he did not lack in sympathy for Paderewski's cause or in appreciation of Paderewski's zeal and courage. When the first troops of Paderewski's army were finally dispatched to Europe, Secretary Baker expressed its ideals as well as Paderewski himself could have. "This American contingent of the Polish army," he wrote, "is made up of men moved by the inspiration of the principles involved on the Allied side in this conflict, and their presence on the Western front representing both their adherence to America as the country of their adoption, and to Poland, free and self-governing, as the country of their extraction, will be a stimulating and inspiring sight."

In the Navy Department likewise Paderewski found support that was invaluable, especially when arrangements had to be made later on for the transportation of the Haller troops. With a great deal of wisdom and foresight, and with the full accord of President Wilson, Josephus Daniels, Secretary of the Navy, had selected for the Assistant Secretaryship a young man who twenty years later was to be one of the great Presidents of the United States, Franklin Delano Roosevelt. The vigorous and liberally endowed young Secretary, then in his thirties, was exactly of the type that would be quick in sympathy with such a cause as Paderewski represented. Besides, as it happened, Roosevelt since his boyhood had not only been an ardent admirer of the Polish artist but had known him personally. Paderewski was one of his heroes. It was not surprising, then, that one of the first to speak out in favor of Poland's claims to a restoration of her seaport rights should be Secretary Roosevelt; nor that, when the occasion rose and President Wilson authorized the help of the American navy in caring for General Haller's soldiers, Roosevelt should enthusiastically carry out the project. His heart was in it and Paderewski was grateful.

In the Haller army a singular tribute was paid to Paderewski, an honor never before given to a civilian in the history of war, and to only one soldier, Napoleon: Paderewski's name was written on the roll of every company. Daily at roll call the name *Ignace Jan Paderewski* was responded to not by one man but by the thunderous chorus of every regiment. There were a hundred thousand Ignace Jan Paderewski's in that army, as there were a hundred thousand who had taken its oath, which in itself was a memorable declaration of the aims for which Paderewski had striven: "I swear before Almighty God, One in Three, to be faithful to my country Poland, one and indivisible, and to be ready to give my life for the holy cause of its unification and liberation. I swear to defend my flag to the last drop of my blood, to observe military discipline, to obey my leaders, and by my conduct to maintain the honor of a Polish soldier." In a hundred different ways Paderewski said to his army, by word and act, what President Poincaré of France said beautifully to them when they first left for the front: "All the future of a nation is wrapped up in the folds of your flags. The White Eagle can once more unfold its wings. It will soon float in the light of a sky once more serene, and in the rays of victory."

While he prosecuted the affair of the army, Paderewski was as active as ever in his capacity of diplomatic plenipotentiary in America of the Polish National Committee at Paris, of which his friend Roman Dmowski was the head. Late the same year of 1917 a new consolidation of his position was reached when Secretary Lansing notified him that on November 10 the United States government had formally recognized the Paris committee. In due time, Secretary Lansing also gave him notice of the official recognition of the new Polish Army. Thus, step by step, Paderewski's work in America succeeded, all leading up to that historic eighth of January, 1918, when President Wilson, addressing a joint session of Congress, delivered his famous Fourteen Points as the "program of the world's peace." The Thirteenth Point was Poland's: "An independent Polish state should be erected which should include the territories inhabited by indisputably Polish populations, which should be assured a free and secure access to the sea, and whose political and economic independence and territorial integrity should be guaranteed by international covenant."

The voice of Paderewski, through President Wilson's declaration of January 8, 1918, was heard unmistakably in Berlin, where it brought forth a rejoinder which showed how sore a point the Polish question was. Unfortunately, Lloyd George, speaking in the British Parliament on January 5, had left the way open for just such a rejoinder, revealing, as the Germans believed, a lack of unanimity among the Allies on the Polish question. "This settlement," said Hertling, the German chancellor, "concerns only the States of Central and Eastern Europe." This was the old Russian plea. Now it was the German plea. But Paderewski had silenced it for all time. The Polish question could never again be a Russian or a German "domestic" question.

The Fourteen Points were the culmination and the crowning event of Paderewski's four-year war struggle in America. From that time until the Armistice was signed, he worked more easily. In this struggle he had encountered mountains of misunderstanding, of division, of delay, of opposition. But he had never given up. His success was, in the words of Lansing, "a triumph of personality." How much it was such a triumph is evidenced by the curious fact that even Cabot Lodge, the Massachusetts

Republican Senator who prosecuted implacable war on President Wilson, yielded to Wilson nevertheless when Paderewski was concerned, as he did when he introduced a resolution in the Senate supporting the Thirteenth Point. Senator Lodge phrased his resolution in the identical words of the President, the words that had been inspired by Paderewski's recommendations through Colonel House, "and I think it will be very well for the Senate," said the Republican leader, "to join itself with the President in regard to Poland. I think nothing is more important than the President's proposition about access to the sea. I have information which I think good," he added, "that there is a movement on foot, a strong movement, though underground, here and abroad, to prevent the establishment of a strong, independent Poland. It would be well to show that the Senate is with the President in his statement in regard to what should be done for Poland." From Senator Lodge this was an almost unbelievable concession. It was unquestionably a Paderewskian "triumph of personality."

Colonel House summed up Paderewski's war success in America in a clear and simple statement: "He gave to the American Poles a single purpose." He was able to do this because he lived himself for a single purpose. *"La patrie avant tout, l'art ensuite."* But he still remained the musician. All that he did was done, it might be said, to the strains of music. It was his art that first of all magnetized the people, gave him free address to multitudes. He dedicated that art to his cause. An incident happened in New York that illustrates how closely music was woven into his war-time work. It was during the visit to America of the French commander Joffre. Joffre, scheduled to be honored by a gala concert at which Paderewski was to play, was inadvertently kept by his American hosts on a sight-seeing tour far beyond the time of the performance. At a late hour, and after Paderewski had come to the piano, the French commander was ushered into his box. The auditorium was packed, and the Marshal's entrance was greeted with a sudden burst of applause, the people standing and cheering him. Paderewski at the piano never turned, but in his own way he joined

in that applause. By a strange coincidence it was Chopin's magnificent Polonaise Militaire that he was playing. How he
played it! The music rang over the plaudits, harmonized them
into an ovation. "I wished to give to Joffre the best that was
in me, my music," Paderewski said afterward. It was then that
he also said, "That was the last time I played. I declared then
that I would never play again until Poland was free."

He definitely ceased his public playing in 1917. In the autumn of that year, after contracts had been signed for a tour
which would have brought a net profit twice the sum of a year's
salary of the President of the United States, he telegraphed
from Paso Robles to Engles, his manager, "Cancel tour. All
my time is needed for Poland." His foresight, his genius for
the ultimate objective, dictated this startling decision. His reasoning was, that although the war victims of his country needed
every cent of the intake of that tour to relieve their suffering,
at the moment they needed still more a defender to save them
from political slavery and national extinction. "I shall not play
again until Poland is free," he told Gutzon Borglum one day
in the sculptor's studio in New York. Besides, the emotional
strain of famine and death in Poland was becoming too great.
"I can't play the piano," he said, "while men, women and children are suffering and the world is aflame." He had tested his
powers as orator and diplomat by this time and knew that by
them better than by giving recitals he could achieve his end.

But if he could not play, he could still compose. In spite of
the complete turnover of his mind from art to public affairs
the poet still strove for utterance. While recruiting his army he
had done a thing characteristically Polish and poetic; he had
had distributed among his soldiers thousands of copies of the
patriotic poems of Mickiewicz, the poet who had inspired his
youth. Perhaps, doing that, a fleeting memory came to him of
the days in his boyhood when, flourishing a wooden sword, he
led his imaginary army in the attic. Now his army was real. In
the midst of his many activities he found time, too, somewhere in the small hours of the night, to compose the words
and music, with orchestral accompaniment, of a War Hymn

for his volunteers, this army of his which had multiplied his name and his power by one hundred thousand. This soldier hymn of Paderewski's breathes the spirit of the words he spoke so many times in his travels over America, pleading for Poland's cause:

"My errand is not of hatred, but of love."

XXXIV

1918: MACHINE GUN STACCATO

IN DECEMBER 1918 Paderewski was once more on the sea, again pacing the decks of a transatlantic liner and facing a problem. The problem this time was more difficult than the one he had faced four years before at the beginning of his struggle in America, more baffling, in fact, than any he had ever faced. "When Europe was tearing herself to pieces," Colonel House has written, "this artist-statesman was formulating plans which later were to mold again his beloved country into a harmonious whole." Now Europe had finished her ghastly job, had literally torn herself to pieces, and Paderewski's task was to formulate plans that would help in putting her together again. Poland, dismembered for a century and more, broken and bleeding in all her parts, was a major wound in the body European. If he could mend that major wound he would indeed be serving to mold the world into a harmonious whole.

World-upsetting things had happened since that for him breath-taking day in January, 1917, when President Wilson had proclaimed as one of the terms of world peace the freedom of Poland.* Austria, by the Treaty of Chelm, had given

---

* A brief chronology of some of these significant happenings overseas, so anxiously watched day by day by Paderewski at work in America, gives an idea of the pressure under which he lived and the preoccupations of his mind as he now returned to Europe. *1917:*— March 17, Russia collapses, revolution begins under Kerensky; July 2, Pilsudski, leader of Polish Legions, resigns from Council of State organized under German military rule; July 9, Legions refuse oath of allegiance to German and Austrian Emperors; July 12, legionnaires interned by Germans; July 22, Pilsudski arrested, imprisoned at Magdeburg; August 15, Dmowski becomes head of Polish National Committee at Paris; August 25, Council of State at Warsaw resigns; September 12, Regency Council established by Germans; October 18, Allies formally recognize Polish National Committee at Paris, of which Paderewski is plenipotentiary in America; December 8, first Polish cabinet, under Regency, formed. *1918:*— January 6, first declaration of Allies

eastern Poland to the Ukrainians. Germany, first taking Russian Poland from the Muscovites, had then sold it back to them by the Treaty of Brest-Litovsk—that is, as much of it as she had decided not to keep for herself; an act which had at least confirmed Paderewski in all that he had prognosticated of the farcical German "independence" of November, 1916. Russia, Lloyd George's "steam roller", had collapsed in the revolution of 1917; the Romanoff dynasty was ended forever. Then at last the monstrous Prussian engine had fallen apart. In Poland the break-down had shown earlier than elsewhere, as early, in fact as October, 1918. It was on the fifth of October that the German Chancellor, Prince Max of Baden, made the Reich's first move toward asking for peace. The significant point is, he asked for negotiations on the basis of the Fourteen Points, whereupon a distinct echo of Paderewski's successful working on President Wilson in the Polish cause, something in fact very much like the voice of Paderewski himself, was heard in the Reichstag. One of the Polish members, Seyda, in the face of furious German opposition, reminded Germany that the Thirteenth Point declared for the freedom of Poland. In Poland itself, so complete was the German breakdown that when the Armistice had been signed scenes almost comic had been enacted on the streets of Warsaw, boys daring to disarm Prussian soldiers and officers, running with their booty to improvised munition depots, the Germans too surprised in the collapse to protest. Such incidents were not altogether surprising, however, for something of the same daring nature had occurred in March, 1917, following the proclamation by the Revolutionary government in Russia recognizing a free Poland. All over the area of German occupation at that time copies of the Russian proclamation were posted one night by

---

favoring independent Poland; February 11, Regency cabinet resigns; June 3, Versailles declaration of Allies on Polish independence; November 1, Ukrainians attack Poles at Lwow; November 7, first Polish Republic proclaimed at Lublin; November 11, the Armistice; Pilsudski, released from Magdeburg prison, returns to Warsaw; German garrisons disarmed, German governor, Gen. Von Beseler, escapes, Pilsudski takes command of all Polish forces, combining his own Legions and others (the Michaelis, the Pulawy) and organizes a Polish Army; November 14, Regency dissolves, Pilsudski becomes Chief of State; November 16, Pilsudski notifies Allies of independent republic.

persons unknown; the German military woke the next morning to find staring them in the face the Russian salutation to "an independent and unified Polish State . . . a solid rampart against the pressure of the Germanic Powers on the Slav peoples." *

As Paderewski, in December, 1918, journeyed back to Europe from America and reviewed the happenings of the past four years and more, he felt that the words of the poet Krasinski were coming true. Back in 1860 Krasinski had written in a letter to General Zamoyski, "We shall be! And if it be not the work of the just, of France and England, it shall be, by God's Will, the work of the devils." The devils, the powers that had sought to destroy Poland, had at last by the weakness of their own overweening power, by their simultaneous fall, restored her to her "to be". But what was she to be? That was the question.

The Allies, like the remainder of the Western world, thought of the war at that time almost exclusively in terms of the Western front, deluding themselves into the belief that Germany defeated in the West was Germany defeated on all sides. Paderewski knew better. He knew Prussia's *Welt Politik* ambitions, he foresaw that Germany would not give up her strangle-hold on Eastern Europe as readily as she withdrew in the West. She had cherished for too many years her *Drang nach Osten* hallucination, her dream of a Hamburg-to-the-Persian-Gulf railway, to give up without a number of last kicks. Had not the Kaiser, on his accession to the throne, proclaimed himself the "Protector of Islam"? The Kaiser had gone, as the Czar had gone, but Kaiserism and Islamism, at least of the Prussian brand, still remained. There was once more a Poland, true enough; but still a threatened Poland. As late as April of 1920, as things turned out, Erzberger, the German Minister of Finance, who had signed the Armistice in November, 1918, was threatening her, saying publicly, "If we succeed in keeping Poland down it will mean enormous gains for us. The way to Russia is open.

---

* *Poland: 1914–1931.* Robert Machray. New York: E. P. Dutton and Company, Inc. 1932. (p. 78.)

Russia is now ripe if planted with German seed to come into the great German future. Poland is the sole but very powerful obstacle. If we succeed in hindering the building up of a strong Poland the future is quite clear for us. We will undertake the restoration of Russia . . . we will be ready within ten or fifteen years to bring France into our power. The march toward Paris will be easier then than in 1914." Even as late as 1921, three years after the signing of the Armistice, General Ludendorff was stirring the students of the University of Königsberg in East Prussia with an inflammatory speech about "sooner or later a battle for that land to our east" (Poland) where "we shall rally round the black, white and red flag of Prussia." Yet this was nothing strange coming from a people who had heard their greatest military leader, Hindenburg, declare in this very year of 1918, a few months before Paderewski returned to Europe, that "Poland must belong either to Germany or the Bolsheviks. There could be no graver danger for Germany"—for Germany's dream of Eastern empire—"than the existence of a Polish state, if that state were destined to continued independence."

Paderewski knew these things in 1918. He knew them because he knew only too well the Prussian mind. As events were later to prove, he knew the "psychology of the war" better than almost any other European statesman knew it. This was due not alone to his intimate knowledge of Eastern Europe and of the Prussian and Muscovite mentalities, but to his knowledge of the statesmen themselves. With Woodrow Wilson and Edward M. House, Paderewski had a perspective impossible to a Lloyd George or even to a Clemenceau.

Crossing the Atlantic in December 1918 Paderewski realized that though his work in America was done his real work was only begun. In 1914 at Morges he had seen Poland's problem as a triple one—military, civilian, political. Time had solved her military problem: the Poles were no longer a conscripted people. The generosity of America had solved her problem of civilian relief or at least had begun the solution of it. Poland was saved from her enemies, gun and famine. But who would save her from herself, unite her lands and people into a responsible state?

Pacing the decks he cast his eye over Poland as she stood at that moment. Poland! He could see the whole land in one glance of his mind's eye, Poland of the rivers, her high level plains stretching from the Oder to the Vistula and beyond to the Niemen, the Dniester and the marshes of the east; from the Baltic and Danzig to the snowy Tatras. A wide and pleasant land, Polska, "land of the plains", the land that he had immortalized in his music; her far horizons rimmed by pines, the plain homeliness of her sober stretches brightened by the variegated green of her patch-quilt fields and by the gay striped violet and orange and crimson and canary of her peasants' garb. Along a path beaten across a wintry meadow he could imagine a band of peasants in their flouncing raiment, colors stolen from their prairie sunsets, crossing the snow, singing . . . they were in rags now, they were hungry, yet they sang because they were free. "Those fields, colored by various grains" that Mickiewicz pictured so lovingly in his poetry, were swept now by freezing winds, but in their hardened bareness the brown succulence of stored-up fertility waited its time. Wide levels of rich soil, soil the richer because it has been fertilized by the blood of its defenders . . . even the snow seemed crimson for a moment . . . old country houses among the trees —Konsnia, how now did beautiful old Konsnia look after four years of war, Konsnia where he had dreamed of a Polish home? . . . Polish homes, lonely thatched cottages by roadsides, villages clustered by stream or pond, towns, cities—Warsaw, "heart of Poland", with its million, royal Cracow crowned by the rusty grandeur of the old Vavel Castle, Lwów with its Italianate robe trailing lost Venetian splendor out of the Adriatic past . . . smoky Lódz with its factories . . . still as death now, the cotton mills denuded, wrecked, their multitudinous chimneys smokeless, standing cold and gaunt, the ghosts of dead industry. . . . Danzig, old Polish Danzig of the high-towered granaries, the canals, the bright-colored roofs . . . the East again, Podolian prairies, Volhynian plains that he had

spent his boyhood on . . . the graves of his people . . . people
. . . his own people—how did they fare? The people of Poland, how did the thirty million fare?

Stupendous task, to save, to secure and stabilize that land,
those millions! And they, those thirty millions of Poles, were
waiting for someone to save them. The clamor of war and the
clamor of voices calling for help, disputing, arguing in their
new release of freedom—it all was stilled now for a moment
while they waited for a leader to come. He had been their deliverer before the eyes of the outside world. Who would be
their leader in the inside world of their own homeland, doing
for them in the sphere of government what Pilsudski and his
soldiers had done for them in the military? As Pilsudski had
held them united in the strength of armed leadership, who now
would renew and unify and strengthen them in the consciousness of political integrity?

Germany was still there, the Germany which Dmowski at
Paris had told House "was passing through its Elizabethan period . . . three hundred years behind the balance of civilized
Europe in her thought . . . it is for that reason she came to
grief." She had come to grief, but she was still entrenched in
Poland. According to the terms of the Armistice she was to
withdraw her troops "within the frontiers of Germany as they
existed on August 1, 1914 . . . as soon as the Allies, taking into
account the internal situation of these territories, shall decide
that the time for this has come." But the German frontiers of
August, 1914 included western Poland, Poznania; and the Poz-
nanian people through their provincial Diet already had demanded, on December 3, before Paderewski had left America,
that they be restored to Poland. Was there a Poland for them
to be restored to? Pilsudski, reorganizing his scattered legions,
had assumed power in Warsaw and had tried to organize a
government. But the Allies were distrustful of him, and in the
meantime Germany stayed on. She stayed on not alone in the
formerly German-ruled territory, but, hoping still to spoil Poland if she could not retain it, she stayed on in Galicia, the former Austrian partition, hidden behind the bayonets of the

Ukrainians whom she abetted in fighting. She was still in the northern and the northwestern territories also, on the Baltic, in Lithuania and Courland, clinging to the empty clauses of the abrogated Treaty of Brest-Litovsk.

Russia was still there. Only a part of the one-time Russian Poland was cleared and in Polish hands, and that part lay stripped naked, without boundaries, threatened on every side. While the Ukrainians attacked her on the southeast the Bolsheviks threatened her on the east, the Lithuanians on the north, the Czechs on the southeast. After all, the military problem was not solved. The Pole was no longer a conscript. But what was he? He was a soldier, yes, a soldier with a great soldier, Pilsudski, to lead him. But to preserve his country the Pole must have more than an army. He must have a government to back that army.

Bad as Paderewski saw the Polish military situation as he journeyed back to Europe in December, 1918, he saw the civil situation as infinitely worse. How many Polish governments had there been? The German "Council of State", invented to preserve the fiction of Polish independence, had given way to a "Regency", both of them handicapped in action and curtailed in law. The Regency had been followed on the withdrawal of the Germans from Warsaw by a socialist government organized November 7 by Daszynski at Lublin. On November 11 Pilsudski, released from German imprisonment at Magdeburg, had returned to Warsaw, assumed power and entrusted Daszynski with the formation of a cabinet to succeed the Lublin coterie. Five days later Daszynski, failing in his effort, had resigned to be followed by another more moderate but still socialist government under Moraczewski. None of these governments had been recognized by the Allies. Assuredly, as Paderewski saw, there was confusion enough, though not for a moment did he lack in appreciation of the patriotic endeavors of the various leaders who, against overwhelming odds, had sought to stabilize the country. Nor were these rapid-fire changes in government at Warsaw all, for, opposing the Moraczewski government had come, on November 18, the Supreme Popular Council in Poznań with a threat to form a separate state unless liberated from the German yoke and from the socialist incubus at Warsaw. This Poznan government had carried out an orderly election and had submitted itself to the Polish National Committee sitting at Paris, with Paderewski's colleague Dmowski at its head; the same National Committee of which Paderewski had been the accepted plenipotentiary at Washington. It was this committee that the Allies recognized. . . . Thus, through the maze of Poland's confusing effort to establish herself Paderewski's mind not only faced the fact that his work, far from being completed was only begun, but tried to trace a line of action which would insure a stable government to Poland, a government acceptable to the Allies. Obviously, whatever the efforts at home in Poland had been or might be, the sanction of the Allies was the *sine qua non* of the situation.

When he landed in England he conferred at once with the British Prime Minister, Lloyd George, and with Balfour, the Secretary of State for Foreign Affairs, with whom he had already counselled in Washington during Balfour's mission to America in 1917. Lloyd George, as usual, was in a captious state of mind concerning things Polish. Whatever the little Welshman's lack of confidence in a pianist as statesman, he had no confidence whatsoever in the soldier-socialist Pilsudski. Lloyd George gave Paderewski a challenge. "If you can pound some sense of harmony into the heads of your compatriots," he said, "you will accomplish wonders." How was it to be done? Balfour, always helpful and sympathetic, knew a way. And it was then that Paderewski heard pronounced his new summons to a new task. The summons came in the form of a question. Would he, backed by the National Committee at Paris and coöperating with the Popular Council at Poznan, go to Poland, organize a coalition cabinet, and get a stable government launched?

This had been House's idea, a coalition government; he had urged it upon Dmowski at their Paris conference on December 4. The French seconded Balfour's proposal when Paderewski arrived in Paris December 15. It was the only way, all agreed, that would insure Poland a voice at the Peace Conference. That voice, Paderewski knew, Poland must have if she was to be restored as a nation instead of as a mere provincial or vassal state.

Paderewski realized that unless something was done and done promptly to win the confidence of the Allies, the Poland that they had rescued was lost. If he refused or delayed there was no telling what might be the outcome. His imagination could run wild picturing the future—civil war in Poland . . . protectorates . . . new partitions. He had to make a decision and a quick one. Yet this proposal was to him appalling in its responsibilities . . . and he wanted to go home . . . a little respite after the four year struggle in America . . . a little breathing spell . . . Christmas at home anyway . . .

He decided. He said "Yes."

On board the British warship *Concord*, with Christmas approaching, significant time of peace and good-will, significant name for the ship that carried him, Paderewski set out on his newest mission, across the North Sea and into the Baltic, headed for the ancient Polish port of Danzig. I have been over the route: no waters can seem so deep, so dark and cold as those black northern waters in winter time, impenetrable and threatening at night, by day sullen, gray and forbidding . . . sleet-laden winds cut like blades and encrust the rigging and decks with ice; if the sun shines it glitters, its rays frosty and brittle. . . . At times the thought must have come to him on that slow journey as the *Concord* plowed its cautious way eastward, that he was fated to be always traveling by sea to some new adventure. This was the most dangerous adventure of all. The sea was full of floating mines; and what lay ahead in Poland? "To venture into Poland at that time," as Colonel House has written, "was a perilous undertaking for one who had played so important a rôle in the humiliation of the governments of which the new Poland had been so recently a part, and to make the venture through Danzig was particularly perilous. But fear for himself had never been a part of Paderewski's character."

Included in Paderewski's staff on this journey was the Polish painter Sigismond Ivanowski. Ivanowski, having gone regularly for twenty years to hear him play, nevertheless had never met Paderewski until he began his "begging" tour in America. He had not wished to meet him; he had wanted to think of him only as the "ideal artist". "I had met other great men and, sooner or later, experience had taught me, flaws were revealed that destroyed preconceived ideals of their characters. My impression of Paderewski was too perfect, too precious, to risk its destruction by personal contact." But after he had heard him speak, he went to him, offered himself as a co-worker, and became one of his chief lieutenants during the five years of political activity that followed. "For five years I was his aide and intimate. The idealistic impression I had had of him was not destroyed by this association. Instead, it was broadened to encompass all that the man did." On board the *Concord* Ivanowski witnessed a little incident which is characteristic.

It is not literally true that Paderewski never opened the piano during his war work after he closed it in 1917. He played once, on the *Concord,* perhaps with memories of the famous rural piano of his runaway tour forty years before, and this, according to Ivanowski's story, is how it happened: "Shortly after the voyage began, a long slow voyage through the minefields still adrift in the Baltic, the commander came to the cabin to say that the officers of the cruiser were all eager to meet their guest and would be pleased if he would receive them in the wardroom later in the day. Paderewski assented graciously and at the appointed time the commander presented his subordinates. During the general conversation which followed, the musician's eyes fell upon a piano in the corner of the wardroom. It was an upright instrument, evidently ancient, and it looked rather as if it had been fished up from the bottom of the sea. The keys were chipped and yellow; the paint clung to it only in patches.

" 'Perhaps,' Paderewski proposed, 'you would like me to play for you a little?' There was consternation among the officers of the *Concord* at his suggestion. 'Oh, Mr. Paderewski, we couldn't think of permitting you to touch this piano. It has not been tuned in the memory of man. Furthermore, there are several keys that do not even respond. No musician would touch it.' But a musician did, nevertheless. Paderewski sat down at that dismal wreck and for the first time since he had vowed to play no more till Poland was free, touched a keyboard—a keyboard from which a half dozen notes were entirely absent and many others scarcely recognizable. He played on that travesty for two hours—favorite compositions in his program—while the wardroom listened with awed delight. Under his masterly touch the battered old instrument seemed to revive and actually uttered music." The stout British ironclad *Concord* felt that day something unknown before to its steel frame, something for its rhythmic engines to remember, unaccustomed vibrations of melodious harmony, a master's music streaming out like warm sunlight over the raw gray wastes of the Baltic.

Through the Skagerrak, along the Jutland Banks, over the waters where in May the year before the naval powers of Germany and the Allies had come to grips, into the Kattegat, past the distant lights of Copenhagen, the *Concord* made careful way. Somewhere in the night along those frostbitten coasts sat Elsinore on its rock, high in the "nipping and eager air" . . . Once there had been a poet prince who journeyed home to find his fatherland shaken to its foundations, the crown of his forefathers despoiled. Did a princely ghost mount the ramparts of Elsinore in December 1918 to hail in passing "the sledded Polack", a new prince of poets, a tall figure, lion-headed, tawny hair blowing in the wind, homeward bound to a despoiled motherland?

There was plenty of time for thought as Paderewski moved slowly forward to his task. He bent close to it, spent long hours in his cabin, long hours pacing the decks, pondering, weighing, measuring . . . but what lay ahead? The problem was one which had no precedents to be measured by. It must be taken at the face. And nothing perhaps could have been more conducive to reflection on that problem, or could have afforded him better opportunity for solitary thought, than this sea-voyage, especially a voyage on a battleship. A battleship, any ship, is not only what some sailor, it may have been Conrad, has called it, "man's noblest handiwork", but a ship is a world in itself, a cosmos, that exists and moves on and has its being on the axis of authority and coordination . . . significant thought for Paderewski journeying toward his uptorn, still disordered, still uncoördinated country. On a ship, disorder means wreck, mutiny means death. But that is not all. Order may be imposed, coördination may be achieved. The ship moves on. But there are the seas that it must ride, elemental forces of disorder, of wreckage and destruction if the ship itself, no matter how manned and ruled, be not built for combat with the deep, its keel truly laid, its rudder firm and flexible. Thoughts for the man voyaging into the unknown seas of new and untried government . . . many thoughts of peril ahead.

Nor were the physical perils of this journey ended when Paderewski set foot on Polish soil on Christmas Day, 1918. The Germans, it will be remembered, on the sufferance of the Armistice, were still in Poznania. Paderewski's party, including Madame Paderewska, and in the escort of a group of British army officers commanded by Colonel Wade, were no longer safe after they left the *Concord* and landed in Danzig. They were unmolested in Danzig but met with serious difficulty in getting to the city of Poznań, so numerous were the obstacles put in their way by the German military. Then, Poznań reached the day after Christmas, real trouble began.

The Germans, entrenched in Poznań, knew why Paderewski had come—to establish peace. This meant the end of their hundred and more years of possession of western Poland. They were desperate, and they acted rashly. They decided on bloodshed. They would stage a fight, and it would have one or possibly two results: either it would be merely a riot which would prove to the Allies how disorderly the Poles were, or it would be a riot which would not only prove the Poles disorderly, but might, accidentally, dispose of Paderewski.

The Poles, receiving him with tumultuous enthusiasm, had arranged a civic demonstration welcoming Paderewski the day after his arrival. The chief feature of this demonstration was a children's parade in which 10,000 children marched. The city was quiet. The Popular Council had impressed on the populace the grave need of order, on pain of incurring discredit with the Allies. Everyone knew that the German military was on all sides of them; all were pledged to provoke no trouble. As the children's parade neared the Bazaar Hotel where Paderewski was housed the Germans began to "rush" the line of procession. On the instant, as if they popped out of the pavement, a battalion of Prussians, composed almost entirely of officers, appeared on the scene, took a machine-gun formation directly opposite the hotel, and opened fire, raking the ranks of the terrified children and only too obviously aiming to get Paderewski. He had retired to his bedroom and had laid down to rest. "I was in the rear of the hotel," Major Ivanowski related afterward, "when the sharp chattering of the guns began, followed by the crash of glass and screams of fright. I ran to Paderewski's room. It had two windows with a mirror hanging on the strip of wall between them. The window-panes had been shot out. I begged Paderewski to come out of the room at once. Instead, he sat on the edge of his bed and began to pull on his clothes, paying small heed to the whizzing spray of steel that dug into the walls only a little above his head, and none at all to my frantic appeals. Then, when I believed that at last he would come with me, he rose and strolled over toward the windows. With bullets pouring past to right and left he stood there before the mirror and tied his tie . . . There is always something almost terrifying in the simplicity of the man's bravery. He literally never considers danger to himself."

This attack of the Prussians resulted tragically, even though it failed to put the Polish leader out of the way. Many were wounded, one killed; a new name, Ratajczak, was added to the long list of Polish victims to Prussian hatred. For a time it looked as if the Germans would get control of the city. Guerrilla warfare raged, and for three days Paderewski lived under fire. Thanks to provisions brought in from the country there was food during the siege. But there was something better than food—the knowledge that the young Poles of Poznań, instead of being a disorderly mob, were capable of action and self-control. Instantly the firing had broken out the first day, without command of any leader, bands of young men rushed to the German barracks, overcame the guards, took possession of all arms and ammunition, returned to the center of the city, established headquarters at Paderewski's hotel, manned it at every window with machine guns, and raised the white and amaranth of the Polish colors over the roof.

The rash act of the Germans proved their undoing. News of the orderly maneuver of the young Poles of Poznań spread like fire through Poznania. New groups of "actionists" followed suit and proceeded to clear the province of the Prussian military. The day after the outbreak in Poznan the city of Gniezno was taken by the young Poles; the next day and the next news was brought to Paderewski of further dispersals. The movement went on, in spite of every effort of Polish officials, who, fearing a revolution and the consequent discredit of Paderewski at Paris, tried to stop it. But there was no revolution. The work was prosecuted in systematic manner, and, what is most remarkable, without leadership. In a short time nothing was left of German power in Poznania but their threat to bomb Poznan from the air.

Paderewski's enthusiastic reception in Poznań had its echo in Berlin. The press was bitter. The *Vossische Zeitung* was scornful, referring angrily to the "common citizens"—Paderewski and his party—"who received in Poznań a triumphal reception such as is usually reserved for crowned heads."

Paderewski spent the last days of 1918 in Poznań, up to midnight of New Year's Eve, every hour crowded with Council conferences. At three o'clock in the morning of New Year's Day, 1919, he set out for Warsaw, he and his wife escorted as far as Kalisz by a party of Poznań citizens. The journey to Warsaw was like a royal progress. Although he was passing through the country in the deep of night and the depth of winter, peasants and townsfolk lined the railway tracks all night long greeting the train at every station. They cheered him, called out to him, cried his name, some wept. At Ostrawa they blocked the tracks and forced Paderewski to speak. By the time he reached Warsaw he had delivered seventeen speeches in one day.

Paderewski entered Warsaw on New Year's day, 1919. The city rose to meet him with a jubilation difficult to appreciate unless one understands what his coming meant to the people of the Polish capital. It meant something better even than freedom. Freedom was won. It meant government, order, an end to apprehension and fear. It meant that at last there was a real Poland, established and secure, a free Polish state recognized by the world. The city was decorated with Allied and American flags, a hundred thousand people crowded the streets and sang and shouted for two days afterward. Some threw flowers at him, wherever they got them, flowers that brightened the snowy pavements with gala colors.

For a quarter of a century the idol and pride of the Polish public, with which he had a spotless record of integrity and patriotism, the Paderewski who had stirred them with hope in 1898, who had prophesied to them in 1910, who had found for them the bread that saved their lives from 1914 to the day of his coming—this Paderewski came home now to his people clothed not only with the authority of a long-established popularity, but with the new record of his American war leadership, and the power of the Allies back of him. He stood to Poland at that moment as the living symbol of all they desired and hoped for, peace, liberty, and security.

He went to work immediately. A suite of rooms had been prepared for him in the Bristol Hotel. He opened his office there January 1, before 1919 was a day old. Outside, the streets still were noisy with the undispersed crowds welcoming him and wishing him "Happy New Year!" It looked like a happy new year for the new Poland.

XXXV

1919: THE STRUGGLE IN POLAND—I

A LETTER written by Paderewski to Colonel House twelve days after his arrival in Warsaw gives a complete impression of the situation which he faced. Under date of January 12, 1919, he wrote as follows*:

I have telegraphed you several times, but evidently not one of my messages has reached you.

The American Food Commission is going to leave Warsaw tonight. My time is very limited and, to my deepest regret, I shall not be able to fully describe to you the situation, which is simply tragic. Mr. J. M. Horodyski will give you the details. I wish, however, to add a few remarks to his verbal report, which will be, I am sure, very exact.

Contrary to the rumors originated by the retiring pro-German propaganda the Poles have been nowhere the aggressive party. Though claiming, most legitimately Danzig as an indispensable condition for their political, commercial, and economic life, they all rely with unshaken confidence on the results of the Peace Conference and do not intend to surprise the delegates by any 'fait accompli'. But could anybody ask them to remain quiet when brutally attacked and not to defend themselves? Surprised by the murderous Ukrainian Bolshevik army the women and children of Lemberg took up arms and defended the city. At the present moment a force of about 80,000 Ukrainians, armed and equipped by the Germans, led by German and Austrian officers under the command of an Austrian Archduke Wilhelm of Hapsburg, is at the gate of Lemberg and the number of Polish soldiers, lacking food and munitions, does not exceed 18,000 men. In Posen, the day after my arrival, during the procession of 10,000 school children marching through the streets, some Prussian companies, mostly officers, opened fire upon the peaceful and unarmed crowd. Quite a number of shots were fired at my windows, some of them at the window of Colonel Wade. Explosive and dum-dum bullets were used. American and British flags

---

* Quoted by special permission of Hon. Edward M. House, from "The Intimate Papers of Colonel House" (Houghton Mifflin Co., Boston).

were insulted. Several eye-witnesses, including the officers of the British Mission, and myself, can testify to these facts.

There is no doubt that the whole affair was organized by the Germans in order to create some new difficulties for the Peace Conference. There is also not the slightest doubt that the present Spartacan movement in Germany and the Bolshevik revolution in Russia are most closely connected. They simply intend to meet on our soil.

The Bolshevik army has already taken Vilna.* The cities of Grodno and Bialystok are in immediate danger. In a few days the invasion of this part of Poland will be an accomplished fact.

Poland cannot defend itself. We have no food, no uniforms, no arms, no ammunition. We have but men, at best 500,000 of them, willing to fight, to defend the country under a strong government. The present government is weak and dangerous, it is almost exclusively radical-socialist.

I have been asked to form a new cabinet, but what could I do with the moral support of the country alone, without the material assistance of the Allies and the United States?

If there were any possibility of obtaining immediate help for my country I would suggest:

(1) To send a collective note to the Ukrainian Directorate at Kief, addressed to Messrs. Petlura, Winnitchenko, and Schwetz, ordering cessation of hostilities in Eastern Galicia and evacuation of the district of Boryslaw, where considerable American, English and French interests are endangered.

(2) To send an interallied military Commission to Warsaw in order to examine the situation and prescribe the means of assistance.

(3) To send as soon as possible some artillery and plenty of German rifle-munitions.

If this action is delayed our entire civilization may cease to exist. The war may only result in the establishment of barbarism all over Europe.

Kindly forgive this chaotic writing.

From this letter it is plain that Paderewski had his work cut out for him. "The question was," in his own later words, "in

---

* Vilna, preëminently Polish, had been turned over by Pilsudski to the Lithuanians, the Lithuanians definitely pledging themselves to defend it for Poland against the Bolsheviks. But the pledge was broken, thanks to the new nationalism of the Lithuanians, a nationalism rooted in social grounds—enmity for the landlords—which had been for decades assiduously nursed by the Germans, in order to make of it an Achilles' heel for Poland. This breach of promise, in Paderewski's opinion, would have justified Poland's openly retaking Vilna. Had this been done the subsequent *coup d'état* of Pilsudski in seizing the city, and thereby putting Poland in the wrong, would have been forestalled. Pilsudski's mistake was not so much in acting as in delaying action, in demurring when action was justified, then resorting to a tardy *fait accompli*.

what character Poland could appear at the Conference, and whether she could appear at all. 'De facto' we were a nation, not a small nation, the sixth largest among the nations of Europe; 'de jure' we were not a state: we had no recognized government." He had, then, just one thing to do—to establish a responsible government which the Allies would recognize. Every other problem, military and civil, of the whole confused and baffling situation was included in that single project. It had to be carried to success promptly, without delay. At present there were actually two governments, the Supreme Popular Council organized at Poznań, functioning locally but still separately until the Peace Treaty was signed and Germany's withdrawal accomplished; and the Socialist government at Warsaw, which, significantly enough, although not recognized by the National Committee at Paris, and therefore not by the Allies, had been recognized by Germany. Berlin had even sent an ambassador to Warsaw, maintaining diplomatic relations until December 15, 1918; a move which obviously certified to Germany's still lingering hope of controlling Poland through the weak radical government fostered by Pilsudski. Besides these two actual governments to be reckoned with, there was the potential military dictatorship of Pilsudski, always in the offing. It controlled the Warsaw cabinet; the probability of it supplanting that cabinet at any moment had to be considered.

Paderewski knew that his first problem was Pilsudski. Pilsudski was popular and he had the power of a rapidly organizing and highly enthusiastic army behind him. Actually Pilsudski had worked miracles since November 11, 1918, in the building up, enlarging and coördinating of the national forces; a characteristic Polish miracle, for the new nation's new army was entirely volunteer—there had been no conscription. From the handful of scattered legions to be drawn together when the Armistice came, the Polish forces had grown to an army of over one hundred thousand men. This fact gave Pilsudski a strong hold on the masses and a complete hold on the military. This was something, at least, to offset his lack of political prestige as Chief of State; for in the eyes of the Allies his authority in that office was not legitimate, since it was derivative from the German power, out of the Regency, which in turn had derived from the German-organized Council of State, which itself derived from the abortive "independence" manifesto of 1916.

Pilsudski was a picturesque man, one of the most romantic figures of the World War, with a record of adventure and patriotic achievement that gave him a powerful grip on popular fancy. He had suffered imprisonment, impoverishment, exile to Siberia, a price had been on his head, he had escaped prison walls, he had done a hundred thrilling story-book things; he was, in short, a popular hero and he was idolized by great masses of the people. But adventure and intrigue had done a certain harm to Pilsudski insofar as his political capacity was concerned; they had made him devious, circumspect, suspicious, not always, in the political arena, capable of the larger view.

He had done much for Poland, more than any other one man actually in Poland. He had given her the nucleus of an army of defense and the national self-confidence that such an army meant. But in the world of international politics he lacked credit. There was a reason for this. He distrusted the Allies, and the Allies distrusted him. Actually he distrusted Dmowski, the chief of the National Democratic Party and president of the National Committee at Paris; and therefore he distrusted the National Committee of which Paderewski was plenipotentiary. The Supreme Council of the Allies at Paris was anathema to him because it had recognized the Polish National Committee but had refused to recognize him through the delegation he had sent them in November. Pilsudski at this time had in fact no credit at all with the Allies. Their feeling toward him obviously was not one based on understanding or appreciation of his motives, although their attitude may be explained by the fact that they were at the moment decidedly nervous and cautious of any man who, like Pilsudski, was tarred with the Socialist stick. It was not alone that France remembered Pilsudski's project of joining Japan against Russia in 1905, a venture on which Paris had frowned at the time, and

of which she had very likely been reminded now, with Pilsudski's political opponent Dmowski on the ground to remind her;
for, as it had happened, it was Dmowski who in 1905 had
scotched that scheme, getting to Tokio ahead of Pilsudski and
convincing the Japanese government of the futility of the plan;
although, as a matter of fact, the Japanese had taken Pilsudski
seriously enough to agree to the separate incarceration of Polish
prisoners of war captured in the Russian armies and to the subsequent release of such prisoners to neutral America. Pilsudski
could hardly be expected to forget that misadventure and
Dmowski's part in it. Nor was it that the Allies, all of them, remembered his earlier Austrian connections during the World
War, when, in 1914, his Riflemen had served the German Command as informers against Russia, then one of the Allies, or
when, in 1917, he had joined the German-organized Council
of State at Warsaw. As a matter of fact, and as the Allies of
course knew, and as we have already seen, Pilsudski had refused
to permit that abortive Council of State, once he had recognized
it as a useless instrument in the Polish cause, to make use of
either him or of his legions; and he had gone to prison for that
refusal. It was none of these things specifically that made the
Allies at Paris reject Pilsudski. What really made him suspect
among them was his political, his Socialistic, background and
activities; that and his well-known career as a revolutionist.
These things smacked of Bolshevism to the Allies, and now his
insistence on a government of the Left, in the organization of
the Moraczewski cabinet, increased their fear of him as a radical. So far as Bolshevism was concerned, the Allies plainly mis-
judged Pilsudski. He could never be a Bolshevik. "Bolshevism," as he himself said to me in Warsaw in 1920, "is a purely
Russian disease. The root idea of it is class vengeance." Class
vengeance was something wholly outside of the Polish psychology. "You accuse me," he once said, after the World War,
to a group of Socialists who reproachfully recalled the time
when he and Lenin were political affiliates, "you accuse me of
having betrayed Socialism. It is this way, gentlemen: we rode
together in a streetcar marked *Socialism*, but I got off at the

stop 'Independent Poland'." "My whole past," he declared to me, "drives me toward governing with the left, but there is something above 'left', and that is Poland." More than that, according to his own expressed purpose, he had design in the emphasizing of the Left in organizing his first government, that design being the forestalling of exactly the kind of trouble the Allies feared, revolution. "Revolution from the Left," he said, "is always more dangerous than from the Right, therefore it was necessary to take the Left into account first and get it to participate in the government of the country." On another and much later occasion he remarked, "They talk to satiety of the Right and the Left. I do not like these categories. They cover different social conceptions, and the solution of social problems is still to seek. We are the neighbors of Russia, who has tried a social experiment on a great scale by putting down the old institutions and replacing them by others. We have no wish to imitate her." Nevertheless, he was suspect of the Allies; they were afraid of him and their fears had not been allayed by the decree which he had published November 22, 1918, calling for the organization of a national assembly which, in his own words, was to be instituted "on the basis even of the most radical bill respecting the mode of carrying out the elections for it."

Thus the Allies, upon whom Poland's political and military security depended, would have nothing to do with Pilsudski as a political leader. Pilsudski very naturally resented this. Such was the situation when Paderewski arrived in Warsaw. He stood between the Allies and Pilsudski, the virtual representative of the Allies in Warsaw, the actual representative of Poland in Paris. However, if the Allies would have none of Pilsudski, he knew that Poland must have much of them. He knew what Allied recognition and backing meant. He knew that Paderewski meant the Allies, their support as well as their recognition. And Paderewski knew that he, Pilsudski, was the first and greatest problem of his task of establishing a government acceptable to the Powers. One of the first moves he made upon his arrival at Warsaw was to call on Pilsudski at the Belvedere Palace.

Paderewski carried on his work in his Hotel Bristol rooms for some time. Later, when he became Prime Minister, he moved to the Zamek, the old Winter Palace, where more commodious quarters were arranged for his staff. It was in his rooms at the Zamek that I first saw him in Poland. As we entered he happened to be standing beyond an open door in front of a long mirror, speaking to someone inside, and there was an excellent opportunity, during the several minutes that elapsed before he joined us, to study him. His figure, which I had last seen on the platform in San Francisco in 1915, seemed unusually gaunt and tall and his leonine mane seemed in that light to have turned almost white. His brow was, as always, very pale. The marks of his care were plainly on his face; but his stride as he came forward, his manner and voice, were strong and alert.

It was with a good deal of natural curiosity as well as with a certain amount of anxiety that Paderewski first approached the famous Legionnaire. He had never seen him. Naturally he had heard much of him, endless things, pro and con. He was neither blind to the Allies' skepticism concerning him nor to Dmowski's intense feeling about him, any more than he was blind to Pilsudski's popularity with the Polish soldiery and with large masses of the people. Nor was he blind to his own difficult situation as an intermediary between antagonized forces. But he and Pilsudski were one at heart in their single aim, the reëstablishment of a Polish State; and in the past, though strangers to each other, they had been of one mind on more than one score—as in 1915 when both of them, he in America, Pilsudski in Poland, had said in unison, "We must resist the Germans"; as in 1916 when they both had resisted the lure of German "independence." Surely, Paderewski said to himself, though he did not minimize the difficulty, surely we can work together. He rehearsed Pilsudski's story to himself as he prepared for their first meeting.

Here was a man born to the rôle of patriot-soldier. Like Kosciuszko, Poland's national hero—whose name Paderewski had joyously found as familiar to American as to Polish ears; like Mickiewicz, the national poet—Pilsudski was a Lithuanian Pole. The Vilna that he had hoped to save to Poland—that he was to seize later—the Vilna that just now had been betrayed by the Lithuanians to the Bolsheviks, this Vilna had been Pilsudski's boyhood home; and Vilna had been for centuries a stronghold of Polish culture and a center of Russian pressure. Pilsudski's earliest years had been, indeed, very much like those of Paderewski. They were both from the Borderlands. He had been born only a few years later than Paderewski himself, four years after the Uprising of '63, which had put its mark on Paderewski's childhood memories, and which had in its aftermath of terrorism shadowed Joseph Pilsudski's youngest years. He had had a patriot father, a patriot mother; it was his mother's name that Sienkiewicz had immortalized as the heroine of his historical novel *The Deluge,* a heroine who was actually one of Pilsudski's maternal ancestors. By both father and mother there had been instilled into his soul love for Poland and hatred of her Russian oppressor. That was one of the keynotes to Pilsudski's character—hatred of Russia. It was that hatred that had put the fatal birthmark of sectionalism on him, and it was that birthmark that explained a great part of his story. Much that had happened: his long conflict with Dmowski, who favored the "Realistic" and compromising attitude toward Russia against Pilsudski's aggressive and revolutionary "Activist" ideal; his Japanese project; his serving the Central Powers against Russia early in the war; his ardent Socialistic politics, because Socialism linked him most warmly with the opponents of Russian rule: all these things were explained in Pilsudski's origin and youth, his hatred for Russia.

His youth had been stormy, tragic. At school in Vilna, under Russian masters, he had been burned with the Muscovite contempt for all things Polish. His brother Bronislas he had seen exiled to Siberia. Studying medicine at the University of Kharkov, he had been drawn naturally into a circle of young revolutionaries who, like himself, chafed under the yoke of Petersburg. Falsely accused of complicity in an abortive plot to assassinate Czar Alexander III, he had suffered, as his brother had, unjust arrest, imprisonment, exile to Siberia. His Siberian sentence served, he had returned to Poland, embittered and revengeful, his life dedicated to revolution and insurrection.

First he had made the pen his instrument; he became the secret and fugitive editor of Socialist journals. He had been caught, arrested, thrown into one of the dungeons of the Warsaw Citadel, that grim prison which the Russians had forced the Polish martyrs of 1831 to build as their own death-house. He had escaped, feigning insanity. He had taken up his secret propaganda work again. He had become the acknowledged leader of the Polish insurrectionists, hunted, "on the run", clever at outwitting the enemy, a secret hero of the people. He moved quickly and furtively, he was to be found anywhere and everywhere, inspiring, leading in the plots and intrigues of his compatriots. He was as well known in London and Paris, among the Polish *émigrés* there, as he was in Russia, Austria, Germany, where the Triple Cormorant sat in the nest of the White Eagle and devoured her young.

From the pen to the sword was an easy, an inevitable transition. His dream of a Polish Legion began; he would fight with the sword as well as with the pen. The Russian Revolution of 1905 supplied him with his first opportunity. The rebuff to his Japanese proposal did not stop him. He organized his first secret fighting corps, held up Russian mail trains, rescued Polish prisoners, captured booty, once to the amount of three million roubles, a million and a half dollars, with which to finance his campaigns, political and military. He became as famous as Robin Hood. Out of that fame and his military experience grew his Riflemen's Clubs, which in due time won the sanction of the Austrian authorities. Out of them came the Legions, which in 1914 swung into action against Russia. And out of all this came Pilsudski's conviction, expressed by him in Paris in 1914, and disturbing, no doubt, to the Allies in 1919, now sick of war, that "the sword alone decides the destinies of nations." "A people which shuts its eyes to this fact," he de-clared, "would irretrievably compromise its future. It must not be that we are that people."

This then was the man to whom Paderewski had come in the hope of joining hands for the building of a Polish state. This was the man who had with his sword, in the words of Stephen Mizwa,* "dug at the foundations for the structure of mod-ern Poland, hewed at her cornerstones, hammered away the obstructions, and chiseled from within"; and he, Paderewski himself, was the man who, in the words of the same author, was to "carve and shape the edifice of Free Poland in the minds and hearts of all the peoples of the earth." There was no ques-tion in Paderewski's mind, as he approached his first meeting with Pilsudski, concerning the man's heroic patriotism; no Pole could question that. But he was highly sensitive to the actuality of the situation which he faced. He knew instinctively what Pilsudski's feelings were and how those feelings had been in-tensified by such happenings at Paris as Marshal Foch's failure to respond to his request, made in November, 1918, to send to Poland the Polish army formed in France, formed in large part by Paderewski's own American recruits. He knew that Pil-sudski was aware of the fact that the French Foreign Office had consulted his, Pilsudski's, political antagonist Dmowski on every telegram and wireless that the Chief of State had dis-patched from Warsaw. He knew that, in November, when Pilsudski had taken office as Chief of State and had sent a dele-gation to Paris, he had also sent a private letter to Dmowski which had said: "I trust that in this case and at such a serious time a few men at least—if, alas, not all Poland—will rise above party politics, cliques and groups; and I should like to think of you as being among those men" . . . and Pilsudski's plea for recognition had been refused. In short, down in the bottom of Pilsudski's heart, Paderewski might well have be-lieved at that moment—if the heart of so secretive a man could be read at all—was the wish, however wisdom and the good

* *Paderewski: His Country and its Recent Progress.* By Stephen P. Mizwa, Executive Director, the Kosciuszko Foundation. Published by the Foundation, New York, 1928.

of the Polish cause forbade its utterance, that Poland might go it alone, that there were no Allied Powers to patronize him and interfere with him, that Poland might be freed from her friends in Paris as she had been freed from her enemies in Berlin, Vienna, Petrograd. The Allies, Paderewski realized, saw Poland from the outside, in; Pilsudski saw from the inside, out. His, Paderewski's, task was to make Pilsudski realize that he, Paderewski, saw both ways, from inside and from without.

The meeting of these two men was one of the most dramatic happenings in modern history. So much depended on it! The prospect of it held the Polish populace in keen suspense, and through the eye of Paris the eyes of the world were on the event. The future peace not only of Poland but of Europe hung on the outcome of this confrontation. What would these two forces do? Would they join in a clash? Would they conjoin and fuse? Each knew his power. Paderewski had the Allied Powers back of him and in his hand he held not only the food that was feeding multitudes, soldiers as well as civilians, but arms as well—a strong hold on the populace. Pilsudski had his army and the hero-worship of the same multitudes. Each knew his responsibility, the welfare of the nation. I can picture that meeting because I have sat in the Belvedere and talked with Pilsudski, perhaps in the same chair that Paderewski sat in as he faced the famous Legionnaire, garbed in his severe military tunic, his brush of iron gray hair standing stiff in a close clip, his deep-set wary eyes quizzing non-committally under bushy brows, his mouth hidden by a drooping mustache. The gentleman who faces him in the picture is free and poised and not surprised because he is received cautiously if not coldly. Paderewski has the ease of a man who has moved all his life in an open world. Pilsudski is calculating, suspicious. Whatever one says to the other, each knows the question in the other's mind: "Will this man work with me?"

Perhaps Paderewski, with his keen instinct for character long trained in public relations, knew the answer first. He may have sensed in a moment that this man would not work with him, not wholeheartedly and unequivocally anyway; that it was impossible for him to work so with anyone. A French political expert, writing in *Le Correspondent* of Paris, recorded in 1920 his impression that "among all Europe's political crowd there is not one less penetrable than Pilsudski." "You could discuss with him for hours the deepest and most fascinating political problems," this French writer said, "listen to him and observe intently, depart thoroughly acquainted with his wishes, hopes and fears, his resources and what obstacles he foresees, but as to what he proposes to do—nothing, absolutely nothing can be gathered. He is shut tight, buttoned up, screwed down." This, as the Paris journalist remarked, is "a powerful asset" when "inquisitive persons and political meddlers" are concerned. But it is a liability, a weakness and a danger, when "those of his own household" are to be dealt with, when friends are regarded as "meddlers". As matters turned out, the secretiveness of Pilsudski served ill to Poland's interests when Paderewski came to deal with him. Once in exasperation Paderewski said to him, "Come out of your subterranea!" But subterranea was too ingrained in Pilsudski's bones for him to come out for anyone. He had lived, of necessity, through his long and tireless struggle for Polish liberty, the subterranean life of the romantic Polish patriots that Mickiewicz had sung of in his poetry:

> Slowly to poison speech;
> To hide with anger underground;
> To make his mind deep as an impenetrable abyss.

During his lifetime Paderewski had encountered many obstacles; the difficult processes of his art to be mastered, the confidence of audiences to be gained, the antagonism of critics to be overcome; in politics the distracting divisions of his people, the hide-bound reluctances of officialdom: his whole life had been a struggle against challenging obstacles. He had taken their challenge, taken life as an instrument to be mastered and played upon. But here, in this fellow patriot, this strong-willed soldier playing a poker-hand at civil government with a poker-face, a poker-soul, he found the most baffling of all the obstacles he had known, the most difficult of all instruments to be played upon. He knew why it was difficult. It had no diapason, it was single-chorded. But its single chord was patriotism, the love of Poland, the major chord of his own, Paderewski's, being. Surely it could be played upon. Played upon it must be if Poland was to be harmonized and saved. And no time must be lost. He kept his single objective constantly before him. "The secret of success is the elimination of the possibility of failure." One thing to do now, everything else afterward—win Pilsudski over to the establishment of a government which the Allies would recognize.

Ivanowski, Paderewski's aide, has said of him after being his intimate associate for five years: "His confidence is absolute. He never doubts himself. Be it a piano or a recalcitrant Diet that he approaches he never questions for an instant whether he will conquer. He knows he will succeed. Failure is never even considered. He is positive that his mental, moral and physical power will enable him to surmount all obstacles. I never saw that confidence misplaced."

It was not misplaced this time. Facing the not-frank and all too secretive Pilsudski, Paderewski's gift of tenacity was put to a test. But he won. Pilsudski agreed. By the fifteenth of January, three days after Paderewski had sent his letter to Colonel House disclosing the situation he was in, Pilsudski's Socialist cabinet was dissolved. By the seventeenth Paderewski's coalition government was organized. He had achieved the first step toward stabilization and unity, toward the fulfillment of the Allies' mandate.

But not without trouble, trouble that seriously endangered his mission. Following his first conference with Pilsudski he went to Cracow to confer with leaders there. Cracow, the ancient capital, gave him a welcome even more passionate and impressive than Warsaw. But in his absence from Warsaw a group of hot-heads, thinking to achieve a *coup d'état*, entirely without his knowledge or sanction attempted to overthrow the Pilsudski dictatorship. They began by seizing, on the night of

January 4, Pilsudski's chief-of-staff. There was excitement in the streets when the tak-tak of machine guns broke through the stillness. In the morning, with the city electrified with apprehension, this, it was learned, was what had happened: The conspirators, surprising their quarry in his room at the Bristol Hotel, had had the tables turned on them. The chief-of-staff had coolly put them under arrest. The tension lasted for a day or two; any noise in the night was for a while taken for the beginning of a revolution. But that was the end of the *coup d'état* and the last thing of its kind to occur while Paderewski was in Poland.

News of this foolhardy conspiracy shook Paderewski to the heart, it roused his anger. Not for a moment would he countenance any illegal or violent attempts to change the government. The fortunate failure of the *coup d'état*, however, resulted in a double victory for him. It saved him from what might have been complete disaster before the Allies, and it apparently made Pilsudski realize not only that his Socialist government lacked the respect of important citizens, but that Paderewski was needed in Warsaw. At any rate Pilsudski sent his chief-of-staff, the officer whom the conspirators had tried to kidnap, posthaste to Cracow to bring Paderewski back to the capital. He was dragged out of bed before dawn to have Pilsudski's urgent offer of coöperation made to him. He hurried back to Warsaw, arriving the same night. The dissolution of the Socialist cabinet and the organization of the coalition government, with Paderewski appointed Prime Minister and Minister of Foreign Affairs, ensued within the week. He was determined to speed things up. The Peace Conference was assembling, ready for its first session. Delay in placing Poland before it would be disastrous.

He had to go over a good deal of ground during these early conferences with Pilsudski before any kind of definite agreement could be reached. His first proposal was that a national committee be appointed consisting of one hundred representative men, twenty-five from Poznania, twenty-five from Galicia, fifty from Congress (formerly Russian) Poland, one half the Congress Poland delegation to be Socialists. Pilsudski, inclined at first to accept this plan, finally rejected it and proposed in turn that Paderewski take the whole burden of forming a new government. Paderewski, refusing to be put in the position of either ousting the existing government bodily or of having one handed to him ready-made by those already in power, would not agree. Pilsudski's next proposal was that nothing be done until an election be held. But Paderewski, with Paris at his back waiting for word of an acceptable government and refusing to accept Pilsudski's weak and unrepresentative Socialist government, urged the necessity of quick action, the grave danger of procrastination. It took ten days to settle the matter with the formation of a coalition cabinet, the best that the two men could accomplish with the material in hand.

While he was still in the throes of organizing a cabinet Paderewski was at the same time taking the next important step toward the establishment of a Poland free in fact as well as in name. He completed plans for a popular election. Here he was obliged to deal with an unwieldy situation. The Socialist government which his coalition cabinet supplanted had begun the election plans, but had elaborated an electoral system that was inclined to be, in its theoretical broadness, actually narrow and discriminating. Pilsudski's decree for "even the most radical bill" had borne fruit. The groundwork had been laid, however, and there was nothing to do but proceed upon it, rather than take the risk of dangerous delay and upset. He went ahead, doing his best to make the country understand that this election was not final, in the sense that its purpose was not the election of a legislative body of supreme power, but for one carrying the sole mandate of voting a budget and a constitution, to pave the way for a regularly constituted parliament.

The high pressure under which Paderewski worked at this time would have soon exhausted a man of ordinary physique, but his magnificently preserved strength kept him fresh and strong. The amazing memory which his career in music had developed likewise served him. "I have seen him sit at his desk with a document before him," his aide Ivanowski had said, "staring at it until I believed that his thoughts must be far away. I could not credit that it would take a man so long to read anything. But, when at length he laid the missive aside, it had become his forever. He had literally photographed it upon his brain and had filed it away in the archives of his mind, from which he could produce it, intact, at need."

That letter which he wrote to Colonel House on January 12 was written, as he said, in chaos. But if he was bringing order out of chaos, he had little time for letters. Madame Paderewska took care of his personal correspondence. A letter which she wrote to her son W. O. Gorski in New York on January 26, Election Day, gives us a detailed picture of what was happening during these first weeks of reconstruction.

"All the political changes in regard to the external and internal policies of Poland," Madame Paderewska related, "have been achieved without the usual accompaniment of disturbances, without the shedding of a drop of blood . . . Today are taking place the elections for deputies to the National Assembly. For the first time in 140 years the Polish people, all of them, without distinction of class, race or religion, have been given the opportunity to vote for their own representatives; and in spite of the fact that many among them are illiterate— thanks to the good care their oppressors took to deprive them of schools—the elections are proceeding without any disturbances, quarrels, or disorders of any kind. In a most orderly way thousands and thousands of Polish citizens, hungry, in rags, are standing patiently in line sometimes for many hours, their bare feet in the snow, shivering from cold, waiting for their turn to cast a ballot . . ."

Zeal and hardihood are in that picture of a people standing barefoot in the snow waiting to cast their vote. I have seen them barefoot in the snow waiting for bread. But ballots were as dear as bread to the Poles who, in 1919, had found in Paderewski a deliverer who fed them "not by bread alone". Besides, ballots were something new in Poland. For over a century the people had had mostly bullets from those governing them. Now they had food and suffrage both. Day by day, during the ensuing months, as he worked—sometimes fifteen hours a day —to stabilize the country, the devotion of the masses to him grew. He became a popular idol. From my diary I draw a picture which shows the two men-of-the-hour in the Poland of that time, Pilsudski the soldier, Paderewski the statesman, greeted by the people who idolized them both.

The occasion was "Soldiers' Day", a national celebration in honor of the Polish arms. Those arms were still, even at this time, in the midsummer of 1919, meager, poorly clad and poorly equipped to defend a country still harassed on every side, but they were the darlings of a liberated people. "The day began," the diary recites, "with a great religious observance, a pontifical requiem mass for the soldier-dead, celebrated in the one-time Russian basilica. Then came the parade, a magnificent military review witnessed by tens of thousands of citizens who thronged the streets. We had a good view from one of the balconies of the hotel. The procession lasted an hour. The band music was splendid, the band located in the reviewing stand just across the street. The appearance of the troops was remarkably fine, the soldiers stepped up with snap and go. The uniforms of many were those purchased from the American army stores after the Armistice, the familiar olive-drab of the A. E. F., but the knapsacks were German and the caps also, refurbished of course. Uniforms! I never saw such a conglomeration of uniforms in my life. It looks as if Poland were the junk-pile of all the discarded military clothes of the world. Besides the "o. d." of the doughboy there is the sage green of the German trooper—much of this, but touched up with new Polish buttons and a bit of cerise-colored braid trimming the cuffs and collars. Among officers one sees a great deal of the German gray-green, but with blue trousers or blue breeches and top boots. Occasionally there is what seems to us a typically Russian outfit, all astrakhan cap, tight-belted full-skirted coat. But the predominating color is the German, a reminder of the servitude these people once suffered. They march freely now under their own flag, though they are too poor to dress themselves in new strictly Polish uniform . . .

"First came the officers and the single company which composed the original Polish army; the men were nearly all in uniform (of various kinds), though a few of them were in civilian clothes. Then followed the infantry. Rifles were decked with green sprays, so were the caps, and every man had a sprig of green or a flower stuck in his belt. The machine guns and the artillery looked trim, the cavalry was magnificent—beautiful horses, full of life, stepping spiritedly to the tune of the band. Finally came the bodyguard of Pilsudski; mounted, carrying guidons and dressed in the historic Legionnaire uniform. Then, to cheers of the crowds, Pilsudski himself in an open automobile, wearing a plain uniform of gray without a sign of decoration or gold braid on his whole outfit. A big laurel wreath rested on the seat of the car in front of him. Other cars and carriages passed. Then the cheering began again. Paderewski was coming.

"He rode bareheaded in a closed car, but we could see him plainly, his long figure, his face white under the mane of coppery whitening hair. His reception was an ovation. His car could hardly pass. Flowers were thrown at him. The cheering went up in waves, drowning out the music of the band . . ."

But it was not all band-music and applause. There was intermittently noise of quite another kind. The radical elements of a capital of over a million population, its population swelled by thousands of refugees, of itinerant unemployed, was bound to be heard from. That element, still feeling the moral support of Pilsudski's ousted Socialist government, was bold and tireless in its demonstrations. One morning while Paderewski was still housed at the Bristol, the Reds began to assemble before the hotel, collecting a horde of the disaffected, obviously bent on mobbing him when he would appear to enter his car which stood at the curb waiting to take him to a cabinet meeting. The crowd grew until the streets were solidly blocked. They began to sing revolutionary songs and to wave red flags and banners with inflammatory slogans. Then in unison they took up a chant, "Chleba! Chleba!" "Bread! Bread! We want bread!", until the whole square rocked with the tumultuous stamping of their feet and the noise of their shouting.

Inside the hotel, members of Paderewski's staff were trying to dissuade him from going out. The Allied envoys had just arrived from Paris—doubtless this fact was the incentive in the minds of the leaders of the mob—and a riot against Paderewski would be a damaging thing to be reported back to Paris. Let him leave the hotel by a rear door and go to the cabinet meeting another way. He refused. "No," he insisted, "I shall go out and talk with them." He appeared at the main door of the hotel and was greeted by a roaring howl. He paused, looked at the mob, ran forward down the steps, and began shouldering his way into the crowd. The chant of "Bread! Bread! We want bread!" rose to a higher and more threatening pitch. Over it women's shrill voices and the bellowing of men screamed and hooted. He went on, straight into the heart of the mob. Then he halted, looked about, raised his hand, removed his hat, began to speak.

Something electrifying in that gesture of dignity with which Paderewski saluted the people and stood bareheaded, struck them into a momentary silence. Then heckling began, a boo here, a hoot there, a shout, more and more shouting and yelling. No one who has not seen a Red mob in full swing can realize the cumulative force of its anger, hatred and scorn, once it finds voice. It is a primitive emotional force almost impossible to face, much less to control. But Paderewski went on speaking. At last they were still. His voice boomed out its ringing changes. They listened, they listened more and more intently. Now there was no sound in that square packed with thousands of rioters save the sound of Paderewski's voice.

He ended. He stood bareheaded among them in the tremendous silence of a silenced mob. Then suddenly the silence was broken—a cheer—a bellowing cheer that swept up to him roaring his name "Paderewski! Paderewski!" The air was black with hats and caps flung high, men and women rushed for-

ward, they threw themselves on their knees, they grabbed his
coat hems and kissed them, they caught at his hands, they knelt
to him. "Paderewski! Paderewski! Vivat! Vivat!" They
opened a lane for him to his car. They lifted him into the car,
shouting, cheering. The car started. They followed it. Paderewski rode to the cabinet meeting that day with thousands of
erstwhile rioters marching before him, beside him, behind him,
shouting "Paderewski! Poland! Vivat! Paderewski!"

But, disturbing as were such incidents as these, behind the
scenes of government other things were happening to give
Paderewski heart. For one thing, that letter which he had written to Colonel House on January 12 bore quick fruit. On re-
ceipt of it Colonel House had written to President Wilson: "I
think that his requests are moderate and I believe that you
should urge the Allied Governments to accede to his wishes
. . . I suggest that you, on behalf of the United States, immediately recognize this government as a *de facto* government.
I believe that we should take the lead in this matter. The British are certain to follow us as they sent Paderewski to Danzig
on a British warship." President Wilson acted promptly on
House's suggestion, and Secretary Lansing, under date of
January 22, sent the following cable to Paderewski:

"The President of the United States directs me to extend to you, as
Prime Minister and Secretary of Foreign Affairs of the Provisional
Polish Government, its sincere wishes for your success in the high office
which you have assumed and his earnest hope that the Government of
which you are a part will bring prosperity to the Republic of Poland.

"It is my privilege to extend to you at this time my personal greetings
and officially to assure you that it will be a source of gratification to enter
into official relations with you at the earliest opportunity. To render
to your country such aid as is possible at this time, as it enters upon a
new cycle of independent life, will be in due accord with that spirit
of friendliness which has in the past animated the American people in
their relations with your countrymen."

"What a joy! What a comfort, what an inspiration that is
for us!" Madame Paderewska wrote in her Election Day letter. "The task which Paderewski has undertaken is superhu-

man, but with the help of God he will accomplish what he has set out to do."

House was right about the recognitions. On February 27 Great Britain's arrived along with that of France. On the 28th Italy came forward. Switzerland followed, then Belgium, Sweden, Spain. Paderewski's struggle in Poland had only begun, but his credit abroad as a statesman grew steadily. Except for an occasional fling in the Berlin papers about "the piano-playing premier", and even one noteworthy jibe of the kind from Lloyd George, Paderewski the musician was all but forgotten now in the record of Paderewski the political harmonizer. Lloyd George's remark was characteristic. "Poland is a mere mask," he said to an American ambassador who was sitting in as an unofficial observer at an Allied conference. "They had to take a pianist as their Premier."

But the report of these particular events anticipates what had happened during the first weeks of Paderewski's régime. He had arrived on New Year's Day. He had swung Pilsudski over to the organization of a new government; he had completed plans for a popular election; he had installed his coalition cabinet. He had accomplished these things under a terrific sense of pressure from the direction of Paris, and amid a cross-fire of separate interests, divergent views, conflicting personalities in Warsaw, that was at times almost maddening, or would have been maddening to a man not trained to keep his head and drive straight forward toward an absolute objective. He was now ready to take the next, all-important step: return to Paris to appear before the Allies and claim for Poland the status of an established state.

XXXVI

1919: AT THE PEACE CONFERENCE

FROM his window in the Zamek Paderewski could look out on the bronze Sigismond, the King who shook his sword. From the eastern galleries he could see the Vistula flowing toward Danzig and the Baltic. If he recalled the legend of Sigismond and his sword, he could remember too the equally strange story of the old peasant "holy woman" who in the eighteenth century had prophesied that Poland would not be free "until the Turk has watered his horse in the Vistula." That prophecy also had been incredibly fulfilled. Germany's *Drang nach Osten*, with the Kaiser the "Protector of Islam", had made the Sultan of Turkey a vassal of Berlin. Certain Turkish troops, brigaded with the Austrian army, had penetrated to the Vistula, and the Turk had literally watered his horse in the historic Polish stream that Paderewski could see from the Zamek rampart. The impossible had come true. He could make the impossible come true again—make harmony out of the triangulated discord of the relations between the Allies, Pilsudski, and himself. Already he had accomplished something with Pilsudski. But beyond the bronze Sigismond and beyond the Belvedere lay Paris, still to be conquered.

He left Warsaw for Paris January 18, the day after the installation of his cabinet.

We are to imagine a spacious room in a palace at Paris, a room about thirty feet long and twenty feet wide, with very high ceilings, a room solidly and richly appointed, with handsome woodwork, high dark wainscoting, the walls above the wainscoting covered with heavy deeply-colored tapestries depicting the life of King Henry IV of France. This room is the

office of the French Minister of Foreign Affairs, M. Pichon. It
is also the meeting-place-in-ordinary of the Supreme War
Council, to which Paderewski, in addition to his offices as Prime
Minister and Minister of Foreign Affairs of Poland, is the Polish delegate. He is due now to arrive from Warsaw.

The room runs east and west. At the west end is a massive
carved mantelpiece; a wood fire blazes in the grate. If we are
facing the fireplace we see an ornamental flat-topped desk a
few feet in front of the grate; a low-backed armchair is behind the desk, its back to the fire. But after all it is not the desk
or the chair but the man that we see—a very striking looking
old man, bulky and round-shouldered—sitting in that chair
behind that desk. He is the kind of an old man who with one
squint of his Chinese-like eyes can make you wonder who you
are without his even putting the question, and with another
squint can make you like him. He has a Ming face, the face of
a Mandarin, high cheek-bones, sallow skin, drooping mustache.
He always wears gloves. It is Clemenceau, the Tiger of France.

To our right, in the center of the long north wall, are two
sets of double doors, one set on the inside of this room, the
duplicate set on the outside; the doors, connected by brass
levers, operate in unison: we have a feeling that with doors
like this and walls so thick as these, whatever goes on in this
room will not be overheard, even though the whole world be
listening—as it is listening. There are chairs ranged by the
north wall near the double doors, and they are filled by distinguished men. To our left the south wall is broken by four
high windows which reach nearly to the ceiling and are set in
deep embrasures; there is a glimpse of shrubbery and trees
outside. With backs to the windows stand eight large chairs; a
small table in front of each, covered with maps and documents.
In these throne-like chairs, beginning at the west end near
Clemenceau, are seated the President of the United States and
his Secretary of State; the Prime Minister and the Secretary of
State for Foreign Affairs of Great Britain; the Premier and
the Foreign Minister of Italy, the plenipotentiaries of Japan.
Behind them, at desks in the large window alcoves, and also

along the east end of the room, are the secretaries and expert advisers of these men.

At Clemenceau's left, between him and Wilson, is M. Pichon, also seated in one of the throne-like chairs; at Clemenceau's right and back of him sits Professor Mantoux, interpreter, and M. Ducasta, secretary-general of the Conference.

This is the famous Council of Ten of the Peace Conference, two delegates each for France, England, the United States, Italy, Japan; that Council which in 1919 was reshaping the European world. It is also the Supreme War Council. It is also the Big Four and the Council of Foreign Ministers; or such it became in March of that year. It is seated in council now, and it is ready to receive the Prime Minister and the Minister of Foreign Affairs of the Republic of Poland, M. Ignace Jan Paderewski. He will enter this sound-proof room from the anxious world outside by those famous double-double-doors in the north wall.

Paderewski had landed in Poland Christmas Day, 1918. It is now January 19, 1919, two days after the organizing of his cabinet in Warsaw. In three weeks he has pacified a politically demoralized country of 30,000,000 people, established a government, arranged for a popular election, set the machinery of government working in a country which through the deprivation of more than a hundred years has forgotten what self-government is. He has worked fast and well, and the members of the Peace Conference at Paris appreciate the fact. They are now ready to receive him and to hear his representations for the recognition of Poland.

As a matter of fact, three days after his arrival, the Conference, having accepted his government, acceded to his request for a political and military mission to be sent to Warsaw. This put the final seal on the Allies' recognition.

Paderewski came to Paris encouraged over his success in Warsaw and ready at last to do what he had said in 1917 he must do, "face the councils of Europe if this fight is to be fought to a finish." Having indeed accomplished the one thing he had set out to accomplish—the establishment of a government in Poland acceptable to the Powers—he might have felt that, once Poland's rightful place at the Conference was assured, his work, his own particular task, was about ended. His co-delegate to the Conference, Dmowski, was on the ground. Dmowski could speak for Poland in the conferences which were to adjust her position and secure her boundaries. In Warsaw the functions of government were at least started. Riond-Bosson, home, his farm and garden, after his four years' absence were waiting for him. And his music? He seldom if ever spoke of it, but it was frequently noticed by friends that when he was seated alone at his desk or engaged in conversation his fingers moved on the arm of his chair or on the table's edge as if he were running an imaginary scale on the keyboard. Questioned one day in Warsaw, when the neuritis had come back, he said that he doubted if he would ever play in public again. He had never sentimentalized about it, however, though there were others who did, who wondered if he did not hear his piano sometimes in the watches of the night, sounding far off as if a sigh passed over the keyboard? If he had any such thoughts he said nothing about them. It is not his way to indulge in verbal dreams.

But "a journey of a thousand miles," said Confucius, "begins with one step." Paderewski, arriving in Paris January 19, had by this time taken at least a dozen forward strides on his long journey of statecraft since that night of his name-day party at Riond-Bosson in 1914. Yet now he learned, with what misgivings we can only guess, that he had a far way yet to go before his ultimate objective, a free Poland, free in every sense and in the fullest meaning of the word, was reached.

"When the Great War broke upon the world and continued so long and with such fury," writes Colonel House, "it was difficult to assess either men or events . . . Some men we exalted beyond their merits and others we appraised at less than their worth. How many of those who led in the council chambers and in the field history will acclaim is yet uncertain. There are some, however, whose ultimate claim to fame is beyond doubt, and one of these is Ignace Jan Paderewski."

The figure of Paderewski stands in a new light as we see it appearing in that room on the Quai d'Orsay. Exactly what was expected of him before he took his place there would be difficult to say. There was hope and expectation among his Allied friends; they could not deny his amazing record since the war began. They marvelled at it. But even some of them were, perhaps, still a little skeptical. Not yet could they get the idea entirely out of their heads that he was "only a musician"; it was almost impossible for them to reconcile art and brains. Nevertheless, whatever was expected of him, he surprised everyone. "Those associated with Paderewski during the stirring days from the time of our entrance into the war until the Peace Conference had finished its labors," says Colonel House, "saw a new and unfamiliar Paderewski. The artist, the composer, the poetic dreamer had left no trace of himself. The old personality had been submerged in the new, and we saw the orator, the executive, the man of action."

Mr. Lansing, President Wilson's Secretary of State, had a perfectly natural prejudice against amateur diplomats, and, as we have seen, he judged Paderewski decidedly as an amateur at first. He changed his opinion completely and avowed his mistake in the handsomest manner. "It was only with time and with a fuller knowledge of the man that I learned how wrong this impression was," Mr. Lansing wrote, "and how completely I had failed to estimate correctly his attainments and his real mental strength. The new impression, which I feel is the true one, did not at once supplant the old. It came by degrees and only overcame the first impression by observation of facts which could not be successfully questioned or denied . . . For a musician of his genius, which necessarily implied a nature sensitive and responsive to emotional influences and to the aesthetic beauties of art, to be transformed, as it were overnight, into a cool hard-headed statesman dealing wisely with rough and ugly facts, seemed to deny all common experience. It was hard to believe that such a complete change and object in life was real. But I was compelled hesitatingly but very gladly to revise my judgment and recognize that my first impression was wrong; I think I may say it was unjust though excusable.

"My second impression, and it is the impression I still hold, was that Ignace Paderewski was a greater statesman than he was a musician, that he was an able and tactful leader of his countrymen and a sagacious diplomat, and that his emotional temperament, while it intensified his patriotic zeal and his spirit of self-sacrifice, never controlled or adversely affected the soundness of his judgment or his practical point of view . . . What others, certainly more experienced than he in public affairs and credited with greater political shrewdness, failed to accomplish, Mr. Paderewski accomplished. Raw amateur though he was in politics, nearly everything that he said and nearly everything that he did seemed to be the right thing."

It was in Paris, at the Peace Conference, that Lansing fully recognized what he called Paderewski's "innate genius for political leadership": "He made few mistakes and he never seemed to be in doubt as to the course which he would take. He was wonderfully resourceful and apparently had an instinctive sense of the possible and the practicable . . . He was not carried away with extravagant hopes of unrealizable dreams. His views were essentially sane and logical . . . He showed a poise of character . . . a conservative judgment . . . an unexcitable manner of discussing matters of difference which gave weight to his words and added greatly to his influence as a negotiator."

It is as a figure standing in the council chamber that he is usually pictured at the Peace Conference. But there is another picture—Paderewski in his Paris hotel, where he established offices for his delegation. Here is where he did the work that, as Lansing remarks, made him seem "never in doubt as to the course he would take." He was never in doubt because he never spoke without the most careful preparation. "His artistic conscience," as Rom Landau, Pilsudski's biographer, remarks, "forbade all improvisation in the matter of responsible acts." Locked in his bedroom at the Hotel Wagram he would work far into the night, writing, rewriting, consulting his files, marshalling his arguments. "In preparing his addresses," Major Ivanowski, close by his side all through this period, said at the time, "he is always deliberate. He writes out the speech he is going to make, fully and carefully. Then, when he goes to deliver it, he never takes the written copy with him. By the act of writing he has also inscribed it on his mind. Several times I have taken the stenographic report of a long address he has delivered and compared it with the document he wrote in preparation and then never looked at again. Always they are alike, word for word, page after page." It was in music that he had learned this art of perfect memorizing. In music, too, he had learned how to be always composed, even though nervous, before an audience—by being always prepared. Now, while many marvelled and a few still scoffed at the "piano-playing premier", he was scoring his points at the Conference simply because he was applying the technique of his art to public affairs.

His career as artist had indeed taught him many things. Among them was the value of criticism, the value of an audience's reaction. After spending the greater part of the night preparing a speech before the Conference, often in the morning he would go over it with Dmowski. With his "exceptional memory, clear expression and controlled, passionate oratory", to quote again from Landau, with the most meticulous preparation behind his utterances, it is not to be wondered at that the Conference room, "crowded with statesmen and famous speakers, sat hushed whenever the Polish pianist spoke."

He was popular in Paris, a familiar figure. Paris had been for years one of his homes. He was especially well known to and liked by the press. Whenever he appeared in public he created more interest among the army of reporters and photographers from newspapers all over the world than any other figure in the whole galaxy of celebrities that crowded the French capital. This popularity was a real asset for his country. It gave him the ear of the world.

Paderewski was now sixty years old and he was working without let-up under a terrific nervous and physical strain, yet he retained his health, except for an occasional attack of neuritis, and he remained youthful in spirits, boyish among his intimates, affable, gracious, easy to deal with. In Warsaw, where he labored at times fifteen hours a day with his cabinet, it was said that he "worked everyone around him to death". But we have the testimony of Ivanowski, of Jan Ciechanowski, his secretary (later Polish Minister to the United States), and others of his staff, that his unfailing good nature and patience, his natural sweetness of temper and his consideration, made anything possible, with him directing. He had kept his health by living as systematically in politics as he had lived in music; in Warsaw and in Paris he followed the same regimen. As unalterable as had been his rule of twenty minutes' seclusion before a recital, was his rule now of twenty minutes' gymnastic exercises daily. Outside of that, or an occasional walk or motor ride, he took no exercise. He would argue that it is not so much the amount of exercise that one takes as the regularity of it that counts. To his mental activities he applied the same rule. "His musical training," writes Landau, "enabled him to systematize and render scientific any interest, geographical, historical or political; it prevented his mind from becoming overburdened with detail, since everything arranged itself almost musically." He had mastered the art of "shutting his mind"; when he closed his bedroom door, either in Paris or in Warsaw, though it might be in the gray dawn after a night-long conference or a never-ending cabinet meeting, he closed the door of his mind to everything, and he slept. He was never distraught nor dishevelled; he was impeccable in his toilet, he knew "the psychology of clothes", he kept his outward person the expression of the orderly man within.

This was the Paderewski, tall, impressive, poised, deliberate, who entered the conference chamber on January 19 and who afterward stood times without number in the midst of the men who were reshaping Europe, as he had stood hundreds of times facing audiences and critics. But now the audience was all critics, the instrument upon which he must play a tremendous and complex one. The questions he had to answer, the problems he had to solve, the quizzing cross-fire of interrogation and opposition he had to undergo, the explanations he had to give to expound and defend Polish ideology, elucidate Pilsudski's attitude, set forth all the intricate movements and confusions of the newly resurrected Polish life—all this was enough to baffle and weaken any but a strong man. Here is a picture of the scene, of which he was so often the center, as Colonel House saw it:

"I well remember his advent upon the world stage as it was then set at Paris. The great and influential of the earth were there playing their several parts. Woodrow Wilson, spokesman for the greater part of mankind, was, because of his great office and his winged words for peace and reason, the most conspicuous of them all. The grim, blunt-spoken, courageous old Tiger, Clemenceau, vied for second place with David Lloyd George, the little Welshman, whose versatile genius had made him practically dictator of the British Empire. Eleutherios Venizelos, the bold and sagacious Greek, Vittorio Orlando, the warmhearted, learned Sicilian, and his cool, diplomatic associate, Sidney Sonnino, Louis Botha, the noble lion of South Africa, and his brilliant colleague, Jan Smuts, were scarcely less in evidence. Balfour, clear-minded philosopher and aristocrat, widely versed in statecraft, was always a conspicuous figure. So also, indeed, were Viscount Chinda and Baron Makino, able and stoical representatives of Japan, who had for their antagonist Wellington Koo, cultured son of the Celestial Kingdom.

"While the accredited statesmen occupied the center of the stage, influential men and women in every walk of life were there in some capacity. Statesmen, soldiers, students of the many questions which were to arise, men of affairs, writers, and artists. Seldom, if ever, was there such a gathering. They came from the four corners of the earth and represented many diversified interests. Never before in the history of the world were there such a variety of questions of so complex and disturbing character to be solved—questions affecting the hopes, the fears, the ambitions of so great a part of mankind. The Conference became as a fiery furnace, and few survived its cruel and relentless flames . . . Of those few I should place Paderewski first. He came to Paris in the minds of many as an incongruous figure, whose place was on the concert stage, and not as one to be reckoned with in the settlement of a torn and distracted world. He left Paris, in the minds of his colleagues, a statesman, an incomparable orator, a linguist, and one who had the history of his Europe better in hand than any of his brilliant associates."

Paderewski's gift for languages was one of his assets. Wilson's and Lloyd George's knowledge of French was meager, Orlando could not speak English, Professor Mantoux's services as interpreter were in constant demand. But Paderewski needed no interpreter for any language spoken in the Council. Viviani, the first war-premier of France and himself a renowned orator once exclaimed, "Oh, if I could play as Paderewski speaks!" An unusual combination of precision and fluency, a low-pitched resonant voice capable on occasion of rolling volume, a gift for noble gesture, spontaneous, simple, and richly illustrative, made him the great orator of the Peace Conference.

It has been said, however, that in spite of his gifts as an orator Paderewski failed in debate. The record of his work at Paris disproves this. We have a scene, reported from the French official record by Owen Wister, which gives a characteristic picture of Paderewski engaged in debate at the Conference. The date is June 5, 1919. The question is of the proposed plebiscite in Upper Silesia, which was one of the most crucial and nerve-wracking questions that Paderewski had to handle at Paris because of the keen and bitter feeling it provoked at home in Poland. Clemenceau is replying to Lloyd George, who wants the plebiscite and who obviously is inclined to favor Germany on this point as against Poland.

"As to Poland," says Clemenceau, "amends are to be made for a historic crime, but also there is to be a barrier between Germany and Russia created. Read the interviews of Erzberger, who wishes Poland to be made as weak as possible, because it separates Germany from Russia. Mr. Erzberger adds that Germany, once she is in touch with Russia, can attack France in far better circumstances than in 1914. Is that what you want? Germany in control of Russia?" Addressing Lloyd

George directly Clemenceau continues: "To decide on a plebiscite and wash your hands of it would be very nice, but it
would be a crime against the Poles . . . Under German rule
Upper Silesia can't make a free choice . . . With inter-Allied
occupation the Germans will claim that the plebiscite was
queered. There are times when the simplest and wisest thing is
to say no. We believe that we have made a fair treaty. Let's
stick to it."

This sets the scene. Lloyd George is stubborn. It is decided
to have the experts draft a *schema*. Paderewski is called in.
President Wilson explains to him and says, "We want your
opinion":

Paderewski: The actual text of the treaty is justice itself. In Silesia
there are two districts where Poland has an undoubted majority, and
one where the majority is German. The part to the west, which is
agricultural, is under the influence of the [German] Catholic clergy,
very dangerous from our point of view; it influences the opinion of the
peasants.* To the east the population is more thoughtful and freer, but
if only the east becomes Polish, the whole industrial region will be close
to the frontier.

Lloyd George: Which zone is the more densely populated?

Paderewski: The east. In the mining region there are 900,000 Poles,
400,000 Germans. In the farming region there are 600,000 inhabitants; it is an indisputably Polish country.

Wilson: The Germans themselves recognize that the population is
Polish.

Paderewski: Yet nevertheless they claim Upper Silesia.

Lloyd George: If we were to speak of Silesia as a whole, and not
merely of Upper Silesia, in its entirety it is mainly German.

Paderewski: Yes, many people were speaking Polish at Breslau when
I was there.

Clemenceau: But as to what concerns Upper Silesia, do you agree to
a plebiscite after the evacuation of the territory by the German troops?
That's what we want to know from you.

---

* Cardinal Bertram, Archbishop of Breslau, later forbade the clergy of his jurisdiction
voting in the plebiscite. The prohibition roused strong feeling among the large numbers
of Polish clergy in the Breslau diocese; they protested to Rome.

Paderewski: Such a change in the treaty would oblige me to resign, for the people to whom the text of May seventh promised Upper Silesia would lose their confidence.

Lloyd George: We promised nothing at all, we wrote the scheme of a treaty, we didn't give it the form of an ultimatum. We reserved our liberty to examine the reply of the Germans, and consequently we have the right to make concessions if they are reasonable. What? Yesterday Poland was divided in three pieces, your fellow countrymen were fighting separately against each other, and all were fighting together against the independence of their own country. To-day you are certain of a resurrected Poland which will have 20,000,000 inhabitants; you're demanding in addition, for example, population in Galicia which is not Polish. You're demanding all this from us; you, whose liberty has been won by the death of 1,500,000 Frenchmen, 800,000 Englishmen and 500,000 Italians. It's our blood that has paid for your independence. If you kick against our decisions we shall have been mistaken in you.

Paderewski: I confined myself to stating that I could not remain in office.

Lloyd George: We have given liberty to Poland, Bohemia, Jugo-Slavia; and those are the countries that kick against the plebiscite. They are much more imperialistic than the great nations themselves.

Paderewski: I cannot admit what you say; you are merely reproducing newspaper talk.

Lloyd George: I say that you want to annex peoples against their will.

Paderewski: Not in the slightest degree. We defend our countrymen when they are attacked.

Clemenceau: I want to come back to the question of the plebiscite. If it is held after some postponement and until that time American troops occupy the country, do you think the vote will be free and favorable to Poland?

Paderewski: Yes, undoubtedly in the eastern part. As for the western part, the threefold influence of the freeholders, the officials and the clericals will make the outcome uncertain. Furthermore the object of the Germans is to provoke a disturbance in order to have to repress it. They have 350,000 men on the Polish frontier.

Paderewski's conduct of even these few moments of debate shows him possessed of the readiness with facts and figures and the control of emotion that make the ideal debater. The short-tempered British politician shows up rather badly beside him, especially when he so far loses his head as to shout such an absurdity as this, that the Poles were "fighting together against the independence of their own country"! The debate was concluded June 14, when President Wilson announced to Paderewski the decision to hold the plebiscite:

Paderewski: I can't pretend that this is not a cruel blow, for we had been promised Upper Silesia. If the plebiscite turned out unfavorable to us it would be the peasants, the workingmen, who would suffer. As to the period of waiting which you have provided, it will create an unwelcome tension. The plebiscite should not be put off longer than six months at the most. Our delegation accepts your decision with the respect it has for you, but not without profound regret.

Wilson: Your words move me deeply; I've gone through many doubts and scruples of conscience.

Clemenceau: You know that my opinion has never changed.

Lloyd George: I was myself much moved by the statements of Mr. Paderewski.

Lloyd George doubtless was really moved. Between him and Paderewski there grew up a personal attachment, in spite of the wily Welshman's obvious anti-Polish sentiment, a sentiment manifestly dictated by political opportunism and not by statesmanship, and caused occasionally by simple geographical ignorance. Lloyd George like everyone else, nevertheless, felt the charm of Paderewski's personality, the force of his sincerity. He disliked Dmowski, but he liked Paderewski so well that more than once he gave him early warning when it looked as if the Big Four were about to make a move unfavorable to him, calling him by telephone sometimes in the middle of the night to post him on the situation. "Those who knew how to talk to the British Prime Minister," André Tardieu wrote in "The Truth about the Treaty," "could always bring him back to fundamental principles . . . The infinite sensitiveness of his mind, his passionate love of success, led him to improvise arguments which did not always bear examination . . . At times his

parliamentary obsession would come over him." Or, as Walter
Hines Page phrased it, "he is too much inclined to yield his
judgment to political motives". Paderewski, "great harmonious
soul making his overflowing heart sing his dream"—thus
Clemenceau described him—knew how to talk to, how to move
this "explosive" little Welshman, "fresh and pink, coming forward with a bright two-fisted smile and gesticulations so violent," as Clemenceau once related, "that one day President
Wilson had to interpose between us." In his relations with
Lloyd George, in his relations with the whole Conference,
which at times resolved itself into as bitter a conflict as ever was
fought on the field of battle, Paderewski continually played
the part of harmonizer. His greatest difficulty on the British
side was not in dealing with Lloyd George, but with Keynes,
the English financial adviser. Keynes, in the words of Tardieu,
was "a man who has understood nothing of the history of
Europe during the past fifty years, and whose insular egoism
cannot grasp what invasion means." Invasion was the story of
Poland, and Paderewski could not make Keynes comprehend it.

One Sunday morning during his 1932 tour of America Paderewski, having heard Mass at the Benedictine Abbey in Oklahoma City, Oklahoma, told to Dom Gregory Gerrer, Custodian of the Art Gallery of Notre Dame University, a little story
about the days of the Peace Conference which illustrates the
companionship which Lloyd George and the Polish leader, in
spite of official differences, enjoyed. To begin with, Paderewski
and Dom Gregory, an authority on art, discussed painting and
painters. Malczewski, one of whose famous triptyches is at
Riond-Bosson, was spoken of, and Styka, whose portrait of
Paderewski he, Paderewski himself, regards as one of the best
that has been done. And Zuloaga. Zuloaga also did a portrait of
Paderewski and it was this portrait that brought Lloyd George
into the conversation. Zuloaga came to Morges, but was taken
ill at his hotel and Paderewski could not pose for him. The
painter asked, nevertheless, for a picture and some clothes and
proceeded to paint the portrait notwithstanding, with the result
that the only thing in the portrait that looked like Paderewski

was the clothes! The head was Lloyd George's—not really intended so, but the effect was unmistakable.

But Paderewski was not as surprised as one might think. The story he told of his Paris days with Lloyd George explains the reason. Lloyd George at the time of the Conference wore his hair fully as long as did the Polish statesman. One afternoon, according to Paderewski's story, the two of them were taking a walk together along the boulevards when Lloyd George proposed that they go into the Trocadero Palace and hear the band concert. Paderewski was delighted with the proposal, but Lloyd George was more than delighted, for he was chuckling all over with the prospect of giving the band director stage fright when he would look down in the audience and see such a distinguished musician as Paderewski before him. So the two bad boys marched themselves up to the ticket office, Lloyd George keeping ahead and taking care to secure front-row seats. They entered and took their places. Of course they were noticed coming in, and of course the people began to look at them and whisper about them.

But that was not enough. One intrepid member of the audience rose and advanced, put out his hand to Paderewski, and said, "Mr. Lloyd George, I am delighted to see you here!" "And I," Paderewski promptly answered with the straightest of faces, "am delighted to see you here. Let me make you acquainted with my friend Mr. Paderewski." The man was overwhelmed as he shook Lloyd George's hand. "Mr. Paderewski!" he exclaimed. "It is a great honor to meet so distinguished a man!" The two solemn statesmen had many a laugh together over that adventure.

The tension of Paderewski's strenuous work at the Peace Conference was relieved by his companionable intercourse with his colleagues. Everyone liked him. He knew how to play as well as how to work. His work was correspondingly effective and fruitful. It is impossible to avoid the conviction that if the others had been more like him, the work of all of them would have been more permanently fruitful of good. Colonel House had this conviction. Paderewski's recommendations at the Conference, he has said, "if accepted, would have brought a fuller measure of peace, not alone to Poland, but to Continental Europe." One of the first advances for peace made to Paderewski was from Tchitcherin, the Soviet Commissar. He offered territorial concessions, amity, and even a musical score of his, as a fellow composer! Paderewski would have at least listened to him, but between Lloyd George and Clemenceau the opportunity was lost. It is possible that the whole terrible Bolshevik War of 1920–21, with its disastrous Pilsudski campaign, its near-wrecking of Poland, its jeopardizing of all Western Europe, might have been prevented if Paderewski's counsel had been acted on, both at Paris by the Powers, and at home in Warsaw by the Chief of State.

He had many ticklish questions, ethnic, territorial, juridical, religious, economic, fiscal, to solve at the Conference; the German boundaries, the minority claims of the Ukrainians and the Jews, the Teschen frontier, the Silesian plebiscite, Danzig, the Vistula, Poland's access to the sea: these were some of them. He stood between two fires, or, as it might perhaps be better stated, between two firing-squads. On the one hand were the Powers, selfish, ready to browbeat, not hesitating to go back on their bond when advantage prompted, in their hearts frequently annoyed at Poland for the troublesome interference of her just claims and the practical idealism of her Prime Minister, an idealism which too often not only blocked their plans but reproached their purposes.* On the other hand was Poland —his country, without frontiers, open to attack and being attacked, lacking not only arms but even the endorsement of her sponsors to defend herself; his people, suffering now in the aftermath of the war as they had not suffered before, ten million of them destitute, all of them inflamed with the hopes and dreams of an unaccustomed liberty; the factional parties, growth of the seed of a hundred years of partition, at war with

---

* Conrad wrote at about this time (January 25, 1919): "If the alliances had been differently combined the Western Powers would have delivered Poland to the German learned pig with as little compunction as they were ready to give it up to the Russian mangy dog." ("Joseph Conrad: Life and Letters", by G. Jean Aubry: Garden City, New York: Doubleday, Page & Co., 1927, Vol. II, p. 216.)

each other and making war on him: all looking to him for everything at once, demanding the impossible, condemning him when the impossible was refused them. "People were unreasoning and unreasonable," says Colonel House. "If a year before the peace was made Poland had been assured of half what was given her at Paris, her citizens would have been wild with joy. In a memorable speech before the Diet at Warsaw Paderewski had the courage to tell them this and more. That was one of his great moments."

In his work at the Peace Conference, as in his war work in America, Paderewski did much more than serve the cause of his own country's freedom. He became in a sense the spokesman for all the "little" countries reaching toward liberty out of the post-war chaos. President Wilson saw him thus. When, addressing the Senate on February 11, 1918, Wilson said, "Peoples and provinces are not to be bartered about from sovereignty to sovereignty as if they were mere chattels and pawns", while he spoke then for others as well as for Poland he undoubtedly was echoing sentiments expressed by Paderewski in his Washington conferences. The same may be said of Wilson's rejection, October 18, 1918, of Austria's "autonomy" proposals, when he refused "to accept the mere autonomy of these peoples as a basis of peace", which refusal was obviously an echo of Paderewski's opposition to autonomy compromise. The old Tiger, Clemenceau, saw Paderewski in the same light, as spokesman for the "little" nations. Recalling him in his "Misery and Grandeur of Victory" he recollected his own youth, the days of '48, when "at Nantes I had seen the Poles set off in arms for the conquest of their country: today I found Paderewski filled with the joy of having found his country again . . . We [France, England] had started out as allies of the Russian oppressors of Poland . . . By the collapse of military Russia Poland found herself suddenly set free and recreated, and then all over Europe oppressed peoples raised their heads." Every time Paderewski, personifying the resurrected Poland, spoke before the Peace Conference pleading for her rights, the voice of all those other oppressed peoples was heard. The problem of none of them was such a problem as Poland's. Each of them was one. Poland was three to be re-made into one. Yet one of the representatives of Czechoslovakia exclaimed to Stojowski during these days of trial and suspense, "Oh, if we only had a Paderewski!"

The Peace Conference had begun its deliberations January 18, the day before Paderewski's arrival in Paris. The Treaty was in the hands of the Germans May 7. Paderewski with the others signed it June 28. But between those dates, travelling back and forth between Warsaw and Paris, Paderewski's struggle for stabilization in Poland went on under high pressure.

XXXVII

1919: THE STRUGGLE IN POLAND—II

"ONLY for a time," in the words of Clemenceau, "do wars destroy the strength of the vanquished." But something worse than even war had sapped the strength of the Poland which Paderewski in 1919 was trying to restore and rehabilitate: a century and a half of subjugation and partition. Paderewski had to deal not only with the literal and physical fact of a devitalized people, but also with the fact that this people was a politically divided people who had been so long deprived of initiative in government that they were virtually helpless before the problems they faced. Without a strong leader to pull them up and out of the by-paths of their confusion and set them on the open road, they were lost.

Life in the Poland of 1919 was lived intensively, dramatically. There was a daily crop of sensations, not an hour was dull, everyone was busy, on the go, from the highest dignitaries of government to the hungriest urchins collecting tomato-tins around the relief kitchens so that they might lick up an extra morsel of flavorous living. The streets of Warsaw swarmed, even in bitter midwinter, barefoot hundreds going to and from work or making for the breadlines, beggars, peddlers, newsboys crying their sheets . . . I remember an American relief worker, fresh from Paris, who was appalled by the way everyone was always saying "Pan!" He thought they spoke French and were crying *pain*, "bread", instead of saying, as they did, "sir", "mister", which in Polish is *pan*. Nevertheless, they were crying for bread. This was one of Paderewski's major problems, the feeding of the starving people.

There was, it is true, a bright surface to Polish life in those trying days. In spite of everything, the impression that one got of Poland at this time was that the people were happy. They were. They had come to life again after a long death of disillusionment and despair. There was real misery, want, hunger, millions were actually destitute, but there was no gloom. Poland was alive and bright, and the radiating point of this new light of life was the Zamek, the old royal castle in the heart of the city. The Zamek, traditional seat of authority, no longer frowned. Its doors were open. Busy men came and went. Sentries paced at its gates. But they were Polish sentries, not Russian gendarmes or German soldiers. The sun flashed on their bayonets, glittered on the snowy red roofs of the Staré Miasto, brightened the broad cold waters of the Vistula sweeping under the bridges, caught gladly at the white and amaranth of the Polish colors fluttering from the flag-pole. I have seen people standing in little groups looking at the Zamek; they seemed to be just looking at it for the satisfaction it gave them. One of their own was in there behind those doors; a Pole, not a Muscovite or a Prussian, was governing them. There was always a crowd to greet Paderewski and raise a cheer for him when he emerged from the old palace.

But under this bright surface of Polish life lay layers upon layers of hunger and disease, and the maimed limbs, the sick face, the feverish eyes, the white, hollowed-out features of Poland just rising from her long prostrations showed through the ragged death-cloth of her suffering. When Paderewski passed through the streets he saw suffering on every hand. He was conscious of it at every turn. He was, in fact, in a position not often falling to the leader of a people, to know intimately and first-hand the real situation; for at his side was his co-worker, his wife, who had come to Poland with him for one sole purpose, to organize relief for the stricken people. Paderewski was not dependent on official and formal reports alone for his knowledge of the people's needs; he had daily behind-the-scene news of their calamitous want. "I also," Madame Paderewska wrote to America in January, "have before me a tremendous task: relief work among the wounded, the sick, the hungry, and the children. I am opening canteens, visiting the hospitals. I am practically at the head of one hundred institutions, with ramifications in Lemberg, Vilna, and the borderlands. It is a huge task, but my whole heart and soul are in it. My efforts are bearing fruit and I am repaid a thousand times by the affection with which the soldiers surround me and the gratitude of the Polish women who are rallying under the sign of the White Cross. The Polish peasant women greet me everywhere as a sister, and I feel happy because I can do good, so much good."

Only one who was there at the time can realize how grave was the need for this work of doing good which Madame Paderewska had instituted; and even when an eye-witness reports it he does so only half credulous of his own senses. There is no word in the dictionary harder to comprehend than the word "starvation". Even though one see it with his own eyes he can still scarcely believe that men, women and children actually do starve, actually do lie down and die for want of food. If a man is hungry he will get food some way. But there is a stage beyond that—"there is no food"—and that is the stage that Poland had reached in 1919, a stage which is best illustrated, perhaps, by the fact that in Poland in 1919 there were few cats and no dogs left; they had been eaten. Had the Germans still been there in 1919 to issue the proclamation which General von Beseler issued in 1916: "If any able-bodied man refuse the order of transportation to Germany to work, let no other Pole give him to eat, not a mouthful, under penalty of military law" —the proclamation would have been a double mockery. There were no mouthfuls.

I have myself lifted up children and grown persons out of the snow and the gutter where they had fallen, too weak for want of food to go another step. I have seen men lying naked with nothing but straw under them and over them for bedding, dying of hunger. I have seen children leaning against walls, fainting for food, sinking to their knees, their bodies bloated with emptiness and water, holding out hands blue as skim-milk, little hands so bony and emaciated that one hesitated to touch

MADAME PADEREWSKA

Original vignette by F. Soulé-Campbell.

them for fear they would fall apart. I have endured the almost insufferable experience of having little children throw themselves at my feet and kiss my shoes in gratitude for a bite to eat. I have picked my way by careful footing through hundreds of diseased men lying in rags on the bare floor of a shed, dying of hunger. No linen, no blankets for hospitals, nothing but straw for covering, paper for bandages to bind up the sores that famine opens on perishing bodies. A single passage from my diary tells of but one hospital instance: "Thirty or forty cases a day here, every imaginable disease, cholera, typhoid, typhus, smallpox . . . the sufferings of the women especially are terrible. They are often delirious when they are brought in and beyond help. Most of them are refugees from the devastated areas who have lived fugitively four and five years in the woods and only now have made their way back to towns. They have become like wild animals, furtive and timid. Through long hiding and bodily weakness many of them no longer walk upright. Their hair is shaggy, like a dog's, their eyes peer through a wild mane that covers their faces."

What Paderewski knew about the things his people were suffering at that moment was enough to unnerve him, for he saw the thing not only intimately and first hand, but he saw it also in its entirety as a national problem of unbelievable dimensions. Yet it was because he saw it in its larger proportions that he had the strength and courage to face it, to carry on and work while he hoped. "We understand," Madame Paderewska said in one of her earlier letters, "that the Poles in America have dispatched a relief-ship with food for their brothers over here, and the very thought of that oncoming relief is keeping alive thousands of unfortunates. The names of the American Poles are on every one's lips. Everyone is blessing them and praying for them. They are our only hope." Already she had help in her work. "Ernest Schelling [the American musician, pupil of Paderewski] is here," she wrote, "working with us for Poland to the very best of his ability. He is putting his whole soul into his work. We are proud of such a collaborator. We have also with us here a few brave American and English army and navy officers. They surround us with affection and care. What wonderful, courageous men they are! They have decided to start to-morrow for Teschen, where terrible events are taking place." But the note of hope always came: "Poland will emerge from all this, powerful and free, nevertheless. But at what cost! The very flower of our youth has already been killed off. Few have survived."

It was burdened with such thoughts as these that Paderewski took up his work again on his first return to Warsaw from Paris, the recognition of his government by the Allies having been achieved. A short time after his return, on the eleventh of February, there was a great stir in the capital. This was an historic day for the new republic, a red-letter day for Paderewski. The first parliament of the new free Poland was opening. The elections had been carried through with speed and order. The delegates were gathered in Warsaw. The hour had come for the inaugural. This congress, named the Seym after the historic national assemblies of the past, was both a provisional parliament and a constituent assembly; its task not alone the immediate government of the country, the providing of emergency statutes, the codifying of existing and conflicting laws left over from the partitions, but, most important, the drawing up of a national constitution.

The elections of January 26 had supplied the man-power of the Seym. Throughout the former Russian Poland and in the western regions of the former Austrian Poland (Galicia) balloting had been easy. But in eastern Galicia—down in the direction of Paderewski's native region—the Ukrainian fighting had made voting temporarily impossible. But Paderewski had found an acceptable remedy for that difficulty: the appointment of the former delegates of this district to the Austrian parliament to serve in the first Seym. Poznania, the province first to establish a local government, was not able as yet, ironically enough, to legally send delegates to the Seym. She must wait until the Treaty of Versailles was signed and the German power definitely ousted in that region.

The scene of the opening of the Seym was an impressive and

picturesque one. The initiating ceremonial was held in the Cathedral of St. John, where, attended by Pilsudski the Chief of State, garbed in his plain old uniform of the First Brigade of the Legions, by Paderewski the Prime Minister, the cabinet members and deputies and the highest military dignitaries, a pontifical mass was celebrated, the Primate, the Archbishops and Bishops of all Poland officiating or assisting. Later, in the hall of assembly, the impressive ceremonies continued. By right of seniority of years the first session was presided over by Prince Ferdinand Radziwill, who was not only the oldest delegate but a prince of one of the oldest Polish families, a venerable and distinguished man of eighty-five. He was, moreover, from Poznania, which province of the republic had not as yet, as has been noted, sent elected delegates; he spoke feelingly in his address of this circumstance and of the significance of his choice as an evidence of the fellowship and good will that was unifying Poland. By tradition also the two vice-presidents of the inauguration were the two youngest delegates. One of these was a Socialist, the other a Catholic priest, both about twenty-five years of age. The eighty-five-year-old prince with the priest and the radical seated on either side of him, and the mixed body of delegates before him, peasants in the bright colors of their countryside garb, aristocrats in formal dress, others in the everyday clothes of business or work; all together made a gathering that was a good deal more than merely picturesque. It was highly significant of the complexity of Polish life and of the intricacies of Paderewski's problem.

Paderewski, Prime Minister, Minister of Foreign Affairs, Delegate to the Supreme War Council of the Allied Powers, Deputy to the Peace Conference—assuredly a man with his hands full—sat with the cabinet members; the two former premiers who had headed the governments which his had superseded had places of honor on the floor of the chamber. Paderewski entered quietly; he permitted no demonstration. After the opening preliminaries various leaders moved quietly to the cabinet box to greet him. His tall figure, topped by the frosted copper of his hair, dominated the scene.

The Chief of State gave the opening address to the assembly. "A century and a half of struggles often entailing blood and sacrifice has found its triumph in this day," Pilsudski said. "A century and a half of dreams of a Free Poland has waited for this moment of realization. Today is a great holiday for our nation—a day of joy after the long dreadful night of suffering. At this moment when all Polish hearts are beating fast I am happy that to me has been given the honor of opening the Polish Seym, which shall be the sole master and ruler of the country's household." Then the moment came for Paderewski to address the deputies. From those words of Pilsudski declaring that the Seym "shall be the sole master and ruler of the country's household" he drew new hope and courage for the task before him. In such an open and unequivocal declaration he could not help but see evidence of progress in the furtherance of his aims, evidence of coöperation from the colleague who had been so hard to win.

This was not by any means the first occasion on which Paderewski had spoken in public in Poland since his coming. His eloquence, such as that shown, for example, in that sensational mob scene in front of the Bristol Hotel, was well known in the capital and it invariably excited interest and discussion. The public was always prepared for something to talk about when Paderewski talked; as on the occasion, shortly after his arrival, in January, when, accepting honorary citizenship of Warsaw, he had told the people some surprising things about themselves and about the right way to achieve order. On that occasion there were many conservatives in the audience strongly opposed to the Pilsudski régime, but Paderewski's words were of no comfort to them. It was not Pilsudski or any other person or party that he attacked, but the common problem they all faced. He summoned all to join together, to hold closely together, to work together, to secure a truly representative government. He denounced and forbade all violent means. His speech was not liked by all his auditors at first, but, as one observer (Dr. Vernon Kellogg of the Hoover Mission) remarked, "they had to like it before he was through."

Now, at the opening of the Seym there was, as he well knew, plenty of opposition, though of a different kind. "On the right side of the Chamber," his adjutant, Major Ivanowski, the portrait artist, an eye-witness, tells us, "were the conservatives, his adherents; on the left, the radical groups that were bitterly hostile to him. They were determined to howl him down. Representatives of the friendly powers were there to hear his address. Disorder would have been extremely damaging to the reputation of the new premier. He stood a minute, arms folded, his splendid head thrown back, gathering his thoughts. His attitude was that of one proudly accepting challenge, and I saw in his face the spirit of the conqueror. This is the best pose I have used in my portrait of him.

"He began to speak, quietly but with a voice that reached to the farthest corner of the room, firm, resonant, with a ground swell of tremendous reserve power. There was neither placation nor doubt in it, only the clear ring of absolute confidence. The Left evidently was surprised. The whole conduct of the man was puzzling. They forebore to heckle at the beginning and the power of his words and the magic of his voice gripped them. He used his voice as he uses the piano, with the surety, grace and dramatic power of a great artist. After his grave beginning, he began to gather warmth and passion. He led his audience on from one climax to another. The Left was scornful no longer. These radicals who had come to confuse him sat forward on their chairs, tense and awed. When he finished speaking, a mighty roar answered him. 'Paderewski! Paderewski!' the chamber bellowed. Every man was on his feet. Every man was shouting for him."

If the opening of the Seym was a dramatic moment in the life of the New Poland, for Paderewski it was one of the profoundest gratification. He had lived to reach this hour, to see Poland free, a Polish congress convened. But anyone observing him at this time would have realized that he had too many preoccupations to indulge in reflection on his satisfactions, for he was, literally, the busiest man in Europe. The aggregate time and mileage that he had to consume travelling back and forth to the Peace Conference at Paris would alone have done him for a lifetime; the work he had to do at both ends of his journeyings was staggering. Here are some of the things he had to do:

Satisfy the Powers at Paris about what was being done in Poland.

Satisfy his people in Poland about what was being done at Paris.

Feed the people, organize their industries, get men back to work, see that the social structure of Poland was not wrecked by destitution and by the disorders of unemployment.

See that her political structure was not wrecked by dissension.

The first of these tasks meant, among other things, convincing the Peace Conference that Poland's boundary claims were just. On this score he had to combat all the clever cupidity of international banking interests favorable to the Central Powers. It meant, furthermore, convincing Paris that the fighting going on on the eastern frontiers of Poland was sheer self-defense against the Bolsheviks and the still active Germans. "Poland is not imperialistic," he declared in the Seym May 21, 1919. "We do not desire annexations. If we are making war, it is to defend Western European civilization against Bolshevism. Our mission today is no different from what it has been for seven hundred years past. We do not desire to force other populations to speak our language or adopt our customs. We wish all our neighbors to develop their own nationalities as they choose. Faithful to the spirit of our nation, faithful to the eternal traditions of our forefathers, we shall never make a war of annexation, of aggression, anywhere. The White Eagle of Poland is no bird of prey. From every side, from every corner of our commonwealth, now once more welding itself into one, people are hastening here to Warsaw, from Warsaw to Paris; they come in coats, in smocks, in old-fashioned doublets, in the dress of the mountaineer, and one and all they cry and implore that their far lands and homes be joined to the Polish State. No bird of prey, assuredly, this White Eagle of ours, when people on every side are so eager to seek shelter under its wings."

Paderewski's championship of the Polish army was nothing short of heroic in the face of the Allies' suspicion at Paris, especially their suspicion of Pilsudski. Here once more Paderewski and Pilsudski were at one in their homage for the Polish soldier. To Paderewski the bleeding breast of the Polish soldier was Europe's only rampart against the Mongolian threat of Soviet Russia, a threat that was doubled by German intrigue which not only roused the Ukrainians in Galicia to attack Poland but opened the Ukraine to Bolshevik incitement. And here came the complex question of using his own army, that Paderewski Army which he had raised in America and which, augmented in France, had fought to bring the Allies' victory to conclusion. Poland was miserably equipped to defend her frontiers, the same frontiers that Paderewski was fighting to preserve on paper while her enemies crowded in on three sides to destroy them in actuality. He wanted that army in Poland, where it belonged. General Haller, its commander, stood waiting his word in France to bring it in. But when, in March, General Nudant of Marshal Foch's staff demanded passage into Poland for the troops through Danzig, the German government balked, delayed, refusing to recognize a Polish army, raising questions as to its composition and numbers, proposing Memel, Libau, Stettin, any place but Danzig, as ports for entry. It was not until April that an agreement was made to ship the force overland via Coblentz. During all this time Paderewski, tortured by the delay, was appealing to the Allies for action. "You cannot fight Bolshevism with Bibles", he told them while they still temporized with the Red Russian menace. The Bolshevists, he declared, were fighting not Poland but civilization. "It is a war against the toothbrush." "Today", he declared, "we are defending 1500 miles of front against Bolshevist forces, and in so doing we stand as the front line in Europe against Bolshevist invasion from the east. We are endeavoring to maintain this front line and at the same time to achieve economic stability, to recuperate our people from the effects of repeated invasions of German and Russian armies. The task is a terrible one. The pressure is upon us on all sides through military action and through Bolshevist propaganda and an intense propaganda from Germany."

The second of Paderewski's tasks during these early months of 1919 meant that he must bring his own people to see that whenever at Paris he made what to them appeared to be concessions, he made them under protest, at the point of threat and always with the hope of future readjustment. He did not always concede, in spite of threats. On the question of Eastern Galicia, which the Allies at Germany's suggestion were inclined to consider an open question, he was adamant. "There cannot be a Polish State without Eastern Galicia," he declared. "Untiringly, bravely, patiently and assiduously we built up that section of our country after innumerable wars, defeats and destructions, and today we are still building it up. We put it on its present level of civilization. Cultivated by us, this land has produced men famous in literature, learning, and art, as well as famous statesmen and leaders. The most decisive battles in the defense of Western civilization have been fought there, and fought by Poland and the Poles, and there many of the most glorious scenes of our national life have been enacted. Are we to resign our right to this land? Are we to leave it to the mercy of foreign intrigues? A large autonomy has been agreed upon, and we shall honorably keep our word. We shall rule honestly and justly. But a temporary settlement of the question would be fatal, fatal politically and morally, because it would make impossible even the commencement of a reconstruction of that devastated country. I therefore declare that neither I nor Mr. Dmowski will ever sign any treaty for such a settlement." And they did not.

The question of Eastern Galicia reminds us of the fact that Paderewski's own native region, beyond Galicia, was involved in the boundary problem. Nevertheless he put aside all personal sentiment in dealing with that problem. "Of course", he said at one time, "I hail from those very regions. But I cannot claim them. To claim too much for Poland would be to bury her cause." As a matter of fact, both Kurylowka, in Podolia, Paderewski's birthplace, and Sudylkow, in Volhynia, his boyhood home, were lost to Poland in the final settlement of the Polish-Russian frontier. The native regions of the Polish leader are no longer Polish; he cannot put his finger on the map of Poland and say, "I was born there."

"When it was possible to confer," he told Poland in the Seym, reporting to it his work at Paris, "we conferred; when it was necessary to fight we fought. Our whole policy may be expressed in the words 'to gain peace and win the war'. For more than four years this was the policy of France, England, Italy, of all the Allied powers; but of us even more has been demanded; it has been required of us that we reconstruct our country without delay, that we immediately reorganize our economic affairs, restart our commerce, settle our currency, solve all our problems and satisfy everybody in a day. It was forgotten that grain cannot be threshed in a burning barn, that hay cannot be made in a thunderstorm."

These two problems, the problems of Paris and Warsaw, would have been enough in themselves to wholly occupy if not to wholly dismay any statesman. But Paderewski faced two other difficulties of stupendous dimensions and immediate urgency, both internal—the question of social welfare and the question of political organization. For the one, social welfare in Poland at that moment meant much more than feeding the starved millions of the country. It meant getting railways running so that food could be transported, getting industries reopened so that people could work and earn. The 250,000 Polish workmen who had been interned in Germany for forced labor must be brought home. There must be coal; coal mines must be rehabilitated; again railways to carry coal as well as coal to carry railways. Telegraphic communication, internal and international, must be established. Money must be found to finance government, to feed and clothe a defensive army. The ramifications of this problem alone were multiple, enormous.

Paderewski, at work at his desk in Warsaw directing, considering, weighing, measuring, found in these appalling days of puzzlement and threatened frustration a new beauty in the golden phrase, "Cast thy bread upon the waters." The friendships that he had made in the past, the honors and prestige that he had won by honesty and integrity and by simple human understanding, they all came back to him now in a rich and generous harvest. Because he had never served himself, but others, because he had devoted his life not to self but to his country, his country now, through him, was remembered and served.

Some twenty-five years before, when young Herbert Hoover at San Jose, California, had been embarrassed before the Polish pianist for lack of funds, Paderewski with an encouraging smile had said to him, "Young man, things in life don't always come out in accordance with our plans." He had been a very young man himself at that time, young in years. But he had lived life fully enough even then to know disappointment. Since then the years had taught him a new wisdom; he could amend his saying now by adding, "Unless you wait long enough." He had not waited; he had worked. And he had long since forgotten the incident of the San Jose concert of the 'nineties. But Hoover had waited and had remembered. On December 22, 1918, while Paderewski was still moving toward Poland through the Baltic sea-mines on the battleship *Concord*, Hoover also moved toward Poland. He arranged on that day to send the first Food Mission to Warsaw. He had not waited for the red tape of the Supreme War Council to untangle itself and authorize the action. Clemenceau had described Hoover at Paris as being "conspicuous for the stiffness of the man whose nerves are at the end of their tether." It is easy to appreciate to what a strain Hoover's nerves had been put by the conflicting deliberations of the Council as to how and when and where interallied relief for the starving should be given. He had got to the point where he must act on his own initiative or not act at all. He went ahead, remembering Paderewski and Poland and remembering also that famine waits on no one, not even statesmen and generals.

On January 4, right on the heels of Paderewski's own arrival on New Year's Day, Dr. Vernon Kellogg and Colonel William R. Grove, representing Hoover's American Relief Administration, reached Warsaw. They presented themselves at once to Paderewski. The joy and relief with which he received them can be imagined, and his joy was increased when he learned that they, like their chief, were determined to act without delay. The initial conferences between Paderewski and Pilsudski had only begun; everything was in chaos. Kellogg and Grove disregarded all that and immediately began their arrangements for bringing food into Poland. They had only one stipulation to make, that "no food," in the words of Dr. Kellogg, "could come from America or the Allies if there was any serious danger that it could not be properly controlled." Paderewski's responsibility was to give the guarantee of control and see that it was carried out. Something of what was soon accomplished in the way of relief is gleaned from a message sent to Hoover by Paderewski in March of that year. "The activity of Colonel Grove and his staff," he wrote, "is beyond praise, goods of higher quality arriving daily, and thousands of people, after four and a half years of terrible suffering, realizing at last what wholesome nutritious bread is."

The problem of relief supplies brought him to the problem of transportation. It was a complicated one. Danzig was the logical port of entry, but Danzig as a receiving point for food presented the same problem as did Danzig as a debarkation point for Haller's army—German objection. I could realize the strength of the German feeling, for I had seen the Red Cross relief train which brought me into Poland stoned as it passed through West Prussian towns. Perhaps such feeling was only human, the bitterness of the vanquished breaking out on seeing the victor, once the victim, being fed. But it was regrettable and it gravely intensified Paderewski's difficulties.

As in the case of the transport of troops, the German objections to food transport were not made outright; they were phrased in such a way as to name apparently only reasonable obstacles, but actually they were designed to block and delay the transport of relief supplies into Poland. They were overcome; and it was in the solution of their problem and all that the whole problem of transportation subsequently entailed in months to come, that Paderewski again showed himself gifted with one of the first attributes of statesmanship, the capacity to seek and use expert counsel. On Hoover's advice he organized a commission of American experts as technical advisers to his government; Colonel A. B. Barber of the American Army Corps of Engineers, Dr. E. Dana Durant, a statistician and economist, Mr. Irving Shumann, a commercial expert, made up this commission. At the same time he established a national board of trade composed of Polish business leaders whose task was to revive industry and help private enterprise by securing foreign credits, buying foreign commodities and selling Polish products in foreign markets.

Paderewski was keen to the psychological effect of the presence of Americans on the ground. Most of them were in uniform; the very appearance of the American uniform on the streets of Warsaw encouraged the public. Soon their number was increased and the spirit of the people grew. President Wilson, through General Pershing, sent Colonel H. L. Gilchrist with a detachment from the U. S. Army Medical Corps. Colonel E. R. Bailey brought the American Red Cross, with Colonel Albert J. Chesley, expert on epidemical diseases, Major Bruce M. Mohler, Sanitary Engineer, Dr. Charles Halliday, and Dr. Placida Gardner, bacteriologist, all of them important figures in the personnel of the peace army that was to fight to save Poland from extinction through typhus and tuberculosis. In time the American Red Cross workers numbered some 200 scattered throughout the country. In the meantime Madame Paderewska developed the work of her Polish White Cross. Into this work Paderewski was pouring funds from his private fortune.

In August, after Dr. Kellogg and Colonel Grove had thoroughly established the A. R. A. relief work, with Captain Maurice Pate in charge since February, Paderewski welcomed Hoover himself to Poland. The artist and the one-time college student met on new and strange ground. Paderewski opened the country to him; they had innumerable conferences. After that visit Hoover issued a statement which is interesting not only as a record of his observations but especially as a compendium of Paderewski's problem. "As a result of seven invasions by different armies," Hoover said, "the country has largely been denuded of buildings. The estates of the larger landowners have been destroyed, and while the peasants are cultivating approximately enough foodstuffs for their own supplies, these regions, which in normal times export large quantities of food, mostly from the large estates, are four-fifths uncultivated. . . .

"In addition to the destruction and robbery which accompanied the repeated invasion of rival armies, these areas have been, of course, through a caldron of Bolshevist revolution, and the intellectual classes either fled from the country or to a considerable extent were imprisoned. Some were executed. The Ruthenian peasants have been stirred up against the great landowners, which accounts for the destruction of the equipment of the large landed properties. It appears to us that it will require years for this region to recover, for animals must be provided, agricultural implements imported and the whole agricultural production restarted."

With the A. R. A. and the A. R. C. help organized and in operation and other help coming or already arrived—the Quakers from America and England, the Young Men's Christian Association, the Joint Distribution Committee representing Jewish benevolence—Paderewski could at last take a free breath when he thought of Poland's 2,400,000 homeless refugees returning that year from their dispersal, her 2,000,000 undernourished children, fifty per cent of them in the industrial centers tubercular, 750,000 of them orphaned. These were thoughts to drive a man mad. The relief from strain was tremendous. His gratitude was deep. The story of these days of struggle and achievement in Paderewski's life is essentially a story of gratitude and friendships. To the world at large Poland meant Paderewski; the world at large loved him and rushed to befriend him. "I was perhaps more intimately in contact with him," President Hoover wrote in a statement * given to me from the White House in 1932, "and with the overwhelming

---

* President Hoover's statement was drawn from a tribute paid by him to Paderewski in 1921; all quotations herein from Hoover relating to the Polish crisis are quoted from this statement.

problems of Poland in the first few months of the re-establish-
ment of the independence of that nation than any other American. I know that it was his high idealism, his high courage and
his high sense of statesmanship that welded renewed independence of the Polish people out of the utter chaos of revolution
and the inherent demoralization of 150 years of enemy occupation." Certainly it was "his high idealism and his high courage"
that brought Hoover to his side so promptly, when delay would
have been disastrous. One day Paderewski tried to express his
feeling. Hoover stopped him. "That's all right, Mr. Paderewski," he said. "I knew the need was great. Besides, you don't
remember it, but you helped me out once when I was a student
in college and I was in a hole." "Herbert Hoover saved us,"
Paderewski said afterward. "He gave us bread, strength and
peace within ourselves." And then he added a specific item
which not only illustrates what Hoover actually had done, but
shows, too, the practical turn of Paderewski's mind in the midst
of the horrors that surrounded him. "Not only did he provide
foodstuffs and clothing for needy multitudes, but, generous,
thoughtful and far-seeing as he is, he enabled my Government
to re-open the idle mills of Lodz by giving me spontaneously
27,000 bales of cotton for that purpose." The question of industrial revival, of work for the people, seed for the farmers, never
left Paderewski's mind.

Of the coming of Hoover, and of all the American and
British aid that followed, Paderewski never speaks but with
deep feeling. The memory of those long days of toil and worry
and longer nights of vigil in the Zamek at Warsaw are brightened for him by the recollection of the friendships they brought
forth. "It was one of the proudest days of my life," he said,
speaking of Hoover's visit to Poland, "when, for the first time
in free and independent Poland, for the first time since Poland's
partition, I could open the doors of our ancient castle of kings
and receive there with royal honors this noble son of American
democracy. Another day," he added, "not of pride but of deep
emotion, was when I had the honor of leading Herbert Hoover

to the castle of Cracow, to the tombs of our kings, among whom the remains of Thaddeus Kosciuszko are laid to rest. Deeply moved, he brought a beautiful wreath and, before depositing it on the sarcophagus containing Kosciuszko's ashes, he uttered a few hardly audible words. It seems still that I have never heard a more eloquent oration."

And yet, despite the intricacies and the pressure of these three problems, the problems of Paris, of Warsaw, and of relief, Paderewski's fourth problem was the most baffling, the most difficult of all. It was not alone that the sudden new release of freedom had loosed the political energies of the nation in a hundred different directions. There was something else for him to combat and overcome. Prejudice. "It is easier," he said in one of his speeches in the Seym, "to storm a hundred fortresses and to burn a thousand towns to cinders than to overcome one prejudice."

At such moments as those when he rejoiced over the Allies' recognition at Paris, the successful holding of the national election, the coming of relief, the opening of the congress—and there he soon had new cause for rejoicing, for on May 3, 1919, the hundred and twenty-eighth anniversary of the historic Constitution of 1791, the making of a new Constitution was begun with the presentation of its first draft;—it was at such happy moments that the thought of these prejudices would have been like a cloud over his mind, so seriously did they threaten the whole framework of the structure he was building, the security of the nation, had he not long ago trained himself to act rather than to brood. It was not in vain that in boyhood he had learned the uselessness of sitting and staring at a keyboard that demanded to be played upon and mastered.

The prejudices he had to combat were of two kinds, political and religious. The religious prejudice was not only both domestic and international, but it was even personal. He himself was attacked by the radicals because he was a Catholic; his government was attacked, inside and out, on the score of being anti-Jewish. The latter charge, invented and exploited by the German press and propagated widely by its agencies in Europe and America, was the cause of grave injury to Poland's good repute and to the progress of Paderewski's administration. It all came out of the ancient feeling engendered by the persecution of the Jews under antisemitic Russian and German rule. Now, in the face of all that the history of Poland offered in refutation, a history of tolerance which had made Poland known in times past as a shelter for the oppressed, Paderewski and his government were blamed, accused of the antisemitic spirit of other times and of other and alien rule, and charged with its continuance.

Paderewski acted promptly and decisively on this. "The time has come," he said, "for the voice of the Polish nation to give the lie to these unfounded foreign accusations." He demanded an investigation by an impartial body. He secured through President Wilson the services of Henry Morgenthau, one of the foremost Jews of America, to head a commission of investigators. This commission exonerated Paderewski and Poland of the unjust charge. In Morgenthau's opinion Paderewski was "infinitely the greatest of the Poles . . . this sheer genius—this unstarred Master." "Twelve or fifteen years ago," he wrote in his memoirs, "there was a picture painted of him . . . it showed him as Orpheus quieting the wild beast with his lyre. It was of this that he irresistibly reminded me . . . He had undertaken the almost impossible task of reconciling the contending factions of his native land, and was eliminating race hatred itself." In his final report, after spending several weeks carefully scrutinizing the situation, travelling over the country and directly questioning the people most concerned, the Jews themselves, Morgenthau gave Paderewski a clear bill.* A separate report made by Mr. Morgenthau's colleagues of the commission, Brigadier General Edgar Jadwin and Mr. Homer Johnson, confirmed the Morgenthau findings, as did also the report of a British commission headed by Sir Stuart Samuel. "During the days of

---

* Morgenthau concluded his findings thus: "Just as the Jews would resent being condemned as a race for the action of a few of their undesirable co-religionists, so it would be correspondingly unfair to condemn the Polish nation as a whole for the violence committed by uncontrolled troops or local mobs."

almost anarchy in the early stages of Polish reorganization," President Hoover wrote later in his statement already quoted from, recalling this phase of Paderewski's problem, "he developed full protection for the helpless elements of the population, particularly the Jews, and laid the foundation for relationships among the people that must be tolerant and enduring."

Direct and prompt action bore its fruits in the handling of this difficulty. But the other, political prejudice, was not to be so readily overcome. It was not merely that political prejudice against Paderewski at Warsaw took the form of violent opposition on the floor of the Seym. That was open and above-board, it could be met and grappled with, he was fully equal to it. But there was subversive opposition too. Paderewski did not need to be clairvoyant to realize that underground forces were working against him, had been so working from the day he came, had been indeed prepared against him before he came. It is difficult to make a record of this aspect of his struggle in Poland without reflecting views which might be confused with Paderewski's, but which are solely those of the observer. From the beginning Paderewski met and dealt with all opposition so fairly and so openly, and he has at all times since been so circumspect and considerate in referring to it,* that when this question of domestic faction and opposition comes to be dealt with by others, the utmost care must be exercised against injustice and misjudgment, and above all against appearing to express opinions which are not Paderewski's. To an impartial observer who was on the ground at the time, and to the same observer looking back at and summing up the situation, the tap-root and true source of the political prejudice which Paderewski had to combat appears to have been, in the last analysis, that power which stood outside the elective responsibility of the people and which still exerted a great and fascinating influence on the country—the military power of Pilsudski. This was a power which had of course been

---

* As late as 1928, speaking in New York City on the tenth anniversary of Polish independence and forced to refer to these matters, all that Paderewski would say was, "In September of that same year (1919) my country found itself in a very difficult position which, at the present moment, I am not free to discuss in all its particulars."

necessary, which still was, within its proper limitations, wholly necessary to the preservation and well-being of the nation. But it had served its specific and initial purpose and was now properly supplanted by the civil power of the suffrage, to which it was rightly subject, that power which, in Pilsudski's own words, was to be "sole master and ruler of the country's household."

From the first, whenever Paderewski faced Pilsudski, whatever their deliberations or decisions, he could not fail to feel that here was something which, like a ghost out of Poland's tragic past, breathed an air of reservation, wariness, and calculation. Whether or not Pilsudski, conceding the situation at the moment of Paderewski's arrival, and agreeing to the dissolution of his, Pilsudski's, Socialist government, had so agreed with reservations, only Pilsudski could have told. Now, reservation or not, Paderewski could only know that there was an impalpable but very real force blocking his way.

If it be true that Pilsudski had indulged in mental reservations in giving way to the organization of a coalition government to replace the Socialist government which Moraczewski had organized under him; if this had been done by him only for expediency's sake, while he bided his time: if this be true, the basis of the truth may be found in the simple fact that Pilsudski at heart not only had no faith in the Allies, but had no real faith in the kind of government Paderewski and the Allies wished to see established in Poland; not for Poland at that stage of her history. On one occasion some years later—it was immediately following the general election of 1928 in which he won a sweeping victory—Pilsudski told his party leaders "that he had always been a partisan of Constitutional regime" and that in his view a parliament "ranged itself alongside the President of the Republic and the Government as an indispensable institution." But in these first days of reconstruction, while there was still no parliament and no Constitution, government meant, as it continued to mean, party government; in the large, the two divisions of Left and Right. "Left" and "Right", as we have seen by his own words, were terms that annoyed Pilsudski. That does not seem to mean, however, that he believed in coalition as a happy medium of representative government. What Pilsudski really believed in, judging him by the record of his past history, that is, before the war, and by his subsequent record, after the war, was military dictatorship. "I am a strong man," he said at one time, "and I like to decide all matters by myself."

Pilsudski may have begun his career in statecraft as a believer in popular government as practicable for Poland. If so, he soon changed. By temperament, by long military training, he was a dictator; and more than ever, as events unrolled, he became a dictator, as he perhaps would have put it, "by necessity." His famous words, "The sword alone decides the destinies of nations," had been spoken at a time when the whole civilized world was turning to the sword. Events seemed to justify those words in 1914; and Pilsudski was one honest man in Europe who spoke the truth that others, Germany above all, believed in, but dissembled about, even while they drew the sword. Now, however, in 1919, while the civilized world, sickened of the sword, was turning from it, Pilsudski still believed in it. Not entirely without reason, as we shall see, for there was still the uncivilized world of Red Russia, egged on by Germany, to deal with; of that, more later. But as time went on and he experimented more and more with tools of domestic governance other than the sword, Pilsudski appears to have more and more lost faith in the franchise and to have grown in his faith in the saber. He had initiated his régime as Chief of Staff, in November 1918, with the sword in hand, but also with at least some avowed adherence to the principles of representative constitutional government. Although he once declared, afterward, that he felt it would have been better if he had assumed an absolute dictatorship in the beginning, he was at the time anxious about the legality of such a procedure. "When I came here from Magdeburg at the end of the war," he said in 1926, "I had absolute power in my hands. I could have kept it, but I saw that Poland must be prudent, because she was new and poor; she had to avoid hazardous experiments." Actually, in 1918, Pilsudski was of a mind with the Allies in questioning the legality of his own power as it derived from the Regency, out of which immediately he had been invested with it, because that power was not genuinely Polish and national, but German. Therefore he had sought the sanction of a popular election which would institute a national assembly, the Seym, which would in turn establish a constitution and elect an executive to supplant the temporary and provisional office of Chief of State, which he now filled. So far, all was well planned, well executed. Poland had the coalition government which, through Paderewski, the Allies had insisted on as being necessary because more representative than the Socialist government Pilsudski had organized. In due time she held her elections, she had her constitutional assembly at work.

But the moment that the national assembly showed signs of limiting the powers of the executive, the moment the Seym disclosed an inclination to draft a constitution which would really give to the deputies that power which Pilsudski declared was rightly theirs, the power to be "sole master and ruler in the country's household," a power which would make impossible for all time anything like a dictatorship; from that moment Pilsudski lost faith in the Seym. There is no question about his disillusionment being genuine. It was not that he desired to dictate merely for the sake of dictating. He sincerely believed that a dictatorship was the best thing for Poland at that time, and that a popular government, no matter how ideally desirable, was the worst thing. He simply did not believe in the present capacity of the Polish people to govern themselves through the type of elected delegates available. And he ardently believed in his own capacity to govern them.

There had been as yet no election, there was as yet no Seym to disillusion Pilsudski, when Paderewski began his first conferences with him. Pilsudski had not yet come to the point, as he did later, of calling the national assembly in his own characteristically original language, "a locomotive drawing a pin", "a sterile, jabbering, howling thing that engenders such boredom as made the very flies die of sheer disgust." He had not yet reached that stage of outraged patience which afterward drove him to declare that "I personally as Dictator called the Parliament together and coöperated with it constitutionally, even though I could have crushed the whole lot under my thumb like a vile worm." But, even though he had not yet antagonized his opponents with such outbursts; even though he had begun by seeking popular sanction for government in Poland, to satisfy his own ideal of legality as well as to satisfy the Allies, nevertheless he commenced his negotiations with Paderewski in a manner scarcely calculated to produce harmony and coöperation. Suspicious of the Allies and suspicious of Paderewski because he spoke for the Allies, he continued those negotiations with growing suspicion, distrust to the point of scorn for the assembly and for the coalition government which Paderewski had organized.

This feeling of impatience with the processes, disbelief in the efficacy, of political deliberations was unquestionably working in Pilsudski when he and Paderewski began their conversations early in January, 1919. It was a feeling rooted in Pilsudski's instincts, in his military training, in his experience with governments and politicians. To his habitude of command-and-obey was joined his ingrained distrust of any who countered his command or questioned his right to demand obedience. In spite of the patriotic zeal and high purpose—in which they were one—which he recognized in Paderewski, he looked upon Paderewski as representing primarily the suspicions and the opposition of the Allies as well as, later on, the antagonism of the Seym. Before long the suspicions of the Seym were to find open expression in such words as "the fear of an abuse of power by a man whose moderation and respect for law were suspect." Pilsudski knew that this feeling concerning him existed, and he responded to it with new suspicion added to his grounded disinclination to trust an opponent. The mistake he made was in suspecting Paderewski. It was, as we have seen, a natural, perhaps it was an unavoidable mistake. In fact Pilsudski's career in politics and war made such a mistake almost inevitable. In the words of Mizwa, "He was wary of politics." It was impossible for him to fully credit the motives and utterances of a politician, any politician, even one so open and above-board as Paderewski. Irked by the law's delays, irritated by what seemed to him only evasion and indirection hampering Poland's progress, Pilsudski balked, held back, let the workings of his mind run in their accustomed channels of noncommittal observance and of reserved acquiescence. This is why Paderewski felt that, do what he might, there still remained an opposing, an impalpable, but a very real, force blocking his way.

It was a plain case of two minds both bent on the same goal, but each going different, almost opposite, directions. Each was sure his way was the right way. One, Paderewski, by natural inclination, showed his way openly. The other, Pilsudski, by inclination equally natural, kept his way hidden. Pilsudski, a champion of the *fait accompli*, must move concealed until time resolved the issue or gave the signal to strike.

Obviously it was not his own way but Poland's way that each of these men struggled and feared for. Paderewski feared for the future of, even for the very existence of, representative, constitutional government in Poland. Pilsudski feared that the future of Poland would be jeopardized by abortive attempts at representative government, for which, in his belief, the country was not yet ready. He believed that the need of the moment was the strong hand of dictatorship and the swift hand of the *fait accompli*. Paderewski feared dictatorship and the *fait accompli* and what such a thing would mean in the relationship of Poland with the Allies. He had written to Colonel House at Paris, "The Poles do not intend to surprise the Delegates of the Peace Conference by any 'fait accompli'." He must keep that word. Pilsudski feared the weaknesses and confusions of coalition; if there must be party government, he would have in power that party which, in his view, was the strongest and the most representative of the mass feeling, the Socialist party, of which he was a leader. Paderewski feared the growth of Socialistic strength. He understood perfectly what Pilsudski's socialism at bottom was, that it was an affiliation subject wholly to the man's love for the good of the country. But just there was the difficulty: Pilsudski did believe that Socialism was good for the country. Paderewski did not, if for no other reason than this: Socialism in Poland at that moment was a tendency toward the radical, which, gaining momentum, and gaining it by very reason of Pilsudski's endorsement and leadership, threatened more and more to join hands with the Soviets of Russia, just across the road, a Red Russia that even then was spending millions in its effort to corrupt the Polish voter and rouse proletarian animosity in Poland. Once when Henry Morgenthau asked him about the complexion of Polish politics Paderewski answered with this apt simile: "You have a bottle and you label it claret; then you paste over that a label declaring it is Haut Sauterne; then you may clean those off and label it Champagne. But all the time the contents of the bottle are home-brew Socialism." Pilsudski stood for home-brew Socialism. There was danger of its growth. It might not indeed grow, in Poland, beyond Pilsudski's control, for the simple reason that he could control it, control it by armed force. But once more that meant dictatorship. One way or the other, the danger of dictatorship threatened, with its inevitable result of ruin for Poland with the Allies, the losing of her hard-won place in the new Europe.

Paderewski said openly in the Seym that he knew his way was being blocked. "I am very well aware," he declared, "that against the government and against me personally there exists a certain feeling." The trouble was, this feeling did not come out into the open; even to the end of the struggle it was as secretive as it was subversive, as sly as it was stubborn. Its manifestations were indirect, so far as its source of origin was concerned. While Paderewski's large constructive policy more and more met in the Seym with a daily crossfire of opposition, from the Belvedere where the real leader of the opposition sat, as if in the dark, watching, came what might have appeared, and what was perhaps designed to appear, as coöperation: more and more frequent calls for conference and counsel. So frequent and so importunate did Pilsudski's demands on Paderewski become that it seems now, in the light of events, almost as if the soldier were trying to wear the statesman down. Day and night, often in the middle of the night, the call would come. To the outsider it might have appeared that the Chief of State was helpless without his Prime Minister.

This may have been the impression that Pilsudski wished Paderewski to get. Pilsudski was crafty, he knew the value of Paderewski at the moment, getting done the things that must be done, above all establishing Poland's credit in her foreign relations. And he knew what Paderewski's popularity was with the masses: he was feeding the masses. That must be done and Paderewski was the one to do it, as he had been doing it since 1914. Pilsudski's game was not to destroy Paderewski but to eliminate him. That done in good time, when the work was completed and the need supplied, he would have a free hand to resume his own exclusive and militaristic way, the only way in which, according to his belief, the salvation of Poland lay.

It is possible for a crafty leader to make his influence felt in a hundred subtle ways without commitment. Such a leader can act negatively, giving the effect that he endorses, without ever openly endorsing—and often. without actually endorsing— movements and expressions which, on the face of it, are incompatible with his position or even with his avowed sentiments. Pilsudski's attitude at this time, scrutinized after the event in the cold atmosphere of fact, appears to have encouraged opposition to the new government which ostensibly he had aided Paderewski in organizing. That mob scene of radicals outside the Bristol Hotel had been an expression of feeling held over from the moment of change from Pilsudski's Socialistic to Paderewski's coalition cabinet. That feeling still existed, and subtly those who cherished it felt back of them, somewhere, behind the scenes, an attitude of sympathy.

One of the manifestations of this feeling of prejudice against Paderewski was the "whispering campaign" which was carried on. This was the real source of that prejudice which attacked him and which found its expression in mocking cartoons and jibes at Paderewski's personality, his art, especially his well-known devotion to his religion and its practices. "He is in league with the Pope!" "He's saying his beads." "He is working for the French clergy!" The fact that Kasimir Lutoslawski, one of the most eminent priests and foremost authorities on constitutional law in Poland, a deputy in the Seym, was likewise active in the framing of the new Constitution, gave added impetus to these attacks. Other utterances of the "whispering campaign" were more sinister and dangerous to the public peace. Because he moved his staff into the Zamek he was accused of royalist ambitions: "Pilsudski lives in a house, Paderewski must have a castle!" "He wants to be King of Poland." * His wife, it was insinuated, nursed dreams of a queenship, a consort's throne. "Queen Helena!" Correspondents sent these stories out, mostly through the Berlin press. They were repeated in England and America. Patent as the absurdity of all such talk was, it existed and it disturbed the public peace, halted progress, and injured Poland's prestige abroad.

Among the extreme and "reddest" of the radicals Paderewski's unpardonable sin was that he was a gentleman. He could not be forgiven that. He was an artist, a "top-hat", he belonged in the parlor. That day at the Bristol mobbing he had swept them off their feet with his physical courage. On another occasion they found out something about his courage that startled them. There was one certain group of radicals which had staged demonstration after demonstration against him. Finally, to quiet them, he agreed to consider their demands if they would send him an orderly delegation. The delegation came, "a group of sneering, noisy louts, big men with expressions of swaggering defiance," as Major Ivanowski described them. The grave dignity of the Prime Minister when he entered the room awed them for a moment, but before the interview was well under way one of the delegates, a burly individual, turned his back upon the Premier and began to talk to his neighbor in offensively loud tones, drowning out Paderewski's voice. Paderewski sprang like a lion. He went through the group of delegates like a cavalry charge, gripped the talker by the collar and spun him around so fiercely that the offender almost fell. "How

---

* By the irony of history, Pilsudski himself had to endure later on, in 1926, the same "King of Poland" canard.

dare you," Paderewski thundered, his blue eyes dark with wrath, "how dare you turn your back on the Prime Minister of the Republic of Poland!" The offender bleated an apology. The rest of the delegates looked on in awe. The conference proceeded as Paderewski wished, in an orderly manner. When the Reds left the Foreign Office that day they left with wholesome fear in their hearts of the "gentleman."

Incidents like these were infrequent, but the whispering campaign, the underground opposition, continued and multiplied, and in the meantime Pilsudski sat in the Belvedere and sent almost daily for Paderewski to come to him. Too often these so frequent conferences came to nothing but talk, with Pilsudski, as his biographer Rom Landau expresses it, playing the Wagnerian rôle of *loquitur*. Landau gives a picture of these conferences. Pilsudski, he says, "spoke in tortuous complicated sentences", Paderewski "was used to clear speech . . . ordered and lucid argument." "In the small hours, after a brief talk on affairs of the State, he would listen to stories of the legions. Those usually selected were concerned with the Pilsudski legend . . . The end would come only in the grey light of breaking dawn. There would be nothing to show but two empty tea glasses, innumerable rounds of lemon-peel, two ash-bowls filled to the brim with cigarette ends."

Pilsudski was younger than Paderewski by seven years, yet Landau's picture gives a rather pathetic impression of an old man, a veteran of the wars, a little hazy with reminiscence who "expressed the mind of yesterday—the last flame in a dying fire of history—the history of the Polish nineteenth century— the great conspirator, the romantic, the Carbonaro," an old man glad of a younger listener. That picture, judging by my own impression, is scarcely true. Pilsudski was anything but a doddering old man; he was a very strong man, vigorous, forceful, far-seeing, keen, of unbending will, of implacable nature, and, as I believe, crafty. Besides, as I remember from my own experience, he was a tremendously interesting talker; there was a glamour of adventure about him, a fascination in his shaggy-browed eyes. He had a rugged charm and Paderewski felt the spell of it. But they were naturally opposed. Paderewski was the Present; he was the modern, the personification of the new age, of the Occidental mind, active and practical in the present, alive with the possibilities of the future, reverent of the past but done with it, except to hold to its inspiration. Pilsudski was the Past. If Pilsudski was the younger man in years, he had the craft of old age and of the East. If Paderewski was the new West, Pilsudski was the ancient East. He was determined on the elimination of this too popular, too successful Lochinvar.

Why? Had he been asked and had he answered frankly he would have said, "Because I love Poland." He lived for Poland, had often risked death for Poland, had suffered and struggled all his life for Poland. Yet, as Landau saw it, "He had never struggled for Poles—always for the idea:—Poland." Pilsudski read Poland in the terms of a heroic dream of the past which must be made come true. The realization of that dream could come, in his belief, only through the sword, through the strong arm of explicit command at home, through soldiering afield, campaigning, battles, bravery, heroism. Through war. Paderewski read Poland in terms more of the every day human equation, the American concept, the people as citizens and voters, their desires, their needs, their rights. To him the realization of the dream of a free Poland meant government, work, industry, security of home life; material prosperity dedicated to spiritual, cultural, betterment. Peace. Pilsudski's ideal was abstract, the State glorified. Paderewski's ideal was concrete, Man in the State.

He was as determined as Pilsudski was. But there was this difference. Pilsudski felt himself indispensable to the country's security. Paderewski counted himself as nothing but an instrument, a mechanic whose job was to repair the machine and get it running. The hand that ran it was incidental. Get it running he would, as he had got it recognized as an actual machine, a working thing. But the minute he would see that his directing hand hindered or interfered with the running, he would withdraw that hand, stand by, and hope for the best. The difference went deeper than that. Paderewski could hope, because he had faith in the popular will and its capacity to achieve. Pilsudski had little or no such faith.

Paderewski might have thought that the moment of with-drawal had come when he had organized a cabinet and had won for it the recognition of the Powers; or later when the national election had been carried off successfully; or still later when the Seym was inaugurated; or again when he had launched the work of relieving destitution. But always there was something else to do. On the thirty-first of July, 1919, however, five years exactly since that memorable name-day party of his at Riond-Bosson, it seemed as if he had actually completed his work.

There had been tremendous excitement two days before, on his arrival from Paris with the Versailles Peace Treaty in his pocket. When he stepped from his train, out from the huge crowd gathered to meet him darted a Bolshevik assassin leveling a pistol at him. The crowd caught the assassin before he could fire and wildly cheered the Premier. This, it must be told, was not the first attempt on Paderewski's life since the Germans had turned machine-guns on him in Poznan. A bomb had been ex-ploded under his train on one of his journeys to the borderlands. Again, one morning when he returned at an early hour to the Zamek to get some rest after a night-long session with Pilsudski, he was amazed to find a man in his bedroom who covered him with a pistol and demanded that he sign a paper containing his resignation as Prime Minister. Paderewski thought fast; he took the paper as if he acquiesced and walked toward a table as if to sign. Suddenly he wheeled, caught the man by the throat, downed him. When Madame Paderewska, asleep in the next room, came running in, hearing a man's screams, she found Paderewski with his would-be assassin pinned to the floor, his steel-like piano fingers throttling his assailant. The man was almost strangled. But when the guard was summoned Pad-erewski simply told him to take the man to the street and release him. He would not permit his arrest.

Now on July 31, all Warsaw, all Poland, was alive over the Treaty, and Paderewski was anxious. Would the Seym ratify it? Or would prejudice and subversive opposition openly conjoin in one final effort to wreck the structure of peace that he had raised? If it did, he was finished. He had struggled bravely at Paris for Poland's rights in that treaty. He knew how he had succeeded, not alone because Poland's name was actually signed to the document, but because her cause was at last understood: a few days before, on July 10, when President Wilson had presented the same Treaty to the United States Senate, he had spoken words that had clearly echoed Paderewski's arguments—"No part of ancient Poland", Wilson had said, "had ever in any true sense become a part of Germany or of Austria or of Russia." Those words, coming to Paderewski across the Atlantic, had put a kind of seal on his efforts. The struggle at Paris was over. But he had to struggle anew in Warsaw.

He won, almost unanimously. The Seym finally ratified the Treaty by a heavy majority. True, the separate agreement imposed by the Allies obliging Poland to pledge herself to their conditions in the matter of national minorities stirred deep resentment. It was manifestly an intrusion on the nation's domestic affairs. But Paderewski felt as everyone else did on that score, and his explanation to the Seym was so frank and so startling that it overcame the opposition. He reiterated the argument that he had always offered concerning the minority populations, specifically the Jews, the argument in which the Morgenthau commission had supported him—that anti-Jewish sentiment in Poland was neither religious nor racial but economic and political. "These conditions," he declared in the Seym, referring to the objectionable Minority Treaty, "so far as they touch upon the Jews, were drawn up before the Armistice was signed and were the work of prominent Jewish Zionists and nationalists in the industrial and financial world." He won the ratification by a vote of 295 to 41. "The Versailles Treaty," he said, "should bring happiness to Poland. It fulfills dreams which five years ago the majority of Poles would have held impossible of fulfillment."

The Poland that Paderewski was building was a well-designed, soundly framed, carefully balanced superstructure, but it was being erected on a foundation which was not yet shaken down to its basic solidity. There were cracks and seams yet to be filled in. To change the figure: there was a machine; he had reassembled its parts, scattered for a century and a half; he had it riveted and belted and oiled and ready to go. Could Pan Pole take charge of it now and make it work? Paderewski believed that he could.

XXXVIII

1919: THE STRUGGLE IN POLAND—III

PADEREWSKI'S life has been a life of decisions. His friend Henryk Opienski, describing him as a boy, spoke of the "extraordinary force" of his mind "every act of which bore the imprint of a powerful lever." The strong leverage of his mind has been used from his earliest years to make decisions. To begin with, he decided at twelve that he would be a musician. It was not merely that he wished to be a musician. He willed it. Still at the same age, and against counsel, he decided that the piano was to be his instrument—not the trombone! At twenty-four, with a certain success already achieved, he decided to begin all over again; to put himself under Leschetitsky and become a master of his instrument. At twenty-seven he decided to challenge the musical world at Paris. At thirty he decided, in the face of the adverse criticism of London, to challenge England—and to include in the terms of his challenge, word for word, the London criticisms that had condemned him. At thirty-one he decided to invade the New World of America. When the World War came he decided promptly, not alone what his part in the struggle should be, but what Poland's eventual rôle must be. Faced with the crisis of the proffered German "independence" of 1916 he decided that it must be rejected, and he rejected it. Facing another crisis in 1918 he decided to go to Poland and establish a government which the Allies would accept.

His entire career as Prime Minister of Poland and Delegate to the Peace Conference was a career of decisions, at Warsaw and at Paris. Now, in the thick of the struggle he was approaching the moment of a new decision, the most responsible and momentous of his life. The time was nearing when he must decide whether to remain at his post and by the pressure of all the concentrated powers which he held available at hand force his will on the nation; or, to save what he had built up, to keep the machine running that he had assembled, withdraw and stand by.

Pilsudski's opposition grew. He continued to summon the Prime Minister to the Belvedere for conferences, but obviously he was working steadily to undermine his partner in government; obviously, for this fact was as manifest now to the man in the street as it was to the initiate. Pilsudski began, in fact, to play something like an open hand. He stated frankly that, once the work of the Peace Conference was concluded, Poland must again have a Socialist government. Such a statement naturally strengthened the opposition to Paderewski, not only because it forecast an end to the coalition government which he had organized, but also because it publicly labeled that government, in the words of his own colleague who had helped him organize it, a makeshift, a mere temporary arrangement designed to meet only immediate needs.

A speech delivered by Paderewski to the Seym on May 21, 1919, if closely studied, offers a key to the explanation of Pilsudski's opposition. In that speech Paderewski did two things; he stated clearly and unequivocally the situation of Poland in relation to her enemies, attacking her borderlands; and he stated just as clearly her position in relation to her friends the Allies, her obligations to those friends. "The Polish nation," he said in this address, "is today living through solemn moments. I suppose that in its eventful history there was never a time more solemn, more fateful than the present. The fate of our country is at stake; powerful people holding in their hands the destiny of the world are building a framework for our independent existence, are deciding the frontiers of our State, and soon will pronounce a final sentence from which, no doubt, for long years there will be no appeal, perhaps for many generations. Violent bursts of hope and of joy and anxiety are strongly shaking our national spirit. . . . What will Poland be like? What will be her frontiers?" Touching then on the two specific points mentioned, Poland's relation to her enemies and to her friends, he said first, as to Poland's enemies (the italics are mine):

The Peace Conference, and especially England and America, with President Wilson at the head, while recognizing the necessity of our defending ourselves against the Bolsheviks, *does not wish for further war on any front.* Mr. Wilson expressed this wish repeatedly and very firmly. Could a Polish Prime Minister, director of the Polish Government, a man upon whose shoulders falls the really dreadful responsibility for the fate of his people in the near future, could such a man wave aside such demands? I did as my conscience prompted me. I acted as my love for my country and my honor as a Pole demanded. *I said I would do all I could to satisfy these demands, and I have kept my word.* An armistice was demanded. I agreed in principle to that. It was demanded that Haller's army should not fight against the Ukrainians. It was withdrawn from the Ukrainian front. Finally it was required that the offensive should stop.*

Although the Ukrainians in their telegram of May 11 asked for a cessation of hostilities, on the 12th, at noon, they attacked us treacherously near Ustrzyki, bombarding the town of Sanok from aeroplanes. In the face of this criminal attack no force could stop the elemental impulse of our young soldiers. Like a whirlwind they threw themselves upon the enemy . . . being joyfully greeted everywhere as saviours by the Polish and Ukrainian population. But . . . a strong Soviet army has entered unhappy Galicia, or rather Ruthenia. Haller's army will probably be obliged to fight on the Ukrainian front, but not against the Ukrainians, only against the Bolsheviks. . . . Our Polish expedition is against bandits from whose oppression both the Polish and Ruthenian population must be set free before law and order can be set up on this immemorially Polish territory.

Second, as to Poland's relationship with the Allies:

We have recognized the authority and dignity of the Peace Conference, as all other civilized nations have done, and we wait for its verdict. Up to the present its verdicts have been favorable to us. *We voted here an alliance with the Entente, that is, with France, England and Italy who are continually sending us the help which is absolutely*

---

* Paderewski did not blame the Ukrainians: "Gentlemen, I am far from blaming the Ukrainian people for such crimes. It was not they who made such an army. Other people made it for them."

necessary to us in present circumstances. We have very much to be grateful for from America and its President. Without the powerful support of President Wilson, whose heart Colonel House, the best friend of the Polish cause, was able to win for us, Poland would no doubt have remained an internal question for Germany and Russia.

The points to be remarked in turning to this speech of Paderewski's for light on the Pilsudski opposition are these: First, that the frontiers of Poland, still unsettled, were being attacked by her enemies, those enemies being the Bolsheviks, whose aims were inspired and whose arms were supported, secretly, by the Germany that had been defeated by the Allies in the West, but that still hoped to wield power in Eastern Europe. Second, that the Allies, while still engaged in the settlement of the Polish frontiers, were willing to supply Poland with defensive arms to protect her borderlands, and were actually doing so, but were unwilling to support Poland in an offensive war. Third, that Paderewski, in the name of Poland, had given guarantees to the Allies that there should be no offensive war on the part of Poland. These three items together give us the sum total of Paderewski's position.

Opposed to this was Pilsudski's position. Pilsudski felt that the incursions of the Bolsheviks justified not only defensive but offensive warfare. The basis of his justification of offensive warfare was his belief that Poland, by striking out, could not only protect herself but could protect the peoples of those Russian borderlands, such as the Ukrainians, the White Russians, the Latvians, whose situation was indeterminate but who had ambitions of independence from Russia. It was not a Polish conquest of these borderland peoples that Pilsudski desired, but a federation of them with the Poles, a federation to be urged and won by Poland's giving them, first, the protection of her arms, and afterward the advantages of political affiliation.

The workings of Pilsudski's mind as it developed this plan were not only quickened by the same dispositions which hindered his work with Paderewski—that is, his militaristic temperament, balking at opposition, and his distrust of both the Allies in Paris and of the home government in Warsaw, but were sped up by the rapid development of hostilities along the eastern frontier, where the Bolsheviks were steadily massing armed forces. Here too, it is not difficult to believe, his ingrained antagonism to Russia, all but born in him, may have come into play. He had fought Russia since boyhood, it was become a natural functioning of his being. With Russia taking the field once more to threaten the life and liberty of Poland, his deepest instincts were roused. He was convinced that Poland could be saved only by a great and swift offensive campaign which would not only sweep the forces of Red Russia out of the borderlands but which would extend, and at the same time hasten the definition of the Polish frontiers and likewise lay the foundations of a cordon of friendly minor states aligned with Poland against the Muscovite. Finally he was convinced that the delays of deliberation in Warsaw and Paris increased daily the danger of Poland being overrun by the Soviet armies. "Freedom," Pilsudski once had declared, "cannot be won by hoping or cheating, it can be bought only with the price of blood."

Pilsudski had a large popular backing for his project of federation; he did not stand alone among Poles in cherishing the ancient Jagellonian theory of a Polish-Lithuanian-Ruthenian union against Russia, a theory as old as these peoples who had lived for centuries opposed to each other on open plains without natural geographic frontiers. Moreover, he was abetted in this theory by the Ukrainian nationalistic agitation aflame at the moment, an agitation sponsored mostly by immature intellectuals and headed by the self-styled "General" Petlura, a former schoolmaster.

Paderewski in his arguments against Pilsudski's ambitious and idealistic scheme, arguments which represented likewise a large popular sentiment in Poland, as well as the view of the Allies, did not discount the attractiveness of a protective hegemony on the Polish frontiers. But he countered the proposal with a practical view which led his supporters to regard the Pilsudski project as romantic. Paderewski's argument was, first, that Poland could not afford such a project: in her present condition she could not prosecute it alone, and since the Allies refused to back it, it was out of the question. Second, desirable as a buffer state in the Ukraine might be, he questioned the capacity of the Ukrainians to establish such a state. His doubt on that score was based largely on the well-known fact that the nationalistic agitation stirring the people of the Ukraine at the time was artificial, that it had its real origin in German propaganda. He went further and argued that whether the Ukrainians had or had not the capacity to establish such a state, they had not the capacity to maintain it, since no Russian government that it was possible to contemplate, Bolshevik or other, would permit such a thing. No Russian government, Red or any other color, he believed, would renounce sovereignty over the most fertile region of the former Russian dominions, a region which possessed moreover the only ice-free seaports available to Russia, those of the Black Sea. To these arguments he added the fear that if Pilsudski insisted on prosecuting his plan he would only provoke the Bolsheviks to a large mass attack, especially since at the moment they asked for nothing better than an excuse of self-defense to move forward against Poland.

The issue between the two men was clear. Paderewski could not for himself in conscience endorse the Pilsudski project. Furthermore he had given his word to the Allies that it would not be carried through, that there would be no *fait accompli* and no offensive warfare. Pilsudski, on his side, convinced that Poland was lost unless she acted, determined to act regardless of the Allies and of Poland's obligations to them. The two leaders came at last to an open clash. In one of their conferences Paderewski said, "At least you must promise me that you will not push toward Kiev." Pilsudski's answer was, "I shall go to Kiev whenever I please."

To Paderewski it seemed impossible to deal with his colleague in such a mood. The temper of Pilsudski's mood at times like this is revealed in his characteristic dictum, "I like to decide all matters by myself," as it is likewise revealed in the words he spoke later to Lord D'Abernon when explaining his choice of action in the defense of Warsaw in 1920: "Moreover," he said, "this thought pleased me . . . I should not be exposed to the suggestions of cowards and the sophisms of the incompetent." These particular words refer, it is true, to his conduct of a specific military operation, but to me they seem in general characteristic of the man when I recall a certain long conversation I had with him several months earlier. The burden of that conversation was the military. I do not rely on memory for this impression, but on a stenographic record of the conversation.

The fears roused in Paderewski by Pilsudski's attitude were shown in a reference which Paderewski made to the issue in this same speech of May 21, 1919, already quoted from. Characteristically he was careful and just in his utterance, naming no names and making no charges, yet no one on the floor of the Seym could mistake his thought. "The foreign press and different political parties abroad," he said, "sometimes accuse Poland of having an imperialistic policy. One of our most prominent Deputies eloquently stated a few days ago that there is a general prejudice abroad against Poland, and, at the same time, said that the responsibility for this falls upon certain classes in our community. I do not go so far. I cannot blame any party for this. I must, however, remark that this prejudice actually exists and is even spreading."

It was spreading. From the days immediately following the Armistice in November, 1918, when Pilsudski had been proclaimed Chief of State and had set up what was virtually a military dictatorship nominally backed by but actually backing a Socialist government, while many of Poland's friends anxiously watched Pilsudski's movements and feared them, her enemies had studiously propagated the idea that Poland was at heart militaristic, imperialistic, greedy for territory and power, on the offensive. Now Pilsudski's attitude toward Paderewski's defensive policy did not tend to lessen the fears of Poland's friends nor the prejudices of her enemies. As that attitude grew more and more manifest the fears grew and the prejudice spread even to friendly circles. Paderewski knew that there was but one way of combating and destroying this prejudice: to develop a sound domestic government and by virtue of a strong defensive policy, backed by the continual sympathy and support of the Allies, secure the country's frontiers.

But in Pilsudski's opinion the merely defensive at such a moment was disastrous. Poland was being attacked, therefore she must attack; invasion must be anticipated by invasion. He was a soldier, a commander. His strategy demanded not talk but the blow, the initial blow, struck far enough forward to insure profit no matter what might be the reckoning afterward. Besides he was tired of politics. The slow movement of national and international deliberation maddened him. For that matter, Paderewski, for at least equally just cause, since he was enmeshed in its intricacies, was as tired of politics as Pilsudski was; but as Paderewski saw things, it was in politics, in political construction, that the solution of Poland's problem lay. He expressed himself forcibly once, years afterward, on the question of political debate, revealing in his words some of the things he had learned in those turbulent days, revealing as well how close he and Pilsudski could come in some opinions. "For years," he said, "the so-called parliamentary system in government has been looked upon as a panacea for all ills. It was felt that when the man in the street was represented in a legislative body, then that man had something to do with the making of the laws and the management of his country. But ideas in regard to this are changing. People are beginning to feel that this system is not altogether what it promised to be. Indeed, it has been my experience that in most bodies of this kind a tremendous amount of time is wasted in useless and futile talk. Hours are used up in listening to speeches of no import or value. In times of economic distress long discussions in parliament only irritate. A hungry man's appetite is not appeased by words. What he wants is food. And when he sees that the words do not give him food, he becomes dissatisfied with that system of representation which does not provide him with necessities, let alone comforts."

In Paderewski's view, what the man in Poland needed most at this time was food; that is, peace, with the stabilized domestic condition that gives him work, the means of earning food. And whatever its drawbacks, political action through popular government was the only means at hand to supply that need. In Pilsudski's view what the Poles needed was the prompt securing of the nation's safety and sustenance by dispersing her enemies and settling her frontiers by force. Agitating this view, blocking and countering Paderewski's efforts for the purpose of advancing this view, he was actually only prolonging the "talk" of which both he and Paderewski were weary. He could not see that wholehearted coöperation from him, even one word signifying such coöperation, would put an end to talk.

Whatever Pilsudski's processes of thought during this time —and they can only be guessed at and judged by the results— there he sat, the veteran leader of the legions, the seasoned old war-horse of battle-attack and cavalry-raid, chafing in the peaceful confinement of the Belvedere Palace, out by the quiet waters of the little Lazienki Lake, impatient to be at the front. His colleague meanwhile stood on the very real and very hazardous battle-front of parliamentary debate and international commitment, struggling to save the lives of the Polish people and the life of the Polish state. And as he struggled, his government moving steadily, in spite of opposition, toward reconstruction of the country, Pilsudski saw that his borderland campaign, his great federalistic project, might never be possible, might be delayed and finally vetoed altogether, if Paderewski remained in power. Poland, in Pilsudski's view, was on the verge of complete disaster. The demand of the Allies, of which Paderewski told the Seym on May 21, that there be no more war on any front, was a challenge to Pilsudski. He was determined to accept that challenge and to carry out his plan. To do so Paderewski must be removed.

The weeks passed, Pilsudski straining in inaction, eager for battle, Paderewski fighting one battle after another on the political front. Paderewski had returned home in midwinter, on New Year's Day; he had tasted once more, after many years, the savour of old-fashioned Polish wintertime, white and glittering, an air sharpened, embittered, it is true, by want and misery, but to him nevertheless the familiar air of home, and full of the tang of hope. Spring had come, the bursting rejuvenescence of a snow-locked land:—the going of the snow and cold, the budding of magnolias in the city gardens, the blooming of the pear-orchards along the Praga banks of the Vistula, visible from the Zamek's windows; the blue lamp of the Madonna shrine, "Queen of Poland", glowing not through frosty filigree now, but through leafy green, the lime trees of the Aleja in full foliage; all this made the more beautiful by the feeling that misery at last was passing from the face of the land; new life coming back to half-dead Poland, work, peace, the fields re-planted, the god-like gesture of the sowers scattering the seed that he, Paderewski, had begged for in America for Polish farmers. Summer had come, harvests to feed the hungry, work and peace . . . Somewhere in the back of his mind his old dream of a Polish home awakened—rest and repose for him here with his fellows in the land of their fathers when his work was done. . . . Summer passed . . . Paderewski was still at his post getting things done in the face of tremendous obstacles. The ratification of the Versailles peace treaty was one of the big things he got done. And Pilsudski still edged at politics and politicians and still dreamed of saving Poland by the sword. "In September of the same year," Paderewski said afterward, reviewing the situation, "my country found itself in a very difficult position. A new military operation was proposed to me, an operation far beyond the means of the exhausted country and dangerous in the extreme." Pilsudski's conviction was that Poland's danger was from the outside. The real danger, as Paderewski saw it, was on the inside. He recognized the gravity of the external threat, but he argued that no outside danger could be permanently withstood unless the country was fortified by stabilization within. Pilsudski argued that there could be no internal stabilization until the threat was removed. And in the meantime, while Paderewski was daily pleading with the Allies for help to aid Poland in meeting the Bolshevik threat—for a settlement of the frontiers and for still more arms with which to defend herself—the Allies, suspicious of Pilsudski, held back and debated.

While the opposition at the Belvedere grew, so did that in

the Seym. By this time it had become a steady campaign of heckling, blocking, stalling, sniping, obstructing. "Don't forget, this isn't one of your concerts!" the socialist deputy Klemensiewicz stupidly shouted at the Prime Minister one day. "If you were playing the piano," he yelled, "we'd all have to be quiet, but we've got just as much right to speak here as you have! And don't you forget it!" Paderewski's response was characteristically courteous and forceful: "Gentlemen, I am paying you respect and to that same respect I am entitled." In Warsaw Paderewski had to endure the same baffling torment that President Wilson at that identical time was suffering in Washington; they were fellows in ideals and in experience. On November 12 it looked as if the break had come; Paderewski that day, addressing the deputies, seemed to be saying his last word. But even yet he was not quite ready. There was still hope, and there still were things that must be done and that he alone could do. But he saw now that to go on in this way much longer was only to provoke dissension to the danger point. The danger point was complete dissolution of representative government, outright precipitation into a military dictatorship. That would mean the undoing of all that had been accomplished, the repudiation of Poland by the Powers, civil war, a total breaking up, with Poland even worse off than before the war. And beyond that possibility was the more fearful possibility of a new world war; for the disruption of the Republic at this time would mean that Poland, weakened by internal conflict, would lie open to attack, East and West, from her ancient partitioners. It would mean Germany roused again on the Prussian frontier, Red Russia overriding the east, Germany and Russia joining hands. . . . Europe in a new chaos.

He had to consider, too, Poland's reputation abroad. Protracted dissension in the Seym meant a bad name for the country in the foreign press. The news bureaus of Berlin influenced the press of both Europe and America, especially the British and American press. Paderewski was so much an American himself, and he felt himself so accountable to the American people, that he dared not, for Poland's sake, take the risk of jeopardizing his country's name before the American democracy. "Poland has set up a democracy under the inspiration of the American people," he said in a statement on September 18. Again: "Laying aside all so-called war literature inspired by strategic motives: boastful appeals, pompous orders of the day, single and double manifestoes occasionally containing indisputable lyric beauty"—obviously a reference to the Russian and the Austro-German manifestoes of Polish "independence"—"all of which has vanished like smoke under the brutal blow of facts, we see clearly that the resurrection of Poland came from the United States and through the United States. It is a truth that only persons of regrettable ignorance or of deplorable bad faith could possibly deny." American backing, the credit of Poland's good name in America, meant everything to him. At this time violent attacks on him were beginning to appear in American and English papers. An article in *The Nation* of New York, which devoted itself to anti-Polish propaganda, called Paderewski's return to Poland a "royal interference", and the same article, significantly enough, linked Pilsudski's name, not Paderewski's, with that of Poland's national hero, Kosciuszko. Silly stories about "King Ignace" and "Queen Helena" were also being reprinted.*

He still maintained a majority in the diet. He might have stayed on, stubbornly insisting on support. He might have made the long fight to win public opinion. But he knew that for the moment partisan opinion was the only public opinion in Poland: the masses whom he was feeding were still too devitalized and too preoccupied with the one terrible problem of escaping starvation to have a voice beyond the voice of their elected delegates or to know that that elected voice was now confused if not corrupted by the military opposition. "The sentiment of the masses, which we usually call public opinion," he once remarked, " is for political action, as for a swimmer the current of the river or for the sailing ship the wind. It is impossible, almost impossible, to

---

* The trivial source of such stories is characterized by one incident: Madame Paderewska remarked of a salad served at an informal luncheon that it was "fit for a king." Her remark was served to the public, garnished by the inspired gossips to regal amplitude!

swim against the current and very difficult to sail against the wind." More and more the current of the Seym, not calmed by the wind off Lazienki Lake, was against him. He saw squalls, a storm, disaster, in the inevitable deadlock ahead and he feared the consequences, which might indeed be complete wreckage of the ship of state. He was by nature a harmonizer, whether in music or politics; and better still he was, in politics, a realist. At all times he kept his head. At Paris, in the words of E. J. Dillon in his "Inside Story of the Peace Conference", he "sank political passion in reason and attuned himself to the role of harmonizer. He held that it would have been worse than useless to have done otherwise." So now at Warsaw.

He might have made out of the situation a personal fight with Pilsudski. He might have declared himself a rival dictator. He had the power to do so. But he had wisdom as well as power, patriotic foresight and unselfishness to see the dangers and disasters that would result from such an issue. As for the power in his hands, there was a time in 1919 when, in the eyes of those who adhered to him, Paderewski might have done any of the things that a dictator would wish to do. One by one he was bringing home to Poland such gifts as could not have been dreamed of. A world-wide sympathy for Poland's cause; prospective Polish boundaries that would make her the sixth largest state in Europe; the alliance of the Powers; a stream of recognitions from foreign governments, ten of them within five months of his coming; free elections, a parliament, a constitution in the making; relief for the hungry and the sick that counted into many millions—food, hospitals, seed for the farmers, rations for the soldiers; the reopening of national universities and of hundreds of schools: these are some of the gifts that poured out of the hand of Fortune into Poland's lap, the fruit of Paderewski's fertile genius for statesmanship; not gifts of his sole making—he would be the last to claim and the first to deny that: he paid all homage to what had been done by Pilsudski and every other one of his compatriots in laying what might be called the physical foundations of his work. Even so, all this accomplished, the task was far from completed. Hardships and difficulties remained which no magic of brain or tongue could exercise. After the first days of popular elation had passed, discontent was smouldering, and there were political enemies who knew how to exploit every sign of such feeling as well as how to take advantage of Paderewski's prolonged absences in Paris to attend the Peace Conference. Not even he, with all his powers of persuasive eloquence, could obtain at Paris all that the newly freed Poles desired: Danzig, Teschen, Upper Silesia, and the rest. In spite of his warnings at Paris the trouble-making plebiscites were decided upon, with the result that the state of uncertainty and discontent in Poland was only prolonged. As one of Paderewski's successors in the Foreign Ministry, Patek, expressed it when speaking of the unsettled frontier problem, "Poland resembled God's mercy, for it knew no bounds."

Paderewski's experiences during these anxious days brought home to him a truth that he had often observed—in politics popular disappointments are almost invariably blamed, regardless, upon leaders. Now it was not alone that fault finding and opposition in the Seym became increasingly vocal; within the cabinet, too, disagreements and dissensions arose. There was the position on finance measures taken by Bilinski, a venerable statesman of the Austrian school. Paderewski saw disaster in certain of Bilinski's decisions, and in the end Paderewski was proved right; but the disagreement stood. The Minister of the Interior, Wojciechowski, was a Socialist and a personal friend of Pilsudski, a colleague of his days of underground struggle against Russia. Wojciechowski's policies opposed Paderewski's. Wojciechowski could not have predicted then the day that was to come when Pilsudski would oust him by force from the office of President of the Republic because he stood, as Paderewski did now, for constitutional order. Thus, in Seym, in cabinet, as in the office of the Chief of State, coöperation grew less and less, dissension and opposition more and more.

Finally, Paderewski, undermined surreptitiously and openly threatened, made his decision to resign. He was convinced that thus only could the Polish State be saved from disaster and ruin.

It is easy to write, "He made his decision." But what he went through in his own mind and heart to make that decision can only be guessed at; weeks, days and nights, with the thought never really leaving him, weeks of cogitation, pondering, considering. It must have seemed to him in many ways a terrible thing for him to give in. The fear must have come upon him at times of being thought a quitter. Not easy to face the charge, bound to be made, of backing down, of failing. The shadow of this care overlaid his mind, the strain of deciding pulled every fibre of his nervous system; he suffered not alone because of the natural feeling of a man in such a situation, but because of the injury bound to be done Poland. Poland, he knew, would be dubbed "impossible" by many as a result of this unfortunate crisis. But he knew that Poland was not "impossible." He had great stores of inner strength, of balance, to draw upon in that belief, of illumination to flood with light the dark crevices that this crisis opened up. He needed all the balance and light that could be given him. He realized this on one occasion especially, when a move was made to humiliate him publicly. On November 27, 1919, the Seym was startled to stunned silence, in spite of the fact that such an announcement was to be expected, by being told by the Marshal (the Speaker of the Seym) that Paderewski had resigned. The surprise was due to the simple fact, known to the deputies, that Paderewski had not resigned. He was at that moment working, still hopefully though with hands shackled, at the formation of a new cabinet. This unpardonable affront, unprecedented in the history of legislatures, gave deep offense to the country. Its repercussion was renewed sympathy for Paderewski. He, on his part, would have been iron and unnatural not to resent it. He was astounded, but he refused to discuss or comment on the outrage, ashamed, no doubt, to think that such a thing could happen in Poland. He continued his work.

In a few days, however, he saw how hopeless the situation was. On December fifth he sent letters to Pilsudski and to the Marshal of the Seym asking to be released from office. He would make the sacrifice, any sacrifice, to forestall disaster to the country. In the words of Colonel House, "No country ever needed the services of one of her sons more than Poland needed those of Paderewski then, but he was never one of those who feel themselves indispensable. Had he been more ambitious and less patriotic and unselfish, he might have continued in power and become an autocrat." It was, as Herbert Hoover commented later, "with rare moral courage" that he made this momentous decision "without complaining . . . refusing to take advantage of the military arm that could have preserved him and his colleagues in office. This he did lest he should do infinite harm to the cause of Democracy."

Pilsudski accepted his resignation. But in the Seym it had a sobering effect. They grew frightened. The Marshal of the Seym was delegated to go that night to Paderewski for a reconsideration. Later that same night two deputies, accompanied by Archbishop Kakowski, followed the Marshal begging that Paderewski at least form a new cabinet. A conference was held with Pilsudski. Paderewski insisted that for the good of the country he must withdraw, that under the existing circumstances he could not be asked to bear the responsibility of government, but he stipulated that in any case it was he who must choose his successors, men whom he had helped train during the past few months in the art of government, an art at that time almost unknown to the Poles after a century and a half of alien despotism.

This grave disturbance in the government had its repercussions in domestic affairs. Within a week there was a street car strike, a strike of the telephone workers and of the gas-plant employees. A potato famine hit the capital, due to a strike of union laborers who refused to unload the supplies which Paderewski had procured. In these disturbances Pilsudski still remained silent. If he dreamed of martial law leading to the proclamation of a dictatorship, such disturbances of course only fed into his hand. Whether or not the rumors were inspired, the streets of Warsaw hummed with talk of a dictatorship.

If Paderewski had had time to read the papers during these days of terrible strain, one item would have interested him.

American dispatches in the Warsaw dailies of December 11 spoke of Herbert Hoover's name being mentioned as a presidential candidate for 1920. Paderewski, wishing well to his old friend, might have smiled grimly at that item of news. He could have given Hoover at that moment some valuable information about the burdens of public office.

It was the eleventh of December, after a week of fruitless conferences, of confusion, of blind staggering on the part of his opponents, that Paderewski finally and definitely put his foot down on the whole affair. It was an impossible situation. He was wanted and he was not wanted. He must organize a new government and no new government could be organized. He saw actual and immediate danger ahead for Poland if this condition continued for even one more day.

By December 15 a new government was at last organized. Paderewski drew a deep breath. For five years he had worked like a wheel ceaselessly turning; he had never dared to be tired. Now he was tired. He wanted to go back home to Riond-Bosson and see how the farm was doing.

Paderewski's largeness of spirit and generosity of temper showed itself at this crucial time. He might have quit angrily, left in a quarrel; there was justification enough. But he stood by, ready for service at the call of his successor in the ministry, ready to give counsel, busy doing so. He accepted the invitation of the Seym to attend its first meeting under the new cabinet. He appeared on that rostrum where a fortnight before the unprecedented offense of his anticipated resignation had been offered to humiliate him. There was no cynicism in his smile when, entering the chamber, he was given an ovation. He was pleased; there was still hope for harmony among his people. If there was sadness in his smile there was also hope. He listened with sincere emotion to the speech of the new Prime Minister who paid him a glowing tribute and who spoke feelingly of the hope of further help from Paderewski's friend Hoover. A few days after Christmas he accompanied Pilsudski to Poznan to join in Poznania's celebration of the anniversary of her liberation from Germany. His reception there was tremendous. Paderewski might have felt at this time, as many felt abroad as well as in Poland, and as the *Outlook* of New York felt when it said "now that he has got all that he could get out of Paderewski, Pilsudski drops him." But no one saw a sign of bitterness or resentment in Paderewski.

Among his intimates it was the same. Those closest to him during those extremely trying days between his resignation and his departure heard no word of repining from him. They felt, as he above all had a right to feel, that affairs would have been in a very different condition had he been given full support in his effort to consolidate the State. This conflict between him and Pilsudski, one of the most dramatic personal conflicts in history—and, as it was to turn out to be, one of the most tragic —might have been avoided. It was based on division as to the methods, not as to the aims, of individual men, although out of it comes striking evidence of how single individuals may personify whole peoples. In this case two individuals, united in ideal but separated in ideas, stand as perfect exemplars of the paradoxical unity and division of the Polish people. Unity was the rightful heritage of the Poles; they had suffered together for over a century for their common ideal of freedom and independence. But the crime of the Partitions had deprived them of practical unity though it could not break their unified spirit of national aspiration and identity. Deeply into the strongly woven texture of united Polish feeling the Partitions had stamped the disfiguring die of division of thought, and division of thought remained their portion. Yet when Paderewski withdrew in 1919 the Poles were a more united people than they had ever been, and that was unmistakably due in very large part to him. Had he been permitted to remain that unity would have increased.

Paderewski would not have been human if, at this crisis, he had not felt these things strongly. But he said nothing of them. He might have easily said, and tens of thousands would have supported him in the saying: "It would have been better if Pilsudski had given me his full support. If Pilsudski, the popular soldier-hero, carrying on his great work of military reorganization and national defense, had openly backed me in the Seym, political dissension in the country would have been reduced, suspicion of Poland would have been lessened among the Allies, larger credits would have been the more readily won from them for defense of the Polish frontiers, the frontiers themselves would have been settled earlier and more willingly. In short, with Pilsudski wholeheartedly backing me from the start, I would have had even greater pulling power at Paris than I had. With no suspicion of Polish imperialism in the minds of the Allies, a suspicion which resulted directly from Pilsudski's Federalism project, with my pledge to Paris kept inviolate that there would be not even the threat of *fait accompli* or of an offensive Polish war, the two of us together could have had from the Allies anything we asked, enough for us to give back to our people the unity which is their right and the peace they crave. . . ."

But these things had not been. He had given his last ounce of strength to make them be. There was nothing to do but go, and still hope that, disastrous as Pilsudski's scheme of action threatened to be, with the Allies alienated and Poland once more almost isolated, unity and peace would come eventually. At least the spectacle of a country divided at its head, a scandal before the world, would not be continued.

He had moved his effects from his official residence in the Zamek and had gone back to the Hotel Bristol. He had paid off his staffs; and it is to be noted that throughout his tenure of office, then and afterward, he paid out of his own pocket all the salaries and expenses of his co-workers both in Paris and Warsaw.

Paderewski's departure from Warsaw was a public event. The people of the capital who had risen in thousands to greet him on New Year's day, 1919, gathered now just one year later, January, 1920, to offer him a homage that all the intrigue of ministers and deputies and all the opposition of Pilsudski could not alter. Twenty thousand people formed into procession and marched to the Hotel Bristol. Hundreds crowded into the hotel. A delegation presented him with a memorial signed by over one hundred thousand citizens.

He went home to Riond-Bosson, tired, perhaps a little discouraged, perhaps even a little disillusioned for the moment, though he is of too strong a nature to cherish disillusionment. The reservoirs of his nature, the wells of his practical idealism, are too deep for that. And even his decision not only to withdraw, but to go away, was a sacrifice made for Poland's sake, for the sake of peace. Wisely he felt that to clear the air, to leave not the least provocation of conflict or dissension, he must withdraw entirely from the scene. It would have been easier to stay, to "play politics" and maneuver a return to his own advantage. There were many to urge him to do this. He would not do it. The last sacrifice of self made, he could stand erect facing his own conscience and say, as he did say to me in October, 1921: "I have done all I could do to obtain for my country the greatest possible advantages with the least possible sacrifice. I have endeavored to spare human life and to save public money. I have opposed all militaristic ventures of those who, holding real power without responsibility, have so completely succeeded in alienating the sympathy and respect of the world for my country and ruining her credit."

These words could be taken as a summing up of Paderewski's career as statesman. In that career of crises and decisions he had made no decision more momentous or to himself more heartbreaking than his decision to withdraw from office and leave Warsaw. But if he regretted the inescapable necessity of making it, he could not regret having made it. He knew that he had done the right thing and that he had done it at the right time. He could only hope that the lessons in self-government and in national and international peace and unity which he had taught his people—which, no matter how unwillingly listened to, he had taught his opponents—would in time bear fruit.

XXXIX

1920: THE DARKEST DAYS

JOSEPH CONRAD wrote to me in March, 1923, a letter concerning the Polish situation which contained the following passage: "You will understand that often I feel cast down when I think of that country's precarious position. A lonely outpost—in the night full of menace to the hard won civilization of Europe. A hard fate, but whatever happens you at least will know that they have been equal to it."

"Whatever happens." What had already happened when Conrad wrote those words, what happened almost immediately after Paderewski's withdrawal from the premiership, was enough to cast him down, down to the depths, enough to make his heart bleed for the "lonely outpost." If we have imagined Paderewski standing in the dawn on the terrace at Riond-Bosson looking out across the Alps as morning broke, wondering when the sun would rise over Poland, we can picture him now watching what must have seemed like a night deeper than any his motherland had ever known, coming down upon her with a dreadful darkness and with the terrible lightnings of death and devastation. Would they, as Conrad said, be equal to it?

Pilsudski had gone ahead with his project amid great popular excitement. With the young Polish Army raised to a force of some 600,000, a tremendous force aflame with patriotic ardor, he had made his dream come true, or at least a part of it. He had driven on into the Ukraine. He had taken Kiev. He had done these things easily. But he had done them too easily, as events proved. He had miscalculated the movements of the Red armies, which were now backed by inflamed popular feeling in Russia, just as Paderewski had feared. "The

capture of Kiev by the Poles," Trotsky wrote later in his book
My Life: the Rise and Fall of a Dictator, "did us great service; it awakened the country." Pilsudski's triumphant advance
into the south had been part of a ruse worked by the Soviets to
draw him on while they massed their attack in the north. At
Kiev he was wakened from his dream. Instead of moving on
toward Moscow he was suddenly turned back to Warsaw in
one of the most disastrous retreats in military history, a retreat
that cost thousands of lives and ended with a Bolshevik nut-
cracker clinched around Warsaw, and all Western Europe
threatened by a Red invasion. The beautiful living Poland
that Paderewski had seen recreated was almost a corpse, hacked
half to death, starved, despoiled, her people wracked by famine and typhus, her army wrecked by dysentery, her two million refugees, who had returned at the summons of peace in
1919 to rebuild their homes and farms, again uprooted and
scattered. Industry was destroyed, epidemic ravaged the country. On March 20 Colonel Gilchrist of the United States Army
Medical Corps reported Poland to be "threatened with one of
the worst typhus fever epidemics in the history of the world",
an epidemic which, he added, "unless checked will prove a
danger that will threaten the whole of Europe."

I was in the Polish retreat of 1920, the greatest retreat since
Napoleon fled from Moscow. I saw the wide march of disease
and death move across the country. I saw the mutilated bodies
of Polish soldier boys who had been captured by the Reds,
young bodies that had breathed with the new Polish life that
peace had brought, now slashed by sabre-blades, salt-tortured,
their heads smashed in by rifle-butts. I saw the brains of Polish
army officers smeared on walls, brains that had leaped to the
new light of freedom, now obliterated in the darkness of
bloody death. I saw villages burning as Paderewski had seen
Kurylowka burn. I saw the whole frantic stampede of a panic-
driven populace fleeing before the Red wave of the Bolsheviks
and the black wave of death. I heard the screams of dying soldiers. . . . I saw Warsaw, swarming with terrorized refugees,
trembling before the onrush of the Reds to its very gates, its

streets at daytime filled with a hundred thousand men, women and children, marching, singing, praying to God for deliverance, its night skies lit by the fire of battle a few miles off. . . .

Paderewski, at Riond-Bosson, heard and saw it all in his tortured mind that saw all, heard all, because he understood it all so terribly.

It is painful to consider what Paderewski went through during these days of blood and disaster, of disappointment and fear and of righteous anger against those who had so injured his motherland. All the powers of his being must have strained to reach over the baffling walls of those snow-clad Alps, over the more baffling walls of circumstance, to fend off this calamity. He had fought valiantly and to his utmost to prevent this fearful thing—nevertheless it had come. But he had fought also against something else that was even worse, civil war; and he had won that fight by the sacrifice of himself. Terrible as this Bolshevik invasion was, and to him terrible as was the thought that in a measure at least it had been invoked and precipitated by the blind idealism of those who should have helped him prevent it, still there was one comforting reflection for him to fall back upon: Poland was not guilty of a fratricidal war. "Perhaps, after all," he might well have said, "the Polish people must go through this new period of suffering and endurance to come to a full realization of their blessings, a full appreciation of the value of unity as well as of freedom. . . . Perhaps after all, in the designs of Providence, Poland's foundations as a state, seamed and cracked through a century and a half of ruin, must be thus violently shaken down to bedrock before a completely stable superstructure can be erected." At least, Poland was still united. He could echo the words that Conrad wrote the twenty-fourth of March that year: "The reborn state has one heart and one soul, one indomitable will, from the poorest peasant to the highest magnate. Those magnates have now no more power and precious little more wealth than the poorest peasant with whom they fight shoulder to shoulder against moral and physical pestilence bred in Russia."

There were glimmers of light in the darkness. It was not

alone the knowledge that Poland was still united, even if in blood, that supported him. There was likewise the knowledge that her friends stood by her. The relief agencies that he had brought in from America and England were still on the ground, working now with redoubled energy; and more than that, Poland's friends were fighting for her, by her side, in her ranks. He had talked once in New York, 1917, with his friend Gutzon Borglum about the artist's part in the making of states; they had spoken of aviation, from the times of Leonardo da Vinci's experiments down to the days of the Wright brothers and the modern flying machine. One day in Paris, in September, 1918, Paderewski was told something that brought that talk back to him. There was a new movement among his American friends to help Poland. A young aviator, Merian C. Cooper, after serving in the World War, had joined Hoover's forces and had come to Poland to work in the administration of relief. He had been assigned to the Galician field; he had seen what Poland needed there to defend her frontiers—aviation; he had gone back to Paris, looked up one of his old pals of the aviation corps, Major Cedric E. Fauntleroy, rounded up a half dozen others, and had organized the Kosciuszko Squadron.* Together they had assembled in Paris for their first review before departing for the Galician front, and happily the one man to whom they wished to offer themselves was also then in Paris—Paderewski. "This amazing genius, beloved of all the world," as Lieutenant Murray of the Squadron recounts the scene, "spoke words of glowing praise for the spirit that brought the group of young pilots before him; and he

---

* The Squadron, recruited from twelve different States of the Union, and from Canada, was highly representative of American sentiment for Poland and admiration for Paderewski. The original members were Merian C. Cooper, Florida; Cedric E. Fauntleroy, Mississippi; Kenneth O. Shrewsbury, West Virginia; George M. Crawford, Delaware; Edward C. Corsi, New York; Carl H. Clark, Oklahoma; E. H. Noble, Massachusetts. The personnel was later augmented by T. V. McCallum, Canada; Elliot W. Chess, and Earl T. Evans, Texas; Kenneth M. Murray and Thomas H. Garlick, New York; J. Inglis Maitland, Michigan; H. C. Rorison, North Carolina; John C. Speaks, Ohio; Arthur H. Kelly, Virginia, and Edmund P. Graves, Massachusetts. Capt. Kelly and Lieut. Graves both gave their lives to the cause. See "Wings Over Poland" by Kenneth Malcolm Murray: New York, D. Appleton Co., 1932.

personally offered them the sum of thirty-five thousand francs from his own fortune to help defray their original organization expenses." The offer was declined; the Americans wished to go wholly on their own. But what Paderewski felt at the moment can be imagined; gratitude beyond words. The ties that bound America and Poland seemed to him stronger then than ever. This was one more gift that he and Poland owed to his friend Herbert Hoover, for it was Cooper's coming to Poland to serve under Hoover that began it. Yet the beginning went far back of that, back to the beginnings of America's and Poland's friendship, for Cooper's ancestral home in Georgia had more than once, during the Revolutionary War, sheltered the Polish patriots Kosciuszko and Pulaski, fighting for American independence.

Now in the dark days of 1920 these glimmers of light came to Paderewski: relief, food, medicine given to his people; the brave and victorious fighting of the Kosciuszko Squadron. "Their bravery, their intrepidity, their dash, their heroism," he said of these American fliers afterward, "were such as to inspire not only terror to the enemy, but to arouse his admiration. Defying danger, challenging death until the victorious end of that terrible campaign, they fought for the safety of our country and the glory of America." But all this time, hungry for the light of hope, he was almost crushed by the thought of what his people were suffering, a suffering all the more painful because renewed after a taste of peace. He could not stop thinking of the Polish soldier-boys, even boys of twelve and fourteen, and of the women legionnaires whose troops he had heard singing as they marched through streets of Warsaw, now butchered by the thousands in this new and calamitous war. In March the thought of them so weighed on him that, although he was now nearing the end of his fortune, his lifetime savings spent, he sent General Haller half a million marks for his invalid soldiers.

Paderewski, no longer Premier of Poland, was still Poland's delegate to the Supreme Council of the Allies, to the Peace Conference and to the League of Nations. "From the Polish point of view," he had said in a statement made September 18, 1919, "our one hope of future security as a State lies in the League of Nations." The time was coming soon, however, when he would have to turn for help back to the Allies, the same Allies who had received his pledges of peace only to see them in effect repudiated by Pilsudski. On the tenth of July, 1920, the then Prime Minister of Poland, Ladislas Grabski, Paderewski's second successor in the premiership within six months, appeared as the spokesman of Poland's humiliation before the Supreme Council at Spa. He came to beg for arms, munitions, money, military advisers, to save the Polish nation from extinction.

Paderewski, in his capacity of delegate to the Supreme Council, was summoned to Spa to help save the desperate situation. He went to the bitter task with grim determination, facing once more his old colleague and sometime anti-Polish adversary, Lloyd George, who was having his moment now of "I told you so." The Poles had gone on this adventure against his counsel, now let them take the consequences: that was Lloyd George's attitude. The whole attitude of the Allies had all along been unquestionably contradictory and unreasonable; they blamed Poland for her so-called imperialism, after the disaster had happened, yet they had refused to let Paderewski make peace with Bolshevik Russia, as he had from the beginning wished to do. A remark of Lloyd George's at one of the peace conferences had been an admission of this contradictory attitude. "We do not want Poland to push beyond her boundaries," he had said, "but we do not want her to make peace." At Spa Paderewski reminded him of those words, much to the British premier's discomfiture. But once more Paderewski knew how to talk the explosive Welshman into reason: in the end Lloyd George spoke openly for England's obligation to protect the integrity of the Polish State. Once more Paderewski saved Poland. He won the promise of Allied arms to support and rescue his country.

But he had to pay a heavy price; a new pledge to renounce all thoughts of conquest (ironical pledge to be given by him who had not only never thought of conquest, but had fought tooth and nail against it in others); a withdrawal to the frontiers set by the Allies; and finally the settlement on the Allies' terms of the Danzig and Teschen boundary disputes. For the latter, one of Poland's long standing and most acute problems, Paderewski was forced, on July 28, to accept a decision of grave disadvantage to Polish nationalistic rights. Pilsudski's adventure in the end cost Poland not only lives and credit, but one of her richest mineral regions. Against this cost was to be balanced, it is true, such advantages as those pointed out by Trotsky afterward. "The Poland of Pilsudski," Trotsky wrote, "came out of the war unexpectedly strengthened. . . . The development of the Polish revolution"—that is, of the proletarian uprising for which the Soviets had hoped—"received a crushing blow. . . . The frontier established cut off the Soviet from Germany, a fact that was later of great importance in the lives of both countries." As to those frontiers, Pilsudski, although he had failed to make federalism good, "succeeded", as Robert Machray states it (in his *Poland: 1914–1931*), "in interposing between the essential or ethnographic Poland and the Soviet a considerable block of territory which, in view of the attitude of the Supreme Council, Poland would probably not have obtained otherwise." In the view of Paderewski all of these benefits could have been obtained in due time without recourse to offensive war.

While the war at home in Poland went on, Paderewski in Switzerland suffered all its agonizing suspense. He needed his home now, its peace and relaxation, to sustain his spirit; but peace only mocked him and relaxation there was none. He needed the occupations of home life to save his health; he had his farm, his stock, his dogs. But everything for him now was a torture, nothing could occupy his mind but the ruin that was destroying the new Poland that he had worked so hard to rebuild out of the older ruins, only to see all swept away. And there was another thing that he needed, too, a thing that was at hand—his music. But he could not take it.

He could not go back to his piano yet. His long absorption

in matters of state had pushed art far into the background of his mind. Habit too played its part. He was out of the habit of music and so deep into the habit of affairs that it might well have been thought at this time that he could never again be interested in anything else. Moreover, this Polish situation, as the months of 1920 went by, became worse and worse; it was a good deal more than a Polish situation, it was a world crisis, and thus all the more painful for him to endure, making all the heavier his burden of fear, anxiety, concern, his profound feeling of responsibility. "If Poland succumbs to the Russian invasion," Colonel House said in Paris on July 11, 1920, "Germany will be the next to go, and largely for the reason that Germany will elect to go. . . . A majority of the Germans will welcome the Russians as deliverers. The Russian army will be enormously strengthened by recruits from the late German army, and together they will make a formidable force, a force that will take all the resources of the Western Powers to reckon with. . . . Already Russian guns are heard along the borders of East Prussia." "Here then," Paderewski might well say to himself, "is the one terrible ruin that I struggled to prevent, the ruin that was bound to come if civil war broke out in Poland. I saved Poland from civil war. But ruin has come anyway."

The Reds drove on and on. They had Poland on her knees asking for an armistice, begging for peace. Pilsudski, though never forgiving Foch for saying of him at this time, *"Il ne fallait pas courir des aventures"*, was big enough to admit his mistake. At any rate, no longer eager to go it alone, he consented to share his power. A Council of Defense was organized. But he was too late, everything now was too late. If there was to be peace it was to be a Bolshevik peace, and the fate of Europe depended on it. "The future peace of the whole world," said Colonel House on the twenty-fifth of July, "as well as the nature of the immediate reconstruction of Europe, depends upon the kind of peace treaty negotiated between the Russians and the Poles. The future color of the governments of Germany, Poland, Czechoslovakia, Austria, Hungary, Roumania and possibly the Baltic States will be largely determined . . . Poland at this moment is the storm-center of the world. The last week has been one of anxiety among the governments of Europe. In fact, the settlement of the Russian-Polish difficulty is more far-reaching than Europe. It is of consequence to the entire world. Without being conscious of it, citizens of the United States, and indeed of every other country, are vitally concerned in what is happening today in central and eastern Europe. The outcome may mean an orderly world, or a disorderly one." The same views were expressed by Poincaré on July 23. "If Poland is beaten," the French President said, "Europe will soon see new Partitions again. Poland will disappear and Germany will be left without a counterpoise in the East. It is then that we shall hear the millions of rifles that she is keeping so jealously, going off of their own accord."

Paderewski was thinking the same thoughts and a thousand others, agonizing nerve-wracking thoughts, as he saw the red ruin advance. Then, black as was the prospect of a Bolshevik peace with a suppliant Poland under its yoke, a still darker turn of uncertainty came. The peace negotiations broke. Fighting was resumed. But Paderewski's credit with the Allies and his pledges made at Spa were now bearing fruit. France hurried war supplies into Poland, Marshal Foch sent General Maxime Weygand to reorganize the forces of defense and strategy, and Pilsudski, once more on his native and familiar ground of military action, redeemed himself as commander and strategist.* Those close to him averred afterwards that he never lost hope, while others about him despaired. Not only

---

* The Battle of Warsaw, of which Lord D'Abernon wrote that "the history of contemporary civilization knows no event of greater importance", caused much debate in military circles, the question being raised as to whom the credit for the victory belonged, the French who helped, or the Poles. General Weygand himself, with characteristic French courtesy, settled the question. "The victory is a Polish victory," he declared; "the military operations were executed by Polish generals in accordance with a Polish plan." "Had the battle been a Bolshevik victory," wrote Lord D'Abernon in his *Eighteenth Decisive Battle of the World*, "it would have been a turning point in European history. . . . Poland saved Europe in 1920." In 1924 Pilsudski's own account of the event appeared in his book *Rok 1920* ("The year 1920"), published in Warsaw. It gives an illuminating picture of the Bolshevik War and tells dramatically how Pilsudski locked himself in his room for many hours struggling with himself and the terrible problem he faced.

Poland's security but his own pride and reputation were at stake. He would have been scarcely human if, over and above his determination to save Poland, he had not been spurred on by the thought of what men like Paderewski, who had warned him of the very disaster now befallen, would say if he lost at the last throw. It was a desperate moment, to Paderewski a maddening moment, when on August 14 the Red armies, within six miles of Warsaw, were closing in, sweeping up from the south, sweeping across the north, cutting off communication with Danzig—where already Allied troops were forced to unload war supplies because of the refusal of German dockworkers to do so—and penetrating even to the Prussian frontier. These perhaps were the blackest moments, the moments nearest to despair, of all Paderewski's life.

On August fifteenth came the "Miracle of the Vistula", with its historic drama of Skorupka, the young Polish priest and scout-master who led his schoolboy soldiers to the attack on Radzymin, his body riddled with bullets but his hand still holding high his crucifix as he sent his companions forward to the victory which turned the course of the whole war. The "Miracle of the Vistula" was a genuine miracle and the news of it was enough to make Paderewski look straight up to Heaven, as if into the Face of God, to utter his unutterable thanks. The Red armies were turned back. Poland was saved. "Seldom in history," Colonel House commented a few days later, "has a change come in an international situation so swiftly."

But that swift change did not release Paderewski's mind from pressure, profound though the relief was of the Bolshevik defeat. Poland's problems were not all solved yet. He was still busy with tasks that exacted every ounce of his strength. The first of these, and the most trying, was the settlement of the Danzig question, which was now referred to the League of Nations. In November, on the fifteenth, he was present at the opening session of the League at Geneva, and shortly afterward he appeared before it to bring to a conclusion its deliberations concerning Danzig. This was another crucial moment in the life of the new Poland that he was still laboring heroically to construct. The Allies by a compromise had made the ancient Vistula seaport a Free City. Historically it was Polish, but, as Paderewski had told the Seym in Warsaw in June, speaking with his characteristic frankness and political realism, "in the course of one hundred and twenty-six years of Prussian oppression and systematic Germanization many Poles have forgotten their native tongue, and there are many real Germans settled in Danzig." The Germans clung tenaciously to it, but Paderewski's statesmanship not only won before the League equal rights for the Poles but established an agreement that resulted in a treaty and a customs union between the Free City and Poland. "In any case," he had said to the Seym, with a wisdom that showed his political foresight and his practical sense, "Danzig's fate will depend on us. Our enterprise, our perseverance, our political understanding will decide whether or not our relations with Danzig and the people of Danzig shall steadily improve and shall finally become such as in the depth of our hearts we wish them to be."

As a matter of fact, they have not become as anyone would wish them to be. But that has not been due, as Paderewski's own words will later show us, to any failure of Polish political understanding.

During all this time the habits of a lifetime of ceaseless activity asserted themselves in Paderewski. It was his nature to be occupied. Work is the keynote of his life. He could never be idle. The tremendous undertow of the happenings of 1920 was bound, however, to have its reaction; if there was a flood-tide there must be an ebb. The ebb-tide of his affairs found him, as 1920 drew to a close, left high and dry on barren sands, not of exhaustion but of inactivity and also of depleted fortune. When once he could find time to consider things personal he discovered himself facing a condition that he had perhaps never thought of during the thirty years of his career. His money was gone. He had always been free in giving. Since the war began he had given lavishly, without a thought of cost. Now, audit his books as he might the fact stood that at the end of the year 1920 his lifetime savings were gone. He must have something to live on. He must have a good deal more than that. He must have much in order to carry on the philanthropies which he and Madame Paderewska had founded and subsidized. They depended on him and they could not be abandoned. And he had actually borrowed money to carry them on and was now bound by debts which he must pay.

He decided to return to America. He had his ranch in California. There were vineyards, walnut and almond orchards, to be looked after. There was work to do. This prospect satisfied the demands of his vitality and energy, and offered him for the time being at least some means of occupation and livelihood. There was perhaps something else to draw him also, a feeling that he belonged now more to America than to any other country. To Warsaw he was determined that he would not return as long as his return would mean even in the slightest degree a stirring among his partisans there. These partisans were many and powerful, and since the tragedy of 1920 they felt their strength, were importunate for his return, and perhaps might be precipitate in action did he return. Peace for Poland was his single thought, a long, quiet, healing peace of sobering and settling. In 1924 he visited Poznan, but the national capital of Poland has never seen him since his departure in 1920.

The comment cannot be avoided here that Paderewski's voluntarily absenting himself from the Polish capital ever since his withdrawal in 1920 has been the action of a large, constructive, farseeing, and unselfish mind. In the case of a man of Paderewski's nature, strong, assertive, self-confident, convinced on principle and by demonstrated fact that he was in the right, it shows extraordinary balance and judgment. Anyone who knows what the conditions in Poland were from 1920 on knows that all Paderewski had to do was to lift his hand, give the signal, and his return to Warsaw would have been acclaimed, perhaps with the unhappy result of renewed political disturbance. In the history of national leaders, therefore, Paderewski's decision to stay away, to keep out, when he might have gone in again to reap new glory and gain new power, is unique.

Back to America, then; the very thought was relieving and expansive. He left Morges early in 1921 for Paris and New York.

It is to be doubted if ever before in his life Paderewski experienced more deeply than he did now his feeling for America and all that it represented of generosity and idealism. Of its generosity he was speaking publicly as soon as he landed. "Long before this mighty Republic decided to join the Allied forces for light and right," he said in his Civic Forum address in New York City in 1921 when he was formally welcomed back to the United States, "long before that I found here friends, many good friends, who most generously enabled me to collect funds for the relief of our war victims. Long before that great event, while still on his mission in Belgium—Belgium without bread because without fear! your Herbert Hoover, our Herbert Hoover, endeavored to bring into Poland the aid needed by our hunger-stricken people. Unfortunately Poland was inaccessible at that time, inaccessible even to American hearts. As soon, however, as the situation had changed and the way to Poland had become a little easier, your unbounded charity began to flow in streams."

But it was not America's generosity alone that stirred him, it was what he called the "American idealism" back of it. "We had had some promises," he said, referring to the early days of Poland's struggle for freedom, "some encouraging words had been spoken to us by other countries. Our best friend, that chivalrous, heroic, glorious France—France whom we have loved for a thousand years—France was desperately struggling for her very existence, and so also were her great and noble allies. What could we expect? The outcome of the gigantic struggle was uncertain. The promises given us were vague. Our prospects were gloomy indeed—until the tremendous weight of your influence was thrown in the balance and decided it at once in our favor. That tremendous weight was something already well known to me. It was your American idealism."

He repeated this sentiment in 1928, when the tenth anniversary of Poland's independence was being observed: "You feel, think and act as you have always felt, thought and acted, in the spirit of your country. So let me incline my head with profound reverence and infinite gratitude before the sanctity and greatness of that spirit." It was American idealism, he declared, that "restored to the Polish plough the ancient soil of my forefathers", that American idealism which, in his words, is expressed in "the sacred symbol of your young nation, the Stars and Stripes, in the folds of which we have found at last, hidden for over a hundred years, the independence of Poland."

XL

1921–1932: THE NEW PADEREWSKI

BUT even an idealistic Pole cannot eat and live on idealism, American or any other kind. For a man past sixty, a man accustomed to large activities and the revenues which they both yield and demand, to begin life over again as a rancher is not practical. And Paderewski the idealist is a very practical man. The new Paderewski that emerged from the strain of the war years is proof of that.

For how long up to this time, in perhaps the vagrant suggestions of thought, he had been considering a return to music, cannot be said. So far, however, he had not been able to even open his piano. The piano was there, and the man was there; but Time must rap and rap persistently for many a long day on the door of his life before the strange silence that had come into the artist's inner being could be broken.

The day came when the silence broke. He lifted the piano cover, he touched the keys. Once that was done, it was not so hard to do again. Soon it would be hard not to do it. A caressing touch . . . a bar . . . a brief phrase . . .

When we seek to reconstruct these moments in Paderewski's life we feel that something sacred and vivifying touches the wellsprings of his being when he touches the piano-keys again. It is not so much the strings of the instrument that vibrate as it is the chords of his heart . . . Before long he is at the piano for hours at a time, not studying yet, just playing, easing his nerves, drinking refreshing draughts, living over again old harmonies. Sometimes he forgets himself entirely, lost in music . . . drifting into intricacies of technique, shading, toning . . . then, like a cloud passing over the wheat fields of Paso

481

Robles—or is it a cloud over the prairies of Podolia?—the thought of Poland comes. What are they doing over there in Poland now? And how is the world judging Poland as she makes her long slow struggle upward toward peace and stability?

With this thought comes a new thought: Poland's debt, his debt, to all the friends of Poland who served her cause. There are not only the needy of his own land still to be cared for; there are broken men in all the hospitals of all the countries that stood by him in his fight. On the shoulders of every one of the Allies who helped Poland lies that burden of caring for ruined manhood. On his own shoulders he feels the burden. Poland has a debt of gratitude to pay . . . How is it to be paid? . . . In the warmth of the California air is a breath of other Californian days, memories of visits to Arden, Modjeska's home . . . memories of earlier days, of youth, of Modjeska at Zakopané . . . Modjeska's voice: "Poland needs you—you as musician."

Was this the answer? Could he still serve Poland in music, still spread abroad her good name, earn a living, retrieve his lost fortune, carry on his work? At sixty-two? After five years of absolute silence? Play again? Be once more the master? A risky undertaking. Failure would mean humiliation, pity, eclipse. It would mean humiliation for Poland.

And the critics. Face all that again? Some of them would be alert, waiting, ready to pounce, the moment word was given of his thinking of a return. There was a challenge in that thought.

Then he decided. And once the decision was made, he went to work as he had perhaps never worked before. He knew what his intimate friends were thinking from the moment that even a hint of his purpose came to them. "Few of us believed," Gutzon Borglum said afterward, "that it would be possible for him to remain away from the instrument for a period of years, and yet return and recover his mastership." But the fond fears of his friends were only another challenge to him. Back to work. Hours on hours of practice. Back to the old regimen of finger-exercise, scales, phrasing, pedaling . . .

The swing came back, the power, the force, sure, delicate, certain, unquestioned. But this does not mean that he became unconcerned or overconfident. Actually, when the time came for him to reappear, he was so nervous that he refused to go out anywhere before the first concert had been given, before, as he expressed it, he had "crossed his Rubicon." Though his will was undaunted there was in him, as there has been throughout his career, the human and natural concern of an uncompromising conscience. He once remarked to the critic Henry Finck that if he was ever nervous while playing in public it was because he feared he might not satisfy himself. Now he must satisfy himself first. If at the Peace Conference he had applied his rule of art in refusing ever to speak until he was sure of all his ground, now he applied his rule of statecraft to his music. He trained himself steadily, tirelessly, mercilessly, for seven months, before he was fully satisfied. "The ultimate necessity is the summoning of mind and will to do their work."

On July 14, 1922, Paderewski made a brief visit to Europe. On that day, before going aboard the S. S. *Savoie* he made the announcement that he would return in the autumn to resume his concert career. The first concert would be given in Carnegie Hall on November 22. The announcement was flashed through the press throughout the country. It created a sensation; not only the news columns were filled with it, but editorial comment throughout the country dilated on it.

There was eagerness, curiosity, skepticism, when he came back. "None of us," Borglum says, "can have forgotten the interest and anxiety felt by every American awaiting his first appearance." Was it to be triumph or failure?

It was a triumph. "A cry of joy," in Borglum's words, "arose throughout the country at the end of his first concert." Critics and public were amazed. This was the real Paderewski of old, and it was something else too. "Five years of politics," wrote Alexander Fried, commenting on the "beautiful physical control of his great and enduring strength", "five years in the purgatory of earthly experience have given Paderewski's art fresh power, new significance. His art is purer than when he left it; his understanding seems broader and more mellow. He resumes his music refreshed and inspirited."

It is not an exaggeration to say that in America the entire country rejoiced in Paderewski's triumphant come-back. He had a deep hold on popular sympathy. Everyone wanted him to win. The opening concert won an ovation from the huge audience which literally fought its way into Carnegie Hall, rising to its feet when he stepped out on the platform, and giving his numbers prolonged applause. It forced him to play a supplementary program of extras, after he had finished his printed list, which consumed nearly three hours.* It crowded about the stage and refused to leave the hall, even after the lights had been extinguished. There was nothing to do but turn them on again.

How did Paderewski feel about all this and all that followed? He could only say over and over again that he was happy. He had put all there was of himself into it; even when returning from Europe to make the venture he had practiced four hours a day on the steamship, according to the violinist Jacques Thibaud, who was on the same boat. He took no chances on past fame, did no leaning on old laurels. He would sacrifice even his beloved bridge game, an especially favorite pastime of his on board steamer, for his regular piano practice. He was happy. "It is wonderful," he exclaimed, "to be back among old friends!" His friends flocked around him, as happy as he; there was a return to the good old days of post-concert "confabs" during which he smokes innumerable cigarettes and lets his mind play like light over the problems of humanity, or else just eases off into reminiscence, as when, at Louisville,

---

* The program, a truly prodigious performance, was as follows: Variations Sérieuses, Op. 54, Mendelssohn; Fantasia, Op. 17, Schumann; Sonata, Op. 57, Beethoven; Ballade in G Minor, Nocturne, Op. 37, No. 2, B Flat Minor Mazurka, Op. 24, No. 2 and C Sharp Minor Scherzo, Chopin; "Au bord d'une source," Etude de Concert in F Minor, and Polonaise in E, Liszt. Encore numbers were a Schubert Impromptu, the Chopin-Liszt "My Joys", the Chopin C Sharp Minor Waltz, Liszt's Second Hungarian Rhapsody, the Liszt transcription of the "Liebestod" from Wagner's "Tristan und Isolde"; Paderewski's own Minuet, played in response to calls from the audience; and the Chopin Etude in E, Op. 10.

Kentucky, he found a veteran piano-tuner, Frederick Jąseck, who had actually studied with him as a boy at the Warsaw Conservatory. "In San Antonio, Texas," Gutzon Borglum reported, "I sat for two and a half hours and listened to his music; listened not only to his music, but listened to all that he meant to mankind . . . he who was willing to step down from his great place among the gods to lead his country to freedom, and then as quietly return to his place as master of the world of music. And after the concert, for three hours—until two o'clock in the morning—we sat and talked. Not a word was spoken of art between us, only the struggling world of humanity in its blind fight for freedom, for immortality."

And the critics? "Music critics," the Minneapolis *Tribune* remarked, "confessed themselves flabbergasted." "Paderewski at the piano again," the New York *World* said editorially, "does more than erase his five years' absence . . . There has been no loss of the magic touch; the consummate artistry is still at his command, potent to recreate the old emotional atmosphere. The years sit lightly on the master who can weave for the younger audience of admirers the same spell he wove for their parents." "The fire, the ardor, the temperament of the man are still there in full measure," was the remark of the Cosmopolitan Service critic, "the magic of poetic vision that conquered the world remains." "Natural misgivings about his powers after so long an absence were quickly allayed," was the verdict from Boston: "His technical powers were undiminished; his bravura was stupendous and electrifying and his finger work in delicate or brilliant passages was superlatively clear and limpid. He played with great spontaneous poetry and epic grandeur and eloquence."

Was there no change in him? "Looking for technical flaws in Paderewski," as Oscar Thompson wrote, "has never been a grateful task:" "Speaking broadly, the pianist seemed in full possession of his resources . . . the first half of his program seemed to present a changed and somewhat chastened Paderewski. There were no visible signs of nervousness . . . The superb and highly individual interpreter spoke in all that he undertook, perhaps a little less volcanically and a little less tenderly than of yore, but with the old power to rivet attention, to fascinate and to enthrall."

It may be that the words "epic grandeur and eloquence" describe and explain as well as any words can the new Paderewski; a moving across the line of the lyric into the epic strain, fruit of his five years' heroic struggle in the arena of human conflict. "He seemed more the philosopher than the poet," Mr. Thompson thought, "and played with an aloofness and sometimes a sense of detachment that were unlike his old self. It was as if he saw a vision afar, more inviting than the precocities of tone and nuance." But then, this critic adds, "something happened. After this feeling of aloofness and of a new approach had become fairly well settled, he brought to his final group the warmer, more romantic, more poetic qualities that had been wanting before." The sum total would seem to be that the new Paderewski was, after all, all that the old Paderewski had been, with a deeper and richer note added.

In the opinion of some, like Alexander Fried, the new was unmistakably an improvement over the old. "His return to the piano," one critic wrote, "revealed him a deeper, riper, more mature artist than ever." Another found his playing "more satisfying than at his last concert during the war." "Liszt's Second Hungarian Rhapsody," according to the Minneapolis *Journal*, "was played with about 100% more vigor and exactness than formerly. His power, balance and elasticity were never so abundant, his famous singing tone never so fluent or silvery."

At the age at which Paderewski was doing this, Liszt had long before retired; the years that Paderewski had now reached had in the history of music marked the disappearance of most artists. But in him there was no evidence that either physical, mental or emotional fatigue bothered in the least. "He played the first three numbers, lasting more than an hour, without leaving the stage for a rest"; so James Davies reported in *The Tribune* of Minneapolis: "That in itself is hard labor. With the prolonged encores, Paderewski did a week's work in a matter of hours." "There was nothing to show a falling off in muscular prowess and endurance. His right hand crashed upon the keys with a force that taxed the dynamic range of the piano, while the swooping energy of his left set the bass booming like a cannon." But again there was "the cembalon effect of trills, executed by one finger of each hand or on one note struck with incredible speed by various fingers"; there were "pearly runs, flute-like octaves"; "the accent of the various 'voices' in the Erlking was a marvel of pianism"; it was as easy to hear "his soft, cajoling, delicate reveries as his famous thunders." His fingering, his pedaling, his apparently inexhaustible and yet perfectly controlled physical strength, were talked of everywhere, as were his "prodigious programs" that would have "tasked the staying powers of the most vigorous among modern players." "But not for a single moment was there the slightest deviation from the highest standards of artistic rectitude." "There is something tremendous", Mr. Davies wrote, "in the sheer mental power of this musician. There is a 'plus' provided by an intellect that penetrates into the farthest recesses of every musical thought he utters . . . fire and imagination of youth balanced by the maturity and depth of experience."

"Youth . . . and experience." Henry Morgenthau's words about the godlike Orpheus come to mind: Paderewski remains the young Orpheus, a god who will have no twilight. "Advancing years mean nothing to the spirit or progress of that great man of the piano," wrote Edward Moore of Chicago in 1932. "When he appears on the stage he becomes an event. . . . Paderewski is a towering personality and forever impressive, at the keyboard or away from it." "The sight of that noble old lion forging on to a shadowy platform," wrote Hiram Moderwell in *The Stage* of New York, "quietly bringing that vast mob to silence with two or three chords, holding it in the hollow of his hand as he played with utter serenity the incomparable Andante of the Appassionata was at once a profoundly human and a profoundly dramatic thing; its memory will bring a retrospective lump to thousands of throats for a long time to come."

The new Paderewski took up his old life of "railroading days" with a relish. Little groups of overalled and oil-smeared workers gathered around his coach once more to listen to him at his practice. He soon reëstablished his title of "champion sleeper of the world", accustoming himself anew to sweet repose while being switched around in noisy railway yards. Big satisfactions came to him, on the practical angle as well as the artistic. For example, his gross earnings during the first tour of his return, in which he traveled 18,000 miles and played in twenty-three cities, brought in a gross of nearly half a million dollars. This was something for a man in the sixties, of depleted fortune, to achieve. Yet no insurance company, not even Lloyds, had been willing to underwrite this tour when it was proposed, so great did they consider the risk. There was a renewal, too, of the old time happy experiences that gladden the life of the artist "on the road." There was the warm friendliness of audiences crowding around him asking for more, and he between numbers exchanging remarks with those nearest to the piano. At the end of a recital in Minneapolis two little girls in pale blue dresses floated down the aisle and deposited a sheaf of lilies at his feet. The youngsters were Polish; he talked excitedly to them in Polish. He found out all about Wanda and Helena Janowska. He even found out that they were related to him!

Paderewski likes people; he is interested in everyone. In Minneapolis again he gives a private recital for ten nuns who cannot attend the public concert. He gives it in his private car in the railway yards, undismayed by the shrill competition of train whistles and the shunting of switch-engines. The recital is very informal; the artist is coatless, in a sports shirt, his hair tousled. Then, the nuns departed and the sports shirt changed for more formal attire, he hurries off to a club luncheon and an afternoon of bridge. He finds time the same day to call on two old Polish veterans, Roman Alexander and George Shunert. Howard Grossman, a boy of eleven, sends him a letter: "I am 11 years old and have studied four years on the piano. My mother was going to get me a $3 seat to hear you play, but the $3 tickets were gone, $5 would be too much to pay for tickets, because we just came from a small town in Montana and we haven't any money. We lost our home there. I can't hear you, so I thought you might send me an autographed photo of yourself and I would appreciate it if you could get me in for $3. I would be glad to stand, for I may never have the opportunity of hearing you again." Howard hears him. Paderewski shows the letter to Mrs. Carlyle Scott, his Minneapolis manager, whom Paderewski calls "an angel"; she arranges things, and Paderewski and his young admirer are both happy.

In 1927 he sails the Pacific from Vancouver. He visits Hawaii and has new adventures there; a rough voyage over, furious wind and sea, and then the "dry" agents at the pier would like to "frisk" him for whisky. He laughs that off, he threatens to go back! He gives a recital in Honolulu, in spite of the fact that he has had not a wink of sleep on the last, the roughest, night of the passage. And after the recital he receives what he says is the most unique tribute of his career. A group of native islanders, dressed in their colorful garb, bring him gifts and wreathe him with *leis*. He is given a new kind of musical instrument, presented by its inventor, George Paele Mossman, a "super-ukulele", constructed on the principle of the violin, and made of koa wood, its design symbolizing a lava flow; there is a silver plate bearing Paderewski's name. He is touched by these gifts and he is pleased when he meets a Honolulu music teacher, Elma Cross, who once climbed up on the roof of a theater in his own Lausanne, Switzerland, to hear him play, and who now presents to him on behalf of her pupils a painting by Hitchcock, the dean of Hawaiian landscape artists.

There are innumerable pleasant experiences, big and little, along the road. On the joint invitation of Governor Christianson of Minnesota, Dr. Coffman, President of the State University, and Elbert L. Carpenter, President of the Orchestral Association, he appears at the University of Minnesota and there the cadet corps musters to honor him, forms a guard at the stage entrance, stands at attention when he arrives for a rehearsal of the Symphony Orchestra. Only to statesmen are such honors paid. He smiles happily, he bares his head in the raw wind to bow to the cadets. It is a cold December forenoon, his attendants are carrying blankets from his car, he is wearing a heavy sweater under his coat; but the lion's mane is uncovered to salute the young American soldiers and his face is bright with pleasure.

This private rehearsal of the Minneapolis Symphony Orchestra, with the cadet corps on guard and with Henri Verbrugghen directing, is the prelude to a real musical event. One of the very rare presentations in America of Paderewski's own Symphony in B Minor, along with his Concerto for Piano and Orchestra, is to be made. He enjoys the rehearsal. He sits in the darkened auditorium listening intently, never missing a phrase, his head nodding vigorously from time to time, his hand occasionally raised, almost unconsciously, to direct. Verbrugghen turns now and then to watch that head, that hand, then faces back to the orchestra with renewed vigor and confidence. All are lost in the music. Paderewski forgets his luncheon engagement, his afternoon bridge engagement, everything but the music. Whereat Eldon Joubert, his traveling companion, piano-tuner and friend for many years, laughingly remarks, "I've waited for him more than I've worked for him in those years!" When it is all over, long past eating time, he answers to an inquiry: "Hungry? Oh no! Why should I be hungry?"

Paderewski seldom appears with orchestra; this event, in 1930, is an exceptional one, a page in American musical history, composer and virtuoso in an orchestral program devoted exclusively to his own works.* But he insists that it is the music alone that matters. Because he himself is to be the soloist after the Symphony is performed he will not consent to come forward for the accustomed composer's bow. "My Symphony must stand on its own merits, must it not? It is responsible for itself.

---

* The Symphony was again performed April 10, 1933, at the Metropolitan Opera House, New York City, with an orchestra of 200 unemployed instrumentalists, Ernest Schelling directing, Paderewski himself at this benefit playing the Schumann Concerto in A Minor.

And I am responsible for myself and for my playing afterward."

But when he does appear there occurs one of those dramatic incidents which, without his foreknowledge, often have characterized a Paderewski concert. When he walks out on the stage the trumpets of the orchestra blow a triumphal welcome. The startled, almost frightened look on his face glows to an expression of deep pleasure as six officers of the Reserve Corps march to the stage bearing American and Polish flags. The immense audience rises spontaneously to its feet; there are five thousand, five hundred people jamming the auditorium, and two thousand have been turned away. The flags are placed to right and left, the officers salute with their sabers. Paderewski, stirred deeply, stands bowing; the audience remains standing, bursts into applause. It is a long ovation. As a matter of fact, this particular ovation was such a long one then and after the concert was over, that his train had to be held for him while he played on for the hungry thousands who would not let him go.

In Europe his return to music is another continuous ovation. There, as in America, the glamour of his personality, instead of being dimmed by the years of absence, is warmer, more compelling than ever. There is a new halo around his once golden, now graying head, a halo the gold of which is fadeless—the nimbus of a tried and tested hero. The old days of popular and royal favor are renewed. In London the audience rises enmasse to receive him, stands in silent tribute. The Queen of England, in spite of the King's serious illness, attends his first recital and has him come to the royal box to converse with him. The critics are nonplussed. "On the ground of virtuosity alone," Ernest Newman, dean of English critics, writes, "he must be justly esteemed incomparable. But not alone can he beat the virtuosi at their own glittering game of legerdemain. There is no other living pianist who can reveal so acute a sensibility to the poetic content of music." The Manchester *Guardian,* speaking of his "amazingly complete" rendition of Chopin, says that "it amounts to a reincarnation." The whole press of England joins in a chorus of acclaim.

On the Continent the same. In Paris, in the Théâtre Des Champs-Elysées, he plays for an hour and a quarter after the recital; in the end, the manager is forced to lower the curtain to dismiss the crowd. Another crowd is waiting for him outside, cheering "Vive Paderewski! Vive la Pologne!" In Brussels in 1932 an unprecedented happening occurs. King Albert and Queen Elizabeth attend the recital. Court etiquette is forgotten; the rulers rise and stand in salutation to the king of musicians. "Only a heroic people," a Brussels editor comments the next day, "could produce the miracle of such a man."

That is the secret of it all, and that is the source of the deeper satisfactions which Paderewski enjoys in his return to the world of music—the thought that his country is glorified. Trumpets and flags, vivats, royal salutations, they mean one thing to him—Poland. Poland is not forgotten; his name, his art, still means Poland to the world. For himself, for his career as a Polish statesman, he has nothing to say; he refers to it, simply and unostentatiously, as he did in talking with Hubert Hughes of the London *Daily Telegraph*, merely as "the time when I was occupied with other affairs." But those "other affairs", Poland's welfare and good name, rest closest to his heart.

One satisfaction of his new life is that he is himself again, at work and earning his living. And he has a remark to make on that score: "Some people appear to be surprised that I need to work, but if a man wants to live he must eat and to eat he must have money—lots of money—and in these times the best way to get it is to work." But it is not that he himself must have "lots of money" that he rejoices in his princely earnings. It is that others may have it. One of the initial impulses back of his return to music, as we have seen, was the desire to carry on the various works of assistance, public and private, that he and his wife had instituted; the private ones are many and unknown, save to the recipients of his bounty. This thought embraced the thought of Poland's debt of gratitude to the soldiers of her allies. Since his return Paderewski has systematically as well as lavishly worked to pay that debt.

In America, France, Great Britain, Belgium, Italy, Switzerland, Paderewski has literally poured fortunes into the coffers of soldiers' hospitals. He is the largest individual contributor to the American Legion's endowment fund for the disabled war veterans; to that fund he turned over the receipts of recitals in New York, Philadelphia, Boston and Washington amounting to $28,600. In France he has played time and time again for the soldiers' benefit, and in addition he has given great sums realized from the receipts of recitals not actually arranged as benefits; one such contribution amounted to 120,-000 francs; again the total proceeds of an entire tour of the French provinces brought two million francs to the war charities of the widow of Marshal Foch. In England the funds of the British Legion have been increased by him by thousands of pounds from recitals in London, Liverpool, Cardiff, Manchester, Glasgow and other cities. In Italy the proceeds of seven recitals have gone to the funds for soldiers' orphans. Two large benefits in Switzerland were tokens of his gratitude for the hospitality shown in that country to his exiled compatriots.

He is incessantly busy wherever he goes, living the life of a man half his years, so far as activity is concerned. Honors are showered upon him. Already at his home at Riond-Bosson there is a brilliant collection of royal, governmental, and civic decorations bestowed upon him; the Great Cross of the Order of the British Empire, the Grand Cross of the French Legion of Honor, the Great Cordon of the Order of Leopold, the Great Cordon of the Order of SS. Maurice and Lazarus, the Great Cordon of the Order Polonia Restituta; a score of others. Now new orders and new decorations are given him by kings, rulers, cities, honorary memberships in humanitarian and artistic societies, degrees from universities. In 1919, while he was Prime Minister of Poland, he had the gratification of seeing the oldest university in his country, Cracow, established six hundred years ago, confer its Doctorate of Laws on Woodrow Wilson. In America, Yale, Columbia, Southern California, New York University, half a dozen others, have paid

Paderewski like tribute; in Great Britain, Oxford, Cambridge, Glasgow. In 1924, on his only reappearance in Poland since he left Warsaw in 1920, Poznan University honored him with its doctorate and all Poznan made a week-long civic *fête* of his return. In 1933 Warsaw awarded him its annual civic music prize. When New York University conferred on him its Doctorate of Music, in April, 1933, he was too ill to leave his hotel, but he joked as he greeted Chancellor Elmer Ellsworth Brown and Dr. Robert Underwood Johnson. "Gentlemen," he smiled, "you have come to a sick man to make a doctor of him."

In Paris he not only plays time and again, welcomed by multitudes, but he makes his first radio broadcast, in order that Poland may hear him on the hundredth anniversary of Chopin's arrival in the French capital. In Rome crowds acclaim him; he sees his old colleagues of Peace Conference days, the King and Mussolini shower him with honors, he and Pope Pius spend happy hours living over again their days together in the Warsaw of 1919. In England, after years of expectation, he meets for the first time his famous compatriot Joseph Conrad. Colonel House arranges the meeting. Conrad, curiously enough, but with characteristic lack of self-conceit, was not certain that Paderewski knew of him, and he was even a little ashamed to meet him. Conrad, it happened, not being conversant with politics and not knowing what was wanted of him, had once failed to respond to a request that he serve on a Polish war-time committee; now he was uncertain of his welcome from the Polish leader. "But I was sure they would like each other," said Colonel House, telling of their meeting. "Paderewski's reception of Conrad was even more cordial and enthusiastic than my assurances that it would be, and they parted friends and admirers." This happened shortly before Conrad's death in August, 1924.

In London there is not only the delight of new artistic triumphs for Paderewski to enjoy, but again the foregathering with war-time and Peace Treaty companions. Lawrence Alma-Tadema, lifelong champion of Poland, is there to greet him. Paderewski and Lloyd George renew their Paris companionship; they have a good laugh over the recollection of the band concert at the Trocadero. Lord Balfour, "the most cultured, the most gracious, the most courteous of adamantine men", as Clemenceau once described him, gives him his warm and courtly welcome. There is a story for them to laugh over too, a story out of the days of Paderewski's war-struggle in America. Balfour visited the United States in 1917, almost immediately after the American declaration of war. He spent all of his time in Washington, and of course he was very busy. One evening, fatigued after a difficult day, he handed the menu card back to the venerable Negro waiter assigned to serve him his dinner and said, "Just bring me a good meal," and he put a generous tip by his plate. A good meal, a very good meal, was served. This happened several times. When Balfour was waited upon for the last time by the Negro veteran, the British statesman tripled the tip as a goodby gesture. Just before he was ready to leave the table his now devoted waiter leaned over his chair confidentially. "Thank you, sah," he said, considerately muffling his voice behind the menu card, "an' if you done got any othah frien's w'at cain't read, you jes' send 'em to me, sah."

Paderewski has a story to match Balfour's. In what American college boys would call his "fan mail" he found one day, among many letters from adoring ladies, a highly scented missive which announced that one of his worshipers was a colored lady, "but if you ain't married, sir, I wouldn't mind if you'd give me a chance."

Wherever he goes, this new Paderewski, back again in the old circles of audiences and intimates, he is welcomed with a feeling that has love in it as well as admiration. Public men, men of affairs, often become entirely impersonal. The manner of their life hedges them about with detachment and aloofness. The secret of Paderewski's charm is that he has remained personal. He has kept "the common touch". True, he has an authority about him, the authority of a dynamic nature and of great achievement, which makes him, in a sense, feared as well as loved. Despite his charm no man would be tempted to take the liberty of too much freedom with him. In business, with all who deal with him his word is law. He disappoints his friends, too, sometimes by apparent indifference, as for instance in the matter of letters. Yet indifference is not in his nature. He simply hates letter-writing, that is all; he will not write letters, even to his intimates, except when absolutely necessary. But if and whenever he can coax or kidnap his friends for a visit in his home he will keep them weeks on end, live with them in joyous companionship. He has also the habit of preoccupation which marks genius, a preoccupation upon which no one would intrude. But above all he is loved. There is no mistaking that feeling among those who know him; and his public, too, cherishes the same feeling for him. It springs from his generous nature. "Paderewski maintains his hold upon his public," a critic once wrote, "because he is a great human personality."

He works as hard as ever at his recitals and his benefits. He has not limited his benevolence to veterans of the war. Artists especially are remembered in his philanthropies. On one occasion, when illness prohibited him from playing at a benefit for the Actors' Fund of America he sent a thousand dollars to the fund along with his note of regret. Everywhere he has gone his fellow musicians have shared, both privately and publicly, his bounty. In London, in January, 1933, in memory of his old friend Lord Northcliffe, he gave in the great auditorium of Albert Hall a large benefit for British unemployed musicians. He brought his 1932 American tour to a brilliant climax in New York City by giving a like benefit, one which attracted the largest crowd that has ever heard a concert in the history of music, 16,000 people. "Hire Madison Square Garden," he said, "and I'll give a concert for unemployed musicians." Something like $50,000 was realized from that one recital. He entertained a number of guests at it, but there were no complimentary seats. He paid for his own tickets; which made one of his friends laughingly recall one of Paderewski's favorite anecdotes, the story of Rubinstein and the importunate lady:

"Oh, Mr. Rubinstein," the lady exclaimed, rushing up to him, "I am so glad to meet you. All the tickets are sold and I have tried in vain to get a seat for your recital. Have you not a seat you could let me take?"

"Madame," replied Rubinstein, "there is only one seat at my disposal—but you are welcome to that if you will take it."

"Oh, thank you, a thousand thanks, Mr. Rubinstein. Where is it?"

"At the piano."

An amusing incident, one of the kind relished by Paderewski, who thoroughly enjoys a good laugh on himself, is told of the 1932 Madison Square Garden benefit. Two strapping "cops", who were "on the door", expected the recital to be some kind of a colossal vaudeville affair. While Paderewski was playing his first number one of them peeped in a foyer door. "What's he doin' now, Bill?" his companion asked. "Nothin' yet, Joe. Just playin' the pianner."

The New York benefit for unemployed musicians was not his final American appearance in 1932, but the comment of Laurence Gilman in the New York *Herald Tribune* on this recital serves as well as any to record the sentiment that Paderewski's return to the piano roused in the heart of the public. "The implications of last night's occasion," wrote Mr. Gilman, "must have stirred deeply his sensitive sympathies and his vivid imagination, and perhaps he was not aware, simple and modest as he is, of the extraordinary atmosphere of veneration and affection which surrounds him, the quickening currents of responsiveness generated by that enormous throng who hung upon every movement of his fingers, and were held by every nuance that they evoked."

Thus, once more, after the long silence, after the dark years when the thunder of guns muted the strings of his music, the old Paderewski magic is at work on the people; men and women by the thousands learn again through the new Paderewski "the art of being good." "Chiefly and most restoringly," in the words of Laurence Gilman, "what one acquires from an experience of Paderewski's playing is the conviction that one has been in contact with a noble and kindled and insuperable spirit." "It is encouraging to think," says Charles Buchanan, "that the world responds to Paderewski in unconscious recognition of his extraordinary morale . . . what a sublime ratification of the theory held by some of us that a valid art is a sublimated record of the human spirit and not a mere negligible puttering around of the emotional unemployed."

During the forty and more years that Paderewski has played in America alone, not to speak of Europe, he has made nineteen tours. He has appeared in every State in the Union, exclusive of his extensive travels in Canada; over 360,000 miles have been covered in his itineraries. More than five million people have heard him in his more than fifteen hundred recitals. Merely from the point of statistics his record is stupendous. It denotes not only a towering genius of art but a physical vigor almost unbelievable when the nervous and bodily strain of his work is considered. How great is that vigor was demonstrated in October, 1931, when, at seventy-one, he was stricken with appendicitis. The world was alarmed when he went under the knife. All recitals were cancelled, his American tour was indefinitely postponed. But he "came back" in 1932 fresh and powerful as ever and he laughed when it was suggested that this latest tour was his "swan song". Earlier than that people had been wondering about Paderewski's swan song. In 1926 Charles Buchanan, writing in *The Outlook* of New York, had told how, to him, "those incredibly intriguing hands linger over certain bits with a tenderness that deceives one almost into thinking he is taking leave of music for the last time . . . one could almost hear the piano saying 'goodby'."

This is the new Paderewski's answer when he is asked about "farewell tours", goodby's, and retirement: "Stop? Quit? When I quit I die!"

XLI

1921–1933: AFFAIRS AND ACTION

PADEREWSKI tells the old story of the five men who competed in writing books about the elephant. He tells it to an American audience with characteristic aptness, a new and timely application, and a humorous apology for its age. "It is to a degree," he says, "like those liquid delicacies which you find sometimes in the houses of your law-abiding friends, and which are offered you with the encouraging remark, 'It will not hurt you. It is pre-war stuff!' "

Here is the story in Paderewski's words: "Once upon a time, somewhere in Utopia perhaps, a large sum of money was offered as a prize for the best description of the elephant. Among the competitors there was a German, a Frenchman, an Englishman, an American and a Pole.

"The efficient German acted very thoroughly. He started on a long, extensive journey, visiting all the most renowned museums and libraries of Europe. He read every book, studied every pamphlet, examined every document pertaining to the huge animal, and after several years of that conscientious work produced two big volumes under the imposing title 'An Introduction to a Monograph on the Elephant.'

"The Frenchman immediately went to the zoölogical garden, visited the elephants' house, made friends with the keeper, invited him to luncheon, took several photographs and after repeating the experience a couple of times, began his work. Within a few weeks a brilliant book was ready under the title, 'L'Eléphant et ses Amours.'

"The Englishman proceeded quite differently. He bought a complete hunter's outfit and in that sporting attire, provided

499

with excellent rifles, supplied with plenty of ammunition, cartridges, biscuits, Scotch whisky, tobacco and pipes, he went to the jungles of India, to the wilderness of Africa, saw thousands of elephants, killed quite a few of them, and upon returning home within six months he wrote a concise graphic essay calling it 'The Elephant in the Jungles of the British Empire.'

"The American worked fast and produced a lively volume, small but unquestionably valuable. Its title was 'Bigger and Better Elephants.'

"As to the Pole, he wrote his book more rapidly than any of the others. He called it 'The Elephant and the Polish Question'."

During the strenuous days of his war-time "begging tours", as he called them, Paderewski was sometimes a little wistful about always coming before his friends to talk on the Polish Question, that and that alone. But his intimates and all who know him know how manifold are his interests, how capacious his mind in embracing ideas about every known human problem, how compelling his gift of utterance to discuss them. He does not limit himself by any means to the Polish Question. Nevertheless this, naturally, is the paramount interest of his life. During the years that have followed his return to music his movements have been extensive, his activities many and engrossing, yet throughout these years he has been at all times at the forefront, on the firing-line, of Polish affairs, alert to every turn of event bearing on Poland's welfare. Nothing happens in his home country or relating to it that does not affect him. His pulse, it might be said, beats and rises or falls with the heartbeat of the young democracy of which he is the father as Washington was the father of the American democracy. In history this will be his fame and rank, "Father of the New Poland". "As time goes on," in the words of Herbert Hoover, "his name will take the position in the minds of the Polish people akin to that of the names of the men we revere in the foundation of our Republic."

There have been moments since his withdrawal from Warsaw when his pulse went up with hope and encouragement. On March 17, 1921, soon after his return to America, the good news came to him that the new Constitution of Poland, the ground work of which he had laid in 1919, the first draft of which he had seen presented to the Seym on May 3 of that year, had been ratified. In November, 1922, he had watched anxiously as the first general election was held for a national legislature to succeed the constituent assembly elected during his premiership. The struggle as to the final nature of this governing body, whether it should have a senate and be bicameral and thus afford balance and check in legislation, or be only unicameral and be more open to radical tendencies, had been a long and exciting one. Paderewski's conservative view had prevailed. Then, in December, 1922, further news of an exciting nature had come. Senate and Seym were locked in a contest over the election of the Republic's first President. Paderewski's name had been proposed for the first presidency of the Republic. His nomination and election would, of course, have been a gracious as well as a grateful gesture on the part of the country in the cause of whose rehabilitation he had served so fruitfully and so unselfishly. But under the circumstances, with the Pilsudski dictatorship still ruling the field, his candidacy was out of the question. He would not consider it, knowing that it would only provoke new dissension. Pilsudski also had declined the candidacy proffered him by parties of the Left; he preferred to back his friend Gabriel Narutowicz, of the Radical Peasant Party. The Radical won, although by the narrowest of margins.

Narutowicz was elected on December 9, 1922. He was inducted into office. Poland had a President, and Paderewski rejoiced. But Poland had a President for just one week, exactly seven days. On December 16 there came over the cables news that was calculated to run Paderewski's pulse down to something like a complete stoppage.

He was giving a recital in New York City that day. In order that he should not be disturbed, the news which all the evening papers published was kept from him. It was not until after the recital that he was told. President Narutowicz had been assassinated.

Paderewski, standing at the moment, all but collapsed into a chair. Grief, chagrin, anxiety, shame, anger, overcame him. Crushed at the thought of what his audience, all the time knowing of the tragedy, must have thought of him, blithely playing at the piano in the face of such a disaster, he felt bitterly at first about not having been told at once. But he appreciated the forethought and concern of his friends. All his own concern now was for Poland. Naturally, one fear above others filled his mind. The murdered President was of the Left. Had the crime been a party crime? Was the Right, the party that had most vigorously supported him, though he belonged to no party, implicated? His relief was immense on learning that the assassin, a youthful fanatic, had had no accomplices, represented no party, no group, no one. Poland was still guiltless of fratricide. "There was never a history more free from political bloodshed, than the history of the Polish State," Joseph Conrad had written in 1919. In the days that followed the shock of the Narutowicz tragedy Paderewski may well have reflected on this fact. "With every incentive present in our emotional reactions," Conrad had said, "we had no recourse to political assassination. In all the history of Polish oppression there was only one shot fired which was not in battle. Only one! And the man who fired it in Paris at the Emperor Alexander II [of Russia] was but an individual connected with no organization, representing no shade of Polish opinion. The only effect in Poland was that of profound regret, not at the failure, but at the mere fact of the attempt. The history of our captivity is free from that stain." Paderewski thanked God that the history of Poland's freedom as well as of her captivity was still stainless. He had sacrificed everything to make sure of that.

The shock of this crime left his nerves unstrung for days. He realized now with renewed anxiety how precarious was the home situation, that it was indeed "a cup of trembling". And the events of the days immediately following the President's assassination were not reassuring. Civil peace was seriously threatened, rumors of a civil war and of a military dictatorship under Pilsudski came over the water. But four days after the murder a new President was elected. He was Stanislas Wojciechowski, old time colleague of Pilsudski in his "underground" days, one of the men who had helped draw up the first draft of the Constitution in 1919, while serving under Paderewski as Minister of the Interior. Paderewski's anxiety was lessened, and as time passed and affairs progressed he became more reassured.

The new President's régime, it is true, was short lived, but it was followed by a "ministry of experts" which gave increasing confidence to Paderewski, so anxiously watching from America every movement and event in the homeland. This ministry was headed by one of the men who had served with him in 1919, a very able man, Ladislas Grabski, the same man who as Prime Minister had come to Spa in 1920 to plead before the Allies for help against the Red invasion. Grabski, back now at the helm, remained in office longer than any other one man since the founding of the Republic, and Paderewski rejoiced to see him accomplishing many of the things that he himself had set on foot. He stabilized finance, established agrarian reform on a more reasonable basis than the radicals had advocated, quieted the minority agitations, especially those of the Jews, from whom he drew an avowal of attachment to "the Polish state and its interests as a Power;" he furthered Paderewski's initial activity in opening schools, achieved an arbitration treaty with Germany, a railway convention with Russia: on the whole, he carried on wisely and efficiently, for two years, the work that Paderewski had inaugurated. To Paderewski it could not fail to be significant, too, that much of this achievement, demonstrating his belief in the capacity of the Poles to conduct themselves under a representative government, came during a period when the public mind was for a while not irritated by interference from Pilsudski; for Pilsudski, no longer Chief of State, since that office had been superseded by that of the Presidency—and increasing in his disgust for the Seym, exclaiming "Serve under such people! Never!"—had resigned his posts

of Chief of the General Staff and President of the Superior
War Council and had retired into private life.

"Happy the country that has no history." These two years
of Grabski's quiet reconstruction, up to nearly the end of 1925,
found Paderewski busier than ever with his music and his be-
nevolences and every day more at ease in his mind. Yet in his
mind also, it might be said, he never really let go of the wheel
of affairs, no matter how removed from active participation in
them. At all times he carried the burden of Poland on his heart
and in his head. Poland's concerns were frequently before the
League of Nations during these years, there was much friction
with Danzig. The ways of peace were slow and difficult.

In November, 1925, Grabski's government fell and Paderewski was naturally disturbed. Then a few months later, a new
shock came, one almost as bad as the assassination of President
Narutowicz. Pilsudski, returning to public life, was again
raising the sword. In May, 1926, he overthrew the coalition
government then in power, gathered troops, marched on Warsaw, and after two days' fighting made himself once more master of the country. His plea was necessity. In Paderewski's
mind the necessity itself had been created more by Pilsudski's
methods than by anything else. Pilsudski's election as President
followed his *coup d'état*, but, again preferring to wield his
power from the outside, he refused the office. The news of this
bloody affair was enough to terrify Paderewski: it looked for
a moment—for two days at least—as if the one unspeakable
thing, civil war, to the prevention of which he had sacrificed
all, himself included, were at last after all to bring ruin to Poland. Happily, things quieted again. A new President, Mościcki,
was elected and peace reigned.

True, it was in a sense an armed peace. It was actually a dictatorship without the name. The nature of the whole situation
during these years may be summed up in the words of Machray: "Pilsudski himself disclaimed dictatorship, but he believed that the mass of the Polish democracy was politically
ill-informed and needed guidance—he was out to educate it."
"Is it necessary that I should be dictator?" he asked. "I am

a strong man and I like to decide all matters by myself." But he did believe that the country could be "educated." "When I consider the history of my country," he said, "I cannot really believe that Poland can be governed by the stick. I don't like the stick. Our generation is not perfect, but it has a right to some respect; that which will follow will be better. No! I am not in favour of a dictatorship in Poland". "Today it would be easy for me," he once told a group of deputies, "to stop you from going into the hall of the National Assembly, but I am still trying to see if the interests of Poland cannot be served except by force." Of course such utterances antagonized the deputies, who felt that their prerogatives as elected represent-atives of the people were at least being threatened, if not tram-pled on, and they responded with opposition. Pilsudski was of the conviction that the Constitution of 1921 had been framed with the set purpose of limiting his powers, and furthermore that it made the function of the Presidency "simply comic." Not the Seym, which he had once declared must be "sole mas-ter of the country's household" should rule—he had, as we have seen, lost all faith in the Seym—but the "only sovereign in Poland should be the President." The Constitution was therefore amended in such a way as to make the Seym sub-servient. Its financial policy was dictated by the military. There was even a new ordinance which required the deputies to stand in a body whenever the President addressed them. This made bad feeling; to the Seym it was "the stick" with a vengeance. An armed demonstration staged by some fifty officers cheering Pilsudski in the corridors of the assembly hall, with the Mar-shal of the Seym defying Pilsudski—"I refuse to open the ses-sion under the menace of swords and revolvers"—brought the conflict at one time to a dangerous crisis. On this occasion an amendment to the Constitution, an amendment which, in the opinion of the Seym, had been forced upon the legislature, served to avert a new civil war by the simple expedient of in-voking a Presidential adjournment of the Seym for thirty days, an adjournment frequently to be made when the Seym's delib-erations countered Pilsudski's wishes. "It is the deputies," he declared, "who most endanger Poland . . . Poland is the victim of her parliamentary system . . . eternal quarrels, eternal discords! Democratic liberty abused to such an extent as to make Democracy hateful!"

The struggle continued, carefully followed in every detail by Paderewski, who at times almost despaired of real internal peace in Poland. At one time eighteen deputies, including Witos, thrice Prime Minister, were summarily arrested by Pilsudski and thrown into the cells of a military fortress. Other arrests followed; some ninety of Pilsudski's opponents were incarcerated. The country hummed with stories of maltreatment of these prisoners. Next there was a scandal over army credits, the Finance Minister being impeached by the Seym, while the Senate, which had been appealed to "because the Seym muddled everything", refused to support Pilsudski. The popular elections brought another scandal, charges being made of what the Warsaw correspondent of the London *Times* called "abuses practised by the Administration in its conduct of the Government's election campaign." Pilsudski's candidates won a sweeping victory at the polls. Nevertheless the Seym did not hold an absolute majority for him, and it began its sessions by electing one of his opponents as Marshal, as well as by staging a scene in which certain Communist deputies had to be expelled by the police for trying to shout Pilsudski down when he appeared in the rôle of Prime Minister to read the President's message . . . To Paderewski, viewing the course of Polish affairs at long distance, these were troubled and anxious times.

All was not anxiety, however, it was not all disturbing news that came to him out of the home country. There were satisfactions emphasizing Poland's basic unity and glorifying her culture. She progressed industrially, weathered financial storms, won new international prestige. In the field of foreign affairs, where he had laid the way for much amity and prestige, Poland's record was especially praiseworthy. The visit of the Polish Foreign Minister, Count Alexander Skrzynski, to the United States in 1925, when he lectured on Poland at the Williamstown Institute of Politics, was one occasion which brought before the eyes of the outside world Poland's "policy of peace and consolidation"; and it was marked especially, in the way of confirming good relations, by his meeting a deputation of American Jews and reassuring them of Poland's liberal treatment of her minorities, an echo of the days when Paderewski had struggled against and overcome prejudice on this delicate question. In the same field of foreign affairs Poland was steadily consolidating amicable relations with her erstwhile enemies Russia and Germany, and growing in credit with her friends. The signing of a Concordat at the Vatican in 1925, with his old-time friend the former Papal Delegate, now Pope Pius XI, in the Pontiff's chair, was another source of stabilization gratifying to Paderewski. In the field of commerce such events as the opening of Poland's new seaport at Gdynia, and the holding of a great national exposition at Poznan in 1929, celebrating the decentennial of liberation, made him rejoice. Four and a half million people came to Poznan to look on the evidences of Poland's progress. In 1924 the occasion of removing the ashes of his friend Sienkiewicz from Switzerland to Poland, in the ceremonies of which he participated, drew new attention to Polish eminence in letters. That eminence was reëmphasized the same year in the award, made for the second time to a Polish novelist, of the Nobel Prize to Reymont, author of "The Peasants." Poland was honoring her past, and she was honoring it most by forging steadily ahead into the future. More and more she enjoyed peace and progress. It was even possible for Paderewski to believe at times that Pilsudski, in spite of his arbitrary conduct of affairs, remembered certain warnings and predictions which he, Paderewski, had made, and that the remembrance was a kind of challenge to him, as such remembrances may well have been during the Bolshevik war of 1920, a challenge to make good, to give no one the opportunity of charging Poland, under his régime, with failure. Opposition is stimulating. Paderewski's influence was still a balancing factor in Polish affairs. Some at least of the lessons in government that he had taught his people were bearing fruit.

When we observe Paderewski in the light of these events

during these years of unofficial but continuously active life, we get the point of his story about the Pole who so readily composed a book on the elephant. There was always the Polish Question. We realize, too, how keenly, how ceaselessly and without let-up, Paderewski felt his responsibility before the world, his country's need of a spokesman. He was ever ready to plead her cause, he was never lacking in eloquence or facts to present her case to the public mind. His readiness and his ability are illustrated by a little happening in Boston in 1930, the account of which is given by the American author Owen Wister. "The Tavern Club of Boston, of which Paderewski has been an honorary member for thirty-seven years," Mr. Wister writes,* "and where in other days he loved to play billiards, gave him a dinner at Christmas time. As I am the president of the Club, he sat at my right. As the time for speeches drew near, I said: 'When I come to introduce you at the end, I am going to refer to three of your appearances in my town of Philadelphia: your first recital there, some forty years ago; your plea for Poland during the war; and your recital this year.'

"Paderewski looked anxious. 'Must I speak tonight?' he asked.

" 'Not a word if you don't wish to. You are here among old and warm friends, who want you to enjoy yourself and to feel at ease.'

"So I called up the two members of the Club scheduled to speak. When the second had finished, Paderewski turned to me: 'I should like to say something, if I may.'

" 'Just as much or as little as you like.' So I introduced him.

"He rose; and he spoke for nearly an hour, and we listened, spellbound, and could have gone on listening . . ."

Wherever he spoke his listeners were spellbound. What may be called one of the great orations of the time was his funeral address delivered at the exhumation of the ashes of Sienkiewicz when the remains of the famous novelist, his lifelong friend and his co-worker in the war, were removed from Vevey, Switzerland, October 20, 1924, and taken to the moth-

---

* In a letter to the author, quoted by permission of Mr. Wister.

erland. Again, his address in honor of Ruskin, delivered at Chamonix, Switzerland, beloved haunt of the English author, was a new demonstration of his oratorical powers; it was eloquent, scholarly, a masterpiece of English diction of which Ruskin the stylist would have been proud. There is an affinity between Paderewski and John Ruskin which occurs to anyone who knows the story of both men. At eighteen Ruskin was called by the editor of the London *Architectural Magazine* what some who knew Paderewski in Warsaw at eighteen had called him: "certainly the greatest natural genius that it has ever been my fortune to become acquainted with." Ruskin loved Switzerland and the Alps, as Paderewski does; Ruskin's bountiful generosity was known to all; before he died he had given away the whole of his immense fortune, "his pensioners were numbered by the hundreds, his charities were as delicate as they were generous." So also his Polish admirer, who has spent his life spending fortunes on others.

In 1925, on July 13, Paderewski made a new impression on England by his London Press Club address. In England he has been known almost altogether as the pianist. He has not spoken there in public often, his powers as orator were little known until his 1925 appearance in St. Bride's House, Salisbury Square. His address on that occasion was widely commented on in the British press, particularly for the reason that he discussed a subject which vitally concerns England and the peace of Europe—the Polish boundaries. The world-picture which he gave, to begin with, of the situation in Poland in 1915 and during the war was a revelation to his hearers; it was something they had never heard before at first hand with such authentic detail. When he came to the matter of the boundaries of the Versailles Peace Treaty and the German agitations to have them revised, he had such men as Lord Stuart of Wortley, Commander Kenworthy, M.P., and Mr. Frank Dilnot "on their toes." He warned his audience against the Berlin boundary propaganda, declaring that already it gave signs of endangering peace on the Continent. He made a strong appeal for the League of Nations and expressed the hope that some day it would "be enabled to meet the greed of some too ambitious people" and that the time would come "when the principles of justice would be applied to all the States of the world, no matter how large or how strong they might be."

Not all of Paderewski's utterances could have found place in the elephant thesis of his humorous story. His interests have been too varied for that; they have reached far beyond the limits of the Polish Question, large and of universal significance as that question is. But they have all been infused with the sincerity and fire and zeal that are the marks of true eloquence, of the born orator. In 1932, however, Paderewski delivered an address on the Polish Question in which he surpassed himself and in which, perhaps more than in any other public utterance of his life, he revealed his gifts of mind, of force and clarity of speech, of fearless conviction. The occasion was a banquet tendered him in New York City, on May 18, by a large group of public men. The speech was broadcast on the radio and created a profound impression throughout the country. Months afterward I heard echoes of it at various scattered points; a business man in Minnesota talked of it, a college student in northern Michigan remembered passages of it verbatim; the press commented widely on it.*

It was on the occasion of this address that Paderewski told his elephant story. His final remark before he launched into his speech gives the key to his theme. "Today," he said, "the patriotic Pole would have to change his title to the more up-to-date 'The Elephant and the Corridor.'" It was the much disputed and still heated question of Poland and her access to the sea that he discussed. At that moment this question was once more alive in the press. One cabinet crisis after another in Germany, Hitlerite disturbances which became definitely alarming in the Danzig area and which seemed to threaten revolution in East Prussia, had brought the matter to a focus in the public eye. Poland's position was questioned, her rights attacked.

For a clear understanding of Paderewski's address we must

---

* Published in full in *Foreign Affairs,* April, 1933; also reprinted in a brochure entitled "Poland's So-Called Corridor."

remind ourselves that Danzig, the ancient seaport of Poland, a maritime centre which formerly, when Poland was free, enjoyed enormous prosperity, a port which is entirely dependent on the Polish hinterland for its commercial existence, had been transformed into a minor German port since the partition of Poland in 1793. During the century and more that Germany was in possession of Danzig and of all Vistula Poland in the West, Danzig had lost its supremacy, due to the fact that Germany had concentrated her Baltic seaport trade at other points, principally Stettin and Königsberg. Danzig, thus deprived of her natural tributary, was changed from a flourishing commercial city to a German naval base, military arsenal and political keystone. When the Peace of Versailles was signed the question was, should Danzig be restored to Poland intact along with those Polish territories which once had fed Danzig as a seaport? Or should Danzig be left in German hands because her population had become predominantly German? And in spite of the fact that the population of the tributary area, right up to the suburbs of the city, was and is Polish? Even before the war, as the story went, trolley car conductors who dared not speak Polish within the city limits, freely spoke it as soon as the car passed out into the suburbs.

The question was a practical one, a clear issue between simple economics and local political sentiment.

Paderewski, as he told the Peace Conference at Paris in 1919, believed that Danzig should be restored to Poland; and not alone did historic right support him in this contention, but common sense looking to the profit of Danzig, her restoration to her natural position as the Vistula seaport. In spite of political complications, the return of Danzig to Poland was the most simple and the logical solution of the matter. Time would have solved the political problem involved, which was at best a local problem. But German propaganda made an international problem of the question, and the Peace Conference was persuaded to a clumsy compromise. Restoring Poland to the Poles, the Conference set Danzig up as a separate Free City, leaving it, although in German hands, isolated both from Germany—which, after all, had already reduced it to the rank of a secondary port —and from its natural source of economical being, Poland. The awkwardness of the compromise was emphasized by the fact that East Prussia, a Germanized agricultural colony to the north of Poland and East of the Vistula, remained a part of the German Reich. This colony is, of course, wholly inadequate to support Danzig as a seaport; besides, it has its own seaport, Königsberg.

Paderewski had been compelled to accept the Conference settlement, and Poland, unable to exist without a free seaport, had to find some other solution for her economic problem. Nor was it purely economic, as later was proved by the refusal of German dock-workers to unload munitions when Poland was overrun by the Bolsheviks. The necessity of Poland having her own harbor, instead of being left at the mercies of her enemies, was obvious. She found the solution in the construction of a new port at Gdynia, a few miles west of Danzig. In ten years Gdynia has grown from a village of three hundred people to a flourishing city of forty-five thousand, equipped with the most modern shipping facilities, and having a greater tonnage and turnover than Bremen. Yet, contradicting by fact the outcry raised by the Danzigers of impoverishment by reason of the new Polish port, Danzig's tonnage has increased fourfold since the war, proof sufficient, assuredly, of the vitality of Poland's commercial life. Nevertheless, even in the face of economic good sense, Danzig still cherishes her political tie with Germany, and, backed by the irreconcilable sentiment of East Prussia, still clamors for reunion with the Reich. Prussian sentiment in these parts was, for some years after the Peace of 1919, intensified by the belief, carefully propagated from Berlin, that the new Polish Republic was only a "seasonal State", that it would soon collapse, and that Germany would regain control of western and northern Poland. Fifteen years of successful if slow political construction in Poland, however, along with a phenomenal economic growth, exemplified particularly in the rise of Gdynia, has dissipated that hope. The only recourse left to the Prussians has been agitation, and to give their agitation point they have invented the term "Corridor", aiming to make the world believe that the restoration to Poland of her western territory was only a cutting into Prussian territory to give the Poles a seaport. The agitation is a part of the larger movement carried on by Germany with a hope of getting the Versailles Peace Treaty boundaries revised.

It is with thoughts such as these that Paderewski addresses his audience. Whatever else is necessary to an understanding of the problem is made clear by his speech; and this speech, moreover, makes clearer than any other utterance of his the practical capacities and workings of his mind. The phenomenon is that this man, a supreme artist, is able to turn immediately— as he did when Colonel House demanded his memorandum for President Wilson in 1917—from the rhapsodic chordings of a nocturne to the baldest statistics of economics and the prosaic facts of history, presenting the one with as great an artistry, force and conviction, as he presents the other. Reading this speech with its marshalling of figures, its breadth of vision and wealth of factual knowledge, it is difficult to believe that it comes from the same man who a few hours before had been rapt in a poetic vision, weaving a spell of melodious magic out of an ivory keyboard. The only explanation is the simple one of which Paderewski's whole career is a demonstration: that to master an art is not to limit but to increase a man's mastery of life with all its divergent interests.

Obviously, into the preparation of this "Corridor" speech, in the midst of a long and arduous recital tour, Paderewski put much care, as much, one might say, as if he were composing a new Concerto. During the time that he was working on it he denied himself to all visitors. He could be seen in his private car, as he moved from one city to another, pacing the floor, exercising his old art of concentration and of a self-discipline which makes it possible for him to say "No" in order that he may say a more important "Yes." The address is, in fact, composed like a piece of music. From its inviting opening it moves on a rising inflection through lucid exposition and merciless argument to a pyramiding climax that is all the more convincing because it is firm, dispassionate and definitely conclusive. Its likeness to a musical composition ends, of course, in the framework. The speech is built of facts, mathematical figures, historical citations, hammer-blow on hammer-blow of convicting argument based on implacable evidence. It is the product of a strong, direct and clear mind.

Paderewski's characteristic evenness of temper and breadth of view are the persuasive keynotes of his "Corridor" speech. He moves away from all possible prejudice by giving at the opening a clear exposition of the historic basis of the confusing problem. His own lack of prejudice accounts for his broad understanding as he shows plainly that the so-called "Corridor" question is not a German question but a Prussian question. He insists on the differentiation and he exposes it categorically, "formally, historically, and logically." "You may read today in the newspapers and magazines," he says, "that the Corridor has been taken away from Germany. This is not correct. When dealing with serious international problems proper terms should be used, proper formally, historically, and logically. Formally, Germany took no active part and found no direct advantage in the dismemberment of Poland. Historically, the territory now called the Corridor was wrested from Poland by Prussia in 1772 . . . Only in 1871, still as a part of a Prussian province, was it included in the possessions of the German Empire. Is it, then, logical," he asks, "to draw the whole of Germany into the conflict and the controversy arising only from an act of violence perpetrated as everybody knows by Prussia, Austria and Russia? . . ."

Insisting on the differentiation between Germany and Prussia, he emphasizes it by historical references, showing that German sentiment, as long as it remained free and until it became shackled by Prussian dominance, favored Poland and repudiated the crime of partition. Even Karl Marx, writing in the *Neue Rheinische Zeitung* "a series of strong and violent articles in favor of Poland and against the Prussian government" felt thus. " 'The partitions of Poland before 1815,' he quotes Marx saying, 'were acts of brigandage. What followed after was theft. Honest German, learn how you have been deceived'." To the real Germany and the real German Paderewski then pays his tribute, not only to the Germans of the Vaterland but to those in other countries, his own Poland included: "There are a great many Germans outside of their densely populated fatherland. The surplus of the population has always endeavored to improve material conditions of life through immigration into foreign countries, and, wherever the Germans by their own free will have established their homes, the inborn qualities and virtues of the race make them soon good, faithful, loyal, model citizens. You see it in your country as we see it in ours. We had a very great number of true loyal Poles bearing German names, good German blood has been flowing in the veins of some of our most ardent patriots . . . The Germans are a very great nation. Their contributions to our modern civilization are of the very highest order. Their achievements in every domain of human activity or thought, in industry or commerce, in science, speculative or practical, in philosophy, poetry, literature, art, and above all, in music, are positively immense. A nation which has produced men like Gutenberg or Reuchlin, Dürer or Holbein, Kepler or Leibnitz, Emanuel Kant, Fuchs, Hegel, Lessing, Goethe, Schiller, Heine, Bach, Händel, Beethoven, Weber, Schumann, Wagner, and so many others—such a nation deserves not only respect but the admiration and gratitude of the civilized world."

Who then are the Prussians, and how did they get into Poland in the beginning? "These people," Paderewski says, "a class apart, however ethnically related to and having a language in common with Germany, are mentally, psychologically, quite different from real Germans. Their ancestors, former Crusaders, were introduced into Poland as evangelists by a pious, too pious, Polish Duke of Mazovia . . . They were the principal trouble makers and peace disturbers in that corner of northeastern Europe. Finally, defeated and obliged to recognize the sovereignty of Poland, they could not forget their past and their not too enviable glory. They could not forgive the humiliation, and as a brilliant English writer says, 'They trained themselves to live in a state of perpetual hate for Poland.'

"Their offspring inherited with large landholdings, with large estates, that fierce hatred for Poland. And that hatred grew from generation to generation. At last the descendants of the Teutonic knights found in Frederick the Great their master avenger as he found in them his most devout disciples and supporters. After the Partition of Poland they became a powerful aristocratic party and the real ruling class of Prussia. Their hatred and contempt and deep scorn for the Polish nation, which they had partly devoured without being able to digest, were practiced as fundamental articles of a political creed. Since 1871 they endeavored to impose that political creed upon the whole of Germany.* It is they who have coined the word 'Corridor', as they have coined that preposterous motto, 'We are the nation of masters; all others are but fertilizers.' "

He goes into the matter of the propagandist term "Corridor", invented for the purpose of confusing and obscuring the question of Poland's access to the sea. "A masterpiece of propaganda has been achieved," he says, "in giving to an old Polish province the name of 'Corridor'. The word 'Corridor' implies the idea of a narrow passage through a solid and more or less homogeneous structure. Applied as it is, it serves its purpose most admirably. It misrepresents and perverts the reality to such a perfection as to convey the impression that in order to comply with the pretentious demands of Poland for an access to the sea, the Peace Conference mercilessly split the national

---

* Paderewski had been much impressed by a certain utterance of President Wilson's in 1917 when, on August 11 of that year, addressing the officers of the Atlantic Fleet, he had said: "The most extraordinary circumstance of modern history is the way in which the German people have been subordinated to the German"—read "Prussian"—"system of authority and how they have accepted their thinking from authority as well as their action from authority. Now, we do not intend to let that method of action and of thinking be imposed upon the rest of the world." But it is to be doubted if Paderewski's realistic mind had ever permitted him to agree with Wilson's idealistic thesis that the German people needed only to be told about democratic government to clamor for it and adopt it.

territorial structure of a great state, thus separating a valuable province from the whole empire.

"The separation has been made, it is true, but it was by no means a new idea, a new operation. It was simply the restoration of a property to its former and legitimate owner. We have not received one inch of German national territory, not one single district where the Prussians or Germans would be or would have been in a majority. Ethnographical principles, ethnical considerations guiding the conscientious and scrupulous territorial readjustments performed by the Peace Conference, were most rigorously observed and were rather prejudicial to our economic and political interest—as in the case of Danzig— than favorable to our national restorations. That territory formerly baptized West Prussia and now so cleverly called the Corridor has never been German national territory. Its name, in German *Pommern*, in Latin and English *Pomerania*, is in both cases only an adaptation of the original Polish name, which is *Pomorze*. *Morze* means the sea in Polish. *Po* is the prefix, which means either 'along' or 'after'. In this particular case both meanings are correct, because they designate the topographical situation and the origin of the land which, according to history and legends in the remote past, had emerged from the sea. From time immemorial it was inhabited by Polish-speaking people and governed by their own Polish rulers."

To bring the definition of terms more closely home to his hearers, he applies the 'Corridor' analogy to America. He refers to the visit of a certain German coal magnate to the United States:

"He tried to appeal to your imagination by asking how you would feel if Mexico, for instance, would be powerful enough to split your country and to establish a wide corridor throughout the United States leading to the Dominion of Canada. What a fantastic figure of speech! It is really too much to ask anyone to imagine that Mexico, having on one side the Atlantic and on the other the Pacific Ocean, would be so ambitious as to pretend to a direct communication with Lake Erie, Lake Ontario or Lake Michigan. That is sheer innocence.

"Americans do not need to be informed about corridors by such hyperbolical arguments. They know corridors. They even have corridors of their own. The first one, and a very big one too, is between the United States and Alaska. Those who look for gold, for sealskins and other valuable furs, those who are fond of fishing or of hunting, go to Alaska by steamers without asking for the annexation of British Columbia. There is another small corridor, a Mexican one, to be crossed, and it is crossed very often—I have crossed it myself several times—from Yuma to Santiago in California. Still another: an American citizen going from Buffalo to Detroit, if he wants to save time, must travel almost the entire way through the Province of Ontario which is at that place many, many times wider than Polish Pomerania. On the other side, a Canadian going from St. John to Ottawa must travel over two hundred miles through the State of Maine and if he goes from Ottawa to Winnipeg, he cannot avoid crossing the State of Minnesota, south of the Lake of the Woods." Does the American, Paderewski asks, demand that the United States take over Ontario, or does the Canadian insist on the annexation of Maine or Minnesota?

Coming to the details of the argument which the Prussian propagandists base on the term "Corridor" he takes them point by point: "Defying or disregarding history, the people who are working for that purpose, for that propaganda, pretend to dwell upon actuality, on economic life and interest. What are their arguments? The German character of the territory taken away from Prussia is the first argument. The second, the unparalleled monstrosity of the 'Corridor' which is preventing normal communications and causing heavy losses to the entire Reich. The third is the unfair treatment of German minorities under the Polish rule, and the fourth is the alleged moral injury inflicted upon the nation by the separation of Prussia from the mother country."

He begins his examination of these arguments by showing that the third, an appeal on behalf of a German "minority" population, contradicts the first, which is a claim of right on the basis of German "majority" population, and he quotes Herr Loeber, President of the Reichsbank, saying to a German audience in the Polish city of Lodz, "We protest in Germany against the Corridor, yet everyone agrees that its population is Polish." He then produces maps, which he has taken from Professor Putzger's German school atlas, of which with characteristic thoroughness he has had numbers of copies made and distributed in his audience, so that everyone of his hearers may follow his arguments readily. Poland's historic rights, he shows, are made apparent on every one of these maps "except the one which simply shows the despoliation performed by Frederick the Great." When he points to the last of the maps, that one which shows the new Poland of today, he calls it "Poland's Magna Charta." And he cannot forget Poland's debt to America for help in securing that charter of liberty. "It is, let me say, the triumph of the American people, for verily, without the generous and great gesture of President Wilson, without the assistance of the members of his cabinet and without the support—the mighty support—of American public opinion, the almost complete restoration of the old Polish republic would not have so easily taken place."

As to the "moral injury" inflicted upon Germany by the separation of East Prussia from the mother country, he reminds his hearers that "East Prussia has never belonged to the German Empire, which finished its existence in 1806. East Prussia has never belonged even to the *Deutscher Bund* which existed between 1815 and 1866. The Peace Conference justly observed that the German historians have never recognized East Prussia as a country of German origin, but merely as a German colony." Are then, he asks, "the ties binding the German nation to East Prussia so strong, so intimate?"

The colonial character of East Prussia, "and of all the Eastern borders of present Prussia," Paderewski shows further, "is still more strongly confirmed by the fact that a provision of over 1,700,000,000 gold marks was voted for the German budget in 1930 for the strengthening of Germanism, or, let us say correctly, of Prussianism in the East during five years. How weak must that be, that pretended Germanism," he remarks, "if over $420,000,000 of borrowed money must be spent for its invigoration! It is no wonder that East Prussia is so dear to some Germans. It is very expensive."

Paderewski is not satisfied with historical citations, even those illustrated by German cartography. "Historical rights, however uncontested," he tells his hearers, "could not produce a rhetorical effect were they not supported by stronger claims, claims based upon actuality, upon life, upon economic conditions and interests. Somebody who could irrefutably prove to be a direct, legitimate descendant of Hannibal Barca, the greatest among the Carthaginians, would have a very little chance to take today possession of Carthage. Carthage is no more, but Poland is there and very much alive." The figures and statistics which he offers are also very much alive. "The element of mathematics may be dry," he remarks, "but it is always persuasive and incontestable." Here he argues two points of alleged losses caused by the "Corridor" through the prevention of normal communication, and of·the alleged "unfair treatment of minorities" by Poland in the "Corridor". As to the Prussian claim that the restoration of Polish territory to Poland, after a century of Prussian confiscation, is ruining Prussian railway traffic, he says: "The only ones to complain are the navigation companies in Königsberg, because they see the volume of their business decreasing. The statistics concerning traffic of goods show that in the year 1913, 47 per cent of merchandise were transported by sea, and 53 by land. In 1925, 32 per cent were transported by sea and 68 by that monstrous, mischievous Polish 'Corridor.' The number of passengers traveling in 1925 between East Prussia and Germany in both directions was 590,-000 by rail, and by steamers only 5,000. These figures fully demonstrate how unfounded and futile are the complaints about traffic difficulties."

He turns finally to the matter of Poland's alleged "unfair treatment of minorities." This too, he says, "may as well be examined in the light of figures": "According to Prussian statistics in 1925 there were in Prussia—I say in Prussia because in Germany there are very, very few Poles indeed—in Prussia there were 985,283 Poles. At the same time there were 884,105 Germans in Poland. I have no more recent figures, but let me suppose, or let us suppose, that the figures mentioned have remained stationary. Well, the 884,105 Germans in Poland have five members in our Seym and three members in our Senate. And do you know how many representatives those 985,283 Poles in Prussia have, either in the Prussian Diet or in the Reichstag? They have none!

"There are 105,861 German children of school age in our country, and they have at their disposal 811 German schools. There are, in round figures, 115,000 Polish children in Prussia, and they have at their disposal the big total of 81 Polish schools. Consequently, 72 per cent of German children in Poland can receive school instruction in their mother tongue, while not quite 2 per cent of all Polish children in Prussia can attend schools where their native language is taught. Which of the two nations has some right to complain about unfair treatment of minors?"

His conclusion, a forceful summing up, is a dramatic fusing of statistical fact and patriotic eloquence. The Prussian argument, he shows, has its sole basis in the ideology of Frederick the Great, that Prussian ruler whose motto was, "God is always on the side of the stronger battalions"; the same Frederick who, when he took his slice of the Polish Partition in 1792, announced with blasphemous irony: "We are going to partake of the Eucharistic Body which is Poland, and if it is not for the good of our souls, it will certainly be a great object for the good of our bodies;" the same Prussian hero who said, "I know that the inhabitants of the Palatinate of Pomerania are of Polish nationality," but who also declared, "Whoever possesses the City of Danzig will be more of a master of Poland than her own government." "It is for their sake," for the sake of the Prussians, then, Paderewski says, "for their comfort, for their political prestige that we are requested now to give up a precious part of our living national body. It is for the chimeric pleasure of a colony, a province, the population of which does not exceed 2,025,000, that we are summoned by some people to sacrifice the real, the vital interests of a state of 32,000,000 inhabitants? Partly, yes, but chiefly, it is in order to restore to Prussia that commanding position of Frederick the Great and to permit her to take all former Polish territories at any time later. What would it mean to us if we consented to such an injury? What would it mean immediately for the whole nation? It would immediately paralyze the entire economic life of the sixth largest state in Europe. It would deprive our country of the only direct connection with the great civilized nations. It would reduce our free and sovereign state to an impotent and pitiable closure between Prussia and Russia. It would make Poland a cripple and a slave.

"We do not wish to be crippled and enslaved again. We will never accept so monstrous an injury, no matter by whom inflicted. The territory restored to us is justly ours. And we will stand by it with all our strength and uphold it by all our means. For if that restoration is wrong, then the partitions of Poland were right—and nobody should expect us to subscribe to such an iniquitous verdict . . .

"We do not want war. Everyone in Poland is longing for peace. We need peace more than any other country in the whole world. Nevertheless, if a war—and I am speaking now not as an official person, because I am not an official; I am a plain citizen, and I assume my own responsibility—if a war, I repeat it, by a formal declaration or by surprise is imposed on us, we shall defend ourselves."

XLII

THE FUTURE

The future of Paderewski may possibly be forecast in his own words, "We shall defend ourselves." The future implied in these words would mean his return to Poland and to active participation in national and international politics. And that, almost assuredly, would mean his definite and final withdrawal from music. As to that, whenever and if ever it comes, it will be an absolute stop, so far as public performances are concerned. "There will be no farewell tour," Paderewski stated in 1932. "The moment I realize that I am no longer making progress in my music I shall stop playing. But you may rest assured that the fact will not be heralded."

What is to be Paderewski's future? It may seem strange to speak of the future of a man over seventy. But there is nothing strange about speaking of the future of a man like this. He was born, it is true, in 1860; he has reached and passed the allotted three-score-years-and-ten of man. Inevitably, too, some of the marks of time are on him. His hair that was a golden mane is a gray mane now. But it is still a mane. His high, dome-like forehead, the most characteristic feature of his fine head, shows some unmistakable furrowings of the years. But it still dominates. The lines of his face may be more deeply incised, but they are firm and clear. There are wrinkles around the blond-lashed eyes with their look of half-mysterious inscrutability, but the eyes have not faded or lost their lustre, they still brighten with laughter or darken and flash with blue fire. The low-pitched voice is clear and rich in tone. The stature of Paderewski's frame may be a little lessened, something of the burden of time and care may be seen on his shoulders, his bodily movement may be not quite so agile and springy as it once was; these things are inevitable. Yet as a matter of fact they do not appear very marked to the casual observer: a New York newspaper described him in 1932, at seventy-two, as "more upright in carriage and more deliberate in speech than ever." And even when the impress of years is discerned it vanishes and is forgotten in immediate contact with the man, a contact which has always had a kind of electrifying surcharge to it. His characteristic handshake, with its special effect of making a man, even an opponent, feel that he takes him wholeheartedly into his confidence, has lost none of its firm grip. And he is not always satisfied with a handshake: the last time I greeted him he seized me by the elbows and lifted me clear off the floor; I was as light in that grip as a suit of clothes on a hanger. At first glance he may appear frail; but Paderewski has always seemed frail: that has been part of his charm, the surprising strength of the frail man. If he tires now more easily than he used to as he moves, with something like velocity, around the world, nevertheless he has reserve forces to pull him up and to keep him going at tremendous momentum and under tremendous pressure. He has great strength of body and great vigor of mind and a nervous system apparently unimpaired. The mainspring of his mentality seems to be unspent. Usage has not touched it save to give it that greater force of cumulative power which comes out of great experience. In short, it is difficult to believe in the calendar-record of Paderewski in the seventies. When he says, "We shall defend ourselves," it is far from being the declamative formula of an aged veteran that we hear. The impact as well as the promise of action is in his words.

A man like Paderewski, even in the seventies, can hardly be denied a future. There is nothing strange, therefore, in calculating the future of such a man. Curiously enough, too, if one wished to calculate outside of the strict circle of literal fact, there is something more than the momentum of Paderewski's past to project him into future activity. Back of his record of achievements, and back of those beginnings of his life with which we are acquainted, is an extraordinary fact that takes us out of the plane of heredity and environment and onto the plane of the mysterious if not the preternatural. There exists something that looks strangely like a prophecy about him.

There was living in Poland in the sixties of the nineteenth century, a poet, Kornel Ujejski, whose songs, as we have seen, were known to Paderewski as a boy, a poet who celebrated in poignant lament the tragedy that swept Paderewski's father into prison in the Uprising of '63. But this poet, born forty years before that event knew nothing of the child of Kurylowka who was only three years old when he saw the village burned to the ground, and who five years later, with his ten-year-old sister Antonina as his playmate, was growing up on the Volhynian prairies. Nevertheless, on the 29th of February, 1868, when Ignace Jan Paderewski was in his seventh year, Kornel Ujejski wrote the following words:

The loftiest and holiest ideals, in order to appeal to the masses and to carry them toward a victorious aim, must become crystallized and embodied in a man. Such a man, hero, victor, representative of the national spirit, such a living, animated shrine of patriotism, we Poles are all awaiting with yearning. *This man will immediately conquer all spirits by his strength and by his kindness.* He will possess the might of a lion combined with the guileless heart of a dove. *To falseness, he will oppose sincerity; to jealousy, a radiant smile; to rebellion, calm and assurance.* His conscience will be his law, and each one of his actions will be as clean as a sword drawn from its sheath, shining in the sun.

And in his soul never will find place that low evil feeling so characteristic of small people, that feeling of egotism which is described in the words: "I, above and before all, I, myself."

He will not crave for power, but it will be bestowed upon him, and he will accept it as a burden and carry it as a cross of self-sacrifice and self-denial.

And when he has fulfilled his mission, he will replace the power into the hands of the nation and efface himself.

Through a mother's suffering, each child is born. Out of the martyrdom of our nation *such a man will arise.* Our sufferings have been, and are, so tremendous, so infinitely beyond conception, that we may trust full well that *such a man already exists on Polish soil. Indeed he exists, he is growing, unaware of what is before him, unconsciously awaiting the moment when God will call him to duty.* Perhaps, as an adolescent youth, *he has seen our villages burning;* perhaps, secretly by night he has been burying our dead. No matter from whence he comes—from a palace or from a workingman's hut—our blessings upon him.

Honor and success to that great unknown.*

Tested by the verification of fact these words would seem to make Paderewski's story "foreordained." The lives of all men are in the foreknowledge of God. As Cardinal Newman once wrote, "each one of us has his own individuality, his separate history, his antecedents and his future, his duties and his responsibilities, his solemn trial, and his eternity"; and all these are in the Mind of God and not in the mind of man, who can ordinarily neither foresee them nor foretell them. But sometimes they are foretold or appear to be, and it is the apparent foretelling that seems to reveal the "foreordination." The Polish people, of which Paderewski is so much the essence and the personification, are, in one way at least, a strange people. They are psychic, given to a mystic apprehension of life, they have a kind of apocalyptical sensitivity that is not known to, or has been lost by, other peoples. Prophets appear among them, "holy men", "holy women", who foretell events; legendary lore has a strong hold on the common mind. Sigismond shook his sword. The Turk watered his horses in the Vistula. In Polish literature the Messianic strain has at times predominated. Krasinski, blind from weeping over his country's woes, foresaw, even in detail, a hundred years before it came, the Bolshevik terror of 1920 and in his "Undivine Comedy" foretold the rising of a world-saviour in Poland. Mickiewicz was definitely mystical. "On the third day," he sang, "the soul will return to the body and the nation will rise from the dead and will free all the nations of Europe from slavery." But Krasinski is vague, and Mickiewicz, with his "man of three faces whose footstool is three cities . . . and his name is forty and four" is obscure. Ujejski's strange utterance, however, is as clear as it is startling. Some of its details, such as those which

---

* The italics are mine. "The prophecy" is from a quotation given in Clarence Edward Le Massena's "Paderewski, the Master of Masters," a typescript copy of which is filed in the New York City Public Library.

I have italicized, are, to say the least, inexplicable to the biographer who would merely rationalize. All that Paderewski's personality represents and all that has happened to him is set forth, as it were prophetically, in these verses, written when he was a child, by a man who, even if he had known the child, could not have penned such words without some occult gift, divination or whatever it might be called. "He exists, he is growing . . . he has seen our villages burning . . . he will not crave for power, but it will be bestowed upon him . . . he will accept it as a burden . . . when he has fulfilled his mission he will replace the power into the hands of the nation. . . ."

As after-the-fact evidence Ujejski's words might be taken seriously, even though they could not be explained. They have come true. As to the future, they could only raise the question, "Has Paderewski's mission been fulfilled?" No question as to what that mission has been and is, prophesied or not: the restoration of his nation. Will he be some day needed in his country once more in person to help stabilize it and secure it? Only time, of course, can tell. There are millions of his countrymen who still feel the need of him in Poland. "I could not help thinking, possibly with some vanity," Gutzon Borglum once exclaimed, "that had I been a Pole, Paderewski would be President of Poland if I had to pull the state apart and rebuild it."

Paderewski would smile gratefully at the zeal of a warm-hearted friend exclaiming thus; but assuredly he would remind his friend that that is the one thing he would never think of, the one thing, in fact, which he refused to permit, which he sacrificed everything to prevent, that the State be "pulled apart." Another friend, one very close to him, possessed of a profound understanding of him as well as of European affairs, Edward Mandell House, has expressed himself on the same question, but more guardedly. "I have been asked many times," Colonel House said, a few years after Paderewski's withdrawal from the government at Warsaw, "whether Paderewski would again be called to Poland as Prime Minister or President. I do not know. Such events lie on the knees of the gods. Clemenceau was called to save France when he was nearing eighty. [Von Hindenburg at eighty was President of the German Reich.] It is unlikely that any national disaster will arise in Poland to make it necessary to call Paderewski back. The tendency of Europe is to become more tranquil year by year, and Poland will doubtless share this tranquillity. He wants no office for the sake of it."

Office for its own sake, true enough, has never meant anything to Paderewski. And unquestionably the tranquil state of Polish affairs during recent years, a tranquillity which has its actual basis on the foundations of state which he laid in 1919, is his greatest source of satisfaction and peace of mind. But if that tranquillity be disturbed; if national disaster do come, contrary to Colonel House's words, which were written before the "Corridor" question sharpened to an issue; if disaster such as at times seems threatened by this issue should come, then Paderewski, if he be alive, will be in the forefront of action. Poland no longer fears Russia. There is peace on that long eastern frontier; there is security in the menace of Japan which for many years to come will be the preoccupation of the Soviets. But Germany's relentless determination to revise the Eastern Peace Boundaries of 1919 is a real threat, one which, as we know from his own words, Paderewski recognizes and is prepared for. In the emergency of disaster may lie his future field of action.

In the meantime, the future interests. The views of Paderewski on the future interest. If he were confronted by the poet's "prophecy" and asked to comment on it, he would very likely refuse to say anything, and his inquisitors would very likely say that he is too modest to talk about such things. The answer he would make to that comment would give them at least a flash of light on the kind of man he is, as he sees himself. No, he would say, as he has said, "I am not a modest man. Frankly, I am not modest before men. But I bow to God and to Art. I am, rather, humble. Humility, my life-long companion, has taught me among other things how to accept events and how to grow old without ever having known conceit."

History has had its men of destiny, so-called, and Paderewski would seem to be one of them. Some men of destiny,
unless they be fortified by sound Christian philosophy, become
outright determinists and fatalists. But most of them, as Paderewski is, are humble men, and few of them are theologians
enough to hair-split on the question of man's free will and the
Divine Will of Providence. There is nothing of the fatalist in
Paderewski. His whole career is a refutation of fatalism. Life
has taught him, it is to be noted, "how" to accept events, not
merely to accept them. He is "joyous in the presence of Infinity", his joyousness expressing itself in action. His nature rejects passivism, and in this he is pre-eminently the Pole as compared to the Russian; he has the divine gift of enthusiasm. As
Conrad wrote to his friend Edward Garnett, Paderewski might
well say, "You remember always that I am a Slav, but you
seem to forget that I am a Pole." And the same Conrad's words
which he penned to describe one of his heroes ("Lord Jim")
might be used to describe Paderewski the Pole: a man "of un-
obscured vision and tenacity of purpose." Nor is there anything of the theologian in him, as there is nothing mystical or
visionary, although his nature is surcharged with that element
of the mysterious which is one of the marks of genius; and vision he assuredly has, though never visions. He is a religious
man, yet anything but pietistic. In the sense that Virgil used the
word, Paderewski is pious, another *pius Æneas; pietas*, love of
patria under the will of God, is the keynote of his life. "I am a
firm believer in God and destiny," he once said; and while he
did not define his meaning of "destiny", what he said immediately following implies nothing but the Christian doctrine of
free will. He was explaining at the time how his experiences
in politics had taught him one thing at least: "to banish the
words 'always' and 'never' from my vocabulary. . . . *It cannot be too late, at any time, to achieve something of real importance in the world.*"

While Paderewski carries on his career in music with only
the words "When I quit I die" to set a limit to his activity in
art; and while those interested in him as politician and states-

man, recalling his own comparative definition of statecraft and art, say that, after all, music, though a great part of his life, is actually only a tributary part to the whole, which is service to his country and humanity: while he still abides and works, busy with his music and occupied with his country's welfare, all who know him or know his story remind themselves that life has taught him things by which they may learn to live. Humility is one of them, that virtue which some poet has beautifully called "the gratitude of the great." And humility has taught him, he tells us, "how to grow old without ever having known conceit." What else has life taught him by which others may live? Carlyle in his "Heroes and Hero Worship" says that "great men, taken up in any way, are profitable company. We cannot look, however imperfectly, upon a great man without gaining something from him." The one thing that we all seek for in the contemplation of the life of a great man is knowledge of life. How does life look to Paderewski? What has he to tell us about it? Is it worth while? How can it be made worth while, and more and more worth while? And what promise does the future hold for those things that make life worth while?

True enough, it is not so much what great men tell us, it is what they are, that counts. The story of a man like Paderewski speaks for itself, and if it says anything it says that life is worth while. Yet we listen eagerly to hear what such a man has actually to say of life. What of Art, assuredly one of the things that make life worth while? And what of success, in art or in anything else?—success, which is the common interest of all of us? Paderewski was once asked what was his secret of success in life. Of material success he said nothing; that after all is an accidental. "If you are kind enough," he answered, "to consider my life successful, I would say this: that I owe whatever success I have had entirely to perseverance and hard work. Any man can succeed in what he undertakes providing he likes his task and spends enough time and energy on it. If you like the work you are doing, then work, work as hard as you can and never allow yourself to be discouraged by any setback. Everything comes to him who tries hard enough." To which he added the story about the father who said to his son, "You may have everything—wealth, fame, ease, anything and everything you wish for—if you'll only work for it." "I just knew there was a catch somewhere!" the son answered. The key to Paderewski's formula, it will be noted, is "tries", not "waits"; moreover "tries hard", and again "hard enough."

The questions of talent and genius are always raised in the face of a career like Paderewski's. Talent in his opinion "is but an instinctive attraction for the things we are doing. It is a feeling Nature has given us for selecting our career and choosing what we are best fitted to accomplish." On one occasion, speaking specifically of talent in music, he mentioned the dangers of misdirected talent. His words have easily a general application: "Misdirected talent is, unhappily, no uncommon thing. It is harder to eradicate faults thus acquired than to learn properly in the beginning, and some trace of these faults is likely to remain behind after the right way is discovered." The responsibility on this score, he pointed out, rests on the parents of talented children, especially the mothers. They must direct.

And genius? "Genius," in the words of Paderewski, "is but an appellation of honor bestowed upon those who have succeeded in doing certain particular things better than anyone else." That definition of genius may be applied to any kind of human endeavor. But it is genius in art that comes to mind when Paderewski speaks. What of art in this age? What opportunities has the artistic genius in the present era? Paderewski discusses these matters with the calm detachment of the philosopher who is content to observe, who neither judges nor condemns, and whose opinions draw their value from the fact that his ideal has never been "Art for Art's sake," but always "Art for Life's sake."

"We are living in a strange age," he says. "It is an age of economics. It is an age of mechanical invention and machine production, and as such has great value, for it has brought greater comfort to the masses. If it be well directed it may later come to be regarded as one of the most valuable epochs of this ever-changing system of human life. I do not underestimate practical things. They make for physical well-being. But with them they bring attendant evils, evils that kill creative genius. Machines tend to destroy culture. The danger is that the more intelligent the machine the less intelligent the man."

"Genius," he goes on, "and therefore the creation of great art, is impossible under the present system of living. Genius is a tender plant which will not thrive in every soil or in all surroundings, and the quiet and peace that are essential to it have been driven out by the mad haste and constant desire for change which marks this era. To have the quiet and intense concentration of mind which are essential to genius, one must retire to a hermitage to live. And even in a hermitage one cannot entirely escape the excitement of movement which is pulsating through the whole world in this age of quick travel, radio diffusion, and political challenge and change."

We have learned already of some of his views on what he calls "the political challenge and change" of the times, for he himself learned much in his political experiences at Washington and Paris and Warsaw, where so often he withstood the impact and pressure of terrific concentrated forces, forces which never broke him but which taught him many things, among them the failure of parliamentary government to fulfill all its promises. "In politics as in the arts, men are not happy. There is a constant desire to get away from existing conditions." Of what might be called the particular mechanical disturbances which art suffers in the twentieth century he has interesting opinions. While he sees, for instance, the development and manifestation of a greater musical appreciation in America than even in Germany, he sees likewise the mechanical handicaps which halt the progress of art. He names especially the automobile. "It is the automobile, the pernicious and dangerous competition of which has caused untold thousands to abandon music for the accelerator. Speed, speed, speed! It is now the habit of those who formerly gained inspiration from the keyboard or the strings to enjoy only the intoxication of swift flight. This requires no art. A difference of skill in driving is all that it requires."

These words, though they are the words of a man of seventy, do not sound like the words of a querulous old man whom the age in which he lives has superannuated. They are the words of a constructive critic of life, at once wise and dynamic, who recognizes the values as well as the faults of a mechanistic age. If he condemns the speed-madness of the automobile era, in the radio of the same era he sees an invention that might contribute to life, through the life of art, could it be rescued from excessive commercialization and be less an instrument tending to demoralize the listener by inducing in him a too passive attitude. The radio listener, he argues, free to turn the dial on and off as he pleases, does not coöperate as an audience does. Yet with those who charge that the radio has done most to lessen the actual practice of music he disagrees emphatically. "This opinion is an error," he insists. "It is the automobile that is the greatest menace to musical education."

"There is another handicap to the creativeness of art in this age," Paderewski says. Individuality and originality are concomitants of genius, "and individuality and originality are being killed by what I might almost call the increasing necessity of collectivism. People are more and more working in groups. They form trusts, corporations and federations, and thereby they accomplish marvels commercially. But no poem or painting was ever created by a syndicate.

"The day of the lone craftsman has passed. One man rarely produces any finished product today. It is the result of many hands, and while better automobiles may perhaps be produced in this way, surely better poems or paintings or sonatas cannot be. And it is this spirit which is pervading everything."

"Art is great," Paderewski tells us, "only when it bears the stamp of the individual. Today the individual is being merged and lost in the group. There are fewer poets and fewer musicians. Those who would come in contact with art are obliged to live on what the great masters of the past have left us. We look in vain for anything to duplicate what Italy gave us in the way of art during the fifteenth and sixteenth centuries. In music we still cling to the old masters. Where is there anyone today who is reaching the heights of Bach, Beethoven, Mozart, or those later romanticists, Schumann and Chopin, or that youngest and most powerful genius, Wagner?"

Paderewski would be the last one to say that he himself has reached those heights. We may be sure he does not believe that, whatever others believe. He simply rests his art on the canons of intelligible form. It is the destruction of the fundamental molds of form in art by the confusions of a mechanized age that he points out. "Great art," he reminds us, "though it is the creation of one man, is also the product and the result of the time in which he lives. Bach could not have written his works in a skyscraper any more than Michelangelo could have decorated one of our modern temples of industry."

Nevertheless, with his eye ahead, Paderewski sees at work in this same age of mechanical speed and syndicated collectivism an impulse which, although he does not name it so, may be taken as a hope for the life of art in future times. "In modern art," he says, "there is a striving for originality. Men are endeavoring to create something new." And he makes us ask if that striving, however undisciplined and misdirected at present, is not actually the protest, even though still unconsciously so, of the individual against the mechanical age, against the undertow of collective effort? "This craving for originality," finding its momentum in a "desire to get away from old forms," a "pulling down of old-time gods," is unmistakably, as he says, "typical of this period of the world's history." May it not, his words raise the question, be seen also as a movement of life in art which needs only to be nurtured, disciplined and directed to result eventually in "great art bearing the stamp of the individual"? True enough, "nothing new," as he has already told us, "was ever created consciously; true originality has its foundations in the soul, not in the mind." Nor was anything new ever created by wiping out consciousness of the old. We come back to the theory that tradition is the ingot-gold of art, the individual the mintman who molds and stamps it into negotiable coin. Ingot alone, stamp alone, are neither one negotiable, mintman without both is useless. All three must be combined to make art. Yet even in his justified criticism of new and purely self-conscious forms in art, Paderewski still recognizes the impulse to create. That impulse is of the individual. Its existence proves that the individual artist still lives. Its recognition implies hope for the life of creative art.

Out of the dictum of this great apostle of art, who is never pessimistic but is at all times clear-seeing, hope for the future comes, even though that hope rest on the outcome of conflict between the artistic individual who creates and the mechanized and collectivistic age which at once produces and tries to submerge the individual. Titans like Paderewski himself must rise in that conflict. Titans of the soul. If his life and his art and the tradition they establish mean anything, they will rise. Man has never wholly rejected tradition. That is impossible. And Paderewski will, in future times, become one of the great traditions of art.

He is a Titan, but he is not the kind of Titan that he is sometimes called. On one of his appearances in 1932 a New York critic spoke feelingly of Paderewski as a "magnificent old Titan playing out the last of his era . . . he stands alone on a mountain-peak of the past, haughtily holding his fort against the cold brilliance of the youthful newcomers." Paderewski's whole attitude, his philosophy, his entire career, belies these words. Among his noticeable attributes is one which can be described in the words of George Meredith as "the Hellenic gift of intellectual sanity." Very much in and of the present, and far from being "alone on a mountain-peak of the past", he has perspective enough nevertheless to look into the future of art. He does so with discernment. What of the future of music? "Music at the present moment," in his opinion, "is in its infancy. It is not yet commenced. Rhythm and vibration are the very basis of life. Where there is rhythm there is order, and where rhythm is lacking there is no order. I feel confident that a time will come when music will be applied in the general broader sense to education, physical as well as mental. Emile

Jacques Dalcroze, for example, working along this principle, followed a line of thought likely to be more fully pursued as time progresses. It points toward the general use of music as a factor in human development. It is through the physical body that everything—the expression of the symmetry hidden within the soul—is awakened into being. By bringing our whole organism under the educational influence of harmony, we should ourselves become finished products of harmony."

He looks to the future for this. But how will modern music serve this end? Of the music of the times, although he has confessed that he "cannot understand the meaning of most of the music that is being written today," he has views which are far from those of a man "haughtily holding his fort against the newcomers." In his own words, he "keeps his mind open." No single characteristic of Paderewski has been more often spoken of than his lively interest in all that is new and promising. But on simple principles of art he is a positivist, as he is a positivist on all principle. Like Dante, he abhors nothing more than the intolerable tolerance of the neutral-minded. He scouts the modernistic thesis, which is one of the sources of confusion and formlessness in musical art, that ideas can be expressed or heard in music, and he scorns the critic who side-steps the question with verbal perambulations. Music is a medium of mood and emotion only. To Paderewski this is a self-evident truth, as is also the fact that there can be in art no such thing as formlessness: the term is self-contradictory. Art and form are synonymous terms. Certain works of modern composers will live, he has said, but, in general, modern music will be "toned down" to become of permanent value. It is this toning down that will give the individual of a collective age, "striving for originality", the discipline that will result in great art.

There is a future for art, in Paderewski's belief, in spite of the handicaps of an age mechanized into comfort and collectivism: "When we pass beyond this age of comfort into an age of luxury, then there may be a renaissance of art. I do not predict that this will happen, for I am no prophet. But art is luxury, and when people can afford luxury they usually look for artistic enjoyment."

The same "Hellenic sanity" which characterizes Paderewski's reflections on art and on the age in which he lives, balances the tone of his comments on human relations. Of him it was once written, "It is because of his integrity as a human being that he endures." There is no man living, perhaps, who has made such close and continuous contacts with life as he has. He has been a dynamo all his life, a machine fueled and driven by human sympathy converting energy into electrical currents of feeling and action, drawing in and giving out power incessantly. There have been shocks and jolts and cross-currents and all the things that make for wear and friction. But the machine still runs evenly and powerfully. It has neither worn down nor blown up nor gone to pieces. It has never been idle and never at rest long enough to be stained by the rust of pessimism or touched by the acid corrosion of cynicism. After seventy years Paderewski still believes in man, likes people, enjoys human companionship with the relish of youth.

Power over multitudes, the adulation, even to the hysterical degree, of millions, the admiration of the great, have all left him unspoiled; and his has been the popular acclaim that sometimes makes men despise those who accord it to them. His natural sweet-temperedness and confidence in the good in others remains. The Marquis de Custine once wrote to Chopin, "When I listen to you I always think myself alone with you and even perhaps with greater than you, or certainly with all that is greatest in you." Paderewski affects people in the same way because he seems conscious not only of "all that is greatest" in others but of all that is. The common denominator of human experience is his integer. He has known and suffered all that all men know. He has been hungry, felt want, been misunderstood, hoped and been disappointed, believed and been deceived. He has loved and lost, buried his dead, heard the fall of grave-sod on the coffin, gone alone from the sepulchre. He has loved and won, he has been loved, felt the warmth of devotion, the supporting strength of loyalty. He has made mistakes and mended them, stumbled and fallen on faults, got up and gone ahead again. He has learned through all this that finest of human arts which Dr. Johnson calls "putting his mind to yours", and years have not lessened in him the practice and the force of that art.

But with sweet-temperedness and faith in fellowmen, something else remains, the balancing quality of keen and incisive insight, born with him in his gift of brains and developed in him through experience. If he knows life and men through sympathy he has learned likewise to weigh motives and measure acts. He speaks, for instance, dwelling on human impulses, of gratitude, "the gratitude of those we do for." He has earned the gratitude of many hundreds. Yet, "I hate the word!" he exclaims. "The man to whom we do a favor recognizes his inferiority and it rankles. A favor is often the poison of friendship." But he does not indict others; he indicts himself. "There are some who have an exaggerated feeling of gratitude. That is an unfavorable trait. I have it. I want to pay a kindness a hundred times. And I have done it." He recalls a friend, an incident, of the past: "There was a man—poor fellow, he is dead now—who once did me a kindness when I needed it. At a banquet given me in Poland he was present. In my speech I told of his act. But I added, 'I do not hold it against him.' And I think he understood what I meant."

It is its balance that makes the strength of Paderewski's character great and lasting. That balance has saved him from the weaknesses of the artistic nature. It has kept him normal. It has kept him from ever being sentimental, in his music or in his human relations, although deep sentiment has been one of the ruling forces of his life. He has not been proud, but he has been assertive. He has not been, in his own words, "modest before men", but he has been humble before God. He has had something better than the gifts of multiple genius; the balance, mental and emotional, to make those gifts work together to good end.

If, in some far-off day to come, the historian and biographer who studies and reports these present times will play, on whatever perfected mechanism the future is to afford, some of the instrumental records of Paderewski's renditions of his own or others' music, and will further play or listen to the playing of some of Paderewski's own compositions; if the historian will then read Paderewski's political speeches and along with them his literary and artistic utterances; if he will do this, and then turn to Paderewski's story in the records of art, where his name shines as player, composer, teacher, critic; and turn further to the records of European and American history during and after the World War, and specifically to the records of Polish history from 1914 on: if the future historian will do these things, he will come to a realization of the fact that there was a man living in this age whose richness of soul, whose protean gifts, whose scope of mind and variation of genius, entitled him to be called a great man, a second Leonardo da Vinci. The comparison of Paderewski with Leonardo has indeed been made in our own time by the musician Edwin Hughes. "In five hundred years," Mr. Hughes has said, "when music lovers of that day and age look backward over the history of the art, they will still find the name of Paderewski looming large among the distinguished world figures of the present, an artist of the type of Leonardo da Vinci, or Rubens, who was not only great in his own art but who was also gifted in many other fields, and who played a significant part in world politics during a historical crisis of the utmost importance."

Ruskin, whom Paderewski admires, once set down what he called the six qualities of legitimate pleasure in artistic execution: truth; simplicity; mystery; apparent inadequacy of the means used to the effect produced; decision; velocity. Paderewski's life, his character, his art, his career, all exemplify these qualities; he has been swift, decisive, mysterious, simple, and true, and he has produced effects out of all measure beyond the apparent adequacy of his means, whether in music or statecraft. But the words spoken by Arthur W. Sewall in New York in 1928, at the celebration of the tenth anniversary of Poland's liberation, are perhaps true, not alone of feeling in America but in every country except his own where his position is doubly unique: "Whatever the course of the world's history may have demanded of Paderewski as statesman, and however practically and brilliantly he may have responded to those demands, he will remain, for the vast majority of his American admirers, the great musician. His place in their admiration and affection is, first, that of the master pianist, the conjurer with the magic of tones; and then that of the composer of strong individuality, tinged deeply with the color of his Polish nationality."

Undoubtedly it will be as a genius of music, as "the musician of the many", that Paderewski will live preëminently and universally in future times. He will live uniquely, too, in Europe and particularly in his native Poland, as a genius of statecraft. But as time goes on and his story is more and more known he will live in the hearts of all people above all as a man: a man whose life tells others how to live, because, no matter what his eminence, he has been at all times that which even the most inconspicuous of us must in some measure be to justify our existence: a contributor to life. Because the dimension of Paderewski's being is greatness, he has contributed greatly.

Summed up, the ultimate characteristic of Paderewski is his balance, a large human balance which has in it no trace of the erratic. He is a rounded circle. Ordinarily genius does not describe a rounded circle; too often genius is only a salient point breaking a common circumference at a sharp angle. It sticks out and thus attracts attention. In this man's case we have, rather, the common circumference of man's basic attributes simply raised to a very high plane, rounded and filled out in a beautiful unity. To change the figure, genius is often a rocket emitting a pyrotechnic blaze that dazzles and snaps and burns away, whereas here we have a large clear flame, something more like a sun than a sunburst, a copious, evenly-glowing, illuminating and fructifying fire the brilliance of which, instead of being angular, is orbital.

In art Paderewski is the fulfillment of what his fellow-Pole Joseph Conrad called "the great aim": "true to the emotions called forth out of the deep encircled by the firmament of stars, whose infinite numbers and awful distance may move us to laughter or tears." In his human relationships, public and private, as a man, a citizen, a patriot, a statesman, he is equally true to "the great aim." Seen thus, Paderewski stands strong and erect, an exemplar of what civilization can produce, of what man at his best can be. With the light of a refulgent past on his lion-like head, the lights of the future playing on his face, he is for our time a kind of luminous figure or symbol, a beacon which makes the words of a good friend of his country, Georg Brandes, glow with meaning: "The future is not to the avenger, nor to the evangel, but to him who labors with genius."

But Paderewski, strong and erect, does not stand still for us to look at him. He moves forward for us to follow him. There is more than a light shining on him, for unmistakably there is a light shining in him. And he is far more than a symbolic picture, a mere flat surface. He is a full-bodied living man, very much alive, and a great man peculiarly different from many of the great, because the nature of his art, and back of that the nature of his character, brings him very close to the masses of people. Leading, he moves among those he leads, all the world over, just as surely as he moved and led that day of the Bristol mob in Warsaw. That was a symbolic as well as a dramatic moment in his life. And this, it seems to me, is the real reason that the future belongs to Paderewski. It belongs to him, paradoxically enough, because he gives it away. The future assuredly is his in the immortality of fame; likewise in the doing of great and good things he can still lay claim to the future as long as he lives. But the future is Paderewski's chiefly because he shares it with others. Not so much by what he says as by what he is, he shares his whole life-long experience with us, his struggles from the obscurity of a prairie farm to world eminence, his contests with poverty, hardships, domestic tragedy, critical opposition, political antagonisms: all telling us that labor is the secret of happiness as well as of success, that everything comes to him who tries hard enough, who never allows himself to be discouraged by any setback; that genius is only an appellation of honor bestowed on those who labor and succeed, and that it is never too late at any time to achieve something of importance in this world. In a story like Paderewski's one truth surely is brought home to us: that art is life, that the artist, be he musician, painter, sculptor, writer, no matter what, is not remote from life nor antagonistic to it, but a living and illuminating part of it. Better still, we learn another truth: that life itself is an art, a fine-art which we all may practice, in which everyone of us may perfect ourselves no matter what our work or our station may be.

No man's story is worth telling unless it has meaning. This is the meaning of the true story of Paderewski which I have tried to tell in the same spirit in which his compatriot Sienkiewicz wrote his historical fictions: "For the comfort of hearts."

POSTSCRIPT

THE biography of a living contemporary cannot be written without direct assistance from the friends of the man whose life-story is told. The author of "Paderewski: The Story of a Modern Immortal" owes a debt of gratitude to a number of Mr. Paderewski's intimates who have generously given effort and time to supply material for the book. To President Roosevelt, former President Hoover, Colonel House, Mr. Sigismond Stojowski, Dr. Francis E. Fronczak, and Mr. Owen Wister he is especially indebted for the use of documents or information. His greatest obligation is to Colonel House and Mr. Stojowski, the latter himself eminent in music, a pupil of Paderewski, and for fifty years his intimate friend. Without Mr. Stojowski's assistance in editing the manuscript, scrutinizing and correcting it minutely (and always with a protest of the most genuine modesty against the inclusion of his own name in the story) the completion of the book would not have been possible. Also to Charlotte Kellogg (Mrs. Vernon Kellogg), who is the author of one of the best books of the time on a Polish historical subject ("Jadwiga, Poland's Great Queen"), for which Mr. Paderewski wrote the preface, the author offers thanks for invaluable help. Others who helped in making researches or otherwise and whose names cannot be overlooked are: Mr. George Engles, director of Mr. Paderewski's American tours; Mr. Henryk Opienski of Warsaw, eminent musician and author of the only other existing biography of Paderewski (published in Polish and French but not in English): from Opienski's work I have drawn copiously and quoted frequently; Mr. Edward Algernon Baughan of London, author of a critical sketch of Paderewski; Mr. Wallace Goodrich, Director of the New England Conservatory of Music, Boston; Mr. James Francis Cooke, editor of *The Etude* and author of "Music Masters New and Old", whose short biographical sketch of Paderewski, originally appearing in that volume, is reprinted in "Beacon Lights of History"; Mr. E. C. Forman, Director of the Victor Company Record Service; Mrs. Eleanor Lansing, widow of the former United States Secretary of State; Mr. Robert Wooley, Director

543

of the United States Mint under President Wilson; Dr. Stephen M. Mizwa, Executive Director of the Kosciuszko Foundation; Col. Albert J. Chesley, formerly head of the American Red Cross Commission to Poland; Dr. Placida Gardner Chesley; Dom Gregory Gerrer, O.S.B., Custodian of the Wightman Memorial Art Gallery, University of Notre Dame; Mr. Roman de Majewski of the Steinway Company; Mr. Gutzon Borglum; Hon. Henry Morgenthau; the Countess Helena Morstyn; Mrs. Carlyle Scott; Mr. George Frederick Wiedman; Mr. Charles Anderson; Miss May S. Brower, for the late Harriette Brower; Miss Helen-Marie Donahue, for library research; Mrs. Mary Byers and Mr. Karol Karnasiewicz for help in translations from the Polish; Mr. John M. Scanlan and Mr. Karnasiewicz for faithful and accurate secretarial work.

For the original portrait of Madame Paderewska I owe a special debt of gratitude to the artist, F. Soulé-Campbell.

To the following named librarians acknowledgment is made for courteous assistance: Miss Gracia Countryman, the Public Library, Minneapolis, Minn.; Miss Ethel G. Baker, the Public Library, South Bend, Ind.; Mr. F. H. Price, the Free Library of Philadelphia; Miss Mary Barsky, the Chicago Public Library; Mr. Paul Byrne, the Library, University of Notre Dame; .Mr. Roberts and Miss Jessica L. Farnum, the Library of Congress, Washington; Mr. Joseph F. Kwapil, the *Public Ledger* library, Philadelphia; Miss Anna Wykes Miller, the Junior College Library, Grand Rapids, Mich.; and the librarian of *The New York Times*.

Acknowledgment is likewise made to various publishers of books and periodicals for permission to use copyrighted material.

Of books:—Gebetner i Wolf, Warsaw; Editions Spes, Lausanne ("I. J. Paderewski": Opienski); Hermann Seeman Nachfolger, Leipzig ("I. J. Paderewski": Alfred Nossig); W. Adlington, London ("Chopin: A Discourse": I. J. Paderewski. Translated from the Polish by Laurence Alma-Tadema); George Allen & Unwin, Ltd., London ("Studies in Polish Life and History": A. E. Tennant; "Outline of Polish History": Roman Dyboski); D. Appleton & Co., New York ("Wings Over Poland": Kenneth Malcolm Murray); Associated Music Publishers, New York ("Little Biographies—Paderewski": Frederick H. Martens); Bobbs-Merrill Co., Indianapolis ("The Truth About the Treaty": André Tardieu); The Century Co., New York and Heinemann, Ltd., London ("Thirty Years of Musical Life in London": Hermann Klein); Doubleday, Doran & Co., Garden City,

N. Y. ("Joseph Conrad—Life and Letters": G. Jean Aubrey; "Notes on Life and Letters", "A Personal Record": Joseph Conrad; "All in a Life-Time": Henry Morgenthau); E. P. Dutton & Co., New York and George Allen & Unwin, Ltd., London ("The Romantic World of Music": William Armstrong; "Poland: 1914–1931": Robert Machray); Harvard University Press, Cambridge ("Some Problems of the Peace Conference": Robert Howard Lord, Charles Homer Haskins); Henry Holt & Co., New York ("Polonaise: The Life of Chopin": Guy de Pourtalès); Harcourt, Brace & Co., New York ("Grandeur and Misery of Victory": Georges Clemenceau); Harper & Brothers, New York ("The New Democracy: Presidential Messages, Addresses and Other Papers": Woodrow Wilson); Houghton Mifflin Co., Boston ("The Intimate Papers of Colonel House": Charles Seymour; "The Big Four": Robert Lansing); Alfred A. Knopf, New York ("Memoirs of Hector Berlioz": edited by Ernest Newman); John Lane, the Bodley Head, London ("I. J. Paderewski": Edward Algernon Baughan); Horace Liveright, New York ("Time Exposures": Waldo Frank); Lincoln McVeagh, the Dial Press, New York ("Pilsudski and Poland": Rom Landau); Minton, Balch Co., New York ("Statesmen of the War in Retrospect": William Martin); The Macmillan Co., New York ("America and the New Poland": H. H. Fisher; "Memories and Impressions": Helena Modjeska); Theo. Presser Co., Philadelphia ("Great Pianists on Piano Playing": James Francis Cooke); Charles Scribner's Sons, New York ("Poland": Roman Dyboski; "Success in Music and How it is Won": Henry T. Finck; "Franz Liszt": James T. Huneker); The University Society, New York ("Modern Music and Musicians"; "Great Composers"). To those reading Polish, *Polska Odrodzona* ("Poland Reborn") by Professor Stanislaw Kutrzeba, late Rector of the University of Cracow, is recommended.

Of periodicals:—*The Saturday Evening Post*, Philadelphia ("Genius Backstage", March 15, 1930; "How One Bomb Was Made": Owen Wister, Dec. 3, 1921); *The Etude*, Philadelphia: numerous critical and biographical articles; *Harper's Magazine*, New York ("Paderewski: the Paradox of Europe"; Edward M. House); *The Ladies' Home Journal*, Philadelphia ("How Paderewski Taught Me to Play": Madame Szumowska-Adamowska and William Armstrong, May, 1905; "Paderewski the Lion Hearted": Sigismond Ivanowski, Nov., 1924); *The Woman's Home Companion*, New York ("What a Little Knowledge of Music Means": Paderewski and William Armstrong, Oct.,

1913); *Good Housekeeping*, New York ("Stars—What They Are Like": Rose Heylbut, Dec., 1932); *The Musician*, New York ("Some Causes of Paderewski's Leadership in Piano Music"; Harriette Brower, Sept., 1926); *Century Magazine* (now *Century and Forum*), New York ("A Conversation on Music": Daniel Gregory Mason, Nov., 1908; "Madame Paderewska": Abbie H. C. Finck, Oct., 1913); *The Living Age*, Aug. 4, 1923; *The Nation*, New York, March 26, 1914, Aug. 4, 1923; *The Outlook*, Feb. 3, 1926; *Poland-America*, New York ("Poland and Peace": I. J. Paderewski, July, 1932; "Paderewski the Unique", "An Outline of Polish Music": Sigismond Stojowski, May, 1932); *World's Work*, New York ("Paderewski: A Great Man": Silas Bent); *The Commonweal*, New York ("Paderewski": Charles Phillips, May 13, 1931); *Pictorial Review*, New York ("Paderewski Says": Konrad Bercovici, May, 1933).

To these formal acknowledgments the author wishes to add a word of thanks to his many personal friends who in innumerable ways aided him in the intricate task of compiling and composing the life-record of a man whose story has never been completely told before and never before in the English tongue—and most happily is far from being yet finished. The task has been a difficult one; at times so delicate a one that the feeling of intrusion into the intimacies of a man's life has all but forced the writer to desist. Again, there has been the fear that the author's interpretation of acts and events, political especially and in particular those relating to the conflict with Marshal Pilsudski, might embarrass the subject of the biography: for all such interpretations the author takes entire responsibility. The author's sole aim in carrying out the work has been to recount truthfully and objectively the history of one of the great human personalities of all time, a man whose character is one of the priceless possessions of our age; of a man, therefore, whose story should be told. "There is no doubt," as Stephen Mizwa has said, "that the story of Paderewski, as artist, patriot, and humanitarian, is a story that has no counterpart in the annals of modern civilization." In the telling of it here Gamaliel Bradford's ideal, as set forth in his book on *The Art of Biography*, has been kept steadily in mind: "The great object of biography must always be the portrayal of character . . . the purpose is always the same, to make us better acquainted with the intimate quality and varied depth and richness of the human soul."

APPENDIX

A: A List of Paderewski's Compositions *

(Unnumbered) Impromptu. (Published by W. Banarski, Warsaw.)

Opus 1. No. 1: Prélude à capriccio for Piano.
No. 2: Minuetto for Piano (G min.).

Opus 2. Three Pieces for Piano:
(1) Gavotte (E min.).
(2) Mélodie (C maj.).
(3) Valse Mélancolique (A maj.).

(Unnumbered) Intermezzi (G min. and C maj.). (Published by Rajchman and Frendler, "Echo Muzyczne," Warsaw.)

Opus 3. Krakowiak for Piano.

Opus 4. Elegy for Piano.

Opus 5. Polish Dances (Tanse Polskie) for Piano; also for piano four hands arrangement:
(1) Krakowiak (E maj.).
(2) Mazurek (E min.).
(3) Krakowiak (B flat maj.).

(Unnumbered) "Powódź" ("Under the Waves"): Published at Warsaw for the benefit of the Polish flood victims, 1884.

Opus 6. Introduction and Toccata for Piano.

(Unnumbered) Moment Musical (Supplement to "Echo Muzyczne," No. 435, Warsaw.)

---

* Unless otherwise noted, published originally by Bote-Bock, Berlin.

Opus 7. Four Songs. Poems by Asnyk; texts in Polish, German, English (English words by Constance Bache):
    (1) The Day of Roses: Gdy ostatnia róża zwiędla.
    (2) To My Faithful Steed: Siwy Koniu.
    (3) The Birch Tree and the Maiden: Szumi w gaju brzezina.
    (4) My Love Is Sent Away: Chłopca mego mi zabrali.

Opus 8. Chants du Voyageur: Five Pieces for Piano:
    (1) Allegro agitato.
    (2) Andantino.
    (3) Andantino grazioso: Melody in B maj. arranged for violin or cello and piano; also for orchestra.
    (4) Andantino mistico.
    (5) Allegro giocoso.

Opus 9. Polish Dances:
    Folio I: (1) Krakowiak (F maj.).
              (2) Mazurek (A min.).
              (3) Mazurek (A maj.).
    Folio II: (4) Mazurek (B flat).
              (5) Krakowiak (A maj.).
              (6) Polonaise (B maj.).

Opus 10. Maytime Album (Album de Mai): Scènes Romantiques for Piano:
    (1) In the Evening (Au Soir).
    (2) Song of Love (Chant d'amour).
    (3) Scherzino.
    (4) Barcarolle.
    (5) Caprice (Valse).

Opus 11. Variations and Fugue on an Original Theme, A Minor, for Piano.

Opus 12. Tatra Album (Dances of the Zakopané Mountaineers) for Piano:
    (1) For four hands (Published by Ries and Erler, Berlin).
    (2) For two hands (Published by Rajchman and Frendler, Warsaw: "Echo Muzyczne").

Opus 13. Sonata for Violin and Piano (A min.).

Opus 14. Humoresques de Concert for Piano:
Folio I (*à l'antique*):
    (1) Menuet Célèbre.
    (2) Sarabande.
    (3) Caprice (genre Scarlatti).
Folio II (*moderne*):
    (4) Burlesque.
    (5) Intermezzo Pollaco.
    (6) Cracovienne Fantastique.

Opus 15. Dans le desert—In the Desert: Musical Tableau in toccata form for Piano.

Opus 16. Miscellanea: Series of Piano Pieces:
    (1) Légende No. 1 (A flat maj.).
    (2) Melodie (G flat maj.).
    (3) Thème varié (A maj.).
    (4) Nocturne (B flat maj.).
    (5) Légende No. 2 (A maj.).
    (6) Moment Musical.
    (7) Menuet (A maj.).

Opus 17. Concerto in A Minor for Piano and Orchestra.

Opus 18. Six Songs from Mickiewicz, with Piano Accompaniment. (Polish, English and German texts):
    (1) Mine Eyes Have Known Tears: Polały się łzy.
    (2) The Piper's Song: Piosnka Dudziarza.
    (3) My Own Sweet Maiden: Moja pieszczotka.
    (4) By Mighty Waters: Nad woda wielka.
    (5) Pain Have I Endured: Tylem wytrwał.
    (6) Might I But Change Me: Gdybym się zmienil.

Opus 19. Polish Fantasy on Original Themes, for Piano and Orchestra. (Published by G. Schirmer, New York.)

Opus 20. Légende, for Piano.

Opus 21. Sonata (E flat min.) for Piano.

Opus 22. Twelve Songs to Poems by Catulle Mendès (Published by Heugel, Paris):
    (1) In the Forest: Dans la forêt.
    (2) Your Heart Is Pure Gold: Ton cœur est d'or pur.
    (3) The Skies Are Very Low: Le Ciel est très bas.
    (4) Not Long Ago: Naguère.
    (5) A Young Shepherd: Le Jeune Pâtre.
    (6) She Walks with Faltering Step: Elle marche d'un pas distrait.
    (7) The Nun: La Jeune Nonne.
    (8) Vacuity: Viduité.
    (9) The Cold Moon: Lune froide.
    (10) Quarrelsome: Querelleuse.
    (11) The Fatal Love: L'Amour fatal.
    (12) The Enemy Reflects: L'Ennemie.

Opus 23. Variations and Fugue for Piano (E flat min.).

(Unnumbered) Canzone (Song Without Words) for Piano.

(Unnumbered) Manru. Opera in Three Acts: Orchestral score; piano score with words; libretto in Polish and German. (Piano score and English text published by G. Schirmer, New York.)

Opus 24. Symphony (B min.) (Full score, orchestral parts and miniature orchestral score, published by Heugel, Paris.)

(Unpublished) Cantata for Chorus and Orchestra to a poem of Tetmajer.
    Violin Concerto (unfinished).
    Series of Etudes for Piano.

B: A List of Paderewski's Recordings

Bandoline, La (Rondeau)—Couperin (6388) *.
Berceuse (Lullaby)—(Op. 57)—Chopin (6428).
By the Brookside—Stojowski (1426).

---

* The numeral at the end of each line, in parentheses, indicates the Victor Record number.

Campanella, La—Paganini-Liszt (6825).
Carillon de Cythère (Chimes of Cythera)—Couperin (88492).
Chant d'amour (Op. 26, No. 3)—Stojowski (6633).
Cracovienne Fantastique (Op. 14, No. 6)—Paderewski (6230).

Dancing Virgins of Delphi (Danseuses de Delphes)—Debussy (1531).

Etude in E Major (Op. 10, No. 3)—Chopin (6628).
Etude in C Minor (Revolutionary)—(Op. 10, No. 12)—Chopin (1387).
Etude in G Flat Major (Black Keys)—(Op. 10, No. 5)—Chopin (1387).
Etude in A Minor—Chopin (6438).
Etude de Concert (F Minor)—Liszt (6438).
Etude in G Sharp Minor (Op. 25, No. 6)—(917).
Etude in G Flat Major (Op. 25, No. 9)—(914).
Etude in C Sharp Minor (Op. 10, No. 4)—Chopin (6448).

Flying Dutchman—Spinning Song, Part 1-2—Wagner-Liszt (1549).
Funeral March—Chopin (6470).

Hark, Hark, the Lark—Schubert-Liszt (6470).
Hungarian Rhapsody, No. 2, Part I—Liszt (6235).
Hungarian Rhapsody, No. 2, Part II—Liszt (6235).
Hungarian Rhapsody, No. 10—Liszt (6231).

Impromptu in A Flat (Op. 142, No. 2)—Schubert (6628).
Impromptu in B Flat, Parts 1-2 (Op. 142, No. 4)—Schubert (6482).

Maiden's Wish (Chant polonais)—(Op. 74, No. 1)—Chopin-Liszt (6231).
Mazurka in C Sharp Minor (Op. 63, No. 3)—Chopin (7416).
Mazurka in A Flat—Chopin (1541).
Mazurka in D Major—Chopin (1541).
Mazurka in F Sharp Minor—Chopin (1027).
Mazurka in A Flat—Chopin (1027).
Mazurka in A Minor—Chopin (6448).
Minstrels—Debussy (1499).
Minuet (Op. 14, No. 1)—Paderewski (6690).

Moonlight Sonata (Adagio sostenuto)—(Op. 27, No. 2)—Beethoven (6690).
Moment Musical in A Flat Major, Part 1-2—Schubert (7508).
My Joys (Chant polonais)—(Op. 74, No. 5)—Chopin-Liszt (6428).

Nocturne in F Sharp Major (Op. 15, No. 2)—Chopin (6825).
Nocturne in E Flat Major (Op. 9, No. 2)—Chopin (7416).
Nocturne in B Flat (Op. 16, No. 4)—Paderewski (6232).
Nocturne in F Major (Op. 15, No. 1)—Chopin (6233).
Nocturne à Raguse, Parts 1 and 2—Schelling (6700).

Polonaise Militaire (Op. 40, No. 1)—Chopin (6234).
Polonaise in E Flat Minor, Parts 1-2—(Op. 26, No. 2)—Chopin (7391).
Prélude in D Flat (Op. 28, No. 15: "Raindrop Prélude")—Chopin (6847).
Prélude in A Flat Major (Op. 28, No. 17)—Chopin (6847).
Prophet Bird (Op. 82, No. 7)—Schumann (1426).

Reflections on the Water—Debussy (6633).

Songs of the Traveler (Chants du Voyageur)—Paderewski (917).

Valse Brilliante (Op. 34, No. 1)—Chopin (6389).
Valse Brilliante, in E Flat (Op. 18)—Chopin (6877).
Valse Caprice—Rubinstein (6877).
Veils—Debussy (1531).
Valse in A Flat (Op. 42)—Chopin (6230).

Waltz in C Sharp Minor (Op. 64, No. 2)—Chopin (6234).
Warum? (Why?) (Fantasiestücke, No. 3, Op. 12)—Schumann (6388).
Wind in the Plains—Debussy (1499).

INDEX